AF663678

VEDIC MYTHOLOGY

Alfred Hillebrandt

ALFRED HILLEBRANDT

Vedic Mythology

Translated from the Original German by
SREERAMULA RAJESWARA SARMA

Volume Two

MOTILAL BANARSIDASS PUBLISHERS
PRIVATE LIMITED • DELHI

3rd Reprint : Delhi, 2016
First English Language Edition: Delhi, 1980
Second Revised Edition, 2 Vols., Breslau, 1927, 1929
First Edition, 3 Vols., Breslau, 1891, 1899, 1902

ISBN : 978-81-208-0799-5 (Vol. I)
ISBN : 978-81-208-0800-3 (Vol. II)
ISBN : 978-81-208-0801-0 (Set)

Also available at :
MOTILAL BANARSIDASS
41 U.A. Bungalow Road, Jawahar Nagar, Delhi 110 007
8 Mahalaxmi Chamber, 22 Bhulabhai Desai Road, Mumbai 400 026
203 Royapettah High Road, Mylapore, Chennai 600 004
236, 9th Main III Block, Jayanagar, Bengaluru 560 011
8 Camac Street, Kolkata 700 017
Ashok Rajpath, Patna 800 004
Chowk, Varanasi 221 001

Printed in India

by RP Jain at NAB Printing Unit,
A-44, Naraina Industrial Area, Phase I, New Delhi–110028
and published by JP Jain for Motilal Banarsidass Publishers (P) Ltd,
41 U.A. Bungalow Road, Jawahar Nagar, Delhi-110007

CONTENTS

CHAPTER FIVE

THE ĀDITYAS

A. VARUṆA

The meaning and origin of Varuṇa, who is connected with Mitra in a dualistic association, has been, in the recent years, the subject of diverse kinds of studies which, however, have led to mutually contradictory results. From the earliest period of mythological studies we inherited the concept of Varuṇa as the god of the sky, as the Indian counterpart of Ouranos. This apart, there are other theories which see in Varuṇa an ancient moon god or also a nocturnal god or which make the ocean the starting point of this personification in accordance with his position in the later period. It will be necessary to re-examine these individual views and to see how far these views are consistent with the material available to us. By the time Varuṇa and Mitra make their appearance in the Vedic hymns, their evolution had passed through a long and, for us, boundless period. We cannot hope any more to penetrate up to the prehistoric times which gave birth to this pair of gods. But by a careful analysis it would certainly be possible to solve many problems, to arrange more correctly many a stone in the edifice of this concept, and to discard as worthless several others which appeared valuable to earlier researchers.

We encounter two difficulties in this task. Firstly, the portrait of Varuṇa exhibits already in the ṚV heterogeneous traits of character that are incompatible with one another. It is not easy to determine which of these is the most original trait. Secondly, he is portrayed in one way in the Brāhmaṇas and in another way in the Ṛgvedic hymns, and the later period deviates not inconsiderably from both the two.

I have stated earlier that the difference in viewpoints between the ṚV and the Brāhmaṇas cannot always be explained away merely with the time difference between the two. Of course, generally speaking, the Brāhmaṇas represent a later stratum of literature; nevertheless they display a tradition which is independent of the ṚV in many respects and which has not been completely obliterated by the mythological speculations of the time. Without this assumption it would not make sense why Mitra and Varuṇa could be interpreted in these works throughout as day and night; for this concept occurs too often to be dismissed as a mere speculation of the Yājñikas and, on the other hand, it is too far removed from the Ṛgvedic concept to be its direct continuation. Naturally we cannot begin our interpretation on the basis of such statements of the Brāhmaṇas. However, we can use them to verify the correctness of the conclusions which we draw from other sources. In this respect, I believe, not enough attention has been paid to the statements of the Brāhmaṇas.

1. Varuṇa and the Sky

The theory that Varuṇa is the sky has by far the greatest number of adherents. Like Roth, Darmesteter and many others earlier, to whom I myself belonged, Hopkins, Bohnenberger and von Schroeder also have recently accepted this view.[1] The arguments cited in support of this view do not convince me any more and I believe with Oldenberg that etymology played a greater role than is admissible in setting up a sky god Varuṇa and that etymological equation is the mother of this concept. But the etymology is uncertain[2] and the concept is alien to the actual material of our texts. No wonder that one of the new adherents of the sky theory admits that we have absolutely no evidence to say "that there were also other traditions among the Vedic people according to which the sky is the naturalistic basis with which Varuṇa was originally identical and from which he evolved further,"[3] that "isolated relics of the special association of Varuṇa with the sky" can be seen [leaving aside the etymology] "only in the notions that the highest heaven and its light are the abode of Varuṇa, that the god is distinguished from the others by his shining and radiant form, probably also in the notion that the sun represents his eye." Except the last point, all these are definitely inadequate arguments for the probability of this hypothesis.

The fact that we do not encounter anywhere—either in the Brāhmaṇas or later —any hint that Varuṇa is the sky demonstrates that Indians themselves were not familiar with this idea and exhorts us to be cautious in our interpretations. Moreover, this equation of Varuṇa with the sky is opposed by the dual formation Mitrāvaruṇau which loses its significance in this interpretation. In our understanding of Vedic mythology the dual gods still lead a shadowy and contrived existence. Instead of attempting to comprehend their significance from the spirit of the Veda and of the ritual, one has so far looked for a neat arrangement. On the basis of such positive examples like Dyāvāpṛthivī, Agnīṣomau, Uṣāsānaktau we can recognize that pairs of this kind are created, as a rule, to reconcile certain contradictions in their intrinsic unity, or to provide the mutually complementary phenomena with the external symbols of unity, whereas in other cases (like Indra-Viṣṇu, Indra-Varuṇa) these associations are merely the products of an artificial process of fusion, brought about by the singers or by the ritualists. It has often been said that the dual form 'Mitrāvaruṇau' is the expression of an intimate connection between the firmament and the sun and that it is an image of the vault of heaven in which the sun traverses along his paths. This association might appear quite obvious to us. But so far as I know Indians have never conceived either in poetry or in mythology the sky and the sun as an intimately connected pair. We search in vain for duals like **dyāvāsūryau*.

Mitra and Varuṇa often appear together. They mount their chariot or their throne in concert. Yet the entire tradition lays stress on the antithesis between the two and not on their identity or affinity. This antithesis is stated in various forms but in such a way that it cannot be explained in all cases from a mythological point of view. We need only to recall the examples where the day is assigned to Mitra and the night to Varuṇa,[4] and the numerous other instances where the two names are employed, without any regard to their meaning, merely as opposites through various turns of expressions.[5] This is also a negative argument but it corroborates our first argument. The antithesis emphasized so sharply in these examples from the Brāhmaṇas can be traced back to the ṚV; it is not so distinct there but it can be still recognized.

Which then are the passages where Varuṇa seems to be the sky god?

First of all we may cite ṚV VII.87.5: "three heavens are deposited within him, below that three earths, forming a row of six;"[6] secondly IX.73.8: "he has set three Pavitras in his heart."[7] If one considers these verses alone as others and I have done earlier and without any reference to related concepts of the ṚV, one may indeed get the impression as though the all-encompassing sky is meant here. But the Vedic poets were inspired by other notions than we are, for quite similar ideas occur again with reference to other gods who have never been regarded as sky gods.[8] Thus it is said of Āditya in

AV XIII. 2. 3: *yád éko víśvaṃ pári bhū́ma jā́yase,*

of Parjanya in

ṚV VII. 102. 4: *yásmin víśvāni bhúvanāni tasthúḥ*
tisró dyā́vas tredhā́ sasrúr ā́paḥ

or of Savitṛ in

I. 35. 6: *tisró dyā́vaḥ savitúr dvā́ upásthāṃ*
ékā yamásya bhúvane virāṣā́ṭ

Although the modes of expression differ slightly, yet I cannot see any substantial difference in these verses. Hence, I think that *tisró dyā́vo níhitā antár asmin* [*váruṇe*] is not much different from *yásmin* [*parjánye*] *víśvāni bhúvanāni tasthúḥ* or from *tisró dyā́vaḥ savitúḥ.*[9] All these passages state much the same thing, namely that Varuṇa, Parjanya and Savitṛ bear the worlds.[10]

Neither do these verses present any convincing evidence nor does ṚV I.50.6,[11] where Varuṇa is said to behold with the "sun's eye," or other passages where the sun is styled as the eye of Mitra-Varuṇa. I admit that I.50.6 appears to be one of the strongest arguments in favour of the sky theory and to justify L. von Schroeder when he poses the question: "Is such a designation conceivable at all if there was even a shadow of moon god in Varuṇa? But it is a very appropriate mythological conception for the sky."[12] However, contrary to the appearance, this argument is not tenable either. For, as we know, Sūrya is called the eye of not only Varuṇa and Mitra but also of Agni.[13] This shows that the sun can serve also gods other than the sky as the organ of vision. On p. 262 of the First Volume, I have cited ṚV IX. 75.1 according to which Soma "mounted the chariot of the mighty sun;" IX. 10. 9 states *abhí priyā́ divás padám adhvaryúbhir gúhā hitám / sū́raḥ paśyati cákṣasā//* No matter whether this should be understood here in a figurative or in an astronomical sense (as an allusion to the new moon), we recall both these verses as counter-argument when I. 50. 6 is cited as evidence to say that Varuṇa must be the sky god. Now Sūrya is not the eye of just Mitra-Varuṇa or of Varuṇa alone. The evolution of Varuṇa as the creator has isolated him completely from his natural basis and made him the creator of the sun whom he sets up in the sky as a golden swing, for whom he opens up the path and so on. Those who share my views on Soma can convince themselves from pp. 260-263 of the First Volume that a god who makes the sun shine and so on need not necessarily be a sky god, for it is said precisely of Soma, the moon, that he causes the sun and the celestial spaces to shine. While the above-mentioned verses, judged by the criterion of Vedic conceptions, do not prove anything in favour of the sky theory, there are others which even raise difficulties for the adherents of the sky theory and to which adequate attention has not been paid; I think they demolish the whole hypothesis; thus

VII. 87. 6: *áva síndhuṃ váruṇo dyaúr iva sthād*
drapsó ná śvetó mṛgás túviṣmān/
gambhīráśaṃso rájaso vimānaḥ

Can one say of the sky god that he descends into the Sindhu "like a white drop, a mighty animal"?[14] Or can we understand

VIII. 41. 8: *sá samudró apīcyàs turó dyā́m iva rohati.../*
sá māyā́ arcínā padā́stṛṇān nā́kam ā́ruhat...//

to mean that Varuṇa resembles a hidden ocean, dispells the attacks with his shining foot and goes up to heaven? I do not think that the difficulties would be nearly as great if we discard the sky theory and look for the explanation of Varuṇa in a different set of conceptions. These become obvious from what I have stated earlier on Soma. Only of Soma it is said *samudráḥ soma pinvase* IX. 64. 8; *tvám samudró asi* 86. 29; *ákrān samudráḥ prathamé vidharman* 97. 40.[15] Soma is an ocean full of amṛta. Even though Soma and Varuṇa are not identical, the line of demarcation is not strictly maintained between these two, who are based on different aspects of the same natural phenomenon.[16]

Finally the sky theory has no answer to the question why Agni is identified with Varuṇa. When it is said that in the evening the sun enters the waters as Varuṇa (KBr XVIII.9), or that Agni becomes Varuṇa in the evening, or that, rising in the morning, he becomes Mitra and goes through the atmosphere as Savitṛ (AV XIII.3.13), the followers of the sky theory would stand quite perplexed about these statements since they cannot account for this confusion in concepts without the aid of the readily available mysticism of the Indians.

2. Ahura and Mithra

An important argument in favour of the old equation between Varuṇa and the sky is the dual formation Mitra-Varuṇa on the one hand and the connection between Mithra and Ahura in the Avesta on the other.[17] It was argued that these two associations cannot be separated from one another and that the sky is the appropriate basis from which Ahuramazda can be abstracted. Particularly the parallelism between the two groups, so ran the argument, speaks against an interpretation of Varuṇa as moon god because then we must be able to see an ancient moon god in Ahuramazda also and this is improbable. This reasoning suffers from one flaw, namely that it starts with the assumption that Ahuramazda and the Ahura who is connected with Mithra are one and the same. This assumption is illusory.[18] Ahura is, as we know, not only the designation of the highest god of Iran but also of a yazata like Apām napå̊, further of the Amešaspəntas and means 'lord' in general.[19] Spiegel has quite rightly recognized the error in the current assumption that the Ahura here must be the same as Ahuramazda.[20] But he missed the chance of comprehending the Iranian god-pair because of his attempt to interpret Ahura as Apām napå̊[21] This equation is completely ruled out because it does not accord with the fact that the association between Varuṇa and Mitra is indeed so ancient and so firmly established that we cannot ascribe a completely new meaning to Ahura; Apām napå̊ who certainly corresponds to the Vedic Apāṃ napāt would be such a new meaning.[22] We can leave Ahuramazda out of the question and still maintain the equation Mithra-Ahura = Mitra-Varuṇa.

We know that Varuṇa is an *ásura*, that he and Mitra are called in I.151.4 *asura* (*asurā* in the Pada text), in VII.36.2 *ásurā*, in 65.2 *devā́nām ásurā*, in VIII.25.4 *devā́v ásurā* and that the epithet *asuryā* is common to them in V.66.2; VII.65.1; 66. 2; VIII.25.3.[23] We cannot do better than to equate these two Asuras with the Iranian Ahura-Mithra. But Ahura is not the same as Ahuramazda; on the contrary, in these few pairs like Ahura-Mithra or Mithra-Ahura the Avesta has preserved a reminiscence of the association between Mitra and Varuṇa which is so familiar to the Veda. The name Varuṇa is either a new accretion in Indian mythology or was lost in the Iranian one. Likewise the Ahura who occurs in this dual has become alien to Iranian mythology except in these few relics. He is on the same level as *nå̊ŋhaithya* or *andra* who are also in the process of fading out. It is not necessary and, in view of the evolution which proceeded in contrary directions in India and Iran, not even probable that the mighty god of India should correspond to an identical being in Iran who is endowed with an equally absolute power. Thus we can remove one obstacle which the Avesta could place in the way of interpreting Varuṇa as some god other than the sky. That Varuṇa as well as Ahuramazda greatly influence the material and moral world is not important here. It is a superficial congruence to which I do not attach any special significance as Oldenberg does (ZDMG, L, p. 48).

If *ahura* in the combination *ahura-mithra* is not necessarily identical with Ahuramazda, then we have full freedom of decision regarding all other interpretations even when they do not see the sky in Varuṇa.

3. Varuṇa and the Waters

Those who interpret Vedic gods on the basis of classical Sanskrit would maintain that Varuṇa is the god of the ocean in classical Sanskrit and claim the meaning for the Vedic period as well. In Vol. I, p. 13, I have pointed out that this view is not compatible with the more numerous attributes of Varuṇa in the ṚV, either in general or with reference to specific traits that are attributed to him. In the ṚV he is endowed with qualities which are not suitable for the ocean even according to Indian concept,[24] and it is precisely these that are discarded later on.[25] From this we may conclude that originally the ocean was not at all the domain of Varuṇa or at least not the only one and that only in course of evolution this trait has won the upper hand to such an extent that the other traits were completely suppressed. In deciding the question it would be necessary to examine the Ṛgvedic concepts about the significance of the ocean and to ask in the end whether the veneration shown to the ocean in the ṚV is so great that an evolution of its presiding deity into the lord of Dharma, into the avenger of sin, into the King and Samrāj, could be a natural consequence of the cult.

a. Samudra in the ṚV[26]

It is commonly held that the Vedic Indians did not know the ocean. We cannot prove that the Vedic tribes reached up to the ocean at that time or were settled on its coast: this much of the prevailing belief could be correct. This belief rests considerably on the negative evidence of the ṚV. But it does not follow from this that the land-locked tribes of the Vedic period were not familiar with the ocean. The tidings of the mighty reservoir of water reach far through commerce and martial expeditions, through travellers and story-tellers and might have reached the inhabitants of Kabul and Swat also. An examination of all the Ṛgvedic passages containing the word *samudrá* would show that in a great number of cases *samudrá* denotes, without doubt, the ocean. There is absolutely no reason to think of any other 'confluence' of waters than the ocean. On the other hand, the ṚV contains so little positive information about the ocean or about its nature and so few traces of a cult that, in spite of the frequency of the mention of the ocean, the Vedic Indians could not have been seafarers in general, nor even a tribe settled on the sea-coast. From the contents of the *Beowulf* one can visualize the difference between the poetry of a seafaring people and that of others. The ṚV contains the following notions about the ocean:

1. Often mention is made—at times directly and at others as comparison—of rivers that flow into the ocean.[27]

2. Or it is Indra who dispatches the streams, the waters, to the ocean. 1.32.2; 130.5; II.19.3; III.33.2 (Vipāś and Śutudrī); VI.17.12; 30.4; VIII.3.10; 6.13 etc.

3. Samudra is the opposite of land. I.163.1: *yád ákrandaḥ ...jắyamāna udyán samudrắd utá vā púrīṣāt.*[28]

4. In one passage the eastern and the western oceans are mentioned. X.136.5: *ubhaú samudrắv ā kṣeti yáś ca pū́rva utắparaḥ.*[29]

5. From this passage other verses should be distinguished which speak of a 'higher' and a 'lower' ocean. Just as our hymns speak of an Agni *paramé sadhásthe* and of another *ávare sadhásthe* (see Vol. I, p. 79) and thus denote the celestial and the terrestrial Agni respectively so do the 'higher' and 'lower' oceans denote the ocean of heaven and that of the earth.

VII.6.7: *ā́ devó dade budhnyā̀ vásūni*
vaiśvānará úditā sū́ryasya |
ā́ samudrā́d ávarād ā́ párasmād
ā́gnír dade divá ā́ pṛthivyā́ḥ ||

X.98.5: *sá úttarasmād ádharaṃ samudrám*
apó divyā́ asṛjad varṣyā̀ abhí |[30]

12: *asmā́t samudrā́d bṛható divó naḥ*
apā́ṃ bhūmā́nam úpa naḥ sṛjehá |[31]

6. Like heaven or earth, the ocean contains concealed treasures. I.47.6: *rayíṃ samudrā́d utá vā divás páry asmé dhattam [aśvinā]*; VII.6.7; IX.97.44.[32] It is immaterial if these verses refer only to pearls and other precious things of the ocean. But from other verses it becomes quite obvious that the poets have heard of the daring sailors who navigated the ocean for the sake of fame and wealth.

I.48.3: *[ráthā] yé asyā [uṣáso] ācáraṇeṣu dadhriré*
samudré ná śravasyávaḥ ||[33]

56.2: *táṃ gūrtáyo nemanníṣaḥ párīṇasaḥ*
samudrā́ṃ ná saṃcáraṇe saniṣyávaḥ |[34]

IV.55.6: *samudrā́ṃ na saṃcáraṇe saniṣyávaḥ*
gharmásvaraso nadyò ápa vran ||

The story of Bhujyu which occurs frequently with many variations is a well known one. Bhujyu had been abandoned by his evil companions and was rescued by the Aśvins from the midst of the ocean.[35] The 'hundred-oared' ship which he boarded (I.116.5) anticipates merchant shipping. Even though we need not exactly take the size of the ship or the number of its oars literally, we need have no hesitation in seeing a reminiscence of a see-going vessel here;[36] for in the same story the Samudra is called *anārambhaṇá*, *anāsthāná*, *agrabhaṇá*, i.e. doubtless an ocean. "Tugra's son invoked you, O Aśvins, as he had crossed the impassable ocean" (I.117.15).[37] Samudra has the epithet *arṇavá* in I.19.7; X.58.5; 190.1,2. In VII.33.8 the epithet *mahimán gabhīrá* is treated as a distinctive characteristic of Samudra just as *jyotíḥ* is regarded as that of Sūryā and *prajavá* of Vāta in the same verse. Mention is made of *samudrásya dhánvan*, the watery waste, in I.116.4,[38] and of *samudrásya viṣṭáp*, "the height of the ocean" or 'surface' in VIII.34.13; 97.5; IX. 107.14. The ocean spreads out, *prathate,* VIII.3.4;[39] it 'swells,' *pinvate,* VIII.12.5.[40] In the story of Bhujyu we can see an ancient seafarer legend which was spread by tribes that were settled on the sea-coast and navigated the oceans. It is significant that the deities of this sole legend of the ṚV that is connected with the ocean are the Aśvins. When we recall that the Dioscuri are in a like manner the protectors of the sailors, then the question whether this group of the Indo-Europeans did not know the ocean[41] can certainly not be dismissed out of hand. The connection between the Aśvins and Sūrya, the relation of the Dioscuri with Helena and the association of the Aśvins as well as of the Dioscuri with the ocean suggest a common background. The rest of the passages which connect the Aśvins with the ocean have little importance.[42] The same is true of the verses which associate other gods with Samudra. For instance, it is said of Indra that he crosses the ocean, that the oceans and mountains cannot encompass his chariot, or he is invoked to come to the singer "from heaven, earth, ocean, land"[43] and so on.

The associations of the Maruts[44] with Samudra or those of Varuṇa yield nothing further. They do not justify the interpretation of Varuṇa as an original god of the ocean.[45] When

I.161.14 states that Varuṇa moves through the waters and oceans, or if one so wishes, "through the waters of the ocean,[46] this can equally mean the ocean of the atmosphere,[47] or we can refer to IV.58.1; VII.55.7; VIII.100.9; X.72.7 and other verses which show that other gods also can be explained in the same way as Varuṇa. What is significant, and with this I come to the purpose of this investigation, is that in the ṚV, Samudra is elevated to the status of a god only quite by chance and that too without attaining any prominent traits. I have noted only few verses where Samudra is invoked (always in conjunction with a series of other gods) and that too without any specia' emphasis.

VI.50.14: *utá nó 'hir budhnyàḥ śṛṇotu*
ajá ékapāt pṛthivī́ samudráḥ /
víśve dévāḥ...
VII.35.13: *śáṃ no ajá ékapād devó astu*
śáṃ nó 'hir budhnyàḥ śáṃ samudráḥ /[48]
VIII.12.2: *yénā dáśagvam ádhrigum...* /
yénā samudrám ā́vithā tám īmahe //
X.66.11: *samudráḥ síndhū rájo antárikṣam*
ajá ékapāt tanayitnúr arṇaváḥ /[49]

We see that the concept of a personal Samudra can hardly be noticed even in its beginnings.

b. Samudra in the Ritual

We come to the same conclusion by examining the ritual literature also. Samudra's worship is mentioned so rarely there that one cannot speak at all of Samudra's position in the cult. I have noticed the following passages: TS IV.6.2.: *samudrāya vayunāya sindhūnāṃ pataye namaḥ / nadīnāṃ sarvāsāṃ pitre juhutā viśvakarmaṇe*; V.7.16: *samudram udareṇa*; TĀr IV.9.1: *samudrāya tvā vātāya svāhā, salilāya tvā* etc.; MS IV.9.8. (128.6); ĀśvGS II.4.14; III.4.1; ŚGS IV.14.2; PGS I.5.10; 16.6; III.3.6; MGS I.13.15; II.8.6; JUBr (ed. Oertel) I.8.7. Most of these are mere enumerations without any special significance.[50] According to ŚSS IV.8.6 the Brahman should fix his thoughts on Ākāśa or Samudra while invoking Ilā and whisper his formula. According to *Kauśika Sūtra* LXXIV.6 Samudra receives a bali along with Dhanvantari, Oṣadhi and others during the Baliharaṇa. The ocean was not an element familiar to the classical period. Manu III.58 places the seafarer, *samudrayāyin*, on the same level as the incendiary, poisoner, pimp, Soma-seller, oil-seller and perjurer.[51] Occasionally the ocean is also personified without however becoming, as far as I can see, an object of worship.[52] The *Rāmāyaṇa*[53] describes how Sāgara emerged from the ocean like the sun from the Mount Udaya. He was surrounded by fire-spitting[54] snakes and resembled a smooth vaiḍūrya. Precious stones were set in his robe, his eyes resembled lotus petals, on his head he wore a splendid wreath made of flowers of all kinds. His was adorned with pure sterling gold, with magnificent ornaments of pearls that originated in him, decorated like the Himālaya with various metals. Stirred by the winds from the dark clouds, his mass of waves tossed to and fro. Gaṅgā, Sindhu and other streams accompanied him, and thus he approached Rāma. If we compare this image, or the description in MBh I.21 or that of the *Jalanidhināthа* by Kālidāsa[55] with the traits of character attributed to Varuṇa in the Veda or in the ritual,[56] we will not find any similarity. The worship of Samudra is unknown to the modern period as it was to the ritual. We find sacred streams, ponds, lakes, but no cult of the ocean. It is true that a special "god of water" is known but, according to Crooke,[57] he is of Muslim origin and "a good instance of a fact ... that Hindus are always ready to annex the deities and beliefs of other races."

One might object to this, saying that a special personification of the ocean was no more necessary because this position was already assigned to Varuṇa. But when we review the information of the ritual which must offer a positive basis, it becomes evident that here also there is absolutely no occasion to interpret Varuṇa as the ocean.[58] To be sure, in the later period fish is regarded as the attribute of the ocean but, as far as I can see, not so in the ritual. During the Varuṇapraghāsa a ram made of dough is offered to the ocean,[59] cattle, preferably black ones, are offered on various occasions but no marine products.[60] All this induces us to exercise great caution with reference to the ṚV.

Its statements, of course, suggest that Varuṇa is distantly associated with the ocean, but never so exclusively or predominantly that we can look for the god of the ocean in him. In the ṚV, Varuṇa is never called *samudrásya páti* or *rấjan*. It is only in the Brāhmaṇa literature that we come across isolated statements like *samudre hy antar varuṇaḥ* (TS VI.6.3.4), *samudro vai varuṇaḥ* (MS IV.7.8). Elsewhere when he is drawn into an association with the ocean,[61] the association is no closer than that of Indra or of the Maruts with the ocean as the verses cited on p. 11 show. His connection with the streams is closer than that with the ocean. However, of all the verses that contain such notions,[62] only one verse from book VIII is of some importance for the interpretation of Varuṇa as the god of the ocean.

VIII.69.12: *sudevó asi varuṇa yásya te saptá síndhavaḥ |*
anukṣáranti kākúdaṃ sūrmyàṃ suṣirám iva ||

When we consider this verse by itself, it looks as though the hypothesis is proved,[63] but when we take the Vedic phraseology into account the verse loses its importance. VIII.69.12 does not differ from VII.87.5; IX,73.8 which we have discussed above: the god who carries three heavens and three earths within himself holds also their streams within him and these streams follow his ordinances.[64] When VIII.69.12 states that the streams flow into Varuṇa's throat as they do in a pipe, I do not see in this any statement of mythological significance but only a variation of the idea expressed in VII.87.5 etc.[65] Against this, one may point to Varuṇa's connection with the stationary waters, e.g., TS VI.4.2.3: *varuṇagṛhītā vai sthāvarāḥ*; ŚBr IV.4.5.10; MS IV.8.5 (112.4 ff.),[66] and the passages which speak in general terms of Varuṇa and the waters like "Varuṇa is in the waters," "his golden mansion is erected in the waters."[67] These waters are not necessarily those of the ocean; as we have seen, Indian thought is familiar with an atmospheric ocean also. It is probable that the waters refer to this. For, the statements of the Brāhmaṇas which could be understood in one sense as well as in the other and which stand midway between the ṚV and the later period should be elucidated here in the light of the concepts of the *preceding* period. In the preceding period it is said that Varuṇa creates the streams (ṚV II.28.4), carves the path for the Sindhu (X.75.2), directs the rivers to the ocean (VII. 87.1) and dwells at the source of the rivers.[68] This can apply only to a god who is not yet exclusively the god of the ocean but a lord of the waters in general, an *apâm ádhipati* (AV V.24.4). We should also keep in mind that in the earliest period Varuṇa is not merely the ruler of the flowing and stationary waters but the lord of heaven as well. He empties the cask "with its opening downward" over heaven, earth and atmosphere; he moistens the sky and earth;[69] along with Mitra, he is the lord of rain. Every explanation that ignores precisely these statements of the oldest texts must be regarded as inadequate.[70] The old hypothesis of Varuṇa as the sky god does, at all events, greater justice to these statements than is the hypothesis of Varuṇa as the god of the ocean.

Moreover, Varuṇa's designation as god of death speaks against the possibility that the conception of Varuṇa as the god of the ocean could be the original one. Varuṇa and Yama appear together in X.14.7; 97.16. During the Vedic period people may have believed that the abode of the dead is situated in heaven or beneath the earth. The dead person who in X.14.7 starts out on the old pathways of his ancestors and "would see the two kings, Yama and god Varuṇa, who enjoy the Svadhā"[71] goes certainly not into the ocean nor into the hell-fire, which the later period placed in the ocean but which is unknown to the entire Veda.

Furthermore, if Varuṇa was already the god of the ocean in the ṚV, we cannot explain the simile *drapsó ná śvetáḥ* (VII.87.6) or the expression *nâkam âruhat* (VIII. 41.8).[72]

An explanation of Varuṇa would do justice to all the claims only when it can account for all the traits that have attained their full development in Varuṇa and seek to explain the transition from one trait to the other. So far we have seen that there are serious misgivings against connecting Varuṇa with the sky or with the ocean. Let us now examine his position in the cult.

4. Varuṇa in the Ritual

Here Varuṇa's character contains specific features. He is

almost always contrasted with Mitra and this contrast is illustrated in manifold ways. But these comparisons are of superficial value only.[73] However, there is one that deserves our attention: namely, the association of Mitra-Varuṇa with day and night, for this association not only occurs again and again with a special regularity but is also supported by the statements of the ritual. Hence the notion of looking here for an old trait of character of the two gods cannot be dismissed so easily as has been done. Above all, here belongs the black colour of the animals assigned to Varuṇa in the cult.[74] On the occasion of a sacrifice which a prince performs in order to be reinstalled in his kingdom, one takes white and black corns of rice; the black corns are employed in making a caru for Varuṇa and the white ones in making a caru for the Ādityas.[75] Colour has a specific meaning throughout in mythology.[76] In Indian mythology black is the colour of night,[77] of Nirṛti,[78] of the Manes and of rain.[79] There is no doubt as to what aspect of Varuṇa is indicated by the black colour. This becomes obvious from the contrast with Mitra for whom white animals are sacrificed[80]— a contrast that is emphasized throughout in the Brāhmaṇas. Just as Mitra-Varuṇa are contrasted in TS II.1.9.2,3 and elsewhere so are Sūryācandramasau contrasted in TBr II.8.9 and receive a white and a black animal respectively; there should be only one sacrificial post for these two.[81] Accordingly Varuṇa is regarded as a sinister god; his form is terrible: *sa yad agnir ghorasaṃsparśas tad asya vāruṇaṃ rūpam / taṃ yad ghorasaṃsparśaṃ santaṃ mitrakṛtyevopāsate tad asya maitraṃ rūpam* (ABr III.4.6). During the Agniṣṭoma when a person returns from the sacrificial bath which releases him from Varuṇa's fetters, he should not look back, *varuṇasyāntarhityai*.[82] In the sacrifices for the Manes, one should, after invoking the Manes, turn away for a while when these are supposed to be absent.[83] During the Traiyambaka sacrifice, one returns without looking back from the tree stump to which baskets are hung which are meant as Rudra's "food for the journey."[84] Thus in the ritual Varuṇa is placed almost on the same level with the Manes and Rudra.[85] In the legend of Śunaḥśepa the memory of human sacrifice is still vivid, and it is precisely Varuṇa who demands it. Hariścandra is set free from the fetters of Varuṇa only when Śunaḥśepa recites verses addressed to Uṣas. The oft-mentioned fetters of Varuṇa denote not only dropsy; diseases of all kinds and even death visit upon him who incurs Varuṇa's wrath.[86] *varuṇo vā etaṃ gṛhṇāti yaṃ vyemānaṃ yakṣmo gṛhṇāti*, says the Kāṭhaka.[87] An Abhiśasyamāna must offer a caru for Varuṇa apart from a puroḍāśa for Vaiśvānara: *apa pāpaṃ varṇaṃ hate, vāruṇenaivainaṃ varuṇapāśān muñcati*.[88] Varuṇa seizes the sacrifice of those who let the sun rise before they have removed the sacrificial fire.[89] According to YV,[90] whatever is 'ill-offered' in a sacrifice belongs to him. Although he is often referred to, Varuṇa as a rule never stands at the centre of the cult, the only exception being the Varuṇapraghāsāḥ.[91] It is true that in the Soma sacrifice a Soma cup is dedicated to him in conjunction with Mitra; however, he does not play any great role and appears primarily as god of fetters, of wrath, of darkness. In this respect, the rites of the bath at the conclusion of a sacrifice are so characteristical that I wish to give below the rules of at least one Sūtra.

The Sacrificial Bath

ĀpŚS XIII.19.1: "He lets the rites of the concluding bath take place.

2: "He prepares the bundle of Veda, encloses the fires [with grass] and begins the rite with the washing of his hands. Arrangement of the vessels according to the need.

3: "At the time when the havis is taken out, he takes out havis for an Ekakapāla-Puroḍāśa for Varuṇa.

4: "He prepares the ājyas that have been taken four times and also the Varuṇa-Puroḍāśa and deposits them [silently] on the northern aṃśa...

7: "With the verse (ṚV I.24.14) 'we deprecate your anger, O Varuṇa, with obeisances, with sacrifices and with the offerings of the havis...,' the sacrificer throws the black skin away into the pit.

8: "Or he should consecrate himself with it, or put it on, or get a pouch made for the ladle out of it or use it [as the base] for husking the havis.

9: "Some [authorities] say that after leaving the bath he should give it to his son or to a brahmacārin.

20.1: "When he wishes to enter into the bath, he should make offerings with the three mantras: 'you bestow life, O Agni, enjoying the sacrificial offerings, O Bath, you who wash...,' and 'salutations to Rudra...'

2: "Reciting the verse (ṚV I.24.8) 'King Varuṇa made a long path for the sun...,' they go there from the vedi or from the pit.

3: " 'O Prastotṛ, sing the Sāman.'

4: "Accompanied by their wives, all sing in chorus the concluding passage of the Sāman thrice. For the second time at half the distance. Having reached the bath, for the third time.

6: "[As in the Varuṇapraghāsāḥ, the rites are repeated] from [Sūtra VIII.7.18] 'the entering of the bath from all directions is mentioned' up to the rite of the puroḍāśa.

7: In the same manner as in the Niṣkāsa (ĀpŚS VIII.7.14) he goes first with the Varuṇa-Puroḍāśa and offers two Anuyājas, having first excluded those meant for barhis.[92]

12: "With the verse 'I throw you away into the ocean,' he throws all the vessels anointed with Soma into the bath.

13: "With the words 'Varuṇa's fetters are loosened,' the sacrificer unties his girdle and his wife the band [around her waist].

14: "Then he throws the girdle, the band, the two garments, the net and the black skin [provided it has not already been thrown into the pit] into the bath."

When the ablutions are completed, the Unnetṛ leads the bathers out of the water. They put on new clothes; the sacrificer puts on the Soma-band and his wife the Soma-cloth. The ĀpŚS describes the next stage thus:

XIII.22.5: "With the formula 'from the darkness we look upward to the higher light,' they worship the sun; with 'Varuṇa's fetter is warded off' they push back the water on the bank [with their feet].[93] Without looking back they return, led by the Unnetṛ. They carry fire-wood in their hands[94] and recite the Mahīyā verse: 'we have drunk Soma and become immortal; we have attained light and discovered the gods. Now what harm can the malice, the wickedness of men, do to us, O Immortal.'[95] This is followed by a formula of atonement,[96] which concludes with these words: 'may we be free from guilt (or debt) in this, free from guilt (or debt) in the other, and free from guilt (or debt) in the third world. May we, free from guilt (or debt), enter all the paths of the gods and the Manes.' "

We have seen earlier that black animals are dedicated to Varuṇa and white ones to Mitra. Now one cannot fail to see that also the fetters of Varuṇa, from which one is released, are conceived as the opposite of *jyotiḥ*, of light and immortality, and that the release from the fetters is akin to the liberation from *tamas*.[97] When we recall that the annual Agniṣṭoma can be regarded as the spring sacrifice, then it would appear that the antithesis in which Varuṇa's fetters are contrasted here with *suvar* and *jyotiḥ* rests on a natural cause.[98]

The Avabhṛtha ceremony is followed by the Udayanīyā, the concluding rite. It consists of sacrificing a *go vaśā anūbandhyā* (ĀpŚS XIII.23.6) for Mitra-Varuṇa. On this occasion the ceremony of the Nirūḍhapaśu is observed. Some teachers of ritual enjoin that in the place of one single cow, three such may be sacrificed: a double-coloured one for Mitra-Varuṇa, a multicoloured one for the Viśve Devāḥ and a red one for Bṛhaspati.[99]

Mitra-Varuṇa are often associated with cattle, not only in the ritual literature[100] but in the ṚV[101] as well. Interesting for us is the fact that at least according to Indian interpretation this has to do with the sacrifice of a barren cow. The commentary on the ĀpŚS explains *vaśā* as *vandhyā*,[102] and ŚBr IV.5.1.9 states: *atha yadā na kaścana rasaḥ paryaśiṣyate tata eṣā maitrāvaruṇī vaśā samabhavat tasmād eṣā na prajāyate*. The texts expound this custom purely from the ritual point of view; they state that whatever is well-offered in sacrifice belongs to Mitra and whatever is ill-offered to Varuṇa.[103] However, this interpretation demonstrates, I think, merely that the ritualists did not know any more what to do with this custom of concluding the spring sacrifice with the offering of a barren cow for Mitra-Varuṇa. Either the choice of such an animal (assuming always that the explanation of the word *vaśā* by the ŚBr and the commentaries is correct)[104] is the first step in eliminating the cow sacrifice inasmuch as a barren cow is substituted for an ordinary one, or this custom is appended to the spring festival that celebrates the end of winter as a reminiscence of the just-concluded winter. In a tropical climate a barren cow is not quite appropriate for a spring sacrifice; it would be a symbol rather of winter, of the barren period, and would well accord with the antithesis between *tamas* and *jyotiḥ* or *svar*, an antithesis that is expressed so clearly at the conclusion of the Agniṣṭoma.

The concluding bath occurs in every Soma sacrifice; of special interest for us is the one at the end of the Aśvamedha, the grand sacrifice performed with special festivities by the king in order to enlarge his kingdom. On this occasion offerings are made "on the head of a man." Several texts see in this man the representative of Varuṇa and attribute to him the physical features of Varuṇa. Here we have the rare possibility of reconstructing the physical features of a Vedic god from the description in the ritual literature.[105] TBr III.9.3.15: *varuṇo vai jumbakaḥ/ antata eva varuṇam avayajate/ khalater viklidhasya śuklasya piṅgākṣasya mūrdhañ juhoti/ etad vai varuṇasya rūpam/ rūpeṇaiva varuṇam avayajate*. Almost the same is stated in ŚBr XIII.3.6.5; TĀr I.2.3. That is to say, Varuṇa is conceived in the form of a bald-headed, leprous, yellow-eyed man;[106] various texts add one trait or the other to this portrait;[107] Thus the description of these physical features is also consistent with the awe which Varuṇa inspires.[108] To complete the picture, we should mention the designation *apsu magna* (KŚS) also, for this man receives the offerings on his head while standing in water.[109]

In all these sources we find the designation *piṅgākṣa*, *piṅgala* or *piṅga*. This attribute of Varuṇa (or of his likeness who is sacrificed to him) is in consonance with the adjective *aruṇa*, attributed to him in TĀr 1.32.2,[110] and also with *hiraṇyaśṛṅga* of the same text.[111] Elsewhere a *khalati* is sacrificed to Dyaus, a *haryakṣa* to Sūrya, a *mirmira* to the moon, a *kilāsa* (leper) to the Nakṣatras, a *śukla piṅgala* to the day and a *kṛṣṇa piṅgala* to the night.[112]

We have seen above that at the end of the spring sacrifice the sacrificer throws his girdle into the water and that all the people return from the water without looking back. The season that is ascertained here during which Varuṇa's fetters are shaken off is not identical with that which is prescribed for the Varuṇapraghāsa ceremony, a sacrifice where Varuṇa alone is the focus of all the rites.[113] Of course, Varuṇa appears as a punishing and avenging god in the Varuṇapraghāsa as well; guilt and confession play a role here and the sacrifice is performed for the release from Varuṇa's fetters. MS I. 10.10 (150.10) states: *yad varuṇapraghāsair yajeta sarvasyāṁhaso 'veṣṭyai.* The ŚBr also contains a similar statement.[114] The concluding bath is performed partly with the same mantras as in the Soma sacrifice.[115] But the season prescribed for this sacrifice differs substantially. According to the ĀśvŚS it is the "fifth full moon" on which the sacrifice falls. Other Sūtras which make more precise statements mention Āṣāḍha or Śrāvaṇa, i.e., the beginning of the rainy season. The statement is so unambiguous and the sacrifice is so firmly incorporated into the framework of the Cāturmāsya ceremonies that any doubt about the time of the sacrifice does not seem to be warranted. This is corroborated by certain other injunctions like, for instance, the employment during the Praghāsas of the Karīra fruits which indicate the rainy season, or the use of wood from flowering trees as fire wood and the employment of fresh twigs as barhis during the Vaiśvadevacāturmāsya that takes place four months earlier. Accordingly, Varuṇa as the god of water might have been assigned this position in the Varuṇapraghāsa and thus would correspond to the conception of the later period which would be quite possible. Yet doubts as to the antiquity of this position are not completely ruled out. For, yava is the prescribed sacrificial material here and in justification of this MS I.10.12 (Kāṭhaka 36.6) remarks thus: *yad vai prajā varuṇo gṛhṇāti śamyaṃ caiva yavaṃ cāpi na gṛhṇāti, hemanto hi varuṇo, yā evāvaruṇagṛhītau tābhyām evainā varuṇān muñcati/varuṇo vai yavo varuṇadevatyaḥ/svenaivainā bhāgadh~yena varuṇān muñcaty anṛtād vai tāḥ prajā varuṇo 'gṛhṇāt/yad ~tā anṛtapaśū anṛtād evainā varuṇān muñcataḥ*...The identification of Varuṇa with winter as given here (*hemantaḥ śītapracuratvena duḥkhatvāt ghoraḥ,* commentai. on the VS) does not occur, as far as I know, anywhere else and it is not necessary either. Indra is the lord of summer but not the summer itself, summer is called his season. Similarly, winter is the domain of the moon—he reaches the culmination in winter—but not the same as the moon. Elsewhere the seasons are distributed differently. For instance, autumn is assigned to Mitra-Varuṇa.[116] Hence, we can treat the isolated statement of the MS and

Kāṭhaka as an occasional fancy of the Yājñikas. But an argument in its favour is the employment of yava which is used even otherwise in sacrifices for Varuṇa.[117] In the rites for the first-born, offerings are made with yava in spring and with rice in autumn.[118] Thus yava is a cereal that ripens in winter. It is probable that the Varuṇapraghāsa, performed for the release from the fetters of Varuṇa, served at first the same purpose as the concluding rites of the Agniṣṭoma, namely, the release from Varuṇa's fetters at the end of winter, before it attained a secure position within the cycle of the Cāturmāsyas at the commencement of the rains.[119] This viewpoint requires a more thorough examination, particularly with regard to the other customs connected with this ceremony, and with regard to the pair of rams designated as *anṛtapaśū*,[120] before it could be treated as anything more than a mere hypothesis.

Thus Varuṇa appears throughout as a sinister god,[121] who shackles men, to whom black animals are assigned, while he himself is represented as a bald-headed yellow-eyed man. Varuṇa is an avenger of sin and protector of law. "When the law is violated Varuṇa seizes," declares TBr I.7.2.6; the titles *dharmapati* and *satyadharman* are attributed to him.[122] Of all the gods of the Vedic pantheon, Varuṇa is closest to Yama who bears the designation *dharmarāj* or *dharmarāja* in the later period.[123] Both are rulers in the realm of death. It is stated as early as in ṚV X.14.7 that the dead person enters the presence of Yama and Varuṇa; both wield the 'staff';[124] both carry in their hands the noose[125] which is the attribute of the night, of the *druh*, of death.[126]

5. Traces of the Varuṇa of the Ritual in the ṚV

Once we have gained an insight into the concept of Varuṇa of the ritual, it will not be difficult to find the traces of the same conception in the ṚV itself. In this context the most important of all the passages is the oft-cited verse of the funeral hymn (X. 14.7), which mentions Varuṇa along with Yama. In X.84.7 *váruṇaś ca manyúḥ* occur side by side. Averting Varuṇa's anger and the expiation of sins play a great role in the hymns to him.[127] He alone of all the gods possesses *dhūrtí* (I.128.7), and thus he is on the same level as the *árarivāṃs* or *árāvan mártya* whose *dhūrtí* is be to feared. Of the nine verses in which *héḍa* or *hé̢das* occurs alone,[128] four speak of Varuṇa's anger. Bergaigne has already noted that Varuṇa's character appears to be "quasi demoniacal,"[129] that there are certain points of contact between Varuṇa and Vṛtra,[130] but "far from being a pure demon," the former is rather the most august of all gods.[131] However, Vṛtra and Varuṇa belong to quite different sets of myths, which should be clearly distinguished.[132] Varuṇa-Mitra stand on one side and Vṛtra-Indra on the other. Mitra and Indra are mythological synonyms although there is a difference in the evolution of their concepts. But Vṛtra and Varuṇa should be held apart both intrinsically and historically, even though the etymon of the two words might in fact be the same and even though a certain degree of relationship, as will be seen later on, can be assumed between the two. When we lay stress on the congruence between the ṚV and the conception of the ritual, this does not imply that the other statements of the ṚV are to be underestimated. It only means that Varuṇa's position in the other statements of the ṚV as the creator of the All and his nature that has become somewhat more benevolent due to the frequent association with Mitra should not induce us to attach little weight to the conclusions which follow from the significant agreement among all the ritual texts in word and rite. The independent tradition of the ritual texts becomes manifest here once again. *No explanation of Varuṇa should be considered adequate which does not do justice to the ṚV, to the ritual and to classical Sanskrit, and which does not explain the connection between the three conceptions* that emanate like radii from a centre which is hidden to us; these conceptions belong to different periods. This is the reason why I do not think that J. J. Meyer—who gladdened me by concurring with the interpretation of Varuṇa as the moon—was right in stating that "the notion of Varuṇa as the god of night is certainly a more original one,"[133] for, starting from this notion, we cannot account for the transition to the other forms of manifestation, to his reign over the ocean, to his identity with Soma; nor can we explain verses like VII.87.6 (*áva síndhuṃ váruṇo dyaúr iva sthād drapsó ná śvetó mṛgás*...) and others.

6. Further Data from the Ritual; Soma and Varuṇa

Our ritual texts take us still a step further. I pass over the diverse kinds of statements which present Varuṇa in some association or other with the 'horse.' Such statements also occur in the ṚV as well as in the later literature.[134] However, there is one point which seems to be quite significant. The notion that Varuṇa could be a designation of the moon suggested itself to me at first through some verses of book IX. In these verses the name of Varuṇa stands for that of Soma, thus suggesting that the poets must have treated the two words as synonyms.[135] Let us take I. 91. 3 [136] first. The verse is addressed to Soma; he is compared with Mitra and Aryaman but identified with Varuṇa. By itself the verse proves nothing, for one can see here an indirect simile in spite of the missing *na* or *iva* in pāda *a*; but that will not do in IX. 95. 4.[137] In this Pavamāna hymn, *váruṇa* is clearly another designation for Soma and is surrounded by the whole terminology which usually characterizes the Soma hymns. The very 'Trita' who carries Varuṇa in the ocean is the mythical sacrificer who presses the Soma; he is frequently mentioned thus in this context.[138] There is no reason to treat these two words, i.e., Varuṇa and Soma, as anything but synonyms here. To this can be added the obviously mystic hymn IX.73 (vv. 3, 9); it refers to Soma who approaches as Varuṇa in the ritual and should be understood in this sense; further VIII.41.8 where Varuṇa is styled *samudró apīcyàḥ*,[139] an expression employed for the nectar-containing moon which makes sense as we have shown in Vol. I, p. 214 ff.;[140] furthermore, other solitary and insignificant points of contact which can serve as illustrations only, e.g., the Kavi-hood emphasized in the case of Varuṇa and Soma,[141] also some verses the content of which is quite in agreement but which prove little by themselves.[142] Bergaigne has already laid stress on the relationship between Varuṇa and Soma but he had been obviously under the misconception that it was the Soma-Sun.[143] As a matter of fact, we cannot ignore the evidence of IX. 95. 4 that the two words, Varuṇa and Soma, are occasionally synonyms. But it must be kept in mind that this linguistic usage occurs but rarely and was not generally very popular. The reason for this is the special individuality connected with the name Soma: just as the concept of the god of death inheres in Yama (=Candramas) and the Kavi-hood and Brahman-hood predominantly in Bṛhaspati (=Candramas), so does the concept of the drink of the gods inhere chiefly in Soma (=Candramas). This concept did not develop in the case of Varuṇa. In his case the emphasis is not on the nectar but on the ominous and avenging god who is the opposite of Mitra, the *priyátama nṛṇā́m,*[144] and who is conceived on the model of a king who is *dhṛtavrata* and *dharmapati* and punishes those who transgress the law. But this is not to suggest that the sphere of influence of one name does not overlap with that of the other; thus Varuṇa, Soma and Bṛhaspati are lords of wisdom; Varuṇa and Soma are lords of the streams, of the waters. In other respects, however, the Veda maintains a clear distinction between Varuṇa and Soma.[145] One may be inclined to think that the occasional designation of the pressed Soma as Varuṇa is a mere poetic fancy and, to support this, may refer to IX. 77. 5, which I have rejected above, and which refers to Soma as Varuṇa in one pāda and as Mitra in another. But my view is corroborated by the ritual the evidence of which is underestimated by Geiger.[146] It is precisely in the ritual that we find Soma represented as Varuṇa directly, or as Vāruṇa, at the beginning of the Agniṣṭoma. The afore-mentioned identification might have originated from such a source. To dismiss this identification as poetic fancy would be, of course, convenient but not objective.[147]

The ĀpŚS has the following on the rites to be observed after the conclusion of the buying of the Soma.[148]

ĀpŚS X. 27. 9: "Reciting the mantra, 'I rose up with life' etc., the sacrificer rises up with the 'King' [Soma] and approaches the cart with the words, 'go along the wide atmosphere.'

10: " 'You are Aditi's seat,' with this mantra the Adhvaryu spreads inside the cart a black skin with its neck to the east and the hair upwards and deposits the King upon it with the words, 'be seated on Aditi's seat,' wraps him in a cloth while saying, '[Varuṇa] has spread the atmosphere in the trees' and ties a black skin in the front [at the door] with its neck upwards and the inner side to the outside, reciting thereby the verse addressed to the sun, 'they lead Jātavedas upwards.'

X. 28. 1: "Now he touches the ends of the yoke as is done in the sacrifice to the new and full moon, lifts the cart up with the mantra, 'you belong to Varuṇa,' props it with the words, 'may Varuṇa prop you,' fixes the yoke-pin with 'you are the prop of Varuṇa,'[149] drives the draught animals towards [the cart] with the words, 'advance, you red ones who bear the yoke,' puts the strap around saying 'you belong to Varuṇa' and ties the halter[150] with 'Varuṇa's fetter is tied.'

2: "Similarly he harnesses the ox on the north side.

3: "Holding two green branches, the Subrahmaṇya crawls between the poles: these are Palāśa or Śamī branches.

4: "Now the Adhvaryu holds the cart and gives the order: 'for King Soma who has been bought and who is being carried forward recite, O Subrahmaṇya, invoke the Subrahmaṇyā."

After this the procession moves forth towards the vedi, while the Adhvaryus carry a chair made in a specific form out of Udumbara wood (quite possibly, a replica of an ancient royal throne).

ĀpŚS X. 29. 9: "[After the arrival] he stops the cart in front of the Prāgvaṃśa, the pole being towards the east or north, lifts [the cart] up in the same way as before, props it up, pulls out the yoke-pin with 'you are the prop of Varuṇa,' unties the strap with 'Varuṇa's fetter is untied,' removes the halter with 'Varuṇa's fetter is removed.'

10: "Thus he unyokes the ox on the north side.

11: "The one on the left is unyoked or remains harnessed."

Then follows the Atithi-ceremony.

ĀpŚS X. 30.14 "After having set his voice free in concert with the Haviṣkṛt and unyoked the ox on the north side [if it had not been done earlier],

15: "he removes the cloth with the words, 'you belong to Varuṇa,' holds the King with the mantra, 'you are Varuṇa who protects the ordinances,' takes him down while reciting the verse: 'Come down with uncurtailed wings to the subjects, longingly to the longing ones, amiably to the amiable, O king Soma' etc., and moves forward saying 'go along the wide atmosphere.'

X. 31. 1: "Carrying the throne, the Pratiprasthātṛ goes in front.

2: "With the verse 'your abodes' (ṚV I. 91. 4) he enters the Prāgvaṃśa[151] through the eastern door, takes the throne behind the Āhavanīya towards the south[152] while reciting 'you are the true seat of Varuṇa,' and installs it to the south of the Āhavanīya.

3: "He spreads a black skin on the throne just as it was spread earlier in the cart, and deposits the King upon it.

4: "You are Varuṇa who protects the ordinances'—thus he greets the king.

5: "You belong to Varuṇa.' With this mantra [addressed to the cloth] he wraps him in the cloth.

6: "'Salute thus the mighty Varuṇa, the wise guardian of amṛta. May he grant threefold protection. O Heaven and Earth, protect me in your lap.[153] He should approach the King always with this verse.

7: " 'Do not walk between Agni and the King.' Thus he directs."

When the Soma is brought to the sacrificial place,[154] a black skin is spread inside the southern cart in the same way as it is spread upon the throne and earlier in the cart, and the Soma is deposited upon this skin. "Now the sacrificer," states ĀpŚS XI.18.1, "gives him over to the gods saying, 'this, O God Savitṛ, is your (plural) Soma.'

2: "He addresses him with 'you went here, O Soma, as a god among the gods'; goes around from left to right with the words 'I here as a man to men'; stretches his hands towards the east with 'salutation to the gods'; towards the south with 'svadhā for the Manes'; goes out with the words 'released from Varuṇa's fetters'; looks to the east saying 'I beheld the Svar'; and surveys the entire Vihāra with 'I wish to behold the Svar,' at the Āhavanīya with 'light of Vaiśvānara.' "[155]

From this we gather that the ritual closely associates Soma and Varuṇa in the preliminary rites. The Brāhmaṇas are no less familiar with these customs than the Sūtras. For example, ABr I.13.26 states: *varuṇadevatyo vā eṣa tāvad yāvad upanaddhaḥ*; similarly ibid. I.30.26; TS VI.1.11.5,6:[156] *varuṇo vā eṣa yajamānam abhyaiti yat krītaḥ soma upanaddhaḥ*, and earlier at 11.1: *vāruṇo vai krītaḥ soma upanaddhaḥ*; ŚBr III.3.4.25: *sa yad āha varuṇasya skambhasarjanī stha iti varuṇyo hy eṣa etarhi bhavati yat somaḥ krītaḥ*.[157] I cannot say why exactly *krītaḥ somaḥ* should be designated thus. But we can surmise why *upanaddhaḥ somaḥ* is called thus if we do not limit ourselves purely to external reasons. The cloth with which Soma is wrapped is told that it belongs to Varuṇa. The commentary on the TS (I, p. 370) states that *upanaddhasya somasya varuṇo devatā*.[158] What does this symbolism denote ? It has been established that the Agniṣṭoma is a spring sacrifice during which Soma returns again to the gods and that the release from Varuṇa's fetters, connected with this, is an antithesis to the light that is heralded in the Agniṣṭoma. In order to evade Varuṇa, one returns from the bath at the conclusion of the sacrifice without looking back,[159] carrying firewood as a symbol of the newly revived sacrifice. We have further seen that in connection with the Varuṇapraghāsāḥ at least the MS interprets Varuṇa as the *hemanta* and that here also the ceremony is concluded with a bath performed with the same rites and mantras. Hence, I conclude that the "wrapped-up Soma" who belongs to Varuṇa or who is designated directly as Varuṇa represents the nectar in the hand of Varuṇa. This is the point where Varuṇa and Vṛtra come close to one another. But not closer than this; they are not identical. Vṛtra is, as I shall attempt to show later on, winter but Varuṇa is not. This is ruled out by many factors; above all, by the dual form Maitrāvaruṇau in which the two gods behave like two mutually complementary beings and supplement one another somewhat like *satyānṛte, dyāvāpṛthivī, uṣāsānaktā*. If Varuṇa were winter, Mitra ought to be summer to assume which there is no ground. Furthermore, an identification of Varuṇa directly with winter is precluded by some epithets which characterize him like *caturānīka*, likewise by the descriptions of his golden robe, throne and chariot, which abound in the ṚV. One could say that Varuṇa is the night and Mitra the day, but from this stage there is no transition to the overlordship of the ocean. For we cannot rest content to let a trait of character arise effortlessly; on the contrary, we must find the path along which the evolution proceeded in a logical way. The moon, above all, fulfills all these conditions.[160] He is the lord of the night, of the waters and of winter, in which season he reaches his highest position in the sky, and makes it possible to understand the various traits in Varuṇa's character, the earlier as well as the later ones. There are two obvious objections to this theory: how does the moon attain by himself the position of the creator of the world and how does he obtain the dismal character which the Veda ascribes to him ? We can dispose of the first objection with a reference to the concept of Soma who holds the worlds apart, creates the sun and upholds the sky.[161] But for the 'ominous' moon god we have no Indian model if we do not draw Yama into this context. Varuṇa and Mitra had come down from a long-forgotten period, before the Indians settled in their new homeland, and were no more at the height of their cult. In the more southern region with its bright nights and its mild winter such a moon god had no significance; the long-inherited nectar aspect asserted itself more and more, pushing aside the severe lord of winter. Either one assigned to him a position which went beyond his original nature and transferred to him a part of the character of Mitra—who was in the process of disappearing completely—as the poets of books V and VII did, or he was restricted chiefly to one of his many realms: to the night in the ritual and to the ocean in classical Sanskrit.

Anthropology is in a position to fill the gap left by Indian sources. At several places we find evidence that the moon god not only assumes the role of the creator and ruler of the world but can also assume the form of a hostile god.[162] It must be conceded that for me also the 'sky' would appear more appropriate as the creator and protector of the world, but the thought process which we assume to be most logical in such things is no criterion for the way a more primitive world looked at things. After all, why should the moon who moves at night in the sky in diverse forms, who occupies a higher position in the sky in winter than he does in summer, not develop into a god who protects the law and avenges the sin that spreads around stealthily ?

The interpretation of Varuṇa which we have presented here has to answer the following question if it is to be correct.

How could he, starting as a moon god, evolve into the god of the ocean ? Does the moon, according to Indian conceptions and more specifically according to the Vedic conception, possess qualities which intrinsically cause such an evolution ? Of course, it is theoretically possible that even without such intrinsic causes new elements accrue to a mythological figure just as the legacy of Mitra who was gradually being replaced passed on, in my view, to a large extent to Varuṇa. But such "deviations and aberrations" which we might be inclined to anticipate here and there[163] leave behind the impression of arbitrariness as long as we do not discover the inner motives for such an evolution. In linguistics we endeavour more and more to look for the reasons for the linguistic deviations; the mythological exegate has the same obligation.

7. The Moon and the Ocean

Earlier we have often remarked on the association of the moon with rain and with all kinds of reservoirs of water. The Indian concepts of this aspect are not unique; they agree completely with concepts of other Aryan and non-Aryan peoples who see in the moon the source of water, the source not only of dew but of rain as well. The close association of Soma to *āpaḥ*, *sindhus* etc. has been thoroughly discussed.[164] We saw that he is sometimes called the "king of streams," sometimes the "drop in the waters," or the "embryo of the waters" and so on, or that "he rules over the rain" (IX.74. 3: *íśe yó vṛṣṭéḥ*). In this respect Varuṇa comes close to Soma.[165] But we also see that Soma had not yet become *rājan* or *pati* "of the ocean." When it is said occasionally that he moves in the waters of the ocean, this quality, by no means, predominates over the others; the same is said of other gods as well. He is called *apā́ṃ śíśu* in VS X. 7; TS I. 8.12.1. This designation is appropriate to the moon, and occurs again and again with one variation or another with reference to Soma, but it would not be a suitable epithet for one who is originally a god of the ocean.

It must be emphasized that of all the Vedic gods Soma alone bears the name *samudríya* in the ṚV.[166] The investigation about the word *samudrá* has shown that this word can denote the ocean of the atmosphere as well as that on the earth. At several places Soma is directly designated as 'an ocean' (of nectar).[167] Almost everything in the Soma cult is symbolical and the passages that are supposed to refer to the Soma vat should not be understood exclusively in this sense; on the contrary, they can denote at the same time either the *úttara* or the *ávara samudrá.* Apart from IX.107.16 I know only the following that refer to the ocean directly.

X.123.2: *samudrā́d ūrmím úd iyarti venáḥ*
IX.35.2: *índo samudramīṅkhaya pávasva viśvamejaya* and
84.4: *índuḥ samudrā́ṃ úd iyarti vāyúbhiḥ*
éndrasya hā́rdi kaláśeṣu sīdati ||

The last passage contributes to the understanding of the second one inasmuch as it prevents us through the additional word vāyubhiḥ from entertaining the possibility that the motion of the ocean caused by Soma can refer to the tides and that a knowledge of the ebb and flow can be anticipated already in the ṚV. But in the case of both the verses we should proceed with the assumption that Soma and moon are identical. These verses would remain unintelligible if we regard Soma there as the plant or as the drink prepared from the plant. The same is true of IX. 86. 8 : *rā́jā samudrā́ṃ nadyò ví gāhate*, where it is not necessary to treat *samudrá* as anything but the ocean.[168] While we notice here only the beginnings of the association between the moon and the ocean, the later period dwelt upon this association with a special predilection. I know only one passage from the Brāhmaṇas,[169] but in the classical period we find the association described so frequently and in such a variety of ways that the moon, rather than any god, appears as the lord, son, friend, and indeed as the god of the ocean. Some examples from quite different branches of literature may be given here.

Pañcatantra I, v. 94 (ed. Kielhorn);
kauśeyaṃ kṛmijaṃ suvarṇam upalād dūrvāpi goromataḥ
paṅkāt tāmarasaṃ śaśāṅka udadher indīvaraṃ gomayāt|
kāṣṭhād agniḥ......

Here the moon and the ocean belong closely together, like silk and the worm that produces it, like gold and the ore, like wood and fire and so on. The moon is called *abdhibandhu*,[170] and at least according to some lexicographers, *abdhinavanītaka*, *samudranavanīta* and *sāgarasūnu*.[171]

Raghuvaṃśa X. 82:

teṣāṃ dvayor dvayor aikyaṃ bibhide na kadācana/
yathā vāyuvibhāvasvor yathā candrasamudrayoḥ//

The *Kādambarī* connects the two in the following similes.

Kādambarī (ed. Peterson, BSS) p. 81, l. 22:[172] *tac ca. sāgarajalam iva candrodayena candrāpīḍanirgamanena sakalam eva saṃcacālāśvīyam.*

p. 148, l. 7:[173] *dūrasthasyāpi kamalinīva savituḥ sāgara-veleva candramasaḥ mayūrīva jaladharasya.*

p. 249, l. 1:[174] *gambhīraprakṛteḥ saritpater iva candramasā sudūram ullāsyamānasyāpi maryādāvaśād ātmānaṃ stambhayataḥ.*

Kathāsaritsāgara I. 39: *tato jātā himādres tvam abdheś candrakalā yathā/*

Ibid. XXXI. 29: *sā dṛṣṭvaivāniruddhaṃ tam uṣā sākṣād upāgatam/ amṛtāṃśum ivāmbodhivelā nāṅgeṣv avartata//*

Vikramāṅkadevacarita[175] XI. 39: *ācakarṣa himadīdhitir uccair miśraṇārtham iva vārdhijalāni//*

Nandivarman's inscription:[176] *mahāguṇa-salilanidhi-salila-saṃvardhanasomarājena.*

Epigraphia Indica II. 3: (besides l. 1: *abdhibandhu*) l. 3: *sūnur devasya saptajalarāśirasāyanasya.*[177]

Indian epigrams contain diverse statements on this association.[178] This shows us the path along which Varuṇa could have evolved into the god of the ocean.

In spite of all the majesty, Varuṇa was originally an ominous god, who gradually deviated from his original traits under a different sky and different circumstances. In favour of the nectar-containing Soma he receded into the background and developed in a direction to which his association with the waters contributed decisively. Starting from this viewpoint we can do complete justice to the three verses that associate him with the ocean as early as in the ṚV, or seem to do so. However, since the *samudrá* in these verses by no means denotes the ocean only but also the atmosphere (see p. 9 above), we cannot assume with certainty that in any of these verses Varuṇa refers to the god of the ocean. VII. 40.3[179] refers through the word *avapáśyan* to the *úttara samudrá*, but the case is doubtful in I. 161.14,[180] and IX. 90.2.[181] But even when we wish to see the god of the ocean in the ṚV, this is only one among the many qualities of Varuṇa on which the ṚV lays emphasis. Hence this quality can claim neither pre-eminence nor any special antiquity.[182]

It is of course understandable if the modern exegete wishes that the Vedic heavens were more plentiful than they actually are and that the Vedic Indians could have given admittance not only to various sun gods, moon gods or wind gods but also to other beings in ample number. But I cannot approve of the courses adopted for the fulfilment of this wish—courses which make the Vedic Indians more interesting than they themselves would have claimed. Nothing would be more gratifying than to rediscover the reflected splendour of Indian life in the Indian sky or to heighten the content of its life with abstract deities. The main thing, however, is that we should also be able to adduce evidence from Vedic literature.

We would gladly surrender several of the many Agni hymns and Indra hymns if only we could exchange these with a more comprehensive view of life of the Vedic period, whereas we have to rest content with the bleak monotony of those hymns and their endless repetitions. If a careful examination of the sources shows that one of the Vedic gods has essentially the same origin as several others and that what is new in him is merely the name and the individual colouring, we have no other way but to accept this and willingly put up with the "dearth of ideas." I think that the monotony of the gods in spite of the many names can be explained from the syncretic nature of Vedic mythology which assimilated the mythologies of different tribes. In future we shall have to enquire more about the diversity of these ethnological foundations than about the variations within the gods themselves. It is true, the threads that partly go back to very ancient times are difficult to disentangle. I do not assert that Varuṇa was familiar to the Indians themselves as the moon god; I maintain simply that all his later traits can be readily explained only from this prehistoric character of his just as the traits of Mitra in the Veda can be explained with reference to the sun. Conjointly with Mitra, he was adorned as the highest god with the emblems of the king as well as with the attributes of sovereignty such as the penal authority and the dispatching of spies.[183]

B. MITRA

Like Varuṇa, Mitra was inherited by the Vedic Indians from the remote period of Indo-Iranian prehistory. We find his name in India and in Iran; he is mentioned along with Auramazdā and Anahata in the old-Persian cuneiform inscriptions.[184] From Iran he reached Armenia, where there was a shrine dedicated to him in the province of Derǰan (Derxene).[185] He also reached Cappadocia and Cilicia. While he thus conquered new domains in the west and even lent his traits to St. George,[186] in the east he faded out completely in a stark contrast to his old companion Varuṇa. In India he plays an insignificant role when alone, and occupies his lofty position solely through the association with Varuṇa. It seems that the qualities of this pair of gods were gradually transferred to one of the two and that Varuṇa attained the glory which he assumes in the eighth maṇḍala solely through the legacy which he obtained as the surviving member of the pair.[187] If Mitra and Varuṇa jointly rule over the day and the night, create and steer the world, it could easily have happened that, while one of the two faded out and the origin of the other was forgotten, what had been once their common domain came now under the sway of the latter. Probably a subordination as suggested by ṚV VII.82.5[188] had preceded this transference of attributes.

The etymology of the word *mitra* or *mithra* is uncertain.[189] Eggers has made a comprehensive study of this deity[190] and held that the appellative meaning 'friend' is a late and derived one whereas the original use of the word was as the name of the god. Unlike von Schroeder and others, I would like to think that Eggers was right insofar as any decision is possible at all on the basis of the available material; thus also Oldenberg.[191] On the other hand, I have nothing much to add to what I have stated earlier and what the above-mentioned scholar states now. But we must refute the theory that Mitra is the lord of contracts and oaths. One neither swears by him nor makes contracts in his presence. I am still inclined to the old view that here we are dealing with an Indo-Iranian sun god who had already lost his vitality on the specifically Indian soil.[192] The ṚV contains only one hymn dedicated to Mitra, composed in a colourless manner by a Viśvāmitra. The ritual assigns the same insignificant position as long as he appears singly without Varuṇa. A rite peculiar to him is the caru offering to him and to Bṛhaspati during the Rājasūya.[193] Here the ritual attempts to bring the distinction between the two gods into bold relief through the ceremonies. For Mitra a vessel is carved out of an Aśvattha branch which grew towards the east or north and which fell off by itself. The vessel is placed upon the one meant for Bṛhaspati. Large undamaged grains of rice are chosen for the portion of caru meant for Mitra; small cast-off grains for Bṛhaspati.[194] Fresh butter is produced in the following manner: one drives round and round on a war-chariot with a leather pouch filled with milk and thus lets the butter form by itself.[195] This butter is thrown into the upper vessel, and also the large grains which will then be cooked there. Here I may add the very clear injunctions given by TS I.8.9.2 for this sacrifice: "in the milk of a white cow with white calf [for Bṛhaspati], in the butter that curdled and formed into butter by itself [for Mitra]; in a vessel with four corners made of Aśvattha wood from a branch that has fallen off by itself. He should sort the husked and unhusked grains.[196] The husked ones in milk are for Bṛhaspati, the unhusked in butter are for Mitra. The vedi is self-made[197] (not artificially constructed), the barhis consists of grass that is self-cut,[198] the fire wood is from branches that have fallen to the ground by themselves,[199] the above-mentioned cow with white calf is the dakṣiṇā."[200]

Here also Mitra makes his appearance in company with another god, although he enjoys certain amount of precedence over Bṛhaspati. Rarely do we come across instances where a sacrifice is prescribed for him alone. I notice only a caru at the conclusion of the Traiyambaka offerings.[201] If the usual homas in these Cāturmāsyas are replaced by animal sacrifices, Mitra also is assigned a victim.[202]

According to all that has been written on this subject so far, only two explanations are possible for the Iranian Mithra as well. He can only be a genius of light or of the sun. While the first view found adherents earlier, recent research is more in favour of the second. To these arguments we should now add Bartholomae's interpretation of Yašt X. 143,[203] which runs in the same direction: "whose (of Mithra) chariot she drives, she who never deceives mankind, she who belongs to the radiant sun god, the Dawn," as well as Lommel's remarks on Yašt X. 136.[204] The statement of the Yašt that Mithra ascends the heights as the first one before the sun does not go against the above contention; as in the Veda so also here the sun god is separated from his natural basis.

1. Mitra-Varuṇa

I have already referred to the duality of Mitra-Varuṇa who were constantly seen by the authors of the ritual literature as a mutually contrasting pair. I have also stated that this aspect should not be ignored, for it is only in the case of these two gods, and not of others, that the antithesis is always stressed. The nature of the one must influence to a certain degree the explanation of the other since we are justified in assuming that they complement one another as *Uṣāsānaktā*, *Dyāvāpṛthivī*, *śuklakṛṣṇa*, *śītoṣṇa*, etc. do. Therefore, we must attempt to look for the explanation of the one in the direction suggested by the interpretation of the other. If Mitra were the day, then it would follow that Varuṇa is the night. If Mitra were the sun, Varuṇa would be the moon. Mitra as the god of summer would imply a winter god Varuṇa. But in actual fact these possibilities are circumscribed by the evidence brought forth for Varuṇa. Neither a god of night nor a god of winter can account for all the qualities that found expression in Varuṇa. Varuṇa as the moon god alone can do justice to all the attributes. This is corroborated also by the description in the Śrauta Sūtras of the "bald yellow-eyed whitish man" who stands in water and receives the offerings on his head, and who was regarded as the very likeness of Varuṇa. This indirectly suggests the solar nature of Mitra, besides there are the positive evidences in its favour.

According to the ṚV, butter-offerings are made to the two gods. They are called *ghṛtáhuti, ghṛtānna, sarpírāsuti.*[205] In the ritual they receive a *payasyā*;[206] in the Soma sacrifice, apart from the *payasyā*, they receive the Maitrāvaruṇagraha offered with special ceremonies.[207] A special vessel called *ajagāva*, 'bock-teat-vessel,' is prescribed for this Graha.[208] The cow is the one animal that is specially assigned to them. ṚV I. 153. 3 states: *pīpáya dhenúr áditir ṛtáya jánāya mitrāvaruṇā havirdé.* According to TS II.6.7.1, Mitra-Varuṇa say to Manu: *gor evāvām īśvarau kartoḥ sva iti| tau tato gāṃ sam airayatām.* On various occasions they receive a *vaśā*: thus at the end of the Agniṣṭoma or in the Rājasūya;[209] or in a milk offering made to them the dakṣiṇā consists, among other things, of a *vaśā.*[210] When a rival offers a *vaśā* in a sacrifice, this sacrifice is counteracted, among others, by a Puroḍāśa Ekakapāla for Mitra-Varuṇa.[211] Also the Graha that is drawn "so that the day breaks"[212] must be mixed with milk.[213] Already during the preparation of the various kinds of milk required in the Soma sacrifice, the command is issued thus: *taptam anātaktam [kuruta] maitrāvaruṇāya.*[214] The Graha is drawn with the words: "this is for you, O Mitra und Varuṇa.[215] Thereupon it is smeared with "boiled milk that has become cold again" and the following mantra is uttered: "May we, gaining much, delight in wealth, may the gods in oblations and the kine in pasture. Grant us for ever and ever, O Mitra and Varuṇa, that cow which does not kick." It is said that whatever milk there is belongs to Mitra, but the Soma to Varuṇa.[216] I cannot ascertain if this statement has a real ancient basis. Of course, Mitra is associated with the cow already from the Indo-Iranian period. According to Yašt X.86, he is the protector of the cow; "the cow driven astray invokes him for help, longing for its pastures." But the cow is assigned to Varuṇa also.[217] Of the other sacrifices, the ritual literature knows a *mitrāvaruṇayor ayana* as a counterpart for *indrāgnayor ayana* and *aryamṇor ayana*, and also pilgrimages which took place on the banks of the Sarasvatī up to its sources; these were briefly described in my *Ritual-literatur*. It is not clear what innate relationship existed between these *yātsattra*-s and the gods whose names they bore.[218]

OTHER DUAL ASSOCIATIONS

2. Varuṇa and Indra

In several instances in the Veda, Indra enters into an association with Varuṇa in the place of the gradually disappearing Mitra. Like Mithra, Indra also liberates the kine. The former is a mighty warrior in Iran, and in this respect also he resembles, to a certain extent, Indra who moved into his place in India.[219] But we should not ignore the fact that the duality of Indra-Varuṇa is not based on the same organic connection as the older duality of Mitra-Varuṇa is. While the last two gods were fused into an inner unity, the association of Indra and Varuṇa may be regarded as an artificial product, the elements of which belonged historically and ethnically to mutually exclusive groups. They are the representatives of two different worlds: on one side a god who holds sway over his kingdom in all his majesty and avenges sin and injustice and on the other a wild warrior and conqueror who is conceived in a different spirit. Varuṇa "has gained the mastery of his old co-partner Mitra, who, while shining in full glory in the West, has lost his importance in the East, and disappears in the rays of his companion. But Varuṇa also is forced to give way before higher authorities. It has correctly been asserted that in the ṚV he enjoys but the last moment of his full fame. ...He has to surrender his power to Indra, who, in his turn, is dethroned by Viṣṇu or Kṛṣṇa. It is interesting to see how the Indian priests and ritualists, facing the rivalry between Indra and Varuṇa, tried to make a compromise with both of them, and directed hymns and oblations to an artificial duality, Indra-Varuṇa, which, like others *flores arte facti* never gained firm ground in Indian mythology."[220] Of course, Indra-Varuṇa are praised in various hymns. Purukutsānī implores them and receives a son called Trasadasyu from them (ṚV IV.42.9). But the association of these two gods did not become animated nor did it gain any great importance in the ritual which furnishes us with a certain criterion for gauzing the popularity of manifestations, although this criterion should be used with caution. The word-index to the ŚŚS lists Indravaruṇau only once (XIV.35.2) and the derivative *aindrāvaruṇa* not at all. We come across the Vedic hymns addressed to the two in the evening savana of the Agniṣṭoma as well as in its varieties and in the different days of the Dvādaśāha, where it is always the Maitrāvaruṇa who recites them verse-wise or hymn-wise.[221] Nevertheless, as far as I can see, oblations are not specially offered to them on these occasions. Hence the recitation of these hymns on the above-mentioned occasions gives the impression of being a late interpolation.

When we look at the hymns themselves, it will be seen that in two hymns Indra and Varuṇa are contrasted with one another; this contrast has been designated as a "dispute over precedence," as Sorensen maintains, hardly with justification.[222] However, even when we discard the designation, there still remains in these hymns, I believe, a factor interesting from the viewpoint of history of religion. We see an old rivalry, though in a diluted form, between the (Mitra-) Varuṇa cult on the one hand and the equally old Indra worship on the other. This rivalry was hardly felt at the time of these poets and was lost in the syncretism of the Vedic period. Occasionally attempts were made, it must be said, in quite a feeble way to retain the distinction between the two gods. We notice a certain amount of uncertainty in the ritual texts as to what should be done with these two representatives of Kṣatra who have been handed down by mythology. For example, the Rājasūya, in which Indra has a prominent position, is also called Varuṇasava. Kātyāyana enjoins that a Kṣatriya should install the fire according to "Varuṇa's ordinance" and a Rājanya according to that of Indra. According to Āpastamba the first rule pertains to a Rājan. The MŚS drops the rule altogether.[223] In the Śunaḥśepa legend, it is Indra who constantly advises Rohita to migrate; this he does in the face of Varuṇa who insists on receiving his sacrifice. Although they come occasionally close to one another in the hymns,[224] yet the lines of distinction cannot be completely effaced. Varuṇa is more of a Kavi, a Brahman; Indra is more of a warrior.[225] Bohnenberger rightly remarks that the ṚV exhibits only the last phase of the full flowering of the Varuṇa worship;[226] his star sinks gradually before the lustre of Indra, who was included in the Vedic pantheon by warlike nomadic tribes. When Indra is placed above all the gods in AV XX. 106, and his laudators include Mitra and Varuṇa also, this is not an instance of 'henotheism,' but a certain phase in the historical evolution, which later on dethroned Indra and let him occupy a position inferior to that of Viṣṇu, or Kṛṣṇa, or made him a worshipper of the Buddha.[227]

The cult of Varuṇa is not treated alike in all the books of the ṚV. In book X, not a single independent hymn is dedicated to Varuṇa. Likewise book VI is noted for the absence of a vigorous Varuṇa cult. Of course, the name of the god is well known to its composers, but remarkably enough the vocative does not occur independently in any single instance;[228] it occurs only in the association Mitrāvaruṇau in hymn VI. 67, which is dedicated to these two gods, and in Indrāvaruṇau in VI. 68. Elsewhere in the sixth book where Varuṇa is mentioned his character is not sufficiently delineated.[229] On the other hand, it cannot be ignored that in the seventh book—its 'composer' Vasiṣṭha regards Mitra-Varuṇa as his progenitors—Varuṇa plays an especially prominent role and is elevated to the status of the demiurge, without, however, Indra losing his position as far as the number of hymns is concerned. Four hymns are dedicated jointly to Indra and Varuṇa. The only thing that I wish to add is that the hymns addressed to Indra are, with the exception of the chronicle VII. 18,[230] barren in content, more barren in comparison to those dedicated to him in the sixth book. The special position which the eighth maṇḍala claims for itself[231] is seen, as in its treatment of the Gandharvas, so also in the characteristics given to Varuṇa in VIII.41. This hymn is closely connected with hymns 39, 40, and 42 through the common refrain *nábhantām anyaké same*. Occasionally its text is disconnected and unintelligible. In the seventh verse, it seems, Varuṇa is designated as Trita. Since IX. 95.4 states that *tritó bibharti váruṇaṃ samudré,* here is probably an instance of confusion on the part of the versifier.[232]

3. Varuṇa and Agni[233]

The diverse images which Agni's form receives in the Vedic period (sun, moon, hearth, fire, etc.) make the treatment of this section specially difficult. Here we enter a very uncertain and less-trodden field and yet, on the other hand, we cannot pass over the questions that have to be answered here because the result we obtain must stand the test here and at the same time throw light into the dark corners.

At times Agni is the guardian spirit who averts Varuṇa's anger, at times the two are contrasted with one another, at others the two are identical. Whosoever examines the relevant and not inconsiderable material cannot escape the conclusion that elements from different sets of ideas found their fusion in Agni.

a. Agni placates Varuṇa's Anger

This notion belongs to the ṚV. It finds a most vivid expression in the propitiatory hymn IV.1, the author of which addresses Agni thus. v.2: *bhrā́taraṃ váruṇam agna ā́ vavṛtsva*; v. 3: *sákhe sákhāyam abhy ā́ vavṛtsva*; v. 4: *váruṇasya vidvā́n devásya héḍó 'va yāsisīṣṭhāḥ*, etc.[234]

The verses of this hymn are recited singly on various occasions. For instance, the fourth and fifth are employed in a Punarādheya where they serve as Yājyāpuronuvākyā verses during an Āgnīvāruṇī oblation (instead of one for Aditi);[235] further during the Prāyaścitta offerings made by the priests at the Āgnīdhrīya at the end of the Soma sacrifice;[236] afterwards during a Vāruṇīṣṭi which follows the concluding bath.[237] The same verses were employed when Śunaḥśepa was led to the sacrificial bath during the Añjaḥsava which was invented by him; thereupon he was made to worship Agni with ṚV V. 2.7.[238] We find them again in the Āgneyakratu of the Āśvinaśastra[239] and other occasions.[240] From the majority of these examples, it is obvious that these deal with oblations for averting the danger, Agni playing the role of a propitiatory fire which wards off calamities.[241]

In these cases we see that the two gods are distinctly separated from one another. The same should be assumed also in a legend—I shall not attempt to explain its mythological character—according to which Agni stealthily creeps up to the waters, who are the wives of Varuṇa, in order to unite himself with them. His seed flowed forth and became gold.[242]

More important than this, it seems to me, is the following ritual procedure.

b. Agnir upanaddhaḥ

The earlier investigations have shown that Soma, on his arrival at the sacrificial place, is still in the possession of Varuṇa and that this idea is expressed symbolically when the Soma plants are wrapped in a cloth. This Soma, who is either Varuṇa himself or has Varuṇa as his deity,[243] is treated like Varuṇa and regarded as a malevolent god whose adverse influence one tries to ward off with a he-goat to which a verse is addressed. A similar procedure with reference to Agni is furnished by the rite of piling up of Agni; when the soil required for the ukhā is brought, it is wrapped up in a lotus leaf[244] as well as in a black skin and the whole thing is tied around with a string.[245] On this TS V.1.5.3 remarks thus: *varuṇo vā agnir upanaddhaḥ;* 5.9: *varuṇo vā eṣa yajamānam abhy aiti yad agnir upanaddhaḥ*; 6.1: *vāruṇo vā agnir upanaddho vi pājaseti vi sraṃsayati, savitṛprasūta evāsya viṣūcīṃ varuṇameniṃ vi sṛjati.* Thus Agni also, who is symbolically represented by the lotus leaf, which is regarded as Agni's womb, approaches the sacrificer in his wrapping as Varuṇa. It seems to me that this ritual episode is not a mere invention of the ritualists but deserves greater attention than it has found so far. Just as the amṛta in Varuṇa's possession comes to the sacrificial place so does Agni who remains in the mother's womb of lotus and will be kindled later in the ukhā through self-ignition. When Soma and Agni are within the wrapping, they are in the possession of Varuṇa. This recalls the antithesis between Varuṇa and Jyotiḥ which finds, expression in the Jyotiṣṭoma at the end of the Pitṛyāṇa or winter. 'Soma' or "Agni in the possession of Varuṇa" seems to be another synonym for the Pitṛyāṇa. Varuṇa might have been divested of his original meaning and conceived merely as the lord of the Pitṛyāṇa, the dark period. The decision, however, is uncertain. The case is somewhat different in X.124.

c. On ṚV X.124

We see Varuṇa, Soma and Agni mentioned side by side in this difficult hymn, to explain which many attempts have been made.[246] Occurring in the midst of a series of hymns containing eight verses each, this hymn with its nine verses arouses doubts, now as before, as to whether all the verses are original. I would, in the first place, consider the seventh verse as an interpolation. The uncertainty regarding as to who the speakers are and how the verses are distributed among them adds to the difficulties. I think that the exegesis should proceed from the idea contained in the verse, that Agni who has remained long in darkness should again come to the sacrifice. The content of the first verse is related to that of hymns X.51 ff.[247] and of other verses which describe in a like manner the renewal of the sacrifice at the end of the Dakṣiṇāyana.[248] Just as Agni is invited in X.124.1 to the *yajñáṃ páñcayāmaṃ trivṛ̥taṃ saptátantum* so have the gods once installed Agni with the desire that for them he *yajñáṃ naḥ kalpayāti páñcayāmaṃ trivṛ̥taṃ saptátantum* (X.52.4). Hence X.124.1 also should probably be understood as referring to the recommencement of the sacrifice after the long period of *tamas*. In the above-mentioned group of hymns it is Varuṇa who replies to Agni (X.51.4,6). Therefore, he must have been sent by the gods to prevail upon Agni to return from the waters and plants into which he had escaped. This is ruled out for X.124 since Varuṇa belongs to the opposite side here. It can be, as Geldner assumes, Indra who speaks in the name of the gods (cf. v. 5 and also V.2.8), but even this is not certain. A second factor that deserves our attention is the antithesis to *pitṛ̥ ásura*, from whose side Agni, Soma and Varuṇa change over to the opposite side headed by Indra (v. 4b: "When I choose Indra, I leave the Father."). My own earlier interpretation, like that of others, has erred in undertaking to identify Varuṇa with the *pitṛ̥ ásura.*[249] However, having reconsidered again and again, I am convinced that my attempt to see here a historical reminiscence which connects the *pitṛ̥ ásura* with the old Indo-Iranian Asura is not at all wrong. I would not know who else could be considered here but the *pratná pitṛ̥* mentioned in other passages (I.87.5; IX.73.8; 86.14), the Asura through whose *māyā* Mitra-Varuṇa cause rain-fall and protect the ordinances, that is to say, the *ádeva* as opposed to the *devá* (v. 2). Indra is opposed to *pitṛ̥-ásura* and Agni, Soma and Varuṇa are on the side of the latter. From this *pitṛ̥* of theirs, the Asuras cannot be separated who, according to v. 5, lose the power of magic and become *nirmāya*.

All this suggests a period which saw the Asuras and the Devas in opposition, which is emphasized so often by the Brāhmaṇas.[250] But it would be wrong to read into the ṚV the entire conceptual framework of the Brāhmaṇas, which occasionally place Vṛtra, the enemy of Indra, at the head of the Asuras. We are cautioned against such an attempt by the position which Varuṇa occupies in our hymn on the side of the "Father Asura" —an old concept, not familiar any more to the later literature. Varuṇa, who is not only an Asura but is also styled as the son of Asura in V.85.5, has been an Asura since the Indo-Iranian period and survives as such in our passage by the side of the *pitṛ ásura.* Apart from him, Agni also owes his loyalty to the *pitṛ ásura*; in III.29.11 Agni is called *gárbha āsuráḥ.*[251] I think we should not dismiss the idea of that Asura who bears the epithet 'Mazda' in Iran and is likewise called the father of fire. When we consider the expression *puthrō ahurahe mazdå*, it becomes obvious that this *ahura* and the *pitṛ ásura* issue from the same concept. While the former stands at the head of the Iranian gods, the later is a mere shadow, projected into the Indian world only through isolated passages.[252] In this *pitṛ ásura*, who shines into the ṚV from afar as it were, I see the ancient Dyaus Asura who has evolved in Iran into the idealized Ahura Mazda through the efforts of Zarathustra.[253] The fusion of the Asuras with Vṛtra was possible only in the later period with the advancing demonization of the Asuras. When Agni changes sides from the 'dear' Father with whom he stayed for years together, from the *ádeva*, to the Devas, this purely calendrical transition from the Pitṛyāṇa to the Devayāna is interwoven with an element—interesting from the viewpoint of the history of religion—which consists in the transference of this period of *tamas* to the historical *pitṛ ásura* who has become an adversary at the time of the poet of X.124.

d. Agni = Mitra; Varuṇa = Soma ?

According to *Maitrāyaṇīya Up.* VI.14, Agni is the representative of the half-year, *maghādyaṃ śraviṣṭārdham*, i.e., the Uttarāyaṇa, and Varuṇa the representative of the Dakṣiṇāyana, *sārpādyaṃ śraviṣṭārdhāntam.* The commentary explains the latter as the rainy season. Probably through this, however, the ancient antithesis between Mitra (=Agni) and Varuṇa (=Soma) is expressed. In the next passage, the Upaniṣad substitutes *vāruṇam* directly with *saumyam.*[254] Nevertheless, the hypothesis is uncertain.

e. Agni and Varuṇa are Identical

We cannot resolve all the problems arising in connection with the relationship of Agni and Varuṇa with the same formula. Here also various elements originating from different sets of concepts are fused together. Already the ṚV equates Agni with Varuṇa as it equates him with other gods.[255] The diversity of Agni's manifestations justifies these identifications, which are by no means based on pantheistic inclinations. Nevertheless, we need not attach great importance to these verses of the ṚV. The case is different with a passage of the KBr where it is said *amum evaitad savanair īpsanti yo' sau tapaty udyantaṃ prātaḥ-savanena madhye santaṃ mādhyandinena savanenāstaṃ yantaṃ tṛtīyasavanena / sa vā eṣo 'paḥ praviśya varuṇo bhavati*[256]—the sun enters into the waters at night and becomes Varuṇa.[257] The idea occurs also in AV XIII.3.13:

sá váruṇaḥ sāyám ágnir bhavati
sá mitró bhavati prātár udyán /[258]
sá savitá bhūtvántárikṣeṇa yāti
sá índro bhūtvá tapati madhyató dívam /

That is to say, Agni becomes Varuṇa in the evening and Mitra in the morning; in other words, Varuṇa and Mitra are two of his manifestations.

In the Agnihotra ceremony there are two kinds of offerings, one for Agni in the evening and one for Sūrya in the morning, provided the offerings are not made exclusively to Agni both the times. **ŚSS II.9.1**:[259] *agnir jyotir jyotir agniḥ svāheti sāyam.* 2: *sūryo jyotir jyotiḥ sūryaḥ svāheti prātaḥ.* Here we see Agni and Sūrya in opposition to one another.[260] In TĀr I.10.5.2 Agni and Āditya are called "the two calves" of the day and night, or it is said that when Āditya goes down he enters into Agni. The ṚV shares this view.[261]

X.88.6: *mūrdhá bhuvó bhavati náktam agníḥ*
tátaḥ sū́ryo jāyate prātár udyán /

Hence the night belongs to Agni: *āgneyī rātriḥ* (TS I.5.9.3); *āgneyī vai rātriḥ ... aindram ahaḥ* (TBr I.1.4.2,3; I.5.3.4; II.1.2.7); *agninā vai tejasā rātris tejasvaty, ādityena tejasāhas tejasvat* (ABr V.29.6).

Now Varuṇa also takes the place of Agni. The Atharva verse according to which Agni becomes Varuṇa in the evening and Mitra in the morning when he rises is quite similar to the one cited from the ṚV. Here Agni and Varuṇa are complete synonyms. Such an occasional synonymity can be seen also in a statement of GDS XXV.9: *ahaś ca mādityaś ca punātv iti prātā rātriś ca mā varuṇaś ceti sāyam* or ABr VI.26.13: *yo vā agniḥ sa varuṇaḥ*. When occasional verses in the ṚV treat Varuṇa as a form of Agni, this is not a frivolous view but is based on a concept that had enjoyed if not a great yet a perceptible popularity.

Who is this Agni to whom oblations are made in the evening and who receives the sun into himself ? This much is clear: the ritual texts see merely an altar fire in him. We may consider TBr I.1.4.3: *naktaṃ gārhapatyam ādadhāti ...... divāhavanīyam*; II.1.2.9: *agniṃ vāvādityaḥ sāyaṃ praviśati tasmād agnir dūrān naktaṃ dādṛśe / ubhe hi tejasī saṃpadyete*; 10: *udyantaṃ vāvādityam agnir anusamārohati*[262] / *tasmād dhūma evāgner divā dadṛśe*;[263] III.7.4.3: *agniṃ gṛhṇāmi ... ya udyantam ārohati sūryam ahne*. In the ṚV also there is no scarcity of passages which speak of a fire that shines at night, e.g., I.127.5;[264] III.9.7;[265] V.7.4;[266] perhaps III.15.3[267] and VI.3.5,6.[268] Furthermore, one may use the close connection between the sun and the altar-fire or the hearth-fire which originates from the sun and can be recognized as such in many passages, to tip the scales in favour of the interpretation of this Agni as the altar-fire into which the sun enters in the evening; perhaps one may also use the minor legends which speak of Āditya in that world and Agni in this world (or the reverse).[269] But this is not adequate. For the sacrificial fires do not shine at night. On the contrary, they are fanned first in the morning by the means of the Prāduṣkaraṇa. I hesitate to refer the statements like ṚV X.88.6a to one of these fires. Also the synonymity between Varuṇa and Agni precisely in the above-mentioned passages refutes the explanation given by the Brāhmaṇas because Varuṇa is never a sacrificial fire. Hence, the interpretations in the ritual texts seem to be a late invention.

We must take the aid of the conclusion of an earlier investigation. From I.95.1; IX.97.9[270] we saw that Agni has two forms: sun and moon.[271] If we assume that these forms of Agni are meant in our passages or were meant originally, then the riddle of these verses is resolved and, above all, the difficulties created in these passages by the switching over from Agni to Varuṇa are removed. The conception of Agni as a manifestation of the moon can still be traced to a certain extent in the ṚV and AV, but it becomes extinct in the subsequent period starting from the Brāhmaṇas, which recognize almost only his nectar-aspect. For this period, the sun is only a representative of the fire and the moon only a representative of nectar, of the waters, etc. The Brāhmaṇas reinterpreted the nocturnal Agni and transferred him to the sacrificial place and thus added to our difficulties in comprehending the true state of affairs. Hence, when Agni becomes Varuṇa in the evening and Mitra in the morning, when Āditya enters into the waters in the evening as Varuṇa, or Āditya enters into Agni in the evening and Agni enters into Āditya in the morning, when Agni is directly called Varuṇa, all these are mythological synonyms, continuations of an ancient concept which is expounded in ṚV I.95.1 in its purest form: "two of different form go forth, pursuing the right goal. Alternately they let the child drink. With one he is golden and endowed with Svadhā, with the other he appears, shining with great radiance." Neither the ocean-theory nor the sky-theory is able to do equal justice to all these facts; hardly any attempt has been made to interpret these facts. If we were to reject these as worthless, then we would have to assume that the transmitted knowledge in India was in a totally confused state, the concepts got thoroughly mixed up in the minds of the Yājñikas and continue their existence only in an undecipherable form in the ritual literature. I, however, deem it our duty to separate the entangled strands to the best of our ability and follow them up to their beginnings. Here one might often go wrong, but one must risk it nevertheless.[272]

C. ARYAMAN

The few passages which refer to Aryaman belong to the debris that lies scattered all over the wide expanse of the ruins of Vedic mythology. So far there has been no work attempting to reconstruct the picture of the god from this debris and, in view of the material which is of course more abundant than has been supposed and yet remains inadequate, we must give up the effort to reach up to the foundations upon which the concept of Aryaman was erected. This is all the more regrettable since the name apparently goes back to the oldest period of Aryan history and there are enough clues to say that it is an old Aryan word. The Indian *aryaman* corresponds to the Iranian *airyaman* as well as to the middle Irish *Airem*, genitive *Areman*, *Eremon*.[273] The equation, proposed at first by Pictet and Stokes, attains still greater significance when it can be shown that on the Indo-Iranian soil the word did not have an exclusively appellative sense but was also a proper noun. I think that the case of *aryaman* would be the same as that of *mitra* which, according to Egger's assumption, was originally a proper noun and, losing its significance gradually, became an appellative. Bergaigne has cursorily touched upon Aryaman a few times,[274] likewise other scholars also passed over him quickly.[275] We can advance slightly further than Darmesteter,[276] or Bergaigne with his notion of the 'beneficent god.' Indian commentators have often explained the name as *sūrya*. But we are justified in doubting that the commentators had inherited an ancient concept and did not rather confer new traits upon an old formation. I shall limit my task to collect the debris and to record the view of the Brāhmaṇas.

1. Aryaman's Path

Two verses deal with Aryaman. These are the only ones which are preserved for us and which might be the fragments from a longer hymn that has been lost:

aryamāyāti vṛṣabhas tuviṣmān
dātā vasūnāṃ puruhūto arhan /
sahasrākṣo gotrabhid vajrabāhuḥ
asmāsu devo draviṇaṃ dadhātu //
ye te 'ryaman bahavo devayānā
panthāno rājan diva ā caranti /
tebhir no deva mahi śarma yaccha
śaṃ na edhi dvipade śaṃ catuṣpade //[277]

In these verses, the words to which emphasis has been added are not without significance. Here we find the epithets *sahasrākṣa, gotrabhid, vajrabāhu* as well as an allusion to "Aryaman's many paths which serve the gods." It looks as though we have before us the fragment of a mythology that is alien to the ṚV. These verses are employed as Yājyā-Puronuvākyās on the occasion of some caru oblations for Aryaman, made in order to reach the celestial world or for other purposes.[278] In the words with which the TS recommends these three oblations, it repeats in each case the following sentence: *asau vā ādityo' ryamā*, that is to say, it sees in Aryaman a synonym of Sūrya. Aryaman's path is mentioned elsewhere also. This path seems to have been thought of as the essential trait of Aryaman just as Indra's chief trait was regarded to be the killing of Vṛtra, Yama's the realm of the dead and Bṛhaspati's the Kavi-hood. It is an oft-seen phenomenon that one specific trait of a god is upheld by the tradition as his characteristic as soon as the god concerned begins to fade out and his original and total significance does not remain vivid any more.[279] In continuation of what is said at TS I.8.12g, it is stated in TBr I.7.6.6: *indro vṛtrāya vajram udayacchat, sa divasam alikhat, so 'ryamṇaḥ panthā abhavat, sa āvinne dyāvāpṛthivī dhṛtavrate iti dyāvāpṛthivī upādhāvat*. Furthermore, while discussing the *aryamṇor ayana*,[280] TMBr XXV.12.3 declares: *yam āhur aryamṇaḥ*[281] *panthā ity eṣa vāva devayānaḥ panthāḥ*. 4: *pra devayānaṃ panthānam āpnuvanti ya etad upayanti*. 5: *tasmād eṣo' ruṇatama iva diva upadadṛśe'ruṇatamo iva hi panthaḥ*. The commentary on the TMBr explains this Aryaman as *āditya*. It describes him as *ādityamūrtibheda* and remarks as follows on the fifth Sūtra, cited just above: *devayānamārgasyārcirādirūpatvāt tena gato'py aryamā aruṇatamo divi dṛśyate, prātaḥkālīna ādityo 'ryamā so 'ruṇatamo bhavati.* We find the same explanation of Aryaman as the sun in the commentary on the ŚBr;[282] further, in lexica and in Sāyaṇa's commentary on the ṚV.[283] At all events, it is significant for the Indian view, no matter whether it was original or not, that from the TS onwards there occurs a specific interpretation which speaks of Aryaman's path as the path of the sun, but not as the milky way, although there have been some attempts to interpret Aryaman's path thus.[284] We learn somewhat more about this path from ĀpDS II.9.23.3 ff. Here Āpastamba quotes two verses from the Purāṇa literature. Bühler has established that these verses are old and widely popular constituents of this branch of literature.[285] In these verses mention is made of the southern and northern paths of Aryaman, i.e., undoubtedly the paths of the sun and of the ecliptic (in the parallel passage cited by Bühler there is also *savituḥ* for *aryamṇaḥ*).

The ṚV, to which we now turn after these enquiries, contains no passage that permits an explanation of Aryaman. In two passages the ṚV also speaks of Aryaman's path. He is called *átūrtapanthan* in X. 64.5: *átūrtapanthāḥ pururátho aryamā́ saptáhotā víṣurūpeṣu jánmasu* / "whose path is not transgressed, unapproachable (Smaller ed. of the PW). Secondly I. 105.6:

kád va ṛtásya dharṇasí kád váruṇasya cákṣaṇam /
kád aryamṇó mahás pathā́ti krāmema dūḍhyò...

Aryaman's path is spoken of in these verses in quite general terms. We may interpret Aryaman as we like; these two passages will not contradict if we wish to transfer the view of the later period to the ṚV which speaks very often of the path or the paths of the sun, but there is no guarantee that it is the original sense. When this path is described as *ánāpta* in ṚV I.100.2 or as *árakṣohata* in TS VI. 1.7.3, this is quite in harmony with Aryaman's epithet, *átūrtapanthan*.[286]

I have shown that the afore-mentioned texts furnish the following, as further epithets of Aryaman: *sahasrākṣá, gotrabhíd, vájrabāhu, pururátha,*[287] *saptáhotṛ* (ṚV X. 64.5). To these we may still add *purujātá* (ṚV VII. 35.2; AV XIX. 10.2), *mandrá* and *sṛprábhojas* (ṚV VI. 48.14), *viṣitastupa*[288] (AV VI. 60.1), and also some quite colourless epithets from other passages,[289] none of which is exclusively peculiar to him or can specially characterize him. None of these epithets attributed to him contradicts, nor does it favour, the interpretation given in the later texts. The designation *saptáhotṛ*, which characterizes Agni also in III. 29.14, deserves a few words. Aryaman is associated with seven Hotṛs once more in TBr II. 3.5.3, where it is said: *yat sapta hotāraḥ sattram āsatu kena te gṛhapatinārdhnuvan kena suvar āyan kenemāṃllokān samatanvann iti / aryamṇā vai te gṛhapatinārdhnuvan tena suvar āyan tenemāṃllokān samatanvan.* Here in this legend it is Aryaman who plays the role of Gṛhapati[290] for the seven Hotṛs who were celebrating a sattra and helps them achieve success and attain heaven.[291]

The epithet *gotrabhíd* suggests another trait from his extinct sagas. Indra who also bears this epithet is assisted by the Manes as he opens the cowpen; Aryaman is closely connected, at least, with the seven Ṛṣis. When the gods granted the cow to Aṅgiras (ṚV I. 139.7; see also Vol. I, pp. 112), it was Aryaman who milked the cow. Thus here also he is associated with the cows and the Manes. It is obvious that Aryaman has several things in common with Agni as well. The latter has a 'chariot,' so does Aryaman. Agni is called *bhūrijanman*, Aryaman *purujātá*. Both are designated as *saptáhotṛ*. This recalls to mind the well-known hymn II. 1, where Agni is identified with Aryaman also (v. 4) as he is with Indra, Varuṇa and Mitra —not quite without any reason, for Agni indeed dwells in all that shines.[292] The similarity in the associations of both the gods can be seen in yet another trait of character which we may regard as the essential feature in the portrait of Aryaman.

2. Aryaman and the Marriage Ceremony

a. God Aryaman

Among the few verses that mention Aryaman, there is a small group belonging mostly to the AV; this group is noteworthy because it makes Aryaman the promotor of matrimony. He procures a husband for the maiden and a wife for the bachelor. According to the sections dealing with the *pativedana* of the twentyfourth chapter of the *Kauśikasūtra*, two of these verses are recited in front of the crow-oracle with the accompaniment of a butter offering for Aryaman. Whence the crow comes, comes also a suitor.

AV VI.60.1: *ayám á yāty aryamá purástād viṣitastupaḥ /*
asyá icchánn agrúvai pátim utá jāyám ajánaye //
2: *áśramad iyám aryamann anyásām sámanaṃ yatí /*
aṅgó nv àryamann asyá anyáḥ sámanam áyati //[293]

Similar verses are employed in marriage ceremonies. Thus

AV XIV.1.17: *aryamáṇaṃ yajāmahe subandhúṃ pativédanam /*
urvārukám iva bándhanāt prétó muñcāmi
nā́mútaḥ //,

furthermore, *Āpastamba Mantrapāṭha* I. 5.7:[294]
aryamáṇaṃ nú deváṃ kanyá agním ayakṣata /
sá imā́ṃ devó adhvaráḥ prétó muñcāti nā́mútaḥ
subaddhā́m amútas karat //

We notice that as in ṚV II.1 so also here Agni is directly identified with Aryaman. Thus we can understand why it is said in

ṚV V.3.2: *tvám aryamá bhavasi yát kanī́nāṃ*
nā́ma svadhāvan gúhyaṃ bibharṣi /
añjánti mitráṃ súdhitaṃ ná góbhir
yád dámpatī sámanasā kṛṇóṣi //[295]

As I.66.8 and other verses demonstrate, it is precisely Agni who is the *jāráḥ kanī́nām*, the *pátir jánīnām*;[296] he is the husband or the lover of Dawn since he follows her as the suitor follows his maiden; she lights up at his glance. The celestial suitor of the daughter of the sky is the archetype for all suitors and the patron deity of matrimony. In view of the antiquity of Aryaman, whose name goes back to the prehistory of the Indo—European peoples, we cannot say whether this activity of his, which coincided here with that of Agni, belongs to the basic elements of his conception. We must limit our task to elicit the picture which the Vedic period had of Aryaman, and this clearly shows traits that are akin to Agni.[297]

b. Aryaman as the Name of the Suitor

In several passages the word Aryaman is also an appellative which designates the suitor or the bridegroom. It is not correct to say with Roth (PW) and other scholars that Aryaman is the match-maker, the Gr. *paranymphios*; on the contrary, he is the bridegroom or the suitor himself. This becomes evident, if not already from AV VI.60.1 to be recited at the time of the crow-oracle, then with all certainty from

AV XIV.1.39: *aryamṇó agníṃ páryetu pūṣan |*
prátīkṣante śváśuro deváraś ca |

'Let her go around the suitor's fire, O Pūṣan. The father-in-law and the brother-in-law are looking on," and from ṚV X.40.12 (=AV XIV.2.5), to be recited during the journey of the newly married couple to their new home:[298]

ábhūtaṃ gopā́ mithunā́ śubhaspatī [*aśvinā*]
priyā́ aryamṇó dúryāṅ aśīmahi ||[299]

Here Aryaman is an honorific of the bridegroom. The bridegroom is designated with the name of the celestial suitor, of *aryamā́ jāráḥ kanīnām*, with a clear allusion to the latter. The marriage has a celestial counterpart. Usually it is the marriage procession of Soma and Sūryā with which the marriage procession of the newly married couple is compared. Here the bridegroom receives his name from another, and as far as the concept is concerned, totally different source, roughly in the same way as the name of Vivasvat, the celestial sacrificer, becomes, *maṅgalecchāyai*, also the name of the earthly sacrificer in the ṚV.[300] In other passages also, excepting those that are in any case difficult for the exegesis, I prefer to replace the meaning 'friend' or "bosom friend" with the more specific 'suitor' or 'bridegroom.' In ṚV V.54.8, for instance, the Maruts are compared to *aryamáṇaḥ*, 'suitors,' who approach laden with ornaments.[301]

As a result of this investigation, we may list the following meanings for Aryaman:

1. [Starting point indeterminate; according to Indian tradition supposedly identical with Sūrya],

2. patron deity of matrimony,
3. suitor.

Aryaman plays no role in the ritual. To be sure, TBr II.3.5.4 states that *yajño vā aryamā*, which is usually said of Viṣṇu. But according to the material at my disposal, Aryaman is not one of the favourite gods of the sacrificial theologians. Apart from the caru offerings which are made "in order to attain heaven," or "to obtain generous subjects," or "to achieve success in an assembly," I can cite only the *aryamṇo ayana*, also called *aryamṇor ayana*, which is a variation of the Sārasvata Sattras. As I have already remarked, I cannot form an idea of their connection with the gods.

Our sources do not make it possible for us to determine the nature and origin of Aryaman more precisely than has been attempted here. But it is possible to recognize that the allusions and verses which are preserved for us are but the fragments of a more glorious past. An intimate association between Aryaman on the one hand and Mitra-Varuṇa or Mitra on the other did not develop in the Veda although they are mentioned together. I find him with Varuṇa alone only once,[302] with Mitra about three times;[303] usually he appears conjointly with that pair of gods, without our being any wiser about his presence there. There are about 62 passages which mention all the three together. In seventeen of these, Aryaman is not at the centre. From this we may perhaps conclude that although he was regarded as a luminous being like Mitra and Varuṇa, it was still vaguely felt that his origin was different.[304] At the most in one passage, he is called Asura.[305]

3. Aryaman in the Avesta

Vīvahvant, Yima and other gods of Iranian mythology advanced a step further than their Indian counterparts in anthropomorphosis. Likewise Airyaman lost more of his divine nature than has been preserved in the Vedic Aryaman. The interpretations given for this Iranian god are diverse. Harlez[306] has seen correctly that Spiegel's explanation of this Iranian Yazata as 'obedient' is not adequate and held the view that Airyaman, who is often closely connected with Aṣa Vahiṣta and Saoka, "the genii of the fire and of the flame," must himself be the personification of one of

"Agni's manifestations," "which brings him singularly close to the Aryaman of the Veda, the son of the grand nature, the agent who separates the day and the night, often also the sun himself."[307] The Avesta does not offer the possibility of obtaining a concrete picture of the Iranian god. The little that it offers, however, suggests in its turn that we are dealing with the remains of a more comprehensive tradition. Only two passages are of some importance. Yasna LIV. 1 (=XXVII.5):

> *ā airyə̄mā išyō rafəδrāi jañtū|*
> *nərəbyas čā nāiribyas cā zarathuštrahē|*[308]
> *vaŋhēuš rafəδrāi manaŋhō...*

"May Airyaman, the desired one, come to the aid of men and women of Zarathustra, to the aid of the good mind."[309] These are words that belong to the *cathrušāmrūta*, the holiest prayers, of the Avesta[310] and are regarded as the most efficacious formula for healing diseases.[311] I do not wish to translate Airyaman in the above passage with Geldner as "dear friend," but, in the light of what has been established from the ṚV, to regard the word as the name of the god of whom it is desired that he should come to the men and women of Zarathustra.[312] If the word usually denotes 'clan' in the Gāthās,[313] then this would only be, inasmuch as it could be determined, an extension of the original linguistic usage to be seen still in its pure form in the Veda, just as the word *mitra* signified at first the god, then 'friend.' That both the stages of the development are present in the Avesta also is proved by the fragment of a Yaśt preserved in *Vendidād* XXII. At first Ahura appeals to Mathra Spenta to heal the 99999 diseases caused by Aṅra Mainyu; then, as the latter was unable to do so, sends his messenger Nairyōsaŋhō to the mansion of Airyaman: "go, drive to the mansion of Airyaman." He promises Airyaman one thousand steeds, swift-running and enduring, if he came to him for healing. "Soon, it did not take long, Airyaman išyō set off on his journey to the mountain of the two Spəntōfrasan, to the tree of the two Spəntōfrasan."[314] We do not learn much from this text either; but a new trait of character, his healing activity, is added to what is known from the Veda.[315] It is worth noting that here also he has the epithet *išyō*, which occurred at the beginning of the first passage and from there passed over to the beginning and to the title of the prayer formula. Therefore, it is quite likely that in the prayer in Yasna LIV.1 also, *ā airyəmō iśyō* refers to the god and that a fragment of the old Airyaman cult is preserved to us in the beginning of this prayer. But no definite conclusion can be drawn. Güntert's theory that Aryaman was connected with civil law more than Mitra was, that unlike the latter he was the "god of the confederation of the Aryan tribes" and that he "protects the bonds of family relationships" does not seem to be well-founded.

D. THE REMAINING ĀDITYAS AND ADITI

1. Bhaga

Of the remaining Ādityas, the one who is described as Aditi's son most often after Varuṇa, Mitra and Aryaman is Bhaga. His name also goes back to a period beyond the Veda and gets lost in a remote antiquity, for we find it in Iran, in the Phrygian *Zeύs Bagaĩos*; it has even reached the Slavonic peoples.[316] In the old Persian cuneiform inscriptions Auramazda is mentioned in company with the *aniyā bagāha tyaiy hantiy* and Auramazda himself is *mathiš̌ta bagānām.* We find the expression *hāda vithaibiš̌ bagaibiš̌*; for our present purpose it is immaterial whether this is rendered as "clan gods" or as "all gods."[317] Even in the Avesta the word possesses no more specific sense than 'god.' Although nothing can be gained directly from the Veda for the Aryan period, yet the Veda ascribes to this Bhaga only such traits which place him on the same level with the Bhaga of other tribes, both representing eudemonist values. Here we have a prehistoric designation that describes not a demon but a good god. The full accord between the Slavonic derivatives which mean 'good, rich'[318] and the Indian Bhaga who grants happiness and wealth and is called *vasuvid* is perhaps not accidental. It is not the major gods and names of the Indo-Iranian world which give information on certain ur-Aryan aspects, but the minor gods who have lost their importance, who have become impoverished but belong to an old aristocracy. Like the old Aryan word *daiva*, which we cannot separate from *div*, *dyaus*, and its amicable sense, the Bhaga in question also has an amicable sense originally. Although I do not wish to attach great importance to the evidence of these word-equations because, besides these, there might also have existed names of ancient demons that are lost now, yet these word-equations demonstrate that the cult of the Aryans was not a mere demon worship, and demolish the theory, as far as such a remote period is concerned, that the lower mythology must necessarily be the preliminary stage for the higher one.

A fresh examination of the scanty material convinced me that the picture drawn by my predecessors, particularly by the PW, is correct. Bhaga is at times an appellative, at others a personal name, and is connected in the former capacity with the names of individual gods,[319] particularly of Savitṛ.[320] However, the lines of demarcation are in flux, for we find Savitṛ and god Bhaga side by side[321] or the Bhaga in the possession of Savitṛ.[322] In some passages Bhaga denotes the sun god.[323] But in view of the wide distribution of the word in Aryan languages, I would think that this was not the original concept but a transference that took place in India owing to the frequent association with Savitṛ. It is true that Bhaga is generally a god of wealth;[324] but it would not be correct to limit him to this aspect only, since he and the appellative noun are connected specially with matrimony and success in love. The old maid living in her parent's house implores Indra for this.[325] In the Traiyambaka sacrifice when the maidens throw the cakes into the air and then put them in the hands of the sacrificer and take them away once again, they say: *bhaga stha bhagasya vo lapsīya.*[326] In ṚV I. 163.8 among those who accompany the sacrificial horse on its journey, *bhágaḥ kanīnām* is mentioned,[327] quite probably a designation for the group of youths who follow the horse, "the success in love," "the hope" of maidens.[328] Bhaga conducts the bridegroom or the bride into the house,[329] and is mentioned in this connection often in the company of Aryaman.[330] Bhaga is also an honorific for the husband, though this is rare.[331]

In some passages the noun occurs beside *várcas* and denotes the power of attraction, the ability to allure.[332] In a formula of exorcism, the malignant woman takes away the *bhaga* and *varcas* of her rival as one takes a garland off the tree;[333] *bhaga* resides in men as well as in women and can be translated at least in one passage as 'fertility.'[334]

Here the appellative noun and the proper noun cannot be separated distinctly because the frontiers between the two meanings are not recognizable. One can say in general that the meanings of the appellative noun denote also the sphere of influence of the god. Everyone invokes him; "even the king," as VII.41, a hymn instructive about the diverse gifts of Bhaga, shows.[235] If Ludwig's translation of I.134.5 is correct Bhaga grants success to the hunter also. By rendering the word as "god of fortune" we would do justice to the nature of Bhaga in its full extent; we may regard *kalyāṇa* and *maṅgala* as the synonyms of the word; according to AV V.26.9 where an individual personal characteristic is ascribed to each god, *āśiṣaḥ* are ascribed to him as *vīrya* is to Indra, *payas* to Soma, *rūpa* to Tvaṣṭṛ, *tapas* to Viṣṇu; *bhagavat* would mean as much as the "blessed one."

2. Dakṣa and Aṃśa

Dakṣa is mentioned less frequently than Bhaga as Aditi's son.[336] The word is employed partly as adjective and partly as noun, and belongs to those words which, like Bhaga, do not exactly maintain the frontiers between the appellative and the proper nouns. Dakṣa's position among the Ādityas or in their vanguard as their father is the outcome of a notion which found a more popular expression in Viśvakarman and Prajāpati in the later times. Agni and other gods are called *sahasaḥ putra*, the Ṛbhus and others *śavasaḥ napātaḥ* or *sūnu*. In the same way a related concept of 'strength' or 'potency' emerged out of semi-philosophical speculations and was elevated to the status of a personage in the highest heaven.[337] Mitra-Varuṇa are called the sons of Dakṣa,[338] so also all the Ādityas (VI. 50. 2) and even the singers themselves in one passage (VIII. 63. 10). In the hymn of creation (X. 72. 4, 5)[339] there is a paradoxical statement of the type one usually meets with in the Upaniṣads: Dakṣa is made the son of Aditi and Aditi the daughter of Dakṣa and the eldest sister of the gods.[340] This belongs more to the realm of philosophy than to that of mythology.[341]

All that can be said about Aṃśa is still less than what has been said of Dakṣa. Aṃśa (share, portion) did not attain any type of importance. As far as the offerings are concerned, I can merely refer to ŚBr V. 3. 5. 9 where an oblation for him is mentioned.[342]

3. The Number of the Ādityas

Of the Ādityas mentioned by name, Mitra, Varuṇa and probably Aryaman have a natural base, but not Bhaga, Dakṣa and Aṃśa. These six are enumerated as Aditi's sons in ṚV II. 27. 1. In VIII. 18.3 only five are mentioned. While Dakṣa and Aṃśa are omitted there, Savitṛ is included as a new member. Elsewhere the name Āditya is applied to Indra or becomes the designation of the sun god.[343] A careful survey of all passages has convinced me of the impossibility of determining the exact number of the Ādityas, or to limit the number to seven. Unlike Oldenberg (ṚdV, 2nd ed., p. 178, n. 2), I do not attach any value to ṚV IX. 114.3, which speaks of seven Ādityas, for the verse mentions, besides the Ādityas, seven different countries with seven suns and seven Hotṛs. I would think that here it is nothing but a play on numbers based on the sacredness of seven. In this I am supported by the context in which our verse is included in TĀr I. 7.1 ff.[344] Mention is made of eight Ādityas as early as in a passage of the ṚV; it is the eighth verse from the cosmogonic hymn X. 72, to which reference is made above in the section on Dakṣa. According to this verse, Aditi approaches the gods with seven of her sons and casts away the eighth. The nature of the hymn and of the verse, which makes a distinction between the gods and the Ādityas who have lost their significance, indicates a source that cannot prove anything for the older conceptions. ŚBr III. 1. 3. 2, 3 speaks of eight Ādityas,[345] TS VI. 6. 1. 2 mentions in all five only (4+1) and in the Brāhmaṇas the usual number of the Ādityas is twelve, so much so the above-mentioned number seven is suggestive only of the beginnings of a system which did not obtain originally and was discarded later on in favour of the number twelve. This system is not in conformity with the first eight maṇḍalas which do not narrow down the concept into numbers anywhere and employ it still quite liberally.[346] At times these maṇḍalas designate only Mitra and Varuṇa as Ādityas, at others Mitra, Varuṇa and Aryaman. X.63.2 classifies the gods into *yé sthá jātā́ áditer, adbhyás pári, yé pṛthivyā́ḥ*. Here Aditi, in contradistinction to the *āpaḥ* and the earth, characterizes the celestial gods. This verse corresponds to the threefold division in VII. 35. 14.[347] In some passages, it seems to me, 'Ādityāḥ' has become the designation for all gods;[348] but this is not the normal usage, provided such an extension of sense is admitted for these verses at all.

The connection of the Ādityas with Indra and with 'Āditya' Sūrya is not without interest for the concept of the Ādityas. Indra who emerged from a completely different area of concepts and myths does not belong to their group from the very beginning but moves towards them gradually. In II. 27. 14; VIII.67.8 we see Indra in the immediate neighbourhood of the Ādityas. Like Varuṇa elsewhere, he is made directly their chief in X. 157. 2, 3 (*ādityaír índraḥ ságaṇo*)[349] and finally designated twice directly as Āditya.[350] But in general Indra's, designation as Āditya has not prevailed. On the other hand, the elevation of Sūrya as Aditi's son met with a good reception throughout and was retained in the classical language. We find this elevation in its beginnings in the ṚV and that too—with the exception of the eccentric eighth maṇḍala—in those parts which are late additions: I. 50. 13; 191. 9; X. 88.11 (*āditeya*).[351] But it occurs far more frequently in the AV;[352] this, I think, is a clear indication of the fact that in the AV, Mitra has completely faded out and was felt only in a vague association with the 'day.' The plural *ādityāḥ* has undergone a total transition to become the designation for a general class of genii of the celestial light, besides whom 'the Āditya' makes his appearence only as an individual manifestation. Even Varuṇa is not called Āditya any more; on the contrary, he is mentioned only in a loose association with the Ādityas as their leader or chief.[353] The dual Ādityau occurs once again. However, these are not Mitra and Varuṇa any more but Sūrya and Candramas. The colourless triad of Ādityas, Vasus and Rudras, which is known to the ṚV but almost only in the tenth book,[354] can be noticed more clearly in its mechanical sequence. The antithesis between the Ādityas and the Aṅgiras, which is noticeable already in the ṚV, becomes more prominent here.[355] In sum, there is a substantial difference between the two Vedas. The difference is still greater between these and the Brāhmaṇa literature, which fixes the number of the Ādityas finally as twelve and identifies them with the twelve months.

Although the understanding of the original meaning of the Ādityas was in a process of disappearing, yet the AV and the later literature held fast, with the ṚV,[356] to the view that they were gods of the celestial world and not of the atmosphere, nor of the earth. The AV demonstrates this through passages like XVIII.4.3: *svargáṃ yátrādityā́ mádhu bhakṣáyanti*; XIX.16.2: *divó mādityā́ rakṣantu*, and the ŚBr corroborates this, for instance, through VI. 1. 2. 8; 5. 2. 5.[357] This is not an insignificant point when we are to define the nature of Aditi. Furthermore, we should remember that with the exception of Dakṣa and Aṃśa it is always the gods of light[358] or those who are close to the former that are reckoned among her sons; even the Brāhmaṇa period does not deviate from this rule.[359]

In the ritual, the Ādityas were given a place in the evening pressing.[360] I do not see why the Ādityas were assigned exactly this position in the evening pressing, which does not seem to be consistent with their undisputed character as gods of light. Not only they, but Savitṛ, the impeller, (this one, of course, for reasons that can be perceived) is also accommodated in the evening pressing. Until others are able to see more penetratingly, I wish to think that the reason lies in the purely superficial connection with their number twelve; for even the metres with their number of eight, eleven and twelve syllables are distributed among the morning, noon and evening pressings respectively. Moreover, the number twelve of the Ādityas corresponds to the twelve months (ŚBr XI. 6. 3. 8). Hence, here in the evening of the day (and symbolically at the end of the year), the ritualists have accommodated besides the three Ṛbhus perhaps also the twelve months. The evening savana and its vicinity have obviously become the collecting centre for such deities who had not yet found a place in the Soma sacrifice and had to be included subsequently.[361]

4. The Ādityas and the Aməsašpəntas

It is an old dogma of Vedic research that the Ādityas are historically related to the seven Aməšaspəntas of Iran. This theory was propounded by Roth[362] and was taken up by various scholars, notably by Darmesteter.[363] In recent times this theory found a strong advocate in Oldenberg who goes still farther than Darmesteter and tries to prove, both in his *Religion des Veda* as well as in his rejoinder to Pischel's and L. v. Schroeder's objections,[364] that these are originally the sun, the moon and the planets. L. v. Schroeder, B. Geiger and Keith also hold the view that the Ādityas and the Aməšaspəntas are identical.[365]

The arguments in favour of a historical relationship between the two groups of gods seemed to me quite inadequate all along. Even after a fresh examination of the arguments and counter-arguments, I can only say that the entire reasoning is based on a weak foundation. Still less do I believe that the five planets have anything to do in the context of the number of the Ādityas and of the Aməšaspəntas. Although the main grounds against a historical relationship between the two groups have been adequately set forth by the other side, I would still like to state my point of view briefly, because Oldenberg, with whom I agree adout the explanation of Mitra-Varuṇa, has not convinced me of the other aspects through his recent statements. "Mitra represents," asserts Oldenberg, "according to innumerable evidences the day and Varuṇa the night. We have established earlier from *material that is totally independent of this*[366] that Varuṇa is precisely the luminous body that illuminates the night...Let us recapitulate once again: seven celestial luminaries and seven luminous gods who reside in the celestial region. Of the luminaries two are large and five small, of the gods two are great and five small."[367]

I think the first flaw in this reasoning lies in the assumption of the number seven. Seven luminous gods ? I have tried to argue that a definite number for the host of the Ādityas cannot be found anywhere in books I-VIII, and that it occurs only in book IX and probably also once in book X. Why then should we not take five as in VIII. 18.3 or six as in II. 27. 1 or eight as one could certainly infer from X. 72 and also AV VIII. 9. 21 or twelve as in the Brāhmaṇas ? Why should we start precisely from IX. 114. 3 which is of doubtful value? Even Barth,[368] who holds that the Ādityas are related to the Aməšaspəntas, does not recognize the evidence of the number seven. Secondly are these really seven luminaries? Only Mitra and Varuṇa and perhaps Aryaman are 'luminaries;' this is precluded for Bhaga, further for Dakṣa and Aṃśa, whom Oldenberg regards as late abstractions. On the other hand, in the Avesta we have admittedly seven genii of light; *aša vahišta, vohumanō, xšathra vairya, haurvatāt,* and *amərətāṭ, spənta ārmaiti* (to whom perhaps *sraoša* can also be added[369]), but all of these with the exception of Ahura himself are merely abstractions or allegories. None of these show an inner or external relationship with even one of the Ādityas. After all, Oldenberg himself admits (ZDMG, L, p. 51) that Vohumanō etc. are Zarathustran abstractions. This cannot be changed. In the Veda, Mitra is always an Āditya, in the Avesta, Mithra is never one of the Aməšaspəntas. Aryaman is mentioned often as Aditi's son, at several places Bhaga also; but neither of these ever belonged to the Aməšaspəntas.

Oldenberg continues further: "Of the two large luminaries one is the sun, of the two great gods one is Mitra, the sun god. The second large luminary rules over the night, the second great god rules over the night. Can all this be accidental?" I cannot see that Ahuramazda rules over the night—this sphere of influence which is attributed to him hangs by the slender thread of a hypothesis, namely the erroneous association between him and Varuṇa. That the two are distinct has been stated long ago by Pischel (GGA, 1895, 448) and established by me from another angle. Thus, the dazzling comparison is without foundation even here. Since the names and character of these two groups do not coincide in any single instance, what remains of the whole thing is the number seven of the Aməšaspəntas (without Sraoša) in Iran and the solitary reference to the seven Ādityas; this congruence is, however, purely accidental. Even if I were to admit that ṚV IX. 114. 3 has certain value, we would have, of course, the number seven on both the sides, but the names and content would still not be identical. The 'edifice,' which Oldenberg (ZDMG. L, p. 57) declares to be ancient, is devoid of any content in Iran; neither the sun and moon, nor the planets are to be found among the beings that fill the edifice in Iran. It is true, in India we come across the sun and the moon and five others besides, but to interpret them as "planets" is without any justification. One might say that probably the place of the five planets has been usurped by the same number of other beings, but that would ultimately be one of those "fanciful visions which miscarry and which must necessarily miscarry if the investigation is not built upon a natural basis."[370] The histories of religion in India and in Iran have, in this respect, nothing in common.[371]

5. Aditi

There remains still the question of the mother of these deities who have attained such importance in the Veda. We can leave aside passages like I.89.10[372] which recall the philosophical hymns of a late period or the Upaniṣads and which have little or no value for mythology.

Like all feminine deities, Aditi too remains, it must be admitted, in the background in the Veda, but the fact that Mitra and Varuṇa are regarded as her sons in all parts of the ṚV testifies to the antiquity of her personification. To compare her with Hera, Dione and Juno, as Colinet[373] does, would be possible, but in my view this would be only an analogy and not a historical relationship.

Although the number of oblations dedicated to her in the ritual is not large, the ritual indirectly attaches a certain amount of significance to her, because during the twelve Ratnahavis-oblations, offerings are made to Aditi in the dwelling of the Mahiṣī: "Aditi is this earth, and she is the wife of the gods,"[374] and the dakṣiṇā here is a cow. On another occasion she is described as the archetype for the housewife. When a girdle is put around the sacrificer's wife, this act is accompanied with the formula *adityai rāsnāsi*.[375]

In my doctoral dissertation,[376] I defined Aditi as "the daylight in its imperishableness" and thus came close to Roth's view (ZDMG, VI, p. 68) according to which this eternal and inviolable principle "which sustains the Ādityas and which constitutes their being" is the celestial light.[377] I still believe even today that this definition is basically correct. On the other hand, Max Müller opines that Aditi denotes "the Infinite"[378] and Oldenberg[379] wishes to recognize in Aditi merely the concept of the "freedom from bondage," not the infinity of space, nor the imperishableness, nor, by connecting the concept with a natural basis, the daylight in its imperishableness; otherwise, says Oldenberg,[379] Aditi would occupy a central position whereas she rightfully belongs, at the most, to the periphery. But were the Vedic Indians already in a position to comprehend the idea of the "freedom from bondage" and that too to such a degree that the idea was elevated to become the name of the mother of the gods? But Oldenberg adduces no evidence for his view and circumscribes his statements to such an extent that the difference between his view and mine becomes in fact quite small.[380] If we were to base our conclusions merely on etymology, the interpretation would hardly be any different from what Oldenberg proposes. But as in the case of Savitṛ there are great limitations to this etymological meaning. Moreover, the verses which speak of Aditi's light are not at all younger than those which beseech her or her sons for freedom from want and oppression. It must be noted here that not all gods but only a specific group among them is made the sons of Aditi. With the exception of Dakṣa and Aṃśa, this group consists exclusively of deities connected with light and celestial region: Savitṛ, Indra and, above all, the sun god who joins the group later (see p. 60 above). We do not find heaven and earth, which are infinite, among her sons, nor any of the storm gods, although this place is due, first of all, to the wind god if Aditi were a goddess of the "freedom from bondage," for of all gods, he is the most eminent son of freedom. ṚV X. 168.4 states: *yathāvaśaṃ carati devá eṣáḥ.* According to TBr III.1.4.13, he achieves *kāmacāra.* In MS II.2. 7 it is said: *na khalu vai kiṃ cana vāyunānabhigatam asti.*[381] Parents and sons are often dissimilar in mythology also. But here Aditi and her sons have a common life principle. Her sons are the gods of light that resides in the sky and Aditi is inseparably connected with that light; it is her innermost essence.[382] All this is consistent with the fact that according to KŚS XV.9.18ff., a reddish yellow cow is sacrificed to Aditi or to the Ādityas, whereas (the Viśvedevāḥ or) the Maruts, who are the sons of Pṛśni, receive a spotted cow.[383]

The possession of freedom can emerge from the possession of light just as easily (or more easily still) as the concept of light emerges from the concept of the freedom from bondage, for the light is directly called *urú,*[384] *ábhaya*[385] and *ávṛka,* and it is the opposite not only of darkness but of restraint and want as well.[386]

Consequently, I do not hesitate to define Aditi as the "eternal light," the imperishable light with its abode in the sky, Ādityas being the sons of this light in contradistinction to others like the Maruts who are called *pṛśnimātaraḥ*. There is one verse which, I think, is a paraphrase of the notion that is personified in Aditi and can be cited here as a parallel, viz., the fifth verse of the Sūrya hymn, I.115:

> *anantám anyád rúśad asya pā́jaḥ*
> *kṛṣṇám anyád dharítaḥ sám bharanti//*

This *anantám anyád ruśad pā́jaḥ* is Aditi.

Colinet[387] had dealt with the same subject before me, and I am glad that my work is in substantial agreement with his conclusions: "we also see in Aditi the empyreal light," says Colinet and adds in another passage that "all the characteristics of Aditi explain themselves if one assumes that she represents the empyreal light in its union with the highest sky. She is then the goddess of the eternal light of which Aurora is the radiant face." Colinet is probably right also when he states that Aditi should not at all be regarded as "the product of individual and fleeting speculations."

On an earlier occasion I have adduced evidence to say that in the Yajus literature Aditi is most frequently identified with the earth,[388] and attempted to ascertain the reasons for this. Even now I think that it is a case of a late transference of attributes. Aditi is the mother of gods, she corresponds to the Mahiṣī and to the Patnī and thus, I believe, the *aditir* might have become the *mātā paramé vyòman* and the *mahī mātā* the designation for the earth, the *gotva* being common to both. "Like Aditi," says Colinet, "the earth is the goddess of fecundity; like Aditi, she is, above all, the wife of Dyaus, not of the empyreal Dyaus, but of the visible sky."[389]

However, if we were to follow the dangerous tendency which is becoming popular now, namely to interpret the mythology of the ṚV in the light of the later literature and to transpose its data into the ṚV, then the view of the YV and Brāhmaṇas that Aditi is the same as the earth would prevail throughout; but the hymns of the ṚV contradict this. Neither Mitra nor Varuṇa, the most eminent of the Ādityas, are earth-born; nor Indra who is occasionally counted among the Ādityas; nor is the earth intimately connected with radiance and light as Aditi is. However, in one passage of the ṚV the above-mentioned identification is already accomplished, viz., in X.70.7[390] where the *dhā́mans*, i.e., the hearths of Agni *vediṣád*, are stated to be situated on "Aditi's lap." Here Aditi means as much as *dhiṣaṇā*, which is a synonym of *vedi*, not in the usual sense of earth but in the sense of consecrated earth. The verse belongs to the tenth maṇḍala. But I cannot draw I.24.1, 2 and I.72.9 into this context as Pischel does.[391] The first passage can easily be explained in a different manner. The second is obscure; I wonder if *áditi* there is not an adjective or if the two verse-halves are not to be separated. On the other hand, IX.26.1 can belong here:

tám amṛkṣanta vājinam upásthe áditer ádhi|
víprāso áṇvyā dhiyā

My earlier rendering as "in the lap of milk"[392] is inadequate.

CHAPTER SIX

SAVITṚ AND THE ṚBHUS

A. SAVITṚ

There are two conflicting views in the interpretation of Savitṛ: one proceeds from the usage of the later period and tries to see the sun god in the Savitṛ of the ṚV as well, the other, advanced by Oldenberg, explains Savitṛ as an abstraction, as a "God Impeller," who was invested subsequently with the character of a god of light. It is not easy to decide between the two because the etymon of the name, of which the composers of the hymns were quite conscious, serves as the basis for many a play upon the words with the verb *su*, and, on the other hand, a somewhat subjective assessment of passages, that are necessary for the interpretation, cannot be avoided completely. Those very verses to which the advocates of the sun-theory attach special value are regarded by the other side as unimportant, and Oldenberg, who does not wish to dismiss those verses altogether, poses the question; "Which statements of the ṚV can actually be regarded as evidence for this (identification of Savitṛ as the sun god)?"[1]

Let us first turn to the ritual.

1. Savitṛ in the Ritual

We encounter Savitṛ regularly in the Agniṣṭoma and also in its other varieties where the Sāvitragraha, accompanied by certain special rules, is offered during the evening pressing. Āpastamba gives the following rules.

ĀpŚS XIII.13.1: "With the mantra, 'fair [wealth], O Savitṛ, today,' he draws [the Graha] by the means of the Antaryāmapātra from the Āgrāyaṇa vessel, but does not deposit it on the ground.[2] 2: The two Sampraiṣas run thus: 'recite for god Savitṛ' and 'summon for god Savitṛ.' 3: The Anuvaṣaṭkāra is prohibited."

According to the ĀpŚS, the Sāvitragraha follows the

Namaskāra to the Manes and, on the other side, precedes the Vaiśvadevaśastra. The hymns inviting Savitṛ are followed by a verse for Vāyu, the Dyāvāpṛthivī-sūkta I.159 and hymn I.111 for the Ṛbhus.

KBr XVI.2 has the following to say on the Sāvitragraha: "Now they proceed with the Sāvitragraha. Earlier one offered it during the Prātaḥsavana. Progeny was not born. [Then it was offered] during the midday savana. Even then [progeny was] not [born]. They offered it here during the third savana. Thereupon progeny was born. Therefore, Savitṛ is fixed at the third savana. Now Savitṛ is one of the Ādityas; the third savana belongs to the Ādityas. Having recited a Triṣṭubh verse as Puronuvākyā for the Sāvitragraha, he employs a Jagatī as the Yājyā verse...He does not make an Anuvaṣaṭkāra (Anuvaṣaṭkāra is the end) with the reflection, 'so that I may not end my life before time.' For the life is harnessed as it were... 3: The Vaiśvadevaśastra begins with Savitṛ. Impelled by Savitṛ, the gods prepared the third savana. Hence 'Pratipad and Anucara, and Sūkta' belong to Savitṛ."

From this statement it follows that the Sāvitragraha was shifted from the morning to the evening, or, since the Agniṣṭoma follows the course of the year and thus is certainly a replica of the year, from the beginning of the year to its end represented by the Tṛtīyasavana. This is closely related to the unusual position of the Ādityas who are accommodated in the evening savana where likewise they also might not have had their place originally.[3]

We cannot separate the worship of the Ṛbhus who obtained a share in the Soma drink from the Sāvitragraha and the Vaiśvadevaśastra. ABr III.30 narrates thus: "They wished to prepare the Soma drink for the Ṛbhus during the Prātaḥsavana. But Agni along with the Vasus pushed them away from the Prātaḥsavana. They wished to prepare [the Soma drink] for them during the midday savana. Indra accompanied by the Maruts pushed them away from the midday savana. They wished to prepare [the Soma drink] for them during the evening savana. The Viśve Devāḥ violently pushed them away saying, 'they should not drink here, not here.' Prajāpati said to Savitṛ: 'They are your pupils (*antevāsa*). You drink with them.' 'So be it,' said

Savitṛ. 'You drink by their side.' By their side Prajāpati drank... The gods were disgusted with them because of their human smell; they inserted the two Dhāyyā verses..." This legend associates the Ṛbhus intimately with Savitṛ and Prajāpati. It has a special significance because the various elements in it are known to the ṚV. For it is impossible to separate this Savitṛ whose *antevāsāḥ* the Ṛbhus are stated to be from that Savitṛ in whose abode, according to some verses of the ṚV,[4] the Ṛbhus stay for twelve days as his guests, i.e., the *savitṛ dāśvaṃs*, the *agohya*. Who is the second one ? I see no reason to differ from Sāyaṇa who in his commentary on I.161.11;[5] IV.33.7[6] explains Agohya as *āditya*. As early as in ṚV I.110.2,3 Agohya is identified with Savitṛ.[7] To look for a mere "god vivifier" or 'impeller' in Savitṛ here is precluded by the situation itself. Even if we wish to ignore Sāyaṇa's testimony, Savitṛ in whose abode the Ṛbhus dwelt is characterized so distinctly that we cannot be satisfied with the notion of a mere abstraction. The appellative has made a progress to become the name of a particular mythological personality here. Moreover, we can obtain a clue to the nature of Savitṛ from the customs of the Agniciti. It is well known that the altar to be constructed there can have different forms: the shape of a *śyena*, of a *śmaśāna* and so on. "Whosoever desires heaven should pile up for Savitṛ."[8] Here the shape of the altar is achieved in the following way. In the centre of the place meant for the Uttaravedi, a peg is driven into the ground and around this peg a circle of the size of a chariot wheel is drawn.[9] I think that this clearly indicates how the Yājñikas conceived Savitṛ. For them Savitṛ was not an abstraction, not a god 'vivifier.'[10] The iṣṭakas used for the construction symbolize the fifteen days or nights of the Pūrvapakṣa, or of the Aparapakṣa, or directly the twelve Pūrvapakṣas or the twelve Aparapakṣas.

Thirdly, the puroḍāśas offered to Savitṛ are not without significance.[11] These occur very frequently in the extensive ritual and are characterized primarily by the specification as *dvādaśakapāla*. Of course, the importance of this statement should not be overrated, for we do not always know for certain why this or another (hardly accidental) number of kapālas is employed. But the regularly recurring number twelve recalls the twelve kapālas in the sacrifices for Vaiśvānara. We have already encountered this Vaiśvānara as a form of the sun god.[12] We should also recall the Savitṛ-oblations that are repeated every day for a year during the Aśvamedha.[13] This period of time also refers to the god who reigns over the year. These three instances which make it possible to define Savitṛ's nature more closely stand *vis-à-vis* those where mention is made of his *sava* or *prasava.* We find a reference to this at the beginning of the major sacrifices[14] which take place "at Savitṛ's command," as well as in the minor rites belonging to them where the expression *devasya savituḥ prasave* occurs innumerable times and denotes the beginning of many acts.[15] Does it follow from this that for those who recited this formula Savitṛ was nothing but a "god impeller"?

Often the formula *devasya tvā savituḥ prasave* has a continuation. It is followed by the expression *aśvinor bāhubhyāṃ pūṣṇo hastābhyām.*[16] Just from this we can see that those words *devasya tvā prasave* have no more significance than "the arms of the Aśvins" or "Pūṣan's hands" have. That is to say, these are simply stereotype phrases which have been borrowed from the set of conceptions of the gods concerned and remain fixed in these formulas without betraying anything of their original connotation.[17]

This judgment will not be shaken even by the fact that *savituḥ prasave* or *save* is stressed quite often. Undoubtedly the meaning of the god's name was still vivid in the minds and became the basis for diverse kinds of plays upon words.[18] But wherever we encounter Savitṛ as the centre of an act in the ritual, this means that Savitṛ has reached beyond the mere form of an impeller.[19] And should it be totally forgotten in the case of the ritual what the vivifying and impelling power was of all sacrifices that were connected with a specific season? I would think that it is quite probable that the abstract conception of *savituḥ prasava* emerged at a later stage from the vivifying power of the sun god[20] who sets the sacrifices as well as the human activity in motion (*mitro yātayajjana*).

2. Savitṛ in the Ṛgveda

The conditions in the ṚV are not different from those in the ritual. In the ṚV also the *prasava* of the god is emphasized equally vividly and, at the same time, Savitṛ is surrounded by all the characteristics of the sun god. If it can be established that those passages which praise the vivifying activity of Savitṛ are older than the others, then Oldenberg's view would be correct. But I find that these passages coexist with the others in the same hymns and that the two aspects of Savitṛ cannot at all be separated from one another in the ṚV. Thus it is said in

V.81.2: *prásāvīd bhadrám̐ dvipáde cátuṣpade |*
5: *utéśiṣe prasavásya tvám éka it |*

and the same second verse states of him in the following words

ví nā́kam akhyat savitā́ váreṇyaḥ
ánu prayā́ṇam uṣáso ví rājati ||

precisely the same as other passages state of Agni, namely "that he follows Uṣas."[21] Names apart, there is no difference here between Savitṛ and Agni-Sūrya. Can we prove that this hymn V.81 in which the solar qualities of Savitṛ are stressed unambiguously is later than the one that follows it, viz. V.82, where his *prasava* is pushed into the foreground? Hence, while discussing the question of the underlying concept of a god, it is impossible to pick out just one quality even when this quality is emphasized much too often. We can recognize the perfect parallelism between Sūrya and Savitṛ, as we do here, in other cases as well.[22]

Besides the fifth maṇḍala, it is the fourth in which the word Savitṛ denotes the sun god most distinctly. Without this assumption, I do not see how else the fiftythird hymn of this book can make sense. We read that Savitṛ lulls the world to sleep and inspires it to activity with his rays,[23] and that he puts on a yellow robe;[24] *niveśayan prasuván...jágat* is unambiguously elucidated by the immediately following word *aktúbhiḥ* (compare this with the ninth verse of the Sūrya hymn, X. 37, or compare v. 3: *ā́prā rájām̐si divyā́ni pā́rthivā* with the words in I.115.1: *ā́prā dyā́vāpṛthivī́ antárikṣam̐ sū́rya.*) If the connotation of a god of light or more correctly of sun god, which Savitṛ had exclusively in the later period, was attributed to Savitṛ only later, then it is evident from this hymn that such an attribution must have been accomplished already before Vāmadeva composed this hymn. I do not see what else can be said about a sun god other than what has been said here, as long as one does not demand that all that is ever stated about Sūrya or Vaiśvānara should be repeated again in this hymn. But such a demand is not justified. In the first volume of this work (p. 81), I have already emphasized that each god is surrounded by a set of concepts that are exclusive to him or predominantly his own and by a specific terminology.[25] Just as the realm of Sūrya is distinct from that of Vaiśvānara so also is Savitṛ's realm different from that of Sūrya. The two names emerge from two different notions. When Oldenberg says: "this much is certain at the first glance: for the Ṛgvedic poets Sūrya and Savitṛ are two different divine personages...they are contiguous but distinct from one another. We should read the Sūrya hymns and the Savitṛ hymns one after the other; the usual content of the one is basically different from that of the other,"[26] this is precisely what is to be expected. One should also read the Sūrya hymns and the Vaiśvānara hymns and one would find here also substantial difference in content although Vaiśvānara and Sūrya are personifications of the same natural phenomenon. I can also fully agree with Oldenberg's statement that "in the ritual Sūrya receives worship at one place and Savitṛ at another and these places cannot be interchanged," for such an interchange, which might appear easy from the exegetical viewpoint, is not quite possible from theological and ritual points of view. Every god is regarded as an individual personality, distinctly marked by his name, and is conceived as a special being. Each name has its special evolution which produced it and ascribed to it certain traits of character. Even Mitra, whom I interpret with Oldenberg as an ancient sun god, cannot be interchanged with Sūrya or Vaiśvānara or any other name which basically denotes the same phenomenon.[27] The freedom which we have with regard to these products of mythological evolution did not exist for the ancient Yājñikas who attempted to incorporate these deities at an appropriate place in the ritual mosaic in such a way that these were in harmony with the tradition. Oldenberg considers Indra and Parjanya as storm gods, but he will certainly not assume that an oblation for one could have been regarded as equal to the oblation for the other from ritual viewpoint, or that Sūrya-sacrifice and Mitra-sacrifice are interchangeable.

Like the poet of IV.53, another Vāmadeva, the composer of IV.13,14, attests to the fact that in his times Savitṛ and the sun were no more distinct. Savitṛ's ray is called *bhānú* or *ketú* there[28] and this is thought of as such a well-established attribute of Savitṛ that it serves as an object of comparison in IV.6.2 where the uplifted ray of Agni is compared to the ray of Savitṛ.[29] This does not preclude the possibility that the same Vāmadevas who see in Savitṛ the sun god can also see in him at the same time the vivifier and impeller who rules over the heaven and earth and grants wealth to men and immortality to the sacrificing gods.[30] But precisely this simultaneous glorification of both the aspects of Savitṛ precludes, as far as the fourth maṇḍala is concerned, the division of his nature into two successive periods, the splitting up into a 'vivifier' Savitṛ and a "god of light" Savitṛ, where the former would have the precedence. The same is true, as hymns 81 and 82 demonstrate, of the fifth maṇḍala. Is something else probable than that the sun god in his capacity as 'impeller' and in his efficacy became the cause for the personification ? Unlike in the case of Indra and Rudra, the poets were still conscious of the etymological meaning of Savitṛ. But is that any reason for making this etymological meaning decisive in the enquiry into the nature of the god who bears this name ? And in addition to these hymns, there are other factors which one cannot, on the basis of our texts, consider as later additions to the personality of Savitṛ as the ṚV conceives him : (1) attributes like *híraṇyajihva*, *híraṇyapāṇi*, *áyohanu* in VI.71.3,4 which would be very inappropriate for a god conceived purely as an abstraction; (2) AV XIII.2.36[31] which adduces evidence that cannot be underestimated and which Oldenberg also recognizes; (3) the designation of Sūryā (i.e., Uṣas), whom we know as the daughter of the sun god, as *sāvitrī* in AV VI.82.2; XIV.2.30; (4) the *sūryā́ śáṃsantī*, given as wife to Soma by Savitṛ in ṚV X.85.9; (5) the marriage procession of Sūryā which Savitṛ releases; though by themselves not significant, all these statements are understandable from the well-known relationship between the sun and Dawn;[32] further the association of Savitṛ with the day and the night. In the Vedic texts we encounter the sun god often in association with the two. Sūrya measures the days with the nights or Uṣāsānaktā are Sūrya's wives.[33] The words employed by the authors of the Savitṛ hymns are, of course, somewhat different, particularly those of the poet of hymn I.35 who speaks of "the black atmosphere" through which Savitṛ moves and sets the day in motion.[34] But this individual colouring which is peculiar to Savitṛ poetry should not lead us astray from the fact that what we have here are essentially only mythological synonyms.[35]

A word that is predominantly distinctive of Savitṛ hymns is *amáti.* It occurs nine times in the ṚV and four of these verses are addressed to Savitṛ: III.38.8; VII.38.1, 2; 45.3;[36] In the Savitṛ concept *amáti* means probably the same as *māyā́ diví śritā́* does in the concept of Mitra-Varuṇa,[37] or Uṣas in the Sūrya hymns. The designations *hiraṇyáyī, urūcī́, urvī́* would be quite befitting to this *amáti.*[38]

The most serious objection that can be raised and has been raised against the identification between the sun and Savitṛ is that occasionally these two are juxtaposed or contrasted with one another.[39] Verses like I. 123.3: *devó no átra savitā́ dámūnā ánāgaso vocati sū́ryāya* appear to support the objection against the identification. However, when we note from other passages that Sūrya is the eye of Mitra-Varuṇa, hence certainly of Mitra also, or when he is addressed in VII.60.1 with the words *yád adyá sūrya brávó 'nāgā udyán mitrā́ya váruṇāya satyám*, we must accept that much that appears improbable becomes probable in the evolutionary process of Indian mythology.[40] This is true also of the Iranian Mithra who is regarded as the sun god by the majority of scholars and yet he "as the first Yazata, rises above the Hara before the undying swift-horsed sun," "whose dwelling was built by the Aməšaspəntas conjointly with the sun in one accord," "for whom the swift-horsed sun awakens worship from afar," "who traverses the breadth of the earth, touches both the ends of the wide round far-reaching earth after-sunset and surveys all that lies between heaven and earth."[41] On the other hand, it is said that for him reddish yoked horses draw the chariot with one wheel which is golden and...which shines upon everything[42] Because of this one could deny Mithra's claim to the title of a sun god just as it has been denied to Savitṛ; for like Savitṛ, Mithra is hardly a mechanically revolving sun, on the contrary he is far removed from the natural basis. Each evolution which does not stop at the stage of crude nature worship is directed towards making a distinction between the agent and the object and towards a search for the spiritual element behind the sensual perception. The solar disc becomes a wheel or one-wheeled chariot on which the sun drives; it becomes the *darśatáṃ vapúr yád āśúr váhati devá étaśaḥ* (VII. 66.14). The god emerges from behind the matter.[43] Thus Savitṛ at times spreads his rays, at others he is called *sūryaraśmí* (X.139 1); or he unites himself with the sun's rays (V.81.4) or the sun is his bird (X.149.3); he impels the sun; he creates the day and the night with his rays; we could say of him: *alme sol, cursu nitido qui promis et celas, aliusque et idem*, "nourishing sun, with your effulgent orbit you reveal and hide, you are different and also the same."[44]

The question where the sun remained at night occupied the Indian mind quite often. The ABr[45] answered it differently from the poets of the Savitṛ hymns who speak of his paths "through darkness." To this refers, as it appears, the epithet *śyāvā́śva* (V.81.5) which refers to the "black horses with white feet" that draw his chariot at night.[46] For the god who moves constantly—through the heavens in the day and through the darkness at night—the ritual dedicated a graha "which must be set down on the ground" and which symbolically suggests his nature.[47]

a. Savitṛ and the Gods

Whosoever goes through the Savitṛ verses of the ṚV will get the impression that Savitṛ occupies a special position *vis-à-vis* the gods. He confers immortality not only upon the Ṛbhus but upon the gods as well.[48] Repeatedly he makes his appearance as the priest or sacrificer who gives the command for sacrifice thrice daily, who rules over *vidátha* ,[49] in whose *sava* Aditi, the Vasus, Mitra among others rejoice,[50] whom all gods follow.[51] He is thus the celestial householder and sacrificer. In the legend of the Ṛbhus who come to his house he is directly called *savitṛ́ dāśvā́ṃs*;[52] in one instance, as in the case of Vivasvat, this expression becomes the honorific for the sacrificer.[53] The epithets *mandrájihva, sujihvá, híraṇyajihva* characterize his priestly activity. One may compare this with III. 54. 11: *devéṣu ca ślókam áśreḥ.*[54] A definite conclusion cannot be drawn from these factors; the verses can very well refer to the "god impeller" just as to the sun god.

I have referred earlier to the diverse roles which the sun plays in the legends of the Brāhmaṇas. I give below some passages from the ṚV which state similar things about the sacrificial activity of Sūrya and Savitṛ. Compare

III. 54. 11: *vidáthe pátyamānaḥ* with
VI. 51. 2: *véda yás trī́ṇi vidáthāny eṣāṃ*
devā́nāṃ jánma sanutár ā́ ca vípraḥ/

or, compare II. 38. 1; IV. 54. 2 with

VI.50. 2: *sujyótiṣaḥ sūrya......vīhi devā́n*

or II. 38. 9; X. 36. 13 with

VII. 5. 4: *táva tridhā́tu pṛthivī́ utá dyaúr*
vaíśvānara vratám agne sacanta/

Here also we should not expect a total congruence in the concepts.[55] Above all, this recalls to mind the Sūrya-stotra in MBh III. 3 16 ff., where Sūrya is elevated above men and gods and glorified as the universal principle.[56]

Let us go back to the ritual once more. We have seen above that Savitṛ receives a graha in the Agniṣṭoma and there he is in the company of the Ṛbhus who are likewise assigned to the Tṛtīyasavana. If we overlook VII. 38 and I. 22 where it can be inferred from the context that Savitṛ is invited to the Soma drink, there is no other mention in the ṚV of Savitṛ's participation in the Soma sacrifice.[57] The ṚV speaks of hymns dedicated to him,[58] of oblations[59] and sacrifices[60] for him but not directly of the Soma draught. We may say that in general Oldenberg's view that the Soma offering to Savitṛ does not go back to antiquity[61] is possible, without however considering this, as Oldenberg does, as an "obvious indication that we are dealing here with a relatively late god." Agni is not a full-fledged *somapā* either as long as he is not in the company of other gods[62] and it is doubtful whether even Mitra-Varuṇa or at least Mitra possessed this attribute originally. Nevertheless it is strange that in the Śrauta ritual Savitṛ has a place in the evening only, and is praised merely as *nivéśano jágatas*, a role assigned to him in conformity with ṚV II.38;[63] for this role is in conflict with his position in the other maṇḍalas like the fourth and the fifth and obviously owes itself to one of those many compromises under which the ritual took its shape. The Yājñikas who gave shape to the Śrauta ritual made a selection from the hymns of different schools[64] and their rituals and conceded a place to Savitṛ in the third pressing as they did to the Ṛbhus. I would think that his association with the Ṛbhus who sojourn in his dwelling as described in the legend—the only legend which is connected with his name—was the reason why Savitṛ and the Ṛbhus were assigned to this place in the ritual.[65] If the Yājñikas had seen in Savitṛ primarily the god 'vivifier,' they would have hardly accommodated him exclusively in the evening pressing.

b. Savitṛ as Appellative

While the names of Agni, Indra, Tvaṣṭṛ and Mitra have lost the connection with their etymons and become exclusively proper names, to a certain extent far removed from their original sense, the original meaning of the word Savitṛ, which as things stand one cannot separate at all from the root *su*, has never been forgotten. On the other hand, a survey of all the verses in the ṚV and the AV shows also that Savitṛ is nowhere a pure appellative, to be used at will somewhat like *kartṛ* or codayitṛ but is already set into narrower paths: either the word has become the designation of a specific god, characterized by the addition of *deva*, of *deva savitṛ*, or it serves as an adjunct to the names of individual gods.[66] We find it often particularly in association with *bhaga*. Either *savitṛ bhaga* or conversely *bhaga savitṛ*[67] occur side by side and amount to one single concept, or we find them as separate entities, though this is rarc.[68] In a few cases Savitṛ occurs similarly along with Dhātṛ[69] and also with Bṛhaspati.[70] But I cannot draw any useful conclusion from the lifeless enumerations and shall avoid repeating what is well known. He is not associated with any god to form a duality, nor is he invoked in any hymn conjointly with another god. The exception is AV. IV. 25, addressed to Vāyu and Savitṛ: but in this hymn there is absolutely nothing useful for the explanation except a half-verse.[71] After the foregoing, there is no need to discuss Güntert's contrary view. He maintains that Savitṛ is only a fragment broken off from Varuṇa, his 'hypostatis,' and that he is the universal monarch conceived from a specific viewpoint in a totally one-sided activity. "The archetype of the Vedic Savitṛ, provided we are on the right track in other respects as well, may thus be given back to us in a plastic and vivid form from the darkest days of prehistory." (Güntert believes, on the basis of the designation of Savitṛ as *pṛthúpāṇi* in II. 38. 2, that this epithet is comparable to a Nordic rock-painting depicting "the god with a huge hand"). It seems to me that at the present stage this historical connection is nothing but a flight into the realm of fantasy. Incidentally we may point out to Indra's epithet *mahāhastín* VIII. 81. 1 which can be compared to Savitṛ's epithet *pṛthúpāṇi*.

B. THE ṚBHUS[72]

These gods or rather spirits of the Vedic world belong undoubtedly to its darkest figures. They had been compared rather precipitately to the Elves of Germanic mythology. But since we possess a more precise knowledge of the texts now, we should treat indifferently this comparison which was suggested by a certain similarity in names. The Vedic hymns contain nothing that would make this class of gods comparable to the dwarves of the Germanic belief or to the hosts of polymorphic Elves. It is true that like Tvaṣṭṛ, the Aśvins and other gods, the Ṛbhus have performed various miracles: they have rejuvinated the parents, created the kine from the skin, produced the steeds for Indra, but they have not, like the nimble spirits of the Germanic world, appeared in diverse manifestations and influenced the human beings in a variety of ways.

When we examine the actual conditions in the Vedas we are struck by one fact. While the ṚV dedicates a number of hymns to the Ṛbhus and particularly the fourth maṇḍala with its five hymns to the Ṛbhus surpasses all other maṇḍalas, the AV shows a different picture: it does not mention *ṛbhukṣán* at all, which occurs 32 times in the ṚV, and *ṛbhú* in eight passages only,[73] without however stating anything significant about them; not a single hymn, not even a verse is addressed to them exclusively. It seems to me that the circle of poets who speak through the AV know very little about these personifications or that the cult of the Ṛbhus was gradually forgotten. They are not mentioned at all in the *Kauśika Gṛhya Sūtra* and of the other Gṛhya Sūtras, only the *Hiraṇyakeśīya*[74] and the *Mānava*[75] mention them in passing. In view of the natural tendency especially of the Gṛhya Sūtras to adapt the names of gods contained in them to the contemporary developments and to show greater flexibility as against the more canonical and conservative character of the Śrauta Sūtras, this silence about the Ṛbhus is not without significance for the history of the evolution of their cult.

1. The Number of the Ṛbhus

Of the series of passages which speak of the Ṛbhus, we should first lay stress on those which refer to them as three. These are the only passages that attempt to differentiate between these spirits and thus state somewhat more than what others do. First of all, we have the differentiation between three brothers in IV.33.5: *jyeṣṭhá*, *kánīyas* and *kaniṣṭhá*.[76] The fourth book has the greatest claim to be discussed here because of its collection of the Ṛbhu hymns (33-37). IV.33.9 from this book takes us a little further:

vā́jo devā́nām abhavat sukármā
índrasya ṛbhukṣā́ váruṇasya víbhvā //

Here we have a threefold distribution which assigns Vāja to the gods, Ṛbhukṣan to Indra and Vibhvan to Varuṇa. The same names recur elsewhere also, but with the difference that *ṛbhukṣán* is replaced by *ṛbhú* alone.[77] Hence, *ṛbhú* besides being a collective name, also designates one of the brothers, the same one who usually bears the name *ṛbhukṣán*.[78]

The plural form is employed side by side with the singular. Here the plural denotes a host, evolved from the personal name, of efficacious forces or helpers, roughly like Agni beside the Agnis.[79] The best illustration is furnished by VII.48.2 despite some obscurities:

ṛbhúr ṛbhúbhir abhí vaḥ syāma
víbhvo vibhúbhiḥ śávasā śávāṃsi |
vā́jo asmā́ṃ avatu vā́jasātau
índreṇa yujā́ taruṣema vṛtrám ||

We find the plural in the place of the singular also, employed, as it seems to me, indeed in an arbitrary manner; at times one name is in the singular, at others another name. But it is worth noting that *víbhvan* is mentioned rather rarely in comparison to *vā́ja* (or *vā́jāḥ*) and *ṛbhú* (or *ṛbhávaḥ*).[80]

2. Indra and the Ṛbhus

Indra is closely associated in IV.33.9 with one of the Ṛbhus. Much more frequently, however, it is all the three who enjoy Indra's friendship or have him as their companion, so much so that he is mentioned often along with them.

III.60.3: *índrasya sakhyám ṛbhávaḥ sam ānaśuḥ*
4: *índreṇa yātha sarátham suté sácām*
IV.35.7: *sám ṛbhúbhiḥ pibasva ratnadhébhiḥ*
sákhīṃr yā́ṃ indra cakṛṣé sukṛtyā́ ||

We may further refer to VII.48.2 given just above or to

IV.33.3: *té vā́jo víbhvāṃ ṛbhúr indravantaḥ*
mádhūpsaraso no 'vantu yajñám ||

and to IV.34.1; 37.6.[81] Hence he is called *ṛbhumát*,[82] *ṛbhuṣṭhirá*,[83] which are almost synonymous with *ṛbhukṣán*, likewise attributed to Indra;[84] further there is the epithet *ṛbhvan*, attributed four times to Indra and twice to Agni.[85]

Hence, it is obvious that of all the gods, Indra is closest to the Ṛbhus. This close connection between them finds expression in the ritual also. In the Praiṣa during the evening savana, Indra is accompanied by the three Ṛbhus, who without having a graha of their own, are mentioned jointly with other gods as partakers in the Soma drink: *tṛtīyasya savanasya ṛbhumato vibhumataḥ prabhumataḥ*[86] *vājavataḥ savitṛvato bṛhaspativato viśvadevyāvatas tīvrāṃ āśīrvata indrāya somān prasthitān preṣya.*[87]

3. The Meaning of the Ṛbhus

When we attempt to interpret the Ṛbhus, we must proceed from the above-mentioned verses which refer to them as three and particularly from IV.33.9 which associates Vāja with the Devas, Ṛbhukṣan with Indra and Vibhvan with Varuṇa. We hear of the "ordinances of the Ṛbhus" in IV.51.6,[88] and elsewhere of their connection with the year.[89] In interpreting their basic character, it is impossible to overlook their connection with the passage of time. They might have been intimately associated with the threefold division of the year and, as Ludwig recognized at first,[90] represented the three seasons which are well known to the Veda.[91] The above-mentioned verse, IV.33.9, has a significant role to play in substantiating this hypothesis; for the grouping into Vāja-Devānām, Ṛbhukṣan-Indra and Vibhvan-Varuṇa has a parallel in the ritual.

The Cāturmāsya ceremonies of the Śrauta ritual are, as is well known, the festivals of seasons and are called by the names Vaiśvadeva, Varuṇapraghāsāḥ and Sākamedhāḥ respectively. One will not fail to notice that Vaiśvadeva corresponds to our Vāja-Devānām, Varuṇapraghāsāḥ to Varuṇa-Vibhvan and in the Sākamedhāḥ Indra or Mahendra is the distinctive god among the deities of the mahāhavis.[92] I think the parallelism is quite evident. With this compare the words of ŚBr II.6.4.1: *sarvair ha tv eva devāś cāturmāsyair vṛtram aghnant sarvair v eva vyajayanta*...2: *te hocuḥ kena rājñā kenānīkena yotsyāma iti... te 'gninā rājñāgninānīkena caturo māsaḥ prājayan*; they gained other four months with Varuṇa as their leader, the last four under Indra's leadership. Thus we see that here also Varuṇa and Indra are in accord with the earlier enumeration (but for the sequence), but in the first of the three sacrifices Vāja is replaced by Agni. However, I do not think that this departure is significant in view of the close association of Agni with All Gods[93], and in view of the name Vaiśvadeva given to the sacrifice.

ṚV I.161.9 belongs in this context:

ápo bhū́yiṣṭhā íty éko abravīd
agnir bhū́yiṣṭha íty anyó abravīt |

vadharyántīṃ bahúbhyaḥ praiko abravīd
ṛtā́ vádantaś camasā́ṃ apiṃśata //

Agni occurs again in the second pāda here. Even though the third pāda is not quite clear, the *vadharyántīm* can only have been derived from *vádhar*[94] which reminds us of Indra, the thunderbolt-bearer. We must assign the *ā́paḥ* to Varuṇa since in this very hymn it is said in v. 14: *adbhír yāti váruṇaḥ samudraír yuṣmā́ṃ icchántaḥ śavaso napātaḥ* and in V.42.12 the streams are called *vibhvataṣṭā́*. Thus by substituting Varuṇa for *ā́paḥ* and Indra for *vádhar* we have again an exact parallel to the earlier passages, namely

(i)	(ii)	(iii)
IV.33.9	Cāturmāsyas	I.161.9
1. vājo-devānām	1. Agni	2. Agni
2. ṛbhukṣan-Indra	3. Indra	3. Vadhar
3. vibhvan-Varuṇa	2. Varuṇa	1. Āpaḥ

Only the sequence in (i) differs from that in (ii) and (iii).[95]

In the light of the conclusion arrived at here, one can understand why Indra, to whom Ṛbhukṣan is assigned, himself bears the same word as an epithet. If the word had really meant 'lord' of the Ṛbhus, it must denote the most important of the seasons, the peak of the year, and this is the most appropriate epithet for Indra. If I am right in assuming that Indra's name is a pre-Vedic designation for the sun, then this epithet draws our attention to this or that passage which shows the sun god as the creator of the seasons or in some other association with them. We may refer to AV VI. 36.1:

ṛtā́vānaṃ vaiśvānarám ṛtásya jyótiṣas pátiṃ
sá viśvā práti cākḷpe ṛtū́ṃr út sṛjate vāśī́[96]

That *vibhvan* and Varuṇa are mentioned rarely as compared to *vāja* and *ṛbhukṣan* seems to correspond with Varuṇa's nature which is certainly dismal on the whole and with the season which was originally his as we have elucidated above.

4. The Ṛbhus in the Ritual

a. In the Agniṣṭoma

Confining the Ṛbhus to the evening pressing, *abhipitvé ahnā́m* (IV.35.6), was already the custom in the ritual of the Ṛgvedic period. This is stated explicitly in the hymns of the Vāmadevas who were close to the cult of the Ṛbhus.[97] This custom of the Vāmadevas, which is quite in agreement with that of the later times, was so well known that AV IX.1.13 could say: *yáthā sómas tṛtī́ye sávana ṛbhūṇā́ṃ bhávati priyáḥ/evā́ ma ṛbhavo várca ātmáni dhriyatām.* An accord between the ṚV and the later ritual can further be seen in the fact that the Ṛbhus are accompanied by Indra in both the cases. Of the verses cited above on p. 80, IV.35.7 deserves to be mentioned once again:

> *prātáḥ sutám apibo haryaśva*
> *mā́dhyaṃdinaṃ sávanaṃ kévalaṃ te/*
> *sám ṛbhúbhiḥ pibasva ratnadhébhiḥ*
> *sákhīṃr yā́ṃ indra cakṛṣé sukṛtyā́ //*

However, we should not overlook one point of difference. We have referred to the formula for summoning to the Praiṣa for Indra during the evening savana. This formula speaks of the savana *ṛbhumat*, *vibhumat* etc. but not of Indra *ṛbhumat* or *vibhumat*. This is a small but not insignificant point of departure. It betrays a difference between the ritual of the Adhvaryus and that of the Hotṛs, between the custom of the former and the wording of the Ṛgvedic hymns which emphatically invite the Ṛbhus to the Soma drink and call them *agrepá* (IV.34.10).[98] In reality they are not *agrepá*; they receive neither their own graha nor any prominent position among the gods. On the contrary, they are mentioned merely in passing by the Adhvaryu in the afore-mentioned formula. Their worship is concentrated among the Sāman-singers who sing the Ārbhavapavamāna-sāman in the evening corresponding to the Bahiṣpavamāna in the morning pressing and the Mādhyandinapavamāna in the midday pressing. The worship takes place among the Hotṛs also, for corresponding to the Ārbhavapavamāna the Hotṛs have the Vaiśvadeva-śastra and this contains for the Ṛbhus hymn,

ṚV I. 111, in which the Nivid formula[99] for these gods is inserted.[100] Before this, during the Camasonnayana the Ṛbhus are invoked in conformity with the above-mentioned command of the Adhvaryu. That is to say, at the command *unnīyamānebhyo 'nubrūhi*, the Maitrāvaruṇa recites hymn IV.35 as *unnīyamānasūkta*[101] and concludes with the Praiṣa: *hotā yakṣad indraṃ tṛtīyasya savanasya...hotar yaja*, whereupon the Hotṛ replies with *ye yajāmahe* and recites verse ṚV III. 60.5.[102] After the Vaṣaṭ call, the Adhvaryu offers the oblation. It is impossible to say whether the ritual of the Adhvaryus has undergone a change or whether the ritual of the Vāmadevas had not once envisaged for the Adhvaryus a more specific invocation of the Ṛbhus than is the case now. The recitations and invocations of the Hotṛs do not seem to be quite consistent with the slight consideration shown to the Ṛbhus by the Adhvaryus.[103]

b. In the Dvādaśāha

Apart from hymns I.111; IV.35 and verse III.60.5 employed in the Agniṣṭoma, the ṚV contains yet other verses dedicated to the Ṛbhus: I.110; III.60 (entirely); IV.33, 34, 36, 37. Of these (excepting the two mentioned above) the majority[104] are recited on the different days of the Dvādaśāha and more precisely during the evening libation of the different days. In this respect the ritual has preserved a characteristic trait. For we know from the ṚV that these very twelve days play a special role in the Ṛbhu myth. This is the duration of their sojourn as guests in the abode of Agohya or *savitṛ dāśvaṃs*.[105] The Dvādaśāha which is the archetype of all sattras, itself originating from the twelve days or nights of the winter solstice,[106] was highly regarded in the Vedic period. TMBr X.5. 15: *oko vai devānāṃ dvādaśāhaḥ*. 16: *gṛhā vai devānāṃ dvādaśāhaḥ* ABr IV.25.6: *jyeṣṭhayajño vā eṣa yad dvādaśāhaḥ sa vai devānāṃ jyeṣṭho ya etenāgre 'yajata| śreṣṭhayajño vā eṣa yad dvādaśāhaḥ*... 7: *jyeṣṭhaḥ śreṣṭho yajeta, kalyāṇīha samā bhavati| na pāpaḥ puruṣo yājyo dvādaśāhena*. TBr I.1.6.7; I.1.9.10: *saṃvatsarapratimā vai dvādaśa rātrayaḥ*.[107] Thus, the Dvādaśāha is a sacred period when the gods take up residence. It is the prototype of the year. And here, in the tranquil evening of the year, the Ṛbhus also receive their share and almost all the hymns dedicated to them in the ṚV are employed in the liturgy.

The Vaiśvadeva-śastra, in which the hymns to the Ṛbhus are inserted, begins, as we shall once again emphasize below, always with the salutation to Savitṛ and is preceded by the Graha offered to this god. This graha on its part is preceded, according to the ĀpŚS, by the Namaskāra to the Manes. This sequence of the Manes, Viśve Devāḥ including Savitṛ and the Ṛbhus attains greater significance when we, for the sake of comparison, look at the Gṛhya Sūtras, in which the sacrificial year is concluded with the Aṣṭakās. Although there are deviations in the Gṛhya Sūtras belonging to different schools, Manes and Viśve Devāḥ are mentioned quite often prominently in their enumerations,[108] and apart from these gods, the Ṛtus are also listed among the alternatives as the deities of the Aṣṭakās by Gobhila and Āśvalāyana.[109] We find an invocation to the Ṛtus precisely in AV III.10,[110] a hymn dedicated to the New Year's Day (Ekāṣṭakā). Thus a certain degree of parallelism can be observed here between the Dvādaśāha-Ṛbhu on the one hand and Ekāṣṭakā-Ṛtu on the other. A statement of ABr IV.25 refers still more distinctly to this innner relationship between the *ṛtu* and *ṛbhu.* Here the Ṛtus themselves are associated with the Dvādaśāha sacrifice. Prajāpati requests the seasons and months to perform the Dvādaśāha for him and gives them *iṣ* and *ūrj* for this purpose: *saiṣorg ṛtuṣu ca māseṣu ca nihitā.*[111] Compare this with the statement that the Ṛbhus, after their stay of twelve days in the abode of Agohya, created fertility, "grass on the mountains and water in the valleys."[112] This also leads us to the assumption that *ṛbhu* was an old name for the seasons and that as an appellative it has been replaced by *ṛtu* as early as in the Brāhmaṇa period.[113]

5. The Ṛtus in the Ritual

In the ṚV, hymns I.15 and II.37, are dedicated to the Ṛtus. The first of these is employed during the Ṛtugrahas of the Agniṣṭoma[114] and the second along with II.36 on the sixth day of the Dvādaśāha; each Ṛtupraiṣa is always followed by a verse.[115] Āpastamba enjoins that one should draw twelve or thirteen or fourteen Ṛtugrahas. If the number chosen is twelve, the first two and the last two are drawn simultaneously; in the case of thirteen the last two are drawn simultaneously and also offered together. If the number is fourteen, the first two and the last two are drawn and offered simultaneously.[116] The custom of the ritual has attempted to symbolize here also, as it does everywhere, the inner nature of the proceedings through certain external acts.

ĀpŚS XII.26.9: "[The Ṛtugrahas] are drawn from the Droṇakalaśa but not deposited on the ground.[117] 10: Into the remains of the preceding grahas, [the Adhvaryu and the Pratiprasthātṛ] draw the subsequent ones. 11: At first the Adhvaryu draws and at last the Pratiprasthātṛ each time with the mantras, *upayāmagṛhīto 'si madhuś ca.*[118] 12: Some [authorities] opine, with *madhave tvā mādhavāya tvā.* 13: Upayāma precedes all [the mantras]. 14: Let one [priest] not follow the other. According to the established custom, the Adhvaryu goes on the south side and the Pratiprasthātṛ on the north side. 15: At the door they pass by one another.[119] 16: When the Adhvaryu enters [the] Havirdhāna hut for drawing], the Pratiprasthātṛ holds the full graha between himself and the Adhvaryu; when he comes out, the empty vessel. 17: During the first three, the Adhvaryu summons to the Praiṣa with the words *ṛtunā preṣya.* Likewise the Pratiprasthātṛ. 18: The Adhvaryu inverts the openings of the two vessels and addresses the two with *ṛtubhiḥ preṣya.* Likewise the Pratiprasthātṛ.[120] 19: The Adhvaryu inverts [the openings] once again and recites once: *ṛtunā preṣya.* Likewise the Pratiprasthātṛ."

We may further add that no Anuvākyā is recited and no Anuvaṣaṭkāra takes place. Furthermore, the Indrāgnīgraha follows immediately after these grahas, and the Adhvaryu sits at the entrance to the hut with the Ṛtu-bowl in his hand in order to lead the recitation of the Ājyaśastra. The drawing of these grahas is regarded as an act that is beneficial to the vegetation[121] and its rightful place is in the morning of the spring sacrifice. At noon the Ṛtus are remembered only indirectly and not all in the evening.[122] But it is remarkable that the Ṛtus are not mentioned at that place where the Ṛbhus have been incorporated in the ritual, for the two names replace one another to a certain extent. It seems that those who systematized the ritual sought to make allowances for various views and introduced into the organism of the ritual, which reconciles between many wishes and directions, the compromise according to which the Ṛtus are invited to the sacrifice mostly in the morning and the Ṛbhus mainly in the evening. We are reminded of the legend in ABr III. 30 according to which the Ṛbhus were excluded from all the three savanas until at last they found a place in the evening libation through the intervention of Savitṛ and Prajāpati.[123] Perhaps this legend reflects the events during the codification of the ritual.

The hymns employed in the Ṛtugraha ceremony are composed by poets other than the authors of the Ṛbhu hymns. When we examine the content of these hymns, it will be seen that they are never actually treated as independent deities, but merely as escorts (*ṛtunā*, *ṛtubhiḥ*) who accompany other gods and it is these other gods who are invited to drink along with the Ṛtus. That is to say, the Ṛtus play a minor role in the ṚV in comparison to the Ṛbhus and their celebrated efficacy. Their name has not developed beyond its appellative sense.[124] There is no mention either of the divineness attained by them or of their special deeds. Only X. 11.1 speaks of *yajñíyān ṛtū́n*; probably the expression *daívya ṛtvíjaḥ* in X.2.1 refers to them. On the other hand, no special value has been attached to the efficacy or to the cult of the Ṛbhus outside the ṚV and its schools.

6. The Name of the Ṛbhus[125]

In the Veda the word *ṛbhú* is used not only as a proper noun but as an appellative also. This is evident from passages like AV IV.7; X.1.8; ṚV VIII.75.5; IX.21.6;[126] X.105.6. Just as one constructs a chariot or a wheel, so does one "manufacture" (*takṣ*) a formula (*dhī́* I.109.1; *bráhman* V.73.10; *mánman* II.19.8; *mántra* I.67.4; VII.7.6; *stóma* X.39.14). Composing such formulas is directly compared to the construction of a chariot.

V.2.11: *etáṃ te stómaṃ tuvijāta vípro*
rátham ná dhī́raḥ svápā atakṣam /

Cf. also I.130.6. In some passages we may interpret *ṛbhú* directly as the priest; thus I.151.2 or X.80.7: *agnáye bráhma ṛbhávas tatakṣur agním mahā́m avocāmā suvṛktím.* It is not necessary to say with Bergaigne (II, p. 422) that the Ṛbhus are artisan-priests."[127] Here *ṛbhú* means as much as "clever, skilled" (cf. *rátham ná dhī́raḥ*);[128] nothing else seems to be the basic sense of the word. German *arb-* in 'Arbeit,' Slavonic *robic* offer still the best parallels to this word; in view of the totally different natures of the Ṛbhus and the Germanic Elves, a phonetic relationship between these two words is improbable although there is certain superficial consonance.[129]

This does not exhaust all that can be said on the Ṛbhus. A certain practice in the ritual takes us slightly further. While installing the fire, it is customary to refer to the method of one's ancestors as the model. An Aṅgiras installs *aṅgirasām vratena*, a Bhṛgu *bhṛgūṇāṃ vratena*. The close connection between the art of chariot-making and the Ṛbhus is expressed in the rule that a *rathakṛt* should install his fire *ṛbhūṇāṃ tvā [devānāṃ] vratena.*[130] We should not overlook the fact that the commentaries are not content with explaining *rathakṛt* as chariot-maker, they also describe him as a half-caste to be placed outside the three castes.[131] It seems to follow from this that these rathakṛts constituted a particular class or a tribe in which the art of chariot-making was specially cultivated and was the common occupation.[132]

We can arrive at this conclusion yet from another angle. In the ṚV the Ṛbhus are often styled as *saudhanvanāsāḥ*, the sons of Sudhanvan. It is precisely in their case—and not in the case of any other name from the ṚV up to the Brāhmaṇa period—that emphasis is laid on the fact that they were once human beings[133] and that they attained immortality or a share in the Soma drink through their skill. I am sure, it would be unjustifiable to dismiss these statements altogether; there is a euhemeristic element in these. A commentary explains *ṛbhu* and *sātvata saudhanvana* as synonyms for *rathakāra*[134] and elsewhere mention is made of *saudhanvanā nāma jātiḥ.*[135] Now we cannot ignore the fact that the Ṛbhus are primarily gods. Only of the gods can it be said that they slept for twelve days in Agohya's house and afterwards granted fertility and that they created, among other things, horses for Indra, the chariot for the Aśvins. We had valid grounds to regard them as ancient genii of the seasons besides the Ṛtus or prior to them. This would be inconsistent with any attempt to explain the Ṛbhus directly from a euhemeristic viewpoint. I think that in the Ṛbhus we have the gods of a tribe in which the art of chariot-making was specially cultivated.[136] It cannot, however, be ascertained whether they were originally regarded in that tribe as the genii of the seasons, or whether they attained this position only after they had been admitted into the Vedic cult; but this is not of importance. Perhaps Ṛbhu was the name of the gods of the tribe and Sudhanvan the name of its mythical progenitor: we cannot decide more exactly.[137] For a long time something of the low origins of their former worshippers stuck to the Ṛbhus; the gods, it was said, were disgusted with their "human smell."[138] The importance of chariot-making and the skill[139] needed for it might have been the basic reason for accepting this tribe and for including their gods in the Vedic cult.

Chapter Seven

INDRA AND THE MARUTS

To describe the character of Indra, the divine champion of the Vedic tribes, and, while doing so, to seek to account for all the details is beyond the realm of possibility and perhaps will remain so for ever. Indra stands at the centre of the sagas of that age. None of the Vedic gods is connected, as he is, with such abundance of names, which might have been of importance in the history and the prehistory of the Vedic peoples. While it is still possible in individual cases to establish the historical basis or the basic mythological concept of a being, there are other names that float past like shadows whose life has been extinguished long ago. Often we do not know whether what we have in front of us is one who was originally a demon or a god, the chief of a hostile tribe or the embodiment of the inclement climate. Even the poets themselves might not have been always aware of the origin of the ideas; for they traditionally took over motifs from older sources, and in their new settlements did not have any more a precise knowledge of the ancient enemies who were gradually disappearing into the darkness of the past.

Before I enter into the description of the god, who has become so important and at the same time fatal to comparative mythology, it would be useful to describe the views upon which the research rests at present. In his exhaustive monograph on Indra, Perry[1] has brought together the views of his predecessors; the majority of them explain Indra as a celestial god. Here it would suffice to discuss only those works on Indra which have appeared since then. Following the PW, Perry himself interprets Indra as a thunderstorm god, likewise Bloomfield.[2] I myself shared this notion for a long time. The same view is professed by Oldenberg. He sees a thunderstorm god in Indra and more precisely one who possesses partly pre-Indian traits.[3] He is of the opinion that the "original exploit of this god, namely the liberation of the celestial waters from the confines of the cloud-mountain which was accomplished in a thunderstorm, was transformed for the Ṛgvedic poets into the liberation of the terrestrial rivers from the rocky enclosure from which they issue forth." For Macdonell also Indra is "primarily the thunder-god, the conquest of the demons of drought or darkness and the consequent liberation of the waters or the winning of light forming his mythological essence. Secondarily, Indra is the god of battle . . ."[4] Thus also L.v. Schroeder in *Herakles und Indra*, (Vienna 1914), p. 20: "He is unquestionably the great thunderstorm god, the ancient thunderstorm giant, and yet likewise unquestionably the solar hero who again and again in his battles recovers the sunlight, gains it by fighting, attains it as a reward of fighting, captures it as booty. . . And finally at several places of the Veda, Indra is straight away identified with the sun, with the sun god Sūrya. There is no adequate reason to make him therefore an old sun god, as Hillebrandt does." Hopkins is less certain: "Indra has been identified with 'storm,' with 'sky,' with the 'year;' also with the 'sun' and with 'fire' in general. But if he be taken as he is found in the hymns, it will be noticed at once that he is too stormy to be the sun; too luminous to be the storm; too near to the phenomena of the monsoon to be the year or the sky; too rainy to be fire; too alien from every one thing to be any one thing. . . ."[5]

Whosoever goes through the great number of Vedic hymns with their diverse statements and similes will be inclined at first to agree with the view of Hopkins. But ultimately Hopkins' view is not satisfactory because he judges Indra on the basis of his superficial appearance but does not attempt to separate the individual strands or to inquire into the supposedly oldest trait of character.

Those of the scholars who saw the sun or lightning in Indra met with little response. Max Müller had advocated the first identification for a while and stated at one time that Indra was "the chief solar deity of India,"[6] but gave up this view. Later on, he says that "Indra was originally a god of the thunderstorm, the giver of rain (*indra* like *indu*, raindrops) . . . but he was soon invested with all the insignia of a supreme ruler, residing in heaven, and manifested no longer in the thunderstorm only, but in the light of heaven and the splendour of the sun."[7] His *Contributions to the Science of Mythology* record a further change in his view: "The two subjects of permanent interest to the Vedic poets were (1) the sunrise, the daily triumph of light over the darkness, and the annual triumph of spring over winter, and (2) the thunderstorm, or the triumph of a bright god over the dark clouds and the rescue of fertilising rain from the prison in which it seemed to be held during the season of heat and drought. The chief actor in the first drama was Agni, as the light in the sun, in the second Indra as the champion of the blue sky. Other gods assisted in these battles, but the chief part devolved on the god of light (Agni), and the god of rain (Indra)."[8] However, the most complicated and yet in my view somewhat more correct than the others is the theory of Bergaigne: "A naturalistic origin of the god Indra may in our opinion be sought in the celestial fire, i.e. the sun and lightning. But this god, continuing all the while to borrow his principal attributes from lightning and the sun, has assumed a distinct personality . . ."[9]

Faced with these divergent theories, it is necessary to build the edifice from the ground anew. Like the majority of scholars, I too proceeded earlier from the notion suggested by the pioneers of Vedic philology that Indra was a thunderstorm god. It is only with an intensification of my own investigations that I have been able to set myself free from the traditional track laid by well-known names. It seems to me that scholars have neglected to examine from different angles the interpretations made till now. They completely neglected a comparison with the ritual. The ritual does not yield absolute data but what it offers on a certain period of mythological conceptions cannot be underestimated, and precisely in one important aspect it contains unchanging data *vis-á-vis* the divergent mass of Vedic statements. In many a respect academic construction played a greater role than the objective study of the Vedic texts which a proper appreciation of the historical evolution ought to have allowed. It is necessary to discard the subjective element more than ever before, to start the investigation from the very beginning and to define criteria that are implied in the historical evolution. In order to achieve this it is first of all imperative to eliminate as far as possible the influence exercised quite often by comparative mythology and, on the other hand, to attach no greater importance to classical Sanskrit than it actually deserves according to its historical position. For many researchers the influences emanating from classical Sanskrit have proved no less disastrous than the theories of comparative mythology.

When comparative mythology began to interest the minds of scholars, neither its foundations were so strong nor Vedic exegesis was so well-established that one could base theories on these with certainty as it happened in the discussion of Indra from various sides, especially by Mannhardt. The only way of expressing our gratitude to these scholars for the great inspiration is to ask them to step aside for a while, and to lay new foundations ourselves. The connecting line which is to lead us from one who is ostensibly an Indo-European thunderstorm god to the Indian or Indo-Iranian Indra is nowhere noticeable or proved. Dragon myths recur here as well as there; but the question is whether dragons and snakes denote one and the same natural phenomenon at all latitudes and whether the subduer of the dragon is always an original thunderstorm god. In the single image of the fight against the dragon, there are various natural phenomena fused together which are to be determined according to the climate of the region and the character of the people among whom the myth had originated. Even though there are undisputed similarities between Thôr, Hercules and Indra, yet these certainly do not prove a historical connection. Indra is not a storm god from the very beginning; it is only in course of his evolution that this extension of his activity took place.

Moreover, there are also benevolent dragons. One of the Chinese travellers to India narrates about one such dragon when he states that "he causes fertilising and seasonable showers of rain to fall within their country; and preserves it from plagues and calamities, and so causes the priesthood to dwell in security."[10]

In introducing the 'cloud-demons' into Vedic mythology, classical Sanskrit and specially the commentaries are not without blame; often they have only one single passage in view and do not examine how far their *megharūpa* Vṛtra or Vala conforms to the general conceptions of the Veda. Notwithstanding the value of classical Sanskrit—I have unambiguously stressed its utility even for our purposes— it is necessary to put a stop to the mixing of Vedic and classical Sanskrit. European scholars of mythology have been influenced and misled by the consideration they had shown to the Vedic exegates who were far removed in time and space from the Vedic poets and who did not have a direct acquaintance any more with the wealth of ancient sagas. We must liberate ourselves from this influence. Vṛtra is neither a 'cloud demon' nor a 'demon of drought.'

A. INDRA AND VRTRA

I have attempted to approach the problem of Indra from a different angle than has been the case so far and sought to define at first the character of Vṛtra, his enemy. There is no doubt even after a careful scrutiny about the naturalistic basis of Vṛtra. Muir[11] speaks of the "hostile powers in the atmosphere who malevolently shut up the watery treasures in the clouds," and of "demons of drought, called by a variety of names as Vṛtra...Ahi, Śuṣṇa..." Darmesteter[12] sees in Vṛtra "the enveloper who shuts them [the light and the waters] up in his cloud-cavern" and describes the name *vərəthra* or *vṛtra* as an "ancient name of the cloud which encloses the light or the cows." Ludwig states thus (III, p. 337): "Most often the celestial rainwater is described as the booty of the battle. Vṛtra withholds it from the world. He is depicted at times as enclosing it or obstructing it, at others as dwelling in it and being dislodged from it," and (III, p. 348) "we cannot easily accept that Vṛtra is the Indian counterpart of Aṃrōmainyuṣ...No doubt Aṃrōmainyuṣ was a celestial god, the god of the wintry sky, and the stark differences between the seasons in ancient Bactria make it conceivable how these differences could be seen as the effects of mutually conflicting elements. We must recognize that a similar notion was certainly embodied in Vṛtra, but the equilibrium of the differences...is missing... at least in the ṚV." At the end of his commentary on ṚV I.56.6, I find this remark: "The battle which bestows the light is the stormy weather that precedes the spring." With this view Ludwig comes very close to the correct interpretation far in advance of his time. So far as I know, nobody paid any attention to this view, and even I myself had to pursue my own path independently before I came to realize that Ludwig went astray at least from the right path. Perry persists in his belief in the cloud-demon: "These different names for Vṛtra, like the large majority of the many and various appellations given to the lesser demons, are but different names for one and the same thing: namely, the cloud, which in its manifold forms presented itself most forcibly to the eye of the poet in the likeness now of this, now of that creature. And it was not alone as hostile and mischievous demons in human or animal form that the clouds were symbolized... we find them described as mountains...or as forts belonging to the demons... or their skilfully fortified dwellings...and in the caves where the evil spirits hide the stolen raincows, as well as the cows themselves...we can discover only clouds."[13] Making a complete departure from this, Bergaigne (II, p. 207) observes: "Does 'the enveloper' of the waters...or, the *paridhi*, 'the enclosure' of the rivers, as Vṛtra is also called, III.33.6, stand for the rain-cloud?...The demon, it is true, might be the rain-cloud which does not give its waters, and it is probable that, as a matter of fact, the rain-cloud has made a certain contribution to the mythical conception of Vṛtra. But the rain-cloud itself is most often in concealment during the dry season and if the 'enveloper' of the waters represents the dwelling where they have been kept prisoners, the demon must be identified rather with this invisible reservoir, with that mysterious world which keeps in bondage, with the waters themselves [and light ...], the cloud which contains them. In fact, a passage, I.54.10, where Indra is represented as delivering the waters contained in an envelope (*vavri*), which is no doubt the same as Vṛtra, situates in the belly of the demon not only the waters, but the 'mountain', that is to say, the rain-cloud. As an animate being Vṛtra is distinguished from the invisible place which apparently he personifies and he has a mysterious (*niṇya*) hiding-place from which the waters escape when they are delivered by Indra...

Briefly, the conception of Vṛtra is reminiscent of that of the mother, or better still, because Vṛtra is a male being, that of the *concealed* father. I cannot say that Bergaigne's thesis is distinguished by clarity of thought or that it advances our appreciation of the Vedic demon. He is strongly influenced by the notion that the 'mountains' are the clouds and the 'rivers' are the celestial waters, for he states (II, p. 206): "In the hymn I.32, where Indra's victory over Vṛtra is described at length, the waters which he causes to flow after splitting the bosom of the mountains, that is to say, the rain-clouds ... are spoken of as cows." Even Oldenberg, who is ever ready to support Bergaigne, does not share this view. Oldenberg himself is far in advance of his predecessors in one point, when he asserts that the mountains are really mere mountains and not clouds and the rivers are not the downpourings of rain but real rivers.[14] However, he was not able to shake himself free from the influence of comparative mythology. A part of what he says is correct but he vitiates the correct understanding with the remark: "The facts of comparative mythology leave us in no doubt that in its original form the myth was certainly a myth of thunderstorm, that it was the cloud-springs where the snake was encamped and that according to its original nature the Vajra was a lightning-weapon." We may well ask: which facts?

Hopkins returns again to the old belief. He refers to ṚV I. 32.2,11 "for the oft-mentioned act of cleaving the cave, where the dragon Vala or Vṛtra (the restrainer or enveloper) had coralled the kine (*i.e.* without metaphor, for the act of freeing the clouds and letting loose the rain)"[15] and elsewhere[16] opposes Oldenberg without adequate reasons. There is no denying the fact that in about six passages of the ṚV, Indra is the bestower of rain. But these passages are in a minority as compared to many others which speak of the release of the waters. Moreover, these passages belong almost wholly to books IV and X with the exception of the eighth maṇḍala which will be discussed separately. I did not notice a single passage in any of the other family books. This point should be kept in mind, for it suggests that the transformation of Indra into a rain god was still in its infancy in the ṚV and was completed only in the subsequent periods. Those who are well-versed in classical Sanskrit must certainly know that a god who sends rain need not necessarily be an original rain god according to Indian conceptions. And so far as the thunderbolt is concerned which Indra wields, the examples of Jupiter, Mithra, Āditya, Bṛhaspati and Vivasvat ought to show that this attribute does not, by any means, indicate an original thunderstorm god. The rising sun god, who gains in strength, needs the thunderbolt to fight his enemies and becomes thus a thunderstorm god at the same time. The birth of the sun and not of the thunderstorm god was the occasion for the solstice festivals. But since thunderstorm is the most important phenomenon in the ascending orbit of the sun god, the latter can easily be regarded as the storm god. From a later period I record another image which describes the sun's battle against winter. In *Kathāsaritsāgara* 91.20-21, the lion of spring slays the elephant of winter.

The scholars who expressed their views after Oldenberg and Hopkins had done so, adhered to the old explanation of Vṛtra, the exception being Max Müller who sees in Vṛtra a demon of darkness as well. He styles Vṛtra as "the coverer, the hider, whether of light or rain" and speaks further of the fact "how, in Vedic phraseology, Vṛtra is the thief who keeps the cows or the rays of the morning shut up in his stable, and how the first peep of day is expressed by Saramā discovering the dark stables of Vṛtra and the Paṇis."[17] In his *Contributions to the Science of Mythology* II, p. 695, he says: "we may find it difficult to understand ... why ... the powers of darkness, whether of the dark night or of the dark clouds, should have been called Coverers (Vṛtra)"; p. 965: "if Vṛtra, from *var*, was the coverer or the genius of darkness" and p. 756: "the coverer, a demon who keeps the rain imprisoned in the cloud, and at the same time keeps the light of the day captive. Hence Vṛtra in later Sanskrit came to be a name for cloud, as well as for enemy in general." Macdonell, as the statement cited on p.91 above shows, thinks of demons "of drought or darkness," but does not express any definite view on their special nature; in the section on Vṛtra of his *Vedic Mythology* (§ 68), where he counts Vṛtra among the individual atmospheric demons only, once he speaks of the "(cloud) mountain (*parvata*) as being within the belly of Vṛtra." About Ahi (Vṛtra), Magoun observes that "he was, originally, probably nothing more than the crest of the approaching thunderstorm, looked upon as a gigantic snake threatening to take away the light of heaven."[18]

This survey does not present a satisfactory picture. It is true, the theories are not far apart from one another, but there is no attempt to subject the nature of Vṛtra to a more precise analysis, to weigh the various statements of the ṚV and of other texts against one another, to resolve the contradictions and, above all, to comprehend Vṛtra in his historical evolution. "Which is the most barren season in India? The summer with its scorching heat which withholds rain and dries up the watercourses. Indra wields the thunderbolt. What is more natural than that he turns against that demon and recovers the waters that are drying up"—this roughly seems to be the reasoning on which the majority of the above-cited interpretations are based. But the "mountains on which Vṛtra is encamped" or "which are in his body" do not quite fit into this scheme. So the mountains become clouds, and the clouds once more become demons in order to take up, on the other hand, the role of the cows which Indra abducts from the fortresses (cloud-fortresses). We need only to keep the inner contradictions in mind in order to be convinced of the want of clarity about the chief enemy of Indra, and secondly we must compare these interpretations with the actual state of affairs in the ṚV in order to realize how little these interpretations agree basically with what we can deduce from the Veda.

Whosoever is of the view that we cannot make any progress on these beaten tracks must be sanguine about the fact that he cannot count on an immediate applause. The old theories which most of us have assimilated in our youth are too widespread and too firmly rooted to be discarded easily. Just as E. H. Meyer wrote even before he had 'examined' the first volume of this work that he would hardly think that I could convince him (about Soma as the moon god),[19] or just as Oldenberg[20] dismissed my interpretation of Indra merely on the basis of my "Vorläufige Mitteilung" so will others oppose this exposition. This cannot be avoided. One should be content if the confidence in the present belief is shaken. We shall avoid a comparison with the legend of Hercules and Gergoneus or of Hercules and Cacus as too uncertain.

The many attempts that were made to interpret Indra's name etymologically did not contribute anything to mythology. We shall leave the older ones aside. Like Grassmann and Bollensen (ZDMG, XLI, p. 505), Bergaigne (II, p. 171) thought of *indh*. Jacobi (KZ, XXXI, p. 316 ff.) construes *indra* as 'man,' 'manly,' the original Indo-European word being **ənro*. According to Güntert, (*Der arische Weltkönig und Heiland*, p. 15) Indra denotes the same as his other epithets like *śakra*, 'strong,' *taviṣa*, etc. do, and is derived from Indo-European **oid*, 'swelling.' The name is based, he says, on his 'swelling virility.' Weber (*Rājasūya*, p. 31, n. 3) adheres to the old etymology of *i*, *inv*. Bezzenberger (BKIS, I, p. 342) cites Avestan *andra*, Pehlavi *andar*, Anglo-saxon *ent* 'giant', Old High German *entisc*, *entrisc* as cognates. All this has little value from the mythological viewpoint.

Indra's name is the epitomé of all energy. Just as Rudra is the lord of animals, Varuṇa of Law, Bṛhaspati of the Brahman, so is Indra *satyaujas*, *ojasāṃ pati*, *balapati*;[21] his arm is the expression of strength,[22] and his symbol is the bull.[23] Indra is the king and reigns over the gods and men. As early as in the ṚV, the gods are occasionally styled as *índrajyeṣṭha*, and the entire Vedic literature treats this motif in the most diverse modes. The gods elect him their king as he is the strongest among them;[24] they put him in the forefront of their battle against Vṛtra[25] or against the Asuras;[26] they give him the thunderbolt,[27] aid him,[28] applaud him,[29] confer the highest power upon him,[30] or abandon him being afraid of Vṛtra.[31] The zenith of his career is the victory over Vṛtra; after he had killed the latter, he is consecrated as the Mahārāja.[32] On the other hand, the gods are older than Indra; the texts describe this in various modes of expression and designate him as *devānām ānujāvara*.[33] Prajāpati created the Devas and the Asuras but not Indra; then the gods said: "create Indra for us."[34] Or Prajāpati creates "the younger brother" of the gods and commands him to become the overlord of the gods. The gods said: "Who are you ? We are more than you are," and Indra became the overlord by means of the heat which resided once in Prajāpati but which now rests in Āditya. Prajāpati made a golden disc out of this heat and tied it to Indra.[35] Elsewhere it is stated that Prajāpati keeps Indra hidden lest the Asuras should kill his eldest son. The gods seek the hidden one with sacrifices, "because for one who has no king a battle is impossible."[36] Or the gods themselves beget Indra.[37] Already in the ṚV, Indra appears as youthful energy emanating from the gods. They arm the new-born;[38] they are afraid of him who was born at a remote distance;[39] they become less strong.[40] He creates freedom for them[41] or he is the champion who destroys the miscreants that transgress against Varuṇa, Mitra and Aryaman.[42] This character of his as the representative of *kṣatra* overshadows his other aspect as Kavi. Of course, in the ṚV also he is occasionally celebrated as Kavi,[43] for the peculiar nature of Vedic poetry has wiped off the clear lines of demarcation; but on the whole, this quality of Indra is indeed met with rarely, and if I am not much mistaken, is almost completely lost in the Brāhmaṇa literature.[44] Here Indra represents the *Imperium* just as Brahmaṇaspati represents the *Sacerdortium*.[45]

As the overlord and champion of the gods, Indra becomes the archetype for the Indian king and also his patron deity. ABr VII. 23.1: *aindro vai devatayā kṣatriyo bhavati*; MS II.1.4 (6.8); 5.8 (58.11): *aindro rājanyaḥ*; ŚBr III.9.1.16, 18: *kṣatraṃ vā indro*; MS III.4.3 (47.10): *yadi rājanyo yajeta indrasavo hy eṣaḥ*. This notion is expressed frequently and particularly in the ceremonies connected with the consecration of the king. Summer, Indra's season, is the period when the Rājanya should install his fire: *indriyāvī bhavati*.[46]

Kings invoke Indra to defeat the enemy in battle. ṚV VI.25 and 26 constitute a prayer to be recited before the battle. The prince in whose house Indra drinks the Soma does not waver;[47] one who is expelled from his kingdom turns to Indra *kṣetraṃjaya* with sacrifices.[48]

On the other hand, he shares with the earthly king the burden of governing fickle subjects. It is said that the gods do not obey him and that he secures their obedience by performing the Dvādaśāha.[49] Or they exclude him from the Soma libation and reproach him for his misdeeds: *viśvarūpaṃ tvāṣṭram abhyamaṃsta, vṛtram astṛta, yatīn sālāvṛkebhyaḥ prādād, arurmaghān avadhīd, bṛhaspateḥ pratyavadhīt*.[50] As weapon Indra wields the thunderbolt in his arms, or "in the right arm." Apart from *vájra*,[51] we find the designations *áśman*,[52] *párvata*,[53] and also *ádri*,[54] and the epithet *adrivat*[55] is employed frequently for Indra. Bloomfield rejects the meaning 'hurler' for *adrivat* because, as he says, Indra carries Vajra and *ádri* does not have the sense of thunderbolt; but I.51.3 supports this sense. Other kinds of names which enlarge our knowledge of ancient Vedic weapons are *paraśú* and *svádhiti*,[56] *aṅkuśá* (listed already by Muir) *hánman*,[57] *vartaní*,[58] (*cakrá* I.53.9 with the addition of *ráthya*), and the bow and arrows.[59] Sometimes the lightning is also Indra's 'chariot.'[60] Also the waters and occasionally the Soma[61] are called Indra's thunderbolt. Several are the beings who fashion the thunderbolt for the thunder god: most often it is Tvaṣṭṛ; furthermore, Indra's 'father' II. 17.6; Kāvya Uśanas I.121.12; Ṛbhu I.121.9 who brings the stone; the singers (*kāru*), the gods and perhaps also Mātariśvan.[62] The Veda has personified the thunderbolt,[63] made it the companion of Indra;[64] occasionally the thunderbolt is praised as Indra's horse[65] and addressed conjointly with Soma.[66]

Apart from the weapon, Indra employs craftiness as well. Like his enemies, he understands *māyā*. He knows how to render innocuous the magic arts of his enemies or even to outwit them.[67] Hence *māyā* is not an exclusive quality of the Asuras. He takes the shape of a woman (Menā),[68] transforms himself into a horse's hair,[69] becomes an ant,[70] approaches Śunaḥśepa as a human being, or as a Brāhmaṇa lays a brick in the altar pile of the Asuras. He does not disdain deceit either. He breaks the compact and the oath which he has sworn to his enemy Namuci and 'steals' the sun from the possession of the enemies. Indra bears not the traits of a Dharmapati like Varuṇa but those of a wilder age, and in this respect also he is the favourite god of myths.[71] In ṚV IV. 24. 10 there is an allusion to an image or a symbol of Indra which was lent in order to make the recipient victorious: "Who will buy my Indra for ten cows? He may give it back to me after killing the enemies."[72]

B. VṚTRA

Indra's main battle was fought for the release of the waters from Vṛtra's control. While making an assessment of this demon, it would be useful at first to discuss the phraseology employed by the ṚV to describe Vṛtra's connection with the waters.

1. Phraseology of the ṚV

gras:

IV. 17. 1; X. 111. 9: *sṛjáḥ síndhūṃr áhinā jagrasānā́n*

dhā+api:

I. 32. 11: *apā́ṃ bílam ápihitaṃ yád ā́sīd*
vṛtráṃ jaghanvā́ṃ ápa tád vavāra ||
IV. 28. 1: ... *ápāvṛṇod ápihiteva khā́ni*
5: *ā́dardṛtam ápihitāny áśnā* ...
On this, cf. III. 33. 6: *ápāhan vṛtráṃ paridhíṃ nadī́nām* |
and X. 139. 6: *ápāvṛṇod dúro áśmavrajānām* (*nadī́nām*)

bādh:

IV. 19. 8: *páriṣṭhitā atṛṇad badbadhānā́ḥ*
sīrā́ índraḥ srávitave pṛthivyā́ ||
V. 32. 1: *ádardar útsam ásṛjo ví khā́ni*
tvám arṇavā́n badbadhānā́m aramṇāḥ |
2: *tvám útsāṃ ṛtúbhir badbadhānā́ṃ*
áraṃha ū́dhaḥ párvatasya vajrin |

rudh:

I. 32. 11: *dāsápatnīr áhigopā atiṣṭhan*
níruddhā ā́paḥ paṇínena gā́vaḥ|

vṛ:

I. 52. 2: *índro yád vṛtrám ávadhīn nadīvṛ́tam*
54. 10: *abhī́m índro nadyò vavríṇā hitā́*
víśvā anuṣṭhā́ḥ pravaṇéṣu jighnate ||
57. 6: *ávāsṛjo nívṛtāḥ sártavā́ apáḥ.*
II.19.2: *áhim índro arṇovṛtaṃ ví vṛścat*|
II.14.2; III.32.6: *vavṛvā́ṃsaṃ pári devī́r* [*apáḥ*] *ádevam* ;
IV.16.7 (VI.20.2): *apó vṛtráṃ vavṛvā́ṃsaṃ párāhan*
IX.61.22: *vavṛvā́ṃsam mahī́r apáḥ*
42 7: *tvā́ṃ vṛtā́ṃ ariṇā indra síndhūn* |
VI.17.12: *ā́ kṣódo máhi vṛtám nadī́nām*
páriṣṭhitam asṛja ūrmím apā́m |

[X.113.6: *vṛtráṃ yád ugró vy ávṛścad ójasā*
apó bíbhrataṃ támasā párīvṛtam //]

stabh:

II.11.5: *utó apó dyā́ṃ tastabhvā́ṃsam*
áhann áhiṃ śūra vīryèṇa //
VIII.6.16: *yás ta indra mahī́r apáḥ*
stabhūyámāna ā́śayat /
96.18: *tváṃ sindhūṃr asṛjas tastabhānā́n*
AV VI.85.3: *yáthā vṛtrá imā́ ā́pas*
tastámbha viśvádhā yatī́ḥ /

sthā+pari:

I.32.8: *yā́ś cid vṛtró mahinā́ paryátiṣṭhat* [*apáḥ*]
II.11.2: *sṛjó mahī́r indra yā́ ápinvaḥ*
páriṣṭhitā áhinā śūra pūrvī́ḥ /

IV.19.8 see s.v. bādh; VI.17.12 see s.v. vṛ
VI. 72. 3: *índrasomāv áhim apáḥ pariṣṭhā́m*
hathó vṛtrám . . .
VII.21.3: *tvám indra srávitavā́ apás kaḥ*
páriṣṭhitā áhinā śūra pūrvī́ḥ/

śī:

I. 121. 11: *tváṃ vṛtrám āśáyānaṃ sirā́su*
mahó vájreṇa siṣvapo varā́hum //
II. 11. 9: *índro mahā́ṃ síndhum āśáyānam*
māyāvínaṃ vṛtrám asphuran níḥ /
III. 32. 11: VI. 19. 2: *áhann áhiṃ pariśáyānam árṇaḥ*
IV. 17.7; 19.3: *tváṃ práti praváta*[73] *āśáyānam*
áhiṃ vájreṇa maghavan ví vṛścaḥ //
V. 30. 6: *áhim ohānám apá āśáyānam* /
32. 2: *áhiṃ cid ugra práyutaṃ śáyānam* /
6: *tyáṃ cid itthā́ katpayáṃ śáyānam*
asuryé támasi vāvṛdhānám
VI. 30. 4: *áhann áhiṃ parisáyānam árṇaḥ* /

Accordingly, Vṛtra is driven out of the waters on which he rests or in which he hides, as well as from the earth and heaven.[74] But almost always it is the terrestrial and not the celestial waters which Vṛtra encloses; it is the terrestrial streams and the terrestrial mountains.

In these examples we see a certain amount of regular repetition of expressions which belong to the oldest repertoire of poets and represent the basic stock of imagery in which Indra's heroic deed of liberating the waters was described from time immemorial. Can these be the images that are inspired by the effects of the hottest period of the year ? Only the word *gras* can be construed in this sense. Can one say of heat that it envelopes the waters and streams, or that it restrains or enchains or surrounds them ? Or can this be said of a cloud-demon of any kind? Although we see now and then that the Vedic imagery is rather primitive or unusual, it is, as a rule, never lopsided. When we compare the description of summer by the classical poets we will see that they never employ such expressions as are used by the RV. I come back to a statement that I have used earlier: "Mythology is poetry." Vodskov strongly disputed this but his counter-example of lotus was not exactly the right one. The sources from which poets in a certain stage of society draw their inspiration are the same for mythology as well. All that moves man, delights or elevates becomes the object of poetry and of belief. Human imagination becomes the energy which is active in the creation of poetry as well as of the gods. And the imagination itself depends on the environment, on the natural phenomena, on the climate and, of course, also on the spiritual factors like the individuality of the peoples. In a tropical country which is usually afflicted by drought, where fever and other kinds of diseases follow the rainy season, the notions, gods and demons will have a character different from a place where winter shackles nature; these traits vary from steppe to seacoast, from hills to plains. Living conditions, vegetation and climate vary from place to place, so do the world of gods and also poetry. Something of the fragrance of the native soil emanates from poetry and mythology. Vedic mythology is not completely indigenous to India. Not only had the long process of natural evolution influenced and transformed Vedic mythology as it did everywhere, but the migrations and the new sky above the heads had also left their mark. As I have stated earlier, some of the gods found in the ṚV are already in the process of extinction, others suddenly rise to the surface, several are arrested in their development and are almost divested of their original nature, whereas others like Soma shine in their full original splendour. But those who are in a process of transformation bear still many a trait which does not match their new clothing. Metaphors that are no more befitting and are merely reminiscent of a former home are carried along for a while like some erratic detritus. Here also poets can be the interpreters of the gods of their tribe to a certain extent. We can ask them: from which sources does the mythology of their native country draw the gods and demons? We can also ask them to a limited degree about what can be autochthonous and what cannot. Even later poets touch upon phenomena which had, in older times, given rise to religious thoughts and conceptions, for these poets share with the ancient singers of myths the inspiration from heaven and earth of one and the same homeland.[75]

With this I come back to Vṛtra. The demon who encompasses the rivers, who lies on the streams or mountains, devoid of hands and feet, who encloses the waters, covers, shackles and obstructs them, who is pierced in his sleep by Indra with his thunderbolt, does not make any sense as a phenomenon on Indian soil and has no analogy in the language of the poets.

2. The Later Poets of India on Vṛtra

In order to obtain the correct yardstick for the appreciation of the Vedic expressions, we would do well to turn to the classical poets of India. These poets are not parsimonious in the descriptions of the seasons and of their impressions and must inform us whether such metaphors as in the ṚV were ever employed in India. I pass over the rainy season of which there are long descriptions in the *Rāmāyaṇa* and the *Mahābhārata*[76]. A survey of such descriptions reveals a complete disparity in ideas and images. We find a description of summer, besides briefly in TĀr I.3.4., in *Raghuvaṃśa* XVI. 43 ff. for example. I give below only relevant expressions that are suitable for comparison.

Raghuvaṃśa XVI. 43: . . . *ājagāma gharmaḥ* . . . .
44: *agastyacihnād ayanāt samīpaṃ*
dig uttarā bhāsvati saṃnivṛtte |
ānandaśītām iva bāṣpavṛṣṭiṃ
himasrutiṃ haimavatīṃ sasarja ||
45: *pravṛddhatāpo divaso 'timātram*
atyartham eva kṣaṇadā ca tanvī |
46: *dinedine śaivalavanty adhastāt*
sopānaparvāṇi vimuñcad ambhaḥ |
uddaṇḍapadmaṃ gṛhadīrghikāṇām
nārīnitambadvayasaṃ babhūva ||

Or *Ṛtusaṃhāra* I. 1: *pracaṇḍasūryaḥ spṛhaṇīyacandramāḥ*
sadāvagāhakṣatavārisaṃcayaḥ|
dināntaramyo 'bhyupaśāntamanmatho
nidāghakālaḥ samupāgataḥ priye ||
10: *asahyavātoddhatareṇumaṇḍalā*
pracaṇḍasūryātapatāpitā mahī | . . .
11: *mṛgāḥ pracaṇḍātapatāpitā bhṛśaṃ*
tṛṣā mahatyā pariśuṣkatālavaḥ |
vanāntare toyam iti pradhāvitā
nirīkṣya bhinnāñjanasaṃnibhaṃ nabhaḥ ||
22: *paṭutaravanadāhāt pluṣṭaśaṣpaprarohāḥ*
paruṣapavanavegāt kṣiptasaṃśuṣkaparṇāḥ |
dinakaraparitāpāt kṣīṇatoyāḥ samantāt
vidadhati bhayam uccair vīkṣyamāṇā
vanāntāḥ ||

Sūryaśataka 14:
āvṛttibhrāntaviśvāḥ śramam iva dadhataḥ śoṣiṇaḥ svoṣmaṇeva |
grīṣme dāvāgnitaptā iva rasam asakṛd ye dharitryā dhayanti ||

The *Kāvyānuśāsana* (V, p. 66) recommends, among others, the following characteristics of summer which poets should mention in their writings: *nadīsaraḥkūpādiṣu nirambhastvam*, *pānthapūrṇāh prapāḥ* or examples like *pacyanta iva bhūtāni*, *kampanta iva toyāni*, *tapyanta iva pāṃsavaḥ*, *ādhmāyanta iva parvatāḥ*—that is to say, here also there are no expressions that correspond to the phraseology of the ṚV, and this difference lies not in the change of style but in the change in attitudes, in the change in the thing itself.[77]

A discussion of the word *parvata* will take us a step further in answering the question about the origin and meaning of Vṛtra.

3. Vṛtra and the Parvata

Where does Vṛtra enclose the waters? The ṚV answers as a rule (in one or another mode of expressions) that it is a *párvata*. Mythologists have interpreted this 'mountain' or these 'mountains' mostly as 'cloud.'[78]

First of all, the following passages are pertinent for our discussion.

I.32.1: *áhann áhim ánv apás tatarda*
prá vakṣáṇā abhinat párvatānām |
2: *áhann áhiṃ párvate śiśriyāṇám...*
51.4: *tvám apā́m apidhā́nāvṛṇor ápa*
ádhārayaḥ párvate dā́numad vásu |
vṛtráṃ yád indra śávasā́vadhīr áhim
ā́d ít sū́ryam divy ā́rohayo dṛśé ||
54.10: *apā́m atiṣṭhad dharúṇahvaraṃ támo*
antár vṛtrásya jaṭháreṣu párvataḥ
57.6: *tváṃ tám indra párvataṃ mahā́m urúṃ*
vájreṇa vajrin· parvaśáś cakartitha
ávāsṛjo nívṛtāḥ sártavā́ apáḥ...
(Cf. IV.17.2: *bhinád giríṃ śávasā vajrám iṣṇám...*
21.8: *vi yád várāṃsi párvatasya vṛṇvé*
páyobhir jinvé apā́ṃ jávāṃsi
V.32.1: *ádardar útsam ásṛjo ví khā́ni* |
tvám arṇavā́n badbadhānā́ṃ aramṇāḥ |
mahā́ntam indra párvataṃ ví yád vaḥ
sṛjó ví dhā́rā áva dānaváṃ han ||
2: *tvám útsām ṛtúbhir badbadhānā́ṃ*
áraṃha ū́dhaḥ párvatasya vajrin |
VI.30.5: *tvám apó ví dúro viṣūcīr*
índra dṛḷhám arujaḥ párvatasya |
VII.79.4: *ví dṛḷhásya dúro ádrer aurṇoḥ* ||
(VIII.64.5 *tyáṃ cit párvataṃ giríṃ śatávantaṃ sahasríṇam*|
ví stotṛ́bhyo rurojitha||

The mere survey shows that these passages (listed by Grassmann, *inter alia*, for the meaning 'cloud') refer only to the mountains. These are sources which Vṛtra besieges and Indra liberates. Certainly, from the heights of the mountains the waters flow downwards (*ápo ná párvatasya pṛṣṭhā́t* VI.24.6), and the mountains possess abundant wealth and nourishment.[79] Let us assume for the sake of argument that it is not the mountains like the Hindukush or the Himalayas upon which Vṛtra lies encamped but 'clouds.' Then it is strange that these 'clouds' are always called *párvata* or *girí*, occasionally also *ádri* or *áśman*,[80] but never *abhrá* or *meghá*. It is certainly surprising that there is not a single authentic passage from which we can deduce that the demon was actually lying on a cloud. Roth follows Grassmann. He lists the following passages for the meaning 'cloud' (however, with the remark that it is impossible to decide between the meaning 'mountain' and the by all means rarer meaning 'cloud'): I.19.7; II.11.7, 8; V.57.3; VIII.7.23; "perhaps also VIII.59.11; VS X.19." But an examination will show that here also *párvata* denotes only the 'mountain.'[81] When it is said in one of these verses that "even the mountain which was about to move came to a standstill" (II.11.7), this can of course be an allusion to the saga according to which the mountains at one time possessed wings but not an evidence to say that the mountains themselves were the clouds. On the contrary, it follows from this very saga that the wings which had been cut asunder by Indra became the clouds and now cling to the mountains for ever;[82] thus a distinction is made between mountain and cloud. It is an old belief that the creator had firmly fixed heaven, earth etc. in their positions. We should understand what has been said about the mountains from this viewpoint. In these verses also *párvata* is occasionally replaced by *girí* but not by any name for the cloud. Furthermore, *párvata* is personified,[83] as in Himavat of Kālidāsa.[84] Then he becomes the *girīśa* and appears as an ally of Indra, associated with him as a dual deity. Together they slay the enemies,[85] ride on a common chariot, bring *vāmī́r íṣaḥ suvī́rāḥ* and enjoy the libations in the sacrifice.[86] When VIII. 70.11 states: *áva sváḥ sákhā dudhuvīta...dásyuṃ párvataḥ*, this is also a personification; it is merely a mythological synonym for the expulsion of the enemy from his rock-fortress. Cf.IV.30. 14: *kaulitaráṃ bṛhatáḥ párvatād ádhi/ávāhann indra śámbaram.*

Since one saw in Vṛtra the hot season or the cloud-demon which withholds the rain, one arrived at the notion that the *párvata* must be the cloud, and the Indian commentators contributed to the fact that the investigations proceeded along the wrong path.[87]

There is not a single reliable passage where *párvata* has the sense of 'cloud.' I think that as far as Vedic mythology is concerned we can safely leave the fanciful notion of the "cloud castles" or of the "cloud-demons" like Vṛtra[88] to its late and not-yet-extinct inventors.[89]

4. Vṛtra and his Season

Which then is the season in which Vṛtra "lies on the mountains," or "holds the mountains in his belly," in which Indra "tears open the channels of the mountains," or lets "the udders of the mountains" flow? Summer is ruled out, so also the "demon of drought" or 'heat.' In the hot season when it is summer on the mountains and the glaciers begin to melt, the rivers do not remain dry; on the contrary, they are full of water.[90] For it is not the 'rain,' nor the 'cloud-waters' which Vṛtra confines, besieges, or imprisons, nor are they ponds or lakes—the ṚV does not speak of these in this context—but merely the 'waters,' the streams and especially the seven streams which Vṛtra holds under his sway. Again and again it is just said that Indra opens the rocks, liberates the waters and lets the streams flow. The root *śuṣ* which would be appropriate for a demon of heat never occurs in the terminology of the myth;[91] at the most we may cite the two occurrences of the root *gras*.

Next, it is impossible to interpret Vṛtra as the demon of the rainy season. From some passage or other according to which Indra, after his conquest over Vṛtra, deposits the sun in the sky or according to which Vṛtra (?) is called *svavṛṣṭi*, if one were to conclude that Vṛtra is the demon of the rains, this interpretation would be totally incompatible with other passages and also with the actual significance of the rainy season. One can entertain such a notion only as a passing fancy.

Thus there would remain the question whether Vṛtra is the same as the 'cloud,' i.e. the 'cloud-covering' of the mountains which rests upon these as a 'demon.' If this was the case, it would be difficult to understand why the destruction of these should be regarded as a great exploit of Indra, since Indians knew as we all do that the cloud is the water-bestower; still less can one understand the inner connection between such a demon represented by the cloud and the fettering of the 'streams.' There is no basis for such an interpretation in any single passage of the ṚV, and even in the later period which preserved for us many a description of the rainy season the clouds are never "hostile monsters," or something else that can resemble the demons who confine the streams or withhold the waters. That occasionally the clouds are compared to various beings like elephants or snakes or conversely various beings are compared to the clouds[92] is a different matter and is not relevant for us here.

5. The Origin of the Vedic Imagery

The analogies to the Vedic imagery, denied to us by classical Sanskrit, can be found elsewhere. They occur—not one or two, but in a considerable number—in the poetry of northern countries where winter shackles the streams and spring victoriously fights with its opponent. It will be easy for anybody to cite examples. I give below only a few, collected at random.[93]

Bartholomae sees the period of stark winter in *brūma*= **mrūma* and compares it with *Vendidād* II. 22: *mrūrō zyå̊*, "the stark frost" (accusative).[94]

Horace, *Odes*, I.9: *geluque flumina constiterint acuto*, "and the streams are frozen with biting cold."[95] Virgil, *Georgica*, III. 354 (about the Skythian nation): *jacet aggeribus niveis informis et alto terra gelu*,[96] "but all/ The region is one frozen continent, / With mounts of snow that rise to seven ells "[97]

Beowulf, 11. 1133-34: *winter yde beléac ȋsgebinde*,[98] "winter locked the waves in its icy bond;"[99] 1. 1608 ff.: *ȋse gelȋcost, thonne forstes bend fäder onloeted, onwinded voelrâpas*, "melted, very like to ice, when as the Father ...loosens the bonds of frost, unwinds the flood ropes."[100]

Andreas 1258: *snâw eordan band wintergewopum*, "the snow bound the earth with the snow-drifts of winter." *Denksprüche* II. 76: *ân sceal inbindan forstes fetre fela-meahtig god*, 'the almighty god alone may loosen the shackles of frost.'

Seefahrer 32: *hrím hrúsan band*, "the hoar frost bound the earth." Cf. Wanderer 102.

Grimm, *Deutsche Mythologie*, 4th ed., p. 634: *die Heide liegt in Banden des Winters*, "the heath lies in the bonds of winter." Ibid, Nachträge III. 231: *der Winter bannt die Heide*, "the winter captivates the hearth."

Graf Snoilsky in a Swedish poem: *se! i vinter tvång sofver forsens sāng under fängelsehvalfven af iskristall*, "Look, under the constraint of winter the song of the waterfall is sleeping under the prison vault of crystal ice." Andreas Aabel. *Friluftsvise*: *Hor fjaeldets stolte fos! Nys brod den vintrens bånd og tvang, nu går den frit sin gang*, "hear the proud waterfall of the mountains; not long ago it broke through the bonds and restraints of winter and now it is running freely on its course."

Thomson, *Seasons*, Spring (ed. Murdoch, p. 4):

"And see where surly Winter passes off,
Far to the north, and calls his ruffian blasts"

and Winter (ed. Murdoch, p. 165):

"with the fierce rage of Winter deep suffus'd
An icy gale, oft shifting, o'er the pool
Breathes a blue film, and in its mid career
Arrests the bickering stream....
.... till seiz'd from shore to shore
the whole imprison'd river growls below."[101]

Or of the more recent writers, notably Goethe in *Faust*, part I:

Vom Eise befreit sind Strom und Bäche
Durch des Frühlings holden, belebenden Blick,—
Der alte Winter in seiner Schwäche
Zog sich in rauhe Berge zurück.
Von dorther sendet er, fliehend, nur
Ohnmächtige Schauer körnigen Eises ...

"River and streams have got rid of their ice in the sweet reviving gleam of spring; the valley is green with hope and happiness; old winter in his weakness has retreated into wild mountains, and from there he can only send impotent showers of hail..."[102]

Raabe, *Unsers Hergotts Canzlei*, II. Cap. 6: *der Schnee ist zergangen, die befreiten Wasser blitzen wie geschmolzenes Silber,* "the snow has melted, the liberated waters are shining like molten silver." We may compare ṚV I. 32. 2: *vāśrā́ iva dhenávaḥ syándamānā áñjaḥ samudrám áva jagmur ā́paḥ* and 8: *nadám na bhinnám amuyā́ śáyānaṃ máno rúhāṇā áti yanty ā́paḥ* with Geibel: *der Schnee im Tal zerschmolz, die Ströme tanzten siegreich durch die Flur*, "the snow melted in the valley, the streams danced victoriously through the meadows."

We can easily add more examples, but let it not be said that I have quoted these unnecessarily. Whosoever reads these and recalls the expression *sindhavaḥ tastabhānāḥ* of the ṚV cannot fail to see the similarity of such images which have their origin not in a southern country but at a place where the *informis hiems* [102a] or the ice-giants enchain the streams and surround the waters. Vṛtra who is described in several passages as asleep and whom Indra awakens with his thunderbolt reminds us of the "winter sleep" of nature.[103] In this respect the Veda is closer to the attitudes of the European poets than to classical Sanskrit; that is to say, the Veda really preserves here a number of images from the earlier periods.

This conclusion is not surprising. We should not forget that Vṛtra's name does not have its origin in Indian mythology. In Iran[104] and Armenia the conquest over Vṛtra is celebrated. Vahagn is an ancient Armenian god of great popularity[105] and, according to Gelzer, of Iranian origin. "His battle with the dragons and his triumph over them was celebrated in song; people sang of him in the same way as they did of the heroic exploits of Hercules."[106] On a coin of Kaniṣka we find *Ordagno* in Skythian dress.[107] The bird Vārəñȷana or Vāragna sits on his helmet.[108] Long ago Benfey had proved that *Ordagno* (there is also the form *Orthágnēs*) is identical with Avestan *Vərəthrajna* and is known to the Greeks as *Oyararánēs*.[109] Lagarde identifies *'Artágnēs* (basic form *Fartágnēs*) with the Avestan *Vərəthragna*.[110] It is not known what the word *vərəthra* "enemy" had originally meant here.[111] The proper name Vṛtra which occurs so often in the Veda does not appear any more in the Avesta, where the ancient pre-Iranian mythology has gone through an advanced stage of corruption. The fact that Vərəthragna was elevated into a deity and was widely popular makes it reasonable to assume that his religious position does not owe its origin to the triumph over an arbitrary enemy as such but over a mythical opponent.[112]

Spiegel[113] is of the opinion that the myth of Indra and Vṛtra has close resemblance to that of Tištrya and Apaoša and that the star Tištrya has replaced Vərəthragno rather late with whom it shares a common cult. I think that the real state of affairs is quite different. Apaoša is a demon of drought; to assume the same for Vṛtra is incompatible with all the relevant passages of the ṚV. When it emerges from the phraseology of the ṚV that the original concept of this enemy of Indra was the "winter giant," the Avesta should have the least objection to this conclusion. For, aside from the scorching heat, the climate of Iran consists also of "the winter which the demons have created."[114] The first Fargard mentions the *ažim ča yim raoiδitəm zyam ča daēvōdātəm*[115] as the counter-creation by Ahriman in the land of Airyana Vaējaṃh and likewise in the lands of *upa aoδēšu raŋhayå*.[116] An etymology first proposed by Noreen[117] would further support the non-Indian origin of the demon. According to this etymology, *vṛtrá = voldrá = vlódra = **Lódurr***, the last one being the epithet of Loki and one of the oldest Aryan manifestations. Unfortunately the meaning and the reason for connecting the epithet with Loki are too obscure to be of any use.

From Kashmir[118] or from the North-West—I shall leave it undecided where the saga took its shape originally—Indians carried the saga of the battle against Vṛtra to their new homelands. The images reminiscent of a Nordic home could still be preserved in the ṚV because its scene of action encompasses the great streams which are in flood in spring and whose sources are situated in the Himalayas. But when we follow the character of Vṛtra in Indian literature, we see a gradual transformation of his traits culminating in the exclusion of all that is reminiscent of the imprisonment and confinement of the waters and so on. If the demon of drought which is well known to the tropical India was personified in Vṛtra then we would expect to find his characteristic features again precisely in classical Sanskrit. But that is not the case. Hence, there remains only this much to say: the change in conceptions is related to the gradual transformation or the replacement of the old tradition. In the chapter on Uṣas (vol. I, p. 26ff.) I have shown how the Vedic poets with their myth of the cowshed in which Vala barricades the cows employed an image which has its origin in some northern country or other, the climate of which forces its inhabitants to barricade their herds in solid stables in the same manner as the Skythians did, about whom Virgil states in *Georgica* III. 352: *illic clausa tenent stabulis armenta*, "There stabled close/The herds they keep."[119] This notion was lost in India later on. In Vṛtra we encounter a further example of recasting of a pre-Indian notion under the Indian sun.

6. Vṛtra and the Rivers of India

I have remarked above that Vṛtra does not besiege the ponds or lakes but—provided what were mentioned are the waters in general—the rivers themselves. Even when we overlook the pre-history of this demon and stand purely on the Indian soil, we should not ignore the above fact. For the lowest waterlevel would by its very nature indicate the zenith of Vṛtra's reign.

Indian rivers attain the highest waterlevel naturally in the rainy season. When do they have the lowest level? One will be inclined to think of the hot season when the beds of the smaller rivers dry up and the land is parched under the scorching heat; but the actual conditions provide a different answer. For we are not dealing with the small brooks of which the ṚV hardly takes any notice but with the major rivers mentioned in our collection of hymns, like the Indus, Vipāś, Śutudrī, Yamunā, Kubhā. With the exception of the Kabul and the Gomatī, all these rivers originate, as the Indus itself does, in the snow-capped ranges of the Himalayas and carry the minimum volume of water not in summer but in winter. "In the winter the streams dwindle away. But as the mountain snows melt on the approach of the Indian summer followed by the rainy season, the waters rise and overflow the surrounding country, at places to a distance of several miles on either bank."[120]

Arrian, *Anabasis*, V.9.4: "Then, besides, about that time all the rivers of India were running with big and turbulent stream, and with a swift current; for it was the season when the sun is just making its bend towards the summer turning;[120a] and at this season heavy rains come down into the land of India and the snows of the Caucasus, whence spring most of the rivers, are melting and greatly increase the volume of water; but in winter the rivers stop again, become smaller and clear in appearance, and fordable in places; except the Indus and Ganges, and possibly another; the Hydaspes at any rate becomes fordable."[121]

It follows from these descriptions that the major rivers reach their lowest level not in May or June, i.e. in the driest period when "the demon of heat" indeed exercises his power, but in winter. Compare with this the following observations on the volume of water in the Indus: "the breadth of the Indus at Attock depends not only upon the season but the state of the river upwards...Its maximum discharge, above the confluence of the Panjab or Five rivers, occurs in July and August, when it is swollen by the seasonal rains, and it then reaches 135 000 cubic feet, falling to its minimum...in December;"[122] or Stein's remark on the Vitastā: "when the river is low as during the winter, the banks rise on an average about 15 feet above the water. But in the spring when the snow melts, the great volume of water brought down from the mountains rises to the top of the banks and often overflows it."[123]

Thornton[124] describes the Chenab (Asiknī) thus: "The Chenaub was here, at the end of June, the season of the greatest height of water, three-quarters of a mile wide...at midsummer, the season of greatest inundation," and about the Vitastā he states: "Von Hügel, at the commencement of January, when the rivers of the Punjab are lowest, crossed at the town of Jhelum, on a bridge of twenty large boats..."[125]

Hence, as far as these rivers are concerned, we cannot say that a demon of drought besieges or confines them in summer, for by this time they have already passed through the state of minimum waterlevel. But we may certainly assume that the tribes and their Kavis who had already descended into the plains of India did not lose, as long as they lived in the vicinity of the great rivers fed by the Himalayas and more particularly in the North-West, the understanding for the Vṛtra saga which they had brought with them from their former homes further in the north. This saga, however, began to lose its original significance already in the ṚV. From a miraculous deed of Indra, confined to a specific period in time, it was gradually transformed into an exploit in general. And when the singers praised the release of the waters by Indra from the power of Vṛtra, they or at least the majority of them need not have been aware any more of the metereological origins of the battle.

This memory gets lost more and more. If Vṛtra was originally winter, his companions were snow and ice. But the old word for 'to snow' is not known to the Veda any more. Occasionally the Veda counts the years in terms of winters; it also knows of the "snow-covered mountains," *himá* is contrasted with heat; VIII.32.26 states that Indra slays Arbuda in winter (See ZII, III, p. 13); TBr III.12.7.2 speaks of *himó yaś ca śīyáte.*[126] But these are only occasional remarks. These phenomena do not govern the life of the poets and are no longer the sources for mythological formations. The seventh book, for which I assume a specifically Indian home in the holy land on the banks of the eastern Sarasvatī for reasons which I have discussed earlier (Vol. I, p. 352), differs from several other books in this respect also. Its Indra-hymns, with the exception of 18 which resembles a chronicle and 19,[127] do not have much content and betray a tradition that has already become quite obsolete. We can see the difference still more clearly in the passages dealing with Vṛtra. The word occurs about fifteen times in thirteen hymns; only in three passages (two of which are uncertain) it is the name of the demon, otherwise it is the designation of the enemy in general. No less typical is the occurrence of the word in the AV; there it occurs disproportionately rarely as compared to the ṚV. If we do not take the compounds *vṛtrahan* and *vṛtrahatya* into account, there remain only fourteen hymns in which the word occurs at all, and the number is still less of the hymns where the word is a proper noun and is of some significance. In Pāli the word has completely disappeared (I know only one passage, *Jātaka* V.153, which speaks of the mighty god who slew Vṛtra) and does not form any more the usual opposite for Sakko who has been transformed into *devānām indo.* This, I think, is an important evidence for the pre-Indian character of Vṛtra, whose original nature could still be comprehended, to a certain extent, only in the north-western part of India.[128]

7. Vṛtra and the Explanation of Indra

The antithesis between Indra and Vṛtra moves along such definite lines that the explanation of the one cannot remain without consequences for the interpretation of the other. Only the sun god, with whose ascending orbit the release and the filling up of the enchained streams begins, can come into question as the opponent of the winter-giant, unless one wishes to be content with a vague etymon. Just as Vṛtra's nature was gradually forgotten in India and continued its existence in solitary myths only, so did Indra's evolution move in new paths under the influence of a new climate. He did not simply transform himself into the sun god of the Indian climate but attained, through paths that will be discussed later, the character of a rain god. His connection to the waters in general might have contributed to this transformation. But in the ṚV his metamorphosis took place only to the extent that he laid aside his character of a personified natural energy. One can already ask whether any poet of the individual books has seen him as a natural phenomenon and will get 'no' for an answer. Indra is no more the sun. As a rule, he is distinguished from the sun and appears as the latter's liberator, or his moderator, or is compared with the sun.[129] On the other hand, he is not yet the rain god either. His transformation in this direction is noticeable only in its very beginnings. As Bergaigne first noted, it is rarely (and that too outside the Vṛtra legend) that Indra is described as the bestower of rain in the ṚV.

One may dispute this by saying that a change could have taken place in the nature of the "thunderstorm god," "an obscuration to remove which is the task or art of the mythologist."[130] However, "the art of the mythologist" stands the test only when it does not deviate from the historical foundations laid by the Indian literature. It is only at a later stage of this literature and not at its beginning that the rain god Indra makes his appearance with a remarkable frequency. We encounter him very rarely in the ṚV.[131] In the classical period, Vedic imagery disappeared and with it the phraseology which is peculiar to the Veda. In order to support one's belief that primarily and originally Indra was a thunderstorm god, one may point, let us say, to a common Indo-European thunderstorm god and say that Indra is an Indian continuation of this common god. To this we can only reply that such a common Indo-European thunderstorm god does not exist if we look at our evidence. Admittedly Thôr and Indra have similar traits. Indra is also described as *aruṇo bhrūmān.*[132] But there is no evidence of a historical relationship and the possession of the thunderbolt proves as little for Indra's original character as thunderstorm god as it does for Zeus or Mithra. Zeus holds the thunderbolt, Mithra the Vazra, but they are not original storm gods because of this. The lightning in Indra's hand merely fecilitates his evolution into a thunderstorm god and finally into a rain god. Even in the Brāhmaṇas we find very few passages which describe him as a storm god as ABr III.4.8 does. Here also we see still allusions to his former nature as a sun god. This is illustrated by Indra's participation in the liberation of the cows from the rock stable, in which exploit he is assisted by the singers and the Manes. His epithet *gotrabhid* which alludes to this exploit survived even later in the classical period. The 'red cows' are intimately associated with Uṣas and their return denotes in a series of hymns, not the dawn of each individual day, but the ascent of the new light out of the winter night.[133] As I have explained earlier, in these verses we have an old inherited image that took its shape in those settlements where the rigours of winter caused the cattle to be shut in solid stables. And now this image continues its existence in a different climate in the saga of the liberation of the cows of Uṣas. If the conception of Indra emanated from the sun god, then his position in these cycles of sagas as the liberator of the cows is quite consistent, even though his character as the sun god began to fade out. The saga of Indra tearing asunder the rock stable and liberating the cows could have its starting point in the sun god who with ever-increasing vigour brings back the light around the New Year;[134] but it does not go well with one who was originally a thunderstorm god.[135] It is not accidental that the Ekāṣṭakā, the New Year's night, who is very closely connected with the Manes, is styled as the mother of Indra in a verse of the AV.[136] This is in conformity with Indra's position at the centre of the major sacrifices like the Agniṣṭoma and Mahāvrata and his connection with grīṣma which is his season.

8. Objections against my Interpretation

So far as I know, my interpretation of Vṛtra and Indra, published in advance in ZDMG, (1896), p. 665 ff., found a response only from A. Barth at first.[137] But the objections raised by him are too obvious to have been overlooked by me. The rivers of India are not the starting point of the Vṛtra legend. I have emphasized already in my "Vorläufige Mitteilung" that "the battle between the demon of winter and the sun has still a great significance in the lands situated to the west and north of the Indus. The word Vṛtra had its origin *there and was inherited along with the concept from the pre-Indian period. But further in the east, in India proper, the origin and significance of the saga was forgotten under different conditions...*"[138] Could I have stated my view any more clearly? Barth does not go into the core of my argument at all. But even if we confine ourselves to the Indian soil, the Vṛtra legend can be valid in relation to the major rivers of India for quite a while. I have not spoken of "all the rivers of India," not even of all which emerge from the Himālayas. Only those known to the ṚV can be considered here. I have mentioned specifically the Indus, to which the Vitastā, Irāvatī, Vipāś and Śutudrī (they themselves extol their release by Indra in ṚV III.33), Yamunā as well as Kubhā can be added. This is clear already from my reference to Arrian and to Hunter's introduction to the maps of "Punjāb, Kashmīr, the NW. Frontier and British Baluchistan." The quotations show that these rivers contain the minimum volume of water in winter and that the "Vṛtra lying on the mountains" has still significance for their waterlevel.[139]

Barth attaches great value to the "thundering god." But Mithra with the Vazra assigned to him demonstrates clearly, as I have already stated, that the sun god can become the bearer of the thunderbolt, and the same is established by some of the verses that I have cited earlier on the relationship between the lightning and the sun in Vol. I, p. 88. But let us for the moment ignore this aspect and confine ourselves to the Indian soil. When do the first thunderstorms of the year occur there? Not just at the beginning of the rainy season but quite earlier still. "The rains in the second half of March and during April and May are thunder-showers or they occur at the end of dust-storms which are frequent in these months. In March and April thunder-storms are often accompanied by hail."[140] Hence, even in India thunderstorms accompany the ascending orbit of the year and reach the climax with the highest position of the sun. Thus it is possible that the thunderbolt could have been placed in the hands of the sun even in India.

Barth speaks of the "caresses of the vernal sun." The vernal sun god displays his love only to the earth and to his friends but not to the powers that are hostile to him. The battles between the summer and the winter in which the latter is treated shabbily are the favourite motifs in popular poetry and drama.[141]

Barth's last objection does not concern me at all, but those who attempt to see in the battle led by Indra's thunderbolt against Vṛtra a reflection of the Indian climate. A large number of my predecessors have invoked the help of the phenomena of the Indian climate to explain the nature of Vṛtra. When Barth states that it is a misconception to look for an exact description of nature in the Vedic myths, he is right to a certain degree, provided such general verdicts are debatable at all. But generally speaking, mythological hymns rarely give expression to the original character of a god in an objective manner. They do so only in a form that has been conditioned by the change in time and circumstances and by the influence of the poets and so on. In the case of Indra also I have taken this into account. However, if we carefully examine the language of the hymns, they can still give us much information, particularly in one instance like here where we can see the entire course of evolution; for language does not keep step with the changing conceptions that gradually gain currency. In every culture area there are formulas, phrases and traditions which belong to the inventory of the priestly poets and which are discarded very gradually by the succeeding generations that do not preserve the tradition with a proper understanding. Thus we have the task of carefully weighing the wording of the Vedic poets, of comparing it with the notions of the later periods and of considering the possibility of purely poetical or mythical evolution by the side of the natural basis. If we encounter in this task formulas which do not fit into the Indian surroundings and yet on the other hand are not subjective since they occur again among totally different poets of older hymns, then we must put these relics into the proper context through which they become vivid once again. Those stereotype statements about Vṛtra that he fetters the streams or confines them or besieges them are the erratic detrital deposits from a pre-Indian period. India of the later period was no longer familiar with them, nor did it know how to explain them satisfactorily. Since we are dealing here with a relic from the past, it is not surprising that snow and ice are not mentioned in the hymns. The poets did not come across snow and ice in India, but the phenomenon of rivers in spate, recurring every year in summer, kept alive the old winter saga for some time. In the later period it became completely extinct or was modified. In India as well as in Iran the word *vṛtra* has long ago advanced far beyond the etymological meaning of "obstructor, encloser, coverer, enveloper" and attained a more lively sense. It would be surprising if those who had emigrated from colder regions did not know that it was the winter which besieged the rivers.[142]

1. More from the Vṛtra Saga

Before I move to the treatment of Indra's position in the ritual, I may discuss here some passages from the ṚV and the Brāhmaṇas, which now come into their own through the result of my investigation so far. First of all there are two verses, 1. 54. 10: *antár vṛtrásya jaṭháreṣu párvataḥ* and I.32.2: *áhann áhiṃ párvate śiśriyāṇám*. These become intelligible as soon as it is realised that they contain a reminiscence of the old saga of Vṛtra as the winter giant. Much more difficult is VIII. 32.26 where Arbuda is described:

> *áhan vṛtrám ṛcīṣama aurṇavābhám ahīśúvam*
> *himénāvidhyad árbudam||*

Sāyaṇa paraphrases *himena* with *tuṣāréṇodakena vā* and explains naturally Arbuda again as 'cloud.' Ludwig translates it as "with winter's cold" and quite rightly finds it strange that the "winter's cold" is Indra's weapon. It seems to me that like *áhnā, divá ghṛṇéva* and *himá* (cf. X. 37.10), *hiména* is only a specification of time: "In winter" Indra struck Arbuda. In view of the peculiar character of the eighth book we never know if we are to attach any value to each of its statements. But since the *dies natalis solis invicti* (birthday of the invincible sun) falls in the winter period and his ascending orbit begins with the winter solstice, I would like to think that also the *hiména* here can be understood as part of tradition.

Furthermore, here belongs a series of verses which speak of the recovery of the sun by Indra, of the sun's shining again in the sky and so on,[143] which we can construe as referring to the time of the winter solstice. If we think of India alone, it might seem that only the rainy season could come into question: *jayati tulām adhirūḍho bhāsvān iha jaladapaṭalāni.*[144] But I may recall what I have stated in Vol. I, pp. 24 ff., 62 ff., 95 ff. In the ṚV there are expressions like *apā́m upásthe* and *támasi.* In the later hymns these two are akin in meaning but by no means identical. *támas* still refers traditionally to the dark period of the year, to that of shorter days, and *apā́m upásthe* to the rainy season. We saw that the Manes discover the light, drive out the cows from the stable and that sacrifice, Sūrya and Agni return again with Uṣas. It is the end of the Pitṛyāṇa, hailed in some of the hymns dedicated to the Uṣas and regarded as the return of the period of the gods by the Indian world also. Here we should not let ourselves be influenced by the conceptions of the later period alone. The Vedic times in which the old and the new intermingled are too complex to be judged from one viewpoint alone. Of course, already in stray passages of the ṚV it is said in conformity with the views of the later period that the gods brought out Sūrya "hidden in the ocean"[145] or that Bṛhaspati cut off the "three together" from the ocean (*udadhéḥ*, Sāyaṇa: *valāt*).[146] But Vṛtra is never connected with *samudrá*, almost never with *vṛṣṭi* or *varṣá*,[147] but always only with *ā́paḥ* or *támas*; nor do we hear that Indra liberates the sun from the womb of the clouds or of the waters. This point ought to be of some importance for our interpretation. The gods who applaud Indra for having killed Vṛtra do not do so because Indra has dispelled the darkness of the rainy season and afterwards placed the sun in the sky; because in this period of the year it is not the gods who exercise their reign but the Manes and these are *deváśatravaḥ*. The applause of the gods would refer to the commencement of the Devayāna. Hence I construe these verses throughout as referring to the period of the Pitṛyāṇa and to the rebirth of the sun at the end of winter.

In his battle against Indra, Vṛtra spreads fog and hail all around.

I.32.13: *nā́smai vidyún ná tanyatúḥ siṣedha*
ná yā́ṃ míham ákirad dhrādúniṃ ca ||
II. 30.3: *mī́haṃ vásāna úpa hīm ádudrot*
tigmā́yudho ajayac chátrum índraḥ ||
X.73.5: *míhaḥ prá tamrā́ avapat támāṁsi* ||[148]

Not only Vṛtra but the host of the Maruts is also associated with *míh* and *hrādúni* (cf. I.38.7; V. 54.3). It is theoretically possible that this is a poetic embellishment which assigns weapons of this nature to Vṛtra without, however, connecting him with any meteorological phenomenon. On the other hand, if we take this literally, it is evident that these weapons of Vṛtra also could have been inherited from a northern region where the fleeing winter sends fog and "impotent showers of hail." Even in India this notion makes sense; hailstorms occur predominantly in the period which corresponds to our spring. "Showers of hail occur almost only in the dry period from February to March. In the rainy season they are almost totally absent. In the Ganges valley extending up to Calcutta, thunderstorms from the NW bring between March and May occasionally a shower of hail also along with them."[149] It is true, hail is mentioned only once as Vṛtra's weapon [150] and therefore this point is not of great significance. But this much can certainly be said: even this factor does not especially favour any attempt to see a demon of the hot season or of the rainy season in Vṛtra.

The last passage I wish to cite here is from the *Satapatha Brāhmaṇa*. There it is said at II.6.1.1: *mahāhaviṣā ha vai devā vṛtraṃ jaghnuḥ| teno eva vyajayanta yeyam eṣāṃ vijitis tām| atha yān evaiṣāṃ tasmin saṃgrāme'ghnaṃs tān pitṛyajñena samairayanta| pitaro vai ta āsaṃs tasmāt pitṛyajño nāma|* 2: *tad vasanto grīṣmo varṣa ete te ye vyajayanta śarad dhemantaḥ śiśiras ta u te yān punaḥ samairayanta*; compare this with II.1.3.1. *vasanto grīṣmo varṣas te devā ṛtavaḥ śarad dhemantaḥ śiśiras te pitaraḥ*. Here the Brāhmaṇa assigns to the gods spring, summer etc., that is, the period between the equinoxes. This is somewhat contrary to the usual definition of the Devayāna, but this small departure is, of no consequence.[151] What is significant is that here the Vasanta, Grīṣma and Varṣāḥ vanquish Vṛtra, and his reign is placed in the dark period of the year and not in summer. The course of my investigation throws light on this passage of the Brāhmaṇa [152] and warns anew that we should not readily dismiss such occasionally absurd-looking statements. Of course, one cannot write Vedic mythology on the basis of such statements, but one can nevertheless explain many of the myths in course of time. And even the oft-discussed eccentric thesis that Vṛtra is identical with Soma[153] makes sense if we remember that here Soma can only be an arbitrarily employed designation for the moon and that the moon is the lord of winter.[154]

Now I can pass on to the treatment of Indra's position in the ritual literature, the statements of which constitute an important endorsement of my interpretation of Indra; for the ritual, in spite of the colourful mixture which owes its existence to the consideration shown to the wishes of different schools and families, nevertheless assigns to Indra an unambiguous position at the centre of the great Soma sacrifice.

C. INDRA IN THE RITUAL

Within the limits of this study, it is neither possible nor necessary to discuss separately all the sacrifices in which Indra has a role. It is sufficient for our purpose to stress the main factors which characterize his position.

The tradition which occupies an important place in the cults of other gods manifests itself quite vividly in Indra's cult as well. The poets of the Vedic hymns allude to their forefathers whose friend Indra was,[155] and like these forefathers the descendants also vie with one another in beseeching Indra's favour with their hymns. "Like unmilked cows" they call out to him,[156] sacrifices strengthen his power,[157] and in return the poet expects the fulfilment of his wishes: *sánti kắmāso harivo dadíṣ ṭvám smó váyam sánti no dhíyaḥ* (VIII. 21.6). The sacrificer and the god have reciprocal relationship. The Veda is still far removed from the belief of the later times that great sacrifices threaten the authority of the king of the gods. [158]

The most important of the sacrifices is the Agniṣṭoma.

1. The Agniṣṭoma

I have already described in Vol. I, p. 328 ff. Indra's participation in the three savanas of this sacrifice. He is entitled to the *Ukthāmadas*, predominantly to the Triṣṭubh among the metres and to the Bṛhat among the Sāmans. He has a share in the morning pressing as well as in that of the evening, pre-eminently, however, in the midday libation. Of course, in another context[159] ŚBr II.4.4.12-13 states: *āgneyaṃ hi prātaḥsavanaṃ . . . aindraṃ hi mādhyandinaṃ savanaṃ . . . vaiśvadevaṃ vai tṛtīyaṃ savanam*, and to this corresponds the distribution of the metres with eight, eleven and twelve syllables respectively. We find the same sequence in the Tryaha which is a prelude to the Dvādaśāha. The three days of the Tryaha belong respectively to Agni, Indra and the Viśve Devāḥ and appear to be an imitation of the three savanas in a single day.[160] But this is only one version. The ṚV, which repeatedly assigns the morning and evening libations to Indra, and also the Sūtras depict Indra as participating in all the savanas. This situation is not changed in the least by the fact that the Grahas of the morning pressing and those of the evening pressing belong in their codified form predominantly to other gods and thus circumscribe Indra's position to some extent. The Prasthitayājyās[161] and the Subrahmaṇyā formula demonstrate that even in the later periods Indra was held to be the real lord of the sacrifice. The formula in its Kaṇva recension is an old constituent of the ritual. It contains a number of allusions to legends that were in vogue among individual gotras.[162] Another remarkable feature of the formula is that it describes Indra as Kauśika[163] and Gautama. All the families who, following Āruṇi's command, invite Indra to the sacrifice with this formula see in Indra the real lord of the entire sacrifice.[164] No matter how we might account for the departures in the case of the morning and evening libations, all the hymns are unanimous in one point: they all assign the midday libation to Indra alone,[165] or as among the Viśvāmitras, to Indra and the Maruts. The later ritual has borrowed the custom from the Viśvāmitras. Hence in the Śrauta Sūtras three of the four Grahas of the midday pressing are dedicated to Indra "accompanied by the Maruts" and one to Mahendra.[166]

The position alloted here to Indra in the middle of the day is of significance for the comprehension of Indra's nature, for it proves that the god who is worshipped specially in the middle of the day is the sun god and thus supports my conclusion. Here Indra has the name Mahendra. According to the testimony of the Brāhmaṇas, the god who triumphed over Vṛtra and was elevated to the status of Mahārāja is entitled to this name.[167] The Agniṣṭoma corresponds to the passage of the year.[168] In ABr III.43.5 the Agniṣṭoma is called a *rathacakram anantam*[169] and in III.44 it is compared to the sun; the manner of recitation imitates his orbit. The individual day is the image of the year and hence the Agniṣṭoma-Ekāha symbolizes the course of the year. Thus Indra is located not only at the zenith of the day but of the year as well. The summer signifies the height of the sun god's reign and the Brāhmaṇas often assign the summer to Indra. For example, MS II.7.20 (105.3): *dakṣiṇā dig grīṣmā ṛtur indro devatā kṣatraṃ draviṇam;* III.15.10 (180.7,8): *indrāya traiṣṭubhāya pañcadaśāya bārhatāya graiṣmāya puroḍāśam ekādaśakapālam;* [170] TS II.1.2.5; *grīṣme madhyandine saṃhitām aindrīm;* VII.5.14; TMBr VI. 1.8: *indro devatā rājanyo manuṣyo grīṣma ṛtuḥ*; ŚBr XIII.5.4.28 :*ṣaḍbhir āgneyair vasante ṣaḍbhir aindrair grīṣme ṣaḍbhiḥ pārjanyair vā mārutair vā varṣāsu.*[171] Statements of the Brāhmaṇas have, it is true, only a limited value. But here they are directly connected with the prevailing custom of the ritual and preserve, in this case, an old tradition. ṚV X.179.2 already depicts Indra in a distinct association with the solstice and the next verse invites him to the midday pressing. It is difficult to say whether the occasional remarks that Indra is the same as Āditya or Sūrya should be construed in this sense or whether they are the results of deduction. The fondness of the Brāhmaṇas for fanciful identifications could have had its influence, although as a rule, this argument should be employed with great caution.[172]

Apart from the Soma libations, Indra receives the Savanīya Puroḍāśas and the Dadhigharma. It does not seem necessary to discuss these in greater detail than has been done in Vol. I, p. 309 ff. But we must add some remarks about the Hāriyojana. During the preparations for the sacrifice, the 'dhānā-s' for "Indra harivat" are also got ready and mixed with butter.[173] On the next step, Āpastamba gives the following injunctions.

ĀpŚS XIII.17.1: "After the Paridhi-sticks have been thrown into the fire [and the Saṃsrāva has been offered], the Unnetṛ draws the Hāriyojanagraha.

2: "With the mantra: *upayāmagṛhīto'si harir asi* [*hāriyojano haribhyāṃ tvā*], he draws with the Droṇakalaśa the entire Āgrayaṇa, but does not deposit it on the ground. He mixes it with plenty of dhānās, places it on his head, goes out and gives the commands thus: *indrāya harivate 'nubrūhi, indrāya harivate preṣya* or *dhānāsomebhyo 'nubrūhi dhānāsomān pratiṣṭhān preṣya*."

It is characteristical that while partaking of this Graha, one does not chew the dhānās but eats them with a 'smacking' sound in an obvious imitation of horses. The formula which follows the Bhakṣaṇa runs thus: *kṛṣyai kṣemāya rayyai poṣāya.*

This ceremony is of some interest insofar as it is a continuation, to a limited extent, of the Ṛgvedic ritual. The ṚV does not yet know of Indra's elephants but it frequently mentions his horses[174] and attributes various qualities to them. Their number varies constantly. Sometimes they are two, sometimes more; even thousands of horses come to the house of the sacrificer, pulling Indra's chariot.[175] This number, which does not have any material significance, varies even within the same hymn.[176] Here I gather the impression as though there exists, as regards the Hari cult, a difference between the individual maṇḍalas, and above all, between the ṚV and the later liturgy. And the cult of Indra's horses seems to have been more prominent in the earlier times than in the later period when it was confined to the evening pressing only. It is said, for instance, in I.62.13: *návyam átakṣad bráhma hariyójanāya...nodhā́ḥ*; 63.9: *ákāri ta indra gótamebhir bráhmāṇy óktā námasā háribhyām| supéśasaṃ vā́jam ā́ bharā naḥ prātár makṣū́ dhiyā́vasur jagamyāt||*

The name of the Graha is particularly conspicuous, for one should expect in the evening savana not a *hariyojanagraha* but rather a *harivimocanagraha* since the former is more appropriate for the libations of the morning pressing.[177] Hence, it seems likely that during the codification of the ritual alterations have taken place: the Hāriyojanagraha was accommodated in the evening but the old name, which had become sacrosanct through the ṚV was retained.

2. Other Soma Sacrifices

The Agniṣṭoma is not the only Soma sacrifice in which Indra has a prominent share. He is honoured still more exclusively in the Mahāvrata, Ṣoḍaśin and Atirātra. The Mahāvrata deserves a more thorough and detailed discussion than has been the case so far.[178] Like the Viṣuvat at which Sūrya is at the centre, the Mahāvrata represents either of the solstitial points in the solar year. It is immaterial whether one interprets it with me as the midsummer festival or as the winter solstice. The Atirātra, known by name already to the ṚV (VII.103),[179] is like the Mahāvrata a gay festival (in the later period Indra's heaven also offered most of the worldly pleasures) and is celebrated all the night long. One should not surrender oneself to sleep and each Graha preceded by the main Graha is dedicated to *indrāya apiśarvarāya*.[180] The Brāhmaṇas leave no room for doubt that this festival also is connected with the New Year: *saṃvatsaró vai samudrás tásyaitát pārám yád atirātraú* (TS VII.5.1.2).[181] The metres help Indra overcome "the night, darkness and death," which he fears.[182] It seems that the Atirātra is also, insofar as one can judge without a close consideration of all the details, one of the forms in which the solstice festival is celebrated When we consider that the ritual is a mosaic put together with the traditions of different families, it is not surprising that the same festival is observed under various names and with different customs.

Of the major Ekāhas, mention must be made of the Ṣoḍaśin; its main features have been described by Eggeling and also by me.[183] Here also the connection with the sun in general is recognizable, although the exact purpose of the ceremony is not clear; in particular, the significance of the number sixteen in this sacrifice defies explanation.[184] While some texts say that the Ṣoḍaśin is Indra, others opine that the Ṣoḍaśin is the Vajra. But when we add all the stipulations together, it becomes evident that firstly the sacrifice is a solar magic and secondly it is a recuperation-sacrifice. That it is a solar magic is suggested by some remarks in the Brāhmaṇas[185] and by the ritual procedure which I shall illustrate with the rules laid down by Lāṭyāyana.

LŚS III.1. 1: "Let the Udgātṛ who wishes to sing the Ṣoḍaśi-sāman look at the Ṣoḍaśigraha with the mantra: *yasmād anyaḥ*[186] 2: Exactly in the same way during the morning pressing. 3: And likewise during the two subsequent savanas also if they were to draw it (Ṣoḍaśigraha) there. 4: 'A black horse should stand at the eastern door of the sacrificial hut, facing the west,' [thus enjoins] Dhānaṃjapya. 5: 'At the western door, facing the east,' opines Śāṇḍilya. 6: If a black horse is not available, a dark-coloured horse.[187] 7: Failing which, any other.[188] 8: If there is no horse, a bullock or a he-goat. 9: Whosoever sings the Aṅga of the Sāman should hold a piece of gold.[189] 10: While they sing the Nidhana, let Udgātṛ hold it. 11: Or all should touch it [during the singing]. 12: When the sun is going down, let him sing the first 'turn'[190] of the Ṣoḍaśin in a low voice. 13: When the twilight is spreading the second in a middle voice. 14: When the sun has set, [let] the third [turn be sung] aloud. 15: [Or] they should sing it when [the Adhvaryus] commence[191] [the Stotra]. 16: [In this case] in a restricted voice during the day and aloud at night. 17: He should give the Udgātṛ horses and gold..."[192]

These statements make it amply clear that the Ṣoḍaśin is a solar magic performed just when the darkness is spreading and this is confirmed by the fact that some texts designate the Stotra as *ekaviṁśa*.[193] Another characteristic feature of the sacrifice is its above-mentioned quality as a recuperation-sacrifice. Indra performs this sacrifice lest he should be the weakest among the gods and the creatures, the gods perform it so that they may attain heaven, so that they may not be inferior to the Asuras,[194] the individual "who desires to excel all others" takes likewise recourse to this sacrifice.[195] We may conclude from this that its symbolic purpose is to make the sun strong[196] and that it symbolizes the evening of the day or more correctly the evening of the year, i.e., the winter solstice.[197]

It has been stated just above that the Ṣoḍaśin is identified by several texts not with Indra[198] but with the "thunderbolt."[199] But I do not think that this difference has any significance. As early as in the ṚV we find the notion that the singers place the thunderbolt in Indra's hands.[200] In connection with the Pṛṣṭyaṣaḍaha, ABr IV.1.1 states that the gods "fashioned the thunderbolt with the first of its days, with the second they consecrated it, with the third they gave it to Indra, who hurled it on the fourth day. Hence he recites on the fourth day the Ṣoḍaśiśastra. The Ṣoḍaśin is the thunderbolt. ..."[201] To the recuperation of Indra belongs the conquest over his enemies and he needs the thunderbolt for the victory. [202] The gods make the thunderbolt for him and the Ṣoḍaśi-day with its ceremonies bestows upon him the strength to wield the thunderbolt.

3. Sacrifices connected with Agriculture

For completeness' sake I add here a short account of the sacrifices connected with agriculture. In the Gṛhya Sūtras, Indra is mentioned during the "furrow-sacrifice" where the furrow is called "Indra's wife,"[203] and during the Navaprāśana he is called the "lord of the plough" in the mantra accompanying the barley offering.[204] The ceremony of yoking the plough has Indra as its presiding deity.[205] To these ceremonies of the Gṛhya ritual we may add the Śunāsīrīya festival of the Śrauta Sūtras.[206] From the dakṣiṇā distributed during this ceremony we can recognize that this is also an agricultural sacrifice. The dakṣiṇā consists of a plough harnessed with six bullocks (according to Āpastamba, twelve or six).[207] And the verses recited during the sacrifice[208] reveal that it has to do with the consecration of the plough, for the words *yuga, lāṅgala and sītā* occur again and again in these verses and the commentary on the *Kauśika Sūtra* calls this act a *Kṛṣiniṣpattikarman.* In our Sūtra texts the Śunāsīrīya sacrifice is preceded by the rules for the Sākamedha and for the ceremony celebrating Rudra's departure. But the statements vary about the day on which the festival is to be actually observed. Some let it follow immediately after the Sākamedha, others recommend the full moon of the month Māgha and again others prescribe shorter intervals.[209] These variations are obviously caused by the different periods at which the tillage was commenced in different regions.

The distinctive feature of this sacrifice is the offering of—apart from the oblations of the Pūrṇamāsa that are frequently made—a puroḍāśa on five kapālas for Śunāsīrau, or a puroḍāśa on twelve kapālas for Indra Śunāsīrīya,[210] a libation of freshly milked ordinary milk, a yavāgū for Vāyu and an Ekakapāla-puroḍāśa for Sūrya.[211] For the last offering, a white horse or also an ox is especially enjoined by some as the sacrificial fee.[212] There are several factors supporting the contention that here we are dealing with an annual sacrifice of agriculturists, which signifies the commencement of ploughing; this is indicated by a rule, ĀpŚS VIII.20.8, which states that an Ekakapāla-puroḍāśa should be offered additionally with the name of the month, saying "you are *saṃsarpa*..."[213] and more so by MŚS I.7.8.4: *prāk sviṣṭakṛto māsanāmāni juhoti.*[214] Likewise the ṚV also seems to allude to this. Relevant here is hymn IV.57; some of its verses are employed in this ceremony. Although in the present version of the ritual, the hymn is dismembered, it may certainly be regarded as one unit, where vv. 6 and 7 cannot be separated from vv. 5 and 8 which serve as Yājyānuvākyās. The ritual which had originally employed them is lost to us. In the words addressed to the 'Sītā': *sá naḥ páyasvatī duhām úttarām uttarāṃ samām*, we may see an allusion to either of the solstitial points. This, of course, does not explain *śúnāsīrau.* According to KŚS V. 11. 5, it means the same as *śuna* and *sīra*, as Eggeling thinks "probably the ploughshare and plough, considered as two tutelary deities of agricultural pursuits..., but by Yāska identified with Vāyu and Āditya."[215]

Sāyaṇa helps no more than Yāska does, whose explanation could hardly have been drawn from tradition.[216] We must distinguish *śúnāsīrau* from Indra. When the latter is called *śunāsīra* in TBr I.7.1.1; II.5.8,[217] the word is merely synonymous with *śunāsīrīya*, meaning Indra accompanied by Śunāsīrau in the same way as these two are called *indravantau* in TBr II.4.5.7. The megre data in the Vedic texts does not permit us to explain these dual deities. ṚV IV.57.5 alone seems to be of some significance:

śúnāsīrāv imáṃ vā́caṃ juṣethāṃ yád diví cakráthuḥ páyaḥ/
ténemā́m [sī́tām] úpa siñcatam//[218]

From the statement that Śunāsīrau make rain in heaven, one may infer that they are some stars which forecast the rain, like Tištrya and Satavaēsa among the Parsees or the Pleiads in the West.[219] This is consistent with the common observation that agriculture is usually connected with heavenly phenomena which forecast the occurrence of the regular atmospheric changes.[220] But we cannot say anything beyond this hypothesis.[221]

4. Other Sacrifices

Although the above-mentioned Soma sacrifices, including the modifications thereof, form the most important constituents of Indra's cult, yet the ritual contains an abundance of minor and major oblations of all kinds from the simple New and Full Moon sacrifice to the Aśvamedha. Special puroḍāśas and other dishes are dedicated to him;[222] various types of animals which are supposed somehow or other to symbolize his energy and colour are sacrificed to him. Thus we encounter among the animals the 'bull,' regarded as Indra's symbol. MS I.10.16 (155.7ff.), for example, states: *teṣāṃ vā ubhayeṣām indraḥ prāvasat/te devā etam indrāya bhāgaṃ ny adadhur asmān śvo nihitabhāgo vṛṇatā ity ṛṣabham āhvayantīndraṃ vā etaṃ nihvayante ruvatho vaṣaṭkāraḥ.*[223] Or we find a "red-coloured animal" because that is Indra's form,[224] or in a sacrifice for Indra the dakṣiṇā consists of a bull—a clear allusion to Indra's strength.[225] TS V.5.1.1 declares in general terms that all male animals belong to Indra: *aindrāḥ paśavo ye muṣkarāḥ.* In individual cases, however, the rules often vary according to the qualities emphasized in that particular case[226] and according to the association with other gods.[227] At the present stage, we can recognize only in rare cases an inner or external reason for the selection of the animal concerned. The few cases that permit a judgement[228] suggest that generally the Yājñikas must have had in view some connection between the deity and the animal even if it be of a quite superficial kind. We may consider it significant that the real animal of the rainy season, i.e. the frog, which is occasionally dedicated to Parjanya [229] is never found in association with Indra.

5. Indra's Epithets

It is a peculiarity of the ritual that it characterizes Indra with a series of epithets and then honours him with special sacrifices. Thus we find *indra aṃhomuc*, *adhirāja*, *adhyakṣa anvṛju*, *abhimātihan*, *abhimātiṣaḥ*, *arkavat*, *aśvamedhavat*, *ādityavat*, *indriyāvat*, *ojasvat*, *gharmavat*, *jyeṣṭha*, *jyeṣṭhānām adhipati*, *trātṛ*, *dātṛ*, *putrin*, *pradātṛ*, *pravabhra*, *bṛhadvat*, *manasvat*, *manyumat*, *vajrin*, *vayasvat*, *viśvadevyāvat*, *vṛtratur*, *vṛtrahan*, *vaimṛdha*, *śākvara*, *sutrāman*, *sūryavat*, *svarājan*. Almost each of these special Indras is invoked for a specific reason. For example, offerings are made to *Indra putrin* when one desires progeny, to *Indra dātṛ* with the desire *dānakāmā me prajāḥ syuḥ* and *an aparuddho vā aparuddhyamāno vā*[230] performs a sacrifice for *Indra sutrāman*. As in the case of Agni so also here in Indra's case these names are not *Sondergötter* who merged with Indra at a later stage, but particularizations of his character. This once again amply demonstrates the untenability of Usener's theory in Indian context.[231] Already in the ṚV we come across the tendency to adorn Indra with epithets; more so in some hymns like II.21 than in others. However, in the ṚV these epithets generally constitute only a fluctuating mass. The emphasis on some special Indras belongs exclusively to the later period. Some of them like *mahendra* and *vaimṛdha* are particularly conspicuous. The former is elevated into a deity whose worship was obligatory in several families of the later period.[232] I give below the rules of Āpastamba. ĀpŚS I.14.9: "One who is not a dignitary (*gataśrī*) should not sacrifice to Mahendra...[233] 10: An Aurva, Gautama or Bharadvāja should worship Mahendra after he has performed the Soma sacrifice. 11: Or anybody." Again others lay down that one who wishes to worship Mahendra should first worship Indra for a year and then, having made an offering to Agni *vratapati*, he may worship Mahendra as he likes. The verses employed in the ceremony, viz. ṚV VIII.6.1; X.50.4 (or any other passages of the ṚV) do not justify such a scholastic individualization of Indra, which clearly belongs to the later times and occurs for the first time, outside the ritual texts, in the AV and in Pāli.[234] The scholastic origins of Indra *vaimṛdha* are still more distinct. From the invocation addressed to Indra, *ví mṛ́dho jahi* (ṚV VI.53.4; VIII.61.13) or *ví ṣū́ mṛ́dho áhan* (V.30.7), there emerged an Indra *vimṛdhá* in ṚV X.152.2 and the ritual provides an Indra *vaimṛdha* with special oblations.[235]

D. THE EVOLUTION OF INDRA AND VṚTRA IN THE LATER PERIODS

1. In the Brāhmaṇas

The theme of the battle against Vṛtra did not yet lose its appeal in the Brāhmaṇas; there it was continued and altered in diverse ways, and in this process its original significance was almost completely pushed into the background. That the battle had been fought for the sake of the waters and streams was quite forgotten. It was stated only in stray passages that Vṛtra had enclosed the waters. With his original myth several others were combined and into this battle gods were introduced whose connection with the battle is hardly perceivable in the ṚV. We can distinguish three episodes: first the prelude, consisting of Indra's battle with Tvaṣṭṛ's son Viśvarūpa, second the battle against Vṛtra himself and third the consequences of this battle which force Indra to flee and deprive him of his strength, etc.

a. Indra and Viśvarūpa

The battle with Viśvarūpa leaves the impression that it is an independent saga which the later tradition merely joined to the Vṛtra saga. Of course, the ṚV is familiar with the three-headed son of Tvaṣṭṛ and relates that Indra slew him and took away his cows.[236] But in the ṚV the saga is complete in itself and is unconnected with the Vṛtra saga. If in some passages of the YV it blends into the Vṛtra saga, again in other passages it has an independent existence and does not need to be supplemented by the latter.[237]

b. Indra and Vṛtra

The shortest and the most simple version of Indra's battle with Vṛtra occurs in TS II.1.4.5 and related texts: *indro vṛtram ahan taṃ vṛtro hataḥ ṣoḍaśabhir bhogair asināt | tasya vṛtrasya śīrṣato gāva ud āyan tā vaidehyo*[238] *'bhavan tāsām ṛṣabho jaghane 'nūd ait tam indraḥ acāyat so 'manyata yo vā imam ālabheta mucyet-āsmāt pāpmana iti.* But I will not maintain that this is, therefore, the oldest version also at the same time. It might have suited the aetiological purpose of the day to reproduce the story only briefly. Moreover, the addition of the story of the recovery of the cows, which is connected with Viśvarūpa's death in the ṚV, creates the impression as though a foreign element has been appended here. On the other hand, ŚBr I.6.3.8 ff. appends the Vṛtra saga to the story of Viśvarūpa. We can identify the following stages in the legend.

1. Tvaṣṭṛ creates Vṛtra from the Soma left by Indra.[239]
2. Vṛtra seizes hold of Agni and Soma, all the sciences, fame and nourishment.[240]
3. Vṛtra grows immensely.[241]
4. Gods, men and the Manes feed him.[242]
5. Indra calls Agni and Soma to his side. On his promising that they shall receive a puroḍāśa they come to him and with them all the sciences, fame and nourishment.[243]

Actually the story should have ended here;[244] for it is said in the next stage. 6. "Vṛtra was struck. He lay there contracted like a leather bottle drained of its contents, like a sack from which the flour has been shaken out." But with the words, *tam indro 'bhyadudrāva haniṣyan,*[245] the Brāhmaṇa immediately combines this version with a totally different second episode which ends in a compact between Indra and Vṛtra.

7. Indra rushes at Vṛtra.[246]
8. Vṛtra says, *mā nu me prahārṣīḥ.*
9. The compact according to which Vṛtra should serve as food for Indra.[247]

From these two versions (1-6 and 7-9), which are in my view parallel to and independent of one another, we can extract the legend of Indra and Agni-Soma at first.

c. Agni and Soma in the Battle against Vṛtra

The legend occurs in three versions.

1. In the legend just narrated above: Agni and Soma were

with Vṛtra. Indra requested them not to support the Dasyu but to come over to him. ŚBr I.6.3.13 (KBr III.6).

2. Or Agni and Soma call out to Indra not to hurl his thunderbolt since they are within the body of Vṛtra. They lose their lustre. TS II.5.2.

3. Or "Indra slew Vṛtra with Agni-Soma [cake]"—a formula used frequently and in connection with the New and Full Moon sacrifice. ABr II.3.12; TBr I.6.1.6; ŚBr II.4.4.15; V.2.3.7;[248] MS II.1.3 (4.17); (5.1).

None of these versions is known to the ṚV. There Agni and Soma do not appear in association with Indra. Of course, Agni ran away from the sacrificial duty out of fear but it is not Indra who calls him back but, at least according to one passage, Varuṇa.[249] Only in hymn X.124, the second part of which (v.6 ff.) in my view is not organically connected with the first, Indra requests (v. 6) Soma to come out and kill Vṛtra. It is likely that this verse is based on a saga akin to the one contained in ŚBr 1.6.3.1. But in the ṚV the circumstances are not yet completely identical since Agni is missing. In vv. 1-5 Agni probably speaks to a person totally different from Indra. Hence, in these three parallel versions there is a tradition which is independent of the ṚV, or a mythological evolution which had developed and combined various strands of the myth.

What the myth implies is clear. It reveals once again the transition from the Pitṛyāna to the Devayāna, from the period devoid of sacrifice and light to the Uttarāyaṇa. The fact that in one of these Vṛtra gives "the Yajus, Ṛks and Sāmans" back to Indra is quite consistant with the above explanation. Like Vṛtra, Indra is divested of his original nature here. The Agni-Soma episode is interwoven with the old battle between Vṛtra and Indra.[250] While Vṛtra himself calls out *mā prahārṣīḥ* to Indra in one version, Agni and Soma do so in another. From the methodological viewpoint such a process of fusion is of great interest. To the same extent as the original significance of certain gods fades away, these gods also enter into new associations with beings who were once homogeneous, and old threads serve for a new fabric.

d. Other Succourers of Indra

Indra has yet other assistants apart form Agni-Soma and Tvaṣṭṛ. In TS II.5.2.5-6 they are Heaven and Earth at whose command Indra hurls the thunderbolt.[251] This is a rare statement and so is the mention of some other gods.[252] More frequently Viṣṇu appears as his assistant; in fact as early as in the ṚV, Indra in company with Viṣṇu subdues not only Vṛtra but other enemies as well.[253] In the YV this martial alliance has taken the following forms.

1. (a) Viṣṇu divides himself into three.[254]
   (b) Viṣṇu marches behind Indra.[255]
   (c) To Indra Viṣṇu shows the Varāha Vāmamoṣa who possesses the wealth of the Asuras. This has nothing to do with Vṛtra, (belongs to a different cycle of sagas).[256]
2. Indra surrenders his strength to Viṣṇu.[257]

Apart from Viṣṇu, we encounter, as we do already in the ṚV, the Maruts who are Indra's old allies. Here also mythological evolution, poets' own mood and the versatality of the possible viewpoint gave occasion to diverse kinds of images. I mention below the most important ones.

1. They dance around Indra who is about to kill Vṛtra,[258] or they help him otherwise in the battle.[259]
2. The gods abandon Indra but the Maruts remain. ABr III. 16.1.[260]
3. After Vṛtra has been killed, the Maruts dance upon his body to see whether he is dead or not. MS I.10.16 (156.1); [261]TBr I.6.7.4.[262]
4. The Maruts also abandon Indra (ṚV; see Macdonell, p. 81).

As a rule, the Brāhmaṇas merely state that Indra killed Vṛtra, without mentioning the place or the circumstances of this exploit. Vṛtra's association with the mountains and the waters, stressed often in the ṚV, is relegated to the background and is merely alluded to in passing. As the sole allusion to the mountains, I can cite at the most MS IV.5.1 (62.14),[263] where Vṛtra is wrongly identified with *giri.* For Vṛtra's association with the waters, apart from the above passage, we may refer also to MS III.6.3 (63.2); TS VI.1.1.6;[264] 4.2.3; TBr III.2.5. These passages are essentially the same. This is a clear indication as to how the origin of the concept gradually faded away and became unimportant.

e. The Consequences of Vṛtra's Death

Several passages, scattered all over the Brāhmaṇa literature but not always connected with the Indra-Vṛtra saga, narrate further what happened to Vṛtra after his death.[265] *Kāṭhaka* XII.3 relates that "Indra killed Vṛtra and pushed him against a human corpse."[266] In one passage it is said that Vṛtra's skull became the Droṇakalaśa-vessel, and the Soma flowing out of it became the Hāriyojanagraha;[267] another passage narrates that Vṛtra's eyeball fell away and became collyrium.[268] It is further stated that Vṛtra's blood flowed into the waters; terrified, they overflowed, and became the Darbha grasses,[269] or the blood flowed upon the earth and hence the earth became ritually impure.[270] Or the limbs of Vṛtra were scattered on earth and heaven, and on a certain occasion (during the Rājasūya) the sacrificer wears a lotus garland representing Vṛtra's limbs in an obscure symbolism.[271]

More often than the fate of Vṛtra, mention is made of the consequences of killing Vṛtra for Indra himself. A characteristic feature of these legends is Indra's flight after his victory over Vṛtra. This is delineated in diverse ways and is known even to the ṚV.[272] Here also we can see how diverse elements, old and new, coming together and, united in a stream, flow further. I notice the following versions:

1. Indra conceals himself as he regards himself to be too weak and fears not to have vanquished Vṛtra. The gods also hide and send Vāyu to check whether Vṛtra is dead or not. ŚBr IV.1.3.1ff.

2. All gods abandon him with the exception of the Maruts. ABr III.16.1.[273]

3. Indra goes *parāḥ parāvataḥ* or *paraṃ parāvatam* as he regards himself too weak [*śithira*, MS II.1.4 (5.14)] and fears not to have vanquished Vṛtra: *nāstṛṣīti bibhyat* (Agni seeks him for the gods, ŚBr I.6.4.1) or since he believes that he had committed a sin: *aparādham*, TS VI.5.5.2; TBr I.6.7.4; TMBr XV.11.9; ABr III.15.1.

4. Indra escapes into the waters (ŚBr VII.4.1.13) or *gāṃ prāviśat* TMBr XII,5.21 (his strength enters into the earth; cf.TS II.5.3.2).

5. [After his triumph over Vṛtra] Indra is consecrated the king (as Mahendra) whereupon his strength deserts him. TBr I.8.2.5; 5.1.

6. After he has killed Vṛtra, the enemies (*mṛdh*) rush at him. TS II.5.3.1.

7. His strength escapes from all his limbs and the light goes out of his eyes. His strength enters into the waters, plants and trees or into the earth. TS II.5.3.1-2; TBr I.6.1.7; MS I.10.5 (146.2); ŚBr V.2.3.8. Almost all these variants are mythological synonyms and emerge from the same basic notion. They become intelligible only when we regard the above-mentioned basic meaning of Indra as their starting point.

The sun, in his passage from the lowest to the highest position and again downwards, passes through all the phases which are denoted by Indra's gradual victory and ultimate flight. At first he is alone without any gods to help him, and repelling Vṛtra, he rises to become Mahendra. The Mādhyandina savana and the Grīṣma belong to him (but never the Varṣāḥ); he goes *parāṃ parāvatam*, but then his orbit starts to sink. One may say that he enters the waters or that his strength escapes from him; these are but variations of the same idea. Thus we have a series of individual traits which are quite consistent with the original—though for the contemporary feelings long ago faded out—nature of the sun god, but which are on the other hand quite incompatible with an original thunderstorm god. The traits attributed in the Ṛgvedic period are in harmony with these: liberating the streams, dispelling the darkness and recovering the cows and the light. That these traits refer to the reappearing of the sun after a thunderstorm is an old fiction of the mythologists, invented in the early stages of mythological studies.

2. In the Mahābhārata, etc.

Here it is neither necessary nor possible to trace all the details of the evolution undergone by the Vṛtra myth in the later period. From the stylistic as well as material point of view it would be of immense interest to study how this myth abandons many an old trait, retains some and acquires some new ones. There are only a few instances in Indian mythology and, as I believe, elsewhere where a myth recurs in three different periods of literary tradition and allows us an insight into the changing destiny of a cycle of sagas. The *Mahābhārata* offers, apart from brief passages, three legends at III.100 ff.; V.9.45 ff. and XII.280 ff.[274] What distinguishes these legends essentially from those of the ṚV is the total lack of any specific association with nature and with the battle of the elements, from which the myth originally emerged. The legends deal no more with the liberation of the streams; now it is merely a battle between Vṛtra and the Dānavas or Kālakeyas who flocked around him on the one hand and Indra and the gods led by him on the other. Of course, we still see the old elements of the saga: the thunderbolt made by Tvaṣṭṛ for Indra and the assistance rendered by Viṣṇu. We still read in III.101.1 that Vṛtra has enveloped the heaven and earth[275] or in V.9.49 that he "arrests the heaven,"[276] that after his death the celestial regions become bright, a mild breeze blows and the creatures are delighted[277]—these are obviously stock phrases from the oldest repertoire. But the saga is fully divested of any association with the mountains and streams on which the ṚV often lays stress. In several verses there are indications of a development which is quite contrary to the original concept. As early as in the Brāhmaṇas, we come across the remark that Indra flees into the waters "out of fear." But when MBh V.10.46 ff. states: "as the lord of the gods vanished [into the waters], fearing the consequences of the Brāhmaṇa-murder, the earth lost its lustre, trees withered, forests became dry, streams suspended their flow, lakes became parched up and men were bewildered at the absence of rain;[278] this is contrary to what we know from the oldest sources, which make Indra precisely the liberator of the waters and streams. Poetry and time have arbitrarily changed the tradition and it would be hazardous if one were to treat the form of the saga as it occurs in the MBh as an old one or to make it the yard stick for judging the oldest period.[279] In other aspects also we can observe the arbitrary treatment of the Vṛtra myth. MBh III.100 takes us to the hermitage of Dadhīca. The gods wish to destroy Vṛtra and under the leadership of Indra they turn to Brahman.[280] This one advises them to approach Dadhīca and ask him for his bones "for the well-being of the three worlds." The bones are meant for the manufacture of the thunderbolt. The hermitage of the Ṛṣi was situated on the banks of the Sarasvatī. There the humming of the bees resounds like that of the Sāman singers, the call of the cuckoo blends with the cry of the Jīvaṃjīvaka; buffaloes, wild boars, sṛmaras and yaks move about without the fear of the tiger; elephants sport in water with their mates. Dadhīca listens to the request of the gods and readily gives up his life.

The saga of the bones of Dadhyañc is on old motif, but his Buddhist readiness to surrender his body for this purpose is the product of the later period. From these bones Tvaṣṭṛ makes the thunderbolt—in the older literature these two motifs, Tvaṣṭṛ making the thunderbolt and the bones of Dadhyañc are not yet combined—and bids Indra to reduce the terrible enemy of the gods to ashes. The battle commences, the gods cannot hold their own before the Kālakeyas and Vṛtra. They flee and Vṛtra grows in size. Then Indra, full of fear, rushes to Viṣṇu who bestows his energy (*tejaḥ*) upon Indra. This the gods see and place their strength also in Indra and the Ṛṣis do likewise. When Vṛtra sees the lord of the gods in possession of the energy, he raises such a terrific roar that heaven and earth tremble. Terrified, Indra lets his thunderbolt go. Struck by the missile, "the great Asura who is adorned with a golden wreath"[281] sinks down. Thereupon Indra, unaware that the thunderbolt has flown away from his hand and slew Vṛtra, runs away to hide in a lake (*saraḥ praveṣṭum*; XII.282.18 on the other hand states that he *nalinyā bisamadhyastha uvāsābdagaṇāṅ bahūn*). Just as here, so also in the second legend (V.9.45 ff.) Vedic motifs are interwoven with later ones. Indra kills Triśiras, the son of Tvaṣṭṛ, and Tvaṣṭṛ creates Vṛtra with the traditional formula: *indraśatro vivardhasva prabhāvāt tapaso mama.* Vṛtra grows into one who is *sūryavaiśvānaropama.* A battle ensues between Vṛtra and Indra whom in the end the former seizes and, full of anger, swallows. Strange as this motif is for the older literature,[282] so is also the *jṛmbhikā vṛtra-nāśinī* who was dispatched by the gods. Through her power Vṛtra is made to yawn and Indra comes out again.[283] A new fight begins in which Vṛtra triumphs. The gods seek counsel, for Vṛtra fills the entire world and arouses the fear in Indra that he might swallow all the three worlds along with the Devas, Asuras and human beings. Viṣṇu advises the gods to make it up with Vṛtra; he himself would invisibly enter into the thunderbolt. Now comes the compact—known from the Brāhmaṇas but there it is made with Namuci—"not to kill him with a dry or wet object, with stone or wood, with weapon or missile, in the daylight or at night." The compact comes to an end, as we know, when Indra kills his adversary not in the daylight nor at night but during the twilight and that too with the "foam resembling a mountain" which he discovers in the ocean. He hurls it along with the thunderbolt at Vṛtra.[284] Viṣṇu had entered into the foam and thus Vṛtra was destroyed.

Śāntiparvan XII.280 goes still further. There Vṛtra is instructed in the Mokṣa doctrine and the old enemy of Indra, who never entertained such thoughts in the Vedic period, listens with devotion: *evaṃgate me na viṣādo 'sti kaścid samyak ca paśyāmi vacas tathaitat | śrutvā tu te vācam adīnasattva vikalmaṣo 'smy adya tathā vipāpmā*[285]—with such and similar sentiments Vṛtra gives up his life and attains the "highest place."[286] In this Parvan he is called *mahātman* (281.13), *dharmabhṛtāṃ varaḥ* (281. 18,), *mahāyogin* (283.60) and so on.[287] Of course, we find old motifs here also. The fire of Maheśvara which turns itself into a fever and attacks Vṛtra recalls the fever marked by alternating cold and heat which Indra produced from within himself (TS II.5.2.2, see n. 243 above). Or when Agni, trees and herbs etc. take upon themselves a part of the sin committed by Indra through the Brahmavadhyā (MBh XII. 282.40 ff.), this is reminiscent of TS II.5.1.1 ff. (see n. 237 above.) But the entire concept is thoroughly altered and reveals to us processes which are instructive from the point of view of history of myths. Had we only the legends of the MBh to go by, every attempt to interpret Indra-Vṛtra would have missed the mark. In the shape assumed by Vṛtra in the MBh and also partly in the Brāhmaṇas there is no trace of the original basic conception. We merely encounter one of the stereotype legends that are far removed from their origins and have reached the final stage of their evolution. This legend demonstrates how the Itihāsas possess little value for the understanding of mythology and at the same time contains a warning to those who attempt to see any value. Only because we can follow the various stages of the myth through different ages and different literary periods, it is possible to arrive at a correct interpretation.

On the basis of the Indian material, I arrive at a conclusion which Boas has reached through an entirely different path. Proceeding from the evolution of the mythology of the Red Indians, he established the following as the result of a comparative study of the sagas of different tribes: "that we must regard the mythology of each and every tribe as the fusion of material, having the most diverse origins. This material is moulded by each tribe according to its genius, its social institutions and the older concepts which govern its thought-process. This removes once and for all the justification for attempts to interpret the myths of primitive peoples as natural phenomena or to see in the myths the results of observations of the primitive life. That the phenomena of the sun, of the vivid animal kingdom, of the roaring ocean have powerfully stimulated the imagination of the primitive peoples admits of no doubt; otherwise we would not find solar myths and animal myths everywhere. But the specific form in which we see these myths today is the result of a long historical development, far removed from the 'elementary notion.' In order to comprehend the elementary conception, it is necessary, not to interpret the myths as found today, but to separate the changes that were caused by historical, social and geographical factors and thus to arrive at the most simple and universally valid basic conception."[288] And on this Ratzel remarks that the interpretation of a myth on the basis of the nature of the place where it obtains today is not admissible.[289]

When the character of Indra and above all that of Vṛtra could undergo a transformation within the framework of this myth itself, it is no wonder that the change was still greater outside this myth. I have already emphasized on p. 116 above that Vṛtra's name does not play any role in the AV and has completely disappeared, as far as one can see, in Pali.[290] Perhaps we may still recognize his form in *Saṃyuttanikāya* XI.3.2, in the *aññataro yakkho dubbaṇṇo okoṭimako,* who approaches the seat of Sakka, the king of the gods, and in the same degree as the 33 gods are vexed with this, he becomes "more handsome, imposing and pleasant."[291] Better preserved is the name of Śambara, who is described in the ṚV still as an Indian king and lord of innumerable fortresses and who makes his appearance in Pali as Asurindo;[292] in another passage Asurindo is called

Vepacitti or Verocana.[293] A demon Virocana is known already to the AV and the TBr but not to the ṚV; hence he belongs to another tradition or to a later development.

While Vṛtra thus completely disappeared in Pali, Indra still continued his existence. But the word became almost a synonym for *rājan*. *Śakra*, which occurs rarely or not at all as a proper noun in the ṚV,[294] became the usual designation here for the ancient king of the gods. Apart from this word, there are *maghavā*, *purindado*, *vāsavo*, *sahassakkho*, *sujaṃpati* and of course *devānām indo*.[295] Buddhism has converted "Indra, the fortress-breaker" into "Indra, the town-bestower,"[296] "who, living once in human shape, gave away town after town as gifts."[297] Generally speaking, here Indra is not a god of importance; he has the character of a Yazata and appears, like the gods, as an ardent Buddhist and an attendant of the Buddha.[298] When the Buddha wishes to wash his clothes, Indra quickly digs a pond with his bare hands and brings for him a big stone to rub the clothes with.[299] He assumes the form of a youth and like a herald goes ahead of the Buddha who is about to enter Rājagṛha with his monks;[300] at the Buddha's death he recites the verse *aniccā vata saṃkhārā*, etc.[301] The Jainas also know him as the worshipper of their great teacher.[302] He has even migrated to other peoples. In the Siamese legends, besides Brahma, no god appears as often as Indra.[303]

Whosoever wishes to study the evolution of the *Sondergötter* in India must not ignore Vajrapāṇi. Grünwedel[304] states thus: "The thunderbolt-wielding god, the *deus ex machina* of the old legends, viz. the god Śakra (sakko) or Indra has given occasion to the most unusual developments. Out of him the Mahāyāna school developed Vajrapāṇi, the protector of the Buddha. Occasionally, however, Indra still remained in specific roles. A reminiscence of him gave birth to a Bodhisattva Vajradhara, and a Dhyānibuddha Vajrasattva, while the irate Vajrapāṇi was designated as a Yakṣa: all are ultimately mere derivations of the old thunderstorm god. And now we see Indra Śatakratu (Tibetan *brGya-byin*, Mangolian *Khormusda*) once more and that too as a god of the later Brahmanical mythology.[305]

It is outside the scope of this work to trace Indra's association with Buddhism further. In the Pāli texts Indra occasionally appears as a rain god also,[306] and in classical Sanskrit we encounter him predominantly in this capacity. His banner is raised and worshipped for the sake of rain.[307] As the snakes began to be burnt under the sun's heat, Śakra covered the entire firmament with clouds and commanded them to rain.[308] Maṇu IX.304ff states that Indra rains for four months and that the sun draws water with his rays for eight months.[309] *Viṣṇupurāṇa* V.10 contains a description of the Indrayajña performed by the cowherds. To Kṛṣṇa who is eager to know, Nanda explains the Indrayajña thus:

19: *meghānāṃ payasāṃ caiṣo devarājaḥ śatakratuḥ|*
tena saṃcoditā meghā varṣanty ambumayaṃ rasam ||
23: *bhaumam etad payo dugdhaṃ gobhiḥ sūryasya vāridaḥ|*
parjanyaḥ sarvalokasya bhavāya bhuvi varṣati ||
24: *tasmāt prāvṛṣi rājānaḥ sarve śakraṃ mudāyutāḥ |*
mahaiḥ sureśaṃ arcanti vayam anye ca dehinaḥ | |[310]

The parallel version in the *Harivaṃśa* II.15[311] reads as follows:

5: *devānām īśvaraḥ śakro meghānāṃ cārisūdana |* . . .
6: *tena saṃcoditā meghās tasya cāyudhabhūṣitāḥ*
tasyaivājñākarāḥ sasyaṃ janayanti navāmbubhiḥ ||
7: *meghasya payaso dātā puruhūtaḥ puraṃdaraḥ |* . . .
12: *dudoha savitur gā vai śakro divyāḥ payasvinīḥ |*
tāḥ kṣaranti navaṃ kṣīraṃ meghyaṃ meghaughadhāritam ||
15: *taj jalaṃ vajraniṣpeṣair vimuñcati nabhogataiḥ |*
bahubhiḥ kāmagair meghaiś śakro bhṛtyair iveśvaraḥ ||[312]

This is the last stage in Indra's evolution. It is true that we notice its first traces in the ṚV but the passages where Indra appears as rain-bestower are still sporadic. Even in the ṚV he is no longer a sun god; on the contrary, he is already divested of that character; but from his exploits we can still recognize him as sun god. Quite gradually he moves into the position which classical Sanskrit assigns to him.[313] Apart from the horses which belong to him in the ṚV and in the entire Vedic literature, there appears the elephant as his animal, and this elephant is regarded as the animal of the east (KŚS XXII.2.23ff.).

3. Indra's Transformation

Just as it has become necessary in linguistics to look for the reasons why a derivation or analogy-formation occurred, so would it be necessary in mythology also to seek the path along which a transformation took place. While Vṛtra, who had no roots in the Indian climate, remained in the saga of the later times merely as an adversary of the gods, an adversary who had been vanquished long ago, Indra's evolution proceeded along other paths. For a long time he remained a vivacious god, but he moved into another sphere of activity and became essentially a rain god.

The culmination of the sun coincides with the commencement of the rains. In our countries also it is established through peasants' beliefs and scientific observations that around the middle of June the rainiest period of the year begins and that the period after the solstice has the maximum number of downpours and floods. In India this period of showers is strengthened into the rainy season. Indians ascribe the birth of this season to the sun himself. Statements of this purport are to be found already in the Saṃhitās. TS II.4.10.2: *yadā khalu vā asāv āditye nyaṅ raśmibhiḥ paryāvartate 'tha varṣati dhāmacchad iva khalu vai bhūtvā varṣati;*[314] III.3.4: *sūryasya raśmayo vṛṣṭyā īśate| ahna eva rūpeṇa sūryasya raśmibhir divo vṛṣṭiṃ cyāvayati;* VS IX.3: *apāṃ rasaṃ . . . sūrye santaṃ samāhitam;* MS II.4.8 (46.1): *agnir vā ito vṛṣṭim iṭṭemaruto 'mutas cyāvayanti tāṃ sūryo raśmibhir varṣati;*[315] TBr I.7.1.1: *sūryeṇa vā amuṣmiṅ loke vṛṣṭir dhṛtā| sa evāsmai vṛṣṭiṃ niyacchati;* ABr IV.25.10: *asāv arvāṅ tapati, arvāṅ varṣati;* TĀr V.10.6; Manu III.76: *ādityāj jāyate vṛṣṭiḥ.*

Viṣṇupurāṇa II.9.8:

vivasvān aṣṭabhir māsair ādāyāpo rasātmikāḥ |
varṣaty ambu tataś cānnam annād apy akhilaṃ jagaı ||

23: *vṛṣṭyā dhṛtam idaṃ sarvam annaṃ niṣpādyate yayā |*
sāpi niṣpādyate vṛṣṭiḥ savitrā munisattama ||

Vāyupurāṇa LI. 13:

sūryaḥ kiraṇajālena vāyuyuktena sarvaśaḥ /
jagato jalam ādatte kṛtsnasya dvijasattamāḥ //
14: *ādityapītaṃ sūryāgneḥ somaṃ saṃkramate jalam* /. . .
23: *ārkaṃ tejo hi bhūtebhyo hy ādatte raśmibhir jalam*/
samudrād vāyusaṃyogād vahanty āpo gabhastayaḥ/
yatas tv ṛtuvaśāt kāle parivartī divākaraḥ/
yacchaty āpo hi meghebhyaḥ śuklāḥ śuklagabhastibhiḥ. . .
51: *sūrya eva tu vṛṣṭīnāṃ sraṣṭā samupadiśyate*/

In his prayer to the sun,[316] Yājñavalkya calls him *himāmbu-gharmavṛṣṭīnāṃ*[317] *kartā hartā ca* and *trikālarūpa*. With the help of these passages it is possible to trace the path along which the transformation of the old sun god Indra took place. The fact that Indra was associated with the waters from time immemorial and that he wielded the thunderbolt might have additionally contributed to this transformation. As in most cases, we must rest content here also with defining the process and the possibility of the development. The process of myth-formation never comes to a rest; it discards outdated elements or moulds the traditional ones into new forms. This process is not governed by any teleological principle that leads to a specific goal but by the restlessness of the human mind, caused no less by psychological factors than by external conditions: migrations, contacts with other tribes, progress or decline in civilization, climate, acceptance of ideas by a new generation, creative power of individuals with far-reaching influence (like poets and priests) and the patterns of thought which emerge from unfathomable depths — these are the driving forces in mythology. Hence, it would be idle to ask why Indians who after all worship the sun with the *Sahasranāmāvalī* did not maintain Indra in this function but chose a different direction for him. We must be satisfied with establishing the inner probability of this evolution from Indian concepts themselves. However, all the glory of the king of the gods was not lost in this process of transformation. When in the *Saṃgāmavacara Jātaka* (II, no. 182) and elsewhere Indra makes his appearance as the king of the gods along with his troop of nymphs, or when his heaven is described as the abode of sensual pleasures, or when mention is made of his *netra-sahasra* in *Kumārasaṃbhava* II.29, the old motifs of his grandeur are still continuing.

E. NAMUCI[318]

In all this discussion I have not paid any attention to Indra's relationship with Namuci. The scarce material which the Veda offers us about this adversary of Indra does not suffice to explain his origin, but it is clear that we are dealing with a cycle of sagas which is totally different from those of Vṛtra and is characterized by its own specific phraseology.[319] In the ṚV, Namuci is mentioned only nine times in eight hymns — quite an insignificant number when compared to the hundreds of passages dealing with Vṛtra. That is to say, even when seen from a purely statistical viewpoint, Namuci lags behind the influence of Vṛtra in the traditions of the Vedic clans. Of the relevant verses, II.14.5; VII. 19.5 and X. 73.7 do not have much to say; V.30.7,8; VI.20.6 have some importance because they contain one of the main catchwords of this cycle of sagas.[320] Considerably more important are VIII. 14.13 and X.131. Like the Brāhmaṇas, VIII.14.13 also mentions *apā́ṃ phéna* as the weapon Indra hurled at Namuci. X.131 is familiar with the elements of the Sautrāmaṇī ceremony, which are in substantial agreement with the custom of the later period. The Sautrāmaṇī was, as I have elucidated earlier,[321] a ceremony in which the Surā occupies the central position as the Soma does in the Soma sacrifice. The *Kāśikā* describes the Prācyas as Surāpāṇas;[322] other tribes had preference for other kinds of draught.[323] In the employment of the Surā and Soma respectively there is expressed what was originally a cult difference. The later period bridges this difference in that it makes the Sautrāmaṇī a healing ceremony for Indra who fell ill after consuming the Soma.[324] Our hymn (X.131) has its place in this ceremony and likewise the name of Namuci who plays the same role among the Surā-drinkers as Vṛtra does among the Soma-pressers. This sacrifice is performed for a person from whose nose, ears etc. Soma flows out, the so-called Somātipūta, further for a brahmin who desires success, for an exiled king, for a Kṣatriya and so on,[325] and is performed in a typical fashion. I have already drawn attention in Vol. I, p. 324 to the fact that some teachers are in the habit of changing all the Praiṣas — a clear indication that the Sautrāmaṇī is fundamentally different from the Soma sacrifice.

Further, we find Namuci's name in a formula; during the consecration ceremony the king, uttering this formula, kicks with his foot a piece of lead that has been kept on the tiger skin.[326] In all the Surā ceremonies lead plays a role. In the Vājapeya and here in the Sautrāmaṇī the Parisrut is bought against lead from a long-haired man.[327] Hence, it must be an integral part of the saga. Indra makes a compact with Namuci also as he did with Vṛtra. These two compacts are different; the later period mixes up between the two. It is the well known compact[328] not to injure Namuci either with a dry object or with a wet one, either in daylight or at night.[329] I think that this is an ancient formula of an oath of allegiance. Indra breaks the oath and kills this opponent *apā́ṃ phénena*, whereas he always employs only the thunder-bolt against Vṛtra. ŚBr XII.7.3.3 interprets the expression, distinctive of the Namuci legend, through the addition of the word *vajra*. Lanman advances another explanation.[330] Frazer takes the expression literally.[331] In the absence of any ascertainable data we cannot make any decision. However, I would think that the *apā́ṃ phéna* should be understood in the sense of some solid material and that it denotes some substance like, e.g. lead, because this very metal serves, as we saw, as the purchasing price in the Surā ceremonies. In the context of removing the old fire, *Kauśika Sūtra* LXXI.15 states that one should place *sīsāni* in the hands of the eldest son, and the commentary explains this word as *sīsaṃ nadīphenaṃ lohamṛttikā. Kauśika Sūtra* VIII.18 lists *sīsa, nadīsīsa,*[332] *ayorajas, kṛkalāsaśiraḥ* among the things called "lead,"[333] but not among the immediately following *rasas* (like *dadhi* and *ghṛta*). This speaks in favour of my assumption.

The whole significance of the Namuci saga remains obscure. Apāṁ phena and sīsa, Surā, the Aśvins and Sarasvatī who heal Indra, and in addition, the proper name Namī Sāpya,[334] described as the opponent of Namuci — these are the only facts we know, but these do not make a complete picture. In the later period Namuci is one of the names of Māra.[335]

But, for the time being, this much is certain: the sagas of Viśvarūpa, Vṛtra and Namuci were not originally connected with one another but belonged to different groups and were brought together at a later stage. Likewise we cannot draw any conclusion about the meaning of Namuci from the interpretation of Vṛtra or Viśvarūpa.[336] There are some, admittedly faint indications to say that Namuci has been borrowed by Vedic mythology from the Dāsa tribes. We shall discuss this point later.

F. VALA

Vala, a third name besides Vṛtra and Namuci,[337] occurs in books I-IV, VI, VIII and X only. The release of the cows and the opening up of the stable is the basic idea that is stated prominently in the episode of the triumph over Vala, in which task the gods help Indra fearlessly (ṚV I.11.5). It is not correct to say that in the ṚV the word *go* means "cloud". It never means "cloud" and very rarely "water". The PW also does not list the meaning "cloud" at all, and for the meaning of "water" (meaning no.13) cites as authorities only lexicons and passages from the later times. On the other hand, Grassmann (meaning no. 13) lists a number of passages where the "cows" are supposed to designate the "rain-clouds," which were shut in the rock of the rainless cloud by Vṛtra and were later released by (Indra Bṛhaspati etc.) and which now let the rain pour down as nourishing milk. My remarks on p. 107 ff. above must have established that Grassmann's theory is based on a misconception. It is not necessary to construe *go* as "rain-cloud" as Grassmann proposes, in any of the passages listed by him. Indra accomplished two exploits that were specially acclaimed: he liberated the waters and set the cows free. In general, these two things are to be separated. The release of the waters refers to the streams and the setting free of the cows to the return of the light, to the return of the "Dawns" (see Vol. I pp. 27-28); it is not ruled out that in a number of passages this refers to real looting expeditions undertaken by Indra-worshippers. The individual concepts of the ṚV are not demarcated so strictly that we do not find constant transition from one to the other, and it shoutd not surprise us to find the lines of demarcation blurred occasionally in the case of the designation *go*. Indra must open up the mountains besieged by Vṛtra in order to release the waters withheld in them. He must open up the rock in battle against Vala in order to bring back the red cows of Uṣas. Both the conceptions occur in the same hymn and even in the same verse. In some cases there is the possibility that the stable of the cows denotes the imprisonment of the waters as well. But such passages are few in number. I can mention only VII.90.4[338] and IX.108.6,[339] and even in these examples the "cows" do not signify "clouds"[340] but "springs" and "streams" which issue forth from the mountains after Indra's exploit of liberation. On the other hand, in the Vala saga *go* refers, as I think, to the cows of Uṣas without any reservation.[341] Passages like

II.24.3: *úd gā́ ā́jad ábhinad bráhmaṇā valám*
ágūhat támo vy àcakṣayat svàḥ ||

demonstrate the direct connection between the ideas.

Generally *valá* is translated as "cave" and for the majority of passages this meaning seems to be appropriate.[342] For we find the verbs *dṛ*, *bhid*, *ruj*, *vṛ+apa* (*apā*) and also *arvāk-nud* connected with *valá*, thus clearly indicating the appellative sense of the word,[343] and in the expressions *valásya bíla* I.11.5; *apadhí* II.12.3;[344] *paridhí* I.52.5;[345] *sā́nu* VI.39.2 also we can recognize the use of the simple appellative.[346]

Besides the liberation of the cows from Vala's cave, there is a second aspect that characterizes the saga. It is the participation of the Aṅgiras' and other Manes in this exploit.

I.62.4: *sá suṣṭúbhā sa stubhā́ saptá vípraiḥ*
svaréṇā́driṃ svaryò návagvaiḥ/
saraṇyúbhiḥ phaligám indra śakra
valáṃ rávena darayo dáśagvaiḥ ||

II.11.20: *bhinád valám índra áṅgirasvān*/
15.8: *bhinád valám áṅgirobhir gṛṇānó*
ví párvatasya dṛṅhitā́ny airat /

VI.39.2: *ayám uśānáḥ páry ádrim usrā́*
ṛtádhītibhir[347] *ṛtayúg yújānáḥ |*
rujád árugṇaṃ ví valásya sā́num
paṇī́ṅr vácobhir abhí yodhad índraḥ ||
X.62. 2: *yá udā́jan pitáro gomáyaṃ vásu*
ṛténā́bhindan parivatsaré valám |

Cf. also X.67, 68.

This association of Vala with the cows on the one hand and with the Manes on the other proves that this saga is a mythological twin of the saga of the liberation of the cows of Uṣas from the mountain-dungeon. In Vol I., p. 360 etc., I have already cited, among others, verses like

IV.1.13: *áśmavrajāḥ sudúghā vavré antár*
úd usrā́ ājann uṣáso huvānā́ḥ ||
15: *té gavyatā́ mánasā dṛdhrám ubdhám*
gā́ yemānáṃ pári ṣántam ádrim |
dṛḷháṃ náro vácasā daívyena
vrajáṃ gómantam uśíjo ví vavruḥ ||
V. 31.3: *prā́codayat sudúghā vavré antár*
ví jyótiṣā saṃvavṛtvát támo 'vaḥ |
VI. 17. 5: *yébhiḥ sū́ryam uṣásaṃ mandasānó*
ávāsayó 'pa dṛḷhā́ni dárdrat |
mahā́m ádrim pári gā́ indra sántam
nutthā́ ácyutaṃ sádasas pári svā́t ||[348]

These verses contain the same notions as the Vala passages. Here *vala, adri, vraja* (*aśmavraja*) are used as mythological and lexical synonyms for the rock-cave in which the cows are shut in.[349]

The sense of "cave" continues in the legends of the Brāhmaṇas as attested by ABr VI.24[350] as well as TS II.1.5.I.[351]

I think it is quite justified to assume with the PW that in all these verses we are dealing with an appellative *valá*. However, this appellative is no longer employed indiscriminately to denote every cave but has already come under the influence of mythology, for the texts use this word in a specific context only.[352] But there is no justification to construe with the PW all the passages of the ṚV in this sense; for in some, particularly in the two hymns X.67 and 68 ascribed to Ayāsya Āṅgirasa, the process of transformation has made further progress and *valá* has become entirely a proper name. Here we have a similar process as in the case of the Paṇis. In the sixth maṇḍala the Paṇis are still people with flesh and blood; but the author of X.108 sees in them only demoniacal beings to whom Indra sends Saramā as messenger. In X.67, 68 Vala is distinctly a demon who has cows in his possession and is described as *góvapus* in one verse.[353] Both the hymns have mythological character and do not allow us to recognize any physical basis for Vala. At the most, it is striking that in X.67.6 Vala is styled as Paṇi. The reputation of the Paṇis, infamous as cattle-thieves, might have been the reason to transpose this name also upon the mythical enemy Vala. In VI.39.2 we find *valá* as an appellative again in association with the Paṇis.[354] In view of the meagre quantity of the material, we cannot draw any conclusions from this. It is likely that the designation *valá* has been borrowed from another dialect and with it also a considerably great number of rare words (*alātṛṇá*, *jásu*, *góvapus*, *phaligá*) which we encounter in these sagas, although not all of these words belong exclusively to them. Of other verses where Vala is a proper name or appears to be so, mention may be made of III.30.10; VI.18.5 and VIII.24.30.[355] In the last passage *gómatī* is conspicuous in its association with Vala. In I.11.5 Vala is called *gómat*; in VIII. 6.23 *gómatī* is an epithet of *púr*. However, I would like to believe, as Sāyaṇa does, that in VIII. 24. 30, *gómatī* refers to the river Gomal, on the banks of which Vala would thus be located. Unfortunately the explanation of this verse is uncertain. In later times Vala becomes Vṛtra's brother (PW).

G. OTHER EXPLOITS OF INDRA

The fact that in some cases it is possible to trace one or the other enemy of Indra back to the natural phenomena is of no consequence for the multitude of other beings who surround him and who have been carried along by the tradition as epic material. The long series of migrations and wars of the Vedic people have left behind an abundance of names which might be of climatological or of historical nature and which must be sought in the character of a country where they had lived earlier or among the people with whom they had come into contact. What the Veda offers is not always the product of an immediate past. Many a hymn leaves the impression as if its author was not in direct contact with the material he was treating; for him it was a mere convention. Here and there we find solitary expressions, vague allusions which we cannot elucidate any more. Several names like those of the Yadu-s are still current in India;[356] others are unintelligible; several others, beginning as proper nouns, have become appellatives. It will take a long time until we can arrange into a certain order the whole expanse of the ruins, in which mythological layers alternate with historical ones and where the relics of the pre-Vedic history lie buried; to be able to sift all of it would probably be impossible. Among the enemies of Indra and, what amounts to the same, among his worshippers, we find despots of the Dāsa tribe like Śambara and Varcin, whose fortresses were destroyed by Indra in company with his worshippers; we find entire tribes like the Paṇis who are still vividly described in the sixth book.[357] Like the name Paṇi, the name of the Dāsas also indicates the West or the North-West. This is supported, inter alia, by the designation given to their fortresses as *śắradīḥ*, which refers to a climate from the rigours of which one sought refuge in "artificial abodes" (*kṛtrímāḥ*).[358] A poet of the eighth maṇḍala changed these autumnal fortresses into "eternal" fortresses (*śáśvatī*)[359]—a typical example which illustrates the value of the eighth book and the relationship of some books to the others within the ṚV. Occasionally the allusions are so fragmentary that it is impossible for me to evaluate them.[360] I do not intend to discuss all the names that are connected with Indra, but shall limit myself to some, where I hope to make somewhat greater progress than others.

1. Dāsa

I have explained in Vol. I, pp. 340-41 that the name Divodāsa means the "Dāsa of heaven." My view has been rejected by

Oldenberg, who, like Bergaigne earlier (II, p. 216), seeks to interpret the name as the "servant of heaven."[361]

Kālidāsa or Śivadāsa, "servant of Kālī or of Śiva" are expressions current in the later times. But to superimpose this upon the Vedic period goes against the principles of name-giving in the Veda in general and against the meaning of the word *dāsa* in particular. It is essential to differentiate between the linguistic usage of each maṇḍala of the ṚV and in the present case to decide the issue on the basis of the usage in that maṇḍala where *dívodāsa* occurs most often and in a most specific sense. Such a maṇḍala is, besides the first, the sixth which I hold to be an earlier compilation.[362] The name does not occur at all in books III, V, VIII and X whose innumerable composers must have been unfamiliar with the name and deeds of king Divodāsa. In the vast seventh maṇḍala, it occurs only once in the eighteenth hymn, which I described as a sort of chronicle.[363] Now, how is the word *dāsa*, which forms the second part of the name Divodāsa, used in books I, II, IV, VI, VII, IX, above all in VI? The answer is that in these books *dāsá* (or *dā́sa*) never denotes a slave[364] but always the "enemy" and that it has the character of a proper noun (or adjective derived from it) occurring sometimes in the plural and other times in the singular. Compare VI. 22.10: *yáyā dā́sāny ā́ryāṇi vṛtrā́ kárah*; 33.3: *tváṃ tā́m̐ indrobháyām̐ amítrān dā́sā vṛtrā́ṇy ā́ryā ca śūra*; 60.6: *ható vṛtrā́ṇy ā́ryā ható dā́sāni*; 25.2: *ā́ryāya víśó 'va tārīr dā́sīḥ*; 20.10: *púraḥ śā́radīr dárd dhán dā́sīḥ purukútsāya śíkṣan*; further, the individual Dāsas, Varcin and Śambara in 47.12; Śambara in 26.5; Dāsa Namuci in 20.6. Nowhere in these passages does *dāsá* denote "slave" or *dā́sa* "slavish."

Or, let us take the first book, where the word and the adjective derived from it occur seven times (in six verses). I.32.11: *dāsápatnīḥ*; 104.2:*devā́so manyúṃ dā́sasya ścamnan*; 158.5: *dāsā́ yád īṃ súsamubdham avā́dhuḥ| śíro yád asya traitanó vitákṣat svayáṃ dāsá úro āṃsāv ápi gdha*; 174.7: *kṣā́ṃ dāsā́yopabárhaṇīṃ kaḥ*; 103.3: *púro vibhindánn acarad ví dā́sīḥ*. Only in one passage, in I.92.8, one may look for the meaning "slave": *úṣas tám aśyāṃ yaśásaṃ. ... dāsápravargaṃ rayím....* Does the word *dāsápravargam* here really mean "inclusive of slaves" or as both the versions of the PW and I myself (in the *Veda-Chresto-*

mathie) have assumed on the authority of Sāyaṇa, "accompanied by a host of servants"? Among the paths that one can take for the explanation of the word *pravarga*, only one leads us to the goal. We cannot separate the word from the root *vṛj* which occurs in the sense of "to knock down" in VI.18.8: *vṛṇák píprum*; 26.3: *śúṣṇaṃ vark*[365] and which is probably implicit in *varga* in KUp II.7 in the sense of "one who averts or removes" (PW). Foy is justified in explaining *vṛj* and *pra+vṛj* in the same way. We find *pra+vṛj*, for instance, in ṚV I.116.24 in the expression *rebhám udáni právṛktam.* Decisive is ŚBr I.3.3.14: *sa hovāca vajro vai tān vaṣaṭkāraḥ prāvṛṇag vajrād vai vaṣaṭkārād bibhemi yan mā vajro vaṣaṭkāro na pravṛñjyād etair eva mā paridhatta*; here *pra+vṛj* clearly means, as Eggeling also translates, "to strike down." We can apply this meaning to our *dāsápravarga rayí.* The singer wishes for himself such wealth that knocks the Dāsas (enemies) down. This is a typically Vedic attitude. One desires undisturbed possession: *aśatrú védas* V.2.12; *vā́ryam ánādhṛṣṭam* VIII.22.18. We may cite in particular VI.20.1 and X.47.4 in this context.[366] Ludwig with his rendering "that which excludes the Dāsa" came closer to the right meaning than any one else did. Under *dāsápravarga rayí* we should understand such "wealth," "which destroys or suppresses the Dāsas (enemies)." Thus in the maṇḍalas where Divodāsa is mentioned most often, the word *dāsa* denotes "slave" in no passage; it means exclusively Dāsa or enemy. From this we have to draw the appropriate conclusion about the meaning of *dāsa* in the king's name.

There remain in the entire ṚV three passages where *dāsá* actually means a "slave": VII.86.7 (probably); VIII.56.3 (Vālakhilya) and X.62.10, i.e. precisely in those books which occupy a special position because of their late origin or special peculiarities.[367] In the last two passages it has to do with tributes.

VIII.56.3: *śatáṃ me gardabhā́nāṃ śatáṃ ū́rṇāvatīnām |*
śatáṃ dāsā́m̐ áti srájaḥ ||
X.62.10: *utá dāsā́ parivíṣe smáddiṣṭī góparīṇasā*
yádus turváś ca māmahe ||

Vanquished peoples supply the slaves. A Roman could ask for ten Ethiopeans, Numidians or Greeks, and an Indian for so-and-so many "Dāsas." After certain major sacrifices like the

Aśvamedha, the booty was distributed among the victorious and in some sacrifices the *puruṣas* were distributed along with goods and chattels (cf. e.g., KŚS XXI.1.14; XXII.1.11). This means that the inhabitants were carried off as captives and distributed. It is however possible that even in the two passages above the word *dāsá* has an additional ethnic meaning just as the word *helot* had among the Spartans and *penest* among the Thessalians. The same is the case in VII.86.7 also.

We see clearly how in the ṚV a differentiation of meaning according to the maṇḍala concerned can be of value; in the present case such differentiation is all the more valuable since it leads to the correct understanding of the name Divodāsa. Of the three likely explanations, the one as "slave of heaven" seems to be completely ruled out; "enemy of heaven" is impossible in itself; now there remains only the third one which I have proposed earlier and which I uphold still. While the solitary word *dāsá* has almost throughout evolved into the name for hostile tribes and later (but only in isolated passages in the ṚV) has acquired the sense of "slave," the ancient tribal designation is preserved in a friendly sense in Divodāsa only and probably in his descendent Sudās as well as in Dāsa Balbūtha (ṚV VIII.46.32.).

From their fortresses the tribes of the Dāsas[368] defended the land against the Vedic Aryans.[369] We have already laid stress on the description of the "Dāsa fortresses" as *śâradīḥ* in VI. 20.10.[370] We should not regard these as the "fortresses of demons" or as "magic fortresses,"[371] but as "autumnal" retreats of the Dāsas, as their winter headquarters. The word *dehyàḥ* in VI.47.2 shows that these are man-made fortifications or "ramparts."

The word *dāsá* occurs, of the 64 cases in the ṚV, eight times in seven hymns in the sixth maṇḍala, four times in four hymns in the seventh maṇḍala, and *dasyu* of the 85 occurrences in 67 hymns, only thrice in the vast seventh maṇḍala and only seven times in the sixth. I have already drawn attention to the fact that this numerical proportion could not have been accidental.[372] The scene of action of the sixth book is in the West, in Arachosia and its neighbouring territories where Divodāsa fought, among others, against the Paṇis and Bṛsaya; the name of the Parthians occurs there alone. The enmity between the Dāsas and the Aryans is felt most strongly in the sixth book; it is geographically closest to the tribes who were known to the Iranians also as the nations of the Dahae. For, of the twelve passages of the ṚV which lay stress on this enmity, four occur in the sixth book alone.[373] Of the enemies of Divodāsa who were designated as Dāsa, we encounter the mountain chief Śambara seven times in five hymns of the sixth book whereas the seventh book mentions him only twice.[374] In all the four passages which mention Varcin,[375] this one is closely associated with Śambara. Both rule over innumerable fortresses which Indra breaks or helps Divodāsa Atithigva to break. Generally they are called *púr*, once (VI.47.2) *dehyàḥ*, as we have stated above. Just as the ṚV exaggerates the number of the fortresses of Śambara and speaks at times of 99 and at others of 100, so might the statement that Indra "discovered Śambara, who lived in mountains, in the fortieth year"[376] be an instance of poetic licence which is supposed to suggest the protracted battles against Śambara. Of the other historical names of the Dāsas, we encounter (if we do not take Kaulitara IV.80.4 into account, which possibly belongs to Śambara) only Pipru, who is called *avratá* in 1.101.2 and lives in fortresses as Śambara does.[377] He is the opponent of Ṛjiśvan Vaidathina.[378] In several passages Pipru is mentioned along with Śambara[379] and generally belongs to a specific group (Śuṣṇa, Vyaṃsa, Namuci, Śambara). However, I cannot pursue this clue further.

In another set of passages, Dāsa has already become the designation of a demoniacal being. Among such passages I count those where mention is made of the *ápo dāsápatnyaḥ* (I. 32. 11; V. 30. 5; VIII. 96. 18[380]), of the *dā́sa tuvīráva ṣaḷakṣá triśīrṣán* (X. 99. 6), of the *śúṣṇa kúyava* (VII. 19. 2) and, above all, of Namuci who is styled as a Dāsa quite frequently (V. 30. 7, 8; VI. 20. 6; X. 73. 7). It is significant that he is described as Dāsa once precisely in the sixth maṇḍala which otherwise reflects a concrete state of affairs.[381] If, in view of the other Namuci passages, one cannot go so far as to declare that Namuci is the name of a historical person, one may at least conclude that this demon must have wandered somehow or other into Vedic mythology from among the Dāsa tribes.[382]

Generally the name Dāsa is interpreted in the sense of the original inhabitant of India. This may be justified in some individual cases, but it would be giving too narrow a sense to the word. Only the second book speaks of the *kṛṣṇáyonīr dā́sīḥ*;[383] from this we cannot immediately draw any conclusion about the other books. For, exactly in this book the word enters the mythological realm and loses its concrete sense.[384] A part of the Dāsas in the later books may be sought among the dark-coloured original inhabitants to whom this name was transferred; another part however is formed by the same tribes whom the Iranians called "the nations of the Dahae."

I have already drawn attention (Vol. I, p. 339 ff.) to the close relationship between the Dahae and the Parnians, which can still be recognized in two passages (Dāsa-Paṇi) of the ṚV also.[385] There among the Śaka (Skythian) tribes would lie the home of the designation which gradually lost its individuality and became the name of the Aryan enemies and finally of the dark-skinned enemies also until the sense of "slave" alone remained. Thus *dāsa* denotes

1. hostile tribe and its members, originally the designation of the Dahae,
2. enemy in general
    a. Aryan as well as dark-skinned
    b. demon
3. slave (vanquished enemy), thrice in the ṚV, exclusive meaning in the later period.

Śambara, who along with Varcin is one of the most famous Dāsas,[386] has also the designation Dasyu in I. 59. 6. Cumuri and Dhuni are called Dasyus and these are Dāsas.[387] The Veda speaks of the troops and forts of the Dasyus[388] and of their expulsion from their settlements.[389]

But the meaning of *dásyu* is not the same.[390] Of course, here also the separateness from the Aryans is clearly emphasized,[391] but the stress is on the religious difference. This is expressed in words like *ákarman*, *ámantu* X. 22. 8; *ádevayu* VIII. 70. 11; *ábrahman* IV. 16. 9; *áyajvan* (I. 33.4); VIII. 70. 11; *áyajyu* VII.6. 3; *avratá* I. 51. 8; 175.3; VI.14. 3; IX. 41. 2 and *anyavratá* "having a different belief" VIII. 70. 11; X. 22. 8; *devapīyú* AV XII. 1. 37. To the two epithets *ádevayu* and *devapīyú* we may add the explicit reference to the enmity towards the Devas in

III. 29.9; X. 95. 7.[392] *dasyuhatya* alternates with *vṛtrahatya* but not with **dāsahatya*; on the other hand mention is made of the *viśaḥ* of the Dāsas[393] but not of the Dasyus.

In discussing this question we should not ignore the testimony of the Avesta. The conditions there are not the same as in the ṚV, but we can gather from the Avesta first of all that the name which Indians apply to their enemies has its origin in the West. *daŋhu* (Old Persian *dahyāuš*) means "region" and denotes Aryan[394] as well as non-Aryan[395] countries. Of the non-Aryan countries mention is made particularly of *tūiryas* (Yašt XIII. 143), *sairimas*, *sāinis* and those of the Dahae (Yašt XIII. 144). In the Veda the word is masculine and used exclusively for enemies. Thus Indians have transferred the regional designation which comes originally from the West to their enemies in a general sense. Some of these enemies are called in V. 29.10 *mṛdhrávāc* and *anā́s*. I think only Max Müller's translation of *anā́s* as "noseless" can be acceptable.[396]

There is only a weak support for the assumption that the Veda distinguishes between the Dasyus of the Dāsa tribe and the Dasyus of other tribes. At the most we may find such support in the fact that Cumuri, Dhuni and Śambara are regarded as Dāsas as well as Dasyus (in the case of Namuci also both the words alternate with one another V. 30. 3). Our material does not permit any positive conclusion. There is one point on which I would go beyond the current theories. All the interpreters understand under the word *dasyu* the original inhabitants of India only—a contention which is not at all confirmed by the statements of the ṚV. The ṚV always lays stress on the separateness from the Aryans and allows us to look for these non-Aryans in Hindusthan as well in the West and North-West. When we see that the Brāhuīs, who are akin to the Dravidians, live even today in the midst of the Aryan tribes, then it is by no means impossible that contacts could have taken place between even these peoples and the Aryans in the West, also outside India proper.

The abundance of historical names in the entourage of Indra is full of variety; so is also the number of myths and sagas connected with this most popular personage of Vedic mythology. Only through a long period of study from various aspects will it be possible to lift the veil of secrecy here and there and to place the individual myths in the right perspective. Thus the saga of Indra rescuing from an anthill the maiden's son who was being eaten by ants,[397] or that of Indra destroying as an "ant" the ramparts of the arrogant one[398] still needs elucidation. Ahalyā and Apālā still remain obscure. What we have inherited is fragmentary and partly obliterated. Much would be based on the subjective fancies of the poets and poetasters.[399] I shall touch upon only a few more points and limit myself to the sagas concerning Etaśa and Kutsa.

2. Etaśa

Besides the saga according to which Indra slew Vṛtra and let the sun ascend the sky, there is another which associates him with *étaśa*. Apart from the occasional use as an adjective like in *rátha étaśa* I.54.6 etc., the word has the meaning "horse."[400] Thus it is employed for Sūrya's horses, sometimes in the singular and sometimes in the plural [401] Among these passages some are particularly conspicuous where Indra encourages or checks the sun's horses or his chariot in some way or other.

IV.30.6: *yátrotá mártyāya kám áriṇā indra sū́ryam |*
prā́vaḥ śácībhir étaśam ||

IV.17.14: *ayáṃ cakrám iṣaṇat*[402] *sū́ryasya*
ny étaśaṃ rīramat sasṛmāṇam |

In mythology the passage of the sun can be expressed in various ways: the change from the day to the night, the two solstices which form the two extremities of the sun's orbit, or the irregular interruption through an eclipse. The ṚV speaks very rarely of the solstices. We can cite only

X.179.2: *śrātáṃ havír ó ṣv índra prá yāhi*
jagā́ma sū́ro ádhvano vímadhyam |[403]

and X. 171.4 (where the last pāda is not quite intelligible) :

tváṃ tyám indra sū́ryaṃ paścā́ sántaṃ purás kṛdhi |
devā́nāṃ cit tiró váśam ||[404]

Also the urging forward or the restraining of the sun's chariot or horses can refer only to the solstices. It is said in *Viṣṇupurāṇa* II.8.33:

kulālacakraparyanto yathā śīghraṃ nivartate |
dakṣiṇe prakrame sūryas tathā śīghraṃ nivartate ||
and 36 : *kulālacakramadhyastho yathā mandaṃ prasarpati |*
tathodagayane sūryaḥ sarpate mandavikramaḥ ||

Since according to these verses the chariot moves slowly in the *udagayana* and swiftly in the *dakṣiṇa prakrama,* the verse X.171.4 (probably) refers to the transition to the Dakṣiṇāyana which opposes the will of the gods. On the other hand, the majority of the passages should be construed as referring to the winter solstice : the passages which speak of the discovery of the sun in darkness, or of winning him in battle and so on. These are akin to those which acclaim the recovery of light and refer distinctly to the commencement of the year. I am not able to say in which sense ṚV IV.17.14; 30.6 should be understood; their allusions are too fragmentary.[405]

étaśa does not always mean the sun's horse. In one passage it denotes a different being. According to some scholars this being conducted a race with the sun.

V.29.5 : *ádha krátvā maghavan túbhyaṃ devā́ḥ*
ánu víśve adaduḥ somapéyam |
yát sū́ryasya harítaḥ pátantīḥ
puráḥ satī́r úparā étaśe káḥ ||

Bergaigne (II, p. 342, n. 1) has construed[406] *étaśe* in the sense of *étaśāya.*[407] Then the verse would mean : "as he, for Etaśa, caused the flying bay horses to lag behind." In support of Bergaigne's contention, we may mention, apart from IV.51.4 : *yénā návagve áṅgire...ūṣá,* cited by Bergaigne himself, also I. 71.2 : *cakrúr gātúm asmé* and VIII.32.17 : *bráhmā kṛṇota pányа ít* (*índre*).[408] If we can render *úparā étaśe káḥ* as "he placed them under" i.e. he brought them under the control of Etaśa, then every difficulty would be removed; but it is doubtful if we can join the locative with *úparā* in this way.[409] Meanwhile, even in the dative construction of Bergaigne, the idea that this verse has to do with a chariot race between Sūrya and Etaśa is by no means indicated. Then what sort of being is this Etaśa supposed to be ? We may rather think of a *ratheṣṭhṛ,* who drives the sun's horses, a *volucrum moderator equorum,*[409a] "driver of winged horses." *étaśa* comes close to *aruṇa* in meaning; the latter is the name of the sun's charioteer in classical Sanskrit. We may cite, besides the *Śakuntalā* (ed. Pischel, p. 149, v. 190[410]), also *Raghuvaṃśa* V.71[411] or *Bhāgavata Purāṇa* V.21[412] for Aruṇa. He is thought of in the *Sūryaśataka* also, in the philosophical teachings of which he is involved, and particularly in the expression *aruṇavarṇa* in v. 50 ff.[413] The MBh narrates in the *Āstikaparvan* (Bombay ed., I. 24) that Aruṇa was made the charioteer of the sun when the latter was about to destroy the worlds.

17 : *mahākāyo mahātejāḥ sa sthāsyati puro raveḥ*
kariṣyati ca sārathyaṃ tejaś cāsya hariṣyati ||
18 : *...tataḥ pitāmahājñātaḥ sarvaṃ cakre tadāruṇaḥ* ||
19 : *uditaś caiva savitā hy aruṇena samāvṛtaḥ*[414]

The attitudes of the ṚV and the MBh are not alike. But the episode in the latter work of the sun burning the worlds and hence being given a charioteer clearly reveals the tendency to look for an explanation for the anomalies in the sun's orbit. With these anomalies the ṚV connects the saga alluded to in V.29.5, viz., Indra brings the swiftly moving horses of the sun under the control of the charioteer. This recalls Ovid's statement : *sponte sua properant, labor est inhibere volentes*, "the horses hasten of their own accord; the hard task is to check their eager feet."[414a] We can also cite I.61.15 : *praítaśaṃ sū́rye paspṛdhānám saúvaśvye sú̄ṣvim āvad índraḥ*. It is a battle for the sun and not with the sun in which Indra helps Etaśa. In view of the meagre quantity of the available material, the proposed interpretation can at best be a mere hypothesis. Nevertheless, it is more satisfactory than the supposed chariot race with an obscure being who is totally different from the sun. To construe the battle for the sun in the sense of the solstice seems to be warranted for yet another special reason. In V.31.11 there occurs the word *páritakmyā* :

sū́raś cid ráthaṃ páritakmyāyām
pū́rvaṃ karad úparaṃ jūjuvā́ṃsam |
bhárac cakrám étaśaḥ sáṃ riṇāti
puró dádhat saniṣyati krátuṃ naḥ ||

páritakmyā is not unrelated to *tak*. I think that Ludwig has correctly interpreted it as the "turning point on the race track."[415] In any case, this could be the original meaning. For further elucidation we may turn to V.30.13,14 where *aktór vyùṣṭau* occurs along with *páritakmyā* :

V.30.13: *...tīvrā́ índram amamanduḥ sutā́so*
aktór vyùṣṭau páritakmyāyāḥ ||

14: *aúcchat sā́ rā́trī páritakmyā yā́ṅ*[416]
ṛṇaṃcayé rā́jani ruśámānām |...

In VI.24.9 we find the same expression with a slight change : *aktór vyùṣṭau páritakmyāyām.* Because of the words *aktór* and *rā́triḥ* here this refers to the end of the year, to the New Year's night which one can call *rā́trī páritakmyā* or simply *páritakmyā*:[417] "at the brightening up of the night of the solstice." This interpretation fits excellently in V.31.11: "the sun's chariot, which lags behind, he drove forward in the decisive night." In these solstitial nights, when the sun's chariot reaches the extreme end of his orbit, Indra could have thus helped the charioteer.[418] Accordingly, *étaśa* denotes

1. horse, particularly the sun's horse,
2. charioteer of the sun.

With this I come quite close to Sāyaṇa who explains *étaśa* at times as horse and at others as a Ṛṣi (however, in a different way); for, keeping Aruṇa in view, one can probably call the sun's charioteer a Ṛṣi.

3. Indra and Kutsa

Anyone who goes through the accounts of the later times about Kutsa, a protégé of the national god of India, will not escape the conclusion that this name refers to a historical gotra whose real or mythical progenitor was elevated by his descendants to the status of a divine being who is closely associated with Indra.[419] In the Brāhmaṇas and Sūtras his clan occupies often a lowly position. Here the tradition of other clans predominates, other clans who were in feud with the Kautsas and who, while codifying the ritual which they themselves popularized, ostracized their opponents.

We encounter this name in the rite of buying the Soma. The

Soma seller is regarded as a contemptible person. In the ritual literature a Kautsa is mentioned as the Soma seller (either alone or alternating with a Śūdra.) Baudhāyana states as follows in the Agniṣṭomabhāga, 15: *athaināṃ [somakrayaṇīm] pradakṣiṇam āvṛtyādbhir abhyukṣyodīcīm utsṛjati | saiṣā kautsasya bhavati | atha kautsād rājānam ādatte ... yajamānam adbhir abhyukṣya kautsāya vā parikarmiṇe voṣṇīṣaṃ prayacchati.*[420]

Kātyāyana also states that the Soma seller is a Kautsa or a Śūdra;[421] on this the commentary remarks that a Kautsa is from the same gotra as Kutsa whereas others opine that a Kautsa is one whose conduct is despicable. Perhaps the two meanings are not far apart. Probably the contempt attached to Kutsa which is expressed in the derivatives like *kutsana*, *kutsay* and also in Pāli *kucchā* has its origin in the despicable position assigned for unknown reasons to the Kutsas by the Vedic clans, in spite of the former's independent participation in the composition of the mantras. We can observe a similar phenomenon in the case of the Kaṇvas who, like the Kaśyapas, were excluded from the distribution of the dakṣiṇās in the Soma sacrifice[422] and who, to judge from the nature of the hymns in the eighth book, did not belong to the elite of the Vedic clans (see Ch. V. n. 232; p. 154 above). In AV II. 25 their name is attributed to a demon and in the *Vārttika* on Pāṇini III.1.14, *kaṇvacikīrṣā* is used in the sense of *pāpacikīrṣā*. Here also the name of a Vedic Ṛṣi clan has acquired a secondary meaning, the reason for which must be sought in the hostility of other clans.

According to a legend in the TMBr, a Kutsa with the surname Aurva was an enemy of Indra. He prohibited sacrifices to Indra and cut off the head of his disobedient chief priest as a punishment.[423] Yāska I.15 mentions the statement of a Kutsa: *anarthakā hi mantrāh.* It is true that some solitary statements reveal the traces of a ritual peculiar to the Kutsas. Gobhila states that the Kutsas perform all the four Aṣṭakās with meat.[424] In TMBr XIV.11.25 and elsewhere Sāmans are mentioned which go back to Kutsa.[325] Lāṭyāyana VII.8.19 reports about their special way of singing the finale. According to ĀśvŚS I.2.5, a Kutsa pronounces the syllable *Hiṃ* aloud and before that limits himself to the whispering of *bhūr bhuvaḥ svar*, he omits the preceding japa completely and so on.[426] ĀpŚS XXIV.8 enumerates *āṅgirasa*, *māndhātra* and *kautsa* as the *tryārṣeya* of the Kutsas. But these evidences of an own cult of the Kutsas cannot conceal the differences that go back to the ṚV; these differences among the Vedic clans and tribes might have been brought about by some member of the Kutsa clan. Kutsa, the progenitor of the clan, was elevated by his sons or followers to the status of a friend and companion of Indra. In Vedic literature we find everywhere the tendency to bring the Ṛṣis into personal relationship with the gods. Through one of his Sāmans Kaṇva reaches an agreement with Indra (TMBr IX.2.6). Turaśravas praises Indra with two Sāmans and in return the latter fetches for him food from the Yamunā (ibid IX.4.10). The Vaikhānasas were Indra's friends (ibid XIV.4.7). The Ṛṣis do not see Indra in person, only Vasiṣṭha acquires the sight of him through the Nihavasāman, and Indra proclaims the Stomabhāgas for him (ibid XV.5.24). Indra enters into a contest with Ruśama, saying that whosoever of the two goes around the earth first will be the winner. Indra goes around the earth and Ruśama around Kurukṣetra (ibid XXV.13.3). By singing the Śakvarī verses aloud, the Vasiṣṭhas make Indra strong (ṚV VII.33.4). Vasiṣṭha himself traces his origin back to Mitra-Varuṇa and receives the Rathaṃtara from Dhātṛ Savitṛ. We find Manu, Indra and the Asuras associated in MS IV.8.1, Bharadvāja and Indra in TBr III.10.11.3, Jamadagni and Viśvāmitra (against Vasiṣṭha) and Indra in TS II.2.12; III.1.7.3; TMBr IX.4.14, Gṛtsamada and Indra in ABr V.2.4. As further examples of such associations we may cite ṚV VII.88.3: *ā́ yád ruhā́va váruṇaś ca nā́vam* and VIII.69.16. Thus Kutsa also was elevated by his descendants to become a companion of Indra on the chariot drawn by the steeds of wind: *índrākutsā váhamānā ráthenā́ vām átyā ápi kárṇe vahantu* (V.31.9). Here we do not need to look for a mythological background as Bergaigne does.[427]

The most significant trait in the family tradition of the Kutsas is the participation of their progenitor in the battle against Śuṣṇa. Just as Atri sets the sun free who has been eclipsed by Svarbhānu and sets him in the sky,[428] so does

Kutsa wrest the sun's wheel from Śuṣṇa. For Atri's exploit, his descendants, with the exception of a few,[429] are honoured still in the ritual; one of them is ceremoniously given a piece of gold during the distribution of the dakṣiṇās (ĀpŚS XIII.6. 12).[430] But the Kutsas had to rest content with the low status of a Soma seller; the "exploit" of their progenitor is forgotten and other Vedic clans did not hold it in esteem.

4. Śuṣṇa

Only in about seven passages Kutsa and Śuṣṇa are mentioned besides Indra.[431] In the majority of passages, however, Kutsa, Śuṣṇa and Sūrya occur together.[432] I think that we would not commit any violence to the tradition if we treat all the verses together and refer them to the same myth.

In the case of a great number of the enemies mentioned in the Indra sagas, the line of demarcation, as Oldenberg rightly emphasizes, between the celestial and the terrestrial, between the historical and the mythological core is so difficult to recognize that often we cannot decide where to look for the locale of the battle. This is true also of Kutsa's adversary Śuṣṇa. While in several places he appears as an earthly adversary whose forts are destroyed by Indra,[433] there are other passages which suggest a nature-myth. The problem would be easily solved if we could simply follow Sāyaṇa who renders the word in the majority of cases as *śoṣaka*[434] and explains him as an Asura. Then the *śoṣaka* would be the "scorcher" who seizes the sun's wheel about the time of the summer solstice and scorches everything. In support of this construction one may perhaps refer to some verses where, besides Śuṣṇa, the word *kuvaya*, "bad harvest" occurs, which could be regarded as an epithet of Śuṣṇa.[435] However, another passage shows that the two words are not related and thus speaks against an identification.[436] But even when the derivation from the root *śuṣ* is correct, other interpretations also are possible besides the one according to which Śuṣṇa is the hot season. In Old Slavonic the month of March is called *suchyj* "dry month" but not the summer months. In Lithuanian *sāusis* means December and January. Or Śuṣṇa could be a celestial phenomenon indicating a bad augury; for instance, a solar eclipse whose occurrence indicates bad harvest, drought or other calamities. But in view of the scantiness of material in the ṚV, we must guard ourselves against any rash conclusion.[437] Anyone who seeks to explain Śuṣṇa as the terrestrial enemy or as one of the solstitial points or as solar eclipse (= Svarbhānu, Ludwig has already discussed this possibility) can cite some argument or other in his favour. I myself would think that the last possibility deserves precedence over the others. In this I am supported by the choice of expressions like *muṣāyá sū́ryam* (I.175.4; IV.30.4; VI.31.3); *pra* +*vṛh* (I.174.5; IV.16.12; V.29.10) which are most apt for the wresting of the sun's wheel from the control of Rāhu;[438] further by the statements of time, *purā́ yát sū́ras támaso ápītes* (I.121.10),[439] "before the sun sinks into darkness,"[440] and *prapitvé áhnaḥ* (IV.16.12)[441] as well as *prapitvám yán*. It was a Brahman or Sāman which Kutsa had invented and to which Indra gave favourable hearing. And this formula might have been tested again on another occasion and thus would explain why in IV.16.12 at first the aorist *ní barhī́ḥ* and then the imperative *prá mṛṇa kutsyéna* ("through the formula of Kutsa"[442]) were employed like an *arthavāda* and *vidhi* as it were.

Of the other enemies of Kutsa, mention is made of Ilībiśa, Tugra, and Tūrvayāṇa.[443] We learn little about Tūrvayāṇa, and Ilībiśa is also quite a rare name. Tugra occurs more often; Baunack[444] has thoroughly discussed all the sagas connected with him. The scantiness of our material does not allow any progress here. However, we may call attention to the fact that in several passages of the ṚV a Kutsa is seen as the enemy of Indra. And the dichotomy of views which we encountered in the later literature belongs thus to the period of the ṚV already. While the Kutsa patronized by Indra is called *ārjuneyá* IV. 26.1; VII.19.2; VIII. 1.11; *atithigvá* I.51.6; VI.26. 3; *yúvan* I.63.3, the Kutsa who had been abandoned by Indra and handed over to his enemies bears the epithet *atithigvá āyú*.[445] Tūrvayāṇa, "the youthful king" is an enemy, so is Suśravas. According to TMBr XIV.6.8 a Suśravas officiates as the Purohita of Kutsa; this Purohita makes sacrifice for

Indra against the order of his master and is decapitated as a punishment for this (see p. 165). In the legend this hostile Kutsa has the epithet Aurava; therefore he is to be distinguished from Kutsa Atithigva Āyu. As a testimony for the fact that several members of the Kutsa gotra had nursed an ancient enmity against Indra and against Suśravas, this passage (TMBr XIV.6.8) is not without significance.

H. INDRĀGNĪ

While the meaning and the origin of the dual association Agni-Soma can easily be understood, it is not so with the *dvandva* Indrāgnī which occurs more frequently. We find the gods in an entirely different relationship to one another and it is difficult to extract the basic notion which gave birth to this dual combination. Agni is supposed to fetch Indra in III.53.4; V.5.3; he roasts 300 buffaloes for Indra in V.29.7 and gives shelter to those who press the Soma for Indra IV.25.4.[446] In VIII.100.1 Agni assures Indra that he would grant strength to Indra if the latter offers him a portion of the sacrifice. Indra agrees, hoping that Agni would become his friend and destroy the enemies in concert with him.[447] In X.52.5 Agni promises to the gods to put the thunderbolt in Indra's hand; then he would win all the battles. In X.32.6 the poet turns to Agni, about whose hiding place Indra has informed him. What is meant here, at least in two of these verses, is the sacrificial fire, the Vaiśvānara Agni, of the gods.[448] But this does not yet explain the significance of the dual association which occurs in several hymns dedicated exclusively or primarily to them and which receives in the ritual a large number of offerings in various major and minor sacrifices. For example, one who desires progeny, one who fights against a kingdom or a rival, one who wishes to march into battle or one who has won a war should sacrifice for Indra-Agni.[449] Indra-Agni (or conversely Agni-Indra also[450]) receive a Graha in the Agniṣṭoma and have their own priest, the Acchāvāka (Latin *calator*, "servant, attendant"), who recites their Śastra.[451] One special Ekāha and one entire Ayana are called after them.[452] In the discussion of the ceremonies, we occasionally come across statements like *indrāgnī vai devānām ojiṣṭhau baliṣṭhau sahiṣṭhau sattamau pārayiṣṇutamau;*[453] *indrāgnī vai devānām ojobhṛtau;*[454] *prāṇāpānau vā etau devānāṃ yad indrāgnī ...ojo balaṃ vā etau devānām*[455] or *yad vahī tenāgneyaḥ yan muṣkaras tenaindraḥ*[456] or also *āgneyī vai rātriḥ..aindram ahaḥ.*[457] Often in the ritual texts[458] as well as in later literature[459] we encounter the notion that Agni denotes the Brahman and Indra the Kṣatra. By and large, these are statements with which we cannot establish much, although it would be wrong to dismiss them as "occasional fancies" or to regard them as emanations of henotheism. Under these circumstances, we should pay attention to a factor that occurs with a great regularity: it is the position occupied by these two gods in the New Moon sacrifice. They are at its centre just as Agni-Soma are at the centre of the Full Moon sacrifice. MS I.5.7 (75.10) states: *agnīṣomīyayā pūrvapakṣa upastheyo 'gnīṣomīyo vai pūrvapakṣo...aindrāgnyāparapakṣa upastheya aindrāgno va aparapakṣaḥ.* Mahendra or Indra can take the place of Indrāgnī but the norm is to worship the latter. We may assume that the ritualists, when they determined this, had a clear notion in their minds, and did not see, like Keith (p. 220), "a curious connexion." Just as it is in the New Moon sacrifice, so is it in the Nirūḍhapaśubandha, an animal sacrifice which does not belong to the Soma sacrifice.[460] Its simple form follows the scheme of the New Moon sacrifice and contains in the place of the Saṃnāyya a sacrificial animal for Indra-Agni as the central point of the offerings; its observance is not limited to the New Moon day.[461] Although there are other possibilities as always in the ritual, where the traditions of different schools are codified, and Sūrya or Prajāpati can alternate with Indra-Agni in the animal sacrifice,[462] yet it is these two gods who are thought of primarily because the mantras accompanying the offerings are first of all addressed to them.[463] Śāṅkhāyana lays down an important rule that the animal sacrifice for Indrāgnī should be performed always at the beginning and end of the Udagayana.[464] This rule demonstrates that the two gods are brought into association with the Uttarāyaṇa or with the transition between the Uttarāyaṇa and the Dakṣiṇāyana. The relationship of the two gods to the year and its seasons, which can be inferred from the above fact, can be recognized also in the Aindrāgnagraha of the Soma sacrifice.

It is drawn after the Ṛtugrahas and according to ŚBr IV.3.1.21 ff., it is directly connected with them: "by drawing the Ṛtugrahas he generates the All. He lays the life in it by drawing the Graha for Aindrāgna after them; Indra-Agni are the life (*prāṇodānau*)." The inner connection between the Grahas is expressed quite clearly in the stipulation that the Acchāvāka, the priest of Indrāgnī, must be seated first before the libations from the Ṛtupātras can begin.[465] One need not attach great value to the speculations of the Brāhmaṇas, yet one may recognize the grain of truth concealed in the close connection between Indrāgnī and the Ṛtus.

Hence, until it is possible to throw more light on the significance of this pair of gods, I draw the following conclusion from the aforesaid : just as Agnīṣomau are the gods of the Full Moon so are Indrāgnī the gods of the New Moon. An animal sacrifice for them begins and (eventually) concludes the Uttarāyaṇa; they are connected with the Ṛtus and generate life for them.

The redactors of the Śrauta ritual found a large stock of sacrifices and ceremonies of all kinds. The ritual had undergone a long process of evolution. The celebrations of the passage of the year were observed with different customs in different families, clans and countries. Among some, certain gods were prominent; among others certain other gods came into the foreground. Those who took upon themselves the task of codifying this material had to take into account the special customs of those families who were most important or close to them; thus they based the Jyotiṣṭoma on several customs of the Viśvāmitras and left the role of Brahman to the Vasiṣṭhas. They assigned a place in the Atirātra to certain peculiar customs of the Kaṇvas,[466] and chose the Subrahmaṇyā formula of the Kauśikas and Gautamas for inviting Indra ceremoniously. They invited the Ṛtus to drink the Soma in the morning, the Ṛbhus in the evening and accommodated Indra chiefly at noon. They placed the other gods of the morning in the foreground. They accommodated Pūṣan with his Karambhas among the Savanīya-Puroḍāśas, and Indra's horses in the Hāriyojana. They named the ceremony Agniṣṭoma following the usage of individual families who invited Agni instead of Indra but they devoted the Agniṣṭoma mainly to Indra. Thus between so many customs they produced a compromise which was an artificial product. To analyse this compromise into its constituents is an important task for the future; it would be at the same time a work of art in a certain sense. They did not select indiscriminately; besides the customs of individual families, they also took into account the character of the gods as far as possible. Their work does not contain everything. What lay beyond their circle and customs and belonged to families without a great reputation must have been excluded as was done by the editors of the hymn-collection. Thus here the Full Moon sacrifice, among other things, was assigned to Agni-Soma, and Indrāgnī receive, besides several minor offerings, the New Moon sacrifice. There must be an inner connection between Indrāgnī and the sacrifice though we cannot define it. It does not however mean that this ceremony gives expression to the full significance of Indrāgnī. Their inclusion in the ritual is one of the solid facts in this uncertain ground and hence we must lay stress on it.[467]

The ṚV devouts a large number of hymns to these two gods in comparison to Agni-Soma.[468] Among these hymns which conceive Indra-Agni always jointly and do not particularly individualize either of them, VI.59 seems to be important because the first verse of this hymn anticipates a situation which the afore-mentioned rule of Śāṅkhāyana calls for.

VI.59.1: *prá nú vocā sutéṣu vāṃ vīryà yā́ni cakráthuḥ |*
hatā́so vāṃ pitáro devásatrava índrāgnī jī́vatho yuvā́m||

It is the end of the Pitṛyāṇa and the beginning of the Udagayana, to which, as I have already remarked in Vol. I, p. 93, this verse refers. Other verses of the same Bharadvāja hymn are also of significance; thus v. 2 where the two are described as sons of the same father and different mothers, as brothers and as twins.[469] Similarly, v. 5, if I understand its content correctly, is more important because it clearly reveals the concept of the New Moon which we encountered in the ritual:[470] "Indra and Agni, which mortal understands this in you? One of you has yoked the unruly horses and drives alone on the common chariot."[471] There is not much to be gleaned from the other hymns. As in the Brāhmaṇas, so also here Indra and Agni are represented as cosmogonic powers. They are worshipped by the Brahman and Rājan, by the Yadus, Turvaśas, Druhyus, Anus, Pūrus (I.108.7,8). They receive astringent Soma (I.108.4), Ukthas (III.12.5; VI.59.10), Nīthas (III.12.5) and Stomas (I.109.2; VI.59.10).[472] Further, verse VIII.40.8 seems to be of some importance (if the statements of the eighth book deserve any importance at all) :

yā́ nú śvetā́v avó divá uccárāta úpa dyúbhiḥ |
indrāgnyór ánu vratám úhānā yanti síndhavo
yā́n sīm bandhā́d amuñcatām...||[473]

because it characterizes the two as "luminous gods" who "will rise" and who set the waters free from their shackles. The cosmogonic activity which comes into bold relief in this verse and which does not need to be interpreted in a metaphorical sense was expressed, as we saw, in the statement of the ŚBr cited above on the connection between the Aindrāgnagraha and the Ṛtus. It leads us to the assumption that Indra and Agni, before a specific place was assigned to them by the redactors of the ritual, were regarded as powers of great efficacy and this is equally reflected in their position at the beginning and end of the Uttarāyaṇa.

I. THE MARUTS OR THE RUDRAS

Two meanings are combined in the name *rudrāḥ*; the word does not always designate the storm-winds who are regarded as Rudra's offspring but also the ubiquitous spirits and demons who come in the wake of the terrible god; they are a part of his being, denoting his influence, maleficence and diseases,[474] and can be regarded as a troop of individual Rudras. These become quite prominent in a ceremony of the Gṛhya ritual. On the occasion of the Śūlagava, blood is offered on Palāśa leaves in all the four quarters to "Rudra and his troops", *rudrāya senābhyaḥ*.[475] In ŚSS IV.19.8 the troops are designated as *āghoṣiṇyaḥ pratighoṣiṇyaḥ saṃghoṣiṇyo vicinvatyaḥ śvasanāḥ kravyādaḥ*; likewise in ĀśvGS IV.8.28,[476] and the next Sūtra, IV.8.29, states: *sarvāṇi ha vā asya nāmadheyāni sarvāḥ senāḥ sarvāṇy ucchrayaṇāni.* That we should not always understand the Rudras as the winds is suggested by the invocations in the Rudrādhyāya, which are addressed to the Rudras, "who are in thousands on the earth." TS IV.5.11.b: *asmin mahaty arṇave 'ntarikṣe bhavā adhī*; c: *nīlagrīvāḥ śitikaṇṭhāḥ śarvā adhaḥ kṣamācarāḥ*; e: *ye vṛkṣeṣu* ... g: *ye anneṣu vividhyanti pātreṣu pibato janān*; h: *ye pathāṃ pathirakṣayaḥ*;[477] i: *ye tīrthāni pracaranti sṛkāvanto niṣaṅgiṇaḥ*... l: *namo rudrebhyaḥ ye pṛthivyāṃ ye 'ntarikṣe ye divi yeṣām annaṃ vāto varṣam iṣavaḥ.*[478] TĀr I. 12.1 speaks in a different way of these countless invisible forms: *ya eko rudra ucyate asaṃkhyātā sahasrāṇi smaryate na ca dṛśyate.* This explains why in several instances the Maruts and the Rudras appear quite separately.[479] Although now and then the scholastic tendency of specialization might have differentiated between the two names purely in a superficial way, there must have been a deeper reason for this distinction.

Frequently the name "Rudras" is attributed to the Maruts.[480] While the above-mentioned troops are only so many parts or multiples of his being, the Maruts are entitled to this name for a different reason. Just as the Kaṇvas are named after their progenitor Kaṇva, the Atris after the Ṛṣi of the same name,[481] so have the Maruts become Rudras as they were the sons of Rudra.[482] But the plural form is not known to all the books of the ṚV. In the sixth book we find *rudrásya putrā́ḥ* but not yet *rudrā́saḥ.*[483] Similarly the fourth book does not contain the plural of *rudra.* It follows from this that this designation slowly gained currency.

Besides the verses which describe Rudra directly as the father of the Maruts, there are some others where Rudra is indirectly alluded to as their father; sometimes it is a "strong one" who goes ahead of them, sometimes a "red one" who draws their chariot.[484]

If I am right in explaining Rudra, in spite of the contrary view held by Arbman, in general terms as the god of the baleful aspects of Indian climate from the beginning of summer up to autumn—I do not think that an attempt at an identification with a specific period of the year is warranted – then with Rudra as the father of the Maruts we have the period of their birth and dominence. It is the time of the South-West monsoon which arrives with turbulent force, accompanied by thunder and lightning. The Maruts are always celebrated as rain-bringers;[485] they yoke the winds as horses and bring the rain from the sea.[486] The earth is like their wife in whom they deposit their seed; the rain is their perspiration.[487] They are clothed with the clouds (V. 63.6) and let the waters of the mountains out (V.59.7: *prá párvatasya nabhanū́nr acucyavuḥ*). Hence they are close to Parjanya, the rain god of the Veda, and are often described as directly associated with him.[488]

The Veda does not mention the same paternity consistently everywhere. In one passage the Maruts are Vāyu's sons,[489] but never Indra's. In II.36.2 we find them described as Bharata's sons. Again it is stated that they were born from the "laughter of the lightning,"[490] that none knows of their birth (VII.56.2) or that they reach heaven *nírṛter avaṃśā́t*[491] (VII.58.1). The views vary in the ṚV about their mother as well. Once they are called *síndhumātaraḥ*, once *gómātaraḥ*, but generally the ṚV prefers the designation *pṛ́śnimātaraḥ*.[492]

1. Pṛśni

The two words *gó* and *pṛ́śni* have been quite correctly regarded as synonyms, but to explain *pṛ́śni* as the "mottled storm-cloud" as Macdonell (p. 125) does, following Roth (on *Nirukta* X.37, p. 145), is supported neither by the actual facts nor by the Vedic conceptions. Even according to Indian views, it is the wind which propels the clouds.[493] Hence I think that Roth's explanation is based on a wrong assumption and that the correct meaning of *pṛ́śni* must be sought elsewhere.[494] Occasionally *pṛ́śni* is a designation for the earth.[495] But such passages are rare, and the Maruts are never styled as earth-born (except in one passage where the earth is mentioned, besides heaven and atmosphere, as the place of their birth[496]). A scrutiny of all Ṛgvedic passages which deal with *pṛ́śni* does not yield any profit either.[497] Therefore, I would like to return to an idea stated in Vol. I, pp. 264-65 that Pṛśni should be contrasted with Uṣas-

Sūryā and that the former signifies the beginning of the rainy season and the latter the commencement of the bright season. Pṛśni is identical with Vaśā, the wife of Parjanya (AV X.10.6). "Her udder is Parjanya, her teats the lightnings" (AV X.10.7).[498] Another synonym is *íḍā*, in whose attribute *yūthásya mātā́* (ṚV V.41.19[499]) we may once again recognize the mother of the Maruts. Just as the Maruts are Pṛśni's sons, so is Vāyu called "the calf of Iḍā."[500] In this connection it is worth noting that a *pṛśni*, a "dappled cow," or the milk of such a cow[501] is offered to the Maruts and that in the sacrifices for the Maruts a *pṛśni* is given as dakṣiṇā. With this *pṛśni* which is dedicated to them regularly, the Maruts are well comparable to the sons of Aditi, of the celestial light, who are entitled to bright-coloured animals.[502] The antithesis that is implied here can also indicate the distinction between the bright half of the year and the dark half and prove that *pṛśni* is the expression for the dark period (*varṣāḥ*) the beginning of which means the oncoming of the Maruts.[503]

2. The "Host" of the Maruts

In the entire ritual literature the Maruts are regarded as a clan, as *devānāṃ viśaḥ*,[504] and seen as the archetype of the Vaiśyas whose fickle relations with their king have their model in those between the Maruts and Indra. If a prince wishes to win over his subjects or secure their loyalty, safeguard his kingdom or recover it, the ritual prescribes offerings which somehow or other should invoke the Maruts and Indra. Occasionally Agni takes Indra's place. For instance, TS II.2.11.1 states: *aindram ekādaśakapālaṃ nir vapen mārutaṃ saptakapālaṃ grāmakāmaḥ* / .. *ājavanīya aindram adhi śrayati gārhapatye mārutam* / . . . *saptagaṇā vai marutaḥ* . . . or quite similarly about Vaiśvānara at II.2.5.6: *vaiśvānaraṃ dvādaśākapālaṃ nir vapen mārutaṃ saptakapālaṃ grāmakāmaḥ . . . māruto bhavati maruto vai devānāṃ viśo devaviśenaivāsmai manuṣyaviśam ava runddhe saptakapālo bhavati saptagaṇā vai marutaḥ* . . .[505] Thus the ritual literature continues a point of view which has been variously expressed in the ṚV already. It is said in V.56.1: *víśo adyá marútām áva hvaye diváś cid rocanā́d ádhi* //[506] and the Maruts occupy a special position in this very maṇḍala as we shall see later on. For the present, we may cite verse V.52.11 in which the poet, at the sight of their splendid forms, recalls the Pārāvatas.[507] In the same book (V.54.8) they are compared to *niyútvanto grāmajíto nárah̤.* Within the fifth maṇḍala as well as outside of it, the Maruts are depicted like the army of a warrior tribe which marches ahead in its battle decorations, with lances and other weapons.[508] *pārāvata* is explained as "people from foreign lands" by the PW and likewise by Sāyaṇa.[509] I do not see why they as aliens should have especially resplendent forms. Hence I think with Ludwig[510] of the warrior tribe of the Pārāvatas who are described as enemies in the sixth book. These now serve our poet, who lives farther in the east, as comparison for the Maruts who are marching forth likewise from the west.[511] These Pārāvatas are mentioned once again in TMBr IX.4.11 (see the PW): in their sacrificial contest with Turaśravas, Indra takes the latter's side and brings him the sacrificial offerings of the Pārāvatas from the Yamunā.[512]

3. The Maruts and the Aśvattha

In several of the Brāhmaṇa texts which describe the relation between Indra and the Maruts, mention is made of their sojourn on an Aśvattha tree, and the use of vessels made of its wood is prescribed. For instance, ŚBr IV.3.3.6 states: *tad yan marutvatīyān gṛhṇāty etad vā indrasya niṣkevalyaṃ savanaṃ yan mādhyandinaṃ savanaṃ tena vṛtram ajighāṃsat / tena vyajigīṣata / maruto vā ity aśvatthe 'pakramya tasthuḥ / kṣatraṃ vā indro viśo marutaḥ / viśā vai kṣatriyo balavān bhavati / tasmād aśvatthe ṛtupātre syātāṃ kārṣmaryamaye tv eva bhavataḥ /* [513]

It seems to me that the oft-attested association of the Maruts with the Pippala tree is based on an old saga and not an erroneous interpretation of ṚV I 135.8.[514] For on another occasion the leaves of the *Ficus religiosa* serve as the containers for the offerings to the Maruts [515] and thus demonstrate that the two are conceived in an intimate association in India. The reason for this becomes evident in a remark of the commentary on the TBr that the Aśvattha is the symbol of the village.[516] The Maruts are Vaiśyas and represent the *viś.* The constant fluttering of the leaves of this tree might have made it an abode for the wind gods in Indian conceptions. [517]

4. The Maruts in the Family Books

Among all the allies who assist Indra in his battle against Vṛtra, the Maruts are the most loyal helpers. A part of the Vedic hymns and the ritual literature bring them so often into association with Indra that this association has been regarded as a common feature of the ṚV. But a closer examination of the state of affairs in the individual family books shows that the above view requires a modification and that the Maruts are not always connected so closely with Indra as is reflected in the customs of the Viśvāmitras and of the ritual literature. This is demonstrated by a review of the individual passages dealing with the Maruts in each of these books.

Maṇḍala II.

11.14 : *rā́si kṣáyaṃ rā́si mitrā́m asmé*
rā́si śárdha indra mā́rutaṃ naḥ |

29.3 : *yūyáṃ no mitrāvaruṇadite ca*
svastím índrāmaruto dadhāta ||

31.3 : *utá syá na índro viśvácarṣaṇiḥ*
diváḥ śárdhena mā́rutena sukrátuḥ[518] |

Hymn 34 is addressed to the Maruts, but Indra is not mentioned (Viṣṇu in v. 11). Thus in this book Indra and the Maruts are mentioned together casually in a few passages only.

Maṇḍala III. The Viśvāmitras invoke Indra conjointly with the Maruts (III. 32.1 ff. midday pressing; 35.9; 47.2; 52.7).[519] They state that the Maruts help Indra in his battle against Vṛtra (32.4; 47.2 ff.; 51.9).

Maṇḍala IV. Maruts' help in the battle against Vṛtra is not recalled. Once Indra is called *marútvat* (IV. 21.3). We find the names of the Maruts only in the litany-like enumeration of the gods (1.3; 2.4; 3.8; [26.4]; 34.7, 11; 39.11; 55.5).[520] Hence, we cannot speak of any significant cult of the Maruts in the family of the Vāmadevas. The plural *rudrā́ḥ* does not occur here.

Maṇḍala V. In 40.4 Indra receives the midday libation without there being a mention of the Maruts. Particularly noteworthy in this fifth book is that the Maruts do not make their appearance as allies of Indra but as his worshippers. They sing in his praise, make offerings to him as though they are a Brahmanical clan devoted to Indra's cult,[521] and help him through their singing. Of course, we find hints of this nature scattered elsewhere also; thus for instance, the Maruts are called *kaváyaḥ* in I.31.1; *brahmakṛ́t mā́ruto gaṇā́ḥ* in III.32.2. They punish him who blames the offering of prayers (VI.52.2); but they do not appear as sacrificers so predominently as they do in the fifth book where they directly resemble the Aṅgiras'.[522]

The word *marútvat* occurs twice in this fifth book. But in one passage (V.87.1) it is not attributed to Indra but to Viṣṇu. In the second passage (V. 42.6) Indra is not expressly mentioned, yet we can infer from the vocative *maghavan* that it is Indra who is meant here. He has his place in the midst of the invocations to other gods in this colourless verse.[523] In this connection we should keep in mind that in all the ten Marut hymns of this book, which bring the character of these gods distinctly into bold relief, Indra's name occurs only once more quite casually.[524] Thus the conclusion is justified that the Atris also did not share with other families the worship of Indra *marútvat*.[525]

As in this point so also in another respect the Atri hymns exhibit a peculiarity. They are of course familiar with the word *vṛtrahan* and its derivatives and twice employ *vṛtra* as an appellative. Nevertheless, they substitute the Vṛtra saga with that of Śuṣṇa (see Ch. VII, n. 437) and betray in this respect also a different tradition. We should consider the home of this tradition during the Vedic times to be the countries to the east of the Indus and more specifically perhaps the banks of the Yamunā.[526]

Maṇḍala VI. The book of the Bharadvājas also differs from its neighbours in a distinctive way. First of all, it is striking that with the exception of the obscure and partly unintelligible hymn VI. 66, no other hymn is dedicated to the Maruts and that they are thought of in a very general sense, often in the midst of invocations to other gods.[527] But the above-mentioned hymn refers neither to Indra nor to Vṛtra, and in the entire maṇḍala the association of the Maruts with Indra is alluded to very casually and in passing.[528] VI.47.5 relates that Indra *marútvat* props up the heavens, but the next verse which invites Indra *samaré vásūnām* to the midday libation does not mention the Maruts. Hence it is not probable that the Bharadvājas had accommodated the Maruts in the midday savana. This accords with the fact that the assistance of the Maruts in the battle against Vṛtra was unknown to the composers of the sixth book as well and that this assistance is merely touched upon only once outside the hymn VI. 66.[529] That Rudra has still less significance in the sixth book and that the Maruts are of course called *rudrasya sūnavaḥ* and once *rudriya*s but not yet *rudrāḥ* is a further peculiarity of this group of hymns. This peculiarity will be discussed further below. It is only in the Marut hymn VI.66 that *pṛśni* is stated to be their mother (vv. 1, 3).

Maṇḍala VII. As in book VI so also here the Maruts are not closely connected with the Vṛtra-killer. Indra and Vâyu are drawn into a close association in three hymns (90-92) but Indra and the Maruts in none. Indra is never called *marútvat* here. Occasionally mention is made of Indra and the Maruts but in such a general way that we realize that the Vasiṣṭhas of course knew the aid rendered to Indra by the Maruts but they did not treat it as an important event.[530] I have already laid stress (see p. 116 above) upon the fact that the Indra hymns of this book are conspicuous by their poverty in content, that the legend of Vṛtra is forgotten to a large extent and that the association *indro rudrebhiḥ* is replaced by *indro vasubhiḥ*.[531]

Thus there are prominent differences between the individual maṇḍalas as regards the worship of the Maruts also; so far attempts have been made in vain to seek such differences in the realm of grammar. By going forward on this hitherto untrodden path, I believe, it will be possible to separate the traditions of the individual Vedic tribes, which were undergoing the process of fusion already in the ṚV. Further, the above discussion may corroborate what I have stated earlier[532] with reference to the Savya and Agastya hymns, however without getting any response, "that in an earlier Vedic period there existed a group, which was somehow or other distinct from others, in which the Marut cult did not meet with a reception or did so at a later stage only."

5. The Maruts as the Manes

The notion that the Maruts are to be regarded as the Manes,

as the spirits and souls of the dead who depart through the air, has been expressed quite often without, however, becoming any more convincing.[533] I have doubted it for long, but now I see that there is much to be said for this theory, and shall attempt to substantiate it in a better way. We can proceed from the statements of the fifth book which clearly characterize the Maruts as the "pious ones" who create the *bráhman,* who like other Kavis worship Indra, who pour out the "well" and so on. Just as the Aṅgiras, who were elevated to the status of gods by the cult of the Manes, get into heat through their penance and cause rain, so is rain the perspiration of the Maruts who accomplish the *bráhman.*

The identification of the Maruts with the Manes finds a rather vague support in the oft-repeated statement that the Maruts receive "sacrificial names,"[534] i.e., they obviously receive cult worship. We come across a similar process in the case of the Ṛbhus whose euhemeristic origin has been discussed on pp. 88-89 above. It is never stated that the Maruts were once human beings. But the reason for this could lie in the fact that their deification in the ṚV was already more advanced than that of the Ṛbhus, Aṅgiras' and Bhṛgus and the character of rain-bringers was imprinted upon them quite definitively.[535] The following evidence has greater significance.

We notice that according to PGS II.15 a sacrifice is performed for Indra on the Full Moon day of the Prauṣṭhapada, and independently of this an offering is made to the Maruts after the food, for which Pāraskara cites the authority of the Śruti: *ahutādo vai devānāṃ marutaḥ.*[536] In conformity with the saga that the Maruts had sojourned on an Aśvattha tree (see p. 177 above), six oblations are made on the leaves of this tree,[537] and these are followed by a seventh during which the Vimukha verse should be recited.[538] The same sacrifice is enjoined by KŚS XVIII.4.23 ff. during the piling up of the altar, with the difference that the oblations to the Maruts are preceded by an offering to Agni Vaiśvānara and not to Indra. In this context the injunction, *vimukhenāraṇye 'nūcyam,*[539] is quite significant; it suggests that the position of the Maruts in the sacrifice is akin to that of the Manes, Rudras or demons.[540] In support of the identification of the Maruts with the Manes, we may also take into account the fact that during the Baliharaṇa (according to Manu III. 88; cf. GDS V. 12 ff.) offerings are made to them in the *dvāra.* Here it is but natural to think of the superstition connected with the threshold. Wuttke, *Der deutsche Volksaberglaube,* 3rd ed., §750, p. 471, states thus about the souls : "... or they are under the threshold. When one enters a new house, one should not step on the threshold because this would injure the poor souls who are underneath the threshold (Upper Franconia) or they are behind the door."

ŚBr IV.5.2.16 (see n. 536) refers to the offering of an embryo to the Maruts. Embryos are regarded as dangerous and not fit for sacrifice otherwise. In the ritual of Baudhāyana, the *patitāḥ garbhāḥ* are specially worshipped with the offering of blood.[541] We should further remember that according to ŚBr IV.5.2.17, the Maruts like the Manes are not entitled to the Svāhā call, which is certainly not denied to Rudra, that they are hostile towards the progeny[542] and sacrifice,[543] that they are able to obstruct the path to the celestial world,[544] and that they have their own priest called the Potṛ, "the Purifier," who belongs to them exclusively in the ṚV but assumes other functions in the later period. Although these above statements belong to the Brāhmaṇa literature only, they certainly contain an old tradition. We find in the ṚV also allusions to the malevolence of the Maruts (see Macdonell, p. 81). Their evolution into pure and simple wind gods in the later period shows that these qualities could have been lost to them rather than added to them, and that what we see are relics of an old tradition.

While Vāyu is never compared to the birds, as far as I know, the Maruts are often thus compared (e.g. I.87.2; 88.1; 165.2; V. 59.7; VII.56.3; 59.7); this must be a relic of the conceptions belonging to the cult of the Manes.[545] Their martial dress, their spears and other weapons recall the *pitáras citrásenā íṣubalāḥ* in ṚV VI.75.9. They rose from the realm of the dead, *nírṛter avaṃśát*, and were made the gods of storm. It is possible that their former realm was the approximate period of twelve nights. The evolution in India has transformed them into the monsoon-storms. Their period begins with the summer solstice and so does the Pitṛyāṇa. Hence, they were regarded as the sons of Rudra and Pṛśni whose reign falls in this period.[546]

In the later period there were occasional attempts to give a new significance to them and to attribute the name Āditya euphemistically. An example of this nature occurs in TS II.3.1.5 where the stake made of the Aśvattha wood and the number seven allude still clearly to the Maruts.[547] This process begins already in the ṚV.[548] We find that they are celebrated *ādityéna nā́mnā* in X. 77.8[549] and likewise probably in I.106.2. I think that it is merely a late continuation of this metamorphosis when the Maruts are designated as the "rays" or as other luminous beings in the Brāhmaṇas and other related texts.[550] There is no deeper reason for this.

6. The Maruts in the Cult

The redactors of the ritual have assigned a place to the Maruts in the midday savana and in the evening savana of the Soma sacrifice,[551] whereas in the morning savana they have accommodated Vāyu and not the Maruts. With the offering of the three Grahas at noon for Indra accompanied by the Maruts, the redactors have taken up a custom that was observed only in some families like the Viśvāmitras. Others did not invoke Indra *marútvat*; they invoked Indra alone for the sacrificial drought at noon. Likewise, the Maruts do not appear alone among the gods invited to the sacrifice in the evening, but always in concert with Agni, who is called *marútsakhi* and *marúdvṛddha*,[552] and receive with him the Āgnimārutaśastra,[553] which consists of the hymns III. 3 (addressed to Agni Vaiśvānara) and I. 43.6, or of II. 33.1 (addressed to Rudra) and I.87 (to the Maruts).[554] Like the association of the Maruts with Indra, their association with Agni also has its starting point in some Vedic hymns; for example, I.19, all the verses of which end in the refrain *marúdbhir agna á gahi*, and I.72; III. 26; V.60 (cf. vv. 7, 8); VIII. 7.32, 36 and some other passages.[555] We have seen above (p. 125 f.) that in the Agniṣṭoma, Agni and Indra change places according to the custom of the family concerned and that in the wish-fulfilment sacrifices performed for securing one's reign there is no basic distinction between these two gods (see Vol. I, pp. 78-79 and II, p. 176). A similarity between Agni *marútvat* and Indra *marútvat* within certain limits cannot be overlooked in the ṚV either. Just as the Maruts sing like pious sacrificers in praise of Indra so do they appear towards Agni, at least in one passage, as ardent worshippers[556] and play the role of the Aṅgiras. The ṚV does not leave us in doubt as to who should be understood by this Agni. V.60.8, which invites him and the Maruts to a common drought, designates him as Vaiśvānara[557] and thus, as is shown in Vol. I, p. 78 f., as the sun god. Hence, we should assume that the associations between Indra and the Maruts on the one hand and between Agni and the Maruts on the other are, despite certain differences, nothing but mythological double formations which had their origin in different areas of culture.

It has been explained before that mythological synonymity does not necessarily imply a complete congruence of two sets of ideas and that the individuality of each set can still be recognized. To these traits which specially characterize the association of Agni with the Maruts belongs the "paternity" of the Maruts which some verses attribute to Agni (see Bergaigne, II, p. 392).[558] The incorporation of this group of Agni and the Maruts in the third savana attests to a certain amount of popularity of their cult. For the explanation of Agni's association with the Maruts, I may cite the testimony of TS II. 4.10.2 : *agnir vā ito vṛṣṭim ud īrayati marutaḥ sṛṣṭāṃ nayanti yadā khalu vā asāv ādityo nyaṅ raśmibhiḥ paryāvartate 'tha varṣati dhāmacchad iva khalu vai bhūtvā varṣati*, or of TBr I.1.3.12 where the same basic idea is expressed through a quite different metaphor: *maruto 'dbhir agnim atamayan.* Both the statements lead us to the rainy season in which, according to VII.103.9, *taptā́ gharmā́ aśnuvate visargám.*

This, however, does not enlighten us as to the reasons why the ritualists have accommodated this group of gods in the evening sacrifice. I would think that there was no other reason except the need to include Agni and the Maruts somewhere. It seems that originally the Maruts did not have a share in the usual Soma sacrifice; from olden times Vāyu had his place in the morning pressing and Indra in the midday pressing. Ancient cult differences might have been resolved when Indra was accommodated besides Vāyu in the morning (see Vol. I. p. 330 f.) and the Maruts were included along with Indra at noon in accordance with the custom of some families. The incorporation into the evening savana of the Āgnimārutaśastra, which being a parallel to the śastra for Indra and the Maruts should have rather found its place in the midday pressing, seems to have taken place similarly out of consideration for the usage of some other families who invoked Agni and the Maruts together in their hymns.

The case is different in the Cāturmāsya ceremonies. In each of these the Maruts are honoured with oblations and therefore they are quite prominent here. In the Vaiśvadeva, the Maruts, characterized by the epithet *svatavas*, receive a puroḍāśa. In the Varuṇapraghāsāḥ they receive without any epithet a sheep,[559] and Varuṇa a male goat and a milk-libation. In the Sākamedhāḥ they receive as *sāṃtapana* a caru at noon and as *gṛhamedhin* a caru in milk in the evening. Finally, before the Mahāhavis they receive an oblation as *krīḍinaḥ*.[560] It is hard to decide whether in these individual rites it is to do with the relics of the cult of the Manes, or whether in the eyes of the ritualists the Maruts have already become full-fledged wind gods and more specifically wind gods belonging to different seasons. The only clue to this is available in the hymns of the Vasiṣṭhas who knew these epithets of the Maruts. In VII. 59 the Maruts are invoked as *sáṃtapanāḥ* (v. 9),[561] *gṛ́hamedhāsaḥ* (v. 10),[562] and *svátavasaḥ* (v. 11) in this order. And as in the Cāturmāsyas so also here in the Vasiṣṭha hymn the invocation to Tryambaka concludes the series. From this it follows that the author of the hymn must have been familiar with the ceremonies known later as the Cāturmāsyas, although what was performed by the Vasiṣṭhas was a Soma sacrifice and although the sequence of the epithets varies.[563] But as far as I can see, any suggestion of an identification of the Maruts with the Manes is already alien to the Vasiṣṭha hymns. From this I would conclude that in this Vasiṣṭha hymn the Maruts are conceived merely as wind gods. Perhaps other scholars can make a better judgement. The present arrangement of the Cāturmāsyas gives occasion to many a doubt concerning their originality (see p. 20 f. above).[564]

J. VĀYU

While in all the Cāturmāsyas the Maruts occupy a prominent position and Vāyu merely receives a cursery attention,[565] in the ritual of the ṚV and in that of the Sūtras the Indo-Iranian god Vāyu has his place at the beginning of the Soma sacrifices as *agrepá*, as *praṇīr yajñānām* (ABr II.34.6), and receives there early in the morning a cup of pure unmixed Soma, either alone or in concert with Indra.[566] It seems that his place in the morning of the spring sacrifice, the Prātaḥsavana of which corresponds to the dawn of the year, is quite justified; for in the ṚV he is called *vasarhán*[567] and one passage (IV. 46.2) describes him as Indra's charioteer. It is his horses which, according to I. 51.10, draw Indra's chariot.[568] It is easy to recognize that the whole set of mythological conceptions which surround Vāyu differs substantially from that of the Maruts. The Maruts are never described like Vāyu as Indra's "charioteers." He is *agrepá*, the Maruts are not, and his nimble step can by no means be compared to the marching tread of the warrior tribe of the Maruts who go about heavily-armed and cause the mountains on their way to shake violently and the earth to tremble. *ojas* belongs to the Maruts (AV III.1.6) and thunder accompanies them on their way like a conqueror's drum.[569] The Maruts come from the ocean and bring rain from there. Vāyu is never associated with the ocean in the ṚV, and in the later times it is even said that he "hates" the ocean.[570] Vāyu is not Rudra's son nor Pṛśni's. Thus between the Maruts on the one hand and Vāyu on the other we can recognize a series of opposing traits, beside which the statement that Vāyu has begotten the Maruts (I. 134.4) does not carry any weight, nor does it suggest any similarity in nature. In this connection, there is one point that deserves attention and scrutiny. In some maṇḍalas which contain verses addressed to Indra-Vāyu, Indra is not invoked together with the Maruts, or at least he is drawn into another type of association. To these belong maṇḍalas IV, V, VII,[571] while the second maṇḍala occupies an intermediate position.[572] The Vasiṣṭhas dedicate three hymns to Indra or Indra-Vāyu as the case may be, but they touch upon the connection between the Maruts and Indra rather superficially (see p. 180 above) and, as is evident from VII. 59 (see p. 185 above), they associate precisely Rudra with different aspects of the Maruts. As against this, the Vaśvāmitras (likewise the Kaṇvas and several poets of the books I and X) have laid special emphasis on the Maruts' association with Indra, described prominently their assistance in battle against Vṛtra and, on the other hand, mentioned Rudra only once in the singular (see below the section, Rudra in the Ṛgveda), so much so that we can notice here also fine lines of distinction between the cults of the two clans. In other respects, I have nothing to add to what my predecessors have said on Vāyu and Vāta. The Brāhmaṇas and the Yajus texts do not add any significant trait to the picture already available. The description of the Vāta given in ṚV X. 168 agrees with the concepts of these texts. Vāyu is not tied to a place and proceeds on his course *yathāvaśam*;[573] he never comes to rest;[574] he is the swiftest of the gods[575] and follows all seasons;[576] his form is not visible.[577] Vāyu is the "breath of the gods;"[578] he is the "spirit." Occasionally troops accompany him. In TĀr I. 9.2 ff. it is eleven male forms and eleven female forms. Atmosphere is his kingdom[579] and hence trees belong to him.[580] He has the purifying power.[581] He is called *stotṛ* and *upaśrotṛ* [582] Naturally he is the cause of the rain,[583] the cause of the fire[584] and, on the other hand, he subdues the heat of the sun (TMBr IV.6.9). To him, the swift and unrestrained one, belong also animals.[585] If an already consecrated animal runs away, it is assigned to Vāyu (KŚS XXV. 9.1). Various kinds of animals are sacrificed to him. Except with Indra, he is rarely associated with other gods.[586]

Vāta is not much different from Vāyu. Macdonell (p. 81) describes the relation quite correctly thus : "Vāyu is chiefly the god and Vāta the element." To this corresponds their treatment in the ritual; there are rarely oblations prescribed for Vāta. On the occasion of the Pravargya ceremony, the Vātanāmajapas are addressed to individual winds identified with various gods,[587] and the Vātahomas are performed during the piling up of the altar.[588] According to TS II.4.9.1, the same homas are to be employed in a rain-making ceremony (of the Kārīriṣṭi): *ramayata marutaḥ śyenam āyinam iti paścādvātaṃ prati mīvati purovātam eva janayati varṣasyāvaruddhyai.*[589]

Naturally, no sharp line of demarcation can be drawn between the appellative *vātá* and the proper noun *vāyú*. For instance, just as Vāyu is the guardian of Soma (ṚV X. 85.5) so is Amṛta in Vāta's house (X. 186.3). Like Vāyu, Vāta is also drawn by horses (I. 121.12; 174.5; IV. 16.11).[590] Generally, these passages do not offer us anything that has not been observed before or that can be mythologically significant. The Veda is not familiar with notions like the one stated in *Śakuntalā*, VII, v. 7, that a wind propels the stars which revolve through it.

K. PARJANYA, ĀPAḤ[591] AND OTHER RELATED MINOR GODS

While Indra, as we have seen, was transformed from a sun god into a rain god, Parjanya, whatever his name might mean,[592] is throughout the god of the rainy season, who "prepares the rain-clouds" and enlivens the voices of the frogs. Even as late as in Pāli, *pajjunna* (*Jātaka* I.75) is the god of rain and thunder as he was in the Veda.

Hymn VII.103, which describes the commencement of the rainy season, takes us into the interior of India, into the land of the Vasiṣṭhas, and Haug's view that this hymn is not a satire[593] does not require substantiation any more. Even today we find that among the Newars of India frogs as well as the Nāgas are worshipped as deities although the time when they observe these rites differs from what is anticipated in our hymn; this difference, however, does not seem to be of any consequence.[594]

1. Āpaḥ

Like fire, water also has retained in the Veda its divineness originating from the times of the most primitive notions. Because of its influence on the growth and prosperity, its beneficent, creative and curative powers, because it washes off the taint of sin, fraud and perjury as well as the impurity of the body, and because it removes the harmful effects of evil spirits of all sorts, Indians like other peoples have placed water among the benevolent gods and worshipped it from the remotest period until the present day. It must be left to others to discuss the Indian water cult as thoroughly as Weinhold has treated the worship of springs in Germany in his article "Die Verehrung der Quellen in Deutschland."[595] For my purpose it would suffice to describe in broad outlines the worship of this element in the Vedic period.

The ṚV differentiates between waters of various kinds; it mentions the waters of the sky, those which flow, those which emanate from wells or springs or those which strive towards the ocean.[596] Distinction is made not only between the waters in the heavens and those in the atmosphere or on the earth but also between those which are beyond and which are beneath the sun.[597] Agni, Kaśyapa and Indra are said to be the offspring of the waters.[598] The gods themselves partake of the waters.[599] In manifold turns of expressions the *mātṛtamāḥ* or *amṛtasya pátnīḥ* (TS I.4.1) are described; even during the ceremonial shaving for the Dīkṣā waters are invoked "for life, longevity and fame·" More than these general turns of expressions, the ritual interests itself in the differentiation of the waters based on their source. For the water is connected with its place of origin through an innate relationship and its powers vary depending upon whether it originates from a lake or a stream, or from rain or from a cremation ground. According to the source, its employment is enjoined or prohibited. Water that collects on the cremation ground is recommended for the rite aimed at the death of the enemy, while on another occasion it is prohibited to draw from "standing water" since it belongs to Varuṇa and Varuṇa might seize the sacrifice.[600] In the Rājasūya, seventeen different kinds of waters are used obviously in order to conduct the secret powers, that are contained in them according to their sources, to the sacrificer: water from the Sarasvatī, that which flows with the stream or against it, that which flows to a side and so on.[601] With the mantra *marutām ojaḥ* the water "flowing against the stream" is drawn (in lieu of which "hailstones" can also be taken); this is supposed to symbolize the recalcitrant nature of the Maruts who represent the *viś.* In the Aśvamedha, one Homa each is offered *kūpyābhyaḥ*, *kūlyābhyaḥ*, *vikaryābhyaḥ*., etc., and these are differentiated minutely as *vahantībhyaḥ*, *parivahantībhyaḥ*, *samantaṃ vahantībhyaḥ*, *śīghraṃ vahantībhyaḥ*, *śībhaṃ vahantībhyaḥ*.[602] In the Soma sacrifice two types of waters are employed, those drawn before sunset from a river that breaks through a mountain and the Ekadhanāḥ collected early in the morning from a flowing stream (see Vol. I, pp. 301-2).

Such fine distinction is not made in minor sacrifices. It is sufficient that water is always available to accompany the various rites. It is employed to consecrate the Havis and the sacrificial vessels. When a mantra is addressed to Rudra, or when the Rakṣas, Asuras or Manes are mentioned, it is necessary to touch the waters as atonement in order to remove the evil effects.[603] Water wards off the demons,[604] hence a jar full of water is kept at the head of the woman in child-bed.[605] In funeral rites, specially noteworthy are the water libations of the Udakakarman meant for the dead; these waters are collected by the relatives during the bath or afterwards. One who takes an oath invokes the *āpo aghniyāḥ* and Varuṇa as witness.[606] Water is poured over the foot-print of the horse, which is caused to be made on the spot from which earth will be dug out for the Ukhā (TS IV.1.2 q). Many are the ways in which the ceremonies are connected with the waters of the sky, with the rain. When one sips water, one employs the words *vṛṣṭir asi, vidyut asi*. . .*jahi* (KŚS IV.15.4-5). When at the end of the sacrifice the Prastara is thrown into fire, it is addressed thus: *divaṃ gaccha tato no vṛṣṭim eraya* (TS I. 1.13 h). The sacrificial formulas *ā śrāvaya, astu śrauṣaṭ, yaja, ye yajāmahe, vaṣaṭ* can be the means for causing rain, for *ā śrāvaya* generates the wind that blows in advance, *astu śrauṣaṭ* the gathering of the clouds, *yaja* the lightning, *ye yajāmahe* the rain and *vaṣaṭ* the thunder (TS I.6.11.3-4). There are several ceremonies whose purpose is to bring rain directly. Then black animals or other black objects are chosen. For example, in TS II.1.8.5 it is a black animal with white spots and horns bent downwards: *prājāpatyaṃ kṛṣṇam ā labheta vṛṣṭikāmaḥ*. . . *kṛṣṇo bhavaty etad vai vṛṣṭyai rūpam* . . . *śabalo bhavati vidyutam evāsmai janayitvā varṣayati, avāśṛṅgo bhavati vṛṣṭim evāsmai ni yacchati*. The stipulation is expressed in a different way in the Kārīrīṣṭi,[607] where a black garment with black fringes, a black skin and a black horse are required (ĀpŚS XIX.25.16 ff.) as well as the pulp of the Kharjūra or Karīra fruits which is mixed with a black sweet syrup. This black colour is regarded as the "form of the rain."[608]

It is worth noting that in India the Manes also are associated with the rain. In the legend of Nakula, the Manes grant life to the *anāstika bhūtas*; the commentary adds *vṛṣṭidvārā* as explanation (MBh XII. 12.4). The reason seems to be the following: all the Aṣṭakās are performed in the dark half of the year.[609] According to a statement of the Brahmapurāṇa cited by Caland (*Über Totenverehrung*, p. 44 ff.), "on the thirteenth day of the dark half of Āśvina and under Maghā in the rainy season, Yama releases the Pretas and Pitaras from his abode and sends them among the human beings," and according to Atri, the Pitaras remain on the earth until the sun enters the sign of Scorpio. Thus the middle of the rainy season is the most appropriate time for the worship of the Manes. When individual families like the Aṅgiras and, as I believe, the Maruts leave the realm of the dead and join the ranks of the gods and then become the bestowers of rain, the rainy season which coincides with the beginning of the Pitṛyāṇa might have given occasion for this. Apart from the commentary cited above, I do not know any other passage which suggests that the Manes were generally regarded as rain-bestowers. But the superstition that a consecrated person should not expose himself to the rain without any covering,[610] that the sacrificial food touched by rain is not fit for sacrifice,[611] may be explained precisely from the association in which the rain and the Manes were conceived.

Just as certain animals and plants are believed to contain fire, similarly certain members of the plant and animal kingdom are close to the waters and these plants or animals are employed in the ceremonies connected with the waters : among the animals, above all, the frog (in ceremonies connected with coolness and rain,)[612] the serpent and the ant; among the plants, apart from Karīra or Kharjūra, Vetasa, Avakā, Maṇḍūkaparṇī, Dūrvā etc.[613] The association of the serpent and of the ant with the waters is well known. In his *Sarpabali*, Winternitz gives examples showing that the serpent is thought of in intimate association with water among all the peoples and that even today. it is worshipped mostly near ponds and trees. In the popular belief of India, the ant has several kinds of significance which are not always definable.[614] It can be seen from various passages that the ant is thought of in association with the subterranean waters also. When the ants were to bite through the chord of the Makha's bow, they expressed the wish, *yatra kva ca khanāma tad apo 'bhitṛṇadāmeti,* and hence wherever they dig they strike water.[615]

In the ṚV itself, i.e., in hymns I.23.16 ff., III.33; VI.50; VII.47,49; X.9,30,75 and in some other passages of less significance, invocations are made to waters of all kinds and particularly to streams. Although the worship of streams does not come directly into the forefront in the Vedic hymns and in their cult, yet the belief in the curative and atoning power of the waters pervades althrough the ritual literature. Even in the hair-parting ceremony one mentions the name of the stream on the banks of which one resides (*Rituallliteratur*, pp. 43-44). ṚV X.17, and more particularly v. 10, alludes to a purificatory bath in the flood waters of the Sarasvatī. We do not know if there were sacred bathing places. But the wide popularity and the reputation of the tīrthas in the later periods—we may refer to the *Anuśāsanaparvan* (MBh XIII.25)—demonstrate that it is not improbable that in the Vedic times also there might have existed specially favoured holy places on the banks of those rivers which were highly esteemed at that time.

Of the gods, Apāṃ napāt is specially associated with the waters, apart from Indra, sun, moon, wind etc. I have set forth my views on Apāṃ napāt in Vol. I, pp. 81 f., 231 ff., and they have not been shaken by the subsequent writings which to a certain extent contradict one another.[616] I would be inclined to see in him rather exclusively a water-demon than the god of lightning about whom one cannot say *yáṃ víprāsa īlate adhvaréṣu*[617] without doing violence to the concepts of the whole ritual. But an exclusive association with the waters will not account for the fact that a, by no means original, luminous aspect is added to Apāṁ napāt, and that in India the moon is a god of the waters and his nature is regarded in the entire Indian literature (and not only there) as *rasātmaka*. On this, compare, apart from what has been said before, also *Sūryasiddhānta* XII.24.

2. Ahi Budhnya

While Apāṃ napāt has become a god of the waters only through an indirect way and even the name makes him only a "son" and not the "lord" of the waters, we can recognize a direct water-demon in another being, namely Ahi budhnya. He is mentioned rarely and that too in verses of no consequence in the company of other gods. But his association with the waters and with the "deep of the waters" becomes at once clear from the name itself.[618]

The ritual does not offer any useful information about the nature of Ahi budhnya, whom it mentions often in the context of the fires. We find him in an address to the Gārhapatya fire that will not be used any more.[619] Just as the serpent lays aside his slough and appears rejuvinated, so does a new fire take the place of an old one here. The invocation in this case is based merely on this symbolism and not on any innate identity between the fire and Ahi budhnya. For the period of the ṚV the oft-repeated association between the "dragon of the deep" and the streams is the decisive factor and, I think, here we have a relic of the cult of the springs whose mysterious gushing out gave occasion to the creation of Ahi budhnya. Although it is occasionally sacrificed to "the celestial serpents," the serpent is a chthonic being and "this earth" is regarded as the mother of the serpents.[620] The mythical serpents like Śeṣa (cf. e.g. Bhartṛhari, I.35), Kumuda (*Raghuvaṃśa* XVI.76: *antarhradavāsin*), Vāsuki to whom oblations are offered "downwards" when a house is being constructed (GGS IV.7.41) are inhabitants of the deep.[621]

On *aja ekapād*—Macdonell (pp. 73-74) has collected all the views on him—I will not express any opinion. The meagre amount of the available material makes me abandon any such attempt. It is striking that he is often invoked beside Ahi budhnya. Is he an antithesis to the latter ? I think that Brunnhofer's view that he is the Pole Star[622] should not be dismissed out of hand as has happened. No great value should be attached to the verses in TBr III.1.2.8.

3. Trita

Until now it has not been possible to define Trita more precisely. Nor do I think that the nature of the passages which mention him would permit an understanding of this prehistoric name. Macdonell has collated conscientiously all the passages and employed them in explaining Trita as god of lightning.[623] But he is not right and the identification between Apāṃ napāt and Trita is not proved. Besides Macdonell, mention must be made of Bloomfield who sees in Trita "the scapegoat of the gods"[624] and Johansson.[625] It does not seem possible to join the scattered relics of the Trita mythology, which continue their existence in stray hymns as vague allusions, into a complete picture. Hence I would limit myself to some aspects which are not sufficiently appreciated. The name *āptya* attributed to Trita in many passages might go back etymologically to *ap*; it is this etymology which gave occasion to the interpretation as god of lightning and which could have aetiologically brought about the stories to be found in TBr III.2.8.10, 11; MBh IX.36.8; XII.13.174 (341.46) and in Sāyaṇa's commentary on ṚV I.105.[626] But in my opinion *āptya* is an ancient proper noun which is ascribed to Trita in the same way as Indra received the designation Kauśika or Gautama and Agni the epithet Aṅgiras. In the ṚV as well as in the later times, the plural form *āptyāḥ* is the name of an entire class of beings—gods or men—who stand in ABr VIII. 12. 4 next to the Sādhyas and between the Vasus, Rudras, Ādityas on the one side and the Maruts and Aṅgiras on the other.[627] Further in the same text (ABr VIII. 12. 14) the Āptyas and Sādhyas are assigned as deities to the same *dhruvā madhyamā pratiṣṭhā diś* in which some kings of the Kurupañcālas, Vaśas and Uśīnaras are consecrated as kings. The ritual also knows their name and enjoins that water libations should be poured for the three Āptyas, namely Trita, Dvita and Ekata, to the north of the Vihāra.[628] The ŚBr (I.2.3.1 ff.) relates that they sprang from the spittle of Agni who, resenting that he had been taken away from the waters, spat upon these waters.[629] The Āptyas, who were thus generated, roamed about with Indra, as a brahmin follows the king, and took upon themselves the guilt when Indra slew Viśvarūpa. When the water with which the dish has been rinsed is poured for them, says the ŚBr, the sacrifice wipes its sin off upon them. The notion that Trita takes the sin and other evil effects upon himself is an ancient one and is known already to ṚV VIII.47.13 ff., howsoever one might interpret the origin and significance of the story. However, in evaluating the individual names, it is worth noting that the ṚV knows only *trita* and *dvita* and the Avesta only *thrita*. Hence *dvita* and *ekata* seem to be freely invented names,[630] formed in analogy to *trita* in order to have a plurality of Āptya names.[631] *Trita āptya* is not the Āptya but an Āptya, that is to say, he is a progenitor of the clan, the most eminent of this class, just as Agni is an Aṅgiras. In ṚV X.120.6, Indra, the ally and friend of Trita, is also included in the group as *inátama āptyá āptyánām.* Āptya cannot be separated from the Avestan Āthwya[632] and Trita is identical with the Iranian Thrita, who is regarded as a healer and who received a thousand healing plants from Ahuramazda. However, as we know since long, the Veda and the Avesta are not entirely parallel in this respect. Vīvahvant was the first man who pressed the Soma and Yima was his son. Āthwya pressed next, Thraētaona was his son. Thrita was the third presser and Urvākhšaya and Kərəsāspa were his sons. Thus Indian mythology and the Iranian one differ from one another in their genealogies insofar as the latter distinguishes between Āthwya and Thrita-Trita. But Āthwya's son Thraētaona and Trita resemble each other through their deeds because the former killed the three-headed Aži Dahāka and the latter *viśvarūpa triśīrṣan.* However, from the fact that Thraētaona is called *vīsō puthrō āthwyānōiš vīsō sūrayå* elsewhere (Yašt V. 33; IX.13; XV. 23), we may conclude that in the Avesta also *āthwya* was a clan name as in the Veda.[633] Trita and Thrita have the common attribute of being Soma pressers. Just as Thrita presses as the third man in the Avesta so is Trita a sacrificer in whose house Indra is received as a guest,[634] and the word has become, like Vivasvat, a honorific name for the ordinary sacrificer.[635] Hence, *vis-à-vis* the ancient line of sacrificers in the Avesta, namely Vīvahvant, Āthwya and Thrita, we can cite from the Veda at least Vivasvat and Trita; *āptya,* on the other hand, is never used in the ṚV independently in the singular.[636]

I do not see how we could proceed beyond this point, namely that there existed an ancient prehistoric clan of the Āptyas to which Thraētaona in Iran and Trita in India belonged. But we cannot say whether Trita was originally a god worshipped in the clan of the Āptyas and later became a hero, or conversely whether he ascended to heaven from the earth as the progenitor of the Āptyas. Here the legends of the gods and heroes merge into one another inseparably. If we were to accept the first possibility, the interpretation of Trita as an old celestial god would seem most acceptable.

IX.37.4: *sá tritásyā́dhi sā́navi pávamāno arocayat|*
jāmíbhiḥ sū́ryaṃ sahá||[637]

Or if he was a human being originally, then it was the ancestor cult of the Āptyas which invented out of its name—as others did out of Manu—a progenitor who, like Kutsa and Kaṇva, received Indra's help[638] and fought the same enemies as Indra did;[639] according to the legend in the Brāhmaṇas, on the other hand, he took Indra's sin upon himself. If we were to adhere throughout to the etymology, then we would have a clan which traced its origin from the water, as the Bhṛgus from the flames of Prajāpati's seed or the Aṅgiras from the "coals." The reminiscence of the clan is preserved in certain water libations offered to them in sacrifice. We may regard these as a kind of libations to the Manes, the original significance of which has been forgotten.

CHAPTER EIGHT

VIṢṆU, PŪṢAN AND LESSER DEITIES

A. VIṢṆU

In relation to the gods who enliven the foreground of Vedic mythology, namely Indra, Soma and Varuṇa, Viṣṇu is quite unimportant although in the later periods he attains precedence over all the others and becomes the most popular deity of India. Of all the etymologies which sought to explain the name, Bloch's attempt to derive the word from *vi* (*+ṣṇu*), as *jiṣṇu* is derived from *ji*, seems to be most reliable. This etymology throws light at the same time on the original nature and significance of the god. His symbol was the bird Garuḍa (*garutmat*) probably even from the very beginning (it became his vehicle only at a later stage).[1] I do not see any connection with the bird that robs the Soma, about which Charpentier speaks.[2] These belong to different sets of myths. Otherwise, Viṣṇu would have found a better place in the Soma sacrifice (see p. 204 ff. below) and his name would have occurred when the Soma thief is mentioned. It should also be kept in mind that in the ṚV mead (*madhu*) is not called Soma when it is connected with Viṣṇu.[3] A scrutiny of the Vedic tradition clearly indicates the distance between the Vedic period and the classical one. Maṇḍalas II, III and IV mention Viṣṇu only seven times in seven hymns, maṇḍala V eight times in five hymns, maṇḍala VI seven times in seven hymns, maṇḍala VII sixteen times in eight hymns, and maṇḍala VIII sixteen times in thirteen hymns.[4] This weak emphasis, which changes considerably in books VII and VIII only, is illustrated by the insignificant content of the majority of passages. The three verses in book II, for instance, have almost nothing to say.[5] With the exception of books I and VII which contain independent hymns to Viṣṇu, there is no other book from which we can glean that Viṣṇu was regarded as an animated energy which governed the thoughts and beliefs and was the favourite god of the Vedic tribes somewhat like Indra.

It does not follow from this that Viṣṇu must have been younger than Varuṇa or Indra. Occasional allusions betray that on the contrary there existed outside the Vedic clans a well-developed Viṣṇu mythology which through specific traditions differed manifestly from the other cults. And this mythology gradually infiltrated—at first only some catchwords—the traditions of the Vedic tribes. An instructive example is the Indra-Vṛtra myth. Here Viṣṇu is actually a dispensable element. In the majority of the passages Indra stands alone in the battlefield; in rare cases Viṣṇu also enters the arena. The three strides which he makes, e.g. in IV.18.11; VIII.12.27; 52.3, for the sake of Indra are quite superfluous here; these were taken over from the sagas connected with Viṣṇu and incorporated in the battle against Vṛtra in order to bring these two gods together for reasons that seemed important to the respective worshippers. Also the hymns which describe the friendship between the two gods[6] allude with this more to the friendship between their worshippers or to the adaptability of the Vedic theologians who were ready for compromise and suggest, through their lack of vivacity, that it was admittedly a difficult task to reconcile between these two gods. For example, VI.69 is a cosmogonic glorification of the two but has no mythological value. In v. 5, the strides of Viṣṇu are transferred to Indra, and the poet, while invoking the two for the Soma sacrifice, has nothing further to say than *ná párā jigye katarā́ś canaínóḥ | índraś ca viṣṇo yád ápaspṛdhethāṃ tredhā́ sahásraṃ ví tád airayethām* (v. 8); this is an allusion, as it appears, to a priestly legend which we find in TS VII.1.5.5; ABr VI.15.10 ff.; MS II.5.3 (50.51).[7] In the Vedic period, in spite of the assurances of the poets to the contrary, Indra needed Viṣṇu still less than the latter needed Indra. This is evident from the legends of the Brāhmaṇa literature cited on p. 137 above. Thus in TS VI.5.1.1 Vṛtra surrenders the Ukthya to his enemy and as Indra raises the thunderbolt for the third time Viṣṇu steps behind him and says *jahi*. In TS II.4.12 it is related that Indra cannot raise the thunderbolt and calls Viṣṇu to help him. We should note the contradiction between the later views and those of the ṚV. The later concepts actually are aimed only at suppressing Indra in order to gain space for Viṣṇu.[8] The change in emphasis begins in some passages of the R̥V. In ŚBr XIV.1.1.5 Viṣṇu appears as the *śreṣṭha* among the gods, in ABr I. 30.19 as *devānāṃ dvārapaḥ.*[9] The transformation is so complete in the subsequent periods that in a legend of the MBh (see p. 141 above) Indra, overcome by fear, hastens to Viṣṇu and receives his energy from him. In another story Viṣṇu advises the gods to make peace with Vr̥tra; he himself would enter invisibly into the thunderbolt. Here Viṣṇu has evolved into the principal character who stands above Indra and offers counsel to the disconcerted gods: again an instructive example for the history of the evolution of myths. Under these circumstances the state of affairs in individual maṇḍalas acquires greater significance. Whenever Indra and Viṣṇu are associated in individual cases, without anything essential being said about them, then we have manifestly before us not the product of a nature myth which had gone through an evolutionary process but an artificial product of cultural and religious history, which emerged through mutual influences of contiguous cults. It is hard to determine where the settlements were of the tribe which spread the Viṣṇu cult. I do not wish to set a high value on the fact that Viṣṇu is called *girikṣít* in the R̥V and is associated with the "mountain" in the YV as Sūrya is associated with the sky and Varuṇa with the waters.[10]

There is another legend which is not so transparent, in which we can see only vague outlines and which defies explanation. This legend also unites the two gods in a common exploit. This is the Varāha myth, the fragments of which are preserved primarily in book VIII, i.e. in the traditions of the Kaṇva family.[11] I hold that any attempt to reconstruct this legend is in vain; I do not wish to express an opinion either on its origin or on its significance.[12] As elsewhere it is possible here also that the legend was transferred from one god to the other and the human fantasy with its fondness for enlarging upon the myths has attempted to connect the two gods with one another. After all, we see that in the words of VI.69.5: *sómasya máda urú cakramā the* such an individual trait as Viṣṇu's "wide strides" are transferred to Indra.

In other cases it is Viṣṇu who presses the Soma for Indra or offers it to him,[13] or along with Mitra-Varuṇa praises Indra.

Here we can clearly see the predominence of the Indra worshippers who make Viṣṇu a Soma presser, while the pressing of the drink is generally alien to the Viṣṇu cult.

1. Viṣṇu Mythology in the Ṛgveda

In the ṚV there are only a few hymns that are addressed to Viṣṇu alone (I.22.16 ff.; 154-156: VII.100) ; nevertheless they offer a well-drawn portrait of the god; these hymns are not rich in characteristic traits or myths but sufficient to show that Viṣṇu was no longer at the preliminary stage of mythological evolution as Savitṛ was.

The most famous trait in the cycle of his sagas is "the three steps." I am of one view with Bergaigne, Oldenberg and others[14] that these steps do not denote the sunrise, zenith and sunset; nor do they denote as a rule the path "across from horizon to horizon" as Hopkins believes,[15] but the three realms of earth, atmosphere and sky. This is borne out, I think, by the imitation of the "three steps" by the sacrificer (or occasionally by other persons as well) who makes these steps in such a way that Viṣṇu's steps are represented either from the sky to the earth or the reverse.[16] Viṣṇu made the first step across the earth, the second in the atmosphere and the third in the sky.[17] However, some passages locate all the three steps on the earth: I. 155.4;[18] VII.100.3;[19] these seem to contradict the former passages to some extent. This contradiction can be explained only by assuming different traditions which were incorporated sometimes even in the same hymn (I.22,155) or through "mythological multiplications" as Bergaigne (II, p. 119 ff.) explains them.

As I have stated at length already, the ritual is made up of the customs of different tribes and clans and can be regarded in a way as an artificial product because of its rational arrangement of all practices. Viṣṇu's steps were a popular trait of the cycle of his sagas and hence were included in the ritual by the redactors. The number three is expressed in other ways also. In the majority of cases where a puroḍāśa oblation is offered to Viṣṇu three kapālas are employed for this.[20] In TS I.7.11 the "three syllables" and the "three worlds" are assigned to him. Viṣṇu's steps are glorified in the ṚV also. It is said that all beings dwell in them;[21] he measured the earth with them; his three steps or footprints are full of honey and inexhaustible.[22] Reverence to the footprints is shown most distinctly in hymns I.22 and 154. Worship of the footprint, which has become very common in the later cults, is generally unknown to the Vedic period.[23] "Viṣṇu's step" is a new element in the Vedic cult and is taken over by it from the circle of the Viṣṇuites. Of interest are particularly some verses which speak of the *paramám padám* and with this reveal the notions of the Viṣṇu-worshippers of that time about the life after death. It is regarded as the abode where the pious rejoice, where there is a well of honey and where many-horned cows roam.[24] It shines down brightly and the pious worshippers wish to attain it.[25] The wise see it for ever like an eye fixed in the sky (I.22.20).

I.22.21: *tád víprāso vipanyávo jāgṛvā́ṃsaḥ sám indhate |*
víṣṇor yát paramáṃ padám ||

takes us still further. It states that the singers light the *paramáṃ padáṃ* vigilantly and are regarded at the same time as the guardians of the celestial fire. Enough attention does not seem to have been paid to this remark. For, it recalls that Viṣṇu conjointly with the fire god is regarded as the guardian of the *dīkṣā*[26] and is the lord of the *tapas*.[27] Thus there seems to exist a connection between these ideas and our verse.

Neither these ideas nor the rest of the material allow us to accept as absolutely correct the widespread explanation that Viṣṇu was a sun god. But this is better than the other theory which sees a god "strider" in him, for the second theory is based only on a single though oft-stressed trait and does not reckon with the possibility, indeed the probability, of a long process of evolution which had preceded and of which the three steps remained behind as a sediment. Also it cannot explain Viṣṇu's association with the *tapas* and the Manes, with the sacrifice, with the Havirdhāna cart and so on. Macdonell (p. 38 f.) has collected systematically all that is in favour of the first interpretation. Besides I. 22.21, I think, I. 154.6; 155.6;[28] AV XIII. 2.31 are particularly of importance, further the fact that all that can be said otherwise of Viṣṇu can best be understood from the sun-theory.

Of the other constituents of the Viṣṇu mythology, the saga that he "firmly fixed the earth with pegs around it"[29] is worth noting because it is a primitive concept and is undoubtedly ancient. Just as Pūṣan possesses a series of specific epithets that are exclusive to him, so does Viṣṇu who is characterized by the obscure words *śipiviṣṭa* and *nikhurya-pa*, *nibhūya-pa* (TS VII. 3.15).[30] In the ṚV, we do not find many epithets of the later period like *śaṅkhacakrapāṇi*, *dharaṇīdhara* etc. *nārasiṃha*, *nārāyaṇa*, *vāsudeva* occur for the first time in the TĀr (X. 1.6-7 and 11.1). The ṚV does not inform us whether it is already familiar with the saga that Viṣṇu "lies in the waters for four months," that he cut off the head of Rāhu, that he drinks nectar and so on.

The later Vedic literature does not conceive Viṣṇu as a god of large physical stature but as a dwarf. Possessing magic powers, the gods have the gift of assuming any form they like. Indra transforms himself into a ram, also into a horse's hair or into a Sālāvṛkī which, in the interest of the gods, runs thrice around the earth and wins it back from the Asuras (TS VI.2.4.4). Viṣṇu becomes a dwarf.[31] "As big as a thumb,"[32] he roams about the earth to kill the Rakṣas'. We find this obviously very popular story of the dwarf Viṣṇu in the *Rāmāyaṇa* (Muir, OST, IV.114) etc., even as early as in the ŚBr (I. 2.5.4) where the Asuras, engaged in a conflict with the Devas, promise to give the latter so much *yāvad evaiṣa viṣṇur abhiśete*. This motif is continued in the ritual when a *vāmana* is chosen as the sacrificial victim for Viṣṇu or as the dakṣiṇā for the priest.[33] Johansson is of the view that "originally Viṣṇu himself is firstly a *pitar* or an *anima* and secondly a higher *pitar* or *anima*, so to say, the basic essence of the *pitaras*" (*Solfågeln*, p. 9).[34] But surely we do not find any evidence for this in the oldest tradition which speaks of the *padáṃ paramáṃ* with its well of honey; we must assume that in the later period new accretions were added to the Viṣṇu cult.

2. Viṣṇu in the Ritual

In the ritual literature we encounter often the formula: *yajño vai viṣṇuḥ*.[35] It is said that the sacrifice assumed the form of Viṣṇu and fled into the earth.[36] This designation of Yajña as

Viṣṇu does not seem to be justified in the present state of the ritual where Viṣṇu's name of course occurs very often during minor offerings or in symbolical comparisons but never occupies a central position in the sacrifice. This identification might owe its origin to other groups of Brahmanical theologians than are known to us, i.e. the Viṣṇuites among whom Viṣṇu occupied the centre of worship.

Viṣṇu receives an oblation in the New and Full Moon sacrifice where the Upāṁśuyāja can be offered to him.[37] The second series of the ten offerings called by the name Tākṣṇī begins with an oblation to Viṣṇu (ŚŚS II.3.14). On other occasions also there are sacrifices prescribed for him, for example, during the Ātithya-iṣṭi of the Soma sacrifice which is dedicated to him,[38] before the Upasad,[39] during the Udavasānīyā of the same (ŚŚS VIII.13.1). Of the Aikādaśina animals one belongs to Viṣṇu[40] and one to Indra-Viṣṇu.[41] Elsewhere distinction is made between three types of Viṣṇu: Viṣṇu, Viṣṇu Urukrama, Viṣṇu Uruga, and these are characterized by the offering of different animals.[42]

What is striking is the scanty attention paid to Viṣṇu during the actual Soma libations as we have already stated. We have cited earlier those passages where Viṣṇu appears like a sacrificer who presses the Soma for Indra. It is true that at several places in the ninth book he is mentioned beside the gods, particularly next to Indra, as a partaker of the Soma draught.[43] On the fourth day of the Aśvamedha, the section intended for recitation begins with the words, *somo vaiṣṇavaḥ* (ŚŚS XVI. 2.10). It is said in ŚBr IV. 3.5.8: *viṣṇa urugāyaiṣa te somas taṃ rakṣasva mā tvā dabhann iti yajño vai viṣṇus tad yajñāyaivaitat paridadāti.*[44] But this statement has no other purpose than to designate Viṣṇu as the guardian of the sacrifice and of the Havis;[45] for in the ritual it is indeed very rare that Viṣṇu takes part in the Soma drink. I have noticed only from ĀpŚS XIV.1.8 ff. that the three rounds of the Ukthya belong to Indra-Varuṇa, Indra-Bṛhaspati and Indra-Viṣṇu[46] and the mantra with which the Ukthya is drawn during the morning savana (ĀpŚS XII.15.11) contains, besides Indra's name, also that of Viṣṇu.[47] The Brāhmaṇa alludes to the help rendered by Viṣṇu to Indra.[48] Hence, probably Viṣṇu is introduced into the Soma sacrifice only through Indra. The little attention paid to the god is all the more striking since during the Soma sacrifice Viṣṇu is not at all mentioned in the verses, but he is drawn into association in this sacrifice, as in others,[49] with various implements, particularly with the Havirdhāna cart.[50] At the individual parts of the cart or of the hut, mantras are recited which contain Viṣṇu's name (ĀpŚS XI. 8.1ff.). Offerings are made on both the wheel tracks of the cart with verses addressed to Viṣṇu (ĀpŚS XI.6.13). From this I can only infer that the Soma offerings to Viṣṇu were not usual among his worshippers from the very beginning. In this I am supported by the fact that in certain cases where one wishes to counteract the Soma sacrifice, it is recommended that one should offer, apart from an Ājyabhāga for Sarasvatī and a caru for Bṛhaspati, one puroḍāśa each to Agni-Viṣṇu and that too upon eight, eleven and twelve kapālas in the morning, midday and evening savanas respectively.[51] Instead of being given a prominent place at the centre of the sacrifice, Viṣṇu was relegated along with Agni to the beginning of the Soma sacrifice when the Dīkṣā was added to the sacrifice as a prelude.[52]

Agni and Viṣṇu are worshipped often outside the Dīkṣā of the Soma sacrifice also. As early as in the AV VII.29.1 they are spoken of as guarding *ghṛtásya gúhyasya nā́ma.* One who wishes to practise or avert witchcraft is advised to offer a puroḍāśa for the two gods.[53] Generally in the sacrifices for the two gods eleven (8+3) kapālas are required; "eight" is the sacred number of Agni and "three" of Viṣṇu.

In the ritual also Viṣṇu is closest to Indra of all the gods. Apart from the common invocations to the two gods which we know from the ṚV, there are sacrifices of various types; for example, an Aikādaśina animal, one of the Ukthyaparyāyas, the Ukrānti sacrifice (ŚŚS XIV.71.1 ff.) etc.[54] There are rare instances of Viṣṇu's association with Varuṇa for which there is no inner reason and which can be seen as a provisional attempt to bring these two different groups together.[55] Even the existence of single verses addressed to Viṣṇu-Varuṇa[56] cannot obscure the fact that this association is a product of theological origin which had no past and which apparantly did not find a response in the subsequent evolution either. One can very well speak of patch-work associations. Viṣṇu's relation to the Maruts is too vague to be discussed here.[57] The connection between Sinīvālī and Viṣṇu which occurs only outside the ṚV[58] is based, as Johansson has demonstrated, on his energy which protects the creation. Hence, I believe that Güntert is justified when he "conceives the solar hero at the same time as a phallic vegetation-demon" and points to ṚV I. 155.3; 156.2; VII. 36.9, besides those cited above.

B. PŪṢAN AND SARASVATĪ

The elements of the Pūṣan cult can still be recognized in their distinct individuality in the ṚV. Here we are dealing with a god of herdsmen, whose worship like that of Viṣṇu was loosely incorporated into the framework of the Soma sacrifice and continued its existence there as one of the many appendages with which the ritual abounds. Soma libations are never offered to Pūṣan. The *karambha*, a gruel made of barley grains, which was apparently connected with his cult from ancient times, followed him into the Soma ritual. In the ṚV a karambha is offered to Indra "accompanied by Pūṣan,"[59] thus clearly indicating that the god who had been once independent was already included in the Indra worship. Following the ritual practice of the Viśvāmitras, the Śrauta Sūtras enjoin among the Savanīya Puroḍāśas a karambha for *indra pūṣaṇvat.*[60] On other occasions we find also a caru in the place of karambha,[61] but our sources leave no doubt that the karambha-meal, taken over from the daily life of the herdsmen, is the foremost characteristic of Pūṣan in the ritual.[62] In the later times this has led to the fact that he was given the name *adantaka*,[63] an epithet which obviously has an aetiological meaning and serves to justify the offering of karambha to the *prapiṣṭabhāga*,[64] the origins of which practice are no more understood.

Animal sacrifices also were made to Pūṣan. During the Aikādaśinapaśus he receives (as ten other gods do) his animal.[65] TĀr III.10.3 mentions a female goat for Tvaṣṭṛ and a sheep for Pūṣan. In connection with the Aśvamedha, TS V.5. 12 states: *āraṇyo 'jo nakulaḥ śakā* and 6.12 : *tisraḥ śyāmā vaśāḥ pauṣṇiyaḥ.*[66] As early as in the ṚV, the male goat for Pūṣan precedes the horse during its sacrifice and announces the sacrifice to the gods (I.162.3-4). But generally animal sacrifices for him are rare.

The descriptions of the ṚV reveal Pūṣan as herdsman who protects his animals from injury and from getting lost,[67] who follows the cows and protects the horses,[68] who as *pathas pati* knows all the paths,[69] drives off the highwaymen and knows the places where the cattle-thieves hide their booty or where treasures are buried.[70]

Neither the horse, still less the elephant, is assigned to Pūṣan. To him belong the cows which are under his protection,[71] the sheep for which he weaves their woollen garment,[72] and above all, the female goat which draws his chariot.[73] Only in one passage the camel is associated with him.[74] Here also the reminiscence of a god is preserved, of a god of a tribe of cattle-breeders who saw their patron deity in him. He was thought of as having a beard[75] and braided hair.[76] The "goad" was placed in his hand,[77] in I.42.6 a golden axe (*hiraṇyavāśī*) and the dagger (*ā́rā*) with which he pierces the hearts of the enemies.[78]

Of special interest is verse VI.54.1. Here Pūṣan is implored to bring a man who knows, and would show the hiding places and say, "here it is." Here the ṚV alludes to a custom and profession which flourishes in India even today. Those "men who knew" of the ṚV are identical with the ancient professional class of the Khoji-s who have preserved themselves till now. On these Khojis Balfour[79] observes thus: "Khoji, a tracker. In the Panjab, professional trackers are employed to trace stolen cattle, by their footprints. . . They do this even for a hundred miles, and their success. . . is very extraordinary, the Panjab Khoji is similar to the Paggi of Gujerat . . ."[80]

Statistical analysis demonstrates that the sixth maṇḍala is the actual seat of the Pūṣan cult which was specially cultivated by the Bharadvājas and the tribe of their native land.[81] In hymns 53-58[82] (to which we may add 48.15-19 as well) we have a small Pūṣansaṃhitā before us which describes the nature of the god quite vividly. It is hardly accidental that in the same book which mentions the much-maligned Paṇis with special emphasis the god of the herdsmen who guards over the herds with goad and dagger plays such a prominent role. Hymn VI.53 is full of special hatred towards the Paṇis: it mentions the enemies four times in its ten Gāyatrī verses. This hymn must be regarded as an accompaniment to a magic as ŚŚS XIV. 22.4 ff. and the *Kauśika Sūtra* describe it.[83] The words employed in the hymn: *ví mṛdho jahi, pári tṛndhi, ví tuda, ārikha, kikirā́ kṛṇu* are *vacāṃsi krūrāṇi*, which usually characterize hostile magic.[84]

In relation to the sixth book with its frequent references to Pūṣan (36 times in 16 hymns), other family books lag much behind. In book II we find Pūṣan thrice only (with the exception of II.40 where Soma-Pūṣan are mentioned), in book III five times in four hymns, in book IV three times in three hymns, (not once in vocative), in book V eight times in six hymns, in book VII six times in six hymns, and in book VIII six times in four hymns. He is mentioned more frequently in book I and especially in book X, whereas the AV (provided the verses are not identical with those of the ṚV)[85] mentions him mostly in indifferent enumerations.

These hymns hand down to us certain traits which must be regarded as the distinctive features of the cycle of sagas which once surrounded the god Pūṣan.

1. The sagas that Pūṣan found "the king on the variegated grass" and drove him back like some lost animal (I.23.13-14),[86]

2. that he loads "the golden wheel of the sun" upon a matted (?) bull,[87]

3. that he is called "his sister's lover" or "his mother's suitor"[88] and that "the gods gave him Sūryā,"[89]

4. and that with his golden ships which move in the air he goes on an embassy to Sūrya.[90]

In my view these allusions are the relics of an extensive Pūṣan mythology which we cannot reconstruct any more.[91] We should not neglect to mention that in a verse of the tenth book, which according to ĀśvŚS VI.10.19 should be recited at the death of a Dīkṣita, Pūṣan appears also as a knowing guide for the dead out of this world.[92] Just as in the bridal hymn (X.85.26) he conducts *hastagṛhya* the bride out of the house[93] so the knower and lord of the paths here is the guide into the kingdom of the dead. In the Aśvamedha, as we have stated, a goat precedes the horse as "Pūṣan's share" and according to AV IX.5.16 it was also a goat which showed the Aṅgiras the way to the world of the gods.[94]

Now the question is how do we explain this god who was introduced into Vedic mythology from a tribe of herdsmen? There have always been attempts to see the sun god in him, and Perry shares this view. Although it cannot be fully substantiated, this theory seems to me to be better than any other, certainly better than the one propounded by Oldenberg who seeks to see primarily "the god of the paths" in him. The ṚV is not completely devoid of allusions to Pūṣan's nature. As I believe, he is undoubtedly a sun god already in hymn II.40 where he is associated with Soma in the dual.[95] One may object to this, saying that the composers of this book know otherwise very little about this clan-god of the goatherds and mention him only in three indifferent passages (II.1.6; 31.4; 41.15) and that therefore the possibility is not completely ruled out that here we have a concept which is not original. The sixth book has the first claim to be consulted on the nature of Pūṣan. Of the epithets attributed to him in this book, only *āghṛṇi*[96] is conspicuous. This epithet is most appropriate for Agni or the sun (cf. IX. 107. 20 : *ghṛṇā́ tápantaṃ sū́ryam*) and in almost all passages Sāyaṇa explains it as related to *dīpti*.[97] According to AV VII.9.2 he constantly moves to and fro along his paths between heaven and earth. I do not see why we should not attach value to this epithet coupled with II.40. I think that this epithet is all the more important since it does not occur in the later literature—only once in the AV (VII.9.2 = ṚV X.17.5) and later, as far as I know, not at all—and thus gives the impression of belonging to a remote antiquity. The solar nature of Pūṣan is expressed in the vague quality which he shares with Agni and Sūrya, namely of being the lover of his sister, i.e. Sūryā or Uṣas.[98] When in the circle of the Pūṣan worshippers there occurs an additional synonym that he is the "suitor of his mother," this is accounted for through the versatile nature of the relationship between Sūrya and Uṣas. When we proceed with the assumption that Pūṣan is a name of the sun god who developed in this form in a clan of herdsmen led by one of the Bharadvājas, then the other qualities attributed to him can easily be explained, whereas it is hardly possible to account for them if he were originally a "lord of the paths." Various types of gods can evolve into "lords of paths" but, as the Veda demonstrates, the gods of light have had a special tendency for this type of evolution.[99]

1. Pūṣan and Indra

I have cursorily touched upon Pūṣan's relation to the Aśvins. This seems to be an invention of the later mythology which made it its business to unite different gods who had been originally separate and firmly rooted in local cults. Examples of this nature are the artificially drawn associations of Indra with Varuṇa and with Mitra-Varuṇa and of Viṣṇu with Indra. This is true of Indra-Pūṣan as well. Even though the two are connected with one another as early as in the sixth maṇḍala and Pūṣan is styled Indra's "brother (VI. 55.5), yet this is a loose inorganic association that became possible through the obliteration of the basic concepts of the two gods. A hymn addressed to them in the sixth book reveals at once the superficial nature of this association. There is no better illustration for this than the remark in VI.57.4: When Indra, the most powerful, led away the flowing mighty waters, Pūṣan was present there."[100] Thus in other verses also, provided they state anything at all, the separateness of the two is fully maintained.[101] Where Indra and Pūṣan make a joint appearance in the ritual, it is the goat which was taken over from the Pūṣan cult that is sacrificed to the two gods. It seems as though the goat, like the karambha, was also transferred in the ritual to Indra who was gradually gaining ground. A goat sacrifice for Indra could not have been an original feature.[102]

2. Sarasvatī

In Sarasvatī the worship of a sacred river attains its fullest expression. She is the most motherly and the most divine of the rivers. She grants progeny (II.41.16 ff.), nourishes with her breast (I.164.49). Her designation as *saptásvasṛ, saptáthī síndhumātṛ* (VII.3.6) raises her above a number of similar streams in esteem.[103] Sarasvatī's association with Pūṣan is based on a historical factor.

1. The worshippers of Pūṣan lived in the vicinity of the Sarasvatī. Book VI takes us to the banks of the western Sarasvatī and book VII, on the other hand, to the area of Kurukṣetra, to the holy Sarasvatī of the middle country. There at the Arghandab in Arachosia, Vadhryaśva's son Divodāsa fought against the Paṇis, Pārāvatas and Bṛsaya, and the river of the country "who consumed the Paṇis" (VI.61) stood by his side as a guardian deity. In the same book which thinks of the Paṇis with special hatred we see Pūṣan "who pierces the Paṇis" at the centre of the cult, and he is mentioned once in the Sarasvatī hymn also (VI.61.6.). Pūṣan and Sarasvatī occur side by side elsewhere too: VI.49.7 Sarasvatī; 8 Pūṣan;[104] X.17.3-6 Pūṣan; 7-9 Sarasvatī; 65.1 (Vāyuḥ) Pūṣā Sarasvatī. Their association has been continued especially in liturgical texts.[105] The fact of the association itself is not without significance and goes back, as I think, to the ancient historical circumstances as they are suggested in book VI. No objection can be raised even from the viewpoint of history of civilization. Goat and sheep-rearing flourished in the mountains of Afghanistan.[106] Pūṣan's chariot is drawn by goats and he weaves the woollen garment for the sheep. As the goat is sacred to Pūṣan so is the ewe, *meṣī*, sacred to Sarasvatī at least in the ritual.[107] The Ṛgvedic period is familiar with the sheep-rearing in Gandhāra, at the Sindhu and perhaps also at the Paruṣṇī.[108] ṚV I.126.7, the only passage which is more significant and speaks of sheep-rearing, mentions a woman "who is hairy like the ewe among the Gandhāris;"[109] the fine wool of sheep and goats from Afghanistan is well renowned even today.[110]

2. But the Sarasvatī of Arachosia alone does not hold good for the entire ṚV. It is likely that the memory of this home of the Vedic clans is preserved in some single passages of the Brāhmaṇa literature as well. But already the seventh book takes us to other surroundings, to the banks of the holy river in the inner India.[111] At the time of the ṚV, the Pūrus were settled there (VII.96.2) and also Nahuṣa (VII.95.2). The sacrificial processions moved along the banks of the Sarasvatī:

eṣa vai devayānaḥ panthās tam evānvārohanti (TS VII.2.1.4). The Ṛṣis held their sacrificial sessions on its banks when they excluded Kavaṣa Ailūṣa, who was not a brahmin but the son of a slave girl, from the sacrifice and drove him into the desert. Its banks resounded with the noise of the sacrifice and were the seat of the sacred knowledge, the *śruti.* For the poet of III.23.4 the Sarasvatī forms, with the Dṛṣadvatī and the Āpayā, the holy region where *vára ā́ pṛthivyā́ḥ* he installs the fire.[112]

In solitary instances even the old Sarasvatī of the West who was worshipped with hymns and sacrifices is alluded to by expressions like *dhíyaṃ dhāt* VI.49.7; *dhīnā́m avitry àvatu* 61.4.[113] In some cases it may be uncertain whether we are to understand the eastern river or the western one. But outside the sixth book it is mostly that Sarasvatī which flows through the land of Brahmanical learning.[114]

3. In hymn X.17 which is included in the Yamasaṃhitā, Sarasvatī is a river endowed with special holiness.

v. 7: *sárasvatīṃ devayánto havante*
sárasvatīm adhvaré tāyámāne
sárasvatīṃ sukṛ́to ahvayanta
sárasvatī dāśúṣe vā́ryaṃ dāt||

vv. 8 and 9 take us to the Manes. v. 8 is particularly important because it states that the Manes, approaching the sacrifice in the south, invoke Sarasvatī.[115] In other words, the verse shows that the Sarasvatī is an object of worship for the Manes. Elsewhere also she is associated with the Manes.

AV VII.68.2: *idáṃ te havyáṃ ghṛtávat sarasvati*
idáṃ pitṝṇā́ṃ havír āsyáṃ yát|

The association is expressed more distinctly still in

AV XIV.2.20: *ádhā sárasvatyai nāri pitṛ́bhyaś ca námas kuru|*

Here the Sarasvatī of the Madhyadeśa will not do either. That hymn X.17 belongs to the cult of the Manes is evident from its position between hymns 16 and 18 and also from vv. 3, 4 and 10 (purificatory verses). But often the ritual does not employ its verses at the right place.[116] However, the funeral rites of some families contain valuable hints. According to the ritual of the Śaunakins, after the funeral pyre is lit some offerings are made to Yama and then some to Sarasvatī,[117] accompanied partly with our three verses. Here she is the stream of the dead. We may recall that the departed souls have to cross a river on their way to the other world.[118] In the later period this is the Vaitaraṇī, the *ghorā nadī*,[119] which divides the dead from the living and flows in the sky as well as on the earth. The Veda does not know the Vaitaraṇī yet; its place is taken by the Sarasvatī in the present hymn. Thus a clear picture emerges of X.17.3 ff.; in vv. 3-6 Pūṣan conducts the departed one safely out of this world; vv. 7-9 invoke the river that separates the dead from the living. The Sarasvatī resembles the Vaitaraṇī of the later period even in the fact that it flows in the sky and on the earth. In Vol. I, pp. 239, 352-53 I have referred to the fact that some Vedic hymns anticipate not only a terrestrial Sarasvatī but a celestial one as well.[120] Apart from some verses from VII. 95-96, I think that also TMBr XXV.10.11[121] as well as AV VII.68.1[122] belong here.

Thus in the ṚV, Sarasvatī has three connotations.

1. Name of the river in Arachosia,
2. name of the river in the Madhyadeśa, and
3. the river of the Manes = Vaitaraṇī (in some cases);

(in addition to these, 4. according to the statements of the ritual texts = *amāvāsyā*.)[123]

3. Soma-Pūṣan

This is the right place to discuss this pair of gods somewhat more closely. The most important description of these gods occurs in II. 40.

v. 1: *sómāpūṣaṇā jánanā rayīṇā́m*
jánanā divó jánanā pṛthivyā́ḥ|
jātaú víśvasya bhúvanasya gopaú
devā́ akṛṇvann amṛ́tasya nā́bhim||

"Soma and Pūṣan, creators of all wealth, creators of heaven, creators of earth; they were born as the protectors of the entire world; the gods made them the centre of the Amṛta."

2: *imaú devaú jā́yamānau juṣanta*
imaú támāṃsi gūhatām ájuṣṭā|
ābhyā́m índraḥ pakvám āmā́sv antáḥ
somāpūṣā́bhyāṃ janad usríyāsu||

"They rejoiced at the birth of these two gods; these two dispelled the loathsome darkness. Through these two Indra produced the ripeness in the raw, through Soma and Pūṣan in the cows."

3: *sómāpūṣaṇā rájaso vimā́nam*
saptácakraṃ rátham áviśvaminvam|
viṣūvṛ́taṃ mánasā yujyámānaṃ
táṃ jinvatho vṛṣaṇā páñcaraśmim||

"Soma and Pūṣan, you drive the heaven-measuring seven-wheeled chariot which does not haul everybody,[124] which turns to everywhere,[125] which yokes itself by the mere thought, the five-reined one."

4: *divy ànyáḥ sádanaṃ cakrá uccā́*
pṛthivyā́m anyó ádhy antárikṣe|
tā́v asmábhyaṃ puruvā́raṃ purukṣúm
rāyás póṣaṃ ví ṣyātāṃ nā́bhim asmé||

"One has made his dwelling high in heaven, the other above the earth in the atmosphere.[126] May these two unite us with precious cattle-wealth and progeny."

5: *víśvāny anyó bhúvanā jajā́na*
víśvam anyó abhicákṣāṇa eti[127]*|*
sómāpūṣaṇāv ávataṃ dhíyaṃ me
yuvā́bhyāṃ víśvāḥ pṛ́tanā jayema||

"One created all beings, the other moves, beholding all. Soma and Pūṣan, help my hymn. With you we may win all the battles."

6: *dhíyaṃ pūṣā́ jinvatu viśvaminvó*
rayíṃ sómo rayipátir dadhātu|...

"May Pūṣan help our hymn, the all-impelling one; may Soma, lord of riches, grant us riches. ..."

One needs only to attempt to understand this hymn, interpreting Pūṣan as the "pathfinder" and Soma as the "beverage" or "plant," to see the futility of the exercise because it would make no sense. Oldenberg (RdV, 2nd ed., p. 237) observes: "If...what is by itself possible... this form of the god has a further prehistory beyond this point, we have no hope of being able to unravel it." I think that this hymn, which was composed in the circle of the Gṛtsamadas, provides us with the key; coupled with this hymn, if we keep in mind the designation *āghṛṇi*, the description of Pūṣan (like that of Agni) as his sister's lover and as his mother's suitor, we can draw no other conclusion but that he is a sun god. Güntert at one point reluctantly decides to admit the possibility of a moon god here, but at the wrong place. For in this hymn the moon is represented already by Soma, who is not subordinated to Pūṣan nor styled as his drink but placed entirely on an equal footing with him, the difference being that the former made his dwelling in the heaven and the latter in the atmosphere. When elsewhere Pūṣan is drawn into association with the Aśvins whom he chooses as his parents, this is an instance of contamination between different sets of myths, a contamination which achieves a balance between various elements and interweaves them.

Soma-Pūṣan occur rarely outside this hymn. We may add

I.23.14: *pūṣā́ rā́jānam ā́ghṛṇir ápagūḷhaṃ gúhā hitám/*
ávindac citrábarhiṣam//

"Pūṣan, the glowing one, has discovered the king, hidden in a deep concealment and resting on a glittering bed of straw [of stars]," and TS III. 3. 9: *somasya drapsam avṛṇita pūṣā.*[128] In the ritual a stew made of grains is often offered to the two gods. The observations made on this point in the Yajus litarature have no value.[129]

C. VIVASVAT AND YAMA

1. Vivasvat

Like Apāṃ napāt, Vivasvat also goes back to the beliefs of the Indo-Iranian period. His identity with the Avestan Vīvahvaṭ as well as the identity between Yama and Yima was recognized by Bopp, Burnouf and Lassen long ago at a time when the mythological studies were still in their infancy, and it required clear-sighted persons to pronounce things which are quite obvious to us today.

At the time when the Vedic hymns were composed the concept of Vivasvat was devoid of any life whatever, and he did not occupy a central position in the cult. Hence, such statements that can be used in interpreting him are quite few. There is general agreement in explaining him as a god of light but not with regard to his specific character. In the later Sanskrit, Vivasvat denotes simply the sun, and thus Kuhn and Spiegel (*Arische Periode*, p. 248 ff.) etc. have explained the Vedic god as well. The PW, on the other hand, explains Vivasvat as "the god of the rising diurnal light, of the morning-sun." Leaning on AV XVIII.2.32, Ludwig[130] explained him as "the bright sky beyond which Yama's realm is situated." Bergaigne connects him with Agni,[131] while Ehni, *Der vedische Mythus des Yama*, pp. 19, 24, observes that Vivasvat appears "predominantly as the morning sky which is gradually becoming bright," or as "the god of the bright sky in general, be it the diurnal sky shining in the radiance of the sun or the nocturnal sky lit by the moonlight." Macdonell (p. 43) sees "the rising sun" in him. He is the "sun" according to Charpentier, *Suparṇasage*, p. 327, while Foy's explanation of Vivasvat as the first sacrificer and of Yama as the first man (AISAK, VIII, p. 30 ff.) seems somewhat ingenious. Should the first man be the son of the first sacrificer?

When we overlook those passages where the word is used as an adjective[132]—not all of them are clear—then from the rest a small group comes into bold relief which speaks of *sádane vivásvataḥ*. According to the PW this means as much as "at the fire-altar," whereas Pischel (VSt, I, p. 242) states that "they show, as it appears to me, quite distinctly that *sádanaṃ vivásvataḥ* is that place where the singers (*víprāḥ, kavávyaḥ, kārúḥ*) stood. *sádanaṃ vivásvataḥ* is 'the chapel of Vivasvat.' That the place was called after Vivasvat might be due to the fact that Vivasvat is Yama's father." Pischel goes on to explain that in the cult of Yama there was much singing, that the Veda of the Udgātṛ was the Veda of the Manes and that *yamásya sádanam* in ṚV X.135.7 is the same as *sádanaṃ vivásvataḥ* which was also called plainly *vivasvat* in I.46.13; V.11.3 etc.

It is improbable that one would readily call the "chapel of Yama" as *sádanaṃ vivásvataḥ*, even though racing contests were held commonly for both. But what we must expect is that in *vivásvataḥ sádanaṃ* Vivasvat or Yama were really worshipped. We see however that in three of the five passages Indra is invoked *vivásvataḥ sádane*,[133] and in the fourth passage (X.75.1) it is the waters. There is no specific name in the last passage (X.12.7); of course, in the sixth verse Yama is mentioned but it is Agni who is invoked, and vv. 5, 8 mention Mitra-Varuṇa, Mitra and Aditi. It is just not probable that in Vivasvat's chapel Indra, Āpaḥ and Agni were invoked but neither he nor his son Yama.

When we turn to Sāyaṇa for the explanation of these passages, which are important for understanding the name, we find in his commentary on I.53.1 the rendering: *paricarato yajamānasya sadane yajñagṛhe* on III.34.7: *viśeṣeṇāgnihotrādikarmārthe vasato yajamānasya sadane gṛhe*; almost the same wording, *manuṣyasya yajamānasya svabhūte sadane vedyākhye sthāne* on III.51.3; X.75.1 as well as I.53.1 and X.12.7. Thus the Indian commentator explains in all passages Vivasvat as the sacrificer. When we ask the ṚV itself as to the usual place of worship the answer is: *dāśuṣo gṛhe*, in the house of the sacrificer. Hence the singers also must have stood there.

III. 25.4 : *ágna índraś ca dāśúṣo duroṇé*
sutā́vato yajñám ihópa yātam
51.3 : [*índro*] *vivásvataḥ sádana ā́ hí pipriyé*
9 : *pibatu . . . sutáṃ sómaṃ dāśúṣaḥ své sadhásthe*
60.5 : *dhiyéṣito maghavan dāśúṣo gṛhé*
saudhanvanébhiḥ sahá matsvā nṛbhiḥ //[134]
IV. 49.6 : *sómam indrābṛhaspatī píbataṃ dāśúṣo gṛhé*

From this answer of the ṚV which is in agreement with Sāyaṇa's explanations we may state as positive inference that here *vivásvat* is a name—of course an honorific name—for the sacrificer and that *vivásvataḥ sádane* has the same purport as *dāśúṣo gṛhé*. Rosen and Myriantheus have recognized this quite early. Having established this, we may expect to see Vivasvat as the designation for the sacrificer in other verses also. VIII. 6.39;[135] IX. 14.5;[136] 99.2[137] offer themselves as examples. Because of the words *dhíyaḥ*, *naptī́bhiḥ* and *matī́*, Vivasvat in these verses must refer to a man and not to a god, and hence Sāyaṇa explained in all the three passages Vivasvat as the "sacrificer." We should put IX.66.8[138] also in the same category for, according to the testimony of the first pāda, the "running race of Vivasvat" mentioned therein is a competition for the favour of the gods, not with chariots and horses but with hymns (*dhībhíḥ*) as it happens for instance, in the Saṃsavas described in Vol. I, p. 168 f. or in IX.94.1 : *spárdhante dhíyaḥ sū́rye ná viśaḥ*.[139] They vied with one another for the favour of the gods in Vivasvat's house.

It is patent that the name Vivasvat must have been transferred from the god to the terrestrial sacrificer and there must have existed a similarity between these two which justified the transference. This similarity, I believe, is stated in X.12.7 (see p. 218 below) where Vivasvat makes his appearance as the celestial sacrificer[140] in whose house the gods rejoice and dwell. He is the householder in heaven just as the sacrificer is one on the earth. In Vālakhilya IV.1 he stands at the head of the Soma pressers of antiquity who were praised as the models.[141] The Avesta knows him only in the form of a pious sacrificer. Now the entire later literature, including the Brāhmaṇas and even the Yajus Saṃhitās,[142] interprets Vivasvat as the sun god with such a degree of unanimity that certain limitations are imposed from the very outset upon our explanation as far as the ṚV is concerned. First of all, it is ruled out that the Vedic Vivasvat can be a designation for heaven. For just as Dyaus had never evolved into a name of the sun nor Pṛthivī into a name of Agni so should we assume that such a transference of meaning is not credible in the case of Vivasvat. In the same degree the view that Vivasvat is a personification of the rising sun is improbable for it receives no support from any passage of our Saṃhitā but is based exclusively on an etymology of *vi-vas* "the shining one," which is correct in itself but semantically misleading. Hence, there is no ground to depart from the linguistic usage of the post-Ṛgvedic period even for the ṚV and look for a meaning other than "sun god" which is adequate in all cases where the god is mentioned, and even necessary in some. The sun god is the lord of the sacrifice. The Brāhmaṇas are fond of stating repeatedly that Viṣṇu is the sacrifice and with this they express a similar idea. Since, according to X.12.7, the gods rejoice in the house of Vivasvat, he must be in possession of the Soma. This is in conformity with statements such as that Soma is a fellow-resident of Vivasvat (IX.26.4, see Vol. I, p. 262), that Indra fetches the Soma jar from Vivasvat (VIII.72.8) and that he deposits his treasure with Vivasvat.[143] In the Avesta also Vīvahvaṭ is indeed the first worshipper of the Haoma. The ṚV repeatedly speaks of the Soma draught which Indra consumes in the house of the sun god. Thus it is said in three passages that Indra rejoices in the Soma in Viṣṇu's abode.[144] These apart, IX.1.6 and 113.3 are worth citing, according to which Sūrya's daughter cleanses the Parisrut or brings the Soma, for this also refers to the dwelling of the sun; further, the legend, to be discussed later, that Indra drinks the Soma in the house of Tvaṣṭṛ or that he seizes the drink by force there.[145] In V.41.8 Tvaṣṭṛ is called a Vāstoṣpati and is probably a sun god.

When the name of the sun, of this celestial householder, is transferred to the earthly one, it is done *boni ominis causa* (for the sake of good augury), *maṅgalecchāyai.* Already in the ṚV, the sacrificial place represents the entire universe. The "ten fingers" are the maidens, the Vedi or Dhiṣaṇā is the earth, Soma the moon and the Pavitra the sky. Hence the sacrificer also, who caused the entire ceremony to be performed, could receive his share in the newly created world. In the ritual such *māṅgalyanāmāni* are often anticipated. According to TBr II.6.6.3. during the Rājasūya the royal Yajamāna must address his court officials with these *māṅgalyanāmāni.* The Gandharvas take a second name in order to achieve success in the sacrifice,[146] and on this the ŚBr remarks thus : "therefore, a brahmin who does not prosper should take a second name; for he certainly prospers who knows this and takes a second name."[147] During the selection of the priests, the potential candidates are compared with gods: "the moon is my divine Brahman, you be my human Brahman; Āditya is my divine Udgātṛ, you be my human Udgātṛ." The deification of the sacrificer himself occurs even in the Soma-consecration, the Dīkṣā, which cannot be traced with certainty in the ṚV[148] but is enjoined by the entire Yajus literature and therefore preserves a true picture of the Indian viewpoint. It is said in ŚBr III. 2.2.19: "One who is consecrated comes close to the gods and becomes one of the gods."[149] III.2.1.39 : "thereupon, some one calls out, 'consecrated is this brahmin, consecrated is this brahmin.' With this he announces him . . . to the gods, 'He possesses great strength who obtained the sacrifice. He has become one of you.'" III.1.4.1: "All the formulas during the consecration are elevatory formulas (*audgrabhaṇāni*) since he who is consecrated elevates himself from this world to the world of the gods." We do not stray away from the circle of proper Indian concepts when we see in *vivasvat* at several passages of the ṚV a sacrificial name for the Yajamāna, through which he makes himself equal to the group which he has entered.[150]

In five passages Agni appears as Vivasvat's messenger. In some of these it is hard to decide whether it is the sacrificer or the god who is meant by Vivasvat. The meaning is plain in I.58.1;[151] V.11.3;[152] VIII.39.3[153] since the rest of the statements in these verses refer to the god Agni who, as the sacrificial fire, brings the oblations of the Yajamāna to the gods; hence Vivasvat here is the sacrificer. I.31.3[154] is slightly more difficult. This verse contains the imperative *bhava.* I am of the view that because of the three imperfect forms *arejetām*, *asaghnos*, *ayajas* that follow *bhava* we are justified in reading with Bergaigne[155] for *bhava* the imperfect form *bhavas*,[156] the final consonant of which could easily have been lost before the initial *s* of the next word. Then the translation would read thus : "O Agni, at first you became manifest to Mātariśvan for the sake of Vivasvat." The doubt whether the last word should not be construed as an adjective of Mātariśvan is removed by VI.8.4 where Mātariśvan and Vivasvat are distinctly independent of one another.[157] Since we know that Mātariśvan as well as the Bhṛgus bring the fire to men from heaven,[158] Vivasvat in our passage must be the man who bears this name, that is to say the sacrificer, probably the mythical first sacrificer who is extolled as the model for the sacrificer. Through this, the same meaning becomes probable for VI.8.4 also; Mātariśvan is the messenger who brings or has once brought the fire to the sacrificer from afar. "As Vivasvat's messenger, Mātariśvan brought Agni Vaiśvānara from afar." The situation in IV.7.4[159] should be understood in a like manner; however, here the friends who fetch Agni are the Āyus : "Once the pious have brought the sacrificer's swift messenger, who is above all men,[160] the son of Bhṛgu, as a token to each clan." The possibility of another construction "they brought the swift messenger from Vivasvat" is not formally ruled out but seems less probable in the context of the first five verses. The interpretation of X.21.5 remains uncertain.[161]

When we look closely, there appears a difference concerning the meaning of Vivasvat between the first group of verses and the second. While in the first group he is plainly designated as the sacrificer, here in the second group, because of the accompanying preterite forms of verbs, the word has more the character of a proper noun and Vivasvat stands almost on the same level as the mythical sacrificer of the Avesta or Manu Vivasvat who is glorified in Vālakhilya IV.1.

When we now turn to the passages which speak of god Vivasvat,[162] it is plain that little information can be obtained from them on his usual nature. For the Vedic period he is just not vivid enough. In I.46.13 the Aśvins who are dwelling with Vivasvat are implored to come down.[163] With this the celestial Vivasvat must have been meant; for this sojourn of theirs with Vivasvat is obviously synonymous with the *pitur yonā* of which VIII.9.21[164] speaks. Who is meant by Vivasvat or *pitṛ* is not clear from either of the two verses. Since the Aśvins are usually described as *divo napātā*, one could believe that here is a passage —it would be the only such one—which demands the equation Dyaus = Vivasvat. However, that would be too rash a conclusion in view of the ease with which the images change in the Vedic kaleidoscope. The moon is said to be the son of heaven as also of earth, of the sun, the offspring of the waters and even of Parjanya. Therefore, we should not lose sight of the possibility that the Aśvins also, whatever their original meaning might be, can very well be the sons of the sun as well as of heaven. One construction does not exclude the other. For me the decisive factor for upholding the interpretation of Vivasvat as the sun here also is, besides the usage in classical Sanskrit and Vivasvat's close connection to the day and to the night (who are the wives etc. of the sun god)[165], the intimate and often underlined[166] relation of the Aśvins to Sūrya's daughter who chooses them as husbands in the Svayaṃvara and climbs into their chariot. This she must have done naturally in the house of her father, Sūrya, where the selection of the husband must have taken place and to this the words of our verse, *vāvasānā́ vivásvati*, are well suited. The suitors of the sun's daughter stay for a while in Sūrya's house. The Aśvins and Vivasvat are associatad in a second passage also; this too fits into the assumption that Vivasvat is the sun.[167] Vivasvat appears as the sun god in VIII.67.20[168] also; here he is mentioned among the Ādityas.[169] IX.10.5 is uncertain. Further perhaps I.96.2[170] as well as I.139.1[171] and X.63.1[172] where man is described as the descendent of Vivasvat. The correctness of this explanation of the last two verses is vouchsafed by the statement in the non-Ṛgvedic literature which distinctly proclaims that the sun god is the progenitor of the human race. Thus TS VI.5.6.2: [*vivasvān ādityas*] *tasya vā iyaṃ prajā yan manuṣyāḥ*; ŚBr III.1.3.4: *sa vivasvān ādityas tasyemāḥ prajāḥ*, while other texts opine that men are the subjects of Manu Vaivasvata.[173] With these statements we should connect the above two verses, I.139.1 and X.63.1, provided that their not very clear wording allows any conclusion at all. As I.109.7 etc. demonstrate,[174] the ṚV is already familiar with the sun's relation to the Manes or to the human race.

To sum up the foregoing enquiry about Vivasvat, the word has the following meanings:

1. sun, sun god,

2. name of a mythical sacrificer (originally the sun god who was degraded to a mythical sacrificer),

2a. honorific name for the ordinary sacrificer.

2. Yama

Yama is the most distinguished member of Vivasvat's clan and the first among the "mortals." He went once in advance of the human beings and showed them the path to heaven. He is *ravitanaya* as *Viṣṇupurāṇa* III.7.35 describes him. ṚV X.14.5 expressly declares Vivasvat as his father: *vívasvantaṃ huve yáḥ pitā́ te*, and the same is implied in Yama's epithet Vaivasvata. Vedic literature contains few passages that throw light on the relationship between the two. The few we have, however, bear witness to a total antithesis. Cf. AV XVIII. 3.61 and more particularly 62.

AV. XVIII.3.61: *vivásvān no ábhayaṃ kṛṇotu*
yáḥ sutrā́mā jīrádānuḥ sudā́nuḥ |
ihémé vīrā́ bahávo bhavantu
gómad ásvavan máyy astu puṣṭám ||

62: *vivásvān no amṛtatvé dadhātu*
páraitu mṛtyúr amṛtaṃ na áitu |
imā́n rakṣatu púruṣān ā́ jarimṇó
mó ṣv eṣām ásavo yamáṃ guḥ ||

"May Vivasvat grant us immortality. May death go away and may immortality come to us. May he protect our men till old age. Let not the life of our [men] go to Yama." Further

XVIII.2.32: *yamáḥ paró 'varo vivásvān*
tátaḥ páraṃ nā́ti paśyāmi kíṃ cana |
yamé adhvaró ádhi me níviṣṭo
bhúvo vivásvān anvā́tatāna ||

"Yama is the higher [one] and Vivasvat the lower; beyond that I see nothing whatever. My sacrifice is deposited on Yama. Vivasvat has spread himself over the worlds."

Though the verses do not throw light on the basic character of the two gods, they do contradict the popular conception that Yama is the first man; if such were the case it is improbable that he would have become the bearer of the sacrifice.[175]

There has been no lack of attempts to probe the nature of the ruler of the kingdom of the blessed dead, of the Indian god of death. Depending on their starting point—a natural phenomenon or the statement of the AV that Yama "died as the first of the mortals"—scholars concluded either that he was originally a god or that he was, on the contrary, a man, a progenitor of the human race. Roth[176] was the one who advocated the second view with determination. He was followed by a number of scholars. One of them, L. Scherman,[177] has discussed in an excellent study the phenomenon of Yama in the later literature. But I cannot share this view.

It is necessary to examine the passages on which this interpretation is based. Prominent of all is

AV. XVIII.3.13: *yó mamắra prathamó mártyānām*
yáḥ preyắya prathamó lokám etám|
vaivasvatáṃ saṃgámanaṃ jánānāṃ
yamáṃ rắjānaṃ haviṣā saparya||[178]

"Him who died first among the mortals, who went forth to this place, Vivasvat's son and assembler of people, king Yama, worship with Havis." Less important, being less intelligible, is

ṚV X.13.4: *priyắṃ yamas tanvàṃ prắrirecīt ||*

"Yama surrendered his dear body."[179] Although the first verse gives no occasion for doubt about its purport, it is necessary to adhere to its wording while interpreting the verse because any slight departure can lead us into wrong paths without our being aware of it. Scholars have departed from this wording when they explained Yama as "the first man" or when they even said that in the ṚV he "was treated always as the first man to die;" but that is not the case at all. It is never said that Yama was the *prathamo janānām* but only that he was the *prathamo martyānām.* Even though the difference between the two words is not considerable because all men are mortal, a difference does nevertheless exist since not all mortals are at the same time human beings. The Veda is quite aware of this distinction, for it refers to Yama as a *martya* but never as *jana or manuṣya.* This is significant. For at the beginning the gods were also *martya* but not *jana*;[180] *martya* were the Ṛbhus,[181] the genii of the seasons, whom Prajāpati raised to immortality but they were not human beings. We must insist on translating the first pāda of the above verse, precisely the way the wording demands: "Yama died as the first of the mortals." It does not follow from this that he had been the first human being. Kastor is called Gr. *thnétós*, a *spérma thnatón* and yet he was one of the Dioscuri.[182] Baldur was killed and yet he was a god. As a matter of fact, in almost all passages[183] a clear distinction is made between Yama and the *pitaraḥ.* Of course, they dwell together and he eats with them,[184] but he is always their king and lord, never quite equal to them. Probably in one passage he himself is called *pitā*, but in a quite different context.[185] One may object by saying that

AV XVIII.4.55[186] distinctly speaks of a "palace" of Yama, which Ehni interprets as a funerary monument.[187] Meanwhile the very expression that "five Mānavas" piled up this *harmya* for him endows the whole thing with a mythical stamp. The grave of Dionysos was known in Greece.[188] In Argos, Kastor 's grave was worshipped.[189] Consequently our verse proves nothing even when the one described there was a real house, a legendary burial place of Yama. But this is not the case. We only know the saga that Yama died once, and to this the legend of his burial was easily appended. Thus the strongest props are taken away from under the theory which sees the first man in Yama.[190] When it is said in ṚV X.14.1-2 that Yama went in advance and found the way for us,[191] the example of Ermes Psychopompos clearly demonstrates that a first man is not necessary for this role.[192] The god who once died in myth could become the guide to the departed into the realm of light.

The arguments developed here against Roth's assumption are supplemented by the fact that this assumption goes against the data in the Avesta. When Zarathuštra asks Haoma as to who among the men pressed him at first, the latter replies: *vīvaŋhå mąm paoiryō masyō hunūta*, and that as reward Yima was born as his son. We have no right to treat this legend from the ninth chapter of the Yasna as less valuable than the passage from the AV. According to the former *Vīvaŋhvaṭ* was the first man. Which is correct ? The answer is: neither of the two.

From the ṚV we know that Vivasvat had been a god once, and the Avesta made him not merely a mortal but even a human being. This offers a glimpse into the evolution of mythical beings and shows the paths taken by the gods to become human beings. When the Iranian saga makes the sun god the first man to press the Soma and Yama his son, the ṚV has of course followed this path but never reached its end. The ṚV has preserved a part of the solar kingdom of the father and also the attributes of the celestial kingship of the son still more than the Avesta did.

Here we have not taken into account hymn X.10 which deals with Yama and Yamī. This hymn is capable of leading the investigation astray and it had done that. Its purpose is to censure the incest into which Yamī tries to seduce her brother. Yama repulses her and suggests other men. Accordingly Yamī is not the mother of the human race which, on the contrary, must have already existed if she were to turn to other men. The expression, *ékasya cit mártyasya*, in the third verse proves nothing. Through this Yamī merely attempts to make her desire appear more urgent. The expression means as much as "with you alone" or "solely with you." Enough attention has not been paid to the fact that Yama and Yamī are not described as the children of Vivasvat but as the descendants of the *gandharvó ápsu* and *ápyā yóṣā*.[193] From both the grounds it follows that in this hymn we are dealing with a set of myths the Yama in which has nothing in common with Vivasvat's son. The hymn was inserted in its place purely on the basis of the superficial consonance between the word *yama* and Yama of the next hymns. It has no relation to the others. L. v. Schroeder is mistaken in assuming that we have a fertility drama in front of us. It is neither this nor an Ākhyāna but its dialogue is "one of the most well-constructed in the entire ṚV" (Charpentier, *Suparṇasage*, *p*. 98). Güntert observes (*Der arische Weltkönig und Heiland*, pp. 319-334) that my separating *yama* from Vivasvat's son "is a valid but impossible radical cure." But this separation is not only possible but also necessary to remove the confusion caused by this hymn.[194] The Avesta does not speak of a sister of Yima; only the *Bundahiš* does. I think it is rash to ignore the creative power of the saga and to invoke this sister of Yima as witness. However, in the Iranian saga (contrary to ṚV X.10) she produced with her brother the first human couple, but she also becomes the mother of monkeys and bears. It remains to be seen whether an ancient trait of a saga can really be proved here. The evidence is much too late.

The above-mentioned antithesis between Vivasvat and his son Yama is seen in the ritual also (in the relation between Sūrya and Yama). It prescribes a white animal for Sūrya and a black one for Yama.[195] From this it follows that the former represents the life, i.e. the day, and the latter the death, i.e. the night, as in the well-known verse X.14.2.

If Vivasvat is the sun—the entire Indian tradition supports this – then the same explanation for Yama is ruled out.[196] He can only go back to another natural phenomenon or he must have been a mythical first man. In the entire Yama mythology there is not a single trace of his earthly origins, with the exception of the verse which describes him as the first mortal to die. We must look for the god whose dying was typical. When we ask who in the realm of Vedic mythology can be the son of the sun and at the same time a "mortal," we realize that the only starting point of this concept can be the actual observation that the moon begins his course every month apparently from the sun and returns to his womb. The moon is *jā́ḥ sū́ryasya*, says IX.93.1. According to ABr VIII.28.14 he is born from the sun (*ādityād vai candramā jāyate*). He is reborn always,[197] hence he must die always. The origin of the dying god is clearly described by X.55.5 which we have cited once before:

> *yúvānaṃ sántaṃ palitó jagāra|*
> *devásya paśya kā́vyaṃ mahitvā́*
> *adyā́ mamā́ra sá hyáḥ sám āna||*

"Yesterday he died and today he lives forth."

With this we enter the realm of anthropology; its experiences support a conclusion which draws the moon into an association with the realm of the Manes. Speaking about the Ipurinas, a Brazilian tribe, Brinton[198] states that they "address the orb as 'our father' and imagine him a little old man who was their ancestor and still watches over their prosperity." Gräbner observes: "It is actually the moon who has aroused the mythological participation of the older cultivators for, with his phases, he appears as the prototype of birth, death and life after death."[199] On the basis of his extensive knowledge of the primitive peoples of India, Crooke states: "the realm of Yama would naturally be fixed in the moon." As among many peoples, the moon is intimately connected among Indians also with the Manes. He is said to be their light, their eye and their abode.[200] What is more obvious than the belief that the realm of light, whence a reflected splendour shines down in the darkness of night upon men, is the land of the dead who roam about for ever in the light of the sun's son, who had preceded them as the first mortal and who rules in their kingdom as the first and the foremost being ?

Now we understand the significance of the words *yamé adhvaró ádhi me níviṣṭaḥ* (AV XVIII.2.32.), cited on p. 222 above. A slightly different statement is made at AV XVIII.2.6: *chándāṃsi súrvā tá yamá árpītā.* To these we should add ṚV VII.33.9-10 according to which the Vasiṣṭhas weave the "frame" or warp which has been stretched out by Yama,[201] i.e., Yama has invented the sacrifice and the Vasiṣṭhas now continue his work. We may recall that the moon announces as messenger the next sacrifice (I.105.4), that he regulates the seasons and assigns the gods their share, that Soma is called *ātmá yajñásya pūrvyáḥ* in IX.2.10 etc., and that Bṛhaspati brings the sacrifice to the unbelieving men,[202] and conclude that similar qualities can be attributed to Yama as well.

It is far from my intention to say that the starting point of the phenomenon of Yama was still vivid in the minds of the Vedic singers. He was the moon god of an Indo-Iranian or still earlier epoch, no longer of the period of the Veda or of the Avesta where he is regarded only as the ruler of the dead or as the founder of a paradisiacal kingdom. It is rarely that a ray of the old majesty illuminates his shadow. But what the ṚV occasionally states —rather incidentally than intentionally— reveals the old god and can be understood only under the assumption that he had been a moon god once. We must realise that different ages and tribes have populated the Vedic Olympus with the creatures of their imagination and that this imagination gave to the same natural phenomenon a different expression according to the current concept. The stream of historical evolution carried these formations to the vast reservoir of the ṚV and built them into a mosaic. Thus we see in the ṚV Viṣṇu, Pūṣan and Savitṛ juxtaposed as sun gods and Yama, Apāṃ napāt, Soma and others as moon gods. Each one of these has his special character but in many cases the point of origin has become obscure. The agent is so far removed from his point of origin that the latter can be perceived in solitary traits only, and *the gods are not only juxtaposed but also can be drawn occasionally into a causal relationship with one another by the ever active mind.* Now Apāṃ napāt is merely the son of the waters and Yama the lord of the departed souls. With a lively empathy, the poetic energies of the period turned to Soma who was fully conceived as the moon god.[203]

When we turn our attention to the Avesta, it is striking that Yima there is no more the ruler of the dead but the king of a paradisiacal kingdom. As in Vivasvat's case, the Avesta has gone a step further than the Veda and has reached the end of the path up to the humanization of the god. The two sources are not fundamentally different but they represent two different stages of mythological evolution. One may perhaps be inclined to see an objection against this in the Iranian saga that Yima lost the splendour of his majesty because he became guilty of false speech. "When he became guilty of falsehood," narrates Yašt XIX.34, "the visible majesty fled away from him in the shape of a bird."[204] The splendour deserts him thrice and is seized by Mithra, Thraētaona, Āthwya and Kərəsāspa. The very wording endows the story with a fabulous character. The god who dies (i. e., who is extinguished) and the god who is robbed of the splendour of his majesty are basically the same beings. With the saga that Yima is robbed of his majesty because of a falsehood, the Iranian mythology has explained the reason—merely in a different way from the Veda—why the moon loses his radiance.

Indian literature relates how Soma, the husband of Prajāpati's daughters, cohabitated only with Rohiṇī of all his wives. "The others became jealous and returned home. Soma followed them and asked for them back, but Prajāpati did not give them any more. 'Swear an oath,' he said, 'that you will cohabit with all of them equally.' Soma took the oath and Prajāpati returned his daughters to him. However, again he cohabitated only with Rohiṇī. Then he was seized by consumption. 'The king was seized by consumption,' this is the origin of Rājayakṣma." Here also mention is made of a falsehood because of which the moon—called Soma here—loses his radiance. The story is narrated in TS II.3.5.1 ff. in order to explain why a person seized by consumption (pāpayakṣma) should offer Ādityacaru on the New Moon's day.[205] On this occasion the stanzas *navo navo bhavati jāyamāno*...and *yam ādityam aṃśum āpyāyayanti*[206] are employed as Yājyā and Puronuvākyā verses respectively;

these speak of the waxing moon, implying thereby that like the moon the sick person may be set free from his chronic disease. It is likely that the story was invented to justify the custom of offering an Āditya-oblation at the time of the New Moon for the recovery of a person attacked by consumption. The notion of a moon who had taken ill has such a homely character and is such a favourite theme of Indian literature[207] that an old folk tale seems to be echoing through it; for the moon with his changing radiance and the spots on his orb was naturally a motif that inspired folk poetry.[208] The Indian legend does not lay claims to be historically related to the Iranian saga. But at this point of discussion it has its value because it shows the myth-creating faculties at work in giving a mythical garb to natural events. With the help of this analogy we can trace the path along which the Iranian saga of Yima who was robbed of his majesty has developed.

When Yima is called *xšaēta* or *hvthąwa*, "rich in herds," this has no special significance because both the words are suited to the earthly king as well as to the sun and the moon; the same is true of the designation *xvarənaŋuhastemō zātanam hvarədaresō mašyānąm*. On the other hand, there is an expression in Vendidād II. 10, which reveals an old moon god:

āaṭ yimō frašūsaṭ raoδāo
ā [upa rapithwąm] hū paīti aδwanəm

"There Yima rose quickly towards the stars [around midday] and against the sun's path."[209] Only one god moves against the sun's path and towards the stars. It is the moon whose apparent motion from the west to the east has been the source of this trait attributed to Yima.[210] This notion could not have arisen either in connection with the sun or with a mere progenitor of men.

In the foregoing discussion we have taken the identity between Yama and Yima, which Bopp had noticed long ago and after him all competent scholars, as self-evident and have substantiated it once again. But we have not paid any attention to etymology. To derive the word from *yam* "to restrain" would be natural but goes against the Vedic accent-system, and we need to assume that here an exception was made. The absence of any material reason speaks against connecting the word with *yama*, "twin." Whose twin brother should we then assume Yama to be? Not of Yamī because a sister of Yama is not known to the Avesta itself but only to Persian literature; not of the sun because from time immemorial he is described as Vivasvat's son. Hence, we would rather abandon any further attempt to comprehend the basic meaning of the word. For often etymological derivations have obscured mythological questions instead of solving them and dislodged the exegesis from its rightful place.

Beyond this I have nothing to add to what has been stated by my predecessors on Yama. The hymns dedicated to him in the ṚV are not many because, as Zimmer and Scherman point out, any reflection about what follows after death is far removed from the general character of this collection of hymns. The first redactors did not pay any regard to the cult of the dead in their compilation. Therefore the hymns connected with this cult were included only in the "book of additions," i.e. the tenth maṇḍala, where they constitute a small Saṃhitā in themselves. We can call this a Yama-Saṃhitā just as the whole ninth book is a Soma-Saṃhitā. We do not know whether the first compilors found this group of Yama hymns already when they began the compilation of the family hymns and therefore excluded them or whether these Yama hymns were the property of a clan devoted to the cult of the dead, so to say, a "grave-diggers' guild." But there is absolutely no reason to assume that the Yama-Saṃhitā is younger because of its inclusion in the tenth book.

In the literature outside the ṚV proper, the features which reveal the old moon god gradually disappeared and Yama was merely the god of the realm of the dead, united with Mṛtyu, death, in a fraternal relationship.

AV XVIII.2.27: *mṛtyúr yamásyāsīd dūtáḥ prácetā*
ásūn pitṛ́bhyo gamayā́ṃ cakāra|

"Death was Yama's wise messenger, he let the life go from the Manes." Cf. AV V.30.12; VI.28.3; 63.2-3; 84.3; 93.1.[211] In VS XXXIX.13 Yama is mentioned next to *ántaka* and *mṛtyú*. In MS II.5.6 (55.13) Yama is directly called *mṛtyú*. He is mentioned along with Nirṛti in AV VI.29.3; MS II.5.6 (55.11).

Even sleep is related to him because it comes from Yama's world AV XIX.56.1;[212] VI.46.1;[213] XVI.5.1; XIX.573. According to ṚV X.97.16; AV VIII.7.28, Yama like Mṛtyu binds his victims with fetters for the feet, *paḍbīśa*,[214] and even otherwise he is regarded as a causer of disasters.[215] He sends his messengers to men,[216] above all, his dogs called *sārameyá*.[217] In AV VIII.1.9 he is styled *śabala* and *śyāma*; thus are described, apart from him, doves[218] and vultures.[219]

Pischel assumes that in ṚV X. 135.7 a chapel of Yama is mentioned.[220] The *yamásya sádana* mentioned therein occurs often. AV II. 12. 7[221]: "I tear out your seven breaths, your eightfold marrow with the Brahman. Go to Yama's seat, well prepared, with Agni as your guide." Here "Yama's seat" means patently as much as Yama's world;[222] likewise in AV XVIII. 2. 56.[223] According to *Kauśika Sūtra* LXXX. 34 it should refer to the cows or men to be sacrificed during the Pitṛmedha along with whom, according to the wording of this verse, the departed is supposed to go to Yama's seat: "Here I fasten to you your draught animals so that they draw you to the realm of the spirits. With these go to Yama's seat and to the council meetings." I think AV III. 29. 1 informs us as to what is meant by the *sámiti*: these are the meetings of the celestial council, of Yama and of the kings.[224] Similarly AV XVIII. 3. 70[225] refers to Yama's kingdom: "Give him back, O Tree, who has been deposited upon you [for burning] so that he may be in Yama's seat, speaking to the sacrificial assemblies(?)"

Of the other passages, verse AV VI. 29. 3 may be considered here which, to judge from vv. 1-2, refers to Nirṛti's messenger whom the author wishes to see powerless in *yamásya gṛhá*.[226]

The word *sādana* has a different meaning in ṚV X. 18. 13, a verse employed in the rite of covering and burying the urn with the bones:

> *etā́ṃ sthū́ṇām pitáro dhārayantu*
> *té 'trā yamáḥ sā́danā te minotu|*

Yama himself prepares the dwelling for the dead. A drink is given to the departed to take with him, during which rite the following words are uttered: *eṣā te yamasādane svadhā nidhīyate gṛhe akṣitir nāma te asau* (TĀr VI.7.2, v. 6). Here *sādana* is the grave.

The survey of the passages shows that it is not probable that *yamásya sádana* in one verse which occurs at the end of an obscure hymn (X.135.7)[227] should have a meaning different from what it has in other passages. Hence I believe that as elsewhere the word denotes in this verse also the place of cremation itself, i. e., *citi* or *śmaśāna*, or that the oft-stressed pleasures in Yama's world are pointed to the departed soul.[228] Music was employed in the Pitṛmedha. In *Kauśika Sūtra* LXXXIV. 8 the command is given "to let the lutes resound" (*vīṇā vadantas*) and tournaments might also have been held.[229]

Postscript: In the above discussion we have not taken into account the two verses, ṚV X. 17. 1 and 2:...*tváṣṭā duhitré vahatúṃ kṛṇoti*..., since they do not contribute anything to the interpretation itself. Nevertheless, they require an explanation. Perhaps these two do not belong together since ṚV X. 17. 1 = AV XVIII. 1. 53 and ṚV X. 17. 2 = AV XIII. 2. 33. Various elements are mixed up in these verses. I shall attempt at the following explanation. Vivasvat is the sun, Yama's mother is the night, as we can infer from AV III. 1. 10, a hymn dedicated to the night of the New Year. The disappearing *saraṇyū* must refer to the substituted wife of Vivasvat; the *savarṇā*, being equal to him in colour, is therefore a goddess of light. Since this second wife is the mother of the twins (cf. ṚV III. 39. 3) and disappears soon after their birth, Dawn—otherwise the beloved of the Aśvins—must be their mother here. Thus Vivasvat has two wives, the day and the night, the unequal sisters (*vírūpe* ṚV I. 113. 3). Thus one wife gives birth to Yama and the other to the Aśvins. Both disappear afterwards. This marriage of Vivasvat is made mythologically dependent upon Tvaṣṭṛ, again another sun god. The author must have been hardly familiar with Tvaṣṭṛ's original significance. Thus in X. 139. 1 Pūṣan goes on Savitṛ's command; the sun is called the eye of Mitra-Varuṇa; Agni-Soma (sun and moon) impel Pūṣan (sun) in AV XVIII. 2. 53. Often Soma and Bṛhaspati are drawn into association or made dependent upon one another. Thus from the ruins of an old mythology a new one is built (on this see my remarks in the Introduction, and Oldenberg, RdV, 2nd ed., pp. 52; 54, n. 2). The original meaning of the Aśvins was forgotten long before. Myriantheus, *Die Aśvins oder arischen Dioskuren*, p. 57, has already explained *saraṇyū* as an adjective. Then the legends connected with *saraṇyū* in the *Nirukta* and *Bṛhaddevatā* might have originated on the basis of this misunderstood passage.

Translation. X. 17.1 : "Tvaṣṭṛ performs the marriage of his daughter. The whole world comes together. Yama's mother (the night), wife of the mighty Vivasvat, disappeared when she was brought home."

2 : "They recovered the immortal woman from the mortals and gave Vivasvat one woman who is equal to him. She gave birth to the Aśvins and when this happened [the swift one] swiftly abandoned the twins."

On the further evolution of this legend, see Blau, ZDMG, LXII, p. 337 ff.

D. TVAṢṬṚ AND HIS SON[230]

In Tvaṣṭṛ we encounter one of the most obscure gods to be exhibited by the Veda. It can be a futile and perhaps even a wrong endeavour to look behind the curtain and to explain his origin. Frequently and most expediently one is satisfied in explaining him as "the master craftsman of the gods." An expert on Indian antiquity like Sylvain Lévi says in his review of Ehni's *Yama* (in *Revue Critique*, 1890, No. 47) : "as far as the true origins are concerned, the wisest thing actually is to give up discovering them." But it seems to me that even at the risk of erring we should not yet lay aside the spade and not yet abandon the attempt even if we cannot unravel the true origin.

Tvaṣṭṛ is not a prominent personage in the ṚV. He belongs to those figures who were already mythical to the Vedic singers themselves or at least lie substantially outside their range of ideas. With the exception of the *tṛca* VII. 34.20-22, not a single hymn is dedicated to him. Outside this indifferent passage, he is not mentioned at all in the seventh maṇḍala; in the eighth only three times in two hymns (26.21, 22; 102.8) and only twice in the ninth (5.8; 81.4). The other family books mention him quite uniformly; both absolutely and relatively he is to be met with most frequently in the first and the last books. What is stated about him is sufficient for us to assume that we have before us the fragments of a bigger mythical cycle which, originating outside the range of the actual Ṛgvedic tribes, was not an object of their special interest.

The customary explanation of Tvaṣṭṛ as the master craftsman of the gods has its ostensible support in the derivation of the word from *tvakṣ* which the Indian lexicographers equate with *takṣ* and in the occasional play upon words like *tvaṣṭā tataksa*. If *tvaṣṭṛ* is really not a loan word from an aboriginal language but goes back to *tvakṣ*, then the basic meaning "shaper" is in keeping with the character of this god, no matter how we interpret him, just as it will be in keeping with the character of any god who is not exactly a god of sleep. Precisely in the same way the name Vivasvat can be applied to each god of light according to its etymology if this universal application was not limited by the actual linguistic usage. One can attempt to explain the traits of Tvaṣṭṛ with reservations only.

1. Tvaṣṭṛ and the drink of the gods. The association with Soma and the Soma drink which is emphasized frequently is important for the appreciation of this god. We read in several passages that he carries a jar full of Soma or bowls from which the gods drink. Thus it is said in

X. 53.9 : *tváṣṭā māyā́ ved apásām apástamo*
bíbhrat pā́trā devapā́nāni śáṃtamā |
śíśīte nūnám paraśúṃ svāyasáṃ
yéna vṛścā́d étaśo bráhmaṇas pátiḥ ||

"Tvaṣṭṛ knew the magic when he, most skilful of the skilful, brought the salutary bowls from which the gods drink. Now he sharpens the axe of metal with which the swift Brahmaṇaspati will carve." Ludwig is right when he connects in his commentary (986) this passage with those which deal with Tvaṣṭṛ's bowl made fourfold by the Ṛbhus. This bowl is the object of a jealous battle between the Ṛbhus and Tvaṣṭṛ, who wishes to kill the former because they find fault with his bowl;[231] Tvaṣṭṛ hides among his wives when he becomes aware of their miraculous achievement. Since, as Ludwig notes, the Ṛbhus are the genii of the seasons, it was probably not an ordinary bowl on which they proved their skill. ṚV X.53.9 says that "the gods drink" from Tvaṣṭṛ's vessels[232] and we see still more clearly in AV IX.4.3-6 that Tvaṣṭṛ carries a bowl full of Soma (see Vol. I, p. 216). The bowl made fourfold by the Ṛbhus has been explained as the "bowl of the year" or as the "nocturnal sky," but neither of the two is probable, for neither would have been described as *devapā́nam* or as *sómena pūrṇám*. The moon contains the drink of the gods, hence the moon is the bowl which Tvaṣṭṛ carries, and his four phases which change in course of time and are mentioned frequently in the Veda[233] are the *camasā́ vibhrā́jamānāḥ* (IV.33.6), the miraculous achievement of the Ṛbhus, the genii of the seasons.

The contest between the Ṛbhus and Tvaṣṭṛ, who is himself a skilful workman like the Ṛbhus, permits us to infer that like them he is also connected with time and, as Ludwig thinks,[234] is the god of the year. This explanation, which is inadequate in itself, contradicts a part of the rest of his activity, above all, his relationship to Indra who drinks the Soma in Tvaṣṭṛ's house.

2. Tvaṣṭṛ is a householder. ṚV V.41.8 states explicitly:

abhí vo arce poṣyā́vato nṝn
vā́stoṣ pátiṃ tvā́ṣṭāraṃ rárāṇaḥ /

"I implore you, O men who grant prosperity, and with rich gifts [I implore] the lord of the house, Tvaṣṭṛ." The ten fingers of the householder produce the fire which is distributed in his abodes.

I. 95.2 : *dáśemáṃ tvā́ṣṭur janayanta gárbham*
átandrāso yuvatáyo víbhṛtram /
tigmā́nīkaṃ sváyaśasaṃ jáneṣu
virócamānaṃ pári ṣīṃ nayanti //

"[the] ten produced the infant of Tvaṣṭṛ, the indefatigable maidens [produced the one who is] much distributed.[235] They carry him around among men, him whose visage is sharp, who is full of fame and shining." Indra seizes the Soma drink in his house and the frightened Tvaṣṭṛ flees away from him.[236] As we saw in Vivasvat's case, the sun is a householder and the moon is also one.[237] The latter does not come into question here. On the other hand, the ṚV mentions often the Soma drink (see p. 218 above) which Indra enjoyed in the house of Viṣṇu, the sun god.[238] Sūrya's daughter cleanses the Parisrut for him. In conjunction with trait no. 1 it is not improbable that Tvaṣṭṛ also, in whose house likewise Indra drinks the Soma, is a former name for the sun god. The following factor also speaks in favour of this : Tvaṣṭṛ's relation to Indra is sometimes friendly and sometimes hostile. On the one hand, he prepares the thunderbolt for Indra and on the other Indra fights him in his own house. Precisely the same is Indra's relation to the sun—the long forgotten point of origin of his own form—who befriends Indra sometimes as Viṣṇu[239] and sometimes as Pūṣan,[240] and who, on the other hand, receives the name of a Dāsa through Indra in V.33.4.[241] This last verse, in translating which I concur with Ludwig,[242] is a parallel to III. 48.4 : *tváṣṭārám índro janúṣābhibhūya* or to I. 80.14: *tváṣṭā cid táva manyáva índra vevijyáte bhiyā́.* Thus also the *pitā́ áśivaḥ* whom Indu, in concert with Indra, robs of the weapons and magic (VI.44.22; see Vol. I, p. 209) is the sun. He is, as far as I can judge, hidden in the names Śuṣṇa and Kayava as well. In the hot countries the sun is the friend or foe of men according to the season and according to the effect of his rays.[243] Hence, the tropical character of India is probably reflected in the twofold conception of the sun in the ṚV. However, the confused strands cannot be disentangled.

3. Madhu and Soma are synonymous in mythological language. Both are designations of the celestial ambrosia. Consequently, like Soma, Madhu is also in the possession of Tvaṣṭṛ.

I. 177.22 : *ātharvaṇā́yāśvinā dadhīcé*
áśvyaṃ śiraḥ práty airayatam |
sá vāṃ mádhu prá vocad ṛtāyán
tvāṣṭráṃ yád dasrāv apikakṣyàṃ vām ||

"To Atharvan's son Dadhyañc you have attached, O Aśvins, the horse's head. The pious [one] revealed to you Tvaṣṭṛ's honey, O wonder-workers, which was hidden even to you." More often than Tvaṣṭṛ's Madhu, mention is made of his possession of cows which are in his son's custody. In X. 49.10 Indra boasts that he has understood better than Tvaṣṭṛ how to deposit the Amṛta in the cows.[244] At Indra's command Trita slays Tvaṣṭṛ's son and drives his cows out.[245]

X. 8.8 : *sá pítryāṇy ā́yudhāni vidvā́n*
índreṣita āptyó abhy àyudhyat |

triśīrṣā́ṇaṃ saptáraśmiṃ jaghanvā́n
tvāṣṭrásya cin níḥ sasṛje tritó gā́ḥ ||
9: *bhū́rī́d índra udī́nakṣantam ójaḥ*
ávābhinat sátpatir mányamānam |
tvāṣṭrásya cid viśvárūpasya gónām
acakrāṇás trī́ṇi śīrṣā́ párā vark ||

"Well-versed in [the use of] the weapons of his father, Trita Āptya, urged on by Indra, attacked him. Then Trita slew the three-headed and seven-rayed [enemy] and freed the cows of Tvaṣṭṛ's son. Indra struck him down who attributed great strength to himself, the true lord [struck] him who considered himself to be such.[246] He seized the cows of Viśvarūpa son of Tvaṣṭṛ and tore off his three heads." Hence in X. 76.3 Tvaṣṭṛ's son is called *góarṇas*, "rich in cows" and *áśvanirṇij*, "adorned with horses" and it is said of him, remarkably enough, that "the sacrifices rest upon him."[247] *go*, *madhu* and *soma* are cognate expressions and denote ambrosia.

An indisputable passage of the ṚV answers the question where then the cows of Tvaṣṭṛ are kept, for it is said in

I. 84.15 : *átrā́ha gór amanvata*
nā́ma tvā́ṣṭur apīcyàm |
itthā́ candrámaso gṛhé ||

"in the moon's house indeed one knew the secret name of Tvaṣṭṛ's cow." From this we may infer that the house of the moon where one knows the cows of Tvaṣṭṛ and his son Viśvarūpa who guards these cows are mythologically the same.

4. Vāyu is regarded as Tvaṣṭṛ's son-in-law.

VIII. 26.21 : *táva vāyav ṛtaaspte tvā́ṣṭur jāmātar adbhuta* |
ávāṃsy ā́ vṛṇīmahe ||
22 : *tvā́ṣṭur jā́mātaraṃ vayám ī́śānaṃ rāyā́ īmahe*
sutā́vanto vāyum.. ||

"Offering Soma, we invoke Tvaṣṭṛ's son-in-law, the lord of riches, Vāyu."[248] The meaning is not clear.

5. Tvaṣṭṛ and Bṛhaspati, Agni. Tvaṣṭṛ has one son in the person of Viśvarūpa; besides him, there is Bṛhaspati whom Tvaṣṭṛ causes to be born from all beings, from every seed,

perhaps in his capacity as the divine master craftsman or perhaps there is another reason for this.

Verse I. 95.2 (*dáśemáṃ tváṣṭur janayanta* etc.) occurs in the middle of a hymn of which single verses like 1, 3, 4 are to be connected with the sun and the moon or with the latter alone. In the same hymn, v. 5 refers to the moon.

I. 95.5 : *āvíṣṭyo vardhate cā́rur āsu*
jihmā́nām ūrdhváḥ sváyaśā upásthe |
ubhé tváṣṭur bibhyatur jā́yamānāt
pratīcī́ siṃhám práti joṣayete ||

"Visible, the lovely one grows in these [waters], rising up with full splendour in the lap of the recumbent ones. Both (heaven and earth) were frightened of [the son of] Tvaṣṭṛ when he was born; turning to him, they fondled the lion." The first two pādas were cited in Vol. 1, p. 235 as a comparison to II. 35.9. It is obvious that Agni "who rises up in the lap of the recumbent ones" and who grows in the waters is none else than the *yúvā kavír góṣu, apsú drapso vāvṛdhānáḥ*, the "one eye which the rivers cause to grow,"[249] i.e. the young waxing moon and that he is a mythological parallel to Apāṃ napāt.

In two more passages Tvaṣṭṛ is said to be the father of Agni.[250] X. 2.7 ought to be the most important of such verses since in this hymn words are employed repeatedly which suggest the lunar character of this Agni,[251] and this seems to corroborate the inference drawn from I. 95.5.

6. Tvaṣṭṛ and women. ṚV I. 161.4 states that Tvaṣṭṛ, envious of the miraculous achievements of the Ṛbhus, hides among the women : *ā́d ít tváṣṭā gnā́sv antár ny ànaje.*[252] This is not the only time in the ṚV that Tvaṣṭṛ is mentioned in association with them.[253] We find a whole series of passages, but an adequate explanation of the nature of these women is given in none of them, not even in the most elaborate passage, viz., MS IV.14.9. Several times they are called the "wives of the gods." In the ritual of the New and Full moon sacrifice also the oblation for Tvaṣṭṛ is followed by one for the *devā́nāṃ pátnyaḥ*. These are, as can be inferred from the sequence in MS IV. 13.10, Indrāṇī, Varuṇānī etc., that is to say, abstractions. Tvaṣṭṛ's association with these divine women is certainly a

late one and proceeds from the conception of his being the genius of procreative power. I think Kuhn[254] is quite justified when he sees the waters as the real wives of Tvaṣṭṛ; these are indeed styled as mothers, wives, women in labour etc. The sun and the waters are connected quite frequently.[255] We may regard the expression is MS IV.12.5 : *sū́ryo apó vigāhate*[256] as synonymous with *tváṣṭā gnā́sv antár ny ā̀naje.*

Tvaṣṭṛ's association with women is regarded so distinctive of the god that all essential rites connected with women, which are in part obscene, are to be performed by the Neṣṭṛ[257] who belongs to the ritual of the Tvaṣṭṛ cult and who is mentioned in ṚV I.15.3 in the place of Tvaṣṭṛ.[258] I cannot account for the unusual role played by Āgnīdhra on this occasion.[259]

In Tvaṣṭṛ's association with women is expressed the notion that he is a genius of fertility. He bestows a pious and god-fearing son VS XXIX. 9 (TS V. 5.1.11); ṚV II. 3.9. He is also called *turī́pa,*[260] *páyasvat,*[261] *bhū́riretas,*[262] *retodhā́,*[263] *surétas,*[264], *sujániman;*[265] he confers procreative power upon human beings[266] as well as upon animals and is the shaper of their manifold forms.

ṚV I. 188.9: *tváṣṭā rūpā́ṇi hí prabhúḥ paśū́n viśvā́n samānajé|*
"Tvaṣṭṛ the mighty has indeed created the forms and all the animals."

III. 55·79 : *devás tváṣṭā savitā́*[267] *viśvárūpaḥ*[268]
pupóṣa prajā́ḥ purudhā́ jajāna |

X. 110.9 : *yá imé dyā́vāpṛthivī́ jánitrī*
rūpaír ápiṃśad bhúvanāni víśvā |
tám adyá hotar iṣitó yájīyān
devám tváṣṭāram ihá yakṣi vidvā́n ||

184.1 : *tváṣṭā rūpā́ṇi piṃśatu |*[269]

The god who creates all the beings and populates the world with them has the claim to be the *apásām apástama,* "the most skilful of the skilful," that is to say, the master craftsman of the gods. Hence he is called *sukṛ́t, supāṇí, sugábhasti, svápas;*[270] he carves the thunderbolt for Indra, sharpens the axe for Bṛhaspati and himself wields, in ṚV VIII. 29.3 as well as in the later literature,[271] a hatchet.[272] To this we may add that he is called *āśuheman* and *aciṣṭu*,[273] that he is the father of the horse and bestows swiftness upon its feet,[274] that with his wives he confers speed upon the chariot.[275] As the progenitor of all creatures he is called *agriyá*,[276] *agrajā́*, *puroyā́van*,[277] *agreyāvan*.[278] That he goes to the abode of the gods (ṚV II. 1.9), moves about between heaven and earth,[279] or as stated in solitary passages that he is extolled by Indra for his wisdom[280] are secondary traits which can be accounted for from every point of view and need not occupy us any further.

It is hard to establish who the two daughters of Tvaṣṭṛ are in the two obscure verses ṚV X.17.1,2. I have stated my views on p. 232 f. In one passage of the *Pañcaviṃśa Brāhmaṇa* (XII. 5.19) mention is made of several of these various daughters of Tvaṣṭṛ who lull Indra to sleep.[281] It is uncertain what Tvaṣṭṛ's union with the Aṅgiras' in ṚV X.70.9; I.186.6 and perhaps also with the Sūris in VI. 47.19 signifies.

The result of this investigation is not much. It is possible that Tvaṣṭṛ had been a sun god once. The later texts and lexicographers have treated him as one. Weber (*Zwei vedische Texte über Omina und Portenta*, p. 391) and others took up the notion. It has inner probability but cannot be proved.

Viśvarūpa

The saga of Tvaṣṭṛ and Viśvarūpa is a favourite motif in the later Vedic literature. Instead of many examples, I give below in an abridged form the legend as contained in ŚBr I.6.3.1 ff. : "Tvaṣṭṛ had a son with three heads and six eyes. This one had three mouths. Because he was shaped thus his name was 'All-shaped' (*viśvarūpa*). One mouth served for drinking the Soma, one for drinking the Surā and the third for other kinds of food. Indra hated him and cut off his heads. From the one with which he drank the Soma a hazel-cock sprang forth; that is why it is reddish brown, for King Soma is reddish brown. From that with which he drank the Surā, a sparrow emerged. Hence it speaks like a besotted person because one who has drunk the Surā speaks like a besotted one. From that which served him for other kinds of food a partridge arose. Hence it is entirely variegated in colour. Tvaṣṭṛ was furious. 'Has he then really killed my son?' He brought the Soma without Indra. Just as this Soma was pressed [without Indra] so it remained without Indra." The Brāhmaṇa goes on to relate how Indra seized the Soma by force and had to vomit it as punishment for this.[282] In the ṚV the word Tvāṣṭra denotes Tvaṣṭṛ's son thrice. To the two passages cited earlier, X.8·8 and 76.3, we should add II.11.19, which is exegetically unintelligible.[283] When we examine the words with which the son of Tvaṣṭṛ is described in this last verse, there is nothing to suggest a demon-like character in him with the exception of his general characteristic of holding the cows imprisoned. In X.8.8 he is described as *triśīrṣán saptáraśmi*; the second word, interpreted by the PW as "roughly seven-tongued," is otherwise an epithet of Agni, Bṛhaspati, Indra and Kāla—all patently gods of light and not demons. Likewise the epithet "three-headed" by itself does not have any hostile sense, for in I.146.1 Agni himself is called *trimūrdhán.* MS IV.13.8 (210.13) attributes to god Narāśaṃsa the epithets which belong to Tvaṣṭṛ's son in the passage from the ŚBr cited above, i.e. *triśīrṣán* and *ṣaḍakṣá.*[284] We may add one more factor. It is said in X.76.3 (see p. 237 above) that the sacrifices rest *goárṇasi tvāṣṭré áśvanirṇiji.* This is also better suited to a god rather than to a demon. Earlier we have come across the expression *yamé adhvaró ádhi me níviṣṭaḥ.*[285] Soma is *ātmā́ yajñásya, ketúḥ, jyótiḥ.*[286] We can assume that Tvaṣṭṛ's son had been at first a god of light and only later underwent the metamorphosis into a demon. It is striking when it is related in TS II.5.1.1 ff. that this Viśvarūpa was the Purohita of the gods[287] and that Indra by slaying him became guilty of brahmin-slaughter, for the luminous nature of the god is dimly visible here.

Thus we have a series of indications which are in agreement with the earlier result gained from I.84.15 and X.8.8, namely that Tvaṣṭṛ's son and the moon are one and the same. Hence Bergaigne was almost on the right path when he said (II, p.340) that "this son of Tvaṣṭṛ appears also to represent Soma, but a Soma assuming the demoniac character, which happens often to the concealed forms of either Soma or Agni."[288] The moon can very well be called Viśvarūpa. In *Bhāgavata Purāṇa* II.1.34 he is styled *sarvavikārakośa* (see PW, s.v. *kośa*, 1g). In TS III.3.10.2 Indu is *viśvarūpa.* "The Finns say that the moon has a peculiar and manifold appearance. Sometimes he is very narrow and some other times again he is much too broad in his face."[289] Keith's view (p.205) that "as Tvaṣṭṛ is himself called more often than any other Viśvarūpa [but still rarely !], it is difficult not to suspect that the connexion of Tvaṣṭṛ with Viśvarūpa of the three heads is due to the similarity of name" is—to use his own words—"not to be taken seriously."

It is difficult to define the correct viewpoint whence the demonization of the moon makes sense. We must underline the fact that this concept is popular in the Brāhmaṇa-like literature to such an extent that it rules out the possibility of its being a mere fanciful notion of the authors. We must state first that no less an authority than Yāska on ṚV I.105.18[290] explains the moon as a *vṛka.*[291] Moreover, ŚBr I.6.3.17 states: *taṃ* [*vṛtraṃ*] *dvedhā anvabhinat tasya yat saumyaṃ nyaktam āsa taṃ candramasaṃ cakārātha yad asyāsuryam āsa tenemāḥ prajā udareṇāvidhyat.* I.6.4.12: *vārtraghnaṃ vai paurṇamāsam indro hy etena vṛtram ahann athaitad eva vṛtrahatyaṃ yad āmāvāsyam / vṛtraṃ hy asmā etaj jaghnuṣa āpyāyanam akurvan.* I.6.4.18: *tad vā eṣa evendro ya eṣa tapaty athaiṣa eva vṛtro yac candramā so 'syaiṣa bhrātṛvyajanmeva* etc. IV.1.4.8: *vṛtro vai somo āsīt taṃ yatra devā aghnaṃs taṃ mitram abruvaṃs tvam api haṃsīti sa na cakame...*[292] 2.5.15: *devo vai somo divi hi somo vṛtro vai soma āsīt tasyaitac charīraṃ yad girayo yad aśmānaḥ...* 4.3.4: *vṛtro vai soma āsīt taṃ yatra devā aghnaṃs tasya mūrdhodvavarta sa droṇakalaśo 'bhavat.* I think we should not ignore the basic notion that "Vṛtra was the moon" which underlies these statements and which was further exploited by the scholiasts, for it reveals the diversity of the sagas connected with the moon and the dissimilarity of the mythical cycles which were interwoven with one another through the fondness for fictitious interpretations during the Brāhmaṇa period. The ŚBr is not alone with the above statement. I find similar expressions elsewhere too, for instance, MS III.7.8 (87.17): *vārtraghnaṃ vā etat somo vai vṛtraḥ pūrvedyur vā indro vṛtram ahan pūrvedyur vāvainam etat sṛtvāthāparedyur abhiṣuṇoti.* 8.2 (93.14): *ghṛtaṃ vai devā vajraṃ kṛtvā somam aghnan ... avadhiṣur vā etat somam.*[293] Hence, there existed, I venture to assume, a cycle of sagas which saw in the moon not the friendly god who causes the waters to flow, not the *yúvānaṃ kavím, vṛṣabháṃ góṣu,* but one who encloses them, namely Viśvarūpa son of Tvaṣṭṛ, by slaying whom Indra releases the waters. The ṚV alludes to this legend in solitary passages only but it attained greater popularity in the Brāhmaṇa period.

E. LESSER DEITIES

In the preceding part of my investigations several lesser deities of the Vedic world have already been discussed in the context of those beings who are akin to them.[294] Some others like Dyāvāpṛthivī do not cause any difficulties from the mythological point of view. I have passed over these because I do not wish to repeat what has already been stated and can recommend Hopkins[295] and Macdonell. Dyāvāpṛthivī are not so neglected in the cult as it might seem to be the case. The cult knows various sacrifices for them and has summarized its attitudes in the Sūktavāka, and in the Nivid formula which is incorporated into the Dyāvāpṛthivīsūkta of the Vaiśvadevaśastra. A *kṛṣamāṇaḥ pratiṣṭhākāmaḥ* offers a sacrificial beast to them; then from the sky Parjanya sends rain for him and plants grow on the earth (TS III.4.3.3). The sacrificial symbolism has seized upon the sky and the earth, and designated them as the *havirdhāne* of the gods (ABr I.29.4) or regarded the earth as the vedi (AV XIII.1.46, 52) and the sky as the dakṣiṇā (AV XIII.1.52).

While we have the impression as though the sky and the earth have meant very little in the mythology of the Vedic tribes, this is not so in the case of lesser deities— plants, professional implements, abstract ideas, all deified—although in comparison to the major gods it is but rarely that even these are mentioned and worshipped with sacrifices.

1. Trees and Plants

Like water and rivers, trees and plants were also objects of worship from time immemorial. As early as in the ṚV, Vanaspati is addressed as the "lord of the trees." Hymn X.97 is dedicated to the plants and X.146 to the forest goddess. At the head of all plants is Soma, the god as well as the plant, and he is regarded as the *oṣadhīpati* even in the later times. *Rukkhadevatās,* the tree and sylvan nymphs, are more prominent in Buddhist and Jaina literatures and in fables than in the literature of the Vedic period.[296] In the ritual also we come across solitary traces of this cult; thus in the expiatory sacrifice when a tree is cut in order to be used as a yūpa. When a man drives on a new chariot and comes across a good tree on the way, he should drive around the tree from left to right and take with him branches and fruit from it (ĀśvGS II.6.9). There are more instances of the tree cult in the magical rites which, to effect the maxim *similia similibus*, employ roots, stalks and fruits. In the short description of the Rājasūya, the *Pañcatantra* speaks of "hundred-and-eight roots that have been gotten ready."[297] Like the entire world, the plant kingdom too falls into two parts according to the evil effects which its members cause or are supposed to cause. While planting good trees is meritorious, it is necessary before one builds one's house to uproot certain plants from the ground (ĀśvGS II.7.5). However, in spite of these traces it is surprising that the tree worship plays a relatively small role in the Veda. Hence the Veda does not seem to share the universal popularity of the tree cult.

The reasons why this tree cult remained in the background must be different from those that can be considered for the meagre worship of the "sky and earth." Those who arranged the Vedic cult and selected hymns for this purpose did not take all that was available but gave preference to the major gods.[298] The elements which, in the eyes of ethnographers, uniformly constitute a mythology were assessed differently and mixed disproportionately by the Vedic redactors. The possibility which I have underlined in the Introduction that the collection of the hymns was primarily for the sake of the Devayāna and its major festivals might have been one of the fundamental reasons why the tree cult etc. were given only minor importance. Also religious differences, which we notice even in the later period, might have played a role. In the *Harivaṃśa* (II.16.2.ff. = LXXI.2) Dāmodara calls upon the people to stay away from Indra's festival and instead worship cows, mountains and forests.

v. 2: *gāvo 'smad daivataṃ viddhi girayaś ca vanāni ca* |
9: *mantrayajñaparā viprāḥ sītāyajñās tu karṣukāḥ*
giriyajñās tathā gopā ijyo 'smābhir girir vane[299] ||

Here we see in a bold relief Kṛṣṇa's distinct opposition to Indra worship, which might have lost its popularity at that time or which began to encroach into Mathurā as well.

2. Animals

Animal cult also finds only a limited place in the ritual. Mostly the animals are supposed to symbolize only that element to which they seem to be related. Frog denotes the coolness of water, goat represents the fire, horse is a symbol of the sun and bull the sign of virility-bestowing Indra. An examination of the ritual literature shows that in the offering or avoiding of certain animals we can notice neither a trace of totemism nor an allusion to the erstwhile animal-shape of the god concerned, that only in solitary instances a specific class of animals is drawn into association with a deity and that the colour of the animal plays a decisive role.[300] The example for such attribution of individual character is the offering of a sheep to Sarasvatī.

Sacrifices are rarely made to animals. Just as there is a "king of the plants" so one invents a "king" of the black ants, of the white ants and of other types of ants.[301] A "king of worms" is imagined and besought to avert the troubles caused by his underlings. An offering is made in the Śravaṇākarman to the Adhipati of serpents of all kinds (PGS II.14.11 ff.), and to the king of mice (*ākhurāj*) for the protection of one's crops and one's fruit (GGS IV. 4.30). Only very rarely sacrificial beasts are dedicated to the representatives of individual species of animals. TS V. 5.11 mentions a *gavaya* for *ṛṣabharājan*, a *gaura* for *śārdūlarājan* and so on. The view has been advanced by various scholars that in the ṚV we find the personification of the "ordinary horses" whose swiftness in the racing contests had paved their way to the gods. I cannot share this view or rather share it with certain reservations, for these hymns, IV.38-40; VII.44; X.178, are a part of the Aśvamedha,[302] well known to the ritual, which was customarily performed by the victorious king as early as in the ṚV. The MBh has dedicated an entire parvan to this phenomenon which had become a significant and characteristic feature in the cultural history of India. There (*Āśvamedhaparvan* 73.27) Arjuna who followed the horse is called *mahāratha*. Just as in the MBh the horse which is destined for the *medha* and which crosses into the territories of the neighbouring kings runs ahead of the young warriors' chariots, so runs Dadhikrāvan in ṚV VII.44.4 *ágre ráthānām*. It is the sacrificial animal which was once given to the Pūrus for victorious battles by Mitra-Varuṇa and is now extolled in the famous sacrificial hymn. It is the custom in India to praise during the great Aśvamedha sacrifice the animal destined for the sacrifice and, as ṚV I.162, 163 demonstrate, to celebrate it in hymns. In the fire-churning rite of Agnyādheya a horse should be present, which is a symbol of the sun, from whom the fire originates, and this horse should touch the place of the Āhavanīya with its hoof; in several sacrifices to Sūrya a white horse significantly enough constitutes the dakṣiṇā. Likewise in the Aśvamedha, the horse represents the swift solar horse, who is the kinsman of the gods. *ātmánaṃ te mánasārā́d ajānām avó divā́ patáyantaṃ pataṃgám / śiro apaśyaṃ pathíbhiḥ sugébhir areṇúbhir jéhamānaṃ patatrí*: thus a sacrificial horse is addressed.[303] Indian texts occasionally join the sun and the Aśvamedha in a dual. TBr III. 9.21.3 : *prāṇāpānau vā etau devānāṃ yad arkāśvamedhau . . . ojo balaṃ vā etau devānāṃ yad arkāśvamedhau* etc. The commentary explains this with the quotation : *arko vā eṣa yad agnir asāv āditya 'śvamedhaḥ*, not quite correctly because what is more probable is that here the sun and the Aśvamedha itself are connected both intrinsically and externally. The sacrificer who takes the Aśvamedha bath hopes to be forgiven for his grave sins, and the poet of IV. 39.3 desires that Aditi may make him free from all sins since he praised Dadhikrāvan at the blazing sacrificial fire early in the morning. In VII.44 Dadhikrāvan is treated quite like a deity. According to TS II.2.5.1, an *abhiśasyamāna* should offer a puroḍāśa for Vaiśvānara, a caru for Varuṇa and another caru for Dadhikrāvan, for which oblation a piece of gold forms the dakṣiṇā. There is no intrinsic difference between the sacrificial horse and the solar horse. What is true of Dadhikrāvan is true also of Daurgaha, called thus probably after the donor,[304] and of Tārkṣya (X.178) who had won thousands for his lord likewise through his swiftness and is being sacrificed now (at the end of a year-long looting expedition which usually precedes the sacrifice). This one is also not a "racing horse" in the ordinary sense of the word.[305]

It might be purely accidental that *bradhná*, which we know as an epithet of the solar horse,[306] has not been used to designate a sacrificial horse as well.

The worship of the ox and cow, attested innumerable times in the AV and notably in the later times, seldom finds a direct expression in the ṚV. But the manifold application of the words *vṛṣabha* and *go* to men and gods (Indra, Uṣas, Pṛthivī, Aditi), the eulogy of the liberation of the cattle etc. are definitely clear indications for this. The inviolability of the cow is proved for the ṚV by the word *aghnyā* (see Macdonell, p. 151), remarkably enough, however not for all its maṇḍalas, but most frequently—in relation to the others—in maṇḍalas VII—X. Of birds only the falcon or eagle is prominent as the bringer of the celestial Soma. Snakes do not yet receive any reverence, the word *sarpa* occurring only once in the ṚV. It is only gradually that offerings to the snakes are included in the Vedic literature and notably in the Gṛhya Sūtras, which were more easily and quickly susceptible to the influences of folk cults than were the Śrauta Sūtras.[307]

3. Mountains

The worship of the mountains also has found only a limited place in the Vedic hymns. Although sacred mountains must have attracted the attention of the pious at all times even in India, none of these are mentioned definitely by name in the Veda. Allusions are made to the cult of the mountains only in vague outlines, in occasional invocations of general nature[308] where "mountains" are mentioned beside forests, waters and plants. The commentary on the *Kauśika Sūtra* speaks of "seven mountain deities."

4. Professional Deities

The Veda informs us about the worship of professional implements at some length, though it is still little in comparison to the magnitude of such cults in the later times. The farmer who worships his furrow, *urvarā khalamālinī*, and plough has his cult hymn in IV.57; VI.28. The warrior invokes the drum, chariot and bow (VI.47.26 ff.; VI.75). It is but natural that the professional deities of the brahmin priests, deities who emerge from the ritual implements, are more numerous. Among these we should count Havirdhāna (X. 13); pestle and mortar (I. 28), Soma press stones (III. 57.4; X. 175 etc.), *aráṇi*, *svárūṇām mitáyaṇ*, *prasvàḥ*, *védi*, *dhiṣáṇā*, *gharmá* (TĀr), last but not least, *yajñá*, the personification of the sacrifice itself. The speculation advanced to such an extent that *bhūtám* etc. have been made mystic priests (TMBr XXV. 18.5) and *úcchiṣṭa* has been elevated to the status of a special deity. In this category we can include also *tápas*, *śraddhā́*, *námas* (X. 92.4), *gír*, *bráhman*, *mántra*, *dhī́*, *matí* and even *vā́c* (X. 125 etc.), perhaps also *dvā́ro devī́ḥ* (I. 142.6 etc.) because all these concepts have been occasionally raised to the rank of independent beings through the priestly activity. This leads us to the next section.

5. Abstractions

Vis-à-vis the host of gods who emerged out of personifications of natural phenomena or of objects which are somehow or other tangible, there appears a floating mass of evanescent forms that rise from the realm of wishes, inclinations and activities. Even these occur sporadically in comparison to the major gods like Agni, Indra, Varuṇa etc.[309] It is rarely that we find hymns like VII.35 with its abundance of names which go back partly to individual gods and partly to abstractions and hymns where Indrāgnī, Indrāvaruṇau etc. are juxtaposed with *śaṁsa*, *satyásya suyámasya śáṃsaḥ*, *dhātṛ́*, *dhartṛ́*, *urūcī́ svadhā́bhiḥ*. *devā́nāṃ suhávāni*, *sukṛ́tāṃ sukṛtā́ni*, *rájasaḥ páti*, *bhavī́tra*, *kṣétrasya páti*, *abhiṣā́caḥ*, *rātiṣā́caḥ*, *satyásya pátayaḥ*.[310] VIII.31.11 mentions *rayí*, *bhága* and *urú ádhvan*. TS IV.1.6 (=VS XI. 61) has besides *devā́nāṃ patnī́ḥ*, also *dhiṣaṇā́ḥ . . . gnā́ḥ . . . varūtrayo janayaḥ*. It is hardly possible to classify these gods into a rigid system because there is a constant transition between the individual classes and because quite different areas are involved. Perhaps it is best to keep the designation "abstractions" for these, for the names that have been proposed more recently have their own drawbacks. Among these we find first of all the personified *deva trātṛ*, *dhartṛ*, *dhātṛ*, *netṛ*, *varūtrīḥ devīḥ* (VS XI.61) who are to some extent agent gods and from whose midst Savitṛ soared up and was raised to a sun god. We find secondly the embodiment of all inclinations, from love to hatred, which have their origin in the innermost feelings of human beings and clothe themselves in magic formulas and sacrificial rites in order to reach their goal : here we should mention primarily *kāma* and *manyu*. As against the objective gods derived from natural phenomena—*prāṇa* also can be counted among these—we can speak here, in the realm of feelings, of subjective gods.[311]

Thirdly we have *Zustandsgötter* (deified states or conditions) arising from appellatives which designate positive or negative states, e.g., Bhaga who became one of the Ādityas, Mahiman, Nirṛti, and inseparable from these the activities like *rāti* and its opposite *arāti*, and finally qualities like fame, industry and energy.[312] Fourthly, here belong the purely abstract words like Prajāpati, Viśvakarman, Hiraṇyagarbha insofar as he is not made abstract from a real basis (X. 121), Brahman himself and finally one of the most unusual gods created by Brahmanism, namely, *ka* (adj. *kāya*) to whom even sacrificial offerings are made.[313]

Though these personifications are often not placed in the foreground and lead a bare existence in the ritual as well, we should not assume that they floated into Vedic mythology very late or from unconnected realms of ideas. The Prajāpati myths contain elements that are familiar to primitive peoples. We may compare for instance, the story of the earth's creation in TBr I. 1.3.6; 2.1.3, 4 etc. (Lang, *Mythes, cultes et religion*, p. 232 ff.). It is well known that *purandhi* which cannot be separated from the Avestan *pārəndi*—as before I adhere to the view that it is not a genius of abundance but of "activity"—and *aramati* (Avestan *ārmaiti*) "the pious thought," have a pre-Indian origin.[314] *kāma, manyu, nirṛti* are invoked often in magic rites. The formation of a sacrificial technique which serves notably the last two notions demonstrates the complete familiarity of the Vedic age with the personification of what are apparently abstract concepts. It would be worth the trouble to follow in detail the notions that surround Nirṛti who is known already to the ṚV as *durvidátrā*, and the adoptation of the sacrificial technique according to these notions. They form a chapter of national psychology that is interesting not merely to students of mythology. Dice, women and sleep are assigned to her realm (MS III. 63.12). Disease (HGS II. 4.1) and all other discomforts are wished away to her. Her ceremonies are performed with black grain or with nail parings. A black cow with faulty horns is given away as dakṣiṇā. In the piling of the fire altar three black bricks, baked with husks, are inserted for Nirṛti. In the Rājasūya the king's barren wife is regarded as the representative of Nirṛti and the oblations to Nirṛti are offered in her house.[315] But the most important of these is the concept of Ṛta which was formed and deified in the so-called Indo-Iranian period.[316]

There is also another factor which testifies to the originality and popularity of these gods, namely their inclusion in the Gṛhya Sūtras which are closer to popular beliefs than the Śrauta Sūtras which developed somewhat farther away from them. PGS I.4.13 speaks of the goddesses who "spun, wove and stretched" (=AV XIV.1.45). In the ceremony of handing over the pupil to the teacher, we encounter names like *antaka, vaśini, subhūta* etc.[317] *Kauśika Sūtra* LVI.13 mentions among others *bhūta, agni, brahman, udaṅkya, śūlvāṇa, śatruṃjaya, kṣātrāṇa, mārtyuṃjaya, mārtyava, aghora, takṣaka, vaiśāleya, hāhāhūhū* (two Gandharvas); this text (like others) even recognizes a distinction between *sarve devāḥ* and *viśve devāḥ*. In ŚGS II.14.10 ff. *śrī, bhadrakālī, sarvānnabhūti, naktaṃcara, ahaścara* make their appearance beside Viṣṇu etc.[318] The "furrow" of the tiller, to which offerings are made, besides to *yajā, śamā* and *bhūti*, is protected by guards, *sītāgoptṛ-s*, of all kinds who are addressed with fanciful names. In the east, for example, the furrow is guarded by *sudhanvan* and *niṣaṅgin*, in the south by *animiṣa* and *varmin*, in the west by *ābhū, prabhū, bhūti, bhūmi, pārṣṇī* and *śunaṃkuri*, in the north by *bhīmā vāyusamā jave*.[319] When the cows go to pasture they are recommended to the protection of the *ghoṣiṇī* (ŚGS III.9.1). There are *devajanāḥ* and *itarajanāḥ*.[320] In the sacrifice for the dead *khyātṛ, apākhyātṛ, abhilālapant* and *apalālapant* are worshipped among others.[321] But seldom has any of these names acquired a general acceptance as in the case of Bhaga, who is included in the ranks of the Ādityas, or of Savitṛ who has become a sun god; Narāśaṃsa belongs to quite a different group and can be drawn into this context only through the confusion with *śaṃsa*, "praise."

However, this process has its limits. I cannot agree with Bloomfield[322] when he seeks to make a deity out of the idea of "red" who is opposed to "yellow" and who becomes the object of worship for all who suffer from jaundice and finally for all who desire health and longevity. It is only "the process of piling upon this very simple fiction all possible myth-making acts derived from the grosser sphere of visible gods" which produces Rohita the god. Similarly, I do not think that the "god yava" who resembles the word *yāvaya* owes his existence to this resemblance. On the contrary, I think that the word-symbolism employed in the exorcism has attached itself conversely with the type of havis and makes use of this superficial resemblance. The word *nyak* is employed in a magic formula but in reality no god of this type is conceived. In a propitiatory formula the symbolizing expression *sam* is fondly employed but it is not elevated to a god with a similar sounding name.

6. Goddesses

Even among the gods the Veda prefers the man and not the woman. Manifestations like Durgā and Śrī with the multiplicity of their synonyms are unknown to it. Such artificial-looking formations like Indrāṇī and Varuṇānī float past us rather feebly without any life whatever.

Basically it is not a correct principle to compare the Vedic goddesses with the gods. For the problem is connected with the question of the origin of the grammatical gender which alone was certainly the reason for the position of, for example, *vāc*, *purandhi* etc. on the feminine side. It is also connected with certain general notions which caused the division into masculine and feminine gender. The winds conceived as men are the Gandharvas, the waters conceived as women are the Apsarases; the ocean is the husband, the rivers are his wives; the sky is the husband, the earth his wife; Sūrya (Savitṛ) the father, Uṣas (=Sūryā) his daughter, beloved etc. Uṣas and Rātrī are sisters just as the Aśvins are brothers. Ambikā is Rudra's sister. We encounter feminine deities based on concrete foundations like Pṛthivī,[323] Sūryā, Uṣas, Rātrī, Paurṇamāsī and Amāvāsyā. Others are fictitious products like Varuṇānī and Indrāṇī. It is difficult to decide about a third group. While at one place Ekāṣṭakā, the night of the New Year, is said to be Indra's mother, at other places Indra joins the ranks of the Ādityas and becomes Aditi's son. In another group, it does not seem to be necessary to look for one or the other specific manifestation in Indra's or Vṛtra's mother (I. 32.9).[324] Often "mother" or "father" is invented purely out of speculative need, from the desire to assign a family tree and origin to each and everybody. Bergaigne (III. pp. 108-10) took great trouble with his enquiry about the father of Indra. These things, based purely on imagination, are not so deep.[325] Similarly the account of Indra's birth as given in ṚV IV.18 reminds us of the many legends about supernatural births the explanation for which cannot be sought in the plane of natural phenomena.[326] The same diversity of origin can be observed in the case of the "wives of the gods." In this context also Indra's evolution offers us instructive examples. For instance, in the ṚV, "the streams" are stated to be Indra's wives, elsewhere *sītā* and *urvarā* occupy this position (see p. 130 f. above); in VS XXVIII.8, on the other hand, *iḍā, sarasvatī* and *bhāratī*; elsewhere *vāc*. Besides these wives, conceived more or less concretely, there are others of quite abstract nature : first of all, Indrāṇī herself, then *śacī, prāsahā, senā.*[327] These names are alike but not synonymous from the very beginning; only at a later stage they were treated as identical. Indrāṇī comes close to Aditi and acquires some traits even from Dawn whose *triṃśataṃ yojanāni* (I.123.8) are transferred to Indrāṇī in MS III.8.4.[328] There are passages where no specific name occurs. It is not at all certain if in such places we are to think of one or the other of the above-mentioned wives and not rather of a "wife" conceived in general terms.[329] In view of such fluid concepts, it is necessary to enquire about the meaning of "mother" or "wife" of Indra separately in each case and not to make one passage the starting point for the explanation of the rest. Among other feminine beings, the *devānāṃ patnyaḥ* occur with relative frequency.[330] In the sacrifice to the New and Full Moon, they have a place at the end of the Patnīsaṃyājas dedicated to Tvaṣṭṛ and receive their oblations behind a veil. Likewise in the evening savana they participate in the fertility rite of the Patnīvratagraha. *gnā́ devápatnīr indrāṇī́, agnā́yyī, aśvínī rā́j, ródasī, varuṇānī́* as well as *ṛtúr jánīnām* are mentioned in the Ṛgvedic verses V. 46.7 and 8 which form the Hotṛ's invocation in the New and Full Moon sacrifice. Besides these names, in the case of special wishes,[331] there occur also Saṃyājas for Rākā, Sinīvālī, Kuhū and probably also for Anumati. From the accompanying verses which are borrowed partly from the ṚV, I cannot infer that the first three denote the phases of the moon as is mostly assumed. I would rather think that they emerged from the sphere of the above-mentioned goddesses "who spun and wove," the *ghoṣiṇī, vāhinī* etc., and have become the midwives for women. We learn still less about names like *mātā́ bṛhaddivā́*. Other beings like Urvaśī[332] (beside her husband Purūravas), who appear among the Apsarases without possessing any individual characteristics and enter the realm of fables, defy in my opinion a definitive mythological interpretation.

CHAPTER NINE

MANES, DEMONS AND ASURAS

A. MANES

Just as the day of the Viṣuvat divides the year into two halves and assigns the Uttarāyaṇa to the gods and the Dakṣiṇāyana to the Manes so is the entire creation divided into two parts : the day belongs to the gods and men, the night to the Manes and evil spirits, the half month with the waxing moon to the gods, that with the waning moon to the Manes, what is on the right belongs to the former and what is on the left to the latter. North is the region of the gods, south that of the Manes : and thus we see further that the opposition between light and darkness, gold and silver, heaven and the interior of the earth correspond to the distinction between the gods and the Manes. Even the duration of human life has a line of demarcation, namely the fiftieth year. While performing the ceremonies, the sacrificer makes allowances for this distinction by wearing the sacrificial thread in different ways,[1] by moving from left to right or from right to left as the case may be,[2] by walking along the course of the sun or against it and so on. The ṚV is not devoted to the cult of the Manes, its aim being the gods of the Devayāna, and so it is not surprising that with the exception of the small Yama-Saṃhitā in book X we learn very little about the Manes from the Veda, but it is obvious that it did not know the concept of a soul detached from the body.[3] The ritual sources which are all the more rich have been discussed so often and so well that, to avoid repeating what has already been stated, I can safely limit myself to some general remarks.

The cult of the dead has its regular place in the afternoon of the New Moon sacrifice, in the Mahāpitṛ sacrifice of the quarterly ceremonies and in the Narāśaṃsa cup of the Soma sacrifices.

As in the Cāturmāsyas so also in the Gṛhya Sūtras their place is in the diminishing half of the year. The Aṣṭakās are devoted to their service. According to a statement of Manu, the Manes wish for a progeny "which offers milk-food with honey and clarified butter on the thirteenth day (of Bhādrapada) and in the afternoon when the elephant's shadow falls into the east."[4] "Whatever one offers mixed with honey on the thirteenth day during the rainy season and under the Maghāḥ is imperishable."

Vedic literature classifies the Manes themselves in quite different ways. Those who have partaken of the Soma drink bear the names *ūmāḥ* or *avamāḥ* in the morning, *ūrvāḥ* at noon and *kāvyāḥ* in the evening.[5] But besides the ancestors of the Soma-sacrificers there are other ancestors who do not have a share in the Soma drink. Already ṚV X. 15.8, 10 mention, apart from the *somyā́saḥ* (*yé...anūhiré somapīthám vásiṣṭhāḥ*), the *havirádaḥ*, *haviṣpāḥ*, *gharmasádaḥ*.[6] Even Manu III.198 divides the ancestors into *somapa*, *haviṣmat*, *ājyapa* and *sukālin*, thus preserving a tradition which probably has been modified but not quite newly invented. Manu adds that the sons of "the Kavi, Aṅgiras, Pulastya and Vasiṣṭha" respectively are called thus. I think that this statement would not be conceivable without certain actual reminiscences of the original differences in the rituals of the different families.[7] Elsewhere in literature mention is made of *pitaraḥ somavantaḥ*, *pitaraḥ barhiṣadaḥ* and *pitaraḥ agniṣvāttāḥ*,[8] and according to the rules of Kātyāyana, in the sacrifice to the Manes during the quarterly ceremonies a puroḍāśa is offered to the first group, grains to the second and a beverage that has been stirred to the third. I think that here also we have the original practices of different families, and the sacrificial offerings have been modified according to the usage of the clan concerned. Also the statement that the *pitaraḥ somapāḥ* are made content in Soma, the *barhiṣadaḥ* in Yama aṅgirasvat and the *agniṣvāttāḥ* in Agni kavyavāhana[9] might be an indication that the erstwhile division of these classes, the so-called *devāḥ pitaraḥ*,[10] is based on clan differences.

Another classification which is occasionally mixed with the former is based on a different point of view, namely on the mode of the disposal of the dead. Here the division is made into *agnidagdha* (*agniṣvātta*) and *anagnidagdha* which is known already to ṚV X.15.14 and is a continuation of the old distinction between cremation and burial (or exposure to the elements as the case may be).

Also the variety of views that occur in the Vedic literature about the abode of the dead need not be the products of a linear historical evolution but could have had, like the differences in the sacrifice, their point of origin in the beliefs of different clans. The theory which assigns the belief in the Manes who dwell inside the earth and are harmful to men to an earlier period and their transference to heaven, on the other hand, to a later period is not adequately proved. Ethnography teaches that the traces of both the concepts can be found in quite primitive peoples. It is also natural that a distinction is made between the spirits of the dead of one's own clan and those of others, in particular those of hostile tribes. In TS II. 4.1.1, for instance, besides the series *devāḥ manuṣyāḥ pitaraḥ* there is a second series of *asurāḥ rakṣāṃsi piśācāḥ*.[11] Moreover, we should take into account the influence of the sacrifice on the transference of the dead from the realm of the shadows to the celestial world.

Death and the realm of the dead are connected with horror. The impurity which emanates from the dead attaches itself to the members of his house for long and makes the departed person himself a danger to the living. Those who return home from the funeral "wipe off" the traces of death; between them and the dead person a stone is placed as a dividing wall and the departed one is addressed with the words *mā́ naḥ prajā́ṃ rīriṣo mótá vīrā́n* (ṚV X. 18.1). When one passes the seven pits after the funeral, stones are thrown into them. The relatives are given seven pebbles each which they are to scatter individually during their return from the funeral (*Ritualliteratur*, p. 89). The remains of the water which is used for sprinkling and which is mixed with barley grains is poured into the pit : *śundhantāṃ lokāḥ pitṛṣadanā iti pitṛdevatyo vai kūpaḥ khātaḥ* (ŚBr III. 7.1.6). Then sacrificial grass is spread into it and during this process the formula *pitṛṣadanam asi* is uttered, for the Manes have that which has been buried as their deity.[12]

One did not remain forever with this notion. At the time of

kindling the cremation fire a pit is dug in which a water plant is deposited and as an explanation for this it is said[13] that the departed one goes from the pit to heaven along with the smoke. Here, I think, the terrestrial concept sought to combine itself with the celestial notion. Already the ṚV speaks in X. 15.1 of the *ávare, párāsaḥ, madhyamā́ḥ pitáraḥ*; v. 2 of the *yé pā́rthive rájasy ā́ níṣattā yé vā nūnáṃ suvṛjánāsu vikṣú*; v. 3 of the Manes and Viṣṇu's step; v. 7 of those who sit in the lap of the dawns (*aruṇī́nām upasthe*). AV XVIII.4.78 divides the Manes into *pṛthiviṣád, antarikṣaṣád, diviṣád.* Besides these, another notion operates in ṚV X.16.3 according to which the eye of the departed one goes to the sun, the mind into the wind and the body into the sky, earth, waters or plants. This recalls the creation of the world out of Puruṣa, from whose eyes the sun springs up and from whose breath the wind takes its shape (ṚV X. 90.13 ff.).

The notion that the dead dwell in the atmosphere occurs more rarely. What I have to say on this has been elaborated already in Vol. I, p. 67 ff. The evolution of the Maruts into the winds of storm and the conception of the Manes as birds (see p. 182 f. above)[14] might be related to this. More frequently we encounter the belief that the heaven is the abode of the departed ones. The departed one who goes forth on the ancient paths joins his fathers and the treasure of his good deeds *paramé vyòman* (X. 14.8) and "those who were cremated in fire as well as those who were not" are delighted *mádhye diváḥ* at the offerings to the dead (*svadháyā*) (X. 15.14; 154.5 etc.).[15] Viṣṇu's "foot-print" shines down from the sky and symbolizes for the Viṣṇuites of the Vedic times the goal of their earthly hope : "let me reach this dear place of his where the pious refresh themselves. The well, filled with honey, at Viṣṇu's step is verily the comrade of the far-striding one" (I. 154.5).[16]

The Viṣṇu cult was the source or one of the sources from which the hope of a future life in the celestial world and in the sun has entered into Indian belief. Other tribes have placed their ancestors euhemeristically among the gods. We cannot cite any definite case where a single historical person was elevated to a god. But the ancestors of the Aṅgiras' and Bhṛgus transfer an entire class from the kingdom of the Manes to the realm of the gods. Frequently the Manes are invoked quite like the gods. Already the ṚV extols their assistance in the opening of the cow-shed, in the recovery of light; it believes that they grant wealth, offspring and protection to their pious descendants.[17] To the category of the deified ancestors belongs, besides the Navagvas and Daśagvas who cannot be defined more precisely, also the group of Āptyas discussed above on p. 194, and perhaps the Sādhyas who are mentioned next to the Devas and Ṛṣis in ṚV X. 90. 7;[18] however, one wonders whether they do not denote an old class of gods. The "five tribes" were also transferred to heaven or at least deified.[19] Conversely, in the later literature it is occasionally stated that the Devas were also once human beings, and according to an ancient statement quoted by Manu, the Vasus, Rudras and Ādityas were also "Manes."[20]

Their relation to the moon has found its religious expression in the myths connected with Soma, Yama and Narāśaṁsa. I have discussed earlier all that can be said on this. The relation is represented in the ritual in the shape of the Dakṣiṇa hearth at which the Manes receive their share. Some remarks made against me by L. von Schroeder make it desirable that I come back to this point once again. In his review of the second volume of the *Vedische Mythologie* (1st ed.), he says: "If we are to believe wholly that in contradistinction to the sun who shines in the sky, the moon is conceived in the atmosphere — thus the triad sky, atmosphere and earth corresponding to the triad sun, moon and earth — then we have before us an impossible assumption. In my knowledge, no tribe on earth entertains such a notion but everywhere the sun and moon both appear as the inhabitants of the heavens, as celestial lights moving in the sky."[21]

This is of course true in the ordinary parlance, L. von Schroeder does not deny his concurrence to my view that the Dakṣiṇa fire seems to refer to the moon or to the wind. Let us consider the layout of the sacrificial place. Above (in the east) is the Āhavanīya fire (=the sun) and below the Gārhapatya (=hearth fire), in the middle to one side in the south the fire of the Manes. Why this arrangement ? The Devayāna, i.e., the period of the Uttarāyaṇa, when the sun reaches the highest point and the moon sinks downwards and belongs to the Antarikṣa, is the period for the sacrifices to the gods. The configuration of the sacrificial place which is set up according to certain cosmological and astronomical principles suggests the conditions in the Uttarāyaṇa. Further, whosoever equates Soma-Pūṣan, as I do, with the moon and the sun can find support in II.40.4: *divy ànyáḥ sádanaṃ cakrá uccā́, pṛthivyā́m anyó ádhy antárikṣe,* "the other has set up his abode above the earth in the atmosphere," or as Sāyaṇa would prefer "on the earth (in the shape of the plant), in the atmosphere (as the moon)." L. von Schroeder states further: "It is impossible and contrary to every naturalistic conception to treat the wind as a form of Agni. The wind has as good as nothing in common with the latter." The objection applies more to the Indians than to me, for their scholars disputed seriously whether one should worship the wind as fire or not (see Vol. I, pp. 69, 98f.) and the Śākāyanins firmly believed that the wind is a form of fire. This notion is expressed in the shape of the hearth of the southern fire which can have, besides the form of the half-moon, also that of a noose. In Punjab *loh* is a designation for the hot winds (Merk, *Acht Vorträge, p.* 73).

The belief that the Manes shine as stars in the sky has likewise its adherents in India.[22] We find that several stars are associated with the changes in nature and that the names of important Ṛṣis occur again in those of celestial stars. "Whenever Agastya rises," says Al-Berūnī,[23] "and the water increases in the rivers and valleys during his time, you see the rivers offering to the moon all that is on the surface of their water..." Agastya, who bears the epithet *kumbhayoni* in classical Sanskrit,[24] is already known from the Veda because of his relation to the Maruts. If we seek to discover further traces of the Vedic star cult, we should refer above all to the testimony of Hiraṇyakeśin (HGS I. 22. 14 ff.) who enjoins the worship of the Nakṣatras, moon, the seven Ṛṣis with Arundhatī, and the Pole Star during the first installation of fire in the domestic hearth.[25] The Pole Star bears the designation *nakṣatrāṇāṃ methī*; it is addressed as *brahman*, *dhruva*, *acyuta*, *avyathamāna*, *nabhya sarvasya*; the first formula for him is followed by *namo brahmaṇaḥ putrāya prajāpataye*, *brahmaṇaḥ putrebhyo devebhyas trayastriṃśebhyo namo brahmaṇaḥ putrapautrebhyo 'ṅgirobhyah.* Thus we find in the Gṛhya ritual a glorification of the Pole Star and of the seven Ṛṣis, i.e. the stars in the Great Bear,[26] and likewise occasionally in the Śrauta ritual as well. One wishes that the sacrifice and the sacrificer may reach "the world of the seven benevolent Ṛṣis"[27] and makes an offering for them in the north-east during the Agnihotra.[28] They are mentioned already in the oldest tradition. It was the "seven Ṛṣis, our fathers," who through sacrifice obtained Trasadasyu as son for the wife of Purukutsa when she was in distress (ṚV IV. 42. 8). They settled down (in the heavens) to practice *tapas*,[29] with the five Adhvaryus they guard "the hidden foot-print of the bird"[30] and are obviously identical with the seven mythical Vipras, Rebhas, Kārus, Hotṛs who stand next to the gods and ancestors,[31] who have taken part in the recovery of the cows,[32] sacrificed at first along with Manu,[33] and are to be regarded as the archetypes for the seven terrestrial Hotṛs who have their place at the seven hearths in the sacrifice.[34] The dhiṣṇyas of the Hotṛ and his companions are constructed with special mantras within the Vihāra, each dhiṣṇya being slightly more to the north than the previous one. It would be worth investigating if these dhiṣṇyas also, like the other constituents of the sacrifice, have a symbolical significance and correspond roughly to the abodes of "the Seven celestial Hotṛs."[35]

In this context another point may be mentioned. In verse III.7.7 cited above "the five Adhvaryus" are mentioned along with the seven Ṛṣis; from this juxtaposition it would seem that this designation too does not refer to the professional priests of the sacrificial place but to certain models in the sky who move to and fro as the Adhvaryus do.[36] It seems to me that here we have an allusion to the five planets. Otherwise we seek in vain for a mention of the planets in the hymns of the ṚV. In view of the ritual origin of the Vedic hymns, this comparison is not unusual.

From these five we should distinguish the other five who "stand in the middle of the sky" (I.105.10).[37] The choice of the words indicates that here it is not the planets which are meant but a never-setting, fixed, hence a circumpolar constellation.

B. DEMONS

The invocations to the higher gods who bestow light and life forms part of the defence and of the battle against hostile beings of all kinds. Behind the arena where the great gods move about, the Rākṣasas, Piśācas and Yātudhānas are up to their mischief—the great host of malevolent hobgoblins who injure the health of man and beast alike, disturb the sacrifice, cause all kinds of calamities to house and property. The nature and the history of the demon cult is yet to be written. The names of the demons are derived from all sources. Whosoever goes through the names of the Vedic demons would observe a confusion of beings of all varieties. Sometimes the designations are chosen according to the momentary impressions and manifestations, sometimes they are products of imagination like Demon "Without-Head," "Vulture-Head," "Piebald-Tummy." In several cases the primitive art of healing must have chosen its technical terms according to the manifestations of the disease and must have lent these names to demonolatry.[38] Among these we find abstractions as well as names of real enemies which become designations of hostile spirits. Mention is made of their father, mother, sometimes with and sometimes without real cause, just as Indra's father and mother are at times real and at others purely fictitious beings. The origin of the demons is as diverse as that of the gods. The bridge which connects the realm of the demons with the kingdom of the gods is constantly crossed by both. Although good gods like Indra and Viṣṇu have never become actual demons in the eyes of their worshippers, there are several borderline cases like Rudra in whose wake terror follows everywhere. Occasionally, as for example in PGS III. 15.7 ff., he is hardly distinguishable from a demon. And even those who are prevented through the whole set of their nature from becoming demons within the same mythical cycle join at least the ranks of the lower gods and serve the art of magic. The mantra one employs when a servant has run away shows Indra in this position,[39] and another mantra that protects the pregnancy[40] invokes the "men," Mitra-Varuṇa, Aśvins, Indra and Sūrya: surely this is no longer an indication of their worship directly as higher gods. We must ask constantly whether a specific name has climbed up from below to the heights or whether it sank down from a god to a demon. Gods and heroes of hostile tribes have the tendency of being regarded as the devils in the mythology of the neighbouring peoples. The demons of one's own clan climb up easily to heaven. New names are joined with the old and broaden the essence of the original god. In the AV, Bhava and Śarva were still independent beings.[41] Later they joined Rudra and became his names. There is no permanent line of division between gods and demons. In the shadow of the official gods there grow and flourish all the spirits who are the offspring of fear, ignorance and the tendency for new interpretations and who cause only harm. Unlike the gods who reward or punish men according to their deeds, these demons are solely the expression of ill-fortune. Their arrival is indicated by the call of disaster-proclaiming animals,[42] jackals, certain kinds of birds, and by the appearance of doves. This double nature is inherent in man also, causing happiness or disaster. The bride whom one brings home may possess inherent powers which make her a calamity to the husband and children, to the home and stable, and may necessitate careful exorcism.[43]

Paṇi, Śambara and Pipru are the names of ancient enemies who have become demons. Whether we can interpret Piśācas and Rākṣasas in the same way is not certain but no less possible. VII. 104 describes the battle against the Rākṣasas in such personal terms that it seems to have been taken from real life. The Yātudhānas mentioned in the same hymn and elsewhere, particularly in X.87, recall the evil of the Yātus which Ahriman created on the banks of Haētumanṭ. They complement the Bheṣajas[44] and represent the magic rites. If I am not mistaken, of all the demons, the Rākṣasas are mentioned most frequently in the ritual. It looks as though the reminiscence of specific enemies who resisted the Brahmanical ritual is continued here.[45] In ABr II.7.1 there is a discussion whether the Ṛākṣasas should be praised or not when their share is offered; the question is settled as follows: if at all the praise should be in undertones, for if it is spoken aloud the voice of the sacrificer might become a Rākṣasa voice. Offerings for them consist in husks of grain[46] and blood libations. As a defence against them a circle is drawn, the enclosing sticks are placed within (TS II.6.6.2), one sprinkles water or takes a firebrand. Or water and fire are replaced by the resounding of the Soma stones, which wards off the evil spirits like Duṣvapnya and Nirṛti (X.36.4) just as the ghosts are driven off elsewhere through metallic sound.[47] When the outline of the resonance hole is drawn, this is done with the words, "here I cut off the necks of the Rākṣasas."[48] An oblation is made in the prepared pit so that no injurious Rākṣasa can rise in it. The resonance holes are called *rakṣohan* and *valahan*.[49] In the Śrāddha "the Asuras, Rākṣasas and Piśācas who dwell on the earth" are driven off before "the fathers" and brahmins are invited.[50] The possibility is not ruled out that here the concept of the Manes is transformed into that of the demons, and that the souls of the departed, especially of the dead enemies (Keith, p.72), and the name of a hostile tribe have entered the realm of mythology again with a hostile sense in the same way as the Aṅgiras and the Bhṛgus are transferred to heaven as the progenitors of the Vedic clans. Of the names of the demons which are prominent mention must be made of Śaṇḍa-Marka who have been discussed in Vol. I, p. 306f. and will be discussed again later. According to the ṚV, in their place the *gṛdhra* drinks the Soma before the Aśvins do. Next comes *aráru* who is perhaps mentioned already in ṚV X.99.10 but who probably attained his full development only later. His name is employed in the mantras, *apārarum pṛthivyai devayajanād badhyāsam* and *araro divaṃ mā paptaḥ*,[51] recited during the construction of the Vedi and of the Utkara. He is regarded as an Asura whom Indra drives away from the earth. TBr III.4.1.5 mentions oblations to the Piśācas and Yātudhānas.[52] The Gṛhya Sūtras acquaint us with demons of all kinds. Just as according to *Milindapañha* the bodies of the dead Yakṣas display all sorts of forms[53] so we encounter here demons in every shape. All the evil spirits who injure property, happiness and life can change their name and shape. Their influence is present everywhere and should be removed from everywhere. Wherever the life of the new-born or of the woman in childbed is in danger, during all the important acts of life, during diseases, there is prescribed the magic which is supposed to arrest their influence. For the protection of the woman in childbed one places a fire at the door, throws the husks of mustard or grain in it and calls out:

śaṇḍa-marka, upavīra, śauṇḍikeya, ulūkhala, malimluca, droṇāsa, cyavana should disappear from here; *ālikhan, animiṣa, kiṃvadanta, upaśruti, haryakṣa, kumbhin, śatru, pātrapāṇi, nṛmaṇi, hantrīmukha, sarṣapāruṇa, cyavana* should disappear from here."[54] Or when a child is attacked by a disease called *kumāra* the demon is exorcised with the formula: "Kūrkura, Sukūrkura, Kūrkura, binder of children! *Cet*! You dog, let go. Reverence to you ... Śīsara, say 'sit down.' Saramā is the mother, Śīsara the father and Syāmaśabalau are your brothers."[55] When the pupil is handed over to the teacher there is a magic formula which averts the harm that can arise from this act.[56] On the day of the ceremonial bath after the completion of one's studentship one invokes [*agni*] *gohya, upagohya, mayūkha, manohan askhala* etc.[57] On the first day of the half-month when the gods have received their share, the housewife thinks of various other beings and shows, outside the house, her reverence "to the woman, to the man of any age, to the white, black-haired husband of evil women who entice my children and who live in the village or in the forest" (PGS I.12.4). To Rudra whose hosts of armies lie in wait everywhere offerings are made as *pathiṣad, catuṣpathaṣad, apsuṣad, giriṣad, pitṛṣad* (PGS III.15.7 ff.). In the formula recommended in TĀr I.28 for warding off the evil spirits from the sacrificial place, it is said: *viśīrṣṇīṃ gṛdhraśīrṣṇīṃ ca apeto nirṛtiṃ hatha paribādhaṃ śvetakukṣaṃ nijaṅghaṃ śabalodaram ...īrṣyāsūye bubhukṣaṃ manyuṃ kṛtyāṃ ca dīdhire.*

C. ASURAS

The history of the Asuras throws special light on the origin and significance of several demons. The problem of the Asuras' relationship with the Devas in the prehistory of Indo-Iranian religion and the reasons for the change in the meaning of the word *asura* are not any clearer today than they were years ago when Haug postulated his thesis that the transition of both the words into the designations of the demons (noticed by Burnouf already) is based on a prehistoric schism in religion, and when Justi and Ludwig (*Der Rigveda*, IV, p. xvii) opposed Haug with important arguments.[58] In recent times Darmesteter's contention that it had nothing to do with religious differences but was a mere change in the meaning of the word and that in later times the names became fixed in a single sense found general acceptance. But it cannot stand the test either. Haug's theory goes against indisputable facts. Darmesteter's contention reminds somewhat of an earlier period of comparative philology when it was the fashion to postulate certain basic rules of universal validity and, according to the exigency, to ignore individual cases when they do not fit in the theory. Like his dating of the Avesta and his identification of the Aməša Spəntas with the Ādityas, this is one of the hypotheses of the learned Iranist which were brilliant but not convincing. Likewise the view of some others that *deva* and *daeva* agree in the meaning "demon" has nothing to recommend for itself; it should be regarded as refuted already by the accord in the Germanic, Greek, Celtic and Indian languages.

I shall take up the discussion again and try to go beyond the dead end where it seems to have stopped. Haug alone was on the right track,[59] but he was certainly wrong in speaking of feuds which, according to him, preceded the invention of the Asura worship and the compilation of the ṚV and which belong to prehistoric times. This is refuted by all the data of the oldest parts in our hymn-collection; there Asura means "lord" and in very rare cases it is the designation of some hostile being. In the ṚV there is little to suggest a familiarity with Zarathuštra's reformation and with his teachings. I am of the view that the period of the ṚV preceded that of Zarathuštra and that the holders of the priestly office offered their services in regions lying far into the West and that the allusion in the ṚV to the generous Parthian prince who rewarded the sacrificial service should not be underestimated. Haug was mistaken also when he attached great significance to names like *nå̊ŋhaithya* and *saurva* which appear on the periphery and are to be met with rarely. On the other hand, I do not wish to dismiss them as Darmesteter does. However, the Iranian parallel forms are too colourless to be of any use as comparison.[60] But Darmesteter's errors are not smaller than those of Haug. They are more hidden among academic constructions and theories and are not so obvious; hence they are more dangerous. having even received much applause. Already the very statement that "in this so-called religious revolution we have nothing but an accident of language, a lexical curiosity"[61] anticipates a peculiar transposition of words, because it creates in Iran "wicked demons" out of the word *deva* which was once unambiguous everywhere and likewise the equally unambiguous designation *asura* is converted into its opposite precisely in neighbouring India. Darmesteter's thought process is stranger still in another passage.[62] I can see nothing but fallacies in this argumentation. He cites Indian examples for the anger of the Devas: *heḍo devānām uta martyānām* etc., which coincide with Iranian examples quite by chance. Otherwise it would be logical that in India also the Devas and Martyas should have become demons. This happened not in India but in Iran. We do not know whether in prehistoric times "the anger of the Devas" was described in the manner as is assumed by Darmesteter to support his theory. "These Indo-Iranian formulas which united in one and the same deprecation the wrath of the gods and men alike"[63] suffer from the infirmity that they probably did not exist. If they did, mention must have been made in prehistoric times of the anger of the Asuras also. But even in the ṚV it is not yet mentioned. And yet precisely in India the Asuras evolved into demons in the later period.[64]

What Tiele[65] states is also erroneous. *asura* does not acquire an unfavourable sense "gradually" and "freely" as Tiele supposes but this sense occurs quite abruptly and suddenly in a distinct opposition to the Devas. Nor does *asura* generally mean "spirits, beings" from which a god or demon can be derived as one likes, but it denotes "lord,[66] god" (and accordingly *asuryà*, overlordship, divineness") or "demon."[67] When Tiele remarks that the "Asuras were after all never evil beings by nature, never actual devils but rather the rivals of gods and tormentors of their worshippers," I wish to dispute this assertion. They are still more malicious than the Rakṣas. They are not appeased like the latter with sacrifices. The Asuras are constant opponents and adversaries during the worship of the gods.[68] In TS II.4.1.1 the Devāḥ, Manuṣyāḥ and Pitaraḥ are opposed by the Asuras, Rakṣas, and Piśācas in that order. Thus the TS sees the enemies of the gods in the Asuras as it sees the enemies of men in the Rākṣasas.[69] Exactly the frequent transference of the battles between the Devas and the Asuras to the realm of ritual seems to me to be an important factor in the explanation of the origin of these feuds.

The Asuras perform other sacrifices than the gods or follow a different custom. They install the three sacrificial fires Āhavanīya, Gārhapatya and Anvāhāryapacana in a different sequence than the gods do and thus are deprived of their luck (TBr I.1.4.4). When a custom has to be rejected as unsuitable it is called an Asura custom.[70] The close religious affinity between Indians and Iranians is indeed demonstrated by the common possession of old sacrificial formulas. Likewise the disputes about the ritual must have a historical origin. The farther one was removed from the point of origin the greater was the tendency to stamp all that was not strictly Brahmanical as Asura-like and to connect every antithesis, even that of day and night with the antithesis between the Devas and Asuras.

In his discussion Darmesteter has underestimated a factor which is very significant for deciding the question, namely that the fate of the Devas who are transformed into devils is shared also by the Kavis, the priests and wise men of India, who are regarded as *śuśruvāṃsaḥ* in the Brāhmaṇas. For even the recent research has not disputed that Kavi is the cognate of *kava*, outlawed in Iran,[71] and of *kāvaya*, the "follower of Kavi." The polemical allusions in gāthās like Yasna XLIV.20 demonstrate clearly his relationship with the Devas, and further with the Karapans and Uśij.

Yasna XLIV.20: *čithenā mazdā huxšathrā daēvā å̊ŋharə*
aṭ īṭ pərəsā yōi pišyeintī aēibyo kám
yāiṣ gam karapā usixš čā aēšəmāi dātā
yā cā kavā anmə̂nī urūdōyatā.[72]

The passage shows the cultural-historical surroundings of the heretical Kavis and Karapans[73] who belong, like the Devas, to the enemies of Zarathuštra and can be as little separated from the Brahmanical belief as the Daēvas whom they serve. Darmesteter tries to explain away the gāthā verse with untenable arguments (*Ormazd et Ahriman*, p. 145, n. 5). Usixš is also mentioned in the gāthā and this very name appears, even though it is not particularly stressed, as the designation of ancient priests precisely in the older texts of the Vedic literature.[74] It is certainly no accident that the famous Kai Kāōs of the Iranian saga exhibits a similarity in name with Kavi Uśanas of India who appears as the teacher of the Asuras in the later literature.[75] To the passages cited by Spiegel we may add the statement of the Brāhmaṇas: *uśanā vai kāvyo 'surāṇām purohita āsīt*,[76] that is to say, directly in the period which follows the ṚV we encounter the name Uśanas on the side of the Asuras, a name which is celebrated in Iran. These facts in their entirety are much more than mere "facts of language" (Darmesteter, *Ormazd et Ahriman*, p. 262); these are the products of a cultural-historical evolution.[77]

When did the separation or the hostile contact take place ? We can rule out the period prior to the ṚV since like the Avesta the ṚV combines the word *asura* mostly with the concept of divineness and sees in *ṛta-aša* the expression of highest holiness. We can draw the line only where *asura* seems to be transformed regularly into a demon, that is between the bulk of the Ṛgvedic hymns on the one side and that of the Brāhmaṇas on the other.[77a] On this side are a few authors of the ṚV who see demoniacal beings in the Asuras just as the Brāhmaṇas do, and on the other side are the bulk of the Ṛgvedic hymns as well as a few scattered passages of the Brāhmaṇas which know the word *asura* still in the good sense.[78]

I have already stated in Vol.I.p. 12, that the traditions of the ṚV are not directly continued in the Brāhmaṇas but that a break can be seen between the two and that two different streams must have joined into a confluence here. "The distance between the tribes who still saw gods in the Asuras (thus predominantly in the ṚV) and those who saw devils in them does not seem to be any smaller than that between the Vedic Indians and Iranians."[79] Zarathuštra is mentioned nowhere, no single passage is directed against him and his reformation, and therefore he should not be regarded as the cause for this enmity. In one of the Asura groups who had fallen out long ago with the Deva worshippers and had protested and fought against their sacrificial cult, the Iranian reformation must have been born long time after the per[illegible] of the Vedic hymns. The Veda and Avesta cannot be connected directly with one another;

many links are missing between the two.[80] The events which took place between the period of the ṚV and that of the Brāhmaṇas are lost for us in obscurity. The state of affairs was not so simple as Haug imagined it years ago. But in the main idea he blundered much less than his successors.[81]

It was observed long ago that there are very few passages in the ṚV which demonize the Asuras. From the ṚV, von Bradke (*Dyaus Asura*, p. 86) lists four occurrences in singular and eight in plural in this sense. Two[82] of the first four and likewise two[83] only of the second eight occur in the family books.

I wish to draw attention to the following fact of which, as far as I know, not much notice was taken and which is not without significance. In the family books the word *asura* occurs relatively rarely and thus suggests the gradual fading out of the Asura cult. It is certainly no accident that in the maṇḍala which according to my theory is closest to the Iranian territories the word *asura* is avoided almost totally,[84] while according to a rough count the word *deva* occurs about 68 times. Here we become distinctly aware of the ascendancy of the Deva religion[85] and of its most excellent representative, Indra, generally still without a perceptible enmity towards the Asuras. Indra is never styled an *asura* in books II to VII[86] but appears in direct enmity towards them particularly in the later legends.[87] On the other hand, book VII, the authors of which lived generally in the territory on the banks of the eastern Sarasvatī, faraway from the possibility of a hostile contact with the Asura worshippers, mentions the word *asura* still seven times, of which only once in connection with Śambara in a hostile sense,[88] and yet rarely as compared with the word *deva*.[89]

It is necessary to obtain an overview of the bone of contention between the Asuras and the Devas, and to examine the names that are prominently mentioned in the battles. All these are by no means of Indo-Iranian origin. On the contrary very few could be from such remote antiquity and those are lost among the multitude of instances which refer only to the disputes with Indian adversaries, hostile clans and priestly families. Already the cry, *he lavo*, attributed to the Asuras in one passage of the ŚBr,[90] demonstrates that under the word *asuras* we should understand purely Indian enemies, in this case, definitely eastern enemies just as enemies from Mazendran (*māzainya*) are included among the Daēvas.[91] But we must hold fast to the notion that the point of origin of the hostile sense lies in the contacts—later forgotten—with western tribes; after all, there had always been contacts with the West to a certain extent.[92]

A systematic classification of the legends and names of the Asuras would have to divide them into three parts. I. Those with a historical core, a) Iranian Asuras, b) Indian Asuras (Aryan or non-Aryan enemies); II. sacrificial speculations; III. mythical opponents: Manes[93] and demons.[94]

Since this system is still uncertain and the material is not yet quite complete, I wish to limit my task to making a beginning of the investigation in the hope that others would continue it. I give below predominantly such material where contacts with Iran can be assumed.[95]

1. TS VI.4.10.1: *bṛhaspatir devānāṃ purohita āsīc chaṇḍāmarkāv asurāṇām . . .*[96] In the course of the Agniṣṭoma both receive two Grahas, the Śukragraha and the Manthingraha, which are late additions in this sacrifice. Originally these Grahas were drawn by the gods in order to entice the two demons, seize them and drive them away. As I have explained in Vol. I, p. 308 *marka* is the same as Avestan *mahrka* and denotes "death" and this is in accord with the belief connected with the Manthingraha that it causes disease and should not be brought close to one who was bound by an oath of allegiance. Such clear etymology does not obtain for *śaṇḍa* but it recalls the name of the Śaṇḍikas, to be found among Indra's enemies, and especially their "vṛṣabha."

ṚV II.30.8: *tyáṃ cic chárdhantaṃ taviṣīyámāṇam*
índro hanti vṛṣabháṃ śáṇḍikānām||

v.4 speaks of the *vṝkadvaraso ásurasya vīráḥ*, soldiers of an *asura vṛkadvaras*, who was probably an Iranian enemy (see n. 82 above)

2. TMBr VII. 5.20 : *uśanā vai kāvyo 'surāṇāṃ purohita āsīt|*[97] *taṃ devāḥ kāmadughābhir upāmantrayanta| tasmā etāny auśanāni prāyacchan.*[98] Uśanas, whom the later Vedic texts associate with Indra a few times and make him a wise man and magician,[99]

is assigned here to the Asuras as the Purohita and likewise in the latter literature (MBh I. 76). Although etymologically somewhat different, he is not distinct from the most famous Iranian, Kai Kāōs, who is equated since long with the Kavi *Kava usa.*[100]

3. TBr I.5.9.1: *devāsurāḥ saṃyattā āsan | sa prajāpatir indraṃ jyeṣṭhaṃ putram apa nyadhatta ned enam asurā balīyāṃso hanan| prahrādo ha vai kāyādhavo*[101] *virocanaṃ*[102] *svaṃ putram apa nyadhatta ned enaṃ devā hanan.* Is there a connection with the Avestan *kayadha* in spite of the fact that the final consonant is different ?

4. MS IV. 2.9 (31.3): *sṛmo vai nāmāsura āsīt tasyeyaṃ pṛthivī paśubhiḥ pūrṇāsīt tān indro 'vṛṅkta.* Possibly the Iranian name *salm, sairima* is borrowed here, who appears, besides Tura and Airya, as the son of Thraētaona and receives the western region.[103]

Besides these there occur other names of the Asuras without, however, offering any grounds for comparison. I give below those I have noticed without venturing any assumption about their origin. Some of these can be quite fictitious names.

Kilāta and Ākuli, priests of the Asuras (ŚBr I.1.4.16); *gaupāyanānāṃ vai sattram āsīnānāṃ kirātakulyāv asuramāye antaḥparidhy asūn prākiratām*[104] (TMBr XIII. 12.5); Araru (TBr III. 2.9.4); Aru (ŚŚS XIV.50.2);[105] Etadu (TS II. 6.9.4);[106] Kālakañja (TBr I. 1.2.4-6);[107] Kustā (the opposite of Aditi, (MS IV 2.3); Jambha (MS III. 8.10). The Devas invoke the Gāyatrī with Viśvakarman, the Asuras with *dābhi* (TS II.4.3; MS II. 1.11). Agni was the messenger of the gods; *daivyo 'surāṇāṃ* (TS II. 5.11.8, cf. ISt X. 39). Asita Dhānva is the king and the Asuras his subjects (ŚBr XIII. 4.3.11). Pūru (definitely from an old proper noun) (ŚBr VI. 8.1.14; VS XII. 34); Vibhinduka (TMBr XV. 10.11); Viṣād (TBr. III. 2.9.2).

Of the other peculiarities attributed to the Asuras, it may be mentioned that according to a legend they do not know the midday savana but only the morning and evening savanas. This seems to me to be a reminiscence of the *fratarəm čiṭ havanəm uparəm ciṭ* of the Avesta.[108] Similarly the mode of piling up the Śmaśāna is regarded as one of the differences between the (eastern) Asuras and the Devas (ŚBr XIII. 8.2.1).[109] The other differences do not seem to be of much significance.[110]

CHAPTER TEN

RUDRA

Rudra, the god with the bow and arrow, who wears dark locks of hair (*nīlaśikhaṇḍa*) or has his hair braided in the shape of a cowrie shell (*kaparda*) and covers himself in a skin, concludes the sacrificial year just as Uṣas commences it. In the costume in which he is traditionally represented we may certainly see the dress of those tribes or groups from whose cult he emerged. Rudra is a god of terror, "the terrible one among the gods."[1] He is never praised as the creator of heaven and earth; very rarely it is said that he sets the streams free.[2] Unlike Indra or other gods, he is never stated to have broken the stables open or performed any other gigantic deeds which men praise. In the majority of sacrifices his place is only at the end. His name is not included in the inventory of ceremonial invocations, no Sāman is sung to him.[3] The ritual places him on the same level as the Rakṣas, Asuras and Pitaraḥ when it enjoins that after uttering any formula which contains his name one should touch the purificatory waters.[4] But elsewhere he is clearly distinguished from the Manes through the Svāhā call and through the northern direction which is assigned to him as regularly as the southern direction to the Manes. Investigation into his nature has been promoted by important contributions, first by L. von Schroeder (WZKM, IX. p. 248 ff.) who sees in him a kinsman of Wodin-Odin and of Dionysos, by Charpentier (WZKM, XXIII, p. 151 ff.) and finally by Arbman.[5]

The least substantiated interpretation is the identification with the lightning. Even today there are scholars who have a special predilection to see the lightning in the Vedic gods. If Rudra were the god of lightning, we would certainly have found quite a different type of characteristics for Rudra in the hymns as well as in the ritual. Indians of those times were as little inclined to the personifications of the lightning as the modern Indians are.[6] What should we make of it when Keith makes the Maruts the sons of Rudra and states that "they are born of the laughter of lightning" (p. 151) ?

A. RUDRA IN THE RITUAL

The two factors which we have mentioned, i.e. the Svāhā call and the northern direction, are important enough but our ritual texts do not stop there; they contain other essential information as well. Thus Rudra is said to be an *uccheṣaṇabhāga*,[7] he is appeased (*niravadayate* is the technical term used in the ritual) with the leavings at the end. To him belong merely the *phalīkaraṇas* (GGS I.4.31) among others; the Agni-sviṣṭakṛt-oblation which completes the main oblations is regarded as his share,[7a] but it should not be added to the main oblations; otherwise the sacrificer would be robbed of his cattle. Outside the paridhi-sticks, on a piece of coal that has been brought there from the north side, the dregs of the Manthingraha are offered to Rudra with the words : "this is your share, O Rudra, for which you asked, enjoy it. Attain the possession of cattle, wealth of food and of men, and a happy year."[8] The rest of the unguents used in the Rājasūya is poured on the Āgnīdhra fire[9] and the TBr adds : "he offers the leavings. Rudra's share are the leavings. He appeases Rudra with a share. He walks off to the north and makes the offerings in the Āgnīdhra fire. That is Rudra's direction."[10] The legend of Rudra's exclusion from the sacrifice by the gods occurs frequently.[11] Among these, a passage of the TS is worth noting which relates that Rudra, upon being excluded, "pierced" the sacrifice,[12] for this feature of the saga occurs again in the *Sauptikaparvan* of the MBh (X.18) also.[13] Rudra's isolation can be seen in the fact that he is rarely associated with other gods. While Indra, Agni and Soma are united with several other gods to form dual divinities, Rudra is associated only with Soma in a quite indifferent hymn, VI.74, of the ṚV and in some wish-fulfilment sacrifices performed for attaining progeny, for warding off diseases etc.[14]

Furthermore, it is considered necessary to avoid various things because Rudra's anger can be aroused through these. Thus for instance, the *iḍā* should not be offered in fire (TS II. 6.8.2), the Ādityagraha should be drawn behind a covering (TS VI.5.6.4), the Anuvaṣaṭkāra is prohibited with this Graha (TS VI.5.6.5).[15] Otherwise, one would surrender one's cattle to Rudra or let him loose upon one's progeny and so on. As a rule, it is the cattle which he, the Paśupati, imperils. When the dakṣiṇās are distributed, the cow is received "for Rudra."[16] When the sacrificial beast shivers or runs away from there or any other mishaps occur, a formula which ends in *namo rudrāya mīḷhuṣe* must be uttered.[17] According to the Gṛhya ritual, an ox is sacrificed to Rudra and his hosts every year during the so-called *śūlagava*, "spit-ox." Among the various supposed purposes of this sacrifice, the most probable seems to be the propitiation of Rudra so that he does not send any diseases and kill the cattle.[18] This sacrifice takes place, according to MGS and Āśvalāyana, in autumn, and according to the latter, possibly in spring as well, outside the village in the north-east, east or north, and under the constellation Ārdrā, which is associated with Rudra even elsewhere.[19] Rudra is fond of blood.[20] When a cow milks blood, an oblation to Rudra is called for.[21] According to MGS eight handfulls of blood should be offered in the eight cardinal points. The autumnal season enjoined by Āśvalāyana and the MGS is in conformity with the former's rule that blood should be poured out for the snakes, which receive also a bali oblation during the Pratyavarohaṇa at the end of the rainy season when the menace of the snakes is past.[22] The fear emanating from the deity is expressed in the prohibition that the members of the sacrificer's family should not approach the sacrificial place and that nothing of the animal should be brought into the village. One may eat from its flesh only on an express command. According to the MGS, only cooked food should be brought into the village and the remnants and the skin should be buried.

So far we have established that Rudra receives the dregs of the sacrifice, that to a certain extent he stands at the end of the sacrifice and that the north is his favourite direction. This position of Rudra is expressed more pointedly and in a more individualistic manner in the Sākamedha, the third of the Cāturmāsya sacrifices, which is performed in Kārttikī or

Mārgaśirṣī or Pauṣī. Just as elsewhere he has his place at the end of the sacrifice as Agni sviṣṭakṛt, so also here his place is at the end of the ecclesiastical year, since the oblation for him follows the great sacrifice for the Manes and completes the Cāturmāsya cycle.[23]

For this Sākamedha the ĀpŚS gives the following rules.

ĀpŚS VIII.17.1 : "man for man, so many as the sacrificer has members in his family including women, for so many cakes upon one kapāla each,[24] the Adhvaryu takes out grains and for one more [cake].[25]

2 : "While they are being taken out the sacrificer whispers : 'As many as we are housedwellers, so many I have pleased.'

3 : "The ceremonies are performed silently.

4 : "On the north side of the Gārhapatya he prepares them for baking.

5 : "He can pour butter over them,[26] he takes them away on to the vedi and throws them all together into a basket with the mantra : 'you are the protection for the animals, protection for the sacrificer; grant me protection.'

6 : "Or into two or more baskets.

(Kātyāyana enjoins a shallow dish).

7 : "Some say that one should carry them upon the lid of a basket.

8 : "With the words, 'there is only one Rudra, he does not yield place to a second,' he (i.e. the Adhvaryu) takes a smoking firebrand from the southern fire.

9 : [Priests and family members] "all go towards the north-east and there he (i.e. the Adhvaryu) throws the extra cake upon a molehill with the words : 'O Rudra, the mole is your animal, enjoy it.'

10 : "Or he thinks thereby of an enemy : 'so and so is your animal.'

11 : "If he does not have any enemy, let him say : 'the mole (*ākhu*) is your animal.'[27]

12 : "He installs a fire upon the cross-roads and adds a fire-brand to it, he throws [grass] all around, takes from the north [or from behind] a part each from all the cakes and offers them with the middle or the last[28] leaf of a Palāśa branch: 'This is

your share, O Rudra, enjoy it with sister Ambikā, Svāhā !'[29]

18.1 : He besprinkles the fire of the cross-roads with water uttering at the same time the two mantras : 'create a remedy for the ox, horse and man, a remedy for us also so that there is happiness, and welfare for the ram and sheep.' The sacrificer whispers : 'we have appeased Rudra, O Amba,[30] we have appeased god Tryambaka[31] so that he makes us better, more prosperous, rich in cattle, so that he sets us free.'

2 : "All circumambulate the fire from left to right and recite the verse (ṚV VII. 59.12) : 'We worship Tryambaka, the fragrant one, who increased the nourishment. Like a fruit from the stalk, I wish to be released from death but not from immortality.'

3 : "If the sacrificer has a marriageable daughter she should go around the fire and say [modifying the wording of the above verse] : 'we worship Tryambaka, the fragrant one, who procured a husband. Like a fruit from the stalk, I wish to be released from here but not from a husband.'

4 : "All throw their cakes high into the air, catch them again and throw them into the hands of the sacrificer with the verse, 'we worship Tryambaka,' whereupon they take them back again : 'you (pl.) are Bhaga. I wish to attain a share of your happiness.'[32] Thus they should do thrice.

5 : "Likewise they should throw them into the hands of the marriageable daughter, who modifies the verse as before.[33]

7 : "Thereupon [the Adhvaryu] throws these cakes into one, two or more baskets.

8 : "With the mantra, 'this is your share, O Rudra, enjoy it. With this as the provision for the journey[34] go beyond the Mūjavat' he suspends the baskets from one, two or more trees.

9 : "Or he throws the cakes into two baskets, suspends these two from a shoulder-yoke and deposits this upon a tree stump or upon an anthill, whereupon they utter thrice the words : 'the one who wields the bow[35] and clothes himself with a skin has loosened his bow,' and hold the breath after each time.

10 : "They pour water around the baskets, return silently without looking back and with the formula: 'thriving are you, we wish to thrive,' they put firewood upon the Āhavanīya and

worship the water with 'I followed the waters.'" This is followed by an oblation to Aditi.

Kātyāyana's rules for the same ceremony agree with those of the ŚBr. From Kātyāyana I add the following features of general importance.

KŚS V.10.4 : "[He performs] all [the rites] with his face turned to the north.[36]

5 : "Also the places [like the cross-roads and molehill, he selects] in the north.

6 : "[The oblations are] Juhoti oblations (i.e. they have neither a Yājyā nor an Anuvākyā).[37]

7 : "Without the Vaṣaṭ call.

8 : "With or without pouring butter.

9 : "He places [the cakes] in a shallow dish, takes a firebrand from the southern fire and makes the offering with the middle leaf of a Palāśa branch upon the cross-roads. ...[38]

15 : "[After returning from the molehill where the extra cake is deposited] all go around the fire three times as in the sacrifice for the Manes[39] (from right to left), while hitting the left thigh with the verse 'we worship Tryambaka.'

16 : "And as in the sacrifice for the gods (from left to right) while hitting the right thigh with the same mantra.

17 : "In the same way (first from right to left and then from left to right) the maidens go around who desire husbands or sexual pleasure with the following mantra.

18 : "The sacrificer throws with his hands the rest of the Rudra cakes so high that a cow with uplifted mouth] cannot reach them.

19 : "He catches them again."

20 : "Should this be not possible for him, then he touches them [after they have fallen down].

21 : "He puts them in two baskets (with ropes to hang), suspends them from the ends of a bamboo staff or of a beam (which is made from the timber of a tree that is pure from the ritual point of view), hangs this beam, in such a way that a cow cannot reach it,[40] to a tree stump, tree, bamboo bush or deposits it upon an anthill with the mantra, 'this is the provision for your journey. . . . ' (VS III.61).[41]

22 : "He whispers the mantra, 'you who are dressed in a skin, go past, without harming, amiably.'

22 : "Without looking back, they return and touch the water."

With Arbman, we may regard the oblation at the cross-roads as a sign of popular cult. The terrible god who is a stranger to other gods is entitled to this place. But the ceremony contains no feature that can be in conflict with the ṚV which also knows Tryambaka. Rudra is not only dangerous, he is friendly as well. He is addressed as the fragrant one and is expected to grant a husband to the sacrificer's daughter. One circumambulates the fire not only from right to left as in the sacrifice for the Manes but from left to right also as in the sacrifice for the gods. The cakes are not deposited on the earth but thrown into the air and afterwards they are hung so high that a cow cannot reach them. We may notice from this popular ceremony that Rudra, just as in the ṚV, is not an implacable god of pure terror and that he is not "earth-bound." In my view this speaks against Arbman's explanation of Rudra as "the god of death."

I think it is hazardous to attempt to force the notions of the later periods upon the ṚV. What would have happened to Varuṇa, Vṛtra and Indra had we attempted to attach more than temporal value to these notions.

We may also stress the fact that in the ritual of the royal consecration, the caru meant for Rudra is connected with three sacrificial remunerations which are after all supposed to symbolize the nature of Rudra partly. According to Weber,[42] these are firstly an ox with white (or black) forelegs or with white (or black) tail, secondly a sword in the shape of a claw and thirdly a dice board bound with a belt made of tail hair. It should be noted that some of these attributes are expressed with obscure words which were variously interpreted (*nakhara*, *pyukṣṇa*).

B. RUDRA AND HIS SEASON

With great unanimity the above-mentioned texts and others[43] assign the concluding part of the sacrifice and the northern direction to Rudra. The texts tell us even more. Rudra is bidden to go past amiably, to go beyond the Mūjavat,[44] and provisions for his journey are suspended from a tree. We can infer from this that he is thought of as departing at the time of this sacrifice, when his reign which endangers man and beast is approaching its end. The Sākamedha sacrifice follows the rainy season. It denotes the approximate beginning of autumn. Hence that would be the period when Rudra's reign is about to end and his departure can be celebrated. Some texts of the Black YV come to our help. TBr I.6.10[45] states thus: "autumn is his sister Ambikā. Through her he kills. . . men propitiate him together with her."[46] The MS is slightly different: "autumn is Rudra's abode. Ambikā is his sister. He sneaks forth behind her. Hence he kills predominantly in autumn. One appeases him jointly with her." It is stated further: "The mountain is Rudra's abode. Hence, sneaking forth from there, he kills the beings. One causes him to go to his abode through one's share which appertains to him."[47]

C. RUDRA'S WEAPONS

What are Rudra's weapons? He is the archer among the gods, called directly *ástṛ* in AV XI.2.7. The verb *as* is specially distinctive of him. In AV VI.90.3 his arrow is revered *prátihitāyai, visṛjyámānāyai, nípatitāyai.* When the gods prepare an arrow out of Agni, Soma and Viṣṇu, and ask who shall shoot it, the reply runs thus: "Rudra! *rudro vai krūraḥ, so 'syatu*" (TS VI.2.3.1; MS III. 8.1). Bow and arrow are quite predominantly his.[48] Somewhere else other than "above us he should shake the celestial branch" (AV XI.2.19). In AV XI.2.26 *vidyút*, among others, is stated to be his missile; Bhāvaśarvau, who are akin to Rudra in nature, wield the same *vidyút* (AV X.1.23: *vidyút devahetí*); elsewhere it is the thunderbolt. The same verse of this hymn, which lists all the calamities caused by Rudra, mentions fever, poison and *divyā́gni.* In AV XI.2.22 *takmán* and *kā́sikā* are mentioned together. AV VI.20.2 reads *námo rudrā́ya, námo takmáne, námo rā́jñe váruṇāya.*[49] In the legends of the MBh fever is just the disease which is caused by him and which rules the world (Muir, OST, 1st ed., IV, p. 314). The commentaries on ĀpŚS VI.14. 11; X.19.2; KŚS XXIII.4.19[50] treat *jvara* as a synonym of Rudra.

When an epidemic breaks out among men or animals sacrifices are made to Rudra.[51] As the climax of his terror may be regarded that season in which diseases, burning fever etc. claim most of the victims, and this season is autumn according to the afore-mentioned texts;[52] of course, not the autumn proper which is the most pleasant period of the Indian year and which is even described by TĀr 1.4.1.2 as "life-giving," but its beginning, i.e. the period of transition from the rainy season to autumn. This period denotes the climax of suffering. "Over a great portion of the Empire the mass of the cattle are starved for six weeks every year. The hot winds roar, every green thing has disappeared, no hot-weather forage is grown; the last year's fodder has generally been consumed in keeping the well-bullocks on their legs during the irrigation of the spring crops; and all the husbandman can do is just to keep his poor brutes alive—. In good years, he just succeeds: in bad years, the weakly ones die of starvation. But then come the rains. Within the week, as though by magic, the burning sands are carpeted with rank, luscious herbage the cattle will eat and over-eat; and millions die of one form or other of cattle disease, springing out of this starvation followed by sudden repletion with rank, juicy, immature herbage."[53] Still more clearly for our purpose, Blanford[54] states the following about Punjab: "the period which immediately follows the rains up to October is the most unhealthy season in the year. Decaying vegetation under an ardent sun generates miasma, the consequences being fever, dysentery, and not unfrequently cholera."[55] The danger of the individual years would vary according to the amount of rainfall. Thus this is roughly the period before the Sākamedha is performed and with it the Tryambakahoma which denotes the end of the terror caused by Rudra.[56]

The sufferings of the tropical country begin with the onset of the hot season. The name of Rudra is interpreted — I think correctly — as "red."[57] More important than the etymology is the following fact to which adequete attention has not been paid anywhere, namely that all the later Vedic texts explain Rudra as a form of Agni and more specifically of the fire in its "terrible" aspect.[58] From the great unanimity of the texts on this point it follows that this explanation should by no means be ignored, all the more so because Agni is styled as Rudra in the ṚV itself and even outside hymn II.1 which identifies Agni with a number of gods.[59] If we hold fast to this fact for the time being, the following picture emerges: Rudra's efficacy is seen to the greatest extent in the diseases of the rainy season and of the beginning of autumn. This is the most productive and also the most dangerous season. It is preceded by summer with its scorching heat. Heat and burning winds scorch the earth and torment its inhabitants. TĀr I.3.3: *śuklavāsā rudragaṇo grīṣmeṇāvartate saha| nidahan pṛthivīṃ sarvāṃ jyotiṣātiprakhyena-saḥ||*[60] It seems quite obvious to me that we should see the god of summer and of the rainy season in the "terrible" or "wrathful" Agni-Rudra. Thus through his overlordship over two successive periods he becomes simultaneously the destroyer and creator and gives expression to the peculiarities of the tropical climate as no other god does. TS V.7.3.3: *rudro vā eṣa yad agnis tasyaite tanuvau ghorānyā śivānyā.* Even if Arbman was right in his explanation of Rudra as the god of death, the season assigned to him here would not be in conflict with such an explanation since this season claims the most victims and the malevolent qualities of Rudra are represented at their best in this season.

D. FURTHER DATA FROM THE RITUAL

Outside the Cāturmāsya sacrifices, Rudra is accommodated yet on other occasions in the ritual, namely in the Rājasūya and in the piling up of the fire-altar. During the royal consecration, wild wheat is brought for Rudra from the lodgings of the royal superintendent of gambling (*akṣāvāpa*) and of the "cow-slaughterer" (*govikarta*)[61] for one of the twelve sacrifices of the royal officers (*ratnahavis*).[62] In the Agnicayana, the first of the major rites to be performed at the altar is the Śatarudriya-homa. This consists of "425 oblations to Rudra and the Rudras for which wild sesamum seeds and Gavedhukā flour or other produce of the forest that grows wildly, possibly also the milk of six goats, are used. These are meant for the Rudras in the earth, atmosphere and heaven..."[63] KŚS XVIII.1.1 states: "The Śatarudriyahoma is performed at the western corner of the north wing of the brick altar,[64] upon the enclosing stones.

With an Arka leaf[65] [which takes the place of the ladle, he makes the offering of] the Gavedhukā gruel mixed with sesamum seeds—some take goat's milk in its stead—which he lets drip down with a piece of Arka wood, reciting the Adhyāya (VS XVI. 1-66) 'Reverence to you,' and standing with the face to the north." The three enclosing stones are buried in the west corner in such a way that they reach up to different heights, up to the thigh, navel and mouth respectively.[66] The sacrifice is performed at these stones in the following manner.[67] At the stone which reaches up to the thigh a Svāhā is uttered at the end of three Anuvākas, at the navel-high stone a second at the end of five Anuvākas and at the stone reaching up to the mouth a third Svāha. Thereupon with the Pratyavarohamantras the oblations are made in descending order starting from the mouth-high stone and ending at the thigh-high stone. For this sacrifice also, as one can see, the direction given is almost exclusively the north or the north-west.

For these oblations many mantras of the YV,[68] known as Rudrādhyāyas, are employed, and these probably represent an important part of the old Rudra cult. In these mantras there occur some words which look as though they belong to some dialect and do not occur elsewhere, such as *giriśanta* (TS IV. 5.1.cd), *giritra* (5.1.d), *giriśa* (5.1.e), *saspiñjara* (5.2.c), *babhluśa* (5.2.d), *bhuvanti* (5.2.1).[69] In one passage (5.1.g) Rudra is depicted as *tāmro aruṇa uta babhruḥ*,[70] in another as blue-necked and golden-armed. It is said that "the one who sneaks down[71] with dark blue neck, bright red, him the herdsmen saw and also the women who carry water, and all beings. He manifested himself. May he be merciful to us." A survey of these passages does not favour the theory of L. von Schroeder[72] that Rudra is the overlord of the departed souls who rush along in the winds. It is true that already in the ṚV, Rudra is a "slayer of men," he possesses arrows that cause ruin, he is also the "father of the Maruts," but nowhere as far as I can see do we find a mention of his realm of the dead as we hear of Yama's world, nowhere does he appear as the *psychopompós*, a conductor of souls to the other world. Kuhn's dubious etymology of the word *marut* from the root *mṛ*, "to die," offers only a shaky bridge. Of course, in the last Cāturmāsya, oblations are made to the Maruts in the morning and evening (incidentally, quite separately from the Tryambakahoma), but they receive oblations also in the first two Cāturmāsyas where Rudra is not accommodated. Nor do I believe with Hopkins and Macdonell[73] that Rudra is a "thunder-storm god" in the ṚV. The "father of the storms" does not need to be a storm god himself. Dyaus is the father of Uṣas and of the Aśvins, Tvaṣṭṛ of Viśvarūpa, Vivasvat of Yama and so on, but in spite of several superficial similarities these fathers are not similar in nature to their offspring. Is Rudra a god of mountains and forests?[74] In support of this one may cite first of all his association with Mount Mūjavat,[75] further his names in the Rudrādhyāya where he is called *giriśanta, giriśa, giritra, girisuta* etc.[76] about six times, further the names given to him there like *vanānāṃ pati, vṛkṣāṇām pati, kakṣāṇāṃ pati* and *oṣadhīnāṃ pati*, to which one may also add his attribute as the patron deity of all sorts of robbers. Against this, I have drawn attention to the fact (on p. 199 of the first edition of this work) that in the same Rudrādhyāya he is also called "the lord of the paths" (VS XVI.17), the lord of the fields, *srutya, pathya, kāṭya*, also *rūpya, kulya, sarasya, nādya, vaiśanta, kūpya* (VS XVI. 37); thus he is associated with all kinds of reservoirs of water so much so that the afore-mentioned names like *girisuta, giriśanta, vanānāṃ pati* etc. form merely one group of the many and cannot claim precedence.[77] I concede to Arbman (*Rudra*, pp. 27, 221 ff.) that all these names do not designate Rudra himself but more or less independent deities who were different from him and were absorbed by him. But in such a case, one would have to assume that these are, or have become, individual names of his ubiquitious hosts in the same way as in the case of the femininely conceived "noisy ones, noise-making ones, searching ones and carrion-devouring ones" who form his army (ŚŚS IV.20.1; Oldenberg, RdV, 2nd ed., p. 218). But after all it cannot be denied that an exclusive and original association of Rudra with the mountains and forests is incompatible with his concept in the oldest of our texts, i.e., the ṚV, which speaks of him in II.1.6 as *ásuro mahó diváḥ*,[78] in I.114. 5 as *divó varāhám aruṣám*[79] and even elsewhere seems to denote precisely him with the expression *divó ásura*.[80] But the ṚV never refers to him as a mountain-prince, nor does the AV. This contradiction cannot be removed with the statement of Arbman that the Vedic texts "far too often express an academic, reflective and speculative mode of thinking and this might be the case also with the instance discussed here," (*Rudra*, p. 227) and "that the world of religious concepts was intermingled with speculative concepts and flashes of inspiration" etc. (ibid, p. 28). The designation of Rudra as the "boar of the sky" does not require any speculative mode of thinking. The evolutionary factor cannot be eliminated yet, in which the theologians had some but not an overwhelming influence. Accordingly the above-mentioned quality could have been added only in the process of later evolution, either independently or through a fusion with other beings.[81] Rudra, the terrible god, is opposed to the home and village, no part of the *śūlagava* should be brought into the village. People wish that he remains far away from them, "beyond the Mūjavat." In ṚV X.155 the inimical Arāyī is told: *girim̩ gaccha*. One curses the enemy that he may live in the mountains (*girīn anupraveśaya*, TĀr IV.39.1). No abode may be alloted to the god of terror in the house or village but, as soon as one began to localize him on the earth, it was far away in the mountains or forests with their oft-described dangers. He is the antithesis of the peaceful cultivation of the village. Hence rice or barley is not used in the sacrificial gruel for him but the produce of the wild plants (see p. 281 above). Offerings are made to him not with a bowl but *arkapatreṇa, āraṇyena*. In ṚV X.146.6 the genius of the forest is called *ákṛṣīvalā*.[82]

E. RUDRA IN THE ṚGVEDA

How do our conclusions accord with the ṚV? It seems to me that the ṚV never contradicts the view put forward by me even though we cannot ignore the disparity between the ṚV and the later period in the description of Rudra. Arbman states that from the ṚV we learn nothing else about Rudra but that he is a terrible god, that from the heavens above he hurls down his death-bringing missiles upon the creatures on the earth, and that nevertheless his nature contains positive aspects as well which can make him a mighty helper and bestower of gifts for man if one knew how to win his favour... and these are, with the exception of his celestial character, only the traits which characterize the later Vedic Rudra-type just as they characterize the epic Śiva as well as the Rudra of the ṚV (*Rudra*, p. 21). For his investigation, Arbman depends upon the later Vedic texts, popular usage and demon cult. Rejecting the Ṛgvedic conception of Rudra as a celestial and luminous being, he explains him as the god of death, "according to his original nature an earth-bound, demoniacal and cruel manifestation arising from the primitive notions about death and its terror" (ibid. p.310). Even the Ṛgvedic Rudra "is only a celestialized form of the Rudra-type that became prominent in the later periods. This origin explains also the dismal and terrible nature of the god. After all even the composers of the hymns see in Rudra primarily and almost exclusively a stern and awe-inspiring form. Uncertainty and fear about his terrible onslaughts, about his gruesome and insatiable urge for murder are prevailing tones of the prayers addressed to him. But with this basic nature of the god, his luminous celestial manifestation is not compatible... Originally he could not have possessed this character."

The same Ṛgvedic poets who described his terrible nature did not hesitate to designate him as a luminous celestial god. Here we are faced with a problem: can we anticipate for the age of the ṚV, the end-product of an evolution which has incorporated various elements into itself as a result of contacts with new tribes and countries, or to put it briefly, can we make the MBh and similar sources the yardstick for the ṚV? But how else could the Vedic poets come to transfer the awesome god to heaven if they had not come across such notions in the popular belief of their time and of their strata in which these notions were indeed rooted! Had he been an earth-bound demon in their time, he would not have been included in the hymn collection. If we put too much reliance on the guidance of the later periods (whose religious conceptions were after all regulated by the priests), we would arrive at notions like the one stated by Arbman (*Rudra*, p. 152) about *deva*, that on the whole in the popular tongue, which obviously has claims to the greatest originality here, the word *deva*, like Gr. *daimon*, seemed to be in the widest and vaguest sense just a designation for a "supernatural being, deity."[83] I think that here also the sense of the word is merely extended to encompass the classes of the minor spirits as well and that the original association with the *dyaus* has been pushed into the background. As for Rudra, he is not only a god of death but a god of fertility also. For the Śiva of the later period, who is identical or has been identified with Rudra, possesses the *liṅga* as the symbol of his fertility. This is the reason why we cannot regard Rudra or Śiva as a mere god of death.

There are very few hymns like I.43.1-6; 114; II.33; VII.46 which are dedicated solely to Rudra. Often in the Viśvadeva hymns like V.41-42;[84] VI.50; VII.36,[85] there are verses that are addressed to him also. I think it is remarkable that the mode of invocation is not the same for him everywhere. In the fourth maṇḍala he is mentioned only in one hymn (IV.3, vv. 1, 6, 7) along with other gods (in v. 1 as the name of Agni) in a row. The few passages of the sixth book where he appears six times in four hymns (28, 49, 50, 66; also *rudriya* in 62) yield little information. In both the books the Maruts are not yet described as the Rudras but merely as *rudrasya sūnavaḥ* (VI.50.4: 66.3,11).[86] The state of affairs in the third book also deserves mention. There the word *rudra* occurs in singular in III.2.5 only, a passage where we may regard the word as a mere epithet of Agni; the Rudras are mentioned indifferently as a class next to the Ādityas and Vasus in III.8.8 and 20.5. Only in III.32.2,3 they appear distinctly as identical with the Maruts who accompany Indra.[87] Maṇḍala VII (singular 9 times and plural 3 times) associates Indra in two of the three passages not with the Rudras but with the Vasus. VII.10.4: *índraṃ no agne vásubhiḥ sajóṣā rudráṃ rudrébhir* ...; 35.6: *śáṃ na índro vásubhir śáṃ no rudró rudrébhiḥ*, while the third passage, 5.9, refers to *vaiśvānara...rudrébhir agne vásubhiḥ*.

Rudra is described as *babhrú, śvityác* (II. 33.8), *aruṣá* (I.114.5). He adorns himself with shining ornaments (II.33.9),[88] carries bow and arrows, lightning or thunderbolt; he is depicted as harmful to man and beast and is "appeased" (*ava+dā*) with oblations. The three hymns dedicated to him are, to a great extent, deprecations (Bergaigne, III, p. 157), but a comparison of the ṚV with the other Vedic texts gives the impression that the older period lays greater stress on his remedies[89] than the later period —the word *jálāṣabheṣaja* is known only to the ṚV and AV—and slightly less emphasis on the terror emanating from him.[90] As the Indian tribes penetrated further into the east and descended deeper into the hot plains of the land, the terrors caused by Rudra might have appeared more concretely before their eyes. The hymns dedicated exclusively to him like I.43 etc. are employed in the ritual in their entirety in the *śūlagava* ceremony only,[91] single verses being used elsewhere also. The content of those hymns suggests a slightly different Rudra cult than what obtains in the ritual, for we find that not only Rudra is called *gāthápati* (I.43.4) but stomas are also assigned to him (I.114.9). As far as I know, our ritual does not list any of these stomas. In I.122.1 Soma is offered to him. X.136.7[92] is specially important. It deals with a man in a wild state of ecstasy and with his orgiastic doings: "Vāyu has churned for him, he pounds for him the Kunannamas, when the long-haired one drank poison with Rudra from the bowl." Arbman has observed pertinently that here we have the earliest trace of the orgiastic Rudra-Śiva cult which becomes very prominent in the later times, specially in this verse where mention is made of the means with which the state of ecstasy is achieved. Thus already in the ṚV, Rudra demonstrates the connection with the Yogi-hood of the later period. However, I see in this hymn not the description of an individual Yogin but of his celestial prototype, who is depicted in the relationship between the Ācārya and the Brahmacārin as well.

F. RUDRA'S NAMES

We do not know from where the seven or eight names of Rudra[93] were borrowed by the later literature. ĀśvGS IV.8.19 adds Hara, Mṛḍa, Śiva and Śaṅkara to these. According to ŚBr I.7.3.8 two of these names have a local origin. Śarva was the name for Rudra among the eastern people and Bhava among the Bāhlīkas (but hardly identical with him at the beginning). In the AV these two are combined into a dual deity, but they are still clearly distinguished from Rudra.[94] In a verse of the ŚŚS (IV.20.1) these two are stated to be Mahādeva's sons who "like wolves with jaws wide open, hunt around in the forest."[95] Neither name occurs in the Ṛ V; this is almost an infallible indication that the mythological area had been extended beyond the range of ideas of the Ṛgvedic poets. His third name, Paśupati,[96] does not require any elaboration. It is taken from Rudra's most favourite area of reign, perhaps in order to seek his protection for the animals, that is to say, for the euphemistic reasons which led to the majority of other names like *ugra, īśāna, mahādeva* and *bhīma*. TBr III. 9.17.3 states : "If the great god waylays, one should prepare a gruel for Rudra," and TMBr VI. 9.7 speaks similarly of "Mahādeva."[97] ABr III.34.7 prescribes a modification of the wording of ṚV II.33.1 in order to avoid the direct mention of Rudra's name, to which the ṚV itself did not have any objection. In an earlier passage of the same text he is referred to simply as *eṣa devaḥ*.[98] In some legends which occur for the first time in the Brāhmaṇa literature, Rudra is stated to have been without name at the beginning. KBr VI.1 ff.[99] narrates thus: "Prajāpati made a golden vessel as high as an arrow and equally wide and laid into it the seed of the gods which they had spilled at the sight of Uṣas who had escaped from them. From it emerged a being with thousand eyes, thousand feet and thousand arrows which were ready to be thrown.[100] He approached father Prajāpati. 'Why do you approach me?' 'Give me a name. Without having obtained a name, I do not wish to eat food.' " Prajāpati gives him at first the name Bhava, and upon his request a second name, then a third name and so on. A motif of these legends which occurs in other texts is Rudra's tears, moved by which Prajāpati grants him a name. "The beings (i.e., the Ṛtus) and the lord of these beings, *saṃvatsara*, laid their seed into Uṣas (his wife); then within a year a boy was born; he cried. Prajāpati said to him : 'Do you cry because you were born from *śrama* and *tapas*?' 'One evil is not yet taken away from me. I have no name...' " (ŚBr VI. 1.3.8 ff.).[101]

The ṚV does not fight shy of mentioning Rudra's name, but it does not contain a single trace of these names mentioned above. In the ṚV we find only "Rudra" and "Tryambaka."[102] Had the poets known other designations, we must expect to meet them, for the god was not at all unknown to them. Hence, we may assume with good reason that these names are the products of a later development or, to be more precise, of non-Ṛgvedic origin. With the gradual expansion of the Ṛgvedic tribes and through their contacts with other Aryan and non-Aryan peoples, their gods also must have gained in name and form.[103]

It has been established that Rudra is a god of the terror of the tropical climate from the onset of the hot season (*kruddha-agni*) up to the transition to autumn. This is roughly the time when the sun stands in the northernmost region in the Tropic of Cancer and therefore north is the direction which is exclusively his. Besides this there is another theory advocated by Oldenberg and Arbman which assigns the north to him because there is a mountain range to the north of the Vedic India and because Rudra dwells in the mountains, in the Himalayas. I have arrived at the interpretation which I have given here on basis of the statements about the time when he is especially furious and on the basis of his identification with Agni. But which form of Agni is meant here? We cannot say that it is the sun, let us say, under the aspect of his devastating power at a specific season. Likewise there is no evidence that he was elevated from a demon of the lower mythology to a celestial god. Would it be possible that he was a constellation the rising of which was the prelude to that period of the year? People generally tend to associate the conception of the seasons with the constellations. Classical antiquity had its "saevus Orion,"[104] the Parsees saw in Tištrya and his companion Satavaesa the enemies of Apaoša, the demon of drought. But here also our material proves itself to be too meagre to allow any precise conclusions. In one passage of the ABr (III.33.5) Rudra of course appears in a stellar saga; but his transference to the sky as a constellation there could have happened only later as in the case of Prajāpati and Uṣas. In ṚV X.64.8[105] he is mentioned along with Kṛśānu who shoots the Soma-eagle, with Tiṣya whose character as a constellation has never been in doubt and with other "archers."[106] In TS II. 2.10.2; MS II. 1.5 (7.5) he is identified directly with Tiṣya. In two verses addressed to Rudra in the TĀr[107] the one "who stands in the heavens like a tree" could refer to the *mṛgavyādha* who plays a role in the aforementioned Aitareya saga.[108] Besides Kārttika and Pauṣa,

Mārgaśīrṣa is the month in which the Sākamedha sacrifice is performed. Not only this but a number of other rites, more or less connected with Rudra, fall in this period or in its vicinity.[109] But this is not adequate to explain Rudra as a star[110] or as a constellation.[111] He remains unidentified.

NOTES

CHAPTER V

THE ĀDITYAS

1. Bohnenberger, *Der altindische Gott Varuṇa*, Tübingen 1893; Hopkins, *The Religions of India*, p. 70 ff.; PAOS, XVI, p. cxlviii; von Schroeder, WZKM, IX, p. 120 ff.; *Arische Religion*, I, p. 322 ff.; Griswold, *The God Varuṇa in the Ṛgveda*, p. 31. F. Knaur, "Über Varuṇa's Ursprung" (*Actes du XIVe Congrès International des Orientalistes*, I) sees the point of origin in the "nocturnal sky." Söderblom, *Das Werden des Gottesglaubens* p. **173,** refuses "to look for the basis of the god in a natural phenomenon." He asserts that "Varuṇa was the mighty *shaman* according to the primitive notions [where is it stated ?] and, in full conformity with the peculiarity of the Indian religion, this character of his has been preserved in the period of the Vedic culture [nowhere !]... He must be a *shaman*, a tribal chief whose power of magic surpasses that of others. We should look for Varuṇa's origin here and not in some aspect of nature ... the naturalistic explanation does not help us any further." Is that really the case with this explanation ? How does it explain the dual Mitra-Varuṇa, the evolution of Varuṇa into a god of ocean and into the *brahmán*, the real *shaman*, with whom Varuṇa has nothing in common ? And how does it explain the many dual divinities in the ritual ? and so on.

2. See, *inter alia*, Joh. Schmidt cited by Macdonell, *Vedic Mythology*, Addenda et Corrigenda. Patrubány, "Armenische Beiträge" in *Ethnologische Mitteilungen aus Ungarn*, V, no. 6, 9 equates Varuṇa with Armenian *garun*, "bright sky". Hübschmann kindly informs me that he does not consider Patrubány's equation to be correct because the Armenian word *garun* does not occur anywhere in the sense of "bright sky," on the contrary, it denotes only "spring," and thus it is certainly akin to Gr. *Géar* but not to Sanskrit *varuṇa*.

3. Bohnenberger, *op. cit.*, pp. 28-29.

4. Muir, OST, V, p. 58; PW, s.v. Mitra; Bergaigne, III, p. 120 ff. Cf. eg., TS VI.4.8.3 : *mitro 'har ajanayad varuṇo rātrim.* TBr 1.7.10.1 : *maitraṃ vā ahaḥ vāruṇī rātriḥ.* TMBr XXV.10.10 etc. ŚBr V. 2.5.17 : *vāruṇaṃ yatkṛṣṇam.*

5. TS V.3.4.2 : *prāṇo vai mitro 'pāno varuṇaḥ*; VII.2.7.1-2; (Savitṛ is substituted for Mitra in TBr I.5.3.1 : *devasya savituḥ prātaḥprasavaḥ prāṇaḥ varuṇasya sāyamāsavo 'pānaḥ*); VI.6.7.3 : *mitraḥ...sviṣṭaṃ yuvate, varuṇaḥ duriṣṭam* (differently in ABr III.38.3 where Viṣṇu is associated with *duriṣṭa* and Varuṇa with *sviṣṭa*); TBr I.7.10.1 : *maitro vai dakṣiṇaḥ vāruṇaḥ savyaḥ*; ABr III.4.5 : *atha yad uc ca hṛṣyati ni ca hṛṣyati tad asya maitrāvaruṇaṃ rūpam*; TMBr XXV.10.10 etc.

6. *tisró dyā́vo níhitā antár asmin tisró bhū́mīr úparāḥ ṣáḍvidhānāḥ* /

7. *ṛtásya gopā́ ná dábhāya sukrátus trī́ ṣá pavítrā hṛdy àntár ā́ dadhe* | Cf. also AV X.10.28 : *tisró jihvā́ váruṇasyāntar dīdyaty āsáni* |

8. Oldenberg, ZDMG, L, p. 61.

9. Cf. also IV.53.5 where it is said of Savitṛ : *trír antárikṣaṃ savitā́ mahitvanā́ trī́ rájāṃsi paribhū́s trī́ṇi rocanā́*. According to the meaning, *trī́ rájāṃsi paribhū́ḥ* here is not much different from *tisró dyā́vo níhitā antár asmin* in VII.87.5. Cf. VIII.41.3: *sá víśvaṃ pári darśatáḥ* and AV IV.16.3: *utéyaṃ bhū́mir váruṇasya rā́jñaḥ utā́sau dyaúr bṛhatī́ dūréantā.*

10. Cf. also V.69.1 : *trī́ rocanā́ varuṇa trī́n utá dyū́n trī́ṇi mitra dhārayatho rájāṃsi*; II.27.8-9; V.29.1.

11. *yénā pāvaka cákṣasā bhuraṇyátaṃ jánāṃ ánu | tváṃ varuṇa páśyasi || 7 : ví dyā́m eṣi rájas pṛthv áhā mímāno aktúbhiḥ | paśyañ jánmānī sūrya ||* For the explanation we may refer to I.95.1; 164.38 (see Vol. I. pp. 215, 431, n. 101).

12. WZKM, IX, pp. 116-117.

13. ṚV I.115.1.

14. Sāyaṇa connects the first simile *dyaúr iva* to the sun. Here *dyaúḥ* denotes the day. Varuṇa sinks down into the stream "like the day," or "like a bright drop." In order to understand the simile, we may cite here TS VI.4.2.4 and MS IV.5.1 (63.6) : *yad vai divā bhavaty apo rātriḥ pra viśati tasmāt tāmrā āpo divā dadṛśe*; *ya naktaṃ bhavaty apó' haḥ pra viśati, tasmāc candrā āpo naktaṃ dadṛśe* and *Kumārasaṃbhava* VIII.42 : *so 'yaṃ [sūrya] astam eti...saṃnidhāya divasaṃ mahodaddhau* |

15. Cf. Vol. I, p. 214 and the connection of the ideas developed there.

16. I should add that I do not lay any special stress upon hymn VIII.41. I do not attach a high value to this hymn as also to most hymns of the eighth book. Cf. Bohnenberger, *op. cit.*, p. 27.

17. Bartholomae, BKIS, X, p. 267 (only a list of the dual associations in the Avesta); Darmesteter, *Ormazd et Ahriman*, p. 65; Eggers, *Der arische Gott Mitra*, p. 31; Spiegel, *Arische Periode*, p. 185 ff. etc.

18. C. P. Tiele, *Geschichte der Religion im Altertum bis auf Alexander den Grossen* (German edition by G. Gehrich), II, p. 69. says of course: "... for, that Ahura [who is connected with Mithra] is a different being from Ahura Mazda is neither proved nor probable." Why "not probable" ?

19. Yašt XIX.77 : *ahurō kava husrava.* Cf. also Yašt V.85.

20. *Eranische Altertumskunde*, I, p. 435; II, p. 25. Before him Windischmann had already recognized it.

21. *Arische Periode*, p. 187.

22. Eggers, *op. cit.*, p. 32 has correctly seen that Spiegel's reasons are not adequate. Ahuramazda and Mithra are not associated in a dual. Cf. Yašt X.1 : *mithrem yim...frādadhąm azem* [*ahurō mazdå*]; 89 : *yim* [*mithrem*] *zaotārem stayata ahurō mazdå aṣava āsuyasnem*; 50.1 or also Yasna I.11. The Ahura who created Mithra and appointed him priest is just not the same as the Ahura who is connected with Mithra in dual form.

23. von Bradke, *Dyaus Asura*, p. 121.

24. Cf. also Oldenberg, ZDMG, L, pp. 56-57; I fully agree with him.

25. Just as the sun and the sky are not combined in Sanskrit to form a dual so are the ocean and the sun a pair which did not attain a dualistic intimacy. Of course, it is occasionally stated that the sun rises from the ocean (TĀr IV.42.33) or that he climbs out of the water and goes into it again in the evening (ABr IV.20.13; cf. AV XIII.2.14). But this does not enable us to understand Mitra-Varuṇa. The same is true of the passage from MBh III.163.11 (Bombay ed. III, folio 171 a), which Pischel cites as authority (GGA, 1895, p. 449). On this cf Oldenberg, *loc. cit*

26. Only in exceptional cases the passages containing the words *salilá, árṇas, arṇavá* have been taken into account. However, an examination of such passages does not alter the result obtained here. How far *ūrvá* denotes the ocean is still uncertain in spite of Geldner (VSt, II, p. 270). That Apāṃ napāt in II.35.3 should have anything to do with the fire of the ocean is shown to be improbable by vv. 10 and 14 of the same hymn.

27. I.55.2 (*arṇavá*); 71.7 : *sacante samudrám ná sravátaḥ saptá yahvī́ḥ*; III.36.7 : *samudréṇa síndhavo yā́damānāḥ* (*samudré ná* VI.19.5); 46.4; V.85.6; VI.36.3; VII.95.2 : *sárasvatī yatī́ giríbhya ā́ samudrā́t;* VIII.6.4 : *sám asya manyáve víśo...namanta kṛṣṭáyaḥ samudrā́yeva síndhavaḥ*; 35; 16.2; 44.25; IX.88.6; 107.9; 108.16. Hence the streams or the waters are also called *samudríya, samudrā́rtha* etc.

28. IV.21.3 : *ā́ yātv índro divá ā́ pṛthivyā́, makṣū́ samudrā́t utá vā púrīṣāt, svàrṇarāt...parāváto vā*; V.55.5 : *úd īrayathā marutaḥ samudrató yūyám vṛṣṭiṃ varṣayathā purīṣiṇaḥ;* VIII.6.29 : *átaḥ samudrám udvátaś* (=land) *cikitvā́ñ áva paśyati.*

29. ṚV IX.33.6 mentions four oceans.

30. The waters flow from the upper ocean, i.e., the ocean of the sky, to that of the earth.

31. Cf. also v. 6 : *asmín samudré ádhy uttarasminn ā́po devébhir nivṛtā atiṣṭhan*; VIII.26.17 : *divó arṇavé*; VI.58.3 : *samudré antárikṣe*, in which Pūṣan's golden ships sail, or V.45.10 : *ā́ sū́ryo aruhac chukrám árṇo áyukta yád dharito vītápṛṣṭhāḥ / udnā́ ná nā́vam anayanta dhī́rāḥ;* cf. also X.89.4 : *ságarasya budhnā́t.*

32. *svā́dasvéndrāya pávamāna, indo, rayíṃ ca na ā́ pavasvā samudrā́t* // VII.6.7, see above under no. 5.

33. Sāyaṇa : *yathā samudramadhye nāvaḥ sajjīkṛtya prerayanti.*

34. Sāyaṇa : *saniṣyavaḥ saniṃ dhanam ātmana icchanto vaṇijo dhanārthaṃ saṃcaraṇe saṃcāre nimittabhūte sati samudraṃ na yathā nāvā samudram adhirohanti.*

35. I.116.5; 117.15; 118.6; VII.68.7; 69.7; VIII.5.22; X.143.5; Baunack, KZ, XXXV, p. 485.

36. Quite correctly Oldenberg, RdV, p. 214; Bühler, *Indische Palaeographie*, p. 17 and even Weber, *Indische Skizzen* p. 135 : "The mention in the ṚV of the sea-voyages and of rescue from shipwreck point out, on the other hand, that Indians also definitely knew how to bustle about on the sea, on the *samudrá*, and it is hardly warranted, as some wished, to see here in

samudrá merely the celestial ocean and in those expressions simple allegories.' See also Myriantheus, *Die Aśvins*, p. 167.

37. *ájohavīd aśvinā taugryó vāṃ próḷhaḥ samudrám avyathír jaganvā́n | níṣ ṭam ūhathuḥ*. I derive *avyathís* from *vyáthis*, "path, course" (cf. *kṛṣṇá-vyathis*) and treat *samudrá* as neuter as it happens once in the Veda (cf. VI. 72.3 : *ā́ samudrā́ṇi paprathuḥ purū́ṇi*). Baunack translates thus : "Tugra's son called you, O Aśvins, (and look), led on, he went his way through the ocean without stumbling" (KZ XXXV, pp. 489, 507). I do not agree with this translation, nor do I believe that here we have a "definite evidence" for the use of "the perfect participle of *vaṃs* supplemented by the auxiliary verb for the finite verb."

38. Baunack, *loc. cit.*, p. 485 : "on the dry [bank], i.e., the strand of the ocean on the other side of the wet bank."

39. Cf. VIII.20.13 : *yéṣām árṇo ná saprátho nāma*; X.109.1 : *ákūpāra salilá*.

40. [Indra] *samudrá iva pinvate*—I.8.7.

41. Oldenberg, RdV, p. 214, n. 2.

42. I.30.18 : *samānáyojano ho vāṃ ráthaḥ...samudré aśvinéyate;* IV.43.5 : *urú vāṃ ráthaḥ pári nakṣati dyā́m ā́ yát samudrā́d abhí vártate vām*; V.73.8; VII.70.2; VIII.10.1.

43. I.174.9 : *prá yát samudrám áti śūra párṣi*; II.16.3 : *ná kṣoṇī́bhyāṃ paribhvè ta indriyáṃ ná samudraíḥ párvatair indra te ráthaḥ;* IV.21.3 : *ā́ yātv índro divá ā́ pṛthivyā́ makṣū́ samudrā́d utá vā púrīṣāt* etc.; VIII.12.17; 13.15; 34.13; X.89.11 etc.; Indra-Soma VI.72.3.

44. I.19.7,8; 167.2; V.55.5 : *úd īrayathā marutaḥ samudrató yūyáṃ vṛṣṭíṃ varṣayathā purīṣiṇaḥ*; VIII.20.25.

45. Lüders, SBKPAW, 1910, p. 931 sees in Varuṇa "the ocean which originally surrounded the earth." I still cannot see that this view can be substantiated.

46. *adbhír yāti váruṇaḥ samudraíḥ*; cf. also VII.49.3; 88.3; IX.90.2. IX.73.3; 95.4 where Varuṇa and Soma are equated will be discussed below.

47. See p. 9 above; cf. also MS IV.3.4 (42.18) : *aham antarikṣād iti varuṇaḥ* [*paśyāmi*]; (43.1); *varuṇo 'ntarikṣe.* See incidentally Oldenberg, ZDMG, L, p. 56, n. 3.

48. VIII.54.4 enumerates Sarasvatī, the seven Sindhus, Āpaḥ, Vāta, mountains, trees and earth but not the ocean.

49. In X.111.4 an *arṇavá* is depicted as the enemy of Indra who destroys the former's *vrata*. In X.67.12 he is styled *mahát arṇavá arbudá*.

50. This collation makes no claim of absolute thoroughness. One may easily find a few additional passages which however do not change the end-result. Samudra receives an animal sacrifice in the Aśvamedha. VS XXIV. 25 enjoins *śiśumāras* and 35 enjoins *nākra, makara, kulīpaya* for Samudra.

51. Holtzmann, *Das Mahābhārata*, I, pp. 38-39; BDS II.2.2.

52. *Rāmāyaṇa* I.1.77-78; *Harivaṃśa* 792 ff.; 6529 (PW). See Hopkins, "The Ocean in Sanskrit Epic Poetry," AJPh, XXI (1900), p. 378 ff.

53. VI.23.18 (*Yuddhakāṇḍa*).

54. *dīptāsyaiḥ.*

55. *Vikramorvaśīyam*, ed. Bollensen, v. 117.

56. See below p. 14 ff.

57. *Popular Religion*, 1st ed., p. 26; 2nd ed., I, p. 47.

58. We cannot attach a high value to the passage ĀpŚS XIII. 20.12.

59. ŚBr II.5.2.16 : *eṣa vai pratyakṣaṃ varuṇasya paśur yan meṣaḥ.*

60. Of the acquatic animals, I have noted only those called *nākra* which are sacrificed to Varuṇa on the occasion of the Aśvamedha. MS III.14.2 (173.2); TS V.5.13.1; VS XXIV.21. According to Mahīdhara it means crocodile.

61. ṚV I.161.14 etc. See n. 46, above.

62. II.28.4; V.85.6 (according to these verses it is due to the *māyā* of Varuṇa that the rivers cannot fill the one ocean. His magic manifests itself in another way also; cf. VIII.41.3 : *ny ùsró māyáyā dadhe*); VII.64.2 : Mitra-Varuṇa are *síndhupatī*; VIII.69.12; IX.90.2; X.124.7. See my *Varuṇa und Mitra*, pp. 85, 146 and my article on Māyā in WZKM, XIII, p. 320.

63. MS IV.7.8 (104. 11,12) connects this verse with the ocean. The context here is an accounting for the sacrifice of a ram (*petva*) for Varuṇa.

64. II.28.4; on this cf. IX.82.5 where it is said of Soma : *táva vratám ánv ā́paḥ sacante*, or I.101.3 about Indra.

65. I leave it undecided whether *kākúd* is correctly understood. Bergaigne, III, p. 133 translates thus : "Thou art a great god, O Varuṇa; from thy mouth flow the seven rivers, as through a deep channel," and interprets the verse quite differently. It is not superfluous to note that here we are dealing precisely with a verse of the eighth book.

66. *āpo hi varuṇaḥ / sthāvarā abhyavayanti tā hi sākṣād varuṇo...āpo vai varuṇo vāto varuṇaḥ* etc. His healing power, which is alluded to in solitary passages, rests perhaps on the waters. ṚV I.24.9 ; *śatáṃ te rājan bhiṣájaḥ sahásram*; TBr II.6.11.9 : *váruṇaṃ bhiṣájāṃ pátim* (cf. also II.6.4.1); III.1.2.7 (*kṣatrasya rājā varuṇo 'dhirājaḥ / nakṣatrāṇāṃ śatabhiṣag vasiṣṭhaḥ*); III.1.5.9.

67. His house is described in detail in MBh, II adhyāya 9.

68. VIII.41.2 : *nābhākásya prā́śastibhir yáḥ síndhūnām úpodayé*
saptásvasā sá madhyamó...

69. V.85.3. For this and other verses, see *Varuṇa und Mitra*, pp. 85-86.

70. Thus also Oldenberg, ZDMG, L, p. 57.

71. *ubhā́ rā́jānā svadháyā mádantā yamáṃ paśyāsi váruṇaṃ ca devám //*

72. In ṚV II.38.8 : *yādrādhyàṃ váruṇo yónim ápyam ániśitaṃ nimíṣi járbhurāṇaḥ*, Roth conjectures *vā́ruṇo*. I have thought, without holding that the conjecture is necessary, that we have here a *deus pro symbolo* and that *váruṇo* means fish. But all this is at least in vain. Here *váruṇo* means "fish" only. If we may draw a conclusion from this it is this : the word is connected etymologically with *vā́r*, "water." Earlier, I had objected to this because fish do not sleep at night and because it is improbable that a fish goes to its place in the evening for sleeping. But that is applying too realistic a yardstick to the poet. If *váruṇo* here means fish and is connected with *vā́r*, this would give for Varuṇa a totally different etymology than what is now quite popular. (The relationship of the moon god with the

waters is adequately discussed in the chapter on Soma in Vol. I). Accordingly Varuṇa would be "the fish" in the celestial ocean. A late verse (cited by Aufrecht, ZDMG, XXXVI, p. 546) styles the moon a carp (*induśaphara*) who, noticing the sun-eagle (*ravikurara*) nearby at the break of dawn, dives out of fear into the sky-ocean and in the evening, accompanied by hundreds of nimble starlets (*caṭulataratārārbhaka*; Aufrecht : starfishes) swims around in the indigo of the flood of darkness. The verse has a graphic value.

73. See n. 5 above.

74. TS II.1.2.1 : *sa etaṃ vāruṇam kṛṣṇaṃ ekaśitipādam ā labheta;* 7.3 : *maitrāvaruṇīṃ dvirūpām ā labheta vṛṣṭikāmo, maitraṃ vā ahar, vāruṇī rātrir, ahorātrābhyāṃ khalu vai parjanyo varṣati*; II.1.9.1 :...*vāruṇīṃ kṛṣṇāṃ vaśām apaśyat*...; 2: *maitraṃ śvetam ā labheta vāruṇaṃ kṛṣṇam apāṃ cauṣadhīnāṃ ca saṃdhav annakāmo, maitrīr vā oṣadhayo vāruṇīr āpo*; V.5.11.1 : *varuṇāya rājñe kṛṣṇaḥ;* 24 : *vāruṇaḥ kṛṣṇa ekaśitipāt petvaḥ*; V.6.11 : *tisraḥ kṛṣṇā vaśā vāruṇyaḥ*; 21 : *vāruṇī kṛṣṇe vaśe*. Somewhat differently V.6.20 : *vāruṇās trayaḥ kṛṣṇalalāmā varuṇāya rājñe trayo rohitalalāmā varuṇāya riśādase trayo 'ruṇalalāmāḥ*; ŚBr V.2.5.17 : *kṛṣṇaṃ vāso vāruṇasya tad dhi vāruṇaṃ yat kṛṣṇaṃ, yadi kṛṣṇaṃ na vinded api yad eva kiṃ ca vāsaḥ syād granthibhir hi vāso varuṇaṃ, varuṇyo hi granthaḥ.*

75. TS II.3.1.4 : *ye kṛṣṇāḥ syus taṃ vāruṇaṃ caruṃ nir vaped, vāruṇaṃ vai rāṣṭram.*

76. Brinton, *Religions of the Primitive Peoples*, p. 237 : "the black and the red are ominous of strife and darkness." Hillebrandt, *Tiere und Götter im vedischen Ritual*, Breslau 1905, pp. 10, 12.

77. Cf. e.g. TS V.5.14 ff. : *mṛtyave 'sitaḥ, pūruṣamṛgaś cāndramase kṛṣṇo rātriyai*; 7.1.2 : *etad vā ahno rūpaṃ yac chveto 'śvo rātriyai kṛṣṇaḥ.*

78. *Ritualliteratur*, p. 144. TS I.8.1.1; TBr I.6.1.3; 7.3,4. The night and Nirṛti cannot be quite separated from each other.

79. *Ritualliteratur*, p. 172. TS II.4.9.1 etc.

80. See n. 74 above. Or bright coloured animals, TS V.6.11 : *tisraḥ śvetā vaśāḥ sauryaḥ;* 12 : *tisro rohiṇīr vaśā maitriyaḥ.*

81. *sūryācandramābhyāṃ yamau śvetaṃ ca kṛṣṇaṃ caikayūpe.* Cf. comm., II, p. 920; ĀpŚS XIX.16.21.

82. TS VI.6.3.5 : *pratiyuto varuṇasya pāśa ity āha, varuṇapāśād eva nir mucyate, 'pratīkṣam ā yanti varuṇasyāntarhityai.* MS IV.8.5 (113.15) : *anapekṣamāṇā āyanti varuṇasyānanvavāyāya, parogoṣṭhaṃ mārjayante, parogoṣṭham eva varuṇaṃ niravadayantā edho 'sy edhiṣīmahīti nirvaruṇā eva bhūtvaidhitum upayanti.*

83. *Ritualliteratur*, p. 115.

84. Ibid., p. 119.

85. Cf. also TBr I.7.1.9 : *apratīkṣam āyanti rakṣasām antarhityai.*

86. His *meni*, TS V.1.6.1.

87. Cf. von Schroeder, ZDMG, XLIX, p. 169.

88. TS II.2.5.1. Cf. also TS II.3.11.1; 12.1 etc.

89. TBr I.4.4.3 : *varuṇo vā etasya yajñaṃ gṛhṇāti yasyāgnim anuddhṛtaṃ sūryo 'bhinimrocati, vāruṇaṃ caruṃ nirvapet* /

90. Cf. n. 5 above and n. 130 below. When the axle of the Soma cart creaks, the "evil-sounding one" is Varuṇa. TS VI.2.9.1 : *varuṇo vā eṣa durvāg ubhayato baddho yad akṣaḥ*. Even "the red-hot glowing Ukhā" belongs to Varuṇa obviously because it is dangerous to touch : *vāruṇy ukhābhīddhā*.

91. In my knowledge, this is the only sacrifice where a confession of sins is made. *Rituallitteratur*, p. 117.

92. Cf. MS IV.8.5 (112). KŚS X.8.19 ff. The second text enjoins in the first place stationary waters situated in the middle of the flowing waters. Offerings are made to Agni and Agni-Varuṇa, to the last two with the remains of the puroḍāśa.

93. Cf. ĀpŚS VIII.8.18.

94. In passages like TS II.6.1.1 *samidh* is brought into an intimate association with *vasanta*, *tanūnapāt* with *grīṣma*, *iḍ* with *varṣāḥ* etc.

95. ṚV VIII.48.3. TS III.2.5.m etc.

96. Here the textual tradition is uncertain. On the wording as given in the ĀpŚS, cf. AV VI.117.3.

97. Cf. also MS IV.1.5 (7.7) : *tān devā etena yajuṣādṛṃhan, yad etad yajur vadaty eṣāṃ lokānāṃ dhṛtyai/ nir varuṇasya pāśād amukṣīti varuṇapāśād eva nirmucyata ātmano 'hiṃsāyai, svar abhivyakṣam iti tama iva vā eṣa prapadyate parīṇāhaṃ / svar evābhivipaśyati, jyotir vaiśvānaram* (I.1.5) *ity asau vā āditya jyotir vaiśvānaram*.

98. That "Varuṇa's fetter" is thrown into water proves nothing in favour of the rainy season. This recalls rather the rites performed in spring for driving the death away, when a figure or a doll which represents the death is thrown usually into water (but rarely cremated). Cf. Grimm, *Deutsche Mythologie*, 4th ed., II, p. 639 ff. Frazer, *The Golden Bough*, I, p. 258 where further citations can be found.

99. ŚBr IV.5.1.11; MS IV.8.6 (114.1); ĀpŚS XIII.23.12; KŚS X.9.12.

100. E.g. TS II.1.7.1; 5.5.4-5; 6.7.4; VI.6.7.4; KŚS IV.11.15 etc.

101. I.153.3; X.65.6.

102. Cf. KŚS XV.8.26 : *vaśā vandhyā ya upagamyamānāpi garbhaṃ na gṛhṇāti*.

103. ŚBr IV.5.1.6; MS IV.8.6 (114.6); TS VI.6.7.4.

104. Johansson has now proved, I think, the correctness of this explanation (*Etymologisches und Wortgeschichtliches*, Uppsala 1927, p. 59 ff.)

105. ĀpŚS XX.22.6 : *avabhṛthena pracaryātreyaṃ śipiviṣṭam khalatiṃ viklidhaṃ śuklaṃ piṅgākṣaṃ tilakāvalam avabhṛtham abhyavanīya tasya mūrdhañ juhoti mṛtyave svāhā, bhrūṇahatyāyai svāhā, jumbakāya svāheti tisraḥ*. ŚŚS XVI.18.18 : *athātreyaṃ sahasreṇāvakrīya yaḥ śuklaḥ piṅgākṣo valinas tilakāvalo viklidhaḥ khaṇḍo baṇḍaḥ khalatiḥ*. TĀr I.2.3 : *paṭharo viklidhaḥ piṅgaḥ*. KŚS XX.8.17 : *piṅgalakhalativiklidhaśuklasya mūrdhani*. Here we may draw attention to the legend of Varuṇa and Bhṛgu (ŚBr XI.6.1). During his wanderings Bhṛgu sees "a black man with yellow eyes and with a staff in the hand," standing between two woman of varying beauty. Here the elements of the saga have undergone a transformation. Johansson,

Dhiṣaṇā, p. 126 ff. discusses this episode in detail but interprets differently. In Varuṇa he sees an original god of vegetation and death, who was "consolidated as 'king' and 'lord' and modelled so to say after human kings..." But Varuṇa's relation to Mitra, to water and the ocean and several others stands in the way of such an interpretation.

106. Some understand *viklidha* as "leprous" (comm. on ŚŚS) and others as *dantura*, "with oversized teeth" (comm. on the KŚS). Again the comm. on TBr, III, p. 708 : *svedanaśilaśarīraḥ, viklinnadeho vā*. TĀr I.2.3 (Ānandāśrama Sanskrit Series ed., I, p. 8) : *vividhakledanayuktaḥ*. The comm. on VS XXV.9 and the KŚS explain *śukla* as *atigaura*, the comm. on the TBr as *citrin*.

107. ŚŚS, for example, adds also the designations *khaṇḍa* (comm. cripple) and *bàṇḍa* (comm. impotent).

108. I do not understand how Keith, p. 96, can say "that we have to deal not with a primitive, but with a mystical, view of the nature of Varuṇa." This becomes evident neither from the context not from the rites. All the ritual texts unanimously give this description. "Mystical" would look quite different. The description is as matter-of-fact as possible.

109. According to the statement of the ŚŚS and ĀpŚS, an Ātreya should be chosen for this ceremony. It is conspicuous that according to the ŚŚS, he is "bought" and that too *sahasreṇa gavām* (cf. TMBr VI.6.11 in a different context : *tasmād ātreyaṃ candreṇecchanty atrir hi tasya jyotiḥ*). This leads us to the notion that this ceremony has preserved a reminiscence of the human sacrifice in which this person who has been bought is regarded as a substitute for another. The mantras which accompany the oblations, *mṛtyave svāhā, bhrūṇahatyāyai svāha*, corroborate this. In Hariścandra's sacrifice also, which was likewise meant for Varuṇa, another man (to be precise, Sunaḥśepa) was brought as the substitute for the king's son. Whosoever has read Frazer's *The Golden Bough* would remember the section on "temporary kings" (I, p. 227 in the chapter, "Killing the Divine King") according to which the king had to be killed at the sign of physical weakness or at the end of a specific period. Among the examples listed by Frazer there are some from India as well. Perhaps we may add the one from the Aśvamedha here : the new victorious king celebrates a grand sacrifice at the conclusion of which the old king is done away with. In the ritual, the place of the king was taken by a man, who had been purchased and whose physical features were supposed to represent the picture of king Varuṇa (cf. my *Alt-Indien*, Breslau 1899, p. 94). Incidentally, Keith is mistaken when he thinks (p. 263) that I "connect" the Sunaḥśepa legend with the Jumbaka. It was cited as an analogy for the purchase of a man as a substitute for another.

110. *varuṇāyāruṇāyeti vratahomāḥ*. (It is however possible that here *aruṇa* is not an attribute but an independent word). Accordingly, we find, besides "black" animals for Varuṇa, also *aruṇababhru, babhru* etc., e.g. in VS XXIV.2.

111. TĀr X.1.47 : *hiraṇyaśṛṅgaṃ varuṇaṃ prapadye tīrthaṃ me dehi yācitaḥ*. The word *maṃścatu* is obscure. Cf. Benfey, *Vedica und Verwandtes*,

p. 57 ff.; von Schroeder on MS IV.11.1 (162.3). Grassmann, *Wörterbuch zum Ṛgveda*, and de Saussure, *Mémoire sur le système primitif des voyelles dans les langues indo-européennes* (p. 120, n. 1) seek to derive the first part from *māṃs*. TĀr I.8.4.11 states *candramāś catur ity ucyate*. Cf. Johansson, *Dhiṣaṇā*, p. 143, n. 2.

112. TBr III.4.17.

113. According to ĀpŚS VIII.4.13, the Vaiśvadeva is performed in *vasanta*, the Varuṇapraghāsāḥ in *prāvṛṣ* and the Sākamedhāḥ in *śarad*.

114. II.5.2.4.: *atha yad eṣa etaiś caturthe māsi yajate tan nāha nv evaitasya tathā prajā varuṇo gṛhṇātīti devā akurvann iti nv evaiṣa etat karoti yāś ca nu evāsya prajā jātā yāś cājātās tā ubhayīr varuṇapāśāt pramuñcati tā asyānamīvā akilbiṣāḥ prajāḥ prajāyante tasmād vā eṣa etaiś caturthe māsi yajate* |

115. ĀpŚS VIII.7.26 : "They step on the edge of the water with the formula 'Varuṇa's fetter is trampled.'" 8.18 : " 'We look upward from the darkness,' with this verse they worship the sun, push back the water on the bank [with their feet] etc." (as described on pp. 17-18 above).

116. TS IV.4.12.g ; ŚŚS XVI.9.31; KŚS XX.8.30 etc.

117. TS I.8.7.1; 8.1; 10.1; ŚBr IV.2.1.11 : *tasmād āhur varuṇyo yava iti*, but probably not always; cf. the *catuṣkapāla* [*puroḍāśa*] in TS II.3.12; *daśakapāla* I.17.8; *caru* II.2.5.1 etc.

118. *Rituallitteratur*, pp. 86, 120; GGS III.8.22 and comm., p. 572; *Śrautapadārthanirvacana*, p. 96 : *yavāgrayaṇakālo vasantaḥ*. KP, p. 159. [Differently TS VII.2.10.1 : *yavaṃ grīṣmāya*]. One may object saying that it is just the custom to make all oblations with yava in spring and in summer. But it is still striking that special emphasis should be laid on the connection with Varuṇa and not on the connection with other gods. Cf. also Vol. I, p. 307; Weber, *Rājasūya*, p. 16, p. 34, n. 4.

119. We should note that the offering is made in the Dakṣiṇa fire; ŚBr II.5.2.25. Oldenberg, RdV, pp. 319-320. If the fetters of Varuṇa should denote the rainy season and its darkness, then a sacrifice for the release from Varuṇa's fetters at the beginning of the rainy season would make as little sense as celebrating the liberation from the fetters of the winter at its beginning. Hence the present position of the Varuṇapraghāsāḥ at the beginning of the rainy season is not in harmony with the signification of this ceremony.

120. Probably they may be substitutes for the sacrifice of real animals. Baking two such animals recalls (without stretching the comparison further) the Yule bread made in the shape of a boar and other such confections.

121. Cf. Oldenberg, *Aus Indien und Iran*, p. 179; RdV, 2nd ed., pp. 193, 194.

122. E.g., TS I.8.10.1; TBr I.7.10.3.

123. Ehni, *Yama*, 2nd ed., p. 98. Their abodes are described in MBh, II, adhyāyas 8 and 9 respectively. Adhyāya 12 however distinguishes the members of Yama's *sabhā* from those of Varuṇa's *sabhā*.

124. Manu IX.245 speaks of Varuṇa as *īśo daṇḍasya, rājñāṃ daṇḍadharaḥ*.

125. Varuṇa is also portrayed thus : Bergaigne, III, p. 118 f. In *Sāmavidhānabrāhmaṇa* III.8.2 the night is called *pāśahasta*. ṚV VII.59.8 speaks of *druháḥ pā́śa*, VII.59.12 and AV XVII.30 speak of *mṛtyór* [*bándhana*]. In the mantra, "may Mitra bind you by the foot," in TS I.2.4.h, Mitra seems to stand for Varuṇa *boni ominis causa*, "for the sake of good augury."

126. They have also the following in common. The majesty (*bharga* or *hvarenaṅh* as the case may be) escapes from Varuṇa according to TMBr XVIII.9.1 and likewise from Yima at least in the Iranian saga. According to TBr I.8.1.1; 8.9.1 the strength (*vīrya*) escapes from him. However, Indra also loses it, TBr I.8.5.1.

127. I.24.11 ff.; 25; VII.86, 89 etc.; *Varuṇa und Mitra*, p. 53; Bohnenberger, *op. cit.*, p. 58.

128. With the exception of *devahéḍana*.

129. III, p. 134.

130. III. pp. 120, 133, 134, 144, 153, 154.

131. III, p. 132.

132. I do not agree with Johansson that these two are identical (*Dhiṣaṇā*, pp. 128 ff., 137, 162). If we equate Vṛtra with Varuṇa, then I do not see how his other qualities and realms of activity can be reconciled with Varuṇa's nature from the evolutionary point of view, whereas with the assumption that he was a former moon god we can easily account for everything. Vṛtra also encloses the streams, but Varuṇa is their friend. Sorensen, "Til sporgsmalet om Ādity'erne," p. 337 ff., also disputes on good grounds the identification first propounded by Bergaigne and now taken up again by Johansson.

133. *Rechtsschriften*, p. 379.

134. *Varuṇa und Mitra*, pp. 34-35; also TMBr I.8.3; TBr III.8.4.1;20.3; 9.16.1. When an offering is made to him, a horse is given away as the dakṣiṇā TS I.8.8. It is not clear what the four-eyed dog signifies which a man of low birth causes in the Aśvamedha to swim under the horse upon a mat. Cf. Oldenberg, ARW, VII, p. 226, n. 1; Hommel, *Festschrift für Kuhn*, p. 422.

135. See Vol. I, pp. 41-43.

136. I.91.3 : *rā́jño nu te váruṇasya vratā́ni*
bṛhád gabhīrám̐ táva soma dhā́ma |
śúciṣ ṭvám asi priyó ná mitró
dakṣā́yyo aryamévāsi soma ||

137. IX.95.4 : *tám̐ marmṛjānám̐ mahiṣám̐ ná sā́nau*
am̐śúm̐ duhanty ukṣáṇam̐ giriṣṭhā́m |
tám̐ vāvaśānám̐ matáyaḥ sacante
tritó bibharti váruṇam̐ samudré ||

138. IX.38.2 : *etám̐ tritásya yóṣaṇo hárim̐ hinvanty ádribhiḥ |*
índum índrāya pītáye ||

"The maidens" are, as the other passages (IX.1.8; 8.4; 38.3; 46.6) show, the fingers. Cf. further IX.34.4 : *bhúvat tritásya márjyo bhúvad índrāya matsaráḥ*; 102.2,3; 37.4; 86.20.

139. *sá samudró apīcyàs turó dyā́m iva rohati.*

140. Not to be taken into account is IX.77.5 where Soma is identified with Varuṇa and Mitra. There for the *hurúg yaté* Soma is a Varuṇa, i.e. an avenging god.

141. On Soma see the passages cited in Vol. I, p. 246 ff., and on Varuṇa those cited in *Varuṇa und Mitra*, p. 79 ff., specially on p. 81.

142. IX.73.8 (Varuṇa) : *trí ṣá pavítrā hṛdy àntár ā dadhe* and IX.97.55 (Soma) : *sáṃ trí pavítrā vítatāny eṣi*; or VI.70.1 : *dyā́vāpṛthiví váruṇasya dhármaṇā víṣkabhite* and one of the verses cited in the *Vedische Mythologie*, 1st ed., I, p. 417, n. 5, like IX.101.15 : *ví yás tastámbha ródasī.*

143. III, p. 135 ff.

144. On the frequency of such epithets like *priyá* etc., see Eggers, *op. cit*, p. 42.

145. Occasionally they are even depicted as enemies, e.g., ŚBr IV.2.1.11.

146. *Aməša Spəntas* p. 214, n. 5.

147. I do not overlook that Soma is identified with yet other gods as well (cf. VS VIII.55 ff.; TS IV.4.9.1), but it seems to me that there is a fundamental difference; such identifications have only a superficial validity and are rather accidental, while the identification with Varuṇa is well developed in the ritual.

148. ĀpŚS X.20.12-27; see Vol. I, p. 160 ff.

149. The commentary on the TS, I, p. 364, explains the *varuṇasya* in one of the mantras as the bull !

150. *abhidhānī*, uncertain. The method of yoking is not clear to me.

151. The hut of the sacrificer, cf. ĀpŚS X.5.

152. The commentary on the ĀpŚS explains *atihṛtya* differently as *rājānam anyasmai pradāya.*

153. TBr II.5.8.4.

154. After the *praṇayana*; ĀpŚS XI.17.10.

155. This last section contains nothing of importance after what has been said on p. 17 above. I have cited it merely for completeness' sake.

156. Cf. *Vedische Mythologie*, 1st ed., II, p. 215.

157. Cf. also MS III.7.8.

158. When a *caru* prepared with barley is offered to Varuṇa in the Rājasūya, the sacrificial fee for this oblation is a black garment. (Weber, *Rājasūya*, p. 19).

159. See p. 17 above.

160. Keith (p. 103) asserts that "the identification of Varuṇa with the moon is absolutely without support." But I do not know of any other explanation which is more well-founded both intrinsically and externally on the basis of the texts and the context. It is better than that of "all encompassing sky," which Keith took up once again but which fails the test in important points.

161. IX.74.2; 101.15; cf. also Bṛhaspati.

162. Tylor, *Anfänge der Kultur*, I, p. 347; II, pp. 299, 323, 326. Cf. also Brinton, *Religions of the Primitive Peoples*, p. 139; Oldenberg, ZDMG, L, p. 67.

163. Oldenberg, *loc. cit.*, p. 66, n. 1.

164. Vol. I, p. 227 ff.

165. Cf. *Varuṇa und Mitra*, pp. 83, 144. As Eggers, *op. cit.*, pp. 68-69 remarks, there is no indubitable evidence that Mitra was regarded as the rain god in the Aryan period. Wherever Mitra and Varuṇa appear jointly as rain gods, the quality which belongs to Varuṇa alone seems to have been extended to the other.

166. IX.107.16 (Besides Varuṇa in I.25.7; yet I think that another explanation is also possible here).

167. Vol. I, p. 214.

168. It has a parallel in IX.73.3 : *mahā́ḥ samudrám váruṇas tiro dadhe*, which must be translated as "Varuṇa concealed himself in the ocean." Oldenberg, *Ṛgveda*, translates thus : "has concealed the ocean." But we may compare, e.g., IX.86.8 : *rā́jā samudrám nadyò ví gāhate*.

169. KBr III.1 : *tenottarāmuttarām upavased uttarām u ha vai samudro vijate somam anu daivatam...*

170. *Epigraphia Indica*, II.3, 5 (Kielhorn).

171. He corresponds to the Agni of the ṚV who was born *samudré* and to the Indu *samudráyoni* of the TS (see Vol. I, p. 86). He is called *samudrávāsas* in ṚV VIII.102.4=TS III.1.11.8=MS IV.11.2 (166) : *aurvabhṛguvác chúcim apnavānavád ā́huve / agním samudrávāsasam //* There can be no question here of an "ocean-fire," which is not a cult object. We can agree neither with Geldner nor with Oldenberg (ZDMG, LV, p. 319).

172. NSP ed., p. 168, line 3.

173. NSP ed., p. 295, line 4.

174. NSP ed., p. 461, line 6.

175. Ed. Bühler. Cf. Haack, *Vikramāṅkadevacaritam*, Ratibor 1897. Anhang 4.

176. Hultzsch, *South-Indian Inscriptions*, II, pp. 350, 358.

177. On this cf. Kielhorn 5.39.

178. Cf. Böhtlingk, *Indische Sprüche*, 2nd ed., and Blau's meticulous Index, s.v. "Mond" : Nos. 436, 1162, 1583, 1774, 1999, 2022, 2594, 3539, 4162, 5764. From the other texts I have noted the following. *Kumārasambhava* III.67; *Raghuvaṃśa* III.17; *Kathāsaritsāgara* XVI.73; *Kalpasūtra*, ed. Jacobi, § 38. See also Hopkins, "The Ocean in Sanskrit Poetry," AJPH, XXI, p. 378 ff.

179. VII. 49.3: *yā́sām rā́jā váruṇo yā́ti mádhye*
satyānṛte avapáśyañ jánānām.

180. *adbhir yāti váruṇaḥ samudraiḥ* (cf. p. 18 above).

181. *vánā vásāno váruṇo ná síndhūn.*

182. Even PGS I.5.10 combines *mitraḥ satyānām, varuṇo apām, samudraḥ srotyānām*, that it to say, it still distinguishes Varuṇa from Samudra.

183. Dr Betty Heimann, *Festschrift für Jacobi*, p. 204. I am not convinced that the notion of the Karman is directly related to that of the Ṛta.

184. Spiegel, *Die altpersischen Keilinschriften*, 2nd ed., p. 68.

185. Gelzer, "Zur armenischen Götterlehre," SBKSGW, XLVIII, 1896, p. 103.

186. von Gutschmidt, *Gesammelte Schriften*, III, p. 173 ff. It is still uncertain whether Mithra reached Assyria. Jensen, *Hittiter und Armenier*, p. 178, n. 1, states : "It may be mentioned here that in vol. III of the *Western Asia Inscriptions*, p. 69, No. 5, 63, *Mi-it* (*t*, *ḍ*)-*ra* occurs as a non-Assyrian name for the sun god. Since, in spite of the ideogramme which corresponds to the name, it is not ruled out that the name is an Iranian one, it could well be the oldest mention we have of the Iranian Mithra and the text could thus show that the latter was in fact a sun god originally. After all, the text is from a period prior to the destruction of Ninives. However, the similarity in sound could equally well be accidental and the *Mi-it* (*t*, *ḍ*)*ra* mentioned in the Assyrian text need not necessarily be the Iranian Mithra." Oldenberg has not adduced any convincing evidence to show that Mitra-Varuṇa were borrowed from the range of Semitic ideas.

187. Bohnenberger, *op. cit*, p. 85 wrongly regards the two as identical : "If we proceed from the ṚV, then in view of the absolutely objective identity between Varuṇa and Mitra there the most simple explanation seems to be to assume that an originally single god had been divided into two gods. Mitra, originally an attributive (!) designation of Varuṇa which has become a name, has developed into an independent deity. Mitra is quite suited as an attribute of Varuṇa."

188. VII. 82.5 : *kṣémeṇa mitró váruṇaṃ duvasyáti*
marúdbhir ugráḥ śúbham anyá īyate ||

189. Attempted variously by Meillet, JA, X (1907), p. 143 ff.; Johansson *Dhiṣaṇā*, p. 136, n. 1 : **mətlo=gmathl*, "place of assembly, market." Originally "coming together, appointment..., "then" friendship, friend." Petersson, *Studier tillegnade Esaias Tegner*, p. 226 ff. etc.

190. *Der arische Gott Mitra*, Dorpat 1894.

191. RdV, p. 186.

192. Apart from this, at the most we may consider whether he does not represent the light as, for example, Windischmann and von Gutschmidt, *loc. cit*, assume. On the whole, this seems less probable to me. See Eggers, *loc. cit*. On the views of Meillet and Sten Konow, see ZII, III, p. 1 ff. What was said there applies also to von Schroeder, *Arische Religion* I, p. 370 ff. ("he was a great god of loyalty, loyalty in friendship and allegiance") and to Güntert. Güntert ignores the fact which is certainly not unimportant that the neuter *mitram* occurs rarely in the ṚV and that too only in the late portions and not in the oldest parts. This fact upsets the entire hypothesis. Again a different explanation by Hüsing, *Die iranische Überlieferung*, p. 49. Although *Mithra* and Homa are very different they both correspond to the Full Moon. I consider that all this is ruled out primarily in view of the entire later tradition and thus in view of his counterpart Varuṇa whose explanation is indirectly determined by that of Mitra.

193. Weber, *Rājasūya*, p. 26, whence I gather the essential information.

194. The injunction that the grain ought to be unbroken, according to Weber, indicates Mitra who injures none and whom none injures.

195. This is a primitive method of extracting butter. Significant here is the "self-originating" of the butter, "self-breaking" of the twig; this obviously symbolizes Mitra *svayambhū*.

196. *karṇa* and *akarṇa* respectively (comm. *khaṇḍita* and *akhaṇḍita*).

197. *svayaṃkṛtā*.

198. *svayaṃdina*.

199. *svayaṃkṛta*.

200. Mention may be made also of the *maitrābārhaspatyā dhūmralalāmās tūparāḥ* TS V.6.11. I do not think it is necessary to cite all the parallel passages either here or later.

201. ŚŚS III.17.10.

202. Ibid., XIV.10.16.

203. IF, V, p. 359, n. 1; p. 360, n. 1 : *yēŋhe vāšəm hangərəwnāiti, aδaviš paoiriš spitama* [*yaθa dāmąn sraēštāiš*], *hū bāmya xšaētāi*. I think that the translation as "mankind" is uncertain.

204. ZII, II, p. 206 : "It seems to me that this [character of Mithra as sun god], which is established for the Avesta by Yašt X.136, is not sufficiently appreciated; the single golden wheel of his chariot (*aeva caxra zaranaena*) can only be explained as the sun." Haug thought that *mitradruh* is "one who deceives the sun."

205. Bohnenberger, *op. cit.*, pp. 79, 81.

206. ŚBr II.4.4.10 ff.; KŚS VIII.9.27 comm.; ĀpŚS XI.5.12 etc.

207. ĀpŚS XII.21.7; 25.1.

208. Ibid., XII.1.11.

209. TBr I.8.2.4; TMBr XVIII.9.13. They have a share in the Ṛtupaśus also; cf. *inter alia*, ŚŚS XVI.9.30.

210. TS I.8.19 : *maitrāvaruṇīm āmikṣāṃ, vaśā dakṣiṇā*. TBr I.2.5.2. A *dvirūpa vaśā* in TS II.1.7.1.3,4.

211. TS II.2.9.7. They receive puroḍāśas on other occasions also; cf. ABr III.47.1.

212. TS VI.4.8.3 : *mitro 'har ajanayad varuṇo rātriṃ tato vā idaṃ vy auchad; yan maitrāvaruṇo gṛhyate vyuṣṭyai*.

213. KŚS IX.6.9.

214. ĀpŚS XI.21.8.

215. ĀpŚS XII.14.12. Later also they receive Soma. The Ukthyasthālī is filled to the brim (ĀpŚS XII.15.11), later it is divided and poured out for the three priests (28.12) : *upayāmagṛhīto 'si mitrāvaruṇābhyāṃ tvā juṣṭaṃ gṛhṇāmi* /

216. ŚBr IV.1.4.9 : *tad yad evātra payaḥ tan mitrasya soma eva varuṇasya*.

217. *Varuṇa und Mitra*, p. 88 f. According to GGS IV.7.24 the Nyagrodha tree belongs to Varuṇa perhaps as a symbol of Ksatra. In the place

of the Soma which is meant for brahmins, the Rājanya and Vaiśya are to be given the juice of the Nyagrodha fruit (*Vedische Mythologie*, 1st ed., II, p. 244).

218. I have discussed Mitra-Varuṇa and Māyā in WZKM, XIII, p. 316 ff, Here I simply refer to this article.

219. Both wield the *vajra* (*vazra*), both fight from war-chariots and so on. See Eggers, *op. cit.*, p. 46.

220. Hillebrandt, *Transactions of the III International Congress of History of Religions*, II, p. 13 f.

221. ṚV IV.41 (ŚŚS XII.11.22); VI.68 (XII.10.10; 11.23); 10 (VIII.2.6); 11 (IX.2.6); VII.82 (IX.2.4; XII.10.8, 12; 11.15; XIV.35.2), VII.83.1-5 (XII.11.7); VII.84 (IX.2.5); 1-3 (XII.10.5); VII. 85.1-3 (XII 10.6); VIII.59 (XII.11.17). Cf. also ABr VI.14, 25, 26; TMBr VIII. 8.6 etc. Of the offerings made to the two, mention may be made of the *ṛtupaśus* at the end of the Aśvamedha. *Vaitānasūtra* XXXVII.8; TS. V.6.14 (*unnata ṛṣabho vāmanas ta aindrāvaruaṇāḥ*). There are several things here which deserve a closer examination.

In *Kāṭhaka Saṃhitā* IV.6 mention is made of drawing a Graha for the two. In the parallel passage at MS I.3.14 they are not expressly mentioned. A payasyā for the two is enjoined in TS 11.3.13.

222. IV.42; (X.124). Sorensen (*Festskrift til V. Thomsen*) says that the hymn is intended for the glorification of the two. We should agree with him. But in the antithesis between the two there is a suggestion that their spheres of influence are different; this can be accounted for not merely on the basis of natural phenomena but also from the historical evolution. Besides the hymns mentioned in the previous note, i.e., IV.41; VI.68; VII.82 ff.; VIII.59; cf. also AV III.4.5 :

ā́ prá drava paramásyāḥ parā́vataḥ
śivé te dyā́vāpṛthiví ubhé stām |
tád ayáṃ rā́jā váruṇas táthāha
sá tvāyám ahvat sá úpedám éhi ||

6 : *indrendra manuṣyā̀ḥ paréhi sáṃ hy ájñāsthā váruṇaiḥ saṃvidānā́ḥ*...and also III.13.1. But I cannot agree with Sorensen when he says that the efficacy of the two is equally necessary and that "they complement one another and cannot do without one another" (*op. cit.* p. 339). It seems to me that they can very well exist without one another.

223. Cf. also Weber, *Rājasūya*, p. 123. However, the commentaries on the KŚS seek to justify the distinction but, as I see, it is a scholastic attempt.

224. Bergaigne, III, p. 145 f. : "it happens very often that while they are thus juxtaposed in the same invocation, their functions are confounded together and that attributes, belonging only to the one or to the other of these two gods, have been mentioned as belonging to the pair." When, for example, it is said : *āpaḥ saṃ pracyutā varuṇena tad āpnod indro vo yatḥ* (MS II.13.1), this is an artificial patchwork without any relevance to mythology.

225. Bergaigne, III, p. 145 ff.; *Varuṇa und Mitra*, p. 101 ff, and the chapter below on Indra.

226. *Op. cit.*, p. 88. See also Hopkins, *The Religions of India*, p. 71 : "...he is too remote to be popular."

227. This is demonstrated in verses like X.113.5 or VII.28.4 etc. (cf. *Varuṇa und Mitra*, p. 103 ff.). Oldenberg refers (ZDMG, XXXIX, p. 71, n. 1) to MBh V. 518 where Varuṇa is installed as the Adhipati by the grace of Indra. Mention must be made also of ṚV IV.5.4 where Agni defends the *dhāmans* of Mitra and Varuṇa. On this Ludwig (IV, p. 314) remarks quite pertinently that according to this verse Mitra and Varuṇa have already suffered the loss of their prestige.

228. Perhaps VI.3.1. : *yáṃ tváṃ mitréṇa váruṇaḥ sajóṣaḥ...pā́sī.*

229. VI.3.1; 21.9; 24.5; 47.28; 48.14 (*māyín*); 49.1; 50.1; 51 (*mitrā-varuṇau*). 3, 10; 62.9; 70.1; 74.4; 75.18.

230. See Vol. I, pp. 347.48; JAOS, XV, p. 261.

231. See Vol. I, pp. 252, 299; Hopkins, "Prāgāthikāni," JAOS, XVII, p. 23ff.

232. In the entire eighth book Varuṇa plays such a minor role that he was probably far remote from the authors. Cf. also Hopkins, *The Religions of India*, p. 64. Of the other absurdities of this book, which might be partly related to the purpose of this book of serving as the libretto, we may underline the unintelligible *sám apsujit* from hymn 36. In VIII.40, vv. 10 and 11 are parallel version (contra Geldner, VSt, III, pp. 63-64; also Oldenberg. *Ṛgveda*, s.v., who does not see any objection), in VIII.35 the pāda c is composed according to the same pattern in all the 23 verses; VIII.45.14 calls Indra a Paṇi perhaps ironically or thoughtlessly. Hopkins made the first attempt to define the precise position of this book. Besides the lexical elements, the content also deserves attention. I shall add some remarks further below. I think a great part of this book is nothing but junk with which we exert ourselves in vain, the other part contains relics of old and quite independent traditions.

233. This section which I have added here deals with the most difficult and tangled aspects of Vedic mythology and is only an attempt to arrange them in some order.

234. IV.1.5 : *sá tváṃ no agne 'vamó bhavotī*
nédiṣṭho asyā́ uṣáso vyùṣṭau /
áva yakṣva no váruṇaṃ rárāṇo...

See *Varuṇa und Mitra*, p. 36, 53. I.128.7; 186.3; V.2.7 also belong here,

235. ŚŚS II.5.30-31.

236. Ibid., VIII.8.10.

237. ĀpŚS VIII.8.8 ff.; ŚŚS VIII.11.2; ĀśvŚS VI.13.6 ff. Cf. TS I.4.45 : VI.6.3.3 : *varuṇaṃ yajatī, varuṇapāśād evainaṃ muñcati / agnīvaruṇau yajati, sākṣād evainaṃ varuṇapāśān muñcati*, ŚBr IV.4.5.1 ff.; comm, on KŚS, p. 479; KP, p. 487.

238. ŚŚS XV.23.

239. ĀśvŚS sV.13.7. ŚŚS VI.4.4 ff. does not choose the verses of IV.1 but those of IV.2 and of other hymns. While discussing the Sūtra schools we must lay stress on this difference in the selection of verses (cf. Vol. 1, p. 358, n. 4).

240. ABr VII.9.5.

241. According to ṚV IV.5.4, Agni burns down those who transgress the ordinances of Varuṇa. Conversely Varuṇa punishes him who removes the fire. TS I.5.2.5 : *vīrahā vā eṣa devānāṃ yo 'gnim udvāsayati / tasya varuṇa evarṇayāt / āgnivāruṇam ekādaśakapālam anu nirvapet.*

242. TS V.5.4; TBr I.1.3.8; 2.1.4.

243. *Vedische Mythologie*, 1st edition, II, p. 215. also see p. 24 above.

244. See Vol. I, pp. 58-59.

245. ĀpŚS XVI.3.4,7; ŚBr VI.4.3.8 etc.

246. To the authors listed in Oldenberg, *Ṛgveda*, II, p. 342, we may now add J. Charpentier, *Suparṇasage*, p. 118. Although I do not agree with him on several points, Sorensen *loc. cit.*, has made a healthy criticism of the existing views, particularly that of Bergaigne. I have the following reservations against the interpretation proposed by Geldner.

1. Geldner explains the "Father Asura" as Vṛtra. Where does Vṛtra, who is mentioned very frequently in the ṚV, bear this name there ? If he stands occasionally in the later Vedic literature in the vanguard of the Asuras, this has to do with their total transformation into demons, which took place in the meantime. This transformation was only in its beginnings in the ṚV and Vṛtra was never an Asura there.

2. Varuṇa's position in the hymn remains as obscure as before. The Itihāsa cited by Geldner is of no use because Varuṇa does not play a role in it, whereas he is at the centre of the hymn. Why was Varuṇa with Vṛtra previously, as we must assume if we accept Geldner's explanation ? Nowhere is it stated that Varuṇa found himself in the power of Vṛtra or in his territory, or that they were friends or something similar.

3. Geldner states on p. 299: "But Indra consents to Varuṇa's change of loyalty only with the proviso that Varuṇa must recognize him as the overlord of his newly acquired kingdom (!) However, in this regard he shows his trust towards Varuṇa (!) since the latter (although an Asura...) distinguishes between truth and untruth, hence must have seen through the deception of the Asura power (5b-d)."

Earlier Geldner observes: "But he [Agni] after all decides to resume his earlier activity which was dedicated to gods and men (3a-b), and bids a peaceful farewell to Vṛtra explaining once again the reasons for the way of his behaviour (3 c-d). He regrets once again (!) that he has to abandon his protector of many years (4a-b) but declares his final desertion as well as that of Soma and Varuṇa, and his going over to Indra's realm (4 c-d)..."

Do these negotiations between the victorious Indra and the powerless Varuṇa which Geldner assumes to have taken place have anything probable in them ? See also Oldenberg, *Ṛgveda*, II, p. 343. Charpentier is of the view that Geldner alone could solve the riddle of the hymn.

247. Oldenberg, ZDMG, XXXIX, p. 68 ff.

248. See Vol. I, p. 91 ff.

249. It is possible that the form of the hymn is a dialogue, an ākhyāna, but this is not so certain as is assumed now. Cf. Sorensen, *op. cit.*, p. 345.

250. v. 5 : *nírmāyā u tyé ásurā abhūvan, tváṃ ca mā varuṇa kāmáyāse |*
ṛténa rājann ánṛtaṃ viviñcán máma rāṣṭrásyā́dhipatyam éhi ||

The verse raises some difficulties. Earlier I understood *nírmāya* wrongly. When Geldner, VSt, II, p. 292ff., rightly lays stress on the reading *ádhipatyam* of the Padapāṭha, it is still doubtful whether 1) we can, with Geldner, draw Pāṇini V.1.128 into this context and whether 2) we are permitted to connect *kāmáyāse* with the far remote *ádhipatyam.* I think we should translate literally: "The Asuras have become powerless, and you, O Varuṇa, may favour me. Discerning between the right and wrong, O king, come for the overlordship of my kingdom." It seems to be Indra's desire to win over Varuṇa just as he invited Soma in v. 6. It is to be noted that v. 4 must have been spoken by some one other than Agni, Varuṇa, Soma, or Pitṛ Asura, hence obviously by the poet.

251. von Bradke, *Dyaus Asura*, pp. 50-51; Oldenberg, ZDMG, XXXIX, p. 69, n. 3. III.29.14 : *yád ásurasya jaṭhárād ájāyata*, and 11 : *tánūnápād ucyate gárbha āsuráḥ*; I.141.4 : *prá yát pitúḥ paramā́n nīyate* [*agniḥ*]. We may also mention the unintelligible hymn AV V. 11 in which "the great Asura," Varuṇa and Agni appear in a certain association.

252. When it is said of Indra in X.138.6 that *ékam akṛṇor ayajñám*, it must be assumed that here also there is a polemical allusion to the Pitṛ Asura, who is contrasted with Indra in X.124.

253. ZII, IV, p. 208 ff.

254. *etasya* [*dvādaśātmakasya saṃvatsarasya*] *āgneyam ardham ardhaṃ vāruṇam | maghādyaṃ śraviṣṭhārdham āgneyaṃ krameṇa, utkrameṇa sārpādyaṃ śraviṣṭhārdhāntaṃ saumyam |*

255. II.1.4; III.5.4; (V.3.1, cf. Oldenberg, ṚdV, 2nd ed., p. 101); VII. 12.3; X.8.5. Cf. *Varuṇa und Mitra*, p. 37.

256. XVIII.9; cf. Weber, ISt IX, p. 358. von Negelein, *Weltanschauung*, § 31 (p. 46) is wrong.

257. Cf. ĀpŚS X.15.6 : *vāruṇīr abhinirmukto japet saurīr abhyuditāḥ.* Sāyaṇa, hitting upon the right explanation, says on ṚV VII.87.1 : *astaṃ gacchan sūrya eva varuṇa ity ucyate | sa hi svagamanena rātrīr janayati* and on I.84.15 : *yad rātrāv antarhitaṃ sauraṃ tejas tac candramaṇḍalaṃ praviśyāhanīva naiśaṃ tamo nivārya sarvaṃ prakāśayati.*

258. Agni is the subject (not Varuṇa as erroneously stated in *Varuṇa und Mitra*, p. 29).

259. ŚBr XI.6.2. Cf. also *Rituallitteratur*, p. 74.

260. Likewise ŚŚS XIV.3.16 : *āgneyaṃ payaḥ pūrvasmin;* 17 : *sauryam uttarasmin.* Cf. also ĀpŚS VI.5.6 : *agnaya ādityaṃ gṛhṇāmy ahne rātrim iti...*; *ādityāyāgniṃ gṛhṇāmi rātryā ahar iti*; 9.4 : *rajatāṃ tvā haritagarbhām agnijyotiṣam*—in the evening; *hariṇīṃ tvā rajatagarbhāṃ sūryajyotiṣam*—in the morning.

261. Thus ŚBr II.3.1.3 : *atha yad astam eti tad agnāv eva yonau garbho bhūtvā praviśati*; 36 : *yadā hy eva sūryo 'stam ety athāgnir jyotir yadā sūrya*

udety atha sūryo jyotiḥ etc. Or ABr VIII.28.9 : *ādityo vā astaṃ yann agnim anupraviśati | so 'ntardhīyate | taṃ na nirjānanti*...13 : *agner vā ādityo jāyate;* TBr III.9. 21.2-3 : *sūryo 'gner yonir āyatanam.*

262. ŚBr II.3.4.24 : *tad yad astaṃ yann āditya āhavanīyaṃ praviśati*...

263. The commentary on TS I.5.3.1 states : *ādityarūpasya gārhapatyasya saṃbandhi triṁśatsaṅkhyākaṃ dhāma muhūrtarūpaṃ tejo...rājate.*

264. *tám asya pṛkṣám úparāsu dhīmahi náktam | yáḥ sudárśataro dívātarāt | áprāyuṣe divātarat |*

265. *tvā́ṃ yád agne paśávaḥ samā́sate sámiddham apiśarvaré*, about the fire of the cattle-pen around which the animals gather.

266. *sá smā kṛṇoti ketúm ā́ náktaṃ cid dūrá ā́ saté*

267. *tvā́ṃ nṛcákṣā vṛṣabhā́nu pūrvī́ḥ kṛṣṇā́sv agne aruṣo ví bhāhi.* But the verse is better suited to the sacrificial fire kindled at the crack of dawn. This is true also of

VI.48.6 : *tirás támo dadṛśa ū́rmyāsv ā́ śyāvā́sv aruṣó vṛṣā́ |* and
VII.9.2 : *hótā mandró viśā́ṃ dámūnāḥ tirás támo dadṛśe rāmyā́ṇām |*

However, a clear decision is not possible.

268. VI.3.5 : *citrádhrajatir aratír yó aktóḥ*
6 : *náktaṃ yá īm aruṣó yó dívā nṝ́n*
ámartyo aruṣó yó dívā nṝ́n ||

269. E.g. TS II.5.8.1-2.

270. Vol I, pp. 216, 437, n. 106; cf. Pischel, VSt, II, p. 221 and ĀpŚS VI. 5.6 (see n. 260 above).

271. AV XIII.3.13 : *sá váruṇaḥ sāyám ágnir bhavati sá mitró bhavati prātár udyán* and ṚV I.95.1 : *hárir anyásyāṃ bhavati, śukro anyásyām* mean the same and are mythological synonyms.

272. Other dual combinations with Varuṇa are to be met with sparingly. For example, Viṣṇu-Varuṇa are mentioned in AV VII.25.1-2; TS II.1.4.3; TBr II.8.4.4 ff. I cannot follow the view of Geiger, *Aməša Spəntas*, p. 191.

273. Brugmann, *Grundriss*, II, § 117, p. 345; Kretschmer, *Einleitung in die Geschichte der griechischen Sprache* p. 131; Zimmer, BKIS, III, pp. 146, 150; Windisch, BGDSL, IV, p. 232; Güntert, *Der arische Weltkönig und Heiland*, p. 180.

274. *Vedic Religion according to the Hymns of the Ṛgveda*, Index; *Manuel pour étudier le Sanskrit védique* (lexicon).

275. Cf. Hardy, *Vedisch-Brahmanische Periode*, p. 56; Hopkins, *The Religions of India.* Oldenberg, ZDMG, L. p. 65 speaks doubtfully of the possibility that Aryaman "denotes the most brilliant of the planets." This can be neither proved nor disproved. Bollensen, ZDMG, XLI, p. 503, regards *devó aryáḥ* in ṚV VII.64.3 as a paraphrase or explanation of the name.

276. *Ormazd et Ahriman*, p. 73, n. 2 : "Aryaman means the friend, that is to say, he is only a duplicate of Mitra, a name for the celestial light (cf. Aṃśa in his relation to Bhaga); he becomes, by inference, the god who is the

intermediary between Mitra and Varuṇa, between the day and the night, that is to say, the god of the twilight (*ubhayor madhyavartī*)." Except for the "friend", I see no evidence for any of this.

277. TS II.3.14. t,u; MS IV.12.4 (190.7ff.).

278. TS II.3.4.1-2 : *aryamṇe caruṃ nirvapet suvargakāmo, 'sau vā ādityo 'ryamāryamaṇam eva svena bhāgadheyenopa dhāvati, sa evainaṃ suvargaṃ lokaṃ gamayati* etc.

279. B. Geiger (*Aməša Spəntas*, p. 147) refers to the fact that mention is made also of the path of other gods, in particular of the Ādityas; yet it is still striking, considering the few passages dealing with Aryaman, his path is mentioned so frequently.

280. Note the dual which is yet to be explained and which occurs in ĀśvŚS XII.6.21 also.

281. The text reads *n* for *ṇ*.

282. On ŚBr V.3.1.2 (=5.1.12) : *tad eṣa upariṣṭād aryamṇaḥ panthāḥ*, the commentary remarks thus : *aryamṇaḥ sūryasya eṣa paridṛśyamānaḥ panthā mārgaḥ sa ca kiraṇasaṃbandhāc chvetaḥ*.

283. Cf. PW, s.v. Aryaman; the smaller ed., Nachträge; Mahīdhara on VS IX.29; Sāyaṇa on I.89.3; 90.1,9 etc.

284. PW (smaller ed.); Weber, *Die Handschriftenverzeichnisse der königlichen Bibliothek zu Berlin. Verzeichnisse der Sanskrit Handschriften*, II, p. 59, n. 1; *Festgruss für Roth*, p. 138. In the last mentioned work as well as in *Rājasūya*, p. 84, n. 2, Weber draws the giving away of a white-backed bull as gift with the milky way into association. Elsewhere the names of the milky way are *suranadī, ākāśagaṅgā, chāyāpatha* (*Raghuvaṃśa* XIII.2) etc. Brunnhofer, *Arische Urzeit*, p. 176 ff. thinks of the milky way.

285. *Indian Antiquary* XXV, p. 323 ff. (ZDMG XXXIX, p. 526). These verses are

aṣṭāśītisahasrāṇi ye prajām īṣirarṣayaḥ |
dakṣiṇenāryamṇaḥ panthānaṃ te śmaśānāni bhejire ||
aṣṭāśītisahasrāṇi ye prajāṃ neṣirarṣayaḥ |
uttareṇāryamṇaḥ panthānaṃ te 'mṛtatvaṃ hi bhejire ||

Cf. Böhtlingk, ZDMG, XXXIX, p. 526.

286. In V.42.1 a *pṝṣadyoniḥ pañcahotā śṛṇotv átūrtapanthā ásuro mayobhū́ḥ* is mentioned. Since Varuṇa, Mitra, Bhaga, Aditi are enumerated in this verse, it is not impossible that the above words apply to Aryaman. (Cf. von Bradke, *Dyaus Asura*, p. 121).

287. The word is obscure. Uṣas drives on a chariot (Vol. I, pp. 26-27; e.g. ṚV I.48.7 : *śatáṃ ráthebhiḥ subhágoṣā́ iyáṃ ví yāti*), so does Agni (I.94.11 : *sugáṃ tát te tāvakébhyo ráthebhyó 'gne;* X.142.5); Indra (or Agni) V.5.3.: *īḷitó agna ā́ vahéndraṃ sukhaí ráthebhir ūtáye*. In the case of Agni it is the flames, in Uṣas' case the rays, hence perhaps in Aryaman's case as well. Yāska (*Nirukta*, ed BI, IV. p. 200) equates *pururátha* with *bahuratha*.

288. Cf. the three Keśins (Fire, sun and wind) in ṚV I.164.44.

289. *abhikṣadā́* VI.50.1; *dakṣā́yya* I.91.3; *dyukṣá* I.136.6; *yātayájjana* I.136.3; *sukrátu* VII.36.4; *suśeva* VI.50.1; cf. *mitró yātayájjana*.

290. *Rituallliteratur*, p. 154.

291. Hence obviously Aryaman is also the chief of the Manes in the later literature. Cf. PW, s.v.; Abegg, *Pretakalpa*, p. 193, n.1.

292. In TBr III.1.1.8 he is a bull (like Agni, Indra etc.): *aryamā rājāparas tuviṣmān phalgunīnāṃ ṛṣabho roravīti.* Cf. also TS II.3.14.t : *aryamāyāti vṛṣabhas tuviṣmān.*

293. For *anyā́ḥ, anyā́* might be the correct reading (Grill) : "may another woman than her go to the rendezvous." Those two verses (VI.60.1,2) are followed by a third which is addressed to Dhātṛ who is similarly supposed to procure a husband for the maiden. Aryaman and Dhātṛ are juxtaposed in TMBr I.1.9.1; TBr XXIV.12.4 (here some other gods also are enumerated).

294. ĀpGS V.3.8. Cf. Winternitz, *Hochzeitsrituell*, p. 56.

295. He functions as Hotṛ during the delivery, AV I.11.1. During the marriage rites other gods are added to these (but due to another development), X.85.23 Bhaga : *sám aryamā́ sáṃ bhágo no ninīyāt;* Aryaman, Bhaga, Dhātṛ AV XIV.1.34; Aryaman, Bhaga, Dhātṛ (Soma, Brahman) AV II.36.2; Aryaman, Bhaga, Savitṛ ṚV X.85.36 (AV XIV. 1.50). Aryaman and Prajāpati Ṛv. X. 85.43. Cf. also AV XIV.2.13.

296. See Vol. I, pp. 28-29.

297. When it is said in AV XIV.2.40 : *ahorātrā́bhyāṃ* [*vāṃ*] *sámanaktv aryamā́,* we can draw the same conclusion from it. Cf. AV XIII.2.5 : *ahorātré vimímāno yád eṣi* [*sūrya*]; 2.32 : *ahorātré pári sū́ryaṃ vásāne.*

298. Cf. Winternitz, *Hochzeitsrituell*, p. 70.

299. Cf. v. 11 : *priyósriyasya vṛṣabhásya retíno gṛháṃ gamema. aryamán* could refer to the bridegroom in X.68.2 also :

sáṃ góbhir āṅgirasó nákṣamāṇo
bhága ivéd aryamáṇaṃ nināya |
jáne mitró ná dampatī anakti...

300. See p. 217 below.

301. V.54.8 : *niyútvanto grāmajito yáthā nárah*
aryamáṇo ná marútaḥ kabandhínaḥ |

What would be the purpose of "bosom friends" here? We may compare V.61.4 where they are called *máryāso bhádrajānayaḥ* and X.77.2 : *śriyé máryāso añjī́ṃr akṛṇvata.*

In the context of a Parṇa amulet, AV III.5.5 says *yáthāhám uttaró 'sāny aryamṇá uta saṃvidaḥ,* "so that I am above the suitor (here rival) and his possession," and not as Weber ISt, XVII, p. 196 wishes, "so that I am above the favour of the friend himself." When it is said in TS II.3.4.1: *yáḥ khálu vai dádāti sò 'ryamṇā́,* and in TBr I.1.2.4 : *aryaméti tám āhur yó dádāti*, this also accords with the picture of the suitor in India who acquires his bride through bride-price or through generous gifts (cf. Hopkins, *Social and mil. pos.*, p. 345; Pischel, VSt, II, p. 78). Here the "suitor" has become the name for the "generous person" in general. X.117.6 rebukes the short-sighted man who consumes his wealth all alone and does not feed a son-in-law or a friend, hence one who is too miserly to marry off his daughter or to acquire a friend :

mógham ánnaṃ vindate ápracetāḥ
satyáṃ bravīmi vadhá ít sá tásya /
nā́ryamáṇaṃ púṣyati nó sákhāyaṁ
kévalāgho bhavati kevalādī́ //

"Since he feeds no suitor (son-in-law) nor even a friend, he alone bears the guilt, he alone consumes his food." *aryamyà* is derived from the name.

ṚV V.85.7 : *aryamyàṃ varuṇa mitryàṃ vā*
sákhāyaṃ vā sádam íd bhrā́taraṃ vā /
veśáṃ vā nítyaṃ varuṇā́raṇaṃ vā
yát sīm ā́gaś cakṛmā́ śiśráthas tát //

I think the word *aryamyà* does not mean "befriended" but, corresponding to the name Aryaman, has a more specific meaning "connected with the suitor (i.e., with the son-in-law and his family)."

The word *aryamán* seems to be an appellative of Indra in some passages like I.174.6 : *prá yé páśyann aryamáṇaṃ śacāyóḥ*; VII.36.4 : *ā́ sukrátum aryamáṇaṃ vavṛtyām*; 40.2 : *dyúbhaktam índro aryamā́ dadātu*; (V.29.1 is not clear). However, the word is undoubtedly independent of Indra in I.40.5; X.92.6.

302. IV.55.4.

303. I.44.13; VI.52.11; 66.4. More often Bhaga is mentioned along with Aryaman, roughly 11 times in the ṚV and 5 times in the AV. Was Bhaga formerly his partner and is *aryamṇoḥ* then as much as *aryamṇo bhagasya ca* ?

304. Aryaman is most remote from the authors of the family books, particularly of the third and eighth books. He is mentioned only once in the third and in the eighth, it is true, 12 times; but these 12 passages are of indifferent kind and contain mere enumerations. Of all the verses only V.3.2 seems to be of some value. Of the verses in the first book (105.6; 139.7; 167.8) the first two are slightly more important. It is patent that Aryaman has become quite a stranger already in the ṚV.

305. V.42.1, cf. n. 286 above.

306. *Avesta, traduit*, I, p. 270.

307. Haug, *Essays on the Parsis*, 2nd ed., p. 273, says that in the Veda and Avesta, Aryaman has a) the sense of "a friend, associate" (in the Gāthās it chiefly means "a client"), b) name of a deity; Darmesteter, *le Zend Avesta*, I, p. 349 : "the word *airyaman* means 'the servant'...and, as a proper name it designates a Yazata who according to the modern Persian usage is 'the Izad of the sky.' This interpretation rests doubtless on the passage of Vendidād XXI.7 where Ahura sends his messenger...Airyaman seems to be an incarnation of the submissive piety, a masculine counterpart of Armaiti (*arya-man=yé arém manyātā*), about whom one thinks as is convenient."

308. Bartholomae, ZDMG, XXXV, p. 158; AF, II, p. 139; Darmesteter, *le Zend Avesta*, I, p. 349; Geldner, *Studien zum Avesta*, I, p. 33.

309. Darmesteter translates *išyo* always with "who is full of desires" and says that "išya is translated as the master of iṣ, of the desires," which is linguistically not probable.

310. Yasna LIV.2 *airyamanəm išīm yazamaide amavañtem vərəthrājanəm viṭbaešaṇhəm mazištem ašahē sravaṇham:* Yašt II.2.7; III.5*: airyamanəm mąthranan mazištem, m. vahištem, m. sraēštem* etc. G. 1.6; Sir. I.3; 2.3; Visp. XXIV. 2; Fragm. (Westergard 332) IV.1.

311. Darmesteter, *le Zend Avesta*, II, p. 288.

312. The employment of the formula in the marriage rites (Haug, *Essays on the Parsis*, 3rd ed., pp. 142. 273; von Schroeder, *Arische Religion* I, p. 387) indicates his character as the god of marriage.

313. XXXII,1; XXXIII. 4; IL. 7.

314. Cf. Geldner, KZ. XXIV, p. 552. On *spəntafrasnāo* as genitive dual see Bartholomae IF, IX, p. 272 ff.; Jackson, JAOS, XX, p. 56. Fritz Wolff (p. 439) "Of the two [Ahura Mazdāh and Zarathustra] who conduct a holy conversation."

315. Cf. from the *Bundahish* (Darmesteter, *le Zend Avesta*, II, p. 319) : "Irmān (Airyaman), the Amshaspend, is the genius who gives the world redemption from all the pains, about whom it is therefore said : '[with] all the remedies which creatures take in order to destroy the pain, if I, Ahuramazd, had not sent Airyaman with his powers of healing, the pain would remain very much there.' "

316. See the compilation (which goes too far as regards the Germanic etymons) of Baynes, in *Actes du 8me congrès international des orientalistes*, Stockholm 1889, II, 1, p. ff., as well as von Schroeder, WZKM, IX, p. 127. In this context it is immaterial whether the Slavonic *bogŭ* is borrowed from Iran as Hirt doubtfully maintains (AISAK, VIII, p. 60, in the review of Kretschmer, *Einleitung in die Geschichte der griechischen Sprache*). Kretschmer, *op. cit.*, p. 81, suggests that Gr. *Phēgōnaios* "oak-god," and Phrygian *Bagaios*, **bhāgā* and Gr. *phāgós* are cognate, but not convincingly.

317. A. V. W. Jackson and Gray, JAOS, XXI, p. 168 ff.; Bartholomae, IF, VIII, p. 252; Justi, *Grundriss der iranischen Philologie* II, p. 427 etc.

318. Cf. also Krek, *Einleitung in die slavische Literaturgeschichte*, 2nd ed., p. 166.

319. With Indra III.36.5; VIII.54.5; Indra compared with him in III.49.3; or he brings the bhaga III.30.18,19; *vásuttaye* VIII.61.7; *bhágaṃ vasuvidam* X.42.3. Pūṣan is called *bhagapati* in ŚBr XI.4.3.15. He is mentioned along with Pūṣan in ṚV I.14.3; 90.4; IV.30.24; V.49.3. He is associated with other gods as well, see n. 303 above.

320. E.g. III.56.6; 62.11; IV.55.10; V.42.5; 48.5; 82.1,3; VI.50.13; VII.15.12; 38.1; 66.4; X.92.4 etc.; see Bergaigne, III, p. 41.

321. VI.50.1; AV VI.53.1.

322. I.24.4-5. VS XX.72 : *váruṇaḥ kṣatrám indriyáṃ bhágena savitā́ śríyam | sutrā́mā yáśasā bálaṃ dádhānā yajñám āśata ||*

323. ṚV I.136.2 : *cákṣur bhágasya* (=the sun); 123.5 : *úṣā bhágasya svásṛ* (AV XIX.49.1 : *yóṣā...rā́trī devásya savitúr bhágasya*). Contra Oldenberg, NGGW, 1915, p. 367.

324. VII.41.6; II.1.7 : *vásva īśiṣe*; cf. n. 319 above; IX.97.44 : *ā́ pavasvā bhágaṃ ca...rayíṃ ca*; VIII.31.11; IX.101.7 : Pūṣan, Rayi and Bhaga.

325. ṚV II.17.7 : *amājū́r iva pitróḥ sácā satī́...ivā́m iye bhágam.* On this, cf. X.39.3 : *amājúraś cid bhavatho yuváṃ bhágo...(nāsatyā).*

326. ĀpŚS VIII.18.4; ŚBr II.6.2.13 etc.

327. I.163.8 : *ánu tvā rátho ánu máryo arvann*
ánu gā́vó 'nu bhágaḥ kanī́nām |

Differently TBr I.5.3.3 : *bhagasyāparāhṇaḥ tat puṇyaṃ tejasvy ahaḥ* | *tasmād aparāhṇe kumāryo bhagam icchamānāś caranti.*

328. During the Rājasūya, oblations are made to Bhaga *vāvātayai gṛhe* and the dakṣiṇā is a *vicitragarbhā paṣṭhauhī*, TBr I.7.3.2. Oldenberg NGGW, 1915, p. 366, says that the allusion is only to fortune in general (in love and in marriage) for the maidens without any specific reference to the youth who follows the horse. This is quite possible.

329. AV VI.74.1 : *sáṃ vó 'yáṃ bráhmaṇaspátir bhágaḥ sáṃ vo ajīgamat* (*mánāṁsi, vratā́*)
82.2 : *yéna sūryā́ṃ sāvitrī́m aśvínohā́thuḥ pathā́* | *téna mām abravīd bhágo jāyā́m ā́ vahatād iti* ||
XIV.1.20 : *bhágas tvetó nayatu hastagṛ́hya, aśvínā tvā prá vahatāṃ ráthena* (Pūṣan takes his place in ṚV X.85.26).
51 : *bhágas te hástam agrahīt*
53 : *ténemā́ṃ nā́rīṃ savitā́ bhágaś ca...pári dhattām*
59 : *bhágo rā́jā purá etu prajā́nan* |

330. ṚV X.68.2 : *sáṃ góbhir āṅgirasó nákṣamāṇo bhága ivéd aryamáṇaṃ nināya* |
31.4 : *bhágo vā góbhir aryamém* (i.e., *aryamaṇam īm* ?) *anajyāt*
85.23 : *sám aryamā́ sáṃ bhágo no ninīyāt*
36 : *bhágo aryamā́ savitā́ púraṃdhiḥ...*
AV XIV.1.34 : *sáṃ bhágena sám aryamṇā́.*

The association of the two gods in ṚV IX.108.14 is quite stereotyped : *aryamaṇā bhagaḥ.* Cf. n. 303 above.

331. AV II.36.4 : *evā́ bhágasya juṣṭéyám astu, nā́rī sáṃpriyā pátyāvirādhayantī* | *bhágasya nā́vam ā́ roha*; XIV.1.31 : *yuváṃ bhágaṃ sáṃ bharataṃ sámṛddham ṛtáṃ vádantāv ṛtódyeṣu.*

332. AV III.22.6; VI.129.2. In TBr III.1.6.3 Uṣas desires "to be agreeable" : *priyādityasya subhagā syām.*

333. AV I.14.1 : *bhágam asyā várca ā́diṣy ádhi vṛkṣā́d iva srájam* | *mahā́budhno iva pārvato jyók pitṛ́ṣv āstām* ||

334. XII.1.25 : *yás te gandháḥ púruṣeṣu strīṣú puṃsú bhágo rúciḥ*
yó áśveṣu vīréṣu yó mṛgéṣūtá hastíṣu

Bloomfield, SBE, XLII, p. 202 : "loveliness and charm"; cf. ṚV I.91. 7 : *tvám soma mahé bhágaṃ tváṃ yū́na ṛtāyaté / dákṣaṃ dadhāsi jīváse.* In ṚV III.30.8 he is called *prajāvat* (cf. PW). Finally the word acquired a concrete sense. PW lists the meaning "pubic region" and Bloomfield, *loc. cit.*, p. 313, recognizes it likewise. It could denote the "masculine organ" in ṚV V.7.8 : *suṣū́r asūta mātā́ krāṇā́ yád ānaśé bhágaṃ*; perhaps in X.11.6 also. The meaning of II.34.8 : *yuñjáte...áśvān ráthеṣu bhága ā́* is not clear to me. Oldenberg, who agrees with my interpretation as "god of fortune" in NGGW, 1915, p. 366, regards the sense of fertility as inadmissible. But it is indeed certain that fertility of man and beast is the most desirable aspect of fortune for Indians.

335. According to AV XIX.7.5 the constellations Revatī and Aśvayujau bring Bhaga. It cannot be determined whether the cycle of sagas connected with Bhaga has been bigger once. In the ṚV, he is mentioned often in comparisons, III.20.4 : *agnír netā́ bhága iva kṣitīnā́m* (cf. that he is called *śreṣṭhī devānām* in TBr III.1.4.10); 54,14 : *bhágasyeva kāríṇaḥ*; III.49.3 (cf. I.141.10) : *bhágo ná kāré hávyaḥ*; X.39.10 : *bhágaṃ ná nṛ́bhyo hávyaṃ mayobhúvam.* He bears heaven and earth I.62.7, and is called *dámūnas.* AV VI.102.3 speaks of his "hands." I do not attach any value to all this. The saga to be found as early as in the ŚBr (I.7.4.6) and well known to the later literature that Bhaga is "blind" seems to me to be rather more significant.

336. II.27.1 and X. 72.

337. X.5.7 : *ásac ca sác ca paramé vyòman*
dákṣasya jánman áditer upásthe
64.5 : *dákṣasya vādite jánmani vraté*
rā́jānā mitrāvaruṇā vivāsasi /

338. VII.66.2 (*dákṣapitṛ*); VIII.25.5 : *nápātā śávaso maháḥ sūnū́ dákṣasya /*

339. X.72.4 : *áditer dákṣo ajāyata dákṣād u aditiḥ pári //*
5 : *áditir hy ájaniṣṭa dákṣa yā́ duhitā́ tava /*
tā́ṃ devā́ ánv ajāyanta...

340. Deussen, *Allgemeine Geschichte der Philosophie*, I, p. 144.

341. The fact that the word is not well established in this sense is demonstrated in expressions like *dákṣasya páti, dákṣapati* and in verses like III.27. 9,10.

342. *aṃśāya svāheti vīryaṃ vā aṃśo vīryeṇaivainam etad abhiṣiñcati bhagāyeti svāhā* etc. TS I.8.13. h. Cf. *Dhammapada* V.72 : *sukkaṃsa* (Comm. *kusalakoṭṭhāsa*).

343. In TBr III.6.2 Tanūnapāt is described as *aditer garbha.*

344. We may compare the numbers like the "five" used in AV VIII.9. 15 ff., or TS I.5.3.2 : *sapta te agne samidhaḥ sapta jihvāḥ, sapta ṛṣayaḥ, sapta dhāma, sapta hotrāḥ, sapta yonīr*; TĀr I.9.5 : seven Parjanyas, seven winds. von Schroeder seeks, as I think in vain, to locate the seventh Āditya (IF, XXXI, p. 178 ff.; *Arische Religion* I, p. 408 ff.); Indians themselves were uncertain. Keith, p. 99, refers to TS II.3.1.5, where mention is made of seven Ādityas. I did not overlook the passage (see further below, the section ;

The Maruts as the Manes) but I do not know if it has any value. Here it has to do with a designation of the Maruts as Ādityas and with a magic. Firstly the number seven occurs more often in the Maruts' case inasmuch as a *puroḍāśa saptakapāla* is assigned to them (see below the sections, Pṛśni, The Host of the Maruts, The Maruts as the Manes) in accordance with their saptagaṇa, secondly the Aśvattha which is distinctive of the Maruts is mentioned here also. Hence, a conclusion that these are "seven Ādityas" is not warranted.

345. Of 7+1; eight indeed are the sons of Aditi, but those who are called "Āditya-deities" are seven. Muir, OST, V, p. 50. TMBr XXIV.12.6. MS IV.6.9; TĀr I. 13.2. All the texts quote the verse of the ṚV.

Cf. also AV VII.9.21 : *aṣṭáyonir áditir aṣṭáputrāṣṭamíṃ rấtrim abhí havyám eti*; TBr I.1.9.1 mentions similarly eight sons. 1. Dhātṛ-Aryaman, 2. Mitra-Varuṇa, 3. Aṃśa-Bhaga, 4. Indra-Vivasvat. TMBr XXIII.15.2 : *trir vai sapta saptādityāḥ.*

346. Darmesteter erred when he connected the verses ṚV VIII.28.4 and 5 with this context; because of the word *ṛṣṭáyaḥ*, the *saptán* in these verses are to be understood as the Maruts.

347. *ādityấ rudrấ vásavo juṣantedáṃ bráhma...|*
śṛṇvantu no divyấḥ pấrthivāso gójātā utá yé yajñíyāsaḥ ||

Compare this with the distinction made in I.139.11 :

yé devāso divy ékādaśa sthá pṛthivyấm ádhy ékādaśa sthá |
apsukṣíto mahinaikādaśa sthá té devāso...

We may cite VI.50.11 : *divyấḥ pấrthivāso gójātā ápyāḥ* also here if we treat *gójātā ápyāḥ* as one single concept as it is necessary to do in my view and equate *gójātā ápyāḥ*=*adbhyás* X.63.2=*gójātā* VII.35.14=*apsukṣít* I.139.11.

348. II.1.13 (thus Bergaigne also III. p. 105); 28.3; X.65.9 : *devấn ādityấn aditiṃ havāmahe yé pấrthivāso divyā́so apsú yé ||*

349. This is at the same time a phenomenon of the Yajus literature; e.g. VS VI.32 (Indra vasumat, rudravat, ādityavat, cf. ṚV X.157.1-2); ŚBr III.9.4.9. The name is transferred a few times to the Maruts; see Kuhn's *Literaturblatt*, II, 5-6, and the sub-chapter on the Maruts further below. In one passage (MS II.2.1; TS II.3.1.1) they play the role of the recalcitrant *viś* as the Maruts usually do. It seems to me that here we have a euphemism which transfers the name of the friendly Ādityas to the wild Maruts and which is supposed to have magical effect. Besides the number seven, the pegs made of Aśvattha wood indicate the Maruts.

350. ṚV VII.85.4 with Varuṇa; Vālakhilya IV.7. I have nothing of importance to add to what I have stated in Kuhn's *Literaturblatt*, *loc. cit.* von Schroeder thinks that there is no justification to apply the word *āditya* to the two gods in VII.85.4, (*Arische Religion*, I, p. 413). Cf. also MS II.1.12 : *aditir vai prajākāmaudanam apacat so 'ñchiṣṭam āśnāt | taṃ vā indram antar eva garbhaṃ santam ayasmayena dāmnāpaumbhat | so 'pobdho 'jāyata |* Bergaigne draws attention to a difference in the nature of the Ādityas and Indra. In their case, he says, the rising of the sun, if it was

their work, is not the result of a fight against the demons of night; "it is an accomplishment of their sovereign will" (III, p. 103).

351. Bergaigne, III, p. 113. As against this, Sūrya appears in VII.60. 4 as the one for whom the Ādityas, i.e., Mitra, Varuṇa and Aryaman, prepare the path. Here the Ādityas are obviously far removed from every natural basis.

352. According to a rough count about 26 times.

353. AV XIX.17.4 : *váruṇo māadityair...pātu;* 18.4 : *varuṇa ādityavát;* 56.4 : *ādityā́so váruṇenā́nuśiṣṭāḥ |*

354. X.66.3,4,12; 98.1; 125.1; 128.9; 150.1. Already in the ṚV we can occasionally notice in solitary instances a separation of the class from Mitra, Varuṇa and Aryaman, V.51,9,10; VI.62.8,9; VII.52.1; VIII.35.13; X.36.1; 72.8; 125.1. They seem to have been quite sublimated in I.105.16 as well : *asaú yáḥ pánthā ādityó diví...|...tám martāso ná paśyatha...||*

355. XII.3.43, 44; XIX.39.5; XX.135.6. Vol. I, pp. 112-113.

356. VI.51.4; X.63.5.

357. Cf. also TBr III.8.18.2.

358. Like Bhaga, cf. pp. 55-56 above.

359. Cf. from the later period, also *Kumārasambhava* II.24 : *amī ca katham ādityāḥ pratāpakṣatiśītalāḥ citranyastā iva gatāḥ prakāmālokanīyatām |*

360. After the offering of the Indra-Varuṇa-graha in the morning oblations (ĀpŚS XII.20.24), the sun (Āditya) is worshipped and the Pratiprasthātṛ pours the rest into the Ādityasthālī with the Āditya-vessel : "you (acc.) for the gods." (21.4). The same thing happens after the offering of the following Dvidevatyagrahas, i.e., the Mitrāvaruṇagraha and the Āśvinagraha, whereupon the Ādityasthālī is covered with the Ādityapātra and remains thus till the evening. Āpastamba lays down the following rules about the evening savana, at the beginning of which the Ādityagraha has in fact its place although all the authorities do not include it there (ŚBr IV.3.5.2). ĀpŚS XIII.9.2 : "Upon a vedi surrounded by many people he draws [the Soma] after the doors of the Havirdhāna cart have been covered. 5 : He draws the Soma from the remainder after the Dvidevatyagrahas have been filled, which remainder he has poured earlier into the Ādityasthālī, with the mantra, *kadā cana starīḥ.* 6 : After this [he adds] the milk, which has been made to curdle in boiled milk (*śṛtātaṅkya dadhi,* see ĀpŚS XI.21.8) earlier for this Graha, with the mantra, *kadā cana prayucchasi.* (In greater detail, in ŚBr IV.3.5.10 ff. I pass over a number of rites which can be added here for magical purposes). 13 : With *ahaṃ parastāt,* the sacrificer holds the Ādityagraha until it is offered. 14 : He brings it there with the mantra *kavir yajñasya vitanoti panthām.* 15 : With the mantra *ā samudrād antarikṣāt* he sets [the liquid] in motion by the means of blades of Darbha. 10.1 : The two Sampraiṣas [for the offering read thus] i. *ādityebhyo 'nubrūhi priyebhyaḥ priyadhāmabhyaḥ priyavratebhyo mahāsvasarasya patibhya uror antarikṣasyādhyakṣebhyaḥ,* ii. *ādityebhyaḥ preṣya priyebhyaḥ*...11.1 : The modification in the mantra during the Sarpaṇa is as follows : *jāgataḥ panthā ādityā devatā avṛkeṇāpariparena pathā svasty ādityān aśiya...*

361. In the distribution of the seasons, autumn (*śarad*) is assigned to these. Winter is regarded as *ṛtūnāṃ svāhākāraḥ*. Since the course of the days corresponds to the passage of the year, a parallelism can be noticed between this position before the winter and before the evening savana.

362. ZDMG, VI., pp. 69, 70.

363. *Ormazd et Ahriman*, p. 82 ff.

364. Pischel, GGA, 1895, p. 447; von Schroeder, WZKM, IX, p. 109 ff; likewise Tiele, *Geschichte der Religion im Altertum bis auf Alexander den Grossen*, II, p. 70 ff. For Oldenberg's rejoinder, see ZDMG, L, p. 43 ff.

365. I have stated my views on Geiger's arguments in ZII, IV, p. 109 ff.

366. The relative clause is stressed in the original.

367. ZDMG, L, p. 64.

368. *Journal des Savants*, 1896, p. 391. I point also to the legitimate reservations which von Schroeder has against the value of the number seven (WZKM, IX, p. 122) although he does not seem to deny the justification in comparing the Ādityas with the Amәša Spәntas (ibid, p. 118).

369. Cf. Jackson, *An Avestan Grammar* XXV.

370. Oldenberg, ZDMG, LIV, p. 57.

371. Another question is whether the Veda knows the planets. Like Oldenberg, I answer this question in the affirmative but believe that they are thought of rather vaguely in general turns of expressions and quite outside the class of gods discussed here.

372. *áditir dyaúr áditir antárikṣam, áditir mātā́ sá pitā́ sá putráḥ...*|

373. *Transactions of the Ninth International Congress of Orientalists* I, pp. 396-410.

374. ŚBr V.3.1.4; also the wife of Viṣṇu only VS XXIX.60.

375. KŚS II.7.1.

376. Doctoral Dissertation, *Über die Göttin Aditi*, Breslau 1876.

377. Roth explains Aditi as "the eternity or the eternal one" but it is clear from the sentences that follow that he circumscribes the general meaning by the reference to the celestial light.

378. SBE, XXXII, p. 241 ff., etc.

379. RdV, 2nd ed., p. 204. von Schroeder, *Arische Religion*, I, p. 395 ff. Neisser, WB, s.v. aditi : "*áditi* denotes the freedom from bondage in the literal sense, i.e., to be free from the bonds which threaten the guilty; when this ethical conception is combined with naturalistic conceptions and the freedom from bondage is associated with the daylight..., then the light can be seen as the liberator from the fetters of darkness, which in their turn are represented through the image of Varuṇa's fetters. By no means can Aditi be understood differently, for as the freedom from fetters..."

380. Oldenberg, RdV, 2nd ed., p. 204 : "At first only this much is correct, indeed obvious, that to the 'freedom' in which she is personified and is associated with Varuṇa and the gods of his class as a relative, now also—perhaps from the very beginning—concrete attributes have been attached which are in harmony with the luminous nature and the regulating and sovereign nature of those deities, so much the more so as the conceptions of

light and of freedom are closely connected with one another." This can only mean the following : it is true that Aditi etymologically means "freedom from bondage" but soon, "perhaps from the very beginning" this word is applied to light. That would be my view also. Still less tenable than the reference to a mere "freedom from bondage," which has after all a superficial support in etymology, is the notion of a cow-fetish in Aditi's casė; I see nothing to support it.

381. Contra Oldenberg, RdV, 2nd ed., p. 203. For further material see the section on Vāyu below.

382. I.136.3 : *jyótiṣmatīm áditim...svàrvatīm ā́ sacete divédive...|*
jyótiṣmat kṣatrám āśāte ādityā́...|
II.27.11 : *yuṣmā́nīto ábhayaṃ jyótir aśyām |*
IV.25.3 : *ká ādityā́ñ áditiṃ jyótir īṭṭe |*
VII.82.10 : *avadhráṃ jyótir áditeḥ |*
X.185.3 : *yásmai putrāso áditeḥ...|*
jyótir yácchanty ájasram ||

In I.113.19 Uṣas is *áditer ánīkam.* Cf. also Bergaigne's remark that we should guard against seeing in Aditi "purely and simply heaven regarded as a female" (III, p. 94). The meaning "freedom from bondage" which is based on those verses where Aditi is implored to release one from guilt and from fetters (von Schroeder, *Arische Religion*, I, p. 399) does not do justice to the other passages which speak of her light; thus this meaning rests solely on etymology.

383. *śyeny ādityebhyo 'dityai vā.* Comm. : *śyenī raktavarṇā...prathame paśubandhe.* 19 : *vaiśvadevī pṛṣatī mārutī vā.* I do not understand the significance of the *avi vaśā* for the Ādityas in TS II.1.2.3 : *yaḥ kāmayeta pratheya paśubhiḥ pra prajayā jāyeyeti sa etām aviṃ vaśām ādityebhyaḥ kāmāya ā labheta.* When the gods sacrificed such an animal, *tato vā aprathata pṛthivy ajāyantauṣadhayaḥ.* VS XXIV.6 : *śvetā avarokiṇa ādityānām nabhorūpāḥ pārjanyāḥ*; TS I.8.19 : *ādityāṃ malhāṃ garbhiṇīm ā labhate mārutīṃ pṛśniṃ praṣṭhauhīm.*

384. I.117.21; II.27.14; VI.3.1; VII.5.6; IX.91.6; 94.5; see Grassmann, *Wörterbuch zum Rigveda.*

385. II.27.14. Cf. VI.47.8 : *urúṃ no lokám ánu neṣi vidvā́n svàrvaj jyótir ábhayaṃ svastí |*

386. III.39.7 : *jyótir vṛṇīta támaso vijānán*
āré syāma duritā́d abhī́ke |
X.36.3 : *víśvasmān no áditiḥ pātv áṃhasaḥ...|*
svàrvaj jyótir avṛkáṃ naśīmahi...|

387. *Transactions of the Ninth International Congress of Orientalists* I, pp. 396-410.

388. *Über die Göttin Aditi*, p. 39; Bloomfield, ZDMG, XLVIII, p. 552.

389. Colinet, *loc. cit.*, p. 402.

390. Vol. I, p. 382, n. 153.

391. VSt, I, p. 217; II, p. 85 ff. Also Johansson, *Dhiṣaṇā*, p. 84, who wishes to see in Aditi an even older earth goddess than Pṛthivī.

392. *Über die Göttin Aditi*, p. 44.

CHAPTER VI

SAVITṚ AND THE ṚBHUS

1. ZDMG, LI, p. 483. See also ibid., LIX, p. 253 f.; RdV, 2nd ed., pp. 63, 240, n. 2.

2. Cf. ŚBr IV.4.1.1 ff. : *mano ha vā asya savitā...*

3. ABr III.29 speaks in the same way as the KBr does. These two texts use partly the same sources and employ the same words. We may add the remark from ABr III.29.5 : "of the two savanas, i.e., the Prātaḥsavana and the Tṛtīyasavana, Savitṛ drinks differently (*vipibati* comm.: *vilakṣaṇatvena pibati*). When a word with *piba* in it precedes the Savitṛ nivid and one with *mad* follows he partakes of it in both the savanas."

4. I.110.2,3; 161.11 etc.; see below.

5. *agohyasyāgrāhyasyādityasya gṛhe maṇḍale yad yāvatkālam...*

6. *agohyasyāgopyasyādityasya gṛha ātithye.*

7. More in the section on the Ṛbhus. Cf. Sāyaṇa on ṚV I.110.3 : *yad yadā yūyam agohyaṃ gūhitam aśakyaṃ sarvair dṛśyamānaṃ savitāraṃ śrāvayanto* etc. Bergaigne, III, p. 54, explains *agohya* as "from whom nothing can be concealed"; it is doubtful.

8. Comm. on TBr III.10.1.

9. Ibid. : *sarvataḥ parimaṇḍalaṃ rathacakramātraṃ sāvitraṃ parilikhya.*

10. Cf. also TBr III.10.9.15.

11. TS I.8.2; 9.1 : *sāvitraṃ dvādaśakapālaṃ kṣattur gṛha upadhvasto dakṣiṇā*; I.8.17; 19; 20; I.8.10.1 : *savitre satyaprasavāya puroḍāśaṃ dvādaśakapālam āśūnāṃ vrīhīṇām*; TBr III.1.4.11; ŚBr II.5.4.5 (*aṣṭākapālo vā*); V.4.5.6 : (or *aṣṭākapāla*); 5.4.29; XII.7.2.19 : *dvādaśakapālaḥ sāvitro bhavati; dvā́daśa vai māsāḥ saṃvatsarasya* etc. Besides these, also eight kapālas as in Agni's case. ŚBr X.4.1 holds a different view : *sa eṣa saṃvatsaraḥ prajāpatir agniḥ / tasyārdham eva sāvitrāṇy ardhaṃ vaiśvakarmāṇi.*

12. On the other hand, Sūrya receives an *ekakapāla puroḍāśa*, ŚBr II.6.3.8.

13. *Rituallitteratur*, p. 150.

14. Cf. e.g., TS IV.1.1 : *yuktvā́ya mānasā devān...savitā pra suvati tān... deva savitaḥ pra suva yajñam, pra suva yajñapatiṃ bhagāya / imaṃ no deva savitar yajñaṃ pra suva devayuvam...*

15. Oldenberg, ZDMG, LI, p. 479.

16. See the index to the TS, ed. Weber, or to the MS, ed. von Schroeder.

17. We may readily concede that mention is made of Savitṛ's *sava* rather frequently, but not *exclusively*. I refer to the "fetters" with which he binds (TS I.1.9.h; 10), or I.1.8.m : *devas tvā savita śrapayatu varṣiṣṭhe adhi nāke*; I.1.5.a : *devo vaḥ savitotpunātu*; 6.k : *prati gṛhṇātu*. Also the passages, somewhat underrated by Oldenberg, ZDMG, LI, p. 482, n. 2, which characterize him directly as the sun. ŚBr III.2.3.18; (6.3.18); IV.4.1.3 :

eṣa vai savitā ya eṣa tapati; in V.3.1.7, in the context of the *puroḍāśa dvādaśa-kapāla* or *aṣṭākapāla* which is offered during the Rājasūya *kṣattur gṛhe*, it is stated : *savitā vai devānāṃ prasavitā, prasavitā vai kṣattā, tasmāt sāvitro bhavati...tasya śyeto 'naḍvān dakṣiṇaiṣa vai savitā ya eṣa tapati, eti vā eṣa, ety anaḍvān yuktas tad yac chyeto bhavati śyeta iva hy eṣa udyaṁś cāstaṃ ca yan bhavati tasmāc chyeto 'naḍvān dakṣiṇā.* His "golden spade" VS XI.11 etc. can also be mentioned. In my knowledge, he is never equated with Vāta or Vāyu but with *manaḥ* in accordance with his intellectual quality (ŚBr III.4.1.1). Incidentally, we may add that Oldenberg seeks to interpret the Aśvins as the morning star and the evening star. We see that here their "two arms" are spoken of. Are these "two arms" in the case of the gods of light more probable or improbable than Savitṛ's "two hands" about which Oldenberg, *loc. cit.*, p. 479, n. 2, thinks with Bergaigne that they do not fit into the picture of countless rays.

18. TS I.1.9.t; ŚBr I.7.4.8 : *sa bṛhaspatiḥ savitāram eva prasavāyopā-dhāvat savitā vai devānāṃ prasavitedam*; 14, 21, II.3.1.38; 4.39; III.9.1.20; IV.6.6.7; V.3.5.8; VI.5.4.11; 6.1 (But cf. also TS I.1.13 : *vājasya mā prasa-venodgrābheṇodgrabhīt;* 2.4 : *tasyās te satyasavaśaḥ prasave vācaḥ* and the Devasū deities).

19. Oldenberg, *loc. cit.*, p. 479, states : "the typical place, however, where we encounter the Savitṛ worship is the beginning of major sacrifices, the intention of their performers being to direct the impelling power of the divine impeller upon themselves so that they may conduct the sacred task correctly. Thus during the Prāyaṇīya of the Soma sacrifice, Savitṛ is invoked besides Pathyā Svasti and others. In the accompanying verses—these are chosen for being *pravatyo netṛmatyaḥ pathimatyaḥ svastimatyaḥ* (ABr I.10.1)—he is revered as *satyasava*, and of him it is said *pra ca suvāti* (ṚV V.82.7, 9) .. so that the purpose which this invocation serves, viz., *prasavāya Savitā*, according to ABr I.8.12, is expressly stated, while nothing is to be discovered of any connection with the solar aspect." Oldenberg does not give due credit to the fact that precisely in the Soma sacrifice Savitṛ has his place in the evening savana and that the Prāyaṇīya is only an auxiliary ceremony which opens the sacrifice just as the Udayanīya closes it (ĀpŚS III.23.1; KBr VII.8) and in both the iṣṭis the deities are the same but for the sequence. In both the iṣṭis we find Agni, Soma and Aditi besides Pathyā Svasti and Savitṛ. In the ABr they are classified according to the points of compass. The south is assigned to Agni, the west to Soma, the north-west to Savitṛ (differently in ŚBr III.2.3.15 ff.). From this occurrence one cannot draw a conclusion about the meaning of Agni and Soma; however, I think a conclusion is admissible about Savitṛ's character. In this context Agni-Soma are described as *cakṣuṣī, prāṇāpānau* and Agni as *annapati* etc. Must Savitṛ then be limited to the position of an abstract deity because he "impels" ? Or do we wish that Indra be interpreted, since the strength of his arms has become proverbial, as the prototype of the strong man from the very beginning without any material basis ? Surely Oldenberg does not hold such view.

20. Cf. *Kāśikā* III.2.21 : *divā karoti prāṇinaś ceṣṭāyuktān iti divākaraḥ* |
21. Vol. I, pp. 28-29.
22.

Sūrya	Savitṛ
I.115.4ab	II.38.4ab
tát sū́ryasya devatvám̐ tán mahitvám	*púnaḥ sám avyad vítataṃ váyantī*
madhyā́ kártor vítataṃ sáṃ jabhāra	*madhyā́ kártor ny àdhāc chákma dhī́raḥ* |
	Cf. *Kumārasaṃbhava* VIII.30
Sun	Savitṛ
I.115.4 cd (also 5cd)	II.38.3bd
yadéd áyukta harítaḥ sadhásthād	*nūnám árīramad átamānaṃ cid étoḥ* |
ā́d rā́trī vā́sas tanute simásmai ||	*...ánu vratáṃ savitúr móky ā́gāt* ||
X.37.9 :	I.35.2 :
yásya te víśvā bhúvanāni ketúnā	*ā́ kṛṣṇéna rájasā vártamāno*
prá cérate ní ca viśánte aktúbhiḥ |	*niveśáyann amṛ́taṃ mártyaṃ ca* |
	or VII.45.1 :
	...antarikṣaprā́ váhamāno áśvaiḥ |
	...niveśáyañ ca prasuváñ ca bhū́ma ||
VIII.25.19 :	VII.76.1 :
úd u ṣyá śaraṇé divó	*úd u jyótir amṛ́taṃ viśvájanyam*
jyótir ayaṃsta sū́ryaḥ |	*viśvā́naraḥ savitā́ devó aśret* |
VII.79.1 :	IV.13.1d, 2a :
susaṃdṛ́gbhir ukṣábhir bhānúm aśret	*út sū́ryo jyótiṣā devá eti* ||
ví sū́ryo ródasī cákṣasāvaḥ	*ūrdhváṃ bhānúṃ savitā́ devó aśret*
	VII.72.4
	ūrdhváṃ bhānúṃ savitā́ devó aśret

23. IV.53.3 cd : *prá bāhū́ asrāk savitā́ sávīmani*
niveśayan prasúvann aktúbhir jágat ||
2a : *divó dhartā́ bhúvanasya prajā́patiḥ*

I admit that instead of "rays" one can translate as "nights." Geldner : "all the nights lulling the world to sleep and (again) awakening." Neisser, WB, is undecided; on p. 6 he renders it as "light" and on p. 7 he is uncertain. Since *aktúbhir* occurs here between *prasúvan* and *jágat*, I adhere to the translation given above. Cf. X.37.9 cited above.

24. IV.53.2b : *piśáṅgaṃ drāpíṃ práti muñcate kavíḥ* |
1cd : *chardír yéna dāśuṣe yácchaté tmánā*
tán no mahā́ṃ úd ayān devó aktúbhiḥ ||

25. The offerings also vary often.

26. ZDMG, LI, p. 482.

27. Vol. I, p. 81; see also my *Vedische Mythologie*, 1st ed., II, p. 237 ff.

28. IV.13.2 : *ūrdhváṃ bhānúṃ savitā́ devó aśred*
drapsáṃ dávidhvad gaviṣó ná sátvā |
ánu vratáṃ váruṇo yanti mitró
yát sū́ryaṃ divy ā́rohayanti ||

14.2 : *ūrdhváṃ ketúṃ savitā́ devó aśret*
jyótir víśvasmai bhúvanāya kṛṇván |
ā́prā dyā́vāpṛthivī́ antárikṣam
ví sū́ryo raśmíbhiś cékitānaḥ ||

29. IV.6.2 : *ūrdhváṃ bhānúṃ savitévāśret*
méteva dhūmáṃ stabháyad úpa dyā́m ||

(Cf. also AV XVIII.3.29 : *ūrdhváṃ bhānúṃ savitā́ dyā́m ivopári*). In this context one may recall the other comparisons between Agni and Sūrya which refer to the radiance of the two.

VI.2.6 : *tveṣás te dhūmá ṛṇvati diví ṣáñ chukrá ā́tataḥ |*
sū́ro ná hí dyutā́ tváṃ kṛpā́ pāvaka rócase ||

VI.4.3,6; VII.8.4 : *ví yát sū́ryo ná rócate bṛhád bhā́ḥ.* VIII.43.32; 69.2d. Furthermore, the adjective *mitramáhas* belongs into this context.

30. IV.54.

31. AV XIII.2.36 : *uccā́ pátantam aruṇáṃ suparṇáṃ*
mádhye divás taráṇiṃ bhrā́jamānam |
páśyāma tvā savitā́raṃ yám āhuḥ...

Also XIII.4.1 : *sá eti savitā́ svàr divás pṛṣṭhé 'vacā́kaśat.* ṚV VII.63.3 belongs here. His designation as *apāṃ napát* (I.22.6; X.149.2) makes good sense in the context of a sun god Savitṛ but not of a mere abstraction.

For completeness' sake I mention here Savitṛ's connection with the cult of the Manes, without however attempting an explanation. ṚV X.17.4 : *yátrā́sate sukṛ́to yátra té yayús tátra tvā deváḥ savitā́ dadhātu* and compare this with ŚBr XIII.8.2.5 : *savitā te śarīrebhyaḥ pṛthivyāṃ lokam icchatu*; 3.3 : *savitā te śarīrāṇi mātur upastha āvapatu.* AV XII.2.48 speaks of a ship of Savitṛ likewise in connection with the cult of the dead :

ā́ rohata savitúr nā́vam etā́m
ṣaḍbhir urvī́bhir ámatiṃ tarema |

The connection with the cult of the dead is intelligible in the case of both Savitṛ and Sūrya alike. Cf. ŚBr II.3.3.7.

32. Vol. I, p. 28 ff.

33. Vol. I, p. 31-32 p. ff.

34. I.35.2 : *ā́ kṛṣṇéna rájasā vártamāno*
niveśáyann amṛ́taṃ mártyaṃ ca |

4 : *ā́sthād ráthaṃ savitā́ citrábhānuḥ*
kṛṣṇā́ rájāṃsi táviṣīṃ dádhānaḥ ||

9 : *...véti sū́ryam abhí kṛṣṇéna rájasā dyā́m ṛṇoti ||*

II.38.3 : *ánu vratáṃ savitúr móky ā́gāt*

IV.53.3 : *prá bāhū́ asrāk savitā́ sávīmani*
niveśáyan prasuvánn aktúbhir jágat ||

7 : *sá naḥ kṣapā́bhir áhabhiś ca jinvatu |*

V.81.4 : *utá rā́trīm ubhayátaḥ parīyase*

82.8 : *yá imé ubhé áhanī purá ety ápraryucchan*
AV XIX.49.1 : *iṣirā́ yóṣā yuvatír dámūnā*
rā́trī devásya savitúr bhágasya

35. Cf. AV XIII.2.43 : *abhy ànyád eti páry anyád asyate*
ahorātrā́bhyāṃ mahiṣáḥ kálpamānaḥ |
sū́ryaṃ vayáṃ rájasi kṣiyántam...
havāmahe |

and ṚV X.37.3,9. Strangely enough, precisely the atmosphere is assigned to Savitṛ. TS VII.5.24a and AV XIII.3.13.

36. III.38.8 : *tád ín nv àsya savitúr nákir me*
hiraṇyáyīm amátiṃ yā́m áśiśret |
VII.38.1 : *úd u ṣyá deváḥ savitā́ yayāma*
hiraṇyáyīṃ amátiṃ yā́m áśiśret |
2 : *vy ùrvī́ṃ pṛthivī́m amátiṃ sṛjānáḥ*
ā́ nṛ́bhyo martabhójanaṃ suvānáḥ ||
45.3 : *viśráyamāṇo amátim urūcī́m*
martabhójanam ádha rāsate naḥ |

On this cf. V.45.2 : *ví sū́ryo amátiṃ ná śríyaṃ sāt.* Further AV VII.14.2 (addressed to Savitṛ) :

ūrdhvā́ yásyāmátir bhā́ ádidyutat sávīmani
hiraṇyapāṇir amimīta sukrátuḥ...||

In the ṚV, *amáti* is directly associated, of other gods, only with the Maruts (I.64.9 comparison) and with Mitra-Varuṇa (V.62.5).

37. ṚV V.63.4; WZKM, XIII, p. 320.

38. Compare this with the designation of Sūryā (i.e. Uṣas who is the daughter of the sun god) as *sāvitrī́,* which we have mentioned on. p. 73 above, or the *sūryā́ śáṃsantī* whom Sūrya gives away to Soma as wife and the bridal procession of Sūryā which Savitṛ started. Geldner, Glossar : "*amáti*= *rūpam. Naigh.* 3.7. Manifestation, image, likeness." He translates ṚV III.38.8 as "his (one ?) golden image." Neisser, WB : "formation."

39. I.35.7,9; 123.3; 157.1; V.81.4; VII.45.2; X.139.1; 149.3. Cf. Muir, OST, V, pp. 169-170; Bergaigne, III, p. 53.

40. Cf. of Agni in X.156.4 :

ágne nákṣatram ajáram ā́ sū́ryaṃ rohayo diví |
dádhaj jyótir jánebhyaḥ ||

or of Rohita in AV XIII.1.25 :

yó róhito vṛṣabhás tigmáśṛṅgaḥ
páry agníṃ pári sū́ryaṃ babhū́va |

Agni Vaiśvānara and Sūrya are basically identical and yet separate in ŚBr VII.5.1.8 : *mā tvā sūryo 'bhitāpsīt, māgnir vaiśvānaraḥ |*

41. Yašt X.13, 51, 90, 95.

42. Yašt X. 136.

43. ṚV I.35 recalls in some respects Mihir Yašt. Compare I.35.8 with Yašt X.15.

44. *Viṣṇupurāṇa* II.8.12 : *ahorātravyavasthānakāraṇaṃ bhagavān raviḥ.*

45. III.44.6. Cf. Weber, ISt, IX, p. 278. Sieg, NGGW, 1923, 1 ff. Hillebrandt, *Festschrift für Scherman* (ZB, VI, p. 114 ff.).

46. See *Abhijñānaśākuntala*, ed. Pischel, p. 121 : *bhānuḥ sakṛdyuktataraṅga eva rātriṃ divaṃ gandhavahaḥ prayāti.* Oldenberg, ZDMG, LI, p. 481, n. 2, thinks that Savitṛ with his two Hari-s (I.35.3) is incompatible with the traditional picture of the sun god with his seven Harita-s. We should not count in this manner. In I.35.5 there is a plural, *śyāvā́ḥ śitipā́daḥ*; likewise in VII.45.1 : *váhamāno aśvaiḥ*. VII.66.14 assigns one horse to Sūrya, another passage seven. It is said in II.11.6 *stávā hárī sū́ryasya ketū́*. The seven Haritas are attributed to Sūrya only; they are not mentioned, for example, in Mitra's case. Similarly I do not attach any value to the occasional allusion to the "two hands" of Savitṛ (see n. 17 above) on which Bergaigne, III, p. 48; Oldenberg, *loc. cit.*, p. 479, n. 2 lay stress. In the case of the Maruts mention is made of *śīrṣásu, tanū́ṣu* and in the same verse also of *áṃsayoḥ, bāhvóḥ* (V.57.6).

47. One could see a reference of a slightly different type to his nature also in the *plāśuka vrīhi-s* employed during the Abhiṣecanīya, ŚBr V.3.3.2 : *savitṛprasūtaḥ sūyā ity atha yat plāśukānāṃ vrīhīṇāṃ kṣipre mā prasuvān.*

48. IV.54.2 : *devébhyo hí prathamáṃ yajñíyebhyo*
amṛtatváṃ suvási bhāgám uttamám |
5 : *índrajyeṣṭhān bṛhádbhyaḥ párvatebhyaḥ*
kṣáyāṁ ebhyaḥ suvasi pastyàvataḥ |
6 : *yé te trír áhan savitaḥ savā́saḥ*
divédive saúbhagam āsuvánti |
cf. also II.38.1 : *nūnáṃ devébhyo ví hí dhā́ti rátnam...*
V.81.1 : *ví hótrā dadhe vayunāvíd ékaḥ*

49. III.54.11 : *híraṇyapāṇiḥ savitā́ sujihvás*
trír ā́ divó vidáthe pátyamānaḥ |
devéṣu ca savitaḥ ślókam áśreḥ...
cf. III.56.6,7 : *trír ā́ diváḥ.*

50. VII.38.4. Compare this with the quotation from MBh III.3.41,43, given below in n. 56.

51. II.38.9 : *ná yásyéndro váruṇo ná mitró*
vratám aryamā́ ná minánti rudráḥ |
V.81.3 : *yásya prayā́ṇam ánv anyá íd yayúr*
devā́ devásya mahimā́nam ójasā |
82.7 : *ā́ viśvádevaṃ sátpatiṃ sūktair adyā́ vṛṇīmahe |*
satyásavaṃ savitā́ram ||
X.36.13 : *yé savitúḥ satyásavasya víśve*
mitrásya vraté váruṇasya devā́ḥ |
100.1 : *devébhir naḥ savitā́ prā́vatu*
cf. also X.139.1 : *tásya pūṣā́ prasavé yāti.*

52. I.110.2 : *saúdhanvanāsaś caritásya bhūmánā ...*
ā́gacchata savitúr dāśúṣo gṛhám |

53. VI.15.16 : [*agne*] *kulāyínaṃ ghṛtávantaṃ savitré*
yajñáṃ naya yájamānāya sādhú ||

54. Cf. V.82.9 : *yá imā́ viśvā jātā́ny āśrāvā́yati ślókena prá ca suvā́ti savitā́*; VII.82.10 : *devásya ślókaṃ savitúr manāmahe.* He is compared to the Upavaktṛ in VI.71.5 (*úd ū ayāṁ upavaktéva bāhū́*) whose functions were transferred in the later ritual to the Maitrāvaruṇa who allots the Praiṣas. His original purpose is not clear.

55. Incidentally there are other points of agreement that can be listed here. We may compare ṚV IX.67.25 : *ubhā́bhyāṃ deva savitaḥ pavitréṇa savéna ca mā́ṃ punīhi viśvátaḥ* with AV VI.62.1 : *vaiśvānaró raśmíbhir naḥ punātu;* TĀr II.6.2 : *vaiśvānaraḥ pavayāt pavitraiḥ* or ṚV I.160.3 : [*sū́ryaḥ*] *pavítravān punā́ti dhī́ro bhúvanāni māyáyā*; *Pitṛmedhasūtra* 130 (ed. Caland) : *sa mā vṛṣabho rohitākṣaḥ sūryo ...manasā punātu.* Cf. also MBh III.3.38 : [*lokaḥ*] *pavitrīkriyate nirvyājaṃ pālyate tvayā* [*sūrya*] and TS I.1.5.a (=I.1.10.p); ŚBr III.1.3.22 : *devo vaḥ savitotpunātv acchidreṇa pavitreṇa vasoḥ sūryasya raśmibhiḥ.*

Further, I wish to add that GGS III.3.9-13 speaks of a Savitṛ-day.

56. v.36 : *tvaṃ bhāno jagataś cakṣuḥ tvam ātmā sarvadehinām |*
tvaṃ yoniḥ sarvabhūtānāṃ tvam ācāraḥ kriyāvatām ||

40 : *tava divyaṃ rathaṃ yāntam anuyānti varārthinaḥ |*
siddhacāraṇagandharvā yakṣaguhyakapannagāḥ ||

41 : *trayastriṃśac ca vai devās tathā vaimānikā gaṇāḥ |*
sopendrāḥ samahendrāś ca tvām iṣṭvā siddhim āgataḥ ||

43 : *guhyāḥ pitṛgaṇāḥ sapta ye divyā ye ca mānuṣāḥ |*
te pūjayitvā tvām eva gacchanty āśu pradhānatām ||

cf. also XII.363.2 ff.

57. From the AV we may mention verse VII.14.4 (to be found elsewhere also) which shows Savitṛ partaking of the Soma drink.

58. *suśastí* I.186.1; *sūktaíḥ* V.49.2; 82.7. Cf. AV. VI.1.1 : *doṣó gāya bṛhád gāya...stuhí savitā́ram.*

59. *ílābhiḥ* I.186.1; *ghṛténa* V.42.3.

60. *yajñáiḥ suvṛktíbhiḥ* III.62.12.

61. RdV, p. 457; ZDMG, LI, p. 479.

62. Oldenberg, RdV, p. 104.

63. The verses at TS I.1.9.h : *badhāna deva savitaḥ paramasyāṃ parāvati śatena pāśair yo 'smān dveṣṭi and* 10.g : *imaṃ vi ṣyāmi varuṇasya pāśaṃ yam abadhnīta savitā suketaḥ* can be included in this context.

64. Cf. Bergaigne, "Recherches sur l'histoire de la liturgie védique," JA, 1889.

65. However, I too think that Savitṛ is one of the younger deities. Besides the still transparent etymology, the absence of any sagas of his own seems to indicate this.

66. Cf Viṣṇu in ṚV X.181.1 : *dhātúr dyútānāt savitúś ca víṣṇo rathaṃtarám;* of Tvaṣṭṛ in X.10.5 : *dámpatī kar devás tváṣṭā savitā́ viśvárūpaḥ.*

67. Cf. Bergaigne, III, p. 40 f. and p. 313, n. 320 above.

68. Besides the examples cited on p. 313, n. 321 above, cf. V.46.3; 49.1; AV XIV.1.53.

69. AV III.8.2 (VII.17.4); V.3.9; VIII.1.15 (IX.7.10, 12 : *dhātā ca savitā cāṣṭhīvantau*); XI.6.3: XIV.1.33; XIX.20.1.

70. AV VII.16.1; VIII.5.5; IX.4.10; XIX.24.8; 31.5.

71. AV IV.25.3 : *táva vraté ní viśante jánāsas*
tváyy údite prérate citrabhāno |

On the connection between the sun and the wind, see MBh XII.362.4 on Sūrya : *yato vāyur viniḥsṛtya sūryaraśmyāśrito mahān*
vijṛmbhaty ambare tatra kim āścaryam ataḥ param ||

72. The dissertation of A. W. Ryder (*Die Ṛbhus im Ṛgveda*. Gütersloh 1901) gives me no cause to modify the following section in any way.

73. Eight times in seven hymns.

74. II.19.1 : *viśvebhyo devebhyaḥ sādhyebhya ṛbhubhyo bhṛgubhyo marudbhyaḥ* etc.

75. II.15.6.

76. IV.33.5: *jyeṣṭhá āha camasā́ dvā́ karéti*
kánīyān trī́n kṛṇavāméty āha |

77. I.161.6 : *ṛbhúr víbhvā vā́jo devā́ṃ agacchata...*
IV.33.3 : *té vā́jo vibhvāṃ ṛbhúr...*
34.1 : *ṛbhúr víbhvā vā́jo índro. . .*
36.5 : *ṛbhutó rayíḥ prathamáśravastamo*
vā́jaśrutāso yám ájījanam náraḥ |
vibhvataṣṭó vidátheṣu pravā́cyaḥ ...

78. The obscure verse X.23.2 dealing with Indra seems to be an exception : *ṛbhúr vā́ja ṛbhukṣā́ patyate* ...

79. Perhaps instances which are analogous to ṚV VII.38.4 : *samrā́jo váruṇo...mitrā́so aryamā́* have contributed to the evolution of such plurals. Cf. incidentally Bergaigne, II, pp. 119-122, 413 ff.

80. All the three :

IV.36.3 : *tád vo vājā ṛbhavaḥ supravācanáṃ*
devéṣu vibhvo abhavan mahitvanám |
6 : *yáṃ vā́jo víbhvāṃ ṛbhávo yám ā́viṣuḥ*
VII.48.1 : *ṛ́bhukṣaṇo vājā mādáyadhvam...*|
ā́ vo 'rvā́caḥ krátavo ná yātā́ṃ
víbhvo ráthaṃ náryaṃ vartayantu ||

Vāja-s and Ṛbhus :

IV.34.4 : *píbata vājā ṛbhavo*
35.3 : *áthaita vājā amṛ́tasya pánthāṃ*
gaṇáṃ devā́nām ṛbhavaḥ suhastāḥ ||
4 : *...ataṣṭendravā́hāv ṛbhavo vājaratnāḥ* ||

36.4,7 : *vājā ṛbhavaḥ*, besides the number three in vv. 3,5,6. *ṛbhukṣán* and *vā́ja* are mentioned together in V.42.5; VI.50.12; X.64.10; 23.2 ?; *vā́jā ṛbhukṣā́ḥ* in IV.34.5; 37.1 (plur ?); *vā́jā ṛbhukṣáṇaḥ* IV.37.3,7,8; VII.37.1; 48.1. There is no ground here to treat one word as the appellative of the other. Cf. also III.60.5 : *índra ṛbhúbhir vā́javadbhiḥ*; 6 : *índra ṛbhumā́n vā́javān*; 7 : *índra ṛbhúbhiḥ vājíbhiḥ*, or I.110.7 : *ṛbhúr vā́jebhir vásubhir vasúr dadiḥ* [*indra*]; 9 : *vā́jebhir no vā́jasātāv aviḍḍhi ṛbhumā́ṃ indra*; ŚŚS III.18.15 : *indra ṛbhubhir...saṃvidānaḥ*. A few times the Ṛbhus are called *vā́jaratna* (cf. also Bergaigne, II, p. 413). Perhaps in this case the Vājas are supposed to be designated thus as the first of the Ṛbhus, according to the season (cf. Vājapeya in autumn) which one prefers.

One could assume that the emphasis on the two Ṛbhus (*vis-à-vis* the third) is based on an antithesis between their nature and that of Vibhvan.

In I.111.4 *ṛbhū́n vā́jān marútaḥ* are mentioned so closely together that one may think of an identity between the last and the Vājas, but the passage is rare; cf. n. 84 below.

81. They laud Indra in VIII.3.7 : *samīcīnā́sa ṛbhávaḥ sám asvaran rudrā́ gṛṇanta pū́rvyam* ||

82. Three times (besides this, *vājavat* also); once the Aśvins.

83. Occurs altogether only once.

84. I.63.3; 111.4; VII.37.4; VIII.96.21; (and some uncertain passages). As regards the meaning of *ṛbhukṣán* we may as well follow Sāyaṇa, who explains the word, with the *Nighaṇṭu*, as *mahannāman* (on I.111.4; 162.1; VIII.7.9 etc.) or as *ṛbhūṇām adhipati* (I.63.3), *pati* (I.186.10); *ukṣan* (I.162.1; 167.10); *jyeṣṭha* (IV.33.9; VII.48.1); *īśvaro* (VII.37.4), *śreṣṭha* (VIII.93.34), that is to say, in a clear relation to *kṣi*, "to govern"; or as *devānāṃ nivāsabhūtaḥ prajāpatiḥ* (I.162.1); *urukṣaya, urunivāsa, ṛbhūṇāṃ vāsayitā vā* (II.31.6; VII.37.4), *ṛbhunivāsaka, ṛbhubhiḥ, saha kṣiyati, nivasati* (VIII.96.21), *vistīrṇasya tejaso nivāsabhūta* (VII.37.1), *urubhāsamānanivāsa* (VIII.20.2), thus on the basis of *kṣi*, "to dwell." *Nirukta* IX.9 : *urukṣayaṇa ṛbhūṇāṃ rājeti vā* |

A few times the Maruts are called *ṛbhukṣán* (exactly in the eighth book which is fond of going its own way, VIII.7.9, 12; 20.2). The Aśvins also bear the epithet *ṛbhumát*; VIII.35.15 : *ṛbhumántā, vā́javantā, marútvantā* (besides X.106.7 where in a hymn full of comparisons, they are called *ṛbhū́* as well). Furthermore, the Ṛbhus themselves are called *pūṣaṇvát* in III.54.12.

85. In some instances Indra himself is obviously a Ṛbhu. Perhaps I.110.7; 121.2; III.36.2; X.23.2 (same as all the three Ṛbhus ?). Agni also is styled a Ṛbhu, II.1.10; III.5.6; V.7.7.

86. *prabhumataḥ* does not occur everywhere. KŚS X.5.9; 8.14.

87. ĀpŚS XIII.12.2; cf. XII.23.4; XIII.4.14. On this cf. ABr VI. 12.1 : *ihopayāta śavaso napāta iti,...tā aindrārbhavyo bhavanti* | 3 : *prajāpatir vai pita ṛbhūn martyān sato 'martyān kṛtvā tṛtīyasavana ābhajat* | *tasmān nārbhavīṣu stuvate 'thārbhavaḥ pavamāna ity ācakṣate* | 6 : *athāha yad aindrābhavaṃ vai tṛtīyasavanam...*

88. IV.51.6: *kvà svid āsāṃ katamā́ purāṇī́*
yáyā vidhā́nā vidadhúr ṛbhūṇā́m |

vidhā́na occurs only once more in X.138.6 (*māsā́ṃ vidhā́na*) besides in the obscure verse X.85.4 : *ācchádvidhānair gupitó bā́rhataiḥ soma rakṣitáḥ.*

89. I.110.4 : *saudhanvanā́ ṛbhávaḥ sū́racakṣasaḥ saṃvatsaré sám apṛcyanta dhītíbhiḥ.* They are awakened from sleep (in Agohya's house) with the call, 161.13 : *saṃvatsara idám adyā́ vy àkhyata* || IV.33.4 : *yát saṃvátsam ṛbhávo gā́m árakṣan yát saṃvátsam ṛbhávo mā́ ápiṃśan, yát saṃvátsam ábharan bhā́so...*

90. III.335. Contra Weber, *Vedische Beiträge* VII (1898, p. 560 and p. 3 of the offprint : "the three Ṛbhus are the three creative genii of time (past, present and future), Agohya, 'who cannot be concealed' is the sun who cannot be deflected from his course even by the winter solstice."

91. Vol. I, p. 25 ff. To the quotations given there under n. 31 we should add VIII.101.6,14 also.

92. *Ritualliteratur*, p. 118.

93. TS II.2.9.1 : *agniḥ sarvāḥ devatāḥ.*

94. Sāyaṇa : *vadhar iti rephānto 'pi vajranāma vadho 'rka iti tannāmasu pāṭhāt...vadharyantī meghapaṅktir ity ucyate* /

95. The distribution is different in TBr I.5.6.3 : Vaiśvadeva—Indra, Varuṇapraghāsāḥ—Varuṇa, Sākamedhāḥ—Soma; for another sequence see p. 80 above. All the three are connected with Indra in ṚV IV.33.3 d : *vā́jo víbhvāṃ ṛbhúr.*

96. AV III.8.1 : *ā́ yātu mitrá ṛtúbhiḥ kálpamānaḥ. Viṣṇupurāṇa* III.5. 19 : *himāmbugharmavṛṣṭīṇāṃ kartā hartā ca yaḥ prabhuḥ / tasmai trikāla-rūpāya namaḥ sūryāya vedhase* //

97. I.161.8; IV.33.11; 34.4; 35.9. On the other hand we cannot conclude from VII.37.11,48 that they are fed exclusively in the third savana.

98. ṚV IV.37.2 mentions their *yajñā́ ghṛtánirṇijaḥ*, which are unknown to the ritual.

99. ŚŚS VIII.20.

100. The hymns ṚV VII.36 (Viśvedevāḥ); VII.37. 1-7 (Indra and Ṛbhus); VII.37.8; 38 (Savitṛ) might together be an old Śastra of the evening pressing.

101. ŚŚS VIII.2.3,5.

102. *índra ṛbhúbhir vā́javadbhiḥ.*

103. Even otherwise they are neglected in the Adhvaryu ritual. With the exception of the Dvādaśāha, which will be discussed soon, I know only one mantra for them during the insertion of the Spṛt bricks in the Agniciti; ŚBr VIII.4.2 : *ṛbhūṇāṃ bhāgo 'si viśveṣāṃ devānām ādhipatyam...*

104. III.60; IV.36; 33; 34; I.110. Cf. ŚŚS X.2.7; 4.14; 5.23; 6.18; 8.18 (I.110 in other sacrifices also, cf. ŚŚS XI.5.4; XVI.20.16).

105. I. 161.11 : *ágohyasya yád áśastanā gṛhé*
tád adyédám ṛbhavo nā́nu gacchatha /

I do not know what the "dog" and *bastá* signify in v. 13 : *śvā́naṃ bastó bodhayitā́ram abravīt.*

VI.33.7 : *dvā́daśa dyū́n yád ágohyasya*
ātithyé ráṇann ṛbhávaḥ sasántaḥ /
I.110.2cd : *saúdhanvanāsaś caritásya bhūmánā*
ágacchata savitúr dāśúṣo gṛhám //
3ab : *tát savitā́ vo 'mṛtatvám ā́suvat*
ágohygaṃ yác chraváyanta aítana /

106. Cf. *Ritualliteratur*, pp. 6, 155. As regards the meaning of the twelve days, Thibaut is of another view (*Astronomie, Astrologie und Mathematik*, Grundriss der indo-arischen Philologie und Altertumskunde III.9,

§ 5). I give the following counter-arguments : i) Thibaut has overlooked or underestimated the connection between I.161.11 and 13. v.11 speaks of the sleep in Agohya's house (through 12 days, IV.33.7) and v. 13 of the awakening with the words : *saṃvatsará idám adyā́ vy àkhyata.* Hence the twelve days fall at the end of the year. ii) There is absolutely no ground to assume that already at the time of the ṚV these twelve days represented a scholastic product from the twelve months. Cf. Vol. I, pp. 62-63. iii) The majority of the Ṛbhu hymns are employed in the Dvādaśāha. Thus there is an inner connection. iv) Thibaut himself has not proved that the number of the months was the primary reason for the formation of the Dvādaśāha. The number twelve is a phenomenon that extends far beyond India.

107. Weber, *Omina und Portenta*, p. 388; ISt X, p. 242; *Vedische Beiträge* VII (1898), p. 559 ff.

108. *Ritualliteratur*, p. 95.

109. III.10 : *aṣṭakā rātridevatā / puṣṭikarma / āgneyī pitryā vā prājāpatya ṛtudevatā vaiśvadevīti devatāvicāraḥ.* ĀśvGS II.4.12 : *tāṃ haike vaiśvadevīṃ bruvata āgneyīm eke sauryām eke prājāpatyām eke rātridevatām eke nakṣatradevatām eka ṛtudevatām eke pitṛdevatām eke paśudevatām eke.* Even elsewhere the Manes and the Ṛtus are thought of in intimate connection. Cf. Manu III.217 : *ācamyodakparāvṛtya trir āyamya śanair asūn / ṣaḍ ṛtūṃś ca namaskuryāt pitṝn eva ca mantravit //*

110. AV III.10.9 : *ṛtū́n yaja ṛtupátīn ārtavā́n utá hāyanā́n*
sámāḥ saṃvatsarā́n mā́sān bhūtásya pataye yaje //

111. Cf. also IV.25.5 : *sa vā ayaṃ prajāpatiḥ saṃvatsara ṛtuṣu ca māseṣu ca pratyatiṣṭhat te vā ima ṛtavaś ca māsāś ca prajāpatāv eva saṃvatsare pratyatiṣṭhaṁs ta ete 'nyonyasmin pratiṣṭhitāḥ / evam ha vāva sa ṛtviji pratitiṣṭhati yo dvādaśāhena yajate /*

112. I.161.11 : *udvátsv asmā akṛṇotanā tṛ́ṇam*
nivátsv apáḥ svapasyáyā naraḥ /
ágohyasya yád ásastanā gṛhe....

IV.33.7 : *dvā́daśa dyū́n yád ágohyasya*
ātithyé ráṇann ṛbhávaḥ sasántaḥ /
sukṣetrākṛṇvann ánayanta síndhūn
dhánvā́tiṣṭhann óṣadhīr nimnám ā́paḥ /

113. On this cf. the following parallels :

ŚŚS III.18.15 : *indra ṛbhubhir brahmaṇā saṃvidānaḥ śunāsīrī havir idaṃ juṣasva /*

ĀpŚS VIII.20.5 : *indra ṛtubhir brahmaṇā vāvṛdhānaḥ śunāsīrī havir idaṃ juṣasva /*

114. ŚŚS VII.8; ĀpŚS XII.26.8. ŚBr I.6.1.1 relates how the Ṛtus wished for a share in the sacrifice.

115. On the day of preparation, the Soma priests are selected with the beginnings of the Ṛtupraiṣas; this is perhaps a reminiscence of the name *ṛtvij* and of his origin. ĀpŚS XI.19.5.

116. ŚBr IV.3.1.3 ff. attaches great value to the rule that these must be

drawn while the Acchāvāka is seated. According to this text it is better to draw 12 Grahas.

117. ŚBr IV.3.1.7 : *taṃ gṛhītvā na sādaya ti tasmād ayam asannaḥ saṃvatsaraḥ* /

118. Adhvaryu—*mādhuś ca;* Pratiprasthātṛ—*madhavaś ca* (Spring). The other pairs are *śukra-śuci* (summer), *nabhas-nabhasya* (rainy season), *iṣ-ūrj* (autumn), *sahas-sahasya* (winter), *tapas-tapasya* (thaw). Moreover, cf. the description by Eggeling, SBE, XXVI, p. 319, n.1.

119. The comm. explains *vyatītaḥ* with *vyatigacchataḥ*, *mithaḥ saṃgatau bhavataḥ.*

120. The vessels are *ubhayatomukha*, ĀpŚS XII.1.13. ŚBr IV.3.1.7. Offerings are made first with the one opening and then with the other.

121. ŚBr IV.3.1.22,23 : *yad v evaindrāgnaṃ grahaṃ gṛhṇāti sarvaṃ vā idaṃ prājījanad ya ṛtugrahān agrahīt, sa...*

122. Ibid., IV.4.1.2 : *ṛtavo vai saṃvatsaro yajñaḥ / te 'daḥ prātaḥsavane pratyakṣam avakalpyante yad ṛtugrahān gṛhṇāti / athaitat parokṣaṃ mādhyandine savane' vakalpyante yad ṛtupātrābhyāṃ marutvatīyān gṛhṇāti* [IV.3.3.12]/ *na vā atra* [*sāyam*] *ṛtubhya iti kaṃ cana grahaṃ gṛhṇanti na ṛtupātrābhyāṃ kaś cana graho gṛhyate* /

ŚBr IV.4.1.3 seeks to explain this by the fact that in the Sāvitragraha, in the view of this Brāhmaṇa, the Ṛtus are included : *eṣa vai savitā ya eṣa tapati / eṣa v eva sarva ṛtavas tad ṛtavaḥ saṃvatsaraḥ / tṛtīyasavane pratyakṣam avakalpyante / tasmāt sāvitraṃ gṛhṇāti* /

123. On this cf. ṚV I.161.8. (According to the *Āryavidyāsudhākara* the five Prājyās are meant for the seasons).

124. Hence also in IV.34.2 : *vidānā́so jánmano vājaratnāḥ utá ṛtúbhir ṛbhavo mādayadhvam* /

125. See on this Neisser, WB.

126. AV IV.12.7 : *ṛbhū́ ráthasyevā́ṅgāni sáṃ dadhat páruṣā páruḥ*
X.1.8 : *yás te párūṃṣi saṃdadháu ráthasyeva ṛbhúr dhiyā́*
ṚV VIII.75.5 : *táṃ nemím ṛbhávo yathā́ namasva sáhūtibhiḥ* /
IX.21.6 : *ṛbhur ná ráthyaṃ návaṃ dádhātā kétam ādiśe* /

127. Only III.54.12 could speak for Bergaigne.

128. In IX.87.2 Soma is called *ṛbhúr dhī́raḥ*. The word *ṛbhú* is used in the sense of wealth in IV.37.5; VIII.93.34; of the various epithets for wealth, probably the designation *ābhū́* comes closest to it. In AV I.2.3 it is an epithet of the arrow.

129. Neisser, WB, is inclined to think, with the PW and Grassmann, of the root *rabh* or of its derivatives.

130. ĀpŚS V. 11.7; KŚS IV.9.5. Weber, ISt, XVII, p. 196.

131. Particularly on KŚS I.1.10; see n. 133 below. Contra the comm. ĀpŚS V.3.18.

132. Cf. Fick, *Die soziale Gliederung im nordöstlichen Indien*, pp. 209-210. We should note that during the Aśvamedha, the body-guards accompanying the horse are instructed to "reside in the kula of a rathakāra." ĀpŚS XX.5.18; ŚBr XIII.4.2.17; KŚS XX.2.16. Weber, ISt, XVII, p. 198.

AV III.5.6 shows that these are a special group of people in the kingdom, whose help is sought by the king :

yé dhī́vāno rathakārā́ḥ karmā́rā ye manīṣíṇaḥ
upastī́n parṇa máhyaṃ tváṃ sáravān kṛṇv abhito jánān ||

133. I.110.4; *mánor nápātaḥ* III.60.3. Other passages in Bergaigne, II, p. 419. ABr VI. 12.3: *prajāpatir vai pita ṛbhūn martyān sato 'martyān kṛtvā tṛtīyasavana ābhajat* |

134. KŚS I.1.11; IV.9.5.

135. KŚS, p. 13.

Cf. Manu X.23 : *vaiśyāt tu jāyate vrātyāt sudhanvā cārya eva ca* |
káruṣaś ca vijanmā ca maitraḥ sāttvata eva ca ||

Jaimini, *Mīmāṃsā Sūtra* VI.1.50 : *saudhanvanās tu hīnatvāt mantravarṇāt pratīyeran* [*rathakārāh*]. Comm. : *na tu sarva eva atraivarṇiko rathakāraḥ, saudhanvanā ity eṣa jātivacanaḥ śabdaḥ, saudhanvanā nāma jātir abhidhīyate, hīnās tu kiṃcit traivarṇikebhyo, jātyantaraṃ, na tu śūdrāḥ na vaiśyā na kṣatriyāḥ* | Yāska's *Nirukta* XI.16 : *ṛbhur vibhvā vāja iti sudhanavana āṅgirasasya trayaḥ putrā babhūvuḥ.* Cf. also Weber, ISt, X, p. 12 ff.; Max Müller, SBE, XXX, p. 316 ff.

136. In V.31.4 it is the Anu-s who build the chariot for Indra (*ánavas te rátham áśvāya takṣan*). As is evident from I.108.8; VII.18.13; VIII.10.5, these are a people. Compare this verse with I.111.1 which speaks of the Ṛbhus : *tákṣan ráthaṃ suvṛ́taṃ vidmanā́pasas, tákṣan hárī...*

137. The admittedly obscure verse I.161.5 seems to allude to the change in names :

anyā́ nā́māni kṛṇvate suté sácāṅ
anyair enān kanyā́ nā́mabhi sparat ||

138. ABr III.30.4 : *tebhyo vai devā apaivābībhatsanta manuṣyagandhāt.* Whosoever wishes to comprehend the difference between the Veda and the later period may read MBh (ed. Bombay), III.261.19 ff.

139. I.110.4 : *viṣṭvī́ śámī taraṇitvéna vāgháto*
mártāsaḥ sánto amṛtatvám ānaśuḥ |
saudhanvanā́ ṛbhavaḥ...

CHAPTER VII

INDRA AND THE MARUTS

1. "Indra in the Ṛgveda," JAOS, XI, p. 2 ff. (Cf. also Muir, OST, V, p. 77 ff. and A. Lang, *Mythes, cultes et religion*, p. 451, n. 3).

2. JAOS, XV (1891), p. 143 : "a storm-god."

3. RdV, 2nd ed., p. 52, and more particularly p. 132 ff. See pp. 95-96 below.

4. *Vedic Mythology*, p. 54.

5. *The Religions of India*, p. 91.

6. *Chips from a German Workshop*, II, p. 91 (see Perry, *loc. cit.*)

7. *Chips from a German Workshop*, new ed., IV, (1895), p. 396.
8. I, pp. 141-2; cf. also pp. 115 (less certain) and 144.
9. II, p. 172.
10. Beal, *Buddhist Records of the Western World*, I, p. xli. Conversely, there are also poisonous dragons, see ibid., p. xcii : "a mischievous dragon took up his residence here and caused calamities. In the summer he rejoiced to dry up the rain, and in the winter to pile up the snow;" cf. also Fā-Hien, p. 24 etc.
11. Muir, OST, V, p. 95.
12. *Ormazd et Ahriman* pp. 97 and 367 respectively.
13. JAOS, XI, p. 20.
14. Oldenberg, RdV, 2nd ed., p. 137, states : "A god fights with a serpent-shaped demon and opens up the inside of the mountains; from there the waters of the rivers flow out towards the sea : this is what the hymns say. One should not confound this simple conception with the explanation that the mountains denote the clouds and the rivers the streams of rain. This was not so. The mountains were real mountains and the rivers real rivers...Where the poets refer to clouds and rain they use different expressions from the stock phrases of the Indra hymns. Magic rites for causing rain are directed chiefly towards other gods than Indra. On the other hand, it is the personified rivers, doubtless personified terrestrial rivers, rivers Vipāś and Śutudrī, ...which speak, precisely through the stock phrases of the Indra hymns, of Indra's exploit of setting them free....Thus it is patent: for the poets Indra's victory had nothing to do with a thunderstorm but with the following : the god has caused the springs to gush forth from the depths of the rocks and these springs growing into rivers bring prosperity to the meadows below."
15. *The Religions of India*, p. 20, n. 3.
16. PJAOS, XVI (1894), p. ccxxxvi ff.
17. *Chips from a German Workshop*, 2nd ed., IV, pp. 249 and 253 respectively.
18. *The Early Religion*, p. 106.
19. AISAK, II, p. 161.
20. ARW, II, p. 184.
21. E.g., TBr I.7.10.3; II.5.7.4; III.11.4; ŚBr XI.4.3.12. Here and in the following cases a few examples should suffice.
22. E.g., TS I.1.2.0 : *indrasya tvā bāhubhyām ud yacche;* 9.b : *indrasya bāhur asi dakṣiṇaḥ sahasrabhṛṣṭiḥ śatatejāḥ*; 11.k etc.
23. ŚBr II.5.3.18 and other quotations given below. He was conceived in the shape of a bull or ram. Oldenberg, RdV, 2nd ed., p. 74; Charpentier, *Kleine Beiträge*, pp. 42, 62.
24. ABr VIII.12.2 : *te devā abruvan saprajāpatikāḥ / ayaṃ vai devānām ojiṣṭho baliṣṭaḥ sahiṣṭaḥ sattamaḥ pārayiṣṇutamaḥ* (VII.16.9). ŚBr III.4.2.2 : *te [devā] indrasya śriyā atiṣṭhanta tasmād āhur indraḥ sarvā devatā indraśreṣṭhā devā iti.* TS III.3.1.
25. ṚV III.51.8; IV.19.1 : *evā́ tvā́m indra vajrinn átra víśve devā́saḥ*

suhávāsa ū́māḥ/...nír ékam íd vṛṇate vṛtrahátye // VI.17.8; VIII.12.22: *índraṃ vṛtrā́ya hántave devā́so dadhire puráḥ*; 25; 89.2; X.49.11. Bergaigne, II, p. 205.

26. TS II.4.2.1.

27. ABr IV.1.1.

28. ṚV I.11.5 : *tvā́ṃ devā́ ábibhyuṣas tujyámānāsa āviṣuḥ*; X.113.2.

29. ṚV I.102.1; 103.7; V.29.8; VI.18.14; X.73.8.

30. ṚV VI.18.15; 20.2; 25.8; 36.1; or bestow the Soma drink V.29.5.

31. ṚV IV.18.11 : *utá mātā́ mahiṣám ánv avenad amī́ tvā jahati putra devā́ḥ*; VIII.93.14 : *ví yád áher ádha tviṣó víśve devā́so ákramuḥ*; 96.7 : *vṛtrásya tvā śvasathā́d ī́ṣamāṇā víśve devā́ ajahur yé sakhā́yaḥ*; ABr III.16.1 : *indraṃ vai vṛtraṃ jaghnivāṃsaṃ nāstṛteti manyamānā sarvā devaıā ajahuḥ*.

32. ŚBr IV.3.3.17; AĀr I.1.1. etc.

33. TS II.3.4.2.

34. TBr II.2.3.3. Cf. also II.2.7.2.

35. TBr II.2.10.1.

36. TBr I.5.9.1.

37. MS I.9.4 (133.3 ff.); 6 (137.14).

38. ṚV III.51.8.

39. V.30.5.

40. IV.19.2 : *ávāsṛjanta jívrayo ná devā́ḥ*.

41. III.34.7.

42. X.89.9.

43. VI.18.14 : *kavítamaṃ kavīnā́m;* 20.3 : *kṛtábrahman;* 45.4.7, 19; VIII.16.7 : *brahmán, ṛṣi*.

44. He is the Purohita during the selection of the Hotṛ, see NVO, p. 91; TBr II.8.4.2. In TBr I.1.2.5 he claims to be a brahmin and approaches Sunaḥśepa in human form as a brahmin (*caraiveti vai mā brāmaṇo 'vocat*)

45. TBr I.7.7.4.

46. Cf. TBr I.1.2.7 and the section below : Indra in the Ritual.

47. ṚV V.37.4.

48. MS II.2.11. Perhaps ṚV VII.37.7 refers to an exiled king.

49. ABr IV.25.8.

50. Ibid., VII.28.1. He himself boasts of his crimes, KUp III.1.ff.; ISt, I, p. 409 ff.; Oertel, "Contributions, II," JAOS, XIX p. 118 ff. He enumerates his exploits in hymn X.49.

51. Muir, OST, V, p. 86, has collected almost all the statements of the ṚV about the qualities of Vajra. I confine myself to a few remarks.

52. IV.22.1; VII.104.19. It is hurled from a sling; I.121.9 : *tvám āyasáṃ práti vartayo gór divó áśmānam úpanītam ṛbhvā*.

53. VI.22.6. Thus Sāyaṇa also.

54. I.51.3 : *ājā́v ádriṃ nartá yan*. Cf. Reichelt, "Der steinerne Himmel," IF, XXXII, p. 45 ff. : *vajrá*, "chopping wedge" or "chopping club."

55. Bloomfield, ZDMG, XLVIII, p. 572: *he who owns the press-stones.*

56. V.32.10; X.43.9; IX.67.30.

57. This includes the bones of Dadhyañc as well. Vol. I, pp. 219, 433,

n. 118; Sāyaṇa on ṚV I.84.13. (Following V. Miller) Ludwig, *Die neuesten Arbeiten*, p. 121, explains differently : bones=stars.

58. Called *téjiṣṭhā* in I.53.8.

59. *dhánus, bundá, íṣu, śáru, sená* (von Bradke, ZDMG, XLVI, p. 456; Bloomfield, ZDMG, XLVIII, p. 459, n, 1); according to Brunnhofer, *sína* also (BKIS, XXVI, p. 105). The notion that the rainbow is Indra's bow is not known to the ṚV.

60. VI.47.27 : *apā́m ojmā́naṃ pári góbhir ā́vṛtam*
índrasya vájraṃ havíṣā ráthaṃ yaja //

On *apā́m ojmā́nam* cf. Vol. I, pp. 88-89, 233. During the Vājapeya and Rājasūya also the war-chariot is addressed as "Indra's thunderbolt." Cf. VS X.21.a; KŚS XIV.3.1,2 etc.; Weber, *Rājasūya*, p. 56, n. 3. The thunderbolt splits into three as Indra hurls it at Vṛtra; "one-third becomes the *sphyaḥ*, one-third the *ratha*, one-third the *yūpa*," TS V.2.6.2. See Vol. I, p. 395, n. 280, where other identifications are listed. Cf : also Oldenberg, RdV, p. 420. The thunderbolt is thought of as "thundering" or "bellowing."

61. Vol, I, p. 434, n. 135.

62. X.105.6,7. Cf. MS II.5.11 (62.7) : *vāyur vajraṃ saṃśyati.* Contra Brunnhofer, BKIS, XXVI, p. 101.

63. VI.41.2. Cf. *Bhaṭṭikāvya* V.25; *Raghuvaṃśa* X.13.

64. I.33.10; VI.21.7; VIII.77.7; X.92.7. Cf. *asidvitīya.*

65. II.11.6.

66. IX.111.3.

67. WZKM, XIII, p. 317 ff.

68. Oertel, "Contributions," JAOṢ, XXVI, p. 176 ff. with important parallels.

69. ṚV I.32.12. Geldner, VSt, II, p. 183.

70. I.51.9 ought to be interpreted in this sense (see below). In the Ahalyā episode he transforms himself into a cat (*Kathāsaritsāgara* XVII.140) or becomes a monkey etc. Oertel, *loc. cit.*, pp. 193, 314. "Fly-whisk," von Negelein, ARW, VI, p. 247 etc. He appears also as an eagle. Thus this incarnation of Indra quite corresponds to the bird Vārəǰan into which Vərəthragna transforms himself. Geiger, *Aməša Spəntas*, pp. 70, 73.

71. I may add that he is also called *nṛtú*; I wish to equate *nṛtú* with *nṛtū́*, i.e., to understand the word as "dancer." Occasionally the god of light is depicted as dancing. Cf. Usener, *Rheinisches Museum*, NF, IL, p. 461; AISAK, V, p. 178. Tylor, *Anfänge der Kultur*, II, p. 297. But I do not think that Indra's dance is derived from this original nature of his. Dance is not merely the expression of delight but also the sign of exorcism and is a custom among warriors. That Indra's dance should be understood in this sense becomes evident, I think, with reasonable certainty from some passages of the ṚV.

I.130.7 : *bhinát páro navatím indra pūráve*
dívodāsāya máhi dāśúṣe nṛto vájreṇa dāśúṣe nṛto /

Here the reference is only to Indra the warrior, and likewise in

II.22.4 : *táva tyán náryaṃ nṛtó 'pa indra prathamám*
pūrvyáṃ diví pravā́cyaṃ kṛtám |
yád devásya śávasā prā́riṇā ásuṃ riṇánn apáḥ |

Sāyaṇa : *raṇe nartanaśīla... gātravikṣepaṇakuśala hastapādādiprakṣepeṇa śatrūṇāṃ hiṃsakaḥ* or *sarveṣāṃ nartayitaḥ*. The idea, suggested to me by a remark of Fay (AJPh, XVII, 11), has been thoroughly examined since then. Besides Indra, the Aśvins also are called *nṛtú* and also the Maruts who dance around Vṛtra (*krīḍanti* etc.) and are designated frequently as *krīḍin*. On dance, see now von Schroeder, *Mysterium and Mimus*, passim; Wundt, *Völkerpsychologie*, 2nd ed., III, p. 419; Hauer, *Anfänge der Yogapraxis*, p. 41 ff.

72. Cf. Kirste, ZDMG, LXXIV, p. 271. Oldenberg, RdV, 2nd ed., p. 84, thinks that a fetish stone which has nothing to do with a carved image is also possible. Arbman, *Rudra*, p. 82.

73. IV.19.3 : *saptá práti pravátaḥ*.

74. Cf. I.54.10 : *apā́m atiṣṭhad dharúṇahvaraṃ támaḥ*
antár vṛtrásya jaṭháreṣu párvataḥ |

I.80.2 :...*vṛtráṃ nír adbhyó jaghántha;* 4 : *nír bhū́myāḥ, nír diváḥ*; VIII. 3.19 : *bṛhatī́bhyo dhánubhyaḥ*; 20 : *nír antárikṣāt*.

75. Others also hold similar views. Laistner "seeks out each saga in ts native place and explains it with the help of natural phenomena which manifest themselves there" (Mogk, *Mythologie*, in Pauls Grundriss, III, 2nd ed., p. 243). Mogk himself states that "this mythological poetry is nothing but a part of the poetry of a people and its transmitted record must be treated as one treats poetry....Here, the scholar must visualize in the first place the nature of the land and the condition of its soil where the myth has its roots; he must draw into account all that under the influence of which primitive man lives" (*loc. cit.*, p. 231).

74. *Rāmāyaṇa* IV.28; MBh III.182.1-18. A description of winter occurs in *Rāmāyaṇa* III.16.1 ff. among others.

77. *Śiśupālavadḥa* VI.22 ff. contains nothing that is useful here, nor does *Sūryasiddhānta* XII.3.

In the creation-sagas of the later period which deal, *inter alia*, with the creation of the rivers (cf. eg., *Harivaṃśa, Bhaviṣyapurāṇa* XVII, XXXI) Indra's participation, as far as I can see, is not recalled any more.

78. I note from Sorensen, *Festskrift til Vilhelm Thomsen*, (1894), p. 336, n. 1, that he advocates the view that the mountains are not clouds but real mountains from which water flows over to the sky as well as to the earth.

79. Besides VIII.64.5 quoted above, cf. also VIII.49.2 : *girér iva prá rásā asya pinvire dā́trāṇi purubhójasaḥ;* 88.2 : *giríṃ ná purubhójasam*, and of other verses, I.73.6 : *ví síndhavaḥ samáyā sasrur ádrim*; X.68.1 : *giribhrā́jo nórmáyaḥ*.

80. I.130.3 : *ávindad divó níhitaṃ gúhā nidhím*
vér na gárbhaṃ párivītam áśmany
ananté antár áśmani ||

81. II.11.8 : *ni párvataḥ sādi*; 7 : *áraṁsta párvataś cit sariṣyán;* X.57.3: *dhūnuthá dyā́m párvatān dāśúṣe vásu*; VIII.73.23 : *ví vṛtrám parvaśó yayur ví párvatāṁ arājínaḥ*; 70.11.

On II.11.7,8, cf. I.61.14 : *giráyaś ca dṛḷhā́ḥ*; II.12.2 : *yáḥ pṛthivī́ṃ vyáthamānām ádṛṃhad yáḥ párvatān prákupitāṁ áramṇāt... yó dyā́m ástabhnāt;* II.17.5 : *sá prācī́nān párvatān dṛṃhad ójasā... | ádhārayat pṛthivī́m ástabhnād ... dyā́m*; VI.31.2; VIII.14.9 : *rocanā́ divó dṛḷhā́ni dṛṃhitā́ni ca*; X.44.8 : *girī́ṁr ájrān réjamānāṁ adhārayat*; 149.1 (Savitṛ) : *pṛthivī́m aramṇād... dyā́m adṛṃhat.* I cannot see why the parvatas in II.11.7,8 should be clouds. Cf. I.39.3 : *vy ā́śāḥ párvatānāṃ* [*yāthana*] |

V.57.3 should be compared with VI.30.5 : *dṛḷhám arjunaḥ párvatasya*; VII.79.4 : *ví dṛḷhásya dúro ádrer aurṇoḥ.* When IV.19.5 states *ráthā iva prá yayuḥ sākám ádrayaḥ*, these are not clouds either but the stones that rolled down from the mountain peaks which had been shattered by Indra (v. 4). The Maruts shake what is firm; V.56.4 : *áśmānaṃ cit svaryàṃ párvataṃ girím prá cyāvayanti yā́mabhiḥ*; I.64.3; 85.4; 168.4 etc.; hence they are *parvatacyút*. *jihīta párvato giríḥ* (I.37.7) denotes nothing but a mountain. I.19.7 : yá ī́ṅkháyanti *párvatān tiráḥ samudrám arṇavám* means "who shake the mountains beyond the sea" and not "toss the clouds" (Max Müller). It is obvious that one can use occasionally the verb *dhū* for this action. Mountains are considered to be rich in wealth and food as verses VIII.49.2; 64.5; 88.2 cited above demonstrate. In the firm stables of the mountains there are cows also. With their chariot tyres the Maruts cleave asunder the mountains : *párvatān* I.64.11; *ádrim* V.52.9, but not the "clouds."

The only passage where *párvata* could mean a cloud is I.57.6 (though not cited by the PW in this sense) : *párvataṃ mahā́ṃ urúṃ vájreṇa parvaśas cakartitha;* but this is only another way of saying *vrajám ūrvā́ṃ bibhidúr.* Cf. VIII.45.30 : *yáḥ kṛntád íd ví yonyám triśókāya girím pṛthúm | góbhyo gātúṃ níretave ||*

82. Kuhn, *Die Herabkunft des Feuers und des Göttertrankes*, p. 157, n. 2; Pischel, VSt, I, p. 174.

83. E.g. III.54.20 : *śṛṇvántu no vṛ́ṣaṇaḥ párvatāso*
dhruvákṣemāsa íḷayā mádantaḥ |
IV.55.5 : *ā́ párvatasya marútām ávāṃsi...avri* |

84. Cf. the *naraḥ parvatāḥ* in the ṚV. Pabbata is the name of a Muni in Jātaka, no. 423.

85. I.132.6 : *yuváṃ tám indrāparvatā puroyúdhā*
yó naḥ pṛtanyā́d ápa táṃ tam íddhatam...

Cf. ŚBr IV.6.9.14.

86. III.53.1 : *índrāparvatā bṛhatā ráthena*
vāmī́r íṣa ā́ vahataṃ suvī́rāḥ |
vītáṃ havyā́ny adhvaréṣu devā...

87. I would like to caution also against the transferring of the later conception of the serpent as it is expressed, for example, in the Śrāvaṇa festival into the ṚV or against the speaking of "cloud-serpents" in the ṚV. Nor should the connection of serpents to rain, as Winternitz emphasizes in his

Sarpabali, (cf. also Ludwig, *Über den Anfang des Mahābhārata, Ādiparvan*, p. 5) be read into the ṚV. We should keep in mind that even in classical Sanskrit there exist no "snake demons" which withhold the rain.

88. Keith, p. 129, even speaks of "the dark mountains of the night" ! Compare this with the hymn to the night.

89. Naturally I mean the proper noun and not the enemies thus referred to with the appellative. Even the most primitive of the peoples would not have been so ignorant as to consider the clouds which bring rain after a long scorching heat as real demons.

90. Cf. the passage from the *Raghuvaṃśa* quoted on p. 106 above.

91. Not even the root *naś* which is used for the rivulets in the summer as in *kriyāḥ sarvā vinaśyanti grīṣme kusarito yathā* (*Hitopadeśa* I.94; *Pañcatantra* II.85).

92. Cf. e.g., *Nirukta*, I, p. 65 : *varāhākāro vā kṛṣṇo megho varāhasādṛśyena vartate;* III.p. 27; or *Harivaṃśa* (ed. Bombay, Śaka 1818) II.10.24 ff.; 95.5 ff. Such descriptions occur in the *Mṛcchakaṭika* as well.

V.2 : *megho jalārdramahiṣodarabhṛṅganīlo*
vidyutprabhāracitapītapaṭottarīyaḥ |
ābhāti saṃhatabalākagṛhītaśaṅkaḥ
khaṃ keśavo 'para ivākramituṃ pravṛttaḥ ||
3 : *keśavagātraśyāmaḥ kuṭilabalākāvalīracitaśaṅkhaḥ*
vidyudguṇakauśeyaś cakradhara ivonnato meghaḥ ||

A series of similes are given in

V.5 : *saṃsaktair iva cakravākamithunair haṃsaiḥ praḍīnair iva* |
vyāviddhair iva mīnacakramakarair harmyair iva procchritaiḥ ||
6 : *tais tair ākṛtivistarair anugatair meghaiḥ samabhyunnataiḥ.*

Cf. also p. 82, 25 ff.; *Ṛtusaṃhāra* II.16 ad; *Śiśupālavadha* VI.26 ff.; *Meghadūta* 2; *Raghuvaṃśa* IV.29; MBh III.134 (on the serpents, cf. Ludwig, *Über den Anfang des Mahābhārata, Ādiparvan*, p. 5).

93. I am indebted to Jiriczek for the quotations from Anglo-Saxon and Norse sources.

94. BKIS, XV, p. 36, n. 3.

95. Horace, *The Odes and Epodes*, with an English translation by C. E. Bennett, London, New York 1914.

96. Cf. Horace, *Odes*, II.10 : *informis hiemes*, "unlovely winters" (tr. by Bennett, see the previous note); ṚV I.121.11 : *vṛtrám āśáyānaṃ sirā́su* and the description of Vṛtra as *vyàṃsa, apā́d, ahastá, vádhri* in I.32.5 ff.

97. *The Works of Virgil*, translated by Charles Rann Kennedy, London 1861, p. 97.

98. Lünig, *Die Natur in der altgermanischen und mittelhochdeutschen Epik*, Zürich 1888.

99. *Beowulf and the Finnsberg Fragment*, a translation into modern English prose by John R. Clark Hall, London, 1911, p. 62.

100. Ibid., p. 85.

101. The images are still more vivid in G. von Swieten's German

translation of this poem, *Die Jahreszeiten,* which formed the basis for Hayden's Oratorio :

Gefesselt steht der breite See
Gehemmt in seinem Lauf der Strom,
Im Sturz von türmenden Felsen hangt
Gestockt und stumm der Wasserfall.

102. *Goethe*, selected verse with an introduction and prose translation by David Luke, Harmondsworth 1964, p. 181.

102a. See n. 96 above.

103. ṚV I.103.7 : *yát sasántaṃ vájreṇắbodhayó 'him*; IV.19.3 : *abudhyám ábudhyamānaṃ suṣupāṇáṃ saptá práti praváta ā́śáyānam.*

104. On Vərəthragna, see Darmesteter, SBE, IV, p. lxiv; Macdonell, "The God Trita," JRAS, XXV, p. 484; Oldenberg, RdV, 2nd ed., p. 132; Geiger, *Aməša Spəntas,* p. 66.

105. Lagarde, *Abhandlungen*, p. 293. Gelzer, BKSGW, 1896, p. 104 : "probably the most national and most popular god of the Armenians." Jensen, *Hittiter und Armenier*, p. 177 ff.; *The Mythology of all Races*, VII (1925), p. 42 ff. : "It is mostly in this capacity [as a god of courage] that he became favourite deity with the Armenian kings....Besides these attributes Vahagn claimed another. He was a sun-god..."

106. Windischmann, *Die persische Anāhitā,* p. 26; Hübschmann, *Armenische Grammatik*, I, pp. 75 ff., 77, 508; Patrubány, *Beiträge zur armenischen Ethnologie*, p. 7 ff.

107. Stein, *Zoroastrian Deities*, p. 5.

108. Hübschmann, KZ, XXVI, pp. 607-8.

109. *Griechisches Wurzellexikon*, II, p. 276; ZDMG, VIII, p. 459; von Gutschmid, *Kleine Schriften*, III, p. 89 ff.; W. Schulze, KZ, XXXIII, p. 214, n. 6.

110. NGGW, 1886, p. 148 ff; *Mitteilungen*, II, p. 28; Niedermann, BKIS, XXV, p. 294.

111. Cf. *vərədra-tauruan*, "overcoming the enemies" (Bartholomae, *Handbuch*, s.v.)

112. Vərəthragna manifests himself in innumerable forms in Bahrām Yašt. On the basis of these forms, Charpentier (*Kleine Beiträge*, p. 25 ff.) has pursued the idea that in his conception there are not only the traits of the old dragon-slayer Vṛtrahan but also accretions borrowed from the treasury of traditions and legends connected with the fire god Ātar-Agni. When in this context Charpentier refers to the parallelism that exists between the Subrahmaṇyā formula addressed to Indra and that to Agni, these two being employed according as the Agniṣṭoma is directed to Indra or to Agni (under the name Agniṣṭut), I believe that in actual fact there existed two different forms of this sacrifice (see below : Indra in the Ritual) and that among many families Agni played the role of a mythological duplicate of Indra. It seems to be a fortunate notion that where Vərəthragna bears the shape of a beautiful reddish horse it is not an incarnation of Indra but of Ātar who, like Agni, was identified with the sun and was conceived in the image of a horse;

similarly the form of the wild ram (the ninth incarnation) refers to Agni rather than to Indra. From this it follows that the form of Vərəthragna which appertains in India primarily to Indra was conferred in the Iranian sagas on several gods, not only on Indra and Agni who are mentioned here. To some extent this is also the view of H. W. Magoun (*Studies in Honor of Maurice Bloomfield*, p. 197 ff.) who unfortunately speaks still of the "sky-dragon" and "cloud-serpent" as well as of Agni as the "lightning" and its different varieties ("a triad of lightning gods will satisfy all the conditions..."). I cannot agree with this, nor with the subtile distinctions he made earlier (JAOS, XIX, p. 144; AJPH, XXI, p. 274 ff.) between the "crest of an advancing thunderstorm" and "stationary crest" etc.

113. *Arische Periode*, p. 197.

114. Geiger, *Ostiranische Kultur im Altertum*, pp. 143-144.

115. Vendidād I.2,3 : *dasa avathra må̊ŋhō zayana dva hąmina...aδa zəmahe maiδīm aδa zərəδaīm aδa čəmahe zyå̊sčiṭ pairipataiti aδa fraēštem vōighnanam* |

116. 19 : *zyām ča daēvōdātəm taožyā ča daiŋhuš-aiwištāra.*

117. *Nordisk tidskrift for filologi*, Ny raekke, IV, p. 28 ff. (Kopenhagen 1879-80). I am indebted to Jiriczek for drawing my attention to it. See now Axel Koch, IF, X, p. 99. If, as Koch reports, Lundgren has laid emphasis on the great similarity of functions between the Indian Vṛtra, the demon of summer's heat, on the one hand and the Norse Loki on the other, this comparison is untenable, for no trace of summer's heat can be proved in Vṛtra's case. I do not know why the heat of summer is supposed to have been regarded by the Aryans as such a frightful demon (unless we place their settlements in the far south) that they should have preserved such a loyal memory of the demon of drought and not of the winter which is the real scourge of all northern countries. Johansson (*Dhiṣaṇā*, pp. 95, 137) looks for Vṛtra in the Norse *Ullr*. Vṛtra : *Ullr*=Anglo-Saxon *wuldor* (Germanic *wulprs*) : *wulpus*. Wackernagel's explanation of *apaoša* from *apvurt* (*Festschrift für Kuhn*, p. 158) does not apply to Vṛtra who has his counterpart already in Vərəthra and is only remotely connected with *apaoša* through the root. The two demons are quite different.

118. On the cold winters in Kashmir, see Stein, *Memoir on Maps illustrating the Ancient Geography of Kaśmīr*, Calcutta 1899, p. 119.

119. *The works of Virgil*, translated by Charles Rann Kennedy, London, 1861, p. 97.

120. Hunter, *Atlas of India*, p. 7.

120a. "An awkward way of expressing the May solstice. Some editors suspect and emend the text," says the translator E. Iliff Robson. See note below.

121. Translation by E. Iliff Robson, B. D. The Loeb Classical Library, vol. 269, p. 31. First printed 1933, reprinted 1958.

122. Balfour, *Cyclopedia of India*, s.v. Indus.

123. Stein, *op. cit.*, p. 99.

124. *Gazetteer of the Countries Adjacent to India*...(London 1844), I, pp. 137 and 291 respectively.

125. Cf. also Merk, *Acht Vorträge über das Pandschab*, p. 8 : "in winter and in spring the water-level is low. In summer when the snow begins to melt in the upper regions, the rivers begin to fill and become full in the rainy season." Bühler (*Detailed Report of a Search of Sanskrit Manuscripts made* [*in* 1875-76] *in Kashmir, Rajputana and Central India*, p. 3) explains that the river name *tohī* means etymologically "a river produced by (the melting of) snow and ice."

126. Cf. the remark of the commentary on it (p. 851) : *himavatparvatādiṣu himaśabdavācyo jalaghanaḥ śīyate adhaḥ patati.* For quotations from the later literature, see PW, s.v. *hima.*

127. See Vol. I, pp. 347-48.

128. See Ungnad, *Die ältesten Völkerwanderungen*, 1923, p. 12.

129. Cf. e.g. III.30.12; VIII.6.10; 70.5. Or VS X.16.a : "With golden forms, you two, Indra and the sun, rise when the dawn lights up." (Mahīdhara explains differently). For further information see below the section on Etaśa. In several places like X.96.11 a definitive interpretation of the relationship is not possible.

130. Oldenberg, RdV, p. 51; ZDMG, XLIX, p. 173 ff.; L, p. 66, n. 1. What Oldenberg says against me in the last mentioned article is based on a misconception.

131. IV.26.2 : *ahám vṛṣṭím dāśúṣe mártyāya* [*adadām*]; 17.2; VIII.4.10 : *niméghamāno...divédiva ójiṣṭhaṃ dadhiṣe sáhaḥ* (?); 6.1 : *mahā́n ... parjányo vṛṣṭimā́m iva*; X.23.4 : *sá cin nú vṛṣṭír yūthyā̀ svā́ sácā̃ índraḥ śmáśrūṇi háritābhí pruṣṇute;* 73.8 (?); 98.4. However, one can also hold a different view about the majority of the verses. Cf. Bergaigne, II, p. 189 f.; Oldenberg, RdV, p. 142; Hopkins, PJAOS, XVI, p. ccxxxviii.

132. TS II.1.6.3 (see below on the sacrificial animals).

133. Vol. I, p. 26 ff.

134. Besides the passages cited in Vol. I, p. 28, cf. the following :

III.31.4 : *tá̄ṃ jānatī́ḥ práty úd āyann uṣā́sah*
pátir gávāṃ abhavad éka índraḥ ||
11 : *sá jātébhir vṛtrahā́ séd u havyaíḥ*
ud usríyā asṛjad índro arkáiḥ |
V.29.12 : *návagvāsaḥ sutásomāsa índram*
dáśagvāso abhy àrcanty arkaíḥ |
gávyaṃ cid ūrvám apidhā́navantaṃ
táṃ cin náraḥ śaśamānā́ ápa vran ||
30.11 : *...índro púnar gávām adadād usríyāṇām* ||

I.32.12; II.19.3 etc. See below the section on Vala.

135. The demon who opposes Indra in these battles is not primarily Vṛtra but Vala. Cf. also Oldenberg, RdV. p. 351, n. 1; p. 149. n. 3.

136. AV III.10.12 (*Mantra Brāhmaṇa* II.3.19):
ekāṣṭakā́ tápasā tapyámānā jajā́na gárbhaṃ mahimānam índram |
téna devā́ vyàṣahanta śátrūn hantā́ dásyūnām abhavac chácīpátiḥ ||

The explanation I have given in my *Sonnenwendfeste*, p. 314, n. 2, that Ekāṣṭakā corresponds only to the end of summer or of the rainy season was still influenced by the conventional notions about Indra and was hence erroneous.

137. *Revue de l'histoire des religions*, XXXIX (1899), p. 69. He sums up his objections in the following words : "He forgets that all the rivers of India, even among those of the Himālayas, do not come from the snowy heights; he forgets also that Indra is first of all the thundering god, that this deliverance of the rivers takes place as a result of a terrible battle which is decided by a great flash of lightning and which does not exactly recall the caresses of the vernal sun; but most of all he forgets...that it is a grave mistake as regards the character of the myths, at least of those myths that have reached the stage in which we find them in the Veda, to look for the exact description and explanation of the circumstances of the natural phenomena in the Veda." I have forgotten none of this.

138. Emphasis added.

139. Here I pass over the question whether the designation "seven streams" is of Indian origin at all or whether it was brought over to India. According to Rawlinson, the name was originally given to the seven chief tributaries of the Oxus (see E. Thomas, "The Rivers of the Vedas," JRAS, 1883, New Series, Vol. No. XV, p. 371 ff.). Narhar Gopal Sardesai (*Bhandarkar Commemoration Volume*, p. 93 ff.) also entertains doubts, but he locates their source in areas which are absolutely impossible.

140. Hann, *Handbuch der Klimatologie*, 2nd ed., II, p. 187. Cf. also Blanford, *Climates and Weather of India*, 'p. 71 : "sometimes the rain of the spring-thunderstorms takes the form of hail."

141. Uhland, *Schriften*, ed. Pfeiffer, III, pp. 17-38; Usener, *Die Sintflutsagen*, p. 195 ff.

142. Oldenberg, RdV, 2nd ed., p. 139, prefers the thunderstorm myth : "Where do we find such a strong interest for the melting of ice in mythologies ?" [Not for the melting of ice but for the liberation of the waters, see pp. 110-112 above]. "Is Indra's appearance compatible with that of a sun god ?" [It is nowhere incompatible and is possible everywhere. The colour of Indra's beard and hair suits the sun god in particular, so does the popular motif of the battle between the summer and winter.] Oldenberg continues : "The water-encompassing mountain plays such a great role in the legend of the battle against Vṛtra and can easily be explained with reference to the thunderstorm as derived from the conception of the cloud. But if we had to do with frozen and thawing rivers, would not then the water-encompassing mountain be an idle and obscure addition ?..." [The mountain withholds the springs and rivers and lets them flow only after the sun's victory and the thaw consequent upon it which breaks the bonds of ice; this, I think, is quite obvious.]

143. I.32.4 : *yád indrā́han prathamajā́m áhinām...|*
ā́t sū́ryaṃ janáyan dyā́m uṣā́saṃ
tā́dī́tnā śátruṃ ná kilā vivitse ||
51.4 : *tvám apā́m apidhā́nāvṛṇor ápa*
ádhārayaḥ párvate dā́numad vásu |

vṛtráṃ yád indra śavasā́vadhīr áhim
ā́d ít sū́ryaṃ divy ā́rohayo dṛśé ||
55.6 : *sá hí śravasyúḥ sádanāni kṛtrímā*
kṣmayā́ vṛdhāná ójasā vināśayan |
jyótīṃṣi kṛṇvánn avṛkā́ṇi yájyave
áva sukrátuḥ sártavā́ apáḥ sṛjat ||
62.5 : *gṛṇānó áṅgirobhir dasma ví var*
uṣásā sū́ryeṇa góbhir ándhaḥ |
100.6 : *sá manyumī́ḥ samádanasya kartā́*
asmā́kebhir nṛ́bhiḥ sū́ryaṃ sanat |
8 : *só andhé cit támasi jyótir vidat...||*
18 : *sánat kṣétraṃ sákhibhiḥ śvitnyébhiḥ*
sánat sū́ryaṃ sánad āpáḥ suvájraḥ ||
III.31.15 : *índro nṛ́bhir ajanad dī́dyānaḥ*
sākáṃ sū́ryam uṣásaṃ gātúm agním ||
32.8 : *jajā́na sū́ryam uṣásaṃ sudáṃsāḥ ||*
39.5 : *satyáṃ tád índro daśábhir dáśagvaiḥ*
sū́ryaṃ viveda támasi kṣiyántam ||
7 : *jyótir vṛṇīta támaso vijānán...*
44.2 : *haryánn uṣásam arcayaḥ*
sū́ryaṃ haryánn arocayaḥ ||
VI.17.3 : *āvíḥ sū́ryaṃ kṛṇuhí pīpihī́ṣo*
jahí śátrūm̐r abhí gā́ indra tṛndhi ||
5 : *yébhiḥ sū́ryam uṣásam mandasānó*
ávāsayó 'pa dṛḷhā́ni dárdrat |
21.3 : *sá it támo 'vayunáṃ tatanvát*
sū́ryeṇa vayúnavac cakāra |

II.11.18; 19.3; III.34.4; VI.32.2; VIII.3.6; 12.9; 89.4,7; 98.2. To these verses we may add the solitary passage in AV IV.10.5 according to which the sun is born from Vṛtra : *samudrā́j jāto maṇír vṛtrā́j jātó divākaráḥ*. This verse becomes intelligible through ṚV I.32.4; 51.4. It is not a "late and absurd legend of the AV," as Keith, p. 104, thinks, but is based on an old tradition. Keith has not understood this or has been prevented from understanding it by his own interpretation of Vṛtra.

144. *Pañcatantra*, V, v. 34.

145. X.72.7, see Vol. I, p. 94.

146. X.67.5. Perhaps the verse is not relevant at all. *udadhi* is a proper name in VII.94.12, and shows another possibility in X.67; v. 3 (*aśmanmáyāni náhanā*), v. 4 (*támas*), v. 7 (*adardar*). This much is certain that *udadhí* does not denote "cloud" in the ṚV (as Grassmann thinks).

147. Perhaps with the exception of *svávṛṣṭi* (I.52.5, 14) which Grassmann and Hopkins (PJAOS, XVI, p. ccxxxviii) refer to Vṛtra. Cf. also Bergaigne II, pp. 186 f., 231.

148. In II.30.3; X.73.5 it can conceivably refer to Indra who knows how to make use of the māyā of his opponent.

149. Hann, *Handbuch der Klimatologie* 2nd., II, p. 200 : "Through the hailstorm of April, 30, 1884, 230 persons died at one place (directly hit, partly also through frost bite)." Blanford, *The India Meteorologist's Vademecum*, vol. II : Meteorology of India, p. 136 : "Hail sometimes falls in north-west, more especially between February and May....The stones are generally of a large size...and the small soft hail, the 'graupel' of the Germans, which is so common in England, is unknown in India...The relative frequency of hail-storms at different seasons of the year is shown in the following table [after Dr Buist] :

January	5	July	2
February	20	August	0
March	31	September	2
April	34	October	3
May	17	November	4
June	4	December	5

Cf. also Balfour, *Cyclopedia of India*, s.v. Hailstorms.

150. Brunnhofer, BKIS, XXVI, p. 101 explains *vépas* in ṚV I.80.12 as hail and connects the word with the Avestan *vafra*, modern Persian *berf* "snow" etc.

151. Cf. Thibaut, *Astronomie, Astrologie und Mathematik* (Grundriss der indo-arischen Philologie und Altertumskunde III, 9), § 6.

152. I should not fail to add here the description of winter which we find in ŚBr I.5.4.5 : *hemanto vā ṛtūnāṃ svāhākāro, hemanto himāḥ prajāḥ svaṃ vaśam upanayate tasmād dheman mlāyanty oṣadhayaḥ pra vanaspatīnāṃ palāśāni mucyante pratitarām iva vayāṃsi bhavanty adhastarām iva vayāṃsi patanti vipatitalomeva pāpaḥ puruṣo bhavati.* The description of the seasons in II.2.3.8 is not so important : *yad eva purastād vāti tad vasantasya rūpam / yat stanayati tad grīṣmasya yad varṣati tad varṣāṇāṃ yad vidyotate tac charado yad vṛṣṭvodgṛhṇāti tad dhemantasya.*

153. See the section on Viśvarūpa below.

154. Some more remarks may be made on this. 1) Here we may think of the name *rauhiṇá* attributed to Indra's enemy in ṚV I.103.2; II.12.12 (*yó rauhiṇám ásphurad vájrabāhur dyā́m āróhantam*); AV XX.128. 13. We are justified in understanding this as the name of a constellation (cf. *Kāśikā* on IV.3.37) or also as a metronymic, "son of Rohiṇī." Contrary to his oath, the moon cohabits only with Rohiṇī of all the 33 daughters of Prajāpati and is cursed with consumption as a punishment for this. (Weber, *Naxatra*, II, p. 277). If Rohiṇī were a constellation which indicated the onset or the climax of winter, then this would explain why the Ahi is called *rauhiṇa.* 2) We should compare the designation of Indra as Ṛbhukṣan and his relationship with the Ṛbhus, see p. 80 above. 3) In the well-known formula *ādityasyāvṛtam anvāvarte, ādityasya* is replaced by *sūryasya, aindrīm,* or all these are juxtaposed. Quotations in Caland, *Een indogermaansch lustratie-gebruik*, p. 10.

155. E.g. ṚV VI.21.5,6,8; 22.2; 34.1; VII.22.9.

156. ṚV VII.32.22.

157. E.g. ṚV VIII.14.5.

158. E.g. *Raghuvaṃśa* III.48 ff.

159. In the Dākṣāyaṇa sacrifice.

160. ABr IV.29.1 : *agnir vai devatā prathamam ahar vahati*...; 31.1 : *indro vai devatā dvitīyam ahar vahati*...; V.1.1: *viśve vai devā devatās tṛtīyam ahar vahanti*. The representation of the metres, stomas, and Sāmans through the three days corresponds to the distribution of the three savanas (I. *trivṛt*, *rathaṃtaram*, II. *pañcadaśa*, *bṛhat* etc.). TMBr VIII.4.5; 5.11 relates that Indra fell ill before the evening pressing.

161. Cf. ĀpŚS XII.23.4 : *prātaḥ prātaḥsāvasya śukravato manthivato madhuścuta indrāya somān prasthitān preṣya;* at noon XIII.4.14 : *mādhyandinasya savanasya niṣkevalyasya...śukravato manthivato madhuścuta indrāya...;* in the evening XIII.12.2 : *tṛtīyasya savanasyarbhumato vibhumato prabhumataḥ vājavataḥ savitṛvato bṛhaspativato viśvadevyāvatas tīvrān āśīrvata indrāya*...

162. ŚBr III.3.4.18 : *indrāgaccha, hariva āgaccha, medhātither meṣa, vṛṣaṇaśvasya mene, gaurāvaskandin, ahalyāyai jāra, kauśika brāhmaṇa, gautama bruvāṇa ahe sutyāṃ devā brahmāṇa āgacchata* (cf. Weber, ISt, I, p. 38; IX. pp. 40, 295; Eggeling, SBE, XXVI, pp. 81, n.1, 2; 82; Hans Oertel, JAOS, XVIII, p. 34 ff.; XXVI, p. 176 ff.; Hillebrandt, *Ritualliteratur*, p. 127) and of other Vedic texts, see MS II.5.5; ABr VI.3.1 ff.; *Ṣaḍviṃśa Brāhmaṇa* I.1.1 ff.; TĀr I.12.3,4. On *meṣá* cf. ṚV I.51.1; 52.1; VIII.2.40; 97.12; on *ménā* cf. I.51.13; 121.2; on *Ahalyā* cf. Weber, SBBAW, 1887, p. 903; *Rāmāyaṇa* I.48.12 ff. (Böhtlingk's *Chrestomathie*, 2nd ed., p. 87). As in the case of *gaurāvaskandin*, we must assume here also that the Nivid formula is made up of material from gotras not belonging to the Ṛgvedic families. J. Charpentier, *Kleine Beiträge*, pp. 67-68, adduces valuable grounds for the antiquity of the Subrahmaṇyā formula but he wishes to ascribe it in its core to the Indo-Iranian period.

An allusion to another form of the Subrahmaṇyā formula occurs in ṚV VIII.17.12 : *śắcigo śắcipūjanāyáṃ rấṇāya te sutáḥ | ắkhaṇḍala prá hūyase ||*

In the ritual I did not come across the secret name borne by Indra; as far as I know he is the only god to whom a secret name is given. Indra's *guhyaṃ nāma* is mentioned as early as in ṚV X.55.1; according to ŚBr V.4.3.7 it is "Arjuna"; cf. Weber, *Akademische Vorlesungen über Indische Literaturgeschichte*, 2nd ed., p. 127; *Naxatra*, II, p. 317; *Rājasūya*, pp. 56-57.

163. He is called thus not only in the ṚV but elsewhere also, e.g., in the *Divyāvadāna* (see the Index, s.v. *Kauśika*).

164. In the Agniṣṭut sacrifice this formula is replaced by another. LŚS I.4.1 says : "In the Agniṣṭut sacrifices the Nigada belongs to Agni. 2 : There the formula of the Gautamas, *agna āgaccha rohitābhyāṃ bṛhadbhāno dhūmaketo jātavedo vicarṣaṇa āṅgirasa brāhmaṇāṅgirasa*, is recited before the reference to the day of pressing (i.e., before the statement, on such and such Soma day). 3 : The word *agnayaḥ* takes the place of *devāḥ*. 4 : The formula of Dhānaṃjapya reads thus : *agna āgaccha, rohitava āgaccha, bharadvājasyāja, sahasaḥ sūno, vārāvaskandin, uṣaso jāra, aṅgirasa* etc."

The choice of the formula was a topic of dispute among the Chāndogyas (cf. KŚS XXII.5.1). The JBr remarks : *tad āhuḥ kiṃdevatyā subrahmaṇyeti / aindrīti brūyād indraṃ hy enayāhvayatīti /...etad dha tat tāṃ ha vā eke yathādevatam āhvayanti sarvāgneyīm agniṣṭuta aindrīm indrastomasya vaiśvadevīṃ vaiśvadevasya aniruktām aniruktasya / tad u śaśvan na tathā* (Hans Oertel, JAOS, XVIII, p. 36).

This difference, which might perhaps go back to an ancient cultural difference in the Vedic clans, is of great significance. According to the canonical ritual, the basic form of all Soma sacrifices is called "Agniṣṭoma" (*Ritualliteratur*, p. 124), not quite correctly since Agni enjoys, by no means, a special position there. The name and content of the sacrifice do not agree with one another. The form inherited from antiquity is as a matter of fact an Indrastoma, not an Agniṣṭoma, and should have also borne this name since Indra is indeed invoked by the means of the Subrahmaṇyā. Among the many Ekāhas known to the ritual there is also one Indrastoma which is not specially remarkable. It seems to me that there occurred a compromise between two schools; one lent the Agniṣṭoma its name, the other the content. The facts of the case might have been as follows : there existed an Agniṣṭut (=Agniṣṭoma) with an Agni-Subrahmaṇyā formula by the side of an Indrastut (=Indrastoma) with its own Indra formula, and these must have been combined in the way as stated above. Lāṭyāyana's statement, I think, is important because it affords us an insight into the history of ritual and into the manner of selection by the ritualists.

165. Vol. I, pp. 328-29.

166. Of the other libations, the following are added : 1) as in the morning sacrifice, the Śukrāmanthinau, 2) as in the morning and in the evening, the Āgrayaṇa, 3) the Ukthya (three Ukthyagrahas); while drawing them and depositing them on the ground at noon, the formula of dedication is addressed to Indra alone, 4) the three Atigrāhyapātras (of which the one for Agni is drawn by the Pratiprasthātṛ, that for Indra by the Neṣṭṛ, the one for Sūrya by the Unnetṛ). *Ritualliteratur*, p. 132. However, Indra remains the chief deity always. Cf. ABr III.27.1 : *tasmin* [*mādhyandine*] *triṣṭubhaṃ chandasām adadhur, indraṃ devatānām*; VI.11.14 : *tāsām etā abhitṛṇṇavatyo bhavantīndro vai prātaḥsavane na vyajayanta, sa etābhir eva mādhyandinaṃ savanam abhyatṛṇat;* 30.10 : *aindro vai mādhyandinaḥ...*

167. ŚBr II.5.4.9 : *indro vā eṣa purā vṛtrasya vadhāt / atha vṛtraṃ hatvā yathā mahārājo vijigyāno evaṃ mahendro 'bhavat;* TS VI.5.5: *mahān vā ayam abhūd yo vṛtram avadhīt;* ABr III.21 : *sa mahān bhūtvā devatā abravīd uddhāraṃ ma uddharateti...sa etaṃ māhendraṃ graham abrūta, mādhyaṃdinaṃ savanāṇāṃ niṣkevalyam ukthānāṃ triṣṭubhaṃ chandasāṃ pṛṣṭhaṃ sāmnām.*

168. ABr III.39.6 : *sa vā eṣa saṃvatsara eva yad agniṣṭomaḥ...*41.1 : *saṃvatsaram evānūkthyo 'gniṣṭomam apyeti;* TBr I.2.2.1 : *agniṣṭomasaṃmitaḥ suvargo loka iti, dvādaśāgniṣṭomasya stotrāṇi dvādaśa māsāḥ saṃvatsaraḥ.*

169. *Ritualliteratur*, p. 124.

170. All the seasons are connected with him in MS III.11.12.

171. KŚS XX.8.30. The months of the Grīṣma are *śukra* and *śuci.*

Hence in the ritual *nabhas* and *nabhasya*, the months of the rainy season, do not belong to Indra. Hence also the occasional remark *grīṣme vā indro vṛtram ahan*. Indra is the archetype for the Kṣatriya. Hence also, summer is the time when a Kṣatriya or one who desires Śrī should instal the fire (KŚS IV.7.6). The later literature also sees the model of the warrior in the sun and not in the thunderstorm god. I cite here once again the characteristic Pāli passage which I have mentioned before in JRAS, 1897.

Dhammapada 387 : *divā tapati ādicco rattim ābhāti candimā |*
sannaddho khattiyo tapati jhāyī tapati brāhmaṇo ||

172. I note the following examples. MS I.10.16 (155.19) : *asau vā āditya indraḥ*; TS V.7.1.c : *asau vā āditya indra eṣa prajāpatiḥ*; ŚBr I.6.4.18 : *tad vā eṣa evendraḥ ya eṣa tapati | athaiṣa eva vṛtro yac candramāḥ;* II.3.4.12; III.4.2.15 etc.; KBr VIII.3 : *yam etam āditye puruṣaṃ vedayante sa indraḥ sa prajāpatiḥ;* JuBr I.28.2 : *sa yas sa indra eṣa eva sa ya eṣa eva tapati*; (comm. on TBr I.5.11.4; II.4.2.4; 4.6.11); TĀr III.118.19,20. Cf. also Ludwig, V, p. 4. We should not overlook AV XIII.3.13 :...*sá mitró bhavati prātár udyán sá savitā́ bhūtvā́ntárikṣeṇa yāti sá indro bhūtvā́ tapati madhyató divam* (a verse which, I think, should be taken literally) and ṚV VIII.52.7; 93.1,2,4 where Indra and Sūrya are treated as synonyms contrary to the common usage of the ṚV (it should be kept in mind that we are dealing with the eighth book).

In the same context belong some passages which assign the day to Indra; TBr I.1.4.3 : *āgneyī vai rātriḥ...aindram ahaḥ*; II.1.2.7. Cf. also VS III.9 : *sajū rātryendravatyā...sajūr uṣasendravatyā*; TBr III.6.2 : *uṣāsānaktā... saṃsmayamāne indreṇa devaiḥ*. Here Indra is the same as Sūrya or Vivasvat with his two wives (Vol. I, p. 366, n. 69).

173. More precisely in ĀpŚS XII.4.6,12.

174. Elephants are the animals of the east, horses of the west, mules of the north. KŚS XXII.2.23, 24. Cf. also *Rāmāyaṇa* I.6.22 according to which the best horses come from Kamboja, Balkh etc.

175. II.18.4 : *ā́ dvā́bhyāṃ háribhyām indra yāhy ā́ catúrbhir ā́ ṣaḍbhír hūyámānaḥ | ā́ṣṭābhir daśabhir* etc.; VI.47.18 : *śatā́ dáśa*; VIII.1.24 : *ā́ tvā sahásram ā́ śatáṃ yuktā́ ráthe hiraṇyáye*...etc.

176. E.g. III.43.3 and 4; VIII.1.9 and 24, 25; 13.10 and 11; X.44.2 and 3.

177. Mention is made of the dhānā-s for Indra I.16.2; IV.24.7; VI.29.4; X.28.1. As far as I can see, it is stated only in book III that the horses are fed. Hence it seems to be chiefly the custom of the Viśvāmitras who make the offering of the dhānās to Indra haryaśva or alone to the horses. The following verses are to be taken into account.

III.35.3 : *grásetām áśvā vi mucehá śoṇā*
divédive sadṛ́śīr addhi dhānā́ḥ |
7 : *kṛtā́ dhānā́ áttave te háribhyām ||*
43.4; 52.1 : *dhānā́vantaṃ karambhíṇam apūpávantam ukthínam |*
indra prātár juṣasva naḥ ||
5 : *mā́dhyaṃdinasya sávanasya dhānā́ḥ...*

6 : *tṛtī́ye dhānā́ḥ sávane...*
7 : *pūṣaṇváte te cakṛmā karambhám*
hárivate háryaśvāya dhānā́ḥ /

We can obviously infer from these verses that the Viśvāmitras did not yet limit the offerings to Indra's horses to the evening savana only as is the case in the later ritual. Of the Ṛgvedic verses, the ŚŚS (VIII.8.1-3) employs only III.53.2; I.82.6 as Anuvākyā and Yājyā respectively. ĀśvŚS VI.11.9 ff. employs III.53.6; I.82.6 in the last days of the Ahīnas (and during the Ekāhas) and on the other days III.53.2 or 5; I.177.4. ĀśvŚS V.4.2 ff. enjoins the verses ṚV III.52.1, 5, 6.

178. *Sonnenwendfeste; Ritualliteratur*, p. 157; Oldenberg, RdV, p. 444.

179. Bloomfield, JAOS, XVII, p. 173 ff.

180. Eggeling, SBE, XLI, p. xvii ff.; *Ritualliteratur*, p. 138. The circumstances are such that we can translate *apiśarvará* here as "nocturnal" only. Bloomfield, JAOS, XVI, p. 37, suggests for the *apiśarvará* in the ṚV the meaning "rather at the end of the night." But the linguistic usage of the Brāhmaṇa passages cited by Bloomfield refers to the night without any qualification. Neisser, WB : "at the beginning of the night" (actually "merging into the night").

181. TMBr X.4.2 : *cakṣuṣī atirātrau, kanīnake agniṣṭomau*; 3 : *saṃvatsarasya vā etau daṃṣṭrau yad atirātrau tayor na svaptavyaṃ saṃvatsarsya daṃṣṭrayor ātmānaṃ ned apidadhānīti;* TS VII.4.1.3. : *atirātrāv abhito bhavataḥ;* KBr XVII.5 : *atha yad atirātram upayanty etāvān vai saṃvatsaro yad ahorātre tad yad atirātram upayanti saṃvatsarasyaivāptyai*; TBr I.3.4.3 : *devayānān eva patha ārohaty atirātreṇa.*

182. ABr IV.5. Like the Mahāvrata, the Atirātra is included in the composition of sacrifices of several days' duration and serves either as the opening day or as the closing day. This is why the texts speak often of two Atirātras.

183. Eggeling, SBE, XXVI, p. 397, n. 2; XI . pp. xvi-xvii; and my *Ritualliteratur*, p. 137. The dispute among the Yājñikas whether the Ṣoḍaśin is an independent sacrifice or not is not relevant for our present investigation (TS VI.6.11 and Weber's note). In the second alternative, it forms the fourth day of the six-day-sacrifice.

184. ABr IV.1.5 : *kiṃ ṣoḍaśinaḥ ṣoḍaśitvam iti / ṣoḍaśaḥ stotrāṇām, ṣoḍaśaḥ śastrāṇām, soḍaśabhir akṣarair ādatte ṣoḍaśibhiḥ praṇauti /ṣoḍaśapadāṃ nividaṃ dadhāti.* The Graha is drawn (according to KŚS XII.5.2) in a square Khādira vessel.

185. KBr XVII.1 : *tad asau vai ṣoḍaśī yo 'sau tapati / etam eva tat prīṇanti/ atho śoḍaśaṃ vā etat stotraṃ ṣoḍaśaṃ śastraṃ tasmāt ṣoḍaśīty ākhyāyate ...atho indra u vai ṣoḍaśī*; TMBr XII.13.8: *ekaviṃśāyatano vā eṣa yat ṣoḍaśī;* ABr III.41.2 : *ekaviṃśaṃ ṣoḍaśi sāma trivṛt sandhiḥ, sā triṃśat sa māsaḥ;* 4 : *so 'sāv ekaviṃśo' dhyāhitas tapati / viṣuvān vā eṣa stomānāṃ / daśa vā etasmād arvāñcas trivṛto daśa parāñco, madhya eṣa ekaviṃśau bhayato 'dhyāhitas tapati* (comm. on 2 : *kiṃ ca ṣoḍaśastotre yat sāmāsti tad ekaviṃśaṃ bhavati*).

186. *yasmān na jātaḥ paro anyaḥ...trīṇi jyotīṃṣi sacate sa ṣoḍaśī* |

187. *śyāva*. The commentary explains this word to the effect that it is of indefinite colour : "neither black nor white; it is in the middle of the two."

188. According to ĀpŚS XIV.3.3 the horse is white or "brown-red" (*aruṇapiśaṅga*); according to KŚS XII.6.1 it is black.

189. TMBr XII.13.25 : *hiraṇyaṃ saṃpradāyaṃ ṣoḍaśinā stuvate* | *jyotiṣmān asya ṣoḍaśī bhavati*. It should be noted that the verses with which the Graha is drawn and praised must contain the word *hari*. ŚBr IV. 5.3.4; TS VI.6.11.4.

190. *Ritualliteratur*, p. 101.

191. ĀpŚS XIV.3.1 : "with a piece of gold [which takes the place of the usual blade of barhis] he leads the stotra for the Ṣoḍaśin when the sun has gone down up to a half." Cf. KŚS XII.6.1; ŚBr IV.5.3.11 : *taṃ vai purāstamayād upākaroty astamite 'nuśaṃśati*. TS VI.6.11.6: *samayāviṣiṭe sūrye ṣoḍaśinaḥ stotram upākaroti*. We may still add a remark of TBr I.5.3.3 : *yat pratīcīnaṃ madhyandināt prācīnam aparāhṇāt tato devāḥ ṣoḍaśinaṃ niramimita* (!) The comm. on TMBr XVIII.6.19 cites from the Śruti the words *nāhno na rātreḥ*; one is inclined to think of the compact between Indra and Namuci.

192. According to ĀpŚS XIV.3.7 the dakṣiṇā consists of a horse or a she-mule. TS VI.6.II : *aruṇapiśaṅgo 'śvo dakṣiṇā*.

193. Cf. TS VI.6.11.4 and n. 185 above. TBr II.2.3.7 : *asāv āditya ekaviṃśaḥ*.

194. TS VI.6.11.1 : *devebhyo vai suvargo loko na prābhavat* | *ta etaṃ ṣoḍaśinam apaśyan* | *tam agṛhṇata...yat ṣoḍaśī gṛhyate suvargasya lokasyābhijityai* | *indro vai devānām ānujāvara āsīt sa prajāpatim upādhāvat tasmā etaṃ ṣoḍaśinaṃ prāyacchat tam agṛṇīta* | *tato vai so 'graṃ devatānāṃ paryait* | *yasyaivaṃ viduṣaḥ ṣoḍaśī gṛhyata agram eva samānānāṃ paryeti*; MS IV.7.6; ŚBr IV.5.3.1 : *taṃ nu sakṛd indraṃ bhūtāny atyaricyanta prajā vai bhūtāni tā hainena sadṛgbhavam ivāsuḥ;* 2: *indro ha vā īkṣāṃ cakre kathaṃ nv aham idaṃ sarvam atitiṣṭheyam arvāg eva mad idaṃ sarvaṃ syād iti sa etaṃ graham apaśyat;* TMBr I.10.4 : *abhijid asi yuktagrāvendrāya tvendraṃ jinva* (*ṣoḍaśin*); XII.13.31 : *aparuddha yajña iva vā eṣa yat ṣoḍaśī* | *kavīyasvina iva vai tarhi devā āsan* | *bhūyasvina asurāḥ*.

195. Besides TS VI.6.11.1 quoted in the previous note, cf. ŚBr IV.5.3.3 : *sarvaṃ ha vā idam atitiṣṭhaty arvāg evāsmād idaṃ sarvaṃ bhavati yasyaivaṃ, viduṣa etaṃ grahaṃ gṛhṇāti* |

196. TS VII.1.5.4 : *ṣoḍaśinaṃ śaṃsaty ahno dhṛtyā aśithilambhanāya*.

197. It should be noted that on the fourth day of the Pṛṣṭya, when the Pṛṣṭhas are sung, fire is churned with the araṇis on the thigh of the Udgātṛ and an oblation is made in the Āhavanīya. KŚS XII.3.10.

198. E.g. TS I.4.37 ff.; TĀr X.1.10.

199. E.g. ABr IV.1.2; TMBr XIX.6.3; TS VI.6.11.4,6 : *aruṇapiśaṅgo 'śvo dakṣiṇaitad vai vajrasya rūpam*.

200. I.63.2; X.44.9; 92.7. Bergaigne, II, p. 245 f.

201. According to KŚS XXII.11.28 the Vajra sacrifice has the form of the Ṣoḍaśin.

202. Originally the weapon is not in his hand. Tvaṣṭṛ or others make it or give it to him; cf. p. 101 above; this also speaks against his being originally a thunderstorm god. ṚV X.43.9 : *új jāyatām paraśúr jyótiṣā sahá*, and also ZDMG, XLVIII, p. 418.

Besides these Soma sacrifices, he receives various others also. It is not necessary to go into these. I mention as examples the *indrasya kukṣī* (LŚS X.18.4; TMBr XXV.11.1; ŚŚS XIII.29.23,25), the fifth of the seven Saptāhas (KŚS XXIII.5.4) etc.

203. PGS II.17.9 : *yasyā bhāve vaidikalaukikānām bhūtir bhavati karmāṇām indrapatnīm upahvaye sītāṃ sā me tv anapāyinī bhūyāt karmaṇikarmaṇi svāhā* (Cf. *Kumārasambhava* V.61). Cf. ṚV VIII.21.3; Indra *urvarāpati* and his connection with the fertility of the field in

V.33.4 : *purū́ yát ta indra sánty ukthā́ gáve cakárthorvárāsu yúdhyan |*
tatakṣé sū́ryāya cid ókasi své vṛ́ṣā samátsu dāsásya nā́ma cit ||

204. PGS III.1.6 : *atha yavānām | etaṃ u tyaṃ madhunā saṃyutaṃ yavaṃ sarasvatyā adhi maṇāv acakṛṣuḥ | indra āsīt sīrapatiḥ śatakratuḥ kīnāśā āsan marutaḥ sudānava iti.* AV VI.30.1.

205. PGS II.13.

206. KŚS V.11; ĀpŚS VIII.20; MŚS I.7.8; ĀśvŚS II.20; ŚŚS III.18; XIV.9; *Kauśika Sūtra* XX.1 ff. Cf. Weber, *Naxatra*, II, p. 334 ff.

207. One or two camels also can constitute the dakṣiṇā.

208. ṚV IV.57; AV III.17; MS II.7.12; TS IV.2.5.5; VS XII.67.

209. Weber, *Naxatra*, II, p. 334 ff.

210. Cf. also TS I.8.7a; TBr I.7.1.1.

211. I do not attach any value to an enumeration of minor deviations in the Sūtras.

212. KŚS V.11.14; ĀpŚS VIII.20. The ŚŚS seems to recommend only one dakṣiṇā for the entire sacrifice. While the Śunāsīrīya is incorporated in the Ṛtusaṃhāra, it is employed also outside the rigid arrangement of the ritual, occasionally in a Naimittika sacrifice. For example, one who "wishes to acquire villages" should choose the Śunāsīrīya and perform it at a pond which has formed by itself through rain. In all the rites for which water is enjoined, he uses rain water. The sacrifice serves also a *prajākāma*, a *paśukāma* etc. for the fulfilment of their wishes. ĀpŚS VIII.22.5 ff.

213. Obviously the name of the thirteenth month, see Weber, *Naxatra*, II. p. 336 ff.

214. Cf. ĀpŚS VIII.21.1 : *anuvatsarīṇāṃ svastim āśāste | divyaṃ dhāmāśāsta iti sūktavākasyāśīḥṣu hotānuvartayati.* MŚS I.7.8.6 : *anuvatsarīyodvatsarīye svastim āśāsa ity āha yajamānaḥ.* TBr I.7.1.1 : *saṃvatsaro vā indraḥ śunāsīraḥ | saṃvatsareṇaivāsmā annam avarundhe |*

TBr II.5.8.12 : *indraḥ śunāvad vitanoti sīram*
saṃvatsarasya pratimānam etat |
arkasya jyotis tad id āsa jyeṣṭhaṃ
saṃvatsaraṃ śunavatsīram etat ||

(Comm. : *vāyuvat sahabhūtam ādityaṃ* (!) *vitanoti vistārayati* / *etad ādityasya vistārarūpaṃ saṃvatsarasya pratimānaṃ pratinidhirūpam* etc.)

215. Eggeling, SBE, XII, p. 445, n. 3.

216. According to Sāyaṇa, Śuna=Indra, Sīra=Vāyu; cf. also ĀśvŚS II. 20..3. The offerings for Vāyu, Indra etc. which are made in the Śunāsīrīya may well be the reason for this explanation.

217. Also ĀśvŚS II.20.3.

218. v. 8 : *śunáṃ parjányo mádhunā páyobhiḥ śúnasīrā śunám asmā́su dhattam.* AV III.17. That the Śunāsīrau are associated with rain is evident from the custom, described above, of using rain water when the sacrifice is performed as a Naimittika sacrifice (n. 212).

Differently TBr I.7.1.1 which regards the participation of Vāyu (*vṛṣṭyai pradāpayitā*) and Sūrya (*sūryeṇa vā amuṣmiṃ loke vṛṣṭir dhṛtā* etc.) as the cause for the rain.

219. Already Max Müller, *Vorlesungen über die Wissenschaft der Sprache*, 2nd ed., II, p. 513, thinks, *inter alia*, of the possibility that a star could have been meant here, "perhaps a very ancient name for Sirius." In principle, it is possible to think of agricultural implements in connection with the name but our texts offer no information on this and speak rather in favour of a constellation.

220. Cf. e.g., on the Pleiades, Andree, "Die Plejaden im Mythus und in ihrer Beziehung zum Jahresbeginn und Landbau," *Globus*, LXIV, p. 362 ff. The remarks of Grierson, *Bihar Peasant Life*, p. 280 ff., and the verses cited by him which are current in the greater part of North India show that Indians observe the position of the constellations with reference to agriculture. I am of the view that in the ṚV also there are various designations of the constellations which were popular until the new terminology (Māgha etc.) replaced them.

221. Are the Śunahotra ceremonies in which oblations are made to Indra and other gods (ṚV II.18.6) connected with the Śunāsīrīya ?

222. I make no claims on completeness and list only the following examples. *odana pañcaśarāva* TBr III.7.1.8; *dadhi* TS I.8.7.b; *puroḍāś* in the Rājasūya, cf. TS I.8.9,10; TBr I.7.3.3 etc.; (a specific sort of rice is used for Indra jyeṣṭha, KŚS XV.4.10); according to some authorities in the morning, at noon and in the evening during the Agniṣṭoma (cf. ABr II.23); ṚV IV. 24.5,7; *caru* KŚS V.7.9 (during the Sākamedhāḥ after the Mahāhavis); ĀśvŚS II.18.18; ĀpŚS VIII.12.3; TS II.2.7.1; ŚBr II.5.4.9; *apūpa* and *dhānā-s* during the Agniṣṭoma; ṚV III.52; IV.24.7.

223. Cf. further MS II.5.8 (58.14); 5.10 (60.16); 5.11 (62.2); ŚBr II. 5.3.18 : *etad vā indrasya rūpaṃ yad ṛṣabhas;* V. 3.1.3: VI.2.1.5; KŚS XX. 10.9 etc. Of animals of other types, mention may be made of TS II.1.2.4 : *saṃhitām aindrīm*; 5.4 : *aindrīṃ sūtavaśām ā labheta bhūtikāmaḥ.* The selection of an ox is in close conformity with the allusions in the ṚV. According to these, Indra is not only a heavy drinker but a great eater as well and consumes 100 or 1000 buffaloes, ṚV VI. 17.11 and VIII. 12.8 respectively. The singer of X.27.2 promises him a *tumraṃ vṛṣabham* (cf. also 28.3).

224. TS II.1.6.2 : *aindram aruṇam ā labhetendriyakāma indram eva svena bhāgadheyenopa dhāvati...aruṇo bhrūmān bhavaty etad vā indrasya rūpaṃ samṛddhyai.*

225. TS I.8.1.2; MS II.6.13 (72.11, 16); TBr I.7.3.3 etc.

226. TS V.6.17: *indrāya rājñe trayaḥ śitipṛṣṭhāḥ, indrāyādhirājāya trayaḥ śitikakuda indrāya svarājñe trayaḥ śitibhasadaḥ;* II.1.3.2: *indrāya manyumate manasvate lalāmaṃ prāśṛṅgam ā labheta saṃgrāme saṃyattaḥ;* likewise 4 : *indrāya vṛtrature...gataśrīḥ pratiṣṭhākāmaḥ indrāya abhimātighne* etc.

227. TS V.6.15 :· *somaindrā babhrulalāmās tūparāḥ;* 16 *aindravaiṣṇavā gauralalāmās tūparāḥ*; 17 : *āgnendrāḥ kṛṣṇalalāmās tūparaḥ* etc.

228. E.g. TS II.1.3.2 : *indrāya marutvate pṛśnisaktham ā labheta grāmakāmaḥ...yad ṛṣabhas tena aindro yat pṛśnis tena mārutaḥ.*

229. Cf. MS III.14.2 (173.1).

230. TS II.2.8.4.

231. Vol. I, p. 54.

232. NVO, pp. iv, 99, 112-113. See also the quotations there.

233. Cf. also TS II.5.4.4. and Eggeling, SBE, XII, p. 183.

234. As we have stated earlier, Indra who receives the midday Graha which is drawn *śukrapātreṇa* is called Mahendra. ĀpŚS XIII. 8.5; KŚS X.3.10; TS I.4.20, 21 (ŚŚS does not mention this Graha in connection with the usual Agniṣṭoma).

235. Cf. e.g., NVO, p. 186.

236. See pp. 230-7.

237. ŚBr I.6.3.1 : *tvaṣṭur ha vai putras triśīrṣā ṣaḍakṣa āsa tasya triṇy eva mukhāny āsus tad yad evaṃrūpa āsa tasmād viśvarūpo nāma.* 2 : *tasya somapānam evaikaṃ mukham āsa surāpāṇam ekam anyasmā aśanāyaikaṃ tam indro vidveṣa tasya tāni śīrṣāṇi praciccheda.* 3 : *sa yat somapānam āsa tataḥ kapiñjalaḥ samabhavat* etc. (A 1). 6 : *sa tvaṣṭā cukrodha kuvin me putram avadhīd iti so 'pendram eva somam ājahre sa yathāyaṃ somaḥ prasuta evam apendra āsa.* 7 : *indro ha vā īkṣāṃ cakre / idaṃ vai mā somād antaryantīti sa yathā balīyān abalīyasa evam anupahūta eva yo droṇakalaśe śukra āsa taṃ bhakṣayāṃ cakāra* (A 2)/ *sa hainaṃ jihiṃsa so 'sya viṣvaṅṅ eva prāṇebhyo dudrāva mukhād dhaivāsya na dudrāvātha sarvebhyo 'nyebhyaḥ prāṇebhyo 'dravat tad adaḥ sautrāmaṇītiṣṭis tasyāṃ tad vyākhyāyate yathainaṃ devā abhiṣajyan* (A 3). This is followed by the narration of Tvaṣṭṛ's renewed anger and of the creation of Vṛtra and then of the battle against the latter in its various phases (B2, B 3).

Slightly different from this is TS II.5,1 : *viśvarūpo vai tvāṣṭraḥ purohito devānām āsīt svasrīyo 'surāṇām / tasya triṇi śīrṣāṇy āsant somapānaṃ surāpāṇam annādanaṃ / sa pratyakṣaṃ devebhyo bhāgam avadat parokṣam asurebhyaḥ...tasmād indro 'bibhed īdṛṅ vai rāṣṭraṃ vi paryāvartayatīti / tasya vajram ādāya śīrṣāṇy acchinad yat somapānam āsīt sa kapiñjalo 'bhavat* etc. (A 1). *tasyāñjalinā brahmahatyām upāgṛhṇāt / tāṃ saṃvatsaram abibhas taṃ bhūtāny abhy akrośan brahmahann iti.* He appeals to the earth, trees and women to take one-third each of the guilt upon themselves (A 1a). II.4.12

and II.5.2.1 (A 2, B). (A 3 is missing here although the Sautrāmaṇī is naturally known to the TS). MS II.4.1 ff. has only A 1-3, B. (In A 1, *inter alia*, the variants : *tena samalabhata tena yugaśaram apatat sa takṣāṇaṃ tiṣṭhantam abravīd ādhāvemāny asya śīrṣāṇi chinddhīti tasya takṣā praskadya paraśunā śīrṣāṇy acchinat,...*).

We find only A 1-3 in ŚBr V.5.4.2 ff.; elaborated in many ways in XII.7.1.1 ff. *Kāṭhaka* XII.10 (with the same variant as in the MS). On this cf. also TMBr XVII.5.1 : Indra kills Viśvarūpa; *tam aślīlā vāg abhyavadat* (cf. above *brahmahan* !); *so 'gnim upādhāvat* etc.

238. Comm. : *viśiṣṭadehasaṃbandhinyo'bhavan.* TS V.4.5.3 (only up to *asināt*); MS II.5.3 (50.7) : *indro vai vṛtram ahant sa prāṅ apadyata sa padyamāna indraṃ saptabhir bhogaiḥ paryagṛhṇāt tasmād viṣvañcaḥ paśavo vyudāyan mūrdhato vaidehīr udāyaṃs tasmāt tāsāṃ puro janma pura okas tāsāṃ jaghanata ṛṣabho vaideho 'nūdait tam acāyad;* III.3.7 (39.17) : *indraḥ ṣoḍaśabhir bhogaiḥ paryagṛhṇāt sa vā agninaiva vṛtrasya bhogān apidahya vaiśvakarmaṇābhyāṃ pāpmanas tamaso niramucyata; Kāṭhaka* XIII.4.

239. ŚBr I.6.3.8 : *sa tvaṣṭā cukrodha kuvin me 'nupahūtaḥ somam ababhakṣad iti sa svayam eva yajñaveśasaṃ cakre sa yo droṇakalaśe śukraḥ pariśiṣṭa āsa taṃ pravartayāṃ cakārĕndraśatrur vardhasveti so 'gnim eva prāpya sambabhūva* [*antaraiva sambabhūvety u haika āhuḥ*]; TS II.4.12 : ...*somam apibat/ tasya yad atyaśiṣyata tat tvaṣṭāhavanīyam upa prāvartayat svāhendraśatrur vardhasveti / sa yāvad ūrdhvaḥ parāvidhyati tāvati svayam eva vy aramata yadi vā tāvat pravaṇam āsīt yadi vā tāvad adhy agner āsīt;* II.5.2 (up to *vardhasveti*); MS II.4.1 (40.4 ff.) : *tato yaḥ somo 'ty aricyata tam agnā upaprāvartayat svāhendraśatrur vardhasva// itīndrasyāhainaṃ śatrum acikīrṣad indram asya śatrum akarot tathā vāk svayam eva vyait /*

240. ŚBr I.6.3.8 :...*so 'gnīṣomāv evābhi sambabhūva sarvāḥ vidyāḥ sarvaṃ yaśaḥ sarvam annādyaṃ sarvāṃ śrīm*; TS II.4.12.2 : *sa sambhavann agnīṣomāv abhi samabhavat.* MS II.4.3 : *sa yaṃ somaṃ prāvartayad yasmiṃś cāgnā upaprāvartayat tā agnīṣomau devate prāṇāpānā abhisamabhavatām.* (In the later period it is Rāhu who swallows the heavenly bodies and has to let them slip out again when Indra slits open his stomach.)

241. ŚBr I.6.3.9 : *sa yad vartamānaḥ samabhavat tasmād vṛtro 'tha yad apāt samabhavat tasmād ahis taṃ danuś ca danāyūś ca māteva ca piteva ca parijagṛhatus tasmād dānava ity āhuḥ.* 11. *atha yad abravīd vardhasveti tasmād u ha smeṣumātram eva tiryaṅ vardhata iṣumātraṃ prāṅk so 'vaivāvaraṃ samudraṃ dadhāv ava pūrvaṃ sa yāvat sa āsa sahaiva tāvad annāda āsa;* cf. ŚBr I.1.3.4. : *vṛtro ha vā idaṃ sarvaṃ vṛtvā śiśye / yad idam antareṇa dyāvāpṛthivī sa yad idaṃ sarvaṃ vṛtvā śiśye tasmād vṛtro nāma.* TS II.4. 12.2 : *sa iṣumātramiṣumātraṃ viṣvaṅṅ avardhata sa imāṅ lokān avṛṇod yad imāṁ lokān avṛṇod tad vṛtrasya vṛtratvam;* 5.2,1-2; *yad avartayat tad vṛtrasya vṛtratvaṃ yad abravīt svāhendraśatrur vardhasveti tasmād asya indraḥ śatrur abhavat / sa sambhavann agnīṣomāv abhi samabhavat / sa iṣumātram... vṛtratvam.* MS II.4.3 (40.10ff.) : *sa vā iṣumātram evāhnā tiryaṅṅ avardhateṣumātram anvaṅṅ atho āhur ahorātre eveṣumātraṃ tiryaṅṅ*

avardhateṣumātram anvaṅṅ ity atho āhur ardhamāsam atho māsam atho saṃvatsaram iti sa vā imāḥ sarvāḥ srotyāḥ paryaśayat /

242. ŚBr I.6.3.12 : *tasmai ha sma pūrvāhṇe devā aśanam abhiharanti madhyandine manuṣyā aparāhṇe pitaraḥ* /

243. ŚBr I.6.3.13 : *sa vā indras tathaiva nuttaś carann agnīṣomā upamantrayāṃ cakre 'gnīṣomau yuvam vai mama stho yuvayor aham asmi na yuvayor eṣa kiṃ cana kaṃ ma imaṃ dasyuṃ vardhayatha upa māvartethām iti.* 14: *tau hocatuḥ kim āvayos tataḥ syād iti tābhyām etam agnīṣomīyam ekādaśakapālaṃ puroḍāśaṃ niravapat.* 15 : *tāv enam upāvavṛtatuḥ / tāv anu sarve devāḥ preyuḥ sarvā vidyāḥ sarvaṃ yaśaḥ sarvam annādyaṃ sarvā śrīs teneṣṭvendra etad abhavad yad idam indra eṣa u paurṇamāsasya bandhuḥ...*

This part of the Agni-Soma episode is lacking in TS II.4.12.2. Tvaṣṭṛ who forges the thunderbolt makes his appearance here and also Viṣṇu (see below !). In II.5.2.2 Indra turns to Prajāpati, who casts the thunderbolt for him, and then follows the slightly changed Agni-Soma legend : *tāv abrūtām agnīṣomau mā pra hār āvam antaḥ sva iti mama vai yuvaṃ stha ity abravīn mām abhyetam iti / tau bhāgadheyam aicchetām... / tāv abrūtām abhisaṃdaṣṭau vai svo na śaknuva aitum iti / sa indra ātmanaḥ śītarūrāv ajanayat...tābhyām enam abhy anayat tasmāj jañjabhyamānād agnīṣomau nir akrāmatām.* When afterwards Indra seizes the thunderbolt, sky and earth call out, *mā pra hār*; they ask and get a boon, and then upon their bidding Indra kills Vṛtra. Agni and Soma lost their radiance because they were inside Vṛtra.

244. Cf. however, *Kāṭhaka* XII.3 : *tasmād āhur hato vṛtro 'stṛtas tv iti* /

245. ŚBr I.6.3.16 : *tad v eva khalu hato vṛtraḥ sa yathā dṛtir niṣpīta evaṃ saṃlīnaḥ śiśye yathā nirdhūtasaktur bhastraivaṃ saṃlīnaḥ śiśye tam indro 'bhyādudrāva haniṣyan.*

246. See the previous note.

247. ŚBr I.6.3.17 : *sa hovāca mā nu me prahārṣīs tvaṃ vai tad etarhy asy yad ahaṃ vy eva mā kuru mānuyā bhūvam iti sa vai me 'nnam edhīti tatheti taṃ dvedhānvabhinat tasya yat saumyaṃ nyaktam āsa taṃ candramasaṃ cakārātha yad asyāsuryam āsa tenemāḥ prajā udareṇāvidhyat.* TS II.4.12 : 1) Vṛtra gives up his strength in three instalments to Indra who passes it on to Viṣṇu. 2) Vṛtra makes a compact with Indra and promises to serve him as his food: *saṃdhāṃ tu saṃ dadhāvahai tvām eva pra viśanti, yan māṃ praviśeḥ kiṃ mā bhuñjyā ity abravīt tvām evendhīya tava bhogāya tvāṃ pra viśeyam ity abravīt taṃ vṛtraḥ prāviśad udaraṃ vai vṛtraḥ* (both are wanting in II.5.2) ...and finally : *yad vā idaṃ kiṃ ca tad asmai tat prāyacchad ṛcaḥ sāmāni yajūṃṣi*; VI.5.1.1 : *sa vṛtro vajrād udyatād abibhet so 'bravīn mā me pra hār asti va idaṃ mayi vīryaṃ tat te pra dāsyāmīti tasmā ukthyam prāyacchat,* thus for the second and the third time.

MS II.4.3 (40 ff.) is like the TS, even as regards the surrendering of the Ṛk, Sāman and Yajus. This last triad seems to be merely a parallel version to the surrendering of the "strength" three times. It occurs in ŚBr V.5.5.1 ff. also quite by itself : *vṛtre ha vā idam agre sarvam āsa yad ṛco yad yajūṃṣi yat sāmāni tasmā indro vajraṃ prājihīrṣat* / 2 : *sa ha viṣṇum uvāca vṛtrāya vai vajraṃ prahariṣyāmy anu mā tiṣṭhasvati / tatheti ha viṣṇur uvācānu tvā sthāsye prahareti / tasmā indro vajram udyayāma / sa udyatād vajrād vṛtro bibhayāṃ cakāra.* 3 : *sa hovāca / asti vā idaṃ vīryaṃ tan nu te prayacchāni mā tu me prahārṣīr iti tasmai yajūṃṣi prāyacchat.* The second time Indra receives the *ṛcaḥ* and the third time the *sāmāni.* In TMBr XX.15.6 we find only the surrendering of *vīrya.* Thus we can distinguish between three aspects. 1) Surrendering of *vīrya,* 2) Surrendering of the Yajus, Ṛk and Sāman (or *vidyā, śrī* in the ŚBr) which I think, is the same as 1), and 3) Vṛtra's promise to serve as Indra's food.

The compact in MS IV.3.4 (42.13 ff.) in violating which Indra is helped by the gods is quite different because it is influenced by the Namuci legend : *devāś vā asurāś cāspardhanta / sa vṛtra indram abravīt tvaṃ devānāṃ śreṣṭho 'sy aham asurāṇāṃ saṃ śaknavāva mā nāv nyo 'nyaṃ vadhīd iti tau vai samām etam anabhidrohāya / te devā vṛtram amanyantāyaṃ vāvedaṃ bhaviṣyatīti / ta indra aicchan / hanāmemam iti / so 'bravīt saṃdhā vai me saṃhitānabhidrohāyeti / tam agnir abravīd aham eva tvetaḥ pāsyāmīti pṛthivyā aham antarikṣād iti varuṇo 'haṃ diva iti rudras tato vai devā vṛtram aghnan...*

248. Cf. also I.6.4.12 : *vārtraghnaṃ vai paurṇamāsam / indro hy etena vṛtram ahan...*;VI.2.2.19.

249. Vol. I, pp. 91-92.

250. On this see Caland (*Festschrift für Jacobi*, pp. 240-41) who sees in this late Vṛtra the form of Rāhu who swallows the sun and the moon and who was, of course, not identical with Vṛtra originally.

251. After Agni and Soma have been won over, Indra raises the thunderbolt. *te abrūtāṃ dyāvāpṛthivī mā pra hār āvayor vai śrita iti / te abrūtām / varaṃ vṛṇāvahai nakṣatravihitāham asānīty asāv abravīt* etc. *sa ābhyām eva prasūta indro vṛtram ahan.* TBr I.7. 6.6 : *sa* [*indra*] *āvinne dyāvāpṛthivī dhṛtavrate iti dyāvāpṛthivī upādhāvat / sa ābhyām eva prasūta indro vṛtrāya vajraṃ prāharat.*

252. E.g. in MS I.10.5 (145.19) Sarasvatī and Pūṣan are mentioned after Agni and Soma; ŚBr II.5.4.

253. Macdonell, pp. 39-40.

254. TS II.4.12 : *tasmai tvaṣṭā vajram asiñcat tapo vai sa vajra āsīt / tam udyantuṃ nāśaknod atha vai tarhi viṣṇur anyā devatāsīt / so 'bravīd viṣṇav ehīdam ā hariṣyāvo yenāyam idam iti / sa viṣṇus tredhātmānaṃ vi ny adhatta pṛthivyāṃ tṛtīyam antarikṣe tṛtīyaṃ divi tṛtīyam abhiparyāvartād dhy abibhed / yat pṛthivyāṃ tṛtīyam āsīt tenendro vajram ud ayacchat viṣṇvanuṣṭhitaḥ / so 'bravīn mā me pra hār asti vā idaṃ mayi vīryaṃ tat te pra dāsyāmīti / tad asmai prāyacchat / tat praty agṛhṇād adhā meti tad viṣṇave 'ti prāyacchat / tat viṣṇuḥ praty agṛhṇād asmāsv indra indriyaṃ dadhātv iti*; this is repeated for the second and third time with *antarikṣa* and *dyauḥ*, whereupon Vṛtra makes the promise of serving as Indra's food (see n. 247 above). Likewise in MS II.4.2 (40 ff.), but not in ŚBr I.6.3.

255. ŚBr V.5.5.1 ff., see n. 247 above. According to TS VI.5.1.1 for the first and second time Vṛtra gives the Ukthya to Indra. As Indra raises the thunderbolt for the third time Viṣṇu steps behind him (quite

without any motive) and says, *jahi.* Now Indra receives the Ukthya for the third time.

256. TS VI.2.4 : *yajño devebhyo nilāyata viṣṇū rūpaṃ kṛtvā sa pṛthivīṃ prāviśat / taṃ devā hastānt saṃrabhyaicchan / tam indra uparyupary aty akrāmat / so 'bravīt / ko māyam uparyupary aty akramīd iti / ahaṃ durge hanteti / atha kas tvam iti / ahaṃ durgād āharteti / so 'bravīt / durge vai hantāvocathā varāho'yaṃ vāmamoṣaḥ saptānāṃ girīṇāṃ parastād vittaṃ vedyam asurāṇāṃ bibharti taṃ jahi yadi durge hantāsīti / sa darbhapuñjīlam udvṛhya sapta girīn bhittvā tam ahan / so 'bravīt/ durgād vā āhartāvocathā etam āhareti/ tam ebhyo yajña eva yajñam āharat*...MS III.8.3 (95.1 ff.) :...*ayaṃ varāha āmukha ekaviṃśatyāḥ purāṃ pāre 'śmamayīnāṃ tasminu asurāṇāṃ vasu vāmanantas... Kāṭhaka* XXV.2 (see Weber on TS, *loc. cit.*)

257. TS II.4.12; MS II.4.2; TMBr XX.15.6.

258. ŚBr II.5.3.20 : *maruto ha vai krīḍino vṛtraṃ haniṣyantam indram āgataṃ tam abhitaḥ paricikrīḍur mahayantaḥ.*

259. From the ṚV, cf. I.30.16; 52.9,15 etc. Macdonell, pp. 80-81.

TS VI.5.5.1 : *indro marudbhiḥ sāṃvidyena mādhyandine savane vṛtram ahan.* MS I.10.14 ((153 ff.): *prajāḥ sṛṣṭvāṃha 'vayajya so 'kāmayata vṛtraṃ hanyām iti sa etābhir devatābhiḥ sayug bhūtvā marudbhir viśāgninānīkenopaplāyata / sa vṛtram etya vṛtraṃ dṛṣṭvoruskambhagṛhīto 'nabhidhṛṣṇuvann atiṣṭhat / tam maruto 'dhyaiyanta / te tyaiṣaṃs, tasya yadā marmāgacchann athāceṣṭat / saṃ vā enaṃ tad atapan...indro vai vṛtrāya vajram udyamaṃ nāśaknot sa etaṃ marudbhyo bhāgaṃ niravapat taṃ vīryāya samatapan... devā vai vṛtrasya marma nāvindaṃs taṃ marutaḥ kṣurapavinā vyayuḥ*...16 : These reflections lead here, as in other texts, to the Cāturmāsyas, the third of which, the Sākamedhāḥ with its "great sacrifice" is specially associated with the slaying of Vṛtra. ŚBr II.5.3.1; 4.1; 6.1.1; 2.1. The time of the year when this sacrifice was originally performed is yet to be discussed.

260. III.16.1 : *indraṃ vai vṛtraṃ jaghnivāṃsaṃ nāstṛteti manyamānāḥ sarvā devatā ajahus taṃ maruta eva svāpayo nājahuḥ /*

261. *devā vai vṛtraṃ hataṃ na vyajānaṃs taṃ marutaḥ krīḍayo 'dhyakrīḍaṃs tasmāt krīḍayaḥ /*

262. *indro vṛtraṃ hatvā parāṃ parāvatam agacchad aparādham iti manyamānaḥ / so 'bravīt ka idaṃ vediṣyatīti / te 'bruvan maruto varaṃ vṛṇāmahai atha vayaṃ vedāma / asmabhyam eva prathamaṃ havir nirupyātā iti / ta enam adhy akrīḍan /*

263. MS IV.5.1 : *apo vai vṛtraḥ paryaśayat / tato yā aty amucyanta tā jīvā yajñiyāḥ / girir vai vṛtro / yā atimumucānā dhāvanti tā jīvā yajñiyāḥ / yad vahantīnāṃ gṛhṇāti yā eva jīvā yajñiyās tāsām eva gṛhṇāti.* Cf. also ŚBr III.9.4.2.

264. MS III.6.3: *indro vai vṛtram apsv adhy ahaṃs tāsāṃ yad yajñiyaṃ medhyam āsīt tad udakrāmat tā imā oṣadhayo 'bhavan*...TS VI.1.1.6 : *indro vṛtram ahant so 'po 'bhy amriyata tāsāṃ yan medhyaṃ yajñiyaṃ sadevam āsīt tad apod akrāmat te darbhā abhavan...*

265. Vṛtra's death is *amedhya* in TS III.3.7.3.

266. *indro vai vṛtraṃ hatvā taṃ śave mānave prauhat / somo vai vṛtra udaraṃ śavo mānavas tasmād udare somaḥ pīyate /*

267. TS VI.5.9.1 : *indro vṛtram ahan tasya śīrṣakapālam ud aubjat sa droṇakalaśo 'bhavat tasmāt somaḥ sam asravat sa hāriyojano 'bhavat.* MS IV.7.4 (97.18).

268. TS VI.1.1.5 : *indro vṛtram ahan tasya kanīnikā parāpatat tad āñjanam abhavat.* MS III.6.3 (62.9)...*parāpatat sā trikakubham agacchat tad āñjanaṃ traikakubham āṅkte.* ŚBr III.1.3.12 : *yatra vā indro vṛtram ahaṃs tasya yad akṣy āsīt taṃ giriṃ trikakudamakarot tad yatraikakakudaṃ bhavati cakṣusy evaitac cakṣur dadhāti* etc.

269. ŚBr I.1.3.4 : *tam indro jaghāna sa hataḥ pūtiḥ sarvata evāpo 'bhiprasusrāva sarvata iva hy ayaṃ samudras tasmād u haikā āpo bībhatsāṃ cakrire tā uparyupary atipupruvire ta ime darbhās tā haitā anāpūyitā āpaḥ / asti vā itarāsu saṃsṛṣṭam iva yad enā vṛtraḥ pūtir abhiprāsravat...*; VII.2.3.2 : *yā vai vṛtrād bībhatsamānā āpo dhanva dṛbhantya udāyaṃs te darbhā abhavan.* MS III.6.3 (63.2); TS VI.1.1.7 are slightly different.

270. TBr III.2.9.2 : *tasya* [*vṛtrasya*] *lohitaṃ pṛthivīm anu vyadhāvat sāmedhyābhavat.* (I prefer to read *sāmedhyā* "impure for sacrifice" for *sāme*).

271. MS IV.4.7 (58.16 ff.) : *indro vai vṛtram ahaṃs tasyeme rūpāṇy upaitāṃ citrāṇīyaṃ nakṣatrāṇy asau / nakṣatrāṇāṃ vā avakāśe puṇḍarīkaṃ jāyate / kṣatrasya vā etad rūpam / kṣatrasyaiva rūpaṃ pratimuñcate / dvādaśa-puṇḍarīkā bhavanti / dvādaśa māsāḥ saṃvatsaraḥ...*TMBr XVIII.9.6. Cf. Vṛtra *kāñcanamālyadhārin* in MBh III.101.15, to be cited below.

272. Cf. ṚV I.32.14 : *áher yātā́raṃ kám apaśya indra hṛdi yát te jaghnúṣo bhī́r ágacchat / náva ca yán navatíṃ ca srávantīḥ śyenó ná bhīto átaro rájāṁsi //*

273. Cf. on this, pp. 92-93, 137 above, and Macdonell, p. 60.

274. Cf. Holtzmann, "Indra nach den Vorstellungen des Mahābhārata," ZDMG, XXXII, p. 305 ff.

275. Ed. Bombay, p. 112 a : *āsasāda tato vṛtraṃ sthitam āvṛtya rodasī.*

276. Ibid., p. 8 a : *so 'vardhata divaṃ stabdhvā sūryavaiśvānaropamaḥ*; XII.281.18 : *tato 'ntarikṣam āvṛtya.*

277. V.10.40 : *nihate tu tato vṛtre diśo vitimirābhavan /*
pravavau sa śivo vāyuḥ prajāś ca jahṛṣus tathā //

278. A winter motif ?

279. Cf. the remarks of L. Feer, "Vritra et Namoutchi dans le Mahābhārata," *Revue de l'histoire des religions*, XIV, p. 291 ff.

280. Cf. Kālidāsa's *Kumārasaṃbhava.*

281. This motif is also old, for in the TMBr the lotus garland is drawn into association with Vṛtra (see p. 138 above).

282. Perhaps TS II.1.4.5 (see pp. 134-135 above): *taṃ vṛtro hataḥ ṣoḍaśabhir bhogair asināt,* is remotely connected with this.

283. *Bhāgavata Purāṇa* VI.12 relates how Vṛtra opens his mouth wide as though he wishes to swallow the three worlds. He swallows Indra but the latter cuts open Vṛtra's stomach and comes out, and then cuts off the head

of Vṛtra. In this episode we find again a motif which is well known to the Brāhmaṇas, viz., that Vṛtra grows each day as much as the range of an arrow (*Bhāgavata Purāṇa* VI.9.13 : *viṣvag vivardhamānaṃ tam iṣumātraṃ dinedine dagdhaśailapratīkāśaṃ sandhyābhrānīkavarcasam*). Besides Holtzmann, cf. Feer, *loc. cit.*, p. 298.

284. As in the form of the compact, this is also a mix-up with the Namuci legend; cf. Feer, *loc. cit.*, p. 297.

285. Ed. Bombay, XII.280.57 (p. 149 a).

286. Cf. XII.283.60 : *dāritaś ca vajreṇa mahāyogī mahāsuraḥ jagāma paramaṃ sthānaṃ viṣṇor amitatejasaḥ.*

287. Cf. also XII.281.1 : *aho dharmiṣṭhatā tāta vṛtrasyāmitatejasaḥ / yasya vijñānam atulaṃ viṣṇor bhaktiś ca tādṛśī //*

288. Boas, Verhandlungen der Berliner Gesellschaft für Anthropologie, *Zeitschrift für Ethnologie*, XXVII, p. 512.

289. "Der Ursprung und das Wandern der Völker geographisch betrachtet", SBKSGW, L, 1898, p. 1 ff.

290. Cf. however, *vatrabhū*, Minayeff, *Grammaire Palie*, § 26; Kuhn, *Beiträge zur Pali Grammatik*, p. 50.

291. *Saṃyuttanikāya*, p. 237 : *abhirūpataro dassanīyataro pāsādikataro.*

292. Ibid., I. 227.

293. Ibid., I.223, 225 ff.

294. VIII.12.17 : *yád vā śakra parāváti samudré ádhi mándase;* cf. VIII. 13.15 also. Nevertheless, in the ṚV, the word is attributed, though not exclusively, still predominantly, to Indra (cf. Grassmann, *Wörterbuch zuṃ Ṛgveda*, s.v.)

295. *Saṃyuttanikāya*, I, p. 229 (XI.2.2)

296. Childers, *Pali Dictionary*, s.v.

297. From this we can draw the appropriate conclusion about the value of such passages like *Assalāyana Sutta*, p. 19 and *Milindapañho*, pp. 123-124 for the explanation of the word *gandharva.*

298. Cf. Bloch, "Buddha worshipped by Indra," PASB, 1898, p. 186 ff. *Sakkapañhasutta* (GIL, II, pp. 32, 41).

299. *Mahāvastu* I.20.4.

300. Ibid., I.22.13.

301. *Mahāparinibbāna Sutta* VI; JRAS, NS, VIII, p. 252. Cf. Rhys Davids, *Buddhist Birth Stories*, XVII, 1.

302. Burgess (*Archaeological Survey of Western India*, 5, 46) : Indra "who plays as great a role in the Jaina as in Bauddha mythological literature, being an interested listener to the teaching of the Jina."

303. Alabaster, *The Wheel of the Law*, p. 171.

304. *Mythologie des Buddhismus*, p. 179.

305. Cf. also I. J. Schmidt, *Forschungen im Gebiete...der Völker Mittelasiens*, St. Petersburg 1824, pp. 176, 237. A silver plate inscription found near Islamabad "is especially noteworthy because it supports the identity of Indra and Chormusda inasmuch as it lets Brahman and Indra perform the same services at the time of the Buddha's birth, the services

which according to the Mangolian texts the Prince of Esrün and Chormusda perform at that time." Robertson, *The Káfirs of the Hindu-Kush*, p. 376 ff., mentions among the gods of the Káfir religions *Imrá* as the chief god. In what is related about him, I find no positive traits which are similar to those of Indra. Besides *Imrá*, a god *Inthr* is mentioned among others without any further information. (Incidentally, we may add that in the context of a sacrifice for *Imrá* the story is narrated of the goat which digs out the sacrificial knife, ibid., p. 385).

306. Oldenberg, RdV, p. 143.

307. *Raghuvaṃśa* IV.3 and Mallinātha on it; *Kumārasaṃbhava* VII.84 : *māhendram ambhaḥ prathamam.*

308. MBh I.25.1 ff. For further material on Indra in the MBh, see Holtzmann, ZDMG, XXXII, p. 315.

309. Cf. also Böhtlingk, *Indische Sprüche*, 2nd ed., 2228.

310. This is followed by Kṛṣṇa's objection against the festival and a dispute between Kṛṣṇa and Indra.

311. II.15=LXX, ed. Bombay, vol. II, 17.

312. According to Wilson, *Viṣṇupurāṇa*, tr., p. 523, no more sacrifices are made to Indra now. The only festival in the Hindu Calendar, the *Śakradhvajotthāna*, is performed on the 12th or 13th of the Bhādrapada, i.e., exactly in the middle of the rainy season. Indra is now subordinated to Kṛṣṇa.

313. That his name is used in exorcisms and that too with formulas which are transferred from mythology to magic (Winternitz, *Sarpabali*, p. 52) might be typical in this case.

314. Cf. also I.4.22.e : *yā divyā vṛṣṭis tayā* [*āditya*] *tvā śriṇāmi.*

315. In my view, ṚV VII.47.4 : *yā́ḥ sū́ryo raśmíbhir ātatā́na* belongs directly here.

316. *Viṣṇupurāṇa* III.5.19 (cf. Böhtlingk, *Sanskrit Chrestomathie*, 2nd ed., p. 102).

317. Cf. also Simon, *Beiträge zur Kenntnis der vedischen Schulen*, Kiel 1889, p. 67. *Rāmāyaṇa* IV.28.3 (ed. NSP) : *navamāsadhṛtaṃ garbhaṃ bhāskarasya gabhastibhiḥ / pītvā rasaṃ samudrāṇāṃ dyauḥ prasūte rasāyanam//*

318. Vol I, p. 487 ff.; Bloomfield, JAOS, XV, p. 143 ff.; Oldenberg, NGGW, 1893, p. 342 ff.; Geldner, VSt, III, p. 164 ff. According to Max Müller, *Academy*, XLII, 1892, p. 364, "waning of the moon;" according to Weber, *Rājasūya*, p. 102, n. 4, "obviously the tenacious morning fog which does not let go." That the name contains a negative was already assumed by Pāṇini (VI.3.75) without substantiation. According to Halévy, *Considér. crit.*, p. 38, Namuci=Namik=Namitch, the form which the Turkish immigrants gave to Namī (=Raṅhā).

319. Bergaigne, II. p. 357 f.; Bloomfield, *loc. cit.*, p. 156.

320. V.30.7 : *dāsásya námuceḥ śíro yád ávartayaḥ*; 30.8; VI.20.6 : *śíro dāsásya námucer mathāyán.*

321. Vol. I, p. 326.

322. Vol. I, p. 469, n. 309.

323. *Kāśikā* III.2.81; VIII.4.9 : *kaṣāyapāyiṇo gāndhārāḥ, kṣīrapāyiṇa uśīnarāḥ sauvīrapāyiṇo bāhlīkāḥ*; cf. *Padamañjarī* on this.

324. I cannot infer from the ṚV that already according to its tradition Indra fell ill after consuming Soma. There Indra drinks the Surā at Namuci's place, falls ill due to it and is cured by Sarasvatī. This, it seems, is the only connection in the ṚV and it differs from the legends of the Brāhmaṇas. It is doubtful whether the verb *vi-pā* has such a special sense as Oldenberg wishes.

325. *Ritualliteratur*, p. 159.

326. *nirastaṃ namuceḥ śiraḥ* TS I.8.14.e; TBr I.7.8.2; ŚBr V.4.1.9; MS IV.4.4 (54.5); Weber, *Rājasūya*, p. 48. The comm. on TS says : *lohitāyasaṃ tāmraṃ pūrvaṃ phenena pātitaṃ yan namuceḥ śiras tad idaṃ tāmrarūpaṃ san nirastaṃ parityaktam.* Cf. Caland, *Altindischer Ahnenkult*, p. 25.

327. Vol. I, pp. 322-323. The MS, *loc. cit.*, mentions a *paṇḍaga*.

328. MS IV.3.4 (43.7) (cf. MBh IX.43.34 ff.) : *indro vai namuciṃ nālabhata sa raśmīn kulāyaṃ kṛtvānvārohad amum ādityam / taṃ vā anvamantrayata / sakhāyā asāveti / so 'bravīt / nāhaṃ haniṣyāmīti / so 'bravīt / saṃdhāṃ te saṃdadhai yathā tvā na divā hanāni na naktaṃ na śuṣkeṇa nārdreṇeti tasya vā upodaye sūryasya nīhāraṃ saṃtatyāpāṃ phenena śiro 'cchinat / tad vā enam anvavartata mitradrug asīti.* TBr I.7.1.6 : *indro vṛtraṃ hatvāsurān parābhāvya namucim āsuraṃ nālabhata / ...so 'smād abhiśunataro 'bhavat / so 'bravīt / sandhāṃ saṃdadhāvahai / atha tvāvasrakṣyāmi / na mā śuṣkeṇa nārdreṇa hanaḥ na divā na naktam iti / sa etam apāṃ phenam asiñcat / na vā eṣa śuṣko nārdraḥ / vyuṣṭāsīt anuditaḥ sūryaḥ /...tasyaitasmiṃ loke apāṃ phenena śira udavartayat.* Cf. also TMBr XII.6.8. The ŚBr weaves various legends together. XII.7.1.1 : Indra kills Viśvarūpa and drinks the Soma by force. Strength and the Soma drink abandon him (1). Thereupon, it is narrated; 10 : *atha ha vai tarhi namucinaivāsureṇa saha cacāra sa aikṣata namucir apunar vā ayam abhūd dhantāsyendriyaṃ vīryaṃ somapītham annādyaṃ harāṇīti / tasyaitayaiva surayendriyaṃ vīryaṃ somapītham annādyam aharat / sa ha nyarṇaḥ śiśye taṃ devā upasaṃjagmire śreṣṭho vai no 'yam abhūt tam imaṃ pāpmāvidad dhantemaṃ bhiṣajyāmeti.* (Sautrāmaṇī) (2). 7.3.1 : *indrasyendriyam annasya rasaṃ somasya bhakṣaṃ surayāsuro namucir aharat / so 'śvinau ca sarasvatīṃ copādhāvac chepāno 'smi namucaye na tvā divā na naktaṃ hanāni na daṇḍena na dhanvanā na pṛthena na muṣṭinā na śuṣkeṇa nārdreṇātha ma idam ahārṣīd idaṃ ma ājihīrṣatheti.* 3 : *tāv aśvinau ca sarasvatī ca apāṃ phenaṃ vajram asiñcan...tenendro namucer āsurasya... śira udavāsayat* / (3). Cf. Mahīdhara on VS X.33 (Muir, OST, V, p. 94).

329. The proviso "neither in the day nor in the night" occurs elsewhere also. TMBr XVI.1.1 : *prajāpatir vā idam eka āsīn nāhar āsīn na rātrir āsīt.* Cf. the Ṣoḍaśin-ceremonies, n. 191, above.

330. JASB, 1889, p. 20 as "waterspout."

331. *The Golden Bough*, II, p. 361 : "...the foam of the sea is just such an object as a savage might choose to put his life in, because it occupies that sort of intermediate or nondescript position between earth and sky or sea in which primitive man sees safety. It is therefore not surprising that the

foam of the river should be the totem of a clan in India ..." Tilak, *Orion*, p. 122, puts forward quite a different point of view.

332. Comm.; *nadīphenapiṇḍa*.

333. Bloomfield, *loc. cit.*, pp. 157-58. Bloomfield thinks that "lead" is a substitute : "foam is too volatile; it does not preserve its character long enough to manipulate successfully in practice. Lead is soft, *mṛdu*..., and has much the same color as foam." I do not think that this assumption is necessary.

334. I.53.7 :... *námyā yád indra sákhyā parāváti*
nibarháyo námuciṃ nā́ma māyínam ||
VI.20.6 : *prā́van námīṃ sāpyáṃ saśantam*...

X.48.9 is obscure. According to TMBr XXV.10.17 Namī Sāpya is the king of Videha.

335. Windisch, *Māra und Buddha*, p. 185.

336. This was a mistake on the part of Tilak, *Orion*, p. 117 ff.

337. In VS XX.68 etc. Namuci and Vala are drawn into association (cf. n. 352 below).

338. *ucchánn uṣásaḥ sudínā ariprā́ urú jyótir vividur dī́dhyānāḥ* |
gávyaṃ cid ūrvám uśíjo ví vavrus téṣām ánu pradívaḥ sasrur ā́paḥ ||

Cf. the *vāśrā́ ā́paḥ* in AV IV.15.

339. *yā́ usríyā ápyā antár áśmano nír gā́ ákṛntad ójasā* |
abhí vrajáṃ tatniṣe gávyam áśvyam...

Quite rightly Oldenberg, RdV, p. 150, n. 1, attaches no value to this passage.

340. Of the passages listed by Grassmann, *Wörterbuch zum Rigveda*, at the most II.23.18 and 34.1 belong in this context.

341. Cf. III.31.4; 39.4,6 as parallels.

342. Sāyaṇa, who is quite responsible for introducing the "cloud-cows" into Vedic mythology in the first place, explains four times Vala also as cloud. The few times he gives an explanation—mostly he is content with describing Vala as Asura—he connects him with *parvata* (X.68.5,9) which is more acceptable than otherwise. (Yāska VI.2; Mahīdhara XX.68 also equate *vala* with *megha*).

343. *dṛ* I.62.4; X.138.1; *bhid* I.52.5; II.11.20; 15.8; 24.3; III.34.10; VIII.14.7; X.62.2; *ruj* III.45.2; IV.50.5; *vṛ+apa* I.11.5; II.14.3; *arvāk-nud* VIII.14.8.

344. Cf. *Veda-Chrestomathie*, s.v. *apadhí*.

345. Here in the sense of "wall."

346. Moreover, the following epithets belong to Vala : the obscure *jásu* X.58.6; *gomā́nt* I.11.5; *alātṛṇá* III.30.10. *phaligá* is an epithet of Vala in I.62.4; IV.50.5 and a "container" for water or some such object in VIII. 32.25; the word must have the sense of "stone" or "stone-like"; this is indicated by I.121.10: *tám adrivaḥ phaligám* (=*aśmānam* ?) *hetím asya*. I think the word belongs to some dialect and means the same as *sphaṭika*.

347. Aṅgiras according to Sāyaṇa.

348. Furthermore I.72.8 : *vidád gávyaṃ sarámā dṛḷhám ūrvám*; III.31.6;

V.29.12; 30.4; 45.1,7,8; VI.17.3,6; 32.2,3; 43.3; 65.5; VII.75.7; 76.4.5; 79.4; 90.4. Geldner, VSt, II, p. 274, translates *antár ádreḥ* or *antár áśman* correctly as "in the mountain" or "in the rock." But he is wrong when he asserts that hence there "cannot be" any reference to the "cowshed" in VI.17.6. On the one hand, exactly in this verse VI.17.6, of which Geldner cites only pāda d, it is said :

(c) *aúrṇor dúra usríyābhyo ví dṛḷháḥ*

(d) *úd ūrvā́d gā́ asṛjo áṅgirasvān* //

and on the other, in this group of sagas, cowshed and mountain-cave are one and the same thing (see Vol. I, p. 28). Cf. also VI.18.5: *hánn acyutacyud dasmeṣáyantam ṛṇóḥ púro ví dúro asya víśvāḥ* //

349. Compare VI.65.5 : *idā́ hi ta uṣo adrisāno gotrā́ gávām áṅgiraso gṛṇánti* / *vy àrkeṇa bibhidur bráhmaṇā ca satyā́ nṛṇā́m abhavad deváhūtiḥ* // with II.24.3 : *úd gā́ ājad ábhinad bráhmaṇā valám* /

350. *devā vai vale gāḥ paryapaśyaṃs tā yajñenaivepsaṃs tāḥ ṣaṣṭhenāhnāpnuvaṃs te prātaḥsavane nabhākena valam anabhayaṃs taṃ yad anabhayān aśrathayann evainaṃ tat* / *ta u tṛtīyasavane vajreṇa vālakhilyābhir vācaḥ kūṭenaikapadayā valaṃ virujya gā udājan* /

351. *indro valasya bilam apaurṇot sa ya uttamaḥ paśur āsīt taṃ pṛṣṭhaṃ prati saṃgṛhyodakkhidat* / *taṃ sahasraṃ paśavo 'nūdāyant* / *sa unnato 'bhavat* / *yaḥ paśukāmaḥ syāt sa etam aindram unnatam ālabheta.* MS II.5.3 (50.16). In spite of the commentary, I cite TMBr XIX.7.1 in this context: *asurāṇāṃ vai valas tamasā prāvṛto 'śmāpidhānaś cāsīt* / *tasmin gavyaṃ vasv antar āsīt* / *taṃ devā nāśaknuvan bhettum* / *te bṛhaspatim abruvann* / *imān na utsṛjeti* / *sa udbhidaiva valaṃ vy acyāvayad valabhidābhinat* / *tān utsedhenaivodasṛjat* ..."the cave of the Asuras was in darkness and was closed with a stone."

352. The verse, *sa bibheda valaṃ maghaṃ namucāv āsure sacā* (VS XX.68=MS III.11.4=TBr II.6.13) combines the Vala saga with that of Namuci.

353. Cf. e.g. X.76.6: *índro valáṃ rakṣitā́raṃ dúghānām*
kareṇéva ví cakartā rávena /
svédāñjibhir āśíram ícchamāno
árodayat paṇím ā́ gā́ amuṣṇāt //

68.6 : *yadā́ valásya píyato jásuṃ bhét*
bṛ́haspátir agnitápobhir arkaíḥ /
dadbhír ná jihvā́ párivistam ā́dad
āvír nidhī́ṃr ákṛṇod usríyāṇām //

9 : *bṛ́haspátir góvapuṣo valásya*
nír majjā́naṃ ná párvaṇo jabhāra //

10 : *himéva parṇā́ muṣitā́ vánāni*
bṛ́haspátinā kṛpayad való gā́ḥ /

354. VI.39.2: *rujád árugṇaṃ ví valásya sā́num*
paṇī́ṃr vácobhir abhí yodhad índraḥ// see also p. 152 above.

355. VIII.24.30 : *yát tvā pṛchā́d ījānáḥ kuhayā́ kuhayākṛte* /
eṣo ápaspṛto való gomatī́m áva tiṣṭhati //

356. Crooke, *The Tribes and Castes...*, III, p. 9.

357. Credit goes to Brunnhofer for having identified for the first time the Paṇis with the Parnians; likewise, as he himself has recognized, Abhyāvartin Pārthavaḥ really refers to a Parthian king. Unfortunately, since some of Brunnhofer's conclusions are far-fetched, his correct notions did not find any acceptance either. His identification of the Hariyūpīya with the Ariōb or Haliāb is comparatively one of the most reliable conclusions that have been put forward so far. But we should not, with Brunnhofer, think of the town Kalliopé in Parthia, but exclusively of the river Iryāb (Haliāb), one of the tributaries of the Kurum (cf. Spiegel, *Eranische Altertumskunde*, I, p. 13; Geiger, *Ostiranische Kultur im Altertum*, p. 85; Darmesteter, *Chants populaires*, CLXX : "situated at a quarter-days' march from Kābul"). At some distance from it flows the Djob (Zhob) (cf. Spiegel, *op. cit.*, p. 15) and the Gomal is its tributary. Perhaps the Yavyāvatī, mentioned in the next verses of the ṚV, is situated here. TMBr XXV.7.1 reports that on the banks of this stream a sacrifice was performed by Gaurivīti Śāktya, who was connected with Ṛṣabha Yājñatura, the king of the Śviknas. This latter one performed the Aśvamedha in a somewhat different form than was adopted by the Pāñcālas, Satvats etc. (ŚBr XII.8.3.7; XIII.5.4.15).

358. Against this Sten Konow remarks that for Indians autumn was the time for martial undertakings, the *vikramakāla*, and that one can say, unlike me, that "Indians would build fortification precisely in autumn." But here we are not dealing with the campaigns of Indians but of western peoples, with the "winter quarters." Even an Indian would not build fortifications just when he has begun an expedition.

359. VIII.18.6 : *tvám hí śáśvatīnām indra dártā púrām asi.* Cf. VIII. 17.4.

360. It is true that many customs of ancient Aryans might lie hidden in these sagas; but I think von Schroeder goes too far with his conclusions in his *Herakles.*

361. RdV, p. 155; ZDMG, XLIX, p. 175; LI, p. 272 ff.

362. I.112.14; 116.18; 119.4; 130.7,10 (plural); II.19.6; IV.26.3; 30.20; VI.16.5,9; 26.5; 31.4; 43.1; 47.22,23; 61.1; VII.18.25; IX.61.2.

363. Vol. I, p. 347.

364. Perhaps with the exception of the passage from the seventh book.

365. Foy, KZ, XXXIV, p. 242.

366. VI.20.1 : *dyaúr ná yá...abhí bhū́māryás*
tasthaú rayíḥ śávasā pṛtsú jánān /
tám naḥ......daddhí vṛtratúram /

X.47.4 : *dasyuhánam pūrbhidam...vṛ́ṣaṇam rayím dāḥ* //

Cf. also VI.49.15.

367. Divodāsa is not mentioned any more in books VIII and X.

368. *víśo dā́sīḥ* II.11.4; IV.28.4; VI.25.2.

369. *púro dā́sīḥ* IV.32.10. *púro dāsápatnīḥ* III.12.6. For other passages, see below the sections on the Dāsa kings Sambara, Varcin and Pipru.

370. Also I.131.4 : *vidúṣ ṭe asyá vīryàsya pūrávaḥ púro yád indra śā́radīr*

avā́tiraḥ; 174.2 : *dáno víśa indra mṛdhrávācaḥ saptá yát púraḥ śárma śā́radīr dárt* |

371. Thus Geldner, VSt, III, p. 125. who is misled by Sāyaṇa. Of course, in I.55.6 *sádanāni kṛtrímā* has already a mythological sense but this is not the original meaning.

372. GGA, 1894, p. 650, n. 1, where the numbers are given. For other differences, see Vol. I, p. 475, n. 57).

373. VI.22.10; 25.2; 33.3; 60.6; one instance in book VII, none in III.

374. Vol. I, pp. 345, 348.

375. II.14.6; IV.30.14, 15; VI.47.21; VII.99.5 where he is promoted to the status of an Asura.

376. II.12.11 : *yáḥ śámbaraṃ párvateṣu kṣiyántam*
catvāriṃśyā́ṃ śarády anvávindat |

377. I.51.5 : *pípror prā́rujaḥ púraḥ;* VI.20.7 : *ví pípror áhímāyasya dṛḷhā́ḥ púraḥ*; X.138.3.

378. IV.16.13; V.29.11; X.99.11; 138.3.

379. I.101.2; 103.8; II.14.5,6; VI.18.8.

380. Or does it refer here to the battles for the fountainheads and rivers?

381. Of the 8 passages in book VI, in four the Dāsas are stated to be opposed to the Aryans; in one passages Dāsa fortresses are mentioned, in two Dāsa Śambara (see n. 373, 386) and finally in VI.20.6 Dāsa Namuci : *śíro dāsásya námucer mathāyán.*

382. When V.30.9 states that Namuci made women into weapons, this can be taken literally. Cf. particularly pāda b : *stríyo hí dāsá ā́yudhāni cakre kíṃ mā karann abalā́ asya sénāḥ* |

383. II.20.7; also II.12.4 *dā́saṃ várṇam.* Cf. also *kṛṣṇágarbha* I.101.1. Because of the situation anticipated in book VI, I refer *kṛṣṇā́ jā́ḥ* in VI.47.21 to the Brāhūī-s (ZII, III, pp. 16-17).

384. Cf. especially II.11.2,4. It is worth noting that in II.24.2 Śambara becomes *śambarāṇi.* See my remarks in Vol. I, p. 474, n. 50

385. Differently Ludwig, *Die neuesten Arbeiten*, p. 77 ff.

386. IV.30.14,15; VI.26.5; 47.21.

387. VII.19.4 : *tváṃ ní dásyuṃ cúmuriṃ dhúniṃ cā́svāpayo dabhī́taye.* Both are opposed to Dabhīti to gain whose favour Indra puts them to sleep (II. 15.9; IV.30.21; VI.20.13; VII.19.4). Otherwise, proper names of the Dasyus are not frequent with the exception of Śuṣṇa and the equally mythical *dā́nu aurṇavābhá* in II.11.18.

388. V.14.4; II.20.8 (*ā́yasīḥ*); X.99.7; AV X.6.20.

389. VII.5.6 : *tváṃ dásyūṃr ókaso agna ājaḥ.*

390. I refer to Zimmer, AIL, p. 109 ff. Ludwig, *Nachrichten*, p. 32, was the first to draw attention to the historical aspect of the two names. Kauffmann, BGDSL, XVIII, p. 155 (cf. AISAK, IV, p. 115), equates *zussa* in Old High German *hagazussa* with Old Iranian, **dasyu* (?).

391. I.51.8; 103.3; II.11.18, 19; III.34.9; VI.18.3; VII.5.6; X.49.3.

292. Among the Dāsas, *avratá* is an epithet of Pipru only.

393. II.11.4; IV.28.4; VI.25.2 etc.

394. Yašt VIII.56, 61; Vedidād XIX.39.

395. Yašt XIX.68. Especially the subjugated countries : Darmesteter, *Ormazd et Ahriman*, p. 270 (§ 219).

396. See the quotations in Zimmer, AIL, p. 115.

397. IV.19.9 : *vamrī́bhiḥ putrám agrúvo adānáṃ nivéśanād á jabhartha* / compare this with 30.16 :...*putrám agrúvaḥ párāvṛktaṃ śatakratuḥ* / *uktheṣv índra ā́bhajat*. Cf. Ludwig, *Über die Anfänge*. pp. 11-12.

398. I.51.9 : *vṛddhásya cid várdhato dyā́m ínakṣata stávāno vamró vi jaghāna saṃdíhaḥ*. Cf. S. G. Oliphant, *John Hopkins University Circulars*, NS, 1906, No. 10, pp. 25-26 (1073-74).

399. The Vṛṣākapi hymn, X.86, demonstrates how many difficulties there arise with regard to the details. Neither Tilak's nor Oldenberg's nor Geldner's (VSt, II, p. 22ff.) explanation is satisfactory. None of these scholars paid attention to the position of this hymn in the Dvādaśāha where it is employed along with the Kuntāpa hymn and the Paṅkti verses (ŚŚS XII.6.13; 8.2; 13.1; ĀśvŚS VIII.3.4). As in the Aśvamedha so also in this sacrifice obscenities are part of the sacrificial repertoire (cf. the *āhanasyā* verses) and demonstrate their connection with the Indra cult, as they do in the Mahāvrata. Tilak thinks of a stellar myth. M. Lindenau's view (*Bhāsa-Studien*, p. 45) that the prototype of the Vidūṣaka existed already in the Vedic period and specifically in the monkey Vṛṣākapi in ṚV X.86 deserves great attention. This would support von Schroeder's hypothesis (*Mysterium und Mimus*, p. 304 ff.) who explains the hymn as a "procreation-mimicry." Cf. Charpentier, *Die Suparṇa Sage*, p. 100. For further bibliographical information see Oldenberg, *Ṛgveda*, II; RdV, 2nd ed., p. 167.

400. II.19.5 : *bhárad áṃśaṃ naítaśo daśasyán* //
VIII.6.38 : *ánu tvā ródasī ubhé cakráṃ ná varty étaśam* /
IX.16.1; 108.2 etc.

401. In the singular :
VII.63.2 : *úd v eti prasavītā́ jánānām*.../
samānáṃ cakráṃ paryāvívṛtsan
yád etaśó váhati dhūrṣú yuktáḥ //
66.14 : *yád īṃ āśúr váhati devá étaśaḥ*
víśvasmai cákṣase áram //

VIII.1.11 etc. Cf. also TS V.6.4 : *sajū́ḥ sū́rya etaśena;* VS XII.74 : *sajū́ḥ sū́ra étaśena*.

In the plural : X.37.3 : *yád etaśébhiḥ patarai rathar yási*; 49.7 (cf. Foy, KZ, XXXIV, p. 237); VII.62.2.

402. Read *ī ṣaṇat* and cf. n. 405 below.

403. Oldenberg, RdV, 2nd ed., p. 448, n. 5. Compare this with the mention of the *mā́dhyaṃdina sávana* in v. 3. Since the midday pressing and the middle of the year correspond with one another, it is not necessary to infer from v. 3 that the second verse refers merely to the midday.

404. Sāyaṇa says : *devānām api tiras tirohitaṃ tair api kva gata iti durvijñātaṃ vaśaṃ kāntam*, but this is an explanation to be arrived at through

round-about ways only. Grassmann and Ludwig find in IV.30.5 an allusion to Indra's fight with the gods :

yátra devā̃ṅ ṛghāyató víśvā̃ṅ áyudhya éka it |
tvám indra vanū́ṃr áhan ||

405. In IF, XLII, Reviews p. 26 (Review of Geldner's *Der Rigveda*), I have attempted an explanation of verse IV.17.14, where I read *ī ṣaṇat* for *iṣaṇat* : "the sun's horse runs too fast; it endangers the sun's chariot and is brought to a halt (summer solstice)." Its counterpart would be 30.6 where Indra helps Etaśa (at the time of the winter solstice).

406. Bergaigne himself translates : "Indra turns, hind part foremost, the Harits..." (II, p. 342) and understands the verse as referring to the bringing back of the sun during the night from the west to the east.

407. Cf. also *Bhāgavata Purāṇa*, V. 21.

408. Cf. also Speyer, *Vedische und Sanskrit Syntax* (Grundriss), 81 b.

409. Delbrück is kind enough to inform me that he knows of no example according to which the locative could have the sense of the ablative in the case of *pū́rva*, *úpara* etc.

410. *kiṃ prābhaviṣyad aruṇas tamasāṃ vadhāya*
taṃ cet sahasrakiraṇo dhuri nākariṣyat |

411. *yāvat pratāpanidhir ākramate na bhānur*
ahnāya tāvad aruṇena tamo nirastam |

412. *Bhāgavata Purāṇa* V.21.16 :
purastāt savitur aruṇaḥ paścāc ca niyuktaḥ sautye karmaṇi kilāste |

413. Cf. v. 53 : *muñcan raśmīn dinādau dināgamasamaye saṃharaṃś ca svatantraḥ*; v. 52 : *yaḥ kāṣṭhādīpano 'gre jaḍita iva bhṛśaṃ sevate pṛṣṭhato 'rkam* etc.

414. In one passage it is said that Indra makes the name of a Dāsa for the sun in his own dwelling (V.33.4 : *tatakṣé sū́ryāya cid ókasi své vṛ́ṣā samátsu dāsásya nā́ma cit*). I think the explanation of the verse must be in conformity with the viewpoints mentioned above. The sun can receive the name of a Dāsa only when, as the saga in the MBh goes, he destroys the worlds through his scorching heat; not only in India but in other tropical countries also the sun has acquired the name of an enemy. In MBh, *Karṇaparvan*, 87.58 ff., Indra and later the gods take Arjuna's side, Sūrya and afterwards the Asuras take the side of Karṇa.

415. Geldner, VSt, II, p. 36 : "the decisive turn around the enemy's chariot, cutting and overtaking the same..."

416. I see no reason to change *páritakmyā yā́ṅ* into *páritakmyāyām* as Pischel (VSt, I, p. 82) proposes (cf. AV III.10.4 : *iyám evá sā́ yā́ prathamā́ vyaúcchat*).

417. X.62.2 : *parivatsaré*, see Vol. I, p. 23.

418. I cannot say for sure what the words *bhárac cakrám étaśaḥ sáṃ riṇāti* in V.31.11 mean. But what Bergaigne, II, p. 342, says is improbable : "Etaśa appears, in his capacity of a nocturnal horse, the opposite of the Harits, although they ... also draw sometimes the sun's chariot from the west to the east." The parallel passage I.121.13 :

tváṃ sū́ro harito rāmayo nṝ́n
bhárac cakrám étaśo nā́yám indra |

does not help any further. Geldner (VSt, II, p. 162) correctly translates pāda a as "you brought to a halt." But *bhárat* in b would perhaps mean only "to take, to snatch away" with the addition *sū́rye paspṛdhānáḥ*. Cf. II.20.6 : *áva...śíro bharad dāsásya*; moreover, *bhar* is used for pulling the cart ("for carrying the yoke")—I.100.16 : *vṛ́ṣaṇvantaṃ bíbhartī dhūrṣú rátham*; X.94.6 : *sākáṃ yuktā́ vṛ́ṣaṇo bíbhrato dhúraḥ*. The word does not seem to be an expression from the terminology of chariot-combat. I do not find it in *Rāmāyaṇa* VI.104.17 ff. where the requisite qualities of a good charioteer are enumerated.

419. *Epigraphia Indica*, II, pp. 22, 364, 365 refer to a Kautsa who studies the VS in the Mādhyaṃdina recension. In ibid., III, p. 342, a Kaucca (Kautsa) is mentioned who has the Āṅgirasa-Āmbarīṣa-Yauvanāśvapravara and studies the Kauthumaśākhā of the SV. Cf. also ibid., V, 100.

420. ĀpŚS X.20.12 : *kautsād rājānaṃ krīṇīyād anyasmād vā brāhmaṇād ity uktvāhāpy abrāhmaṇād iti.*

421. VII.6.3.4 (cf. Vol. I, p. 418, n. 129). On the connection between the Kaśyapas and the "tortoise" see Charpentier, *Die Suparṇa Sage*, p. 322.

422. ĀpŚS XIII.7.5.

423. XIV.6.8 : *upagur vai sauśravasaḥ kutsasyauravasya purohita āsīt | sa kutsaḥ paryaśapad ya indraṃ yajātā iti | sa indraḥ suśravasam upetyābravīd yajasva māśanayāmi vā iti | tam ayajata | sa indraḥ puroḍāśahastaḥ kutsam upetyābravīd ayakṣata mā kva te pariśaptam abhūd iti | kas tvāyaṣṭeti |suśravā iti | sa kutsa aurava upāgoḥ sauśravasasyodgāyata audumbaryā śiro 'cchinat | sa suśravā indram abravīt | tvattanāt vai medam īdṛg upāgād iti.* See ISt, X, p. 32.

424. GGS III.10.6.

425. Weber, *Die Handschriftenverzeichnisse der königlichen Bibliothek zu Berlin*; *Verzeichnis der Sanskrit Handschriften*, II, p. 22.

426. Cf. also ĀśvŚS I.4.6; VII.1.19; LŚS X.2.9 etc.

427. II, p. 347 : "The identity of Kutsa with Agni or Soma, already suggested by his character as a sacrificer and as a mythical ancestor, appears to have been moreover confirmed by certain direct arguments...Kutsa may moreover represent also the other celestial form of Agni or Soma, that is to say, the sun." It is not the question of Soma, Agni or the sun, but of a mythical or real chief of a tribe who was elevated to a semi-divine status and whom we cannot distinguish from his gotra.

428. Cf. ṚV V. 40. Lanman, *Festgruss für Roth*, p. 187.

429. Namely the Hāleyas, Vāleyas, Kaudreyas etc. KŚS X.2.21. In the *Nāgānanda* an Ātreya plays the role of the Vidūṣaka.

430. Cf. ŚBr IV.3.4.21 and Eggeling on the same. The Brāhmaṇa, however, connects the gift of gold not with this exploit but in general with the dispelling of "the darkness of the Asuras who broke into the sacrificial

place." Ludwig, *Über die Erwähnung von Sonnenfinsternissen* pp. 7-8. See ABr VIII.22 where the Purohita is an Ātreya.

431. I.51.6; 63.3; II.19.6; (V.31.7); VII.19.2; X.49.3; 99.9. What is striking is that even in those hymns which are traditionally ascribed to Kutsa himself (I.94-98; 101-115; IX.45-58,97; X.105) Śuṣṇa is mentioned rather perfunctorily (I.101.2; 103.8).

432. I.121.9,10; 175.4; IV.16.12; 30.3; V.29.9,10; VI.20.5; 31.3.

433. I.33.12 : *ny àvidhyad ilībíśasya dṛḷhā́*
ví·śṛṅgínam abhinac chúṣṇam índraḥ |
51.11 : *ugró yayíṃ nír apáḥ srótasāsṛjat*
ví śúṣṇasya dṛṁhitā́ airayat púraḥ |
IV.30.13 : *utá śúṣṇasya dhṛṣṇuyā́...* | *púro yád asya sampiṇák* ||
VIII.1.28 : *tvā́ṃ púraṃ cariṣṇvàṃ vadhaiḥ śúṣṇasya sáṃ piṇak* |

(Is *púr cariṣṇū́* a "mobile fortress," i.e., a sort of war-chariot ?)

434. I.11.7 : *bhūtānāṃ śoṣaṇahetum* (=*piprum*); 33.12 : *jagataḥ śoṣakaṃ vṛtram*; 56.3 : *sarvasya śoṣakam asuram*; 63.3 : *śoṣayitāram;* 54.5 : *rasānāṃ śoṣayitur ādityasyāpi* etc. (Cf. Yāska V.16), but also I.121.10 : *tamasas tamorūpasya śuṣṇasyāsurasya...phaligaṃ megharūpeṇāvṛṇvantam.*

435. II.19.6; IV.16.12; VI.31.3; VII.19.2.

436. I.103.8 : Śuṣṇa, Pipru, Kuyava. VII.19.2 : *dā́saṃ yác chúṣṇaṃ kúyavam* is, according to Sāyaṇa, *śúṣṇaṃ ca kúyavaṃ ca.* I.104.3 mentions the two wives of Kuyava who bathe in milk and about whom it is wished that they drown in the stream of the Siphā.

437. In the fifth book, in the two passages where the word *vṛtra* occurs (37.4; 42.5) it is an appellative. Of course *vṛtrahan* occurs more often (29.7; 35.6; 38.4; 40.1,4; 86.3) but the saga of Vṛtra is unknown to this maṇḍala. Here Vṛtra's place is occupied by Śuṣṇa who, at least in V.32, is described just as Vṛtra is usually described and is even killed *vajreṇa* by Indra. Whether it was an original version or a late interpolation cannot be determined at the present state of our research. But by itself the Śuṣṇa saga in V.32 looks like a duplicate of the Vṛtra myth of other families; but this does not mean that therefore Vṛtra and Śuṣṇa must be interpreted as identical. The Atris and Kutsas glorify just the enemy of Śuṣṇa in Indra and not the Vṛtra-slayer. To this can be added III.30.8 where Śuṣṇa is connected with the Aṅgiras saga and perhaps represents Vala. We may also note that in I.174.2 Indra hands over Vṛtra *yū́ne purukútsāya* just as he hands over Śuṣṇa *yū́ne kútsāya* in I.63.3. On this point the tradition seems to be confused. Oldenberg, NGGW, 1915, p. 373; RdV; 2nd ed., p. 93, n. 1, refutes what I have said here. But the only passage which describes the battle in detail calls the dragon *śuṣṇa* and not Vṛtra and attributes to him moreover epithets like *dānavá, mṛgá* which suggest the traces of a special Śuṣṇa mythology. In other passages the Ahi (without name) is spoken of in general terms. Wherever the word *vṛtra* occurs in this maṇḍala it is an appellative. The maṇḍala is familiar already with the battle against the dragon (who is however called *śuṣṇa*) but not with the saga of Vṛtra.

In V.32.3 Śuṣṇa is styled a *mahā́n mṛgá*. (In I.33.12 he is *śṛṅgín*). Apart from in this verse, the demoniacal gazelle appears also in 29.4; 34.2 of the same book but rarely elsewhere (I.80.7 *māyín* and VIII.93.14, besides *mṛ́gaya* twice). As I stated already in WZKM, XIII, p. 316 ff., a direct line can be drawn here from the Veda to the sorcerer Mārīca of the *Rāmāyaṇa* who transforms himself into a gazelle.

438. We find the same terminology in I.130.9 :

sū́raś cakrám prá vṛhaj jātá ójasā
prapitvé vā́cam aruṇó muṣāyati
īśāná ā́ muṣāyati | uśánā yát...

Here *aruṇó* can denote Indra but also the charioteer Aruṇa; the uncertainty about the word *vā́cam* next to it does not permit any conclusion.

439. I.121.10 *purā́ yát sū́ras támaso ápītes*
tám adrivaḥ phaligáṃ hetím asya |
śúṣṇasya cit párihitaṃ yád ójo
divás pári súgrathitaṃ tád ā́daḥ ||

440. Oldenberg, RdV, p. 160, n. 2 (cf. Sāyaṇa : *tamorūpasya śuṣṇasya*, n. 434 above).

441. It may not be necessary to combine IV.16.12 (*prapitvé áhnaḥ*) and IV.28.2,3 (*purā́ madhyáṃdināt*). These may be dealing with events of different nature belonging to different times. In IV.16.12 it is Indra-Kutsa who are active and in the latter passage it is Indra-Indu. As it happens often in the Kutsa tradition, the first verse has *prá+vṛh*, whereas the second has *ni+khid*. But it seems to me that Bloomfield's explanation of the expression *prapitvé* (JAOS, XVI, p. 24 ff.) as "at the morning pressure of the day" is appropriate and that therefore no real difficulties do arise when the two passages are combined. Neisser, WB, p. 48 : *prapitváṃ yan=prātaḥsavanam*.

442. The interpretation of *kutsya*, as far as I can see, is always off the mark. Kutsa does not have a weapon or some similar object. It is Indra who wields a weapon while a Ṛṣi would possess a mantra or a Sāman of his own.

443. I leave *smadibha* aside which one can treat with Baunack as an adjective ("having followers"). Luśa is Kutsa's rival in sacrifice. See TMBr IX.2.22 and Hans Oertel, JAOS, XVIII, p. 31. Indra goes to Kutsa who holds him by the testicles. The saga is an old one and occurs, as is well known, in ṚV X.38.5.

444. KŚS, XXXV, p. 485 ff.

445. I.53.9 : *tvám etā́ñ janarā́jño dvír dáśa*
abandhúnā suśrávasopajagmúṣaḥ |
ṣaṣṭíṃ sahásrā navatíṃ náva śrutó
ní cakréṇa ráthyā duṣpádāvṛṇak ||
10 : *tvám āvitha suśrávasaṃ távotíbhis*
táva trā́mabhir indra tū́rvayāṇam |
tvám asmai kútsam atithigvám āyúm
mahé rā́jñe yū́ne arandhanāyaḥ ||

II.14.7 : *kútsasyāyór atithigvásya vīrā́n*
ny ā́vṛṇag bháratā sómam asmai ||
VI.18.13 : *prá tát te adyā́ káraṇaṃ kṛtáṃ bhūt*
kútsaṃ yád āyúm atithigvám asmai |
purū́ sahásrā ní śiśā abhí kṣā́m
út tū́rvayāṇaṃ dhṛṣatā́ ninetha ||
VIII.52.2 (Vāl) : *yá āyúṃ kútsam atithigvám árdayo*
vāvṛdhānó divédive ||

In view of the constant combination of these ree words (Sāyaṇa explains them as three kings), I think, we must distinguish the Kutsa thus designated from the mere Kutsa Atithigva. Atithigva is an epithet, also of Divodāsa (Oldenberg, ZDMG, XLII, pp. 210-11). But those who do not wish to separate this Kutsa Atithigva Āyu from Kutsa Atithigva must assume that in this hymn I.53 (vv. 8-10) two different traditions merged, one of which knew Kutsa Atithigva triumphing with Indra's help over Karañja and Parṇaya (v. 8) while the second tradition let Kutsa Atithigva fall into the hands of Tūrvayāṇa; this would be certainly possible. Suśravas also plays in v. 9 a role different from that in v. 10. In principle there is nothing to object to in Oldenberg's remarks, *loc. cit.*, n. 7. Then the changing destinies of one and the same Kutsa would have served the poet of our hymn —tradition calls him Savya Āṅgirasa—in describing the might of Indra. Cf. also Ludwig, *Rigveda*, III, p. 157 and Perry, "Indra in the Ṛgveda," JAOS, XI, p. 65.

446. Cf. Bergaigne, II, pp. 305-6.

447. Cf. Oldenberg, ZDMG, XXXIX, p. 54 ff.

448. Vol. I, p. 90 ff.

449. TS II.2.1.1 : an oblation during the Varuṇapraghāsāḥ; moreover *aindrāgnaṃ punarutsṛṣṭam ālabheta ya ā tṛtīyāt puruṣāt somaṃ na pibet*, TS II.1.5.5; if the horse sniffs at the *svayamātṛṇṇa-iṣṭikā* he recites the verse : *indrāgnī avyathamānām iṣṭakāṃ dṛṃhatam* etc. TS IV.3.6 (V.3.2). Whosoever installs the fire should afterwards make oblations to Indra-Agni and to Aditi, TBr I.1.6.5. When Indra was deprived of his strength, he performed an Aindrāgna sacrifice, I.6.1.7. In connection with the Viśākhā nakṣatra, see TBr III.1.1.11.

450. ŚŚS III.12.3.

451. ABr II.36.4; ŚBr III.6.2.13; IV.3.1.1 ff. See Vol. I, p.471, n. 332.

452. *ekāha*—TMBr XIX.15.1; 17.1; LŚS IX.4.30; ŚŚS XIV.29.1. *ayana*—TMBr XXV.11.1; ŚŚS XIII.29.28. The two *paurṇamāvāsye* which follow the Abhijit-Viśvajit are regarded as Indrakukṣī and on these days the key words are *ubhā kukṣī pṛṇatām, vārtraghnaṃ ca māghonaṃ ca.*

453. ABr II.36.4; TBr III.8.7.1.

454. TS V.3.2.

455. TBr I.6.4.3. Hence, the two are equated with *sarve devatāḥ*. ŚBr IX.5.2.10; XIII.5.3.2 or *ete vai devate anv anye devate* in XI.8.3.3 etc.

456. MS IV.3.1 (40.12); TBr I.6.1.7.

457. TBr I.1.4.3; II.1.2.7; see n. 172 above.

458. ŚBr II.5.4.8; X.4.1.5,9; TS II.1.5.6; TMBr XV.4.8. *āgneyī pṛthivy āgneyo brāhmaṇaḥ | aindrī dyaur aindro rājanyaḥ;* XIX.17.4; LŚS IX.4.30; KŚS XXII.11.19. Cf. Weber, ISt, X, pp. 26, 31.

459. Holtzmann, ZDMG, XXXII, p. 313.

460. This is the Agnīṣomīya and the Prakṛti of all animal sacrifices.

461. Schwab, *Tieropfer*, p. xv.

462. Ibid., p. xvi, n. 3; *Rituallliteratur*, p. 121.

463. Schwab, *op. cit.*, p. 143 ff. In other cases they should naturally be modified.

464. ŚŚS VI.1.33 : *udagayanasyādyantayor aindrāgno nirūḷhapaśubandhaḥ | sāṃvatsaro vā.* Cf. on this, the rules of other Sūtras collected by Schwab (*op. cit.*, p. xiii, n. 2) which recommend chiefly the same periods (every six months, or annually).

465. *sa vai sanne 'chāvāka ṛtugrahaiś carati | tad yat sanne 'chāvāka ṛtugrahaiś carati mithunaṃ vā acchāvāka aindrāgno hy acchāvāko dvau hīndrāgnī dvandvaṃ hi mithunaṃ prajananaṃ sa etasmān mithunāt prajananād ṛtūn saṃvatsaraṃ prajanayati.* IV.3.1.3; III.6.2.13.

466. See Bergaigne, "Recherches sur l'historire de la liturgie védique" JA, huit. série, tome XIII, Paris 1889. *Rituallliteratur* p. 16.

467. Our treatment of the dual gods lacks, as I have stated on p. 3 above, still very much the sharpness. It will be necessary in each case to pose the question whether the two deities denote, as Agni-Soma, brahmakṣatra etc. do, the fusion of two opposites, or of two mutually complementary aspects or whether they are based on priestly combinations.

468. I.21, 108, 109; III.12; V.86; VI.59, 60; VII.93, 94; VIII.38, 40; and also a number of single verses like III.25.4.

469. *samānó vāṃ janitā́ bhrā́tarā yuvā́m yamā́v ihéhamāturā ||* (Cf. on this I.144.4 : *yā́ṃ dvā́ sávayasā saparyátaḥ samāné yónā mithunā́ sámokasā*). Sāyaṇa : *iha ceha ca sarvatra mātā yayoḥ...*

470. VI. 59.5: *índrāgnī kó asyá vāṃ dévau mártaś ciketati |*
víṣūco áśvān yuyujānā́ īyata ékaḥ samānā́ ā́ ráthe ||

471. Sāyaṇa : *yuvayor eka indraḥ sūryātmanā vartamāno.* Ludwig, V, p. 295 : "Sūrya goes on the chariot which is common to Indra and Agni." What the poet finds as marvellous is that they are only "one," that one does not see both but only one into which they have united, that is to say, "the new moon." Cf. IX.75.1 (Vol. I. p .262) : *ā́ sū́ryasya bṛható bṛhánn ádhi rátham viṣvañcam aruhad vicakṣaṇáḥ |*

472. VII.94.1 : *pūrvyástuti*; 2 : *hávaḥ, giraḥ, dhiyaḥ*, VII.96.6 : *giraḥ, práyas*; VIII.38.6 : *gāyatrávartani-suṣṭuti.*

473. As I have stated on p.306, n. 232 above, vv. 10 and 11 in this hymn are variations on the same theme; v.10 : *ójasā* for *óhata, śúṣṇasyāṇḍā́ni* for *āṇḍā́ śúṣṇasya* , *jéṣat* for *ájaiḥ, ṛgmíyam* for *ṛtvíyam.* Geldner's interpretation, VSt, III, p. 63, is erroneous.

474. MS I.8.4 (120.11) : *oṣadhīr vā imā rudrā viṣeṇāñjan.* I agree with Arbman, *Rudra*, p. 164, that they "are to be understood as the designations of a motley crowd of demons and other sinister beings of all kinds who are

conceived as the entourage or the subjects of the great demon god. From the last mentioned relation the designation *rudrāḥ* makes sense; with this is meant simply the demon-folk."

475. PGS III.8.11.

476. ĀśvGS addresses them as "serpents" and lets the oblations be offered to the serpents : *śoṇitaṃ ninayec chvāsinīr ghoṣiṇīr vicinvatīḥ samaśnuvīḥ sarpā yad vo 'tra tad dharadhvam iti* (IV.8.27).

477. HGS I.16.7 ff. enjoins offerings to Rudra *pathiṣad, paśuṣad, vāteṣu, sarpasad, antarikṣasad.*

478. Cf. VS XVI.6 : *ye cainaṃ rudrā abhito dikṣu śritāḥ sahasraśo 'vaiṣāṃ heḍa īmahe.* In TS I.4.11 the name is transferred to the Viśve devāsaḥ : *triṃśat trayaś ca gaṇino rujantaḥ divaṃ rudrāḥ pṛthivīṃ ca sacante| ekādaśāso apsuṣadaḥ sutaṃ somaṃ juṣantām...||*

479. ṚV VIII.13.28 : *abhí svarantu yé táva rudrā́saḥ sakṣata śríyam |*
utó marútvatīr víśo abhí práyaḥ ||

TĀr I.3.3 : *śuklavāsā rudragaṇo grīṣmeṇāvartate saha nidahan pṛthivīṃ sarvām* as opposed to the Maruts mentioned in I.4.2 who are assigned to autumn. PGS III.3.6 : *viśve ādityā vasavaś ca devā rudrā goptāro marutaś ca santu.* TS II.1.11.3 (AV VI.74.3) : *yathādityā vasubhiḥ sambabhūvur marudbhī rudrāḥ samajānatābhi.*

480. Arbman, *Rudra*, p. 18, shows that in the ṚV the Maruts, and in the late Vedic texts on the other hand a host of demons who are quite different from the Maruts, appear under the same designation of "Rudras" when they are associated with Rudra. In the late Vedic period it is forgotten that the Maruts were the Rudras.

481. Delbrück, *Grundriss*, III, p. 169.

482. I.64.2 : *té jajñire diváḥ...ukṣáṇo rudrásya máryā ásurāḥ*; 12 : *rudrásya sūnúm...mā́rutaṃ gaṇám*; 85.1; 114.6,9,11; V.60.5 : *yúvā pitā́ svápā rudrá eṣām*; 52.16; VI.50.4; 66.3 : *rudrásya yé mīḷhúṣaḥ sánti putrā́ḥ*; 11 : *mā́rutaṃ rudrásya sūnúm*; VII.58.5.

483. Only VI.62.8 : Ādityas, Vasus, Rudriyas (but not Rudras).

484. I.39.6 : *úpo rátheṣu pṛ́ṣatīr ayugdhvaṃ prā́ṣṭir vahati róhitaḥ |*
VIII.7.28 : *yád eṣāṃ pṛ́ṣatī ráthe prā́ṣṭir váhati róhitaḥ |*
20.9 : *śárdhāya mā́rutāya. . .vṛ́ṣaprayāvṇe*

Cf. II.33.6 : *vṛṣabhó marútvān*; 15 : *bábhru vṛṣabhá*=Rudra. This recalls the *divó varāhá aruṣá kapardín* in I.114.5 who is called *pitṛ́ marutā́m* in the next verse. When one dedicates a bull and sacrifices the old one, the verses at TS III.3.9 are employed ; b : *namo mahimna uta cakṣuṣe te marutāṃ pitas tad ahaṃ gṛṇāmi*; e : *tvāṃ gāvo 'vṛṇata rājyāya tvāṃ havanta marutaḥ svarkāḥ ||*

It is not certain whether the verses I.6.1 : *yuñjánti bradhnám aruṣám*; V.56.7 : *utá syá vājy àruṣás tuviṣváṇir ihá sma dhāyi darśatáḥ* also belong here or on p. 175 below.

485. E.g. I.38.9 : *dívā cit támaḥ kṛṇvanti parjányenodavāhéna |*
yát pṛthivī́ṃ vyundánti |
64.5 : *duhánti ū́dhar divyā́ni...|*

V.55.5 : *yūyáṃ vṛṣṭiṃ varṣayathā purīṣiṇaḥ* /
59.7 : *prá párvatasya nabhanū́ṃr acucyavuḥ* //
85.4 : *sám abhréṇa vasata párvatāsaḥ*
taviṣīyántaḥ śrathayanta vīrā́ḥ //
TS II.4.10 : *agnír vā itó vṛ́ṣṭim úd īrayati, marutáḥ sṛṣṭā́ṃ nayanti*;
III.5.5 : *marúto varṣayantu* etc.

Their activity is described through specific images.

1. ádri, párvata etc.

I.85.5 : *vā́je ádriṃ maruto raṃháyantaḥ* /
10 : *ūrdhváṃ nunudre 'vatáṃ...*
dādṛhāṇáṃ cid bibhidur vi párvatam /
V.52.9 : *pavyā́ ráthānām ádriṃ bhindanty ójasā* //
54.4 : *áśmānaṃ cit svaryàṃ párvataṃ giríṃ*
prá cyāvayanti yā́mabhiḥ /

(on this and on the whole question, cf. my review in *Asia Major*, I, p. 785, cf Hertel's *Himmelstore* and also of Reichelt's *Der steinerne Himmel.*)

2. píppala :

V.54.12 : *rúśat píppalaṃ maruto ví dhūnutha* /

3. avatá :

I.85.10 : *ūrdhváṃ nunudre 'vatám*; 11.

4. útsa : I.64.6; 85.11;

VIII.7.16 : *útsaṃ duhánto ákṣitam* (AV IV.27.2 : *vyácanti.*)
V.52.12 : *útsam ā́ kīríṇo nṛtuḥ*; 54.8 : *pínvanty útsam*;
AV IV.15.9 plural (exceptionally means cloud).

5. kóśa :

V.53.6 : *diváḥ kóśam ácucyavuḥ* /
ví párjanyaṃ sṛjanti ródasī
ánu dhánvanā yanti vṛṣṭáyaḥ // 59.8.

6. ū́dhar :

I.64.5 : *duhánti ū́dhar divyā́ni* / (see above)
II.34.10 : *pṛ́śnyā yád ū́dhar ápy āpáyo duhúḥ* /

(*ū́dhaḥ* in V.32.2 : *áraṃha ū́dhaḥ párvatasya* refers to the waters of the mountain range.)

7. véḥ śī̀rṣán :

I.164.7 : [*véḥ*] *śīrṣṇáḥ kṣīráṃ duhrate gā́vo asya*
vavríṃ vásānā udakáṃ padā́puḥ /]

8. vājín, vṛ́ṣan etc. :

I.64.6 : *átyaṃ ná mihé ví nayanti vājínaṃ*
85.5 : *utā́ruṣásya ví ṣyanti dhā́rāḥ*...(Cf. V.56.7 : *utá syá vājy àruṣás tuviṣváṇir ihá sma dhāyi darśatáḥ*/)
AV IV.15.11 : *prá pyāyatām vṛ́ṣṇo áśvasya rétaḥ*;
[1 : *maharṣabhásya nádato nábhasvato*
vāśrā́ ā́paḥ pṛthivíṃ tarpayantu]

ṚV I.160.3 : *dhenúṃ ca pṛ́śniṃ vṛṣabháṃ surétasam*
viśvā́hā śukráṃ páyo asya dukṣata |

With this we should compare the black horse which is made to stand at the sacrificial place with its face towards the west during the Kārīrīṣṭi. (*Rituallitcratur*, p. 120 and, *inter alia*, TS II.4.9). Cf. further ṚV I.79.2 :

ā́ te suparṇā́ aminantām̐ évaiḥ
kṛṣṇó nonāva vṛṣabhó yádīdám |

I cannot venture to decide who is meant in each individual case. It seems to me that several completely different things were imagined as the container or the source of rain. Partly (but not always) the cloud (*ū́dhar divyā́ni*), partly Agni (sun), partly the mountain (*párvata*), partly Parjanya. I have discussed (Vol. I, p. 213 ff.) *útsa*, *kóśa* and *pippala*, which occur almost always in the singular only, and see no reason to change my views. I would like merely to add a reference to AV XVIII.4.35, 36; the *sahásradhāra útsa ákṣita* mentioned there whom the Manes worship permits of only one explanation since it is to do with nectar there.

486. ṚV I.167.2 : *ádha yád eṣāṃ niyútaḥ paramā́ḥ*
samudrásya cid dhanáyanta pāré ||
V.55.5 : *úd īrayathā marutaḥ samudrató*
yūyáṃ vṛṣṭíṃ varṣayathā purīṣiṇaḥ |
AV IV.15.5 : *úd īrayata marutaḥ samudratás*
tveṣó arkó nábha útpātayātha |
27.4 : *apā́ḥ samudrā́d dívam údvahanti*
divás pṛthivī́m abhí yé sṛjanti |

487. ṚV V.58.7 : *vā́tān hy áśvān dhury àyuyujré*
varṣáṃ svédaṃ cakrire rudríyāsaḥ

Occasionally they "create" the winds and lightnings (I.64.5), or they have the epithet *vā́taviṣ*. In an isolated passage the poet assigned the sky to them and the atmosphere to Vāta, I.161.14 : *divā́ yānti marúto bhū́myāg-nír ayáṃ vā́to antárikṣeṇa*. On the other hand, I.187.4 says : *diví vā́tā iva śritā́ḥ*. Their character as rain gods brings them into association with the individual streams, cf. II.30.8; III.54.13; X.75.5.

488. ṚV I.38.9; V.53.6; AV IV.11.4; 15.4, 6; VIII.7.21.

489. I.134.4 : *ájanayo marúto vakṣáṇābhyo divá ā́ vakṣáṇābhyaḥ* || Cf. IX.25.1 : *marúdbhyo vāyáve mádaḥ*. In VIII.7.3, 4, 17 Maruts are different from Vāyus, the latter being regarded as companions of the former; e.g., v. 17 : *úd u svānébhir īrata úd ráthair úd u vāyúbhiḥ* |

490. I.23.12 : *haskārā́d vidyútas páry áto jātā́ avantu naḥ* |
marúto mṛḷayantu naḥ ||

491. "From the abyss of the Nirṛti." Sāyaṇa explains differently. Arbman explains Nirṛti as the underworld, hell.

492. Cf. the *sabardúghā dhenú* VI.48.11 ff.

493. ṚV I.116.1 : *stómām̐ iyarmy abhríyeva vā́taḥ*; X.68.5 : *abhrám iva vā́ta ā́ cakra ā́ gā́ḥ*; AV IV.15.1 : *abhrā́ṇi vā́tajūtāni*; 7 : *marúdbhiḥ prácyutā meghā́ varṣantu*; VIII.6.19 : *vā́to abhrám ivājatu;* X.1.13 : *yáthā vā́taś cyāváyati bhū́myā reṇúm antárikṣāc cābhrám*. In the ceremonies

connected with the rain, the commands contain the sequence *purovāta, vidyut, abhra, stanayitnu, varṣa.* KŚS IV.5.17 ff. On this cf. ŚBr I.5.2.18 : *oṃ śrāvayeti vai devāḥ purovātaṃ sasṛjire 'stu śrauṣad ity abhrāṇi samaplāvayan* etc. TS I.6.11.3; IV.4.6 d. Of the variants, I know only ṚV IV.17.12: *vā́to ná jūtá stanáyadbhir abhraíḥ.*

494. Wherever the clouds have the designation *dhenú* and are associated with the Maruts, they are not their mothers. II.34.5 : *índhanvabhir dhenúbhī rapśádūdhabhir...ā́ gantana.* V.52.3 : *áti ṣkandanti śárvarīḥ* (see Max Müller, SBE, XXXII, p. 73). 55.5 : *ná vo dasrā úpa dasyanti dhenávaḥ...*

495. ṚV VI.6.4. Cf. TBr I.4.1.4, 5 : *devā vai pṛśnim aduhan | tasyā ete stanā āsan | iyaṃ vai pṛśniḥ | tām ādityā ādityasthālyā catuṣpadaḥ paśūn aduhan* etc.

496. ṚV V.52.7. Macdonell, p. 78.

497. Hymn VI.66 which deals with the birth of the Maruts and which von Bradke has sought to explain in *Festgruss an Roth,* p. 116, is too obscure to be of any use.

498. Compare also ṚV VIII.94.1 (about Pṛ́śni) :

gaúr dhayati marútāṃ śravasyúr mātā́ maghónām |

and v.2 : *yásyā devā́ upásthe vratā́ víśve dhāráyante |*

with AV X.10.5 : *ye devā́s tásyāṃ* [*váśāyām*] *prāṇánti te...*

499. V.41.19 : *abhí na iḷā yūthásya mātā́*

smán nadī́bhir urváśī vā gṛṇātu |

500. TS I.7.1.2 : *ete vā iḍāyai stanāḥ | iḍopahūteti vāyur vato* [*iḍāyai*]; 2.2. *vṛṣṭir vā iḍā*; cf. the *iḍāhvāna* (NVO, p. 125): *vāyav iḍā te māteti hotāraṃ īkṣamāṇo vāyuṃ manasā dhyāyet* (ĀpŚS IV.10). Of course, *iḍā* cannot be separated from *iḍ.* We have the names for the seasons in the sequence *samidh* (=*vasanta*), *tanūnapāt* (=*grīṣma*), *iḍaḥ*(=*varṣāḥ*) etc. ŚBr I.5.4.1ff.; TS.II.6.1.1; KBr III. 4. The *éni* (ṚV X. 12.3; AV XVIII. 1.32) also is to be regarded as a synonym.

My explanation is only an attempt. It is not completely satisfactory since some peculiarities in II.34.2 (*vṛ́ṣājani pṛ́śnyāḥ śukrá ū́dhani*) and in VI.66.1 (*sakṛ́c chukráṃ duduhe pṛ́śnir ū́dhaḥ*) remain obscure.

501. TS I.8.9.1 (=TBr I.7.3.4) : *mārutaṃ saptakapālaṃ grāmaṇyo gṛhe, pṛśnir dakṣiṇā*; 8.19 : *mārutīṃ pṛśniṃ paṣṭhauhīm;* II.1.3.2; 2.11.4 : *pṛśniyai dugdhe praiyaṃgavaṃ caruṃ...marudbhyo grāmakāmaḥ, pṛśniyai vai payaso maruto jātāḥ*; V.6.12. On the other hand, in TBr II.7.11 Agastya sacrifices bulls to them which Indra seizes. Larger victims (kine) for them have been listed in *Ritualliteratur*, pp. 148-49.

It may be mentioned that at the beginning of the rainy season, cows have the most milk (ĀpŚS VIII.22.3 : *yasminn eva prāvṛḍādau prabhūtakṣīrā gāvaḥ sampadyante*).

502. See p. 319, n. 383 above. In *Rāmāyaṇa* I.47.1 ff. and also in *Viṣṇu Purāṇa* I.21 (at the end), the seven Maruts are made the descendants of Diti. Thus they are on the same level there as the Aṅgiras' who are often contrasted with the Ādityas.

503. Lindenau, ZII, I, p. 34, speaks of her as "cloud cow." I think

this is too narrow an explanation. Rodasī should be distinguished from Pṛśni. As Bergaigne aptly remarks (II, p. 400), *rodasī* belongs to the Maruts in the same way as Sūryā to the Aśvins and Sarasvatī to the Manes, but her significance is not patent.

504. In ABr I.9.5 etc.; TBr I.7.10.6 they receive an Ekaviṃśatikapāla; in TBr III.4.1 a Vaiśya is offered to them. During the Rājasūya, oblations are made to the Maruts *grāmaṇyo gṛhe* and the dakṣiṇā is a *pṛśni*. TS I.8.9; TBr I.7.3.4 (see n. 501 above).

505. Cf. also TS VI.1.5.3; 6.5.3 : *aindram ālabhya mārutam ālabhate viḍ vai maruto viśam evāsmā anu badhnāti*; during the royal consecration when he draws the waters *yāḥ pratīpaṃ gacchanti hrādunīnāṃ vā*, he recites *marutāṃ ojaḥ* TS I.8.11. Here belongs also the verse ṚV V.58.4 : *yūyáṃ rā́jānam íryaṃ jánāya vibhvataṣṭáṃ janayathā yajatrāḥ / yuṣmád eti muṣṭihā́ bāhújūto yuṣmát sádaśvo marutaḥ suvī́raḥ*, which refers to the brave hero.

506. VIII.12.29 : *yadā́ te mā́rutīr víśaḥ túbhyam indra niyemiré*
13.28 : *marútvatīr víśaḥ...*

507. V.52.11 : *ádhā náro ny óhaté 'dhā niyúta ohate /*
ádhā pā́rāvatā íti citrā́ rūpā́ṇi dárśyā //

508. E.g. ṚV I.64.4 : *citraír añjíbhir vápuṣe vy àñjate*
vákṣassu rukmā́ṅ ádhi yetire śubhé /
áṃseṣv eṣāṃ ní mimṛkṣur ṛṣṭáyaḥ
sākáṃ jajñire svadháyā divó nárah //

11; 88.1 ff.; 166.4,9,10; 172.2; V.54.11 (*aṃśeṣu va ṛṣṭáyaḥ patsú khādáyaḥ* etc.); 57.6; VII.56.11, 13 etc. The Maruts are the epitomé of strength and give strength to the Viś (VII.56.4 ff.). They also constitute *vrātas, gaṇas* (ṚV III.26.6; Hauer, *Vrātya*, p. 184). In these words I see old military expressions (cf. *Lieder des Ṛgveda*, p. 67, n. 2).

509. *parāvad dūradeśaḥ / tatsambandhinaś cāntarikṣādidūradeśe grahatārāmeghādidhārakāḥ santa ohata ity arthaḥ /*

510. No. 686 : "as though they were Pārāvatas."

511. Beyond Rasā, Kubhā, Krumu, Sarayū etc. V.53.9.

512. Thus here the Pārāvatas are placed already further towards the east. V.52.9 states that the Maruts put on woollen clothes on the banks of the Paruṣṇī : *utá sma té páruṣṇyām ū́rṇā vasata śundhyávaḥ*. Already in my *Varuṇa und Mitra*, p. 92, I have explained this as a river; Pischel, VSt, II, p. 208 looks for it quite rightly on the earth. The home of the poet of V.52 (and probably of the Atris in general) is situated on the banks of the Yamunā (v.17). The poets of the eighth book refer especially to the mountain range in their descriptions (VIII.7.1, 2, 4, 23; cf. also AV V.24.6).

Of proper names, only Dyutāna Māruta (VS V.27.b; ŚBr III.6.1.16; TMBr XVII.1.7) and Marutta (ABr VIII.21.14 : *marutaḥ pariveṣṭāro maruttasyāvasan gṛhe*) are associated with the Maruts.

513. In the Vājapeya, when one throws bags of salt at the victorious person, these are done up in Aśvattha leaves. ŚBr V.2.1.17 : *āśvattheṣu palāśeṣūpanaddhā bhavanti / sa yad evādo 'śvatthe tiṣṭhata indro maruta upāmantrayata tasmād āśvattheṣu palāśeṣūpanaddhā bhavanti viśo 'nūdasyanti /*

viśo vai maruto 'nnam viśas tasmād viśo 'nūdasyanti. (Even elsewhere salt symbolizes fortune and fertility; for example, bags of salt are thrown upon the Yūpa so that the sacrificer acquires many heads of cattle); V.3.5.14 : *āśvattham bhavati tena vaiśyo 'bhiṣiñcati sa yad evādo 'śvatthe tiṣṭhata indro maruta upāmantrayata tasmād āśvatthena vaiśyo 'bhiṣiñcati* (a brahmin takes Palāśa wood, a Rājanya Nyagrodha wood and so on); TS III.5.7.2 : *brahma vai parṇo viṇ maruto...maruto 'śvattho...rāṣṭram vai parṇo viḍ aśvatthaḥ:* II.3.1.15; TBr I.7.8.7 : *āśvatthena vaiśyaḥ.*

514. Eggeling, SBE, XXVI, p. 334, n. 2. It is not ruled out that in vv. 8, 9 of this hymn it is the Maruts who are addressed as *jāyú ukṣán* and that accordingly this saga was known to the ṚV as well.

515. PGS II.15.

516. I.1.9.5 : *aśvatthagrāmo 'śvatthacitraka ity ucyate yo 'śvattho grāmādeśe cihnībhūtas tadīyāḥ samidha ādadhyāt* (cf. I.2.1.7 : *citriyād aśvatthād sambhṛtā bṛhatyaḥ*). We can rest content with this explanation and do not need to think, with Güntert, of the tree with the thick foliage under which Yama holds a feast for the departed souls. Cf. my *Vedische Mythologie* (Kleine Ausgabe), p. 104.

The quality of the Aśvattha (Vol. I, p. 96 f.) which has been discussed in the context of the fire cult is not relevant here.

517. Crooke, *The Popular Religion and Folklore of Northern India*, 2nd ed., II, p. 97 : "Pīpal (ficus religiosa), which is connected with old temples, as it forces its roots into the crumbling masonry, grows to a great age, and, like the poplar, moves its leaves at the slightest breath of wind...the Pippala or Aśvattha is said by some to be the abode of Brahmā, and is sometimes invested with the sacred thread by the regular Upanayana rite. Others say that in it abide Brahmā, Viṣṇu and Śiva, but specially Viṣṇu in his incarnation as Kṛṣṇa." (Cf. also Lassen, IAK, I, p. 305 ff.).

Like the village, the sky also has its Aśvattha. AV V.4.3; XIX.39.6 : *aśvatthó devasádanas tṛtī́yasyām itó diví; Kāṭhaka Up.* VI.1 : *ūrdhvamūlo 'vākśākha eṣo 'śvatthaḥ sanātanaḥ;* BhG XV.1. We may also recall the tree with thick foliage in ṚV X.135.1 : *vṛkṣá supalāśá*, on which Yama drinks in the company of the gods, and of the sweet Pippala fruit of the Universal Tree in ṚV I.164.21, 22 to which the "birds" (=stars=Manes) fly (see Vol. I, pp.440-41) Even the Maruts are associated with the sky and its Pippala fruit, V.54.12 : *tám nā́kam ágṛbhītaśociṣam rúśat píppalam maruto ví dhūnatha.*

518. Also 3.3; 36.1, 2; II.11.3 :
ukthéṣv ín nú śūra yéṣu cākán stómeṣv indra rudríyeṣu ca |

519. Cf. also AV VI.47.2.

520. For example, in IV.34.11 (a hymn addressed to the Ṛbhus) :
sám índreṇa mádatha sáṃ marúdbhiḥ |
sáṃ rā́jabhī ratnadhéyāya devāḥ ||

521. V.29.1 cd : *árcanti tvā marútaḥ pūtádakṣās*
tvám eṣām ṛ́ṣir indrāsi dhī́raḥ ||

2 ab : *ánu yád īṃ marúto mandasānám*
ā́rcann índraṃ papivā́ṃsaṃ sutásya |
3 ab : *utá brahmā́ṇo maruto me asya*
índraḥ sómasya súṣutasya peyāḥ |
6 : *árcantī́ndraṃ marútaḥ sadhásthe*
traíṣṭubhena vácasā bādhata dyā́m |
30.6 : *túbhyéd eté marútaḥ suśévāḥ*
árcanty arkáṃ sunvánty ándhas |
áhim ohānám...sākṣad índraḥ ||
31.4 : *brahmā́ṇa índraṃ maháyanto arkaír*
ávardhayann áhaye hántavā́ u ||
10 : *víśve te átra marútaḥ sákhāyaḥ*
índra bráhmāṇi táviṣīm avardhan ||
45.4 : *ukthébhir hí ṣmā kaváyaḥ suyajñā́*
āvívāsanto marúto yájanti ||

(*marúto*=Nominative in view of 29.3; 30.6).

On this and on the emptying of the well caused by them, cf. the parallel dealing with the Gotamas,

I.88.4 : *bráhma kṛṇvánto gótamāso arkaír*
ūrdhváṃ nunudra utsadhíṃ píbadhyai |

522. On the Maruts as the sacrificers, see Bergaigne, II, p. 393 ff., and specially ṚV X.122.5 where as fire priests they are on the same level as the Bhṛgus. Cf. also I.165.11 : *ámandan mā maruta stómo átra yán me naraḥ śrútyaṃ brahma cakrá*; 72.3 : *tisró yád agne śarádas tvā́m íc chúciṃ ghṛténa śúcayaḥ saparyā́n | nā́māni cid dadhire yajñíyāni.*

523. He is mentioned alone in v. 4 and along with other gods in v. 5. But it is not ruled out that Viṣṇu could have been meant in V.42.6 as well. Viṣṇu and the Maruts are mentioned together in II.34.11; VIII.20.3 also.

524. V.57.1 : *rudrāsaḥ indravantaḥ.*

525. Occasional references to Indra and the Maruts can be found also in V.5.11 : *svā́hendrāya marúdbhyaḥ, svā́hā devébhyo havíḥ*; 30.8; 36.1-5 Indra; 6 Maruts; 41, 42 among other gods.

526. V.53.9 and 52.17 (see n. 512 above). On V.52.7 ff., cf. Hauer, *Der Vrātya*, p. 141.

527. Eg. VI.21.9; 49.11; 48.12; 50.4 :
ā́ no rudrásya sūnávo namantām
adyā́ hūtā́so vásavo ádhṛṣṭāḥ |
yád īm árbhe mahati vā hitā́so
bādhé marúto áhvāma devā́n || and 5.

528. VI.17.11 : *várdhān yáṃ víśve marútaḥ sajóṣāḥ*
pácac chatáṃ mahiṣā́m̐ índra túbhyam |
pūṣā́ víṣṇus tríṇi sárāṃsi dhāvan
vṛtrahánaṃ madirám aṃśúm asmai || and 40.5; 52.11.

529. VI.48.21 : *sadyáś cid yásya carkṛtíḥ pári dyā́ṃ devó naiti sū́ryaḥ |*
tveṣáṃ śávo dadhire nā́ma yajñíyam
marúto vṛtraháṃ śávo jyéṣṭhaṃ vṛtraháṃ śávaḥ ||

530. VII.31.8 : *táṃ tvā marútvatī pári bhúvad vā́ṇī sayā́varī |*
nákṣamāṇā sahá dyúbhiḥ ||
32.10 : *índro yásyāvitā́ yásya marúto gámat sá gómati vrajé ||*
82.5 : *marúdbhir ugráḥ śúbham anya īyate ||*
93.8 : *méndro no víṣṇur marútaḥ pári khyan...*

531. See the section, Rudra in the ṚV below. We may still add VII. 47.2. In 56.17 the Maruts are called *vasavàḥ*—"the good ones'=Manes, Eumenides ?—instead of *ghorāḥ*.

532. GGA, 1889, No. 10, p. 422.

533. Kuhn, Benfey, E. H. Meyer, *Indogermanische Mythen*, I, p. 218; Mogk, *Germanische Mythologie*, p. 119; von Schroeder, WZKM, IX, p. 248 ff.

534. I.72.3 : *nā́māni cid dadhire yajñíyāni*
ásūdayanta tanvàḥ sújātāḥ ||
87.5 : *yád īm índram śámy ṛkvāna ā́śata*
ā́d ín nā́māni yajñíyāni dadhire ||

V. 43.10;52.10 : *ā́pathayo vípathayó 'ntaspathā ánupathāḥ | etébhir... nā́mabhir yajñám...ohate;* VI.48.21 (n. 529); VII.56.14; 57.6 (*víśvebhir nā́mabhiḥ*); X.77.8. I.6.4 is difficult :
ā́d áha svadhā́m ánu púnar garbhatvám eriré |
dádhānā nā́ma yajñíyám ||

Max Müller's explanation of the verse (SBE, XXXII, p. 36) is hardly correct. Since they are often depicted as pious ascetics who practise *tapas* etc., I would rather think of the *dīkṣā* the observer of which must become an embryo. Geldner, *Der Rigveda*, thinks that the Aṅgirases or the patriarchs are the subject; that is not necessary, *marútaḥ* is sufficient.

535. That the Manes can be thought of in association with the rain has been shown above in the context of the Aṅgirases (Vol. I. pp. 111-112). Like the Manes, the Maruts are also celebrated as bringers of light. Compare I.86.10 (*gū́hatā gúhyaṃ támo...jyótiṣ karta*); VII.56.20 and more particularly also verses from the eighth book (7.8; 29.10; 76.4; 89.1) where Indra kills Arbuda "in winter" (see p. 122 above). AV XIII.3.23 states that the Maruts sang when the gods created Rohita (on this, about Indra himself, cf. ṚV I.6.3 : *sám uṣádbhir ajāyathāḥ*).

536. ŚBr IV.5.2.16. This portion of the Brāhmaṇa is about the sacrifice of the Vaśā, belonging to Mitra-Varuṇa, with its embryo. One can deposit this embryo upon a tree, in water, or throw it upon a mole-hill or sacrifice it for the Maruts upon the Paśuśrapaṇa fire (the Kāṇva text says :" the common people are eaters of raw flesh, and the Maruts are people," Eggeling, SBE, XXVI, p. 396, n. 2). The following remark of the ŚBr is also important, IV.5.2.17 : *na svāhākaroty ahutādo vai devānāṃ maruto viḍ ahutam ivaitad ayad asvāhākṛtaṃ devānāṃ vai marutas tad enaṃ marutsv eva pratiṣṭhāpayati.* The statement in TBr I.8.3.2 : *garbhiṇy ādityā bhavati...agarbhā mārutī* is based on a different notion, namely, the antithesis between the "fertile" and the "unfertilized." Cf. also Segerstedt, *Revue de l'histoire des religions*, LVII, p. 198 ff.

537. VS XVII.80-85.

538. VS XVII.86; XXXIX.7 : *ugraś ca bhīmaś ca dhvāntaś [ca dhuniśca sāsahvāṃś ca...*

539. *araṇye 'nūcya* is the name of the Puroḍāśa. Mahīdhara on VS XXXIX.7.

540. The designation of the verse as *vimukha* is characteristical. This can only mean that while reciting the verse one should turn one's face away. The fertility of the Maruts is obvious from their Mane-like quality; in the case of a real sacrifice for the Manes, it is enjoined : *apaparyāvṛtya* and *abhiparyāvartamāna* (GGS IV.3.12, 13). If besides this mantra of the Āraṇyaka, there are six others which have nothing to do with forest as Oldenberg remarks in NGGW, 1915, p. 388, this can be adequately explained by assuming various kinds of Manes who were partly friendly and partly dangerous. According to Pāraskara and Kātyāyana, the ceremony is concluded with a mantra, *indraṃ daivīr viśo maruto 'nuvartamāno 'bhavan;* this seems to be rather without any motive in the Sūtras of the second authority since he is dealing with a Vaiśvānara sacrifice.

541. Ludwig, V, 421; on I.6.4 (445) Ludwig points out to ŚBr IV.5.2. 10; KŚS XXV.11.18 : *ayajñiyā garbhāḥ;* Caland, *Altindischer Ahnenkult*, p. 32; Oldenberg, RdV, p. 569.

542. TBr I.6.2.2 : *tāḥ prajā jātā maruto 'ghnan| asmān api na prāyukṣateti | sa etaṃ prajāpatir mārutaṃ saptakapālam apaśyat;* 4 : *yāḥ pūrvāḥ prajā asṛkṣi marutas tā avadhiṣuḥ katham aparāḥ sṛjeyeti...*

543. TBr I.3.4.4 : *maruto yajñam ajighāṃsan prajāpateḥ | tebhya etāṃ mārutīṃ vaśām ālabhata |*

544. ABr I.10.2 : *maruto ... 'ntarikṣabhājanās tebhyo ha yo 'nivedya svargaṃ lokam etīśvarā hainaṃ ni vā roddhor vi vā mathitoḥ.* TS VII. 1.5.4 : *tad antarikṣaṃ vy avairyata | tasmād rudrā ghātukā anāyatanāḥ.* We shall discuss soon below the fact that they are often compared with the birds (cf. BDS II.14.10). I attach less weight to AV XVIII.2.22 : *út tvā vahantu marúta udavāhā́ udaprútaḥ;* here it is only about carrying away the dead body and keeping it cool. Even the etymology is uncertain, no matter whether one thinks with Kuhn of the root *mar* or with Grassmann (KZ, XVI, p. 190) of *Umbr. Serfo Martio.* More acceptable is Güntert, *Der arische Weltkönig und Heiland*, p. 198, *marut=maru+t,* where *maru* is related to *marú*, desert, *māra*, death, *morior* etc. I would rather agree with the derivation of the name from the Dravidian *marutta*, "medicine man, sorcerer" (ZDMG, XXIII, p. 518).

545. On the conception of the Manes as birds, see Caland, *Die altindischen Todten- und Bestattungsgebräuche*, p. 78, n. 288, and von Negelein, "Seele als Vogel," *Globus*, LXXIX, 1901, p. 357 ff., 381 ff. The position of the Maruts originally as the Manes is quite compatible with Arbman's view that "they were creatures of lower mythology, originally of sinister and hostile character" (*Rudra*, p. 309).

546. Whosoever thinks, besides of the "piety" of the Indra-worshipping Maruts, also of their designation as *gaṇa* and their number seven (always expressed through the *saptakapāla*)—this apart, 3 times 60 Maruts are also

mentioned, e.g., in VIII.96.3—would consider the following notion at least worth stating, viz., if they are not a star-cluster denoting rain, corresponding in this respect to the (feminine) Kṛttikāḥ of the later times. Their worshipper Agastya, who receives the name *kumbhayoni* in classical Sanskrit, becomes as is well known the Canopus. Just as the progenitors of the Vedic clans were transferred to the sky as "seven Ṛṣis" and were located in the constellation of the Great Bear so the Maruts as a pious group could have been raised to the sky and identified with a constellation that indicates storm and rain. On the manifold images to which the Pleiades gave occasion, see Andree, *Ethnographische Parallelen.*

547. If one does not recover one's kingdom after an oblation to the sun, one should do the following : *āśvatthān mayūkhān sapta madhyameṣāyām upa hanyād idam aham ādityān badhnāmy āmuṣmād amuṣyai viśo 'vagantor ādityā evainam baddhavīrā viśam ava gamayanti / yadi nāvagacched etam evādityaṃ caruṃ nirvapet / idhme 'pi mayūkhān saṃ nahyed anaparudhyam evāva gacchati / āśvatthā bhavanti marutāṃ vā etad ojo yad aśvatthaḥ /*

548. See my discussion in Kuhn's *Literaturblatt*, II, p. 6 ff.

549. X.77.8 : *té hi yajñéṣu yajñíyāsa ū́mā*
ādityéna nā́mnā śámbhaviṣṭhāḥ /

550. E.g. ŚBr IX.3.1.26 cites from VS XXVII.80 as names for the Maruts (as opposed to those of the Vimukha verse) : *śukrajyotiś ca citrajyotiś ca satyajyotiś ca jyotiṣmāṃś ceti* [etc.] *nāmāny eṣām etāni.* TMBr XIV.12.9 : *māsā vai raśmayo maruto raśmayaḥ; maruto vai devānāṃ bhūyiṣṭhāḥ.* TĀr V.4.8.26 : *asau khalu vā ādityaḥ pravargyaḥ tasya maruto raśmayaḥ.* Compare also the connection of the Ādityas in VS XXI.25; TĀr I.3.4 with the rainy season which is not original. On the other hand, the Maruts as the sons of Diti are diametrically opposed to the sons of Aditi (n. 502 above).

551. ĀpŚS XIII.2.3 ff.; 8.1 ff.; Vol I, pp. 328-29.

552. VIII.103.14 and III.13.6 respectively.

553. ĀpŚS XIII.15.12; ĀśvŚS V.20.2 ff.; ŚŚS VIII.6; ABr III.34-35; Eggeling, SBE, XXVI, p. 369.

554. Other hymns are employed in the Dvādaśāha and in the Abhiplava week at the corresponding places.

555. I do not take hymns like V.56, 58 (cf. v. 6 : *ayáṃ yó agnír marutaḥ sámiddha etáṃ juṣadhvam)* into account; they deal merely with a *devatāhvāna.*

556. I.72.3 : *tisró yád agne śarádas tvā́m ic*
chúciṃ ghṛténa śúcayaḥ saparyā́n /
nā́māni cid dadhire yajñíyāni
ásūdayanta tanvàḥ sújātāḥ //

Cf. I.58.3 where they (according to Bergaigne, II, p. 391) appoint Agni as the priest.

557. V.60.8 : *ágne marúdbhiḥ śubháyadbhir ṛ́kvabhiḥ*
sómaṃ piba mandasānó gaṇaśríbhiḥ /
pāvakébhir...vaiśvānara pradíva ketúnā sajū́ḥ //

He is designated as Agni Vaiśvānara elsewhere too like TS II.2.5.6 (see p. 176 above); V.4.7.7 : *vaiśvānaraṃ hutvā mārutāñ juhoti rāṣṭra eva viśam anu badhnāti* etc.

558. I.71.8 : *agníḥ śárdham anavadyáṃ yúvānaṃ*
svādhyàm janayat sūdáyac ca ||
VI.3.4 : *dhā́yobhir vā yó yújyebhir arkaír*
vidyún ná davidyot svébhiḥ śúṣmaiḥ |
śárdho vā yó marútāṃ tatákṣa
ṛbhúr ná tveṣó rabhasānó adyant ||
Cf. also I.31.1 : *táva vraté kaváyo vidmanā́paso*
ájāyanta marúto bhrā́jadṛṣṭayaḥ |

In III.2.5 Vaiśvānara is called *rudra*.

559. The juxtaposition of these gods with Varuṇa is rare and obscure (see n. 564, below). If I am right in my conjecture about the position of Varuṇa in the Praghāsāḥ (see p. 20 ff. above) then the fact of the Maruts being accommodated there can be explained from their character as the Manes.

560. Cf. also TS I.8.4.1. TBr I.6.6. The observance of the Cāturmāsyas with animal sacrifices makes no difference here. ŚŚS XIV.10.16.

561. In AV VII.77.3 they are designated as *saṃvatsarī́ṇa.*

562. Cf. VII.56.14 : *bhāgám etáṃ gṛhamedhī́yaṃ maruto juṣadhvam.*

563. According to the ritual, one could perform the Cāturmāsyas with the Soma also. In the ṚV, the "playing" Maruts are not yet mentioned in connection with this sacrifice. We find them described as *prakrīḍín* (*vatsā́so ná*), *krīḍí* and *krīḍá*, but they have not yet found a place in the ritual. Cf. the story in *Āryavidyāsudhākara*, p. 73.

564. Of the other gods, Varuṇa is associated with the Maruts in ṚV VIII.41.1 (and in the Cāturmāsya ceremonies, cf. p. 185 above); so also Soma (see Vol. I, pp. 225-27) and Bṛhaspati (see Vol. I, p. 105). In most of the cases it must be the Aṅgirases' who are meant although Sāyaṇa on X.67.3 thinks that it is the Maruts.

565. He receives a milk libation during the Śunāsīrīya which is appended to the Cāturmāsyas, ŚŚS III.18.3; *Ritualliteratur*, p. 119.

566. Bergaigne, *Histoire de la littérature védique*, p. 125. Vol. I, pp. 298, 330 (to which we may add, I.135.1; VII.92.1). Besides these, I find him accommodated in the evening on one more occasion, ĀpŚS XIII.13.12 : *niyudbhir vāyav iha tā vimuñca.* When the Pratiprasthātṛ hears these words, he removes the Dvidevatyapātras from their place with the words, *vāyur vo vimuñcatu*, carries them away through the back door and so on.

567. I.122.3 : "he who leaves the spring behind" (Ludwig). Cf. I.134. 3: *vāsayoṣásaḥ*; 4 : *túbhyam uṣā́saḥ śúcayaḥ parāváti bhadrā́ vástrā tanvate;* VIII.46.26 : *yó áśvebhir váhate vásta usrā́s tríḥ saptá saptatīnā́m;* VII.90.1-3 Vāyu; 4 Uṣas; 5 ff. Indra-Vāyu.

568. Cf. also I.174.5; V.31.10. This pair of gods did not give occasion for ritualistic speculation as often as the other pairs did. I have noticed

only ABr III.4.4 : *atha yad dvaidham iva kṛtvā dahati dvau vā indravāyū tad asyaindravāyavaṃ rūpam* /

569. ṚV I.23.11 : *jáyatām iva tanyatúr marútām* etc. Cf. X.103.8 : *devasenā́nām abhibhañjatīnā́ṃ jáyantīnāṃ marúto yantv ágram* //

570. Cf. the unusual passage in the commentary on KŚS XXV.14.27 : *śrūyate vāyuḥ samudraṃ sadā vidveṣṭi...ayaṃ vāyuḥ samudraṃ sadā dveṣṭi śoṣayitum icchati / samudraś ca sarvadā snehaparaḥ / ata eva mahān bahula eva vāyukṛtena dveṣeṇa samīpa eva sthitasya tasya kim api na hīyate* /

571. Indra-Vāyu IV.21.4; 24.4; 46; 47; V.51; VII.90-92 (from the other books, cf. I.2, 23, 135).

572. Indra-Vāyu II.41; Indra-Marutaḥ II.3.3 etc., cf. p. 178 f. I am not taking the eighth book into account. I wish to say merely this much that the association between Indra and the Maruts becomes more prominent here. Cf. VIII.76.1 ff.; 89; 96.

573. MS II.2.7 (20. last line) : *na khalu vai kiṃ cana vāyunānabhigatam asti*; ŚBr VIII.2.3.2 : *sarvāsu dikṣu vāyuḥ*; 3.1.11 : *yābhir ado vāyur digbhir anantarhitābhir upait tā etās...*; X.3.3.8 : *vāyau diśaḥ pratiṣṭhitā vāyor evādhi punar jāyante*; XIV.9.4.21 : *vāyur diśāṃ yathā garbhaḥ*. AV II.10.4 : *pradíśaś cátasro vā́tapatnīḥ*; (sometimes the north-west is assigned to him). Cf. here and in the following notes, Eggeling's Indices to the ŚBr.

574. AV X.7.37 : *katháṃ vā́to nélayati*. ABr V.25.17 : *na hy eṣa kadā canelayati*; ŚBr XIV.4.3.33 : *mlocanti hy anyā devatā na vāyuḥ saiṣānastamitā devatā yad vāyuḥ*. TBr III.1.4.13 : *vāyur vā akāmayata kāmacāram eṣu lokeṣv abhijayeyam*; 9.4.1 : *vāyur vai caran* as well as the fact that in the later period the wind is called *sadāgati*.

575. *kṣepiṣṭha* TS II.1.1.1; III.4.3.2 : *āśuḥ sārasāritamaḥ javaṃ ... dadhāti*, TBr III.8.7.1. Hence *anāśú* in ṚV I.135.9 must be changed into *anāsú*. It would be meaningless if the swiftest of the gods is assigned "slow" bulls. His bulls know no rest, "they do not sit down." Therefore, Geldner on ṚV I.135.9; and Sieg, GGA, 1925, p. 130, are wrong.

576. TS V.3.1.3 : *sarvān ṛtūn anu vāyur ā varīvartti*.

577. ṚV X.168.4; ŚBr XI.8.3.8 : *rūpam eva vāyor ādatta / tasmād etasya lelayata ivaivopaśṛṇvanti na tv enaṃ paśyanti*.

578. ṚV X.168.4; ŚBr XIV.3.2.7 : *vāyur vai sarveṣāṃ devānām ātmā*; XI.5.3.11 : *vāyuṃ hy eva sarvāṇi bhūtāny apiyanti vāyoḥ punar visṛjyante*. In AV VI.10.2 *prāṇa*, *antarikṣa*, *vayaḥ* and *vāyu* are mentioned together. The examples here and in the following notes can easily be increased.

579. TS III.4.5 etc. According to AV IV.39.4 "the atmosphere is the cow, and Vāyu its calf."

580. MS III.9.4 (120.9) : *vāyugopā vai vanaspatayaḥ*.

581. TS II.1.10.2 : *vāyavyaṃ gomṛgam ālabheta yam ajaghnivāṃsam abhiśaṃseyuḥ / apūtā vā etaṃ vāg ṛcchati...vāyur vai devānāṃ pavitram*; VI.4.7.1; MS II.5.2 (49.11 ff.); TBr III.2.4.5.

582. TBr III.9.4.4 and III.7.5.4 respectively.

583. TS II.4.9.1 : *vāyur vai vṛṣṭyā īśe*; V.1.5.1; 3.1.3 : *vāyupracyutā divo vṛṣṭir īrte*. TBr I.7.1.1 : *vāyur vai vṛṣṭyai pradāpayitā*; III.7.1.5 : *vāyur*

vai payasaḥ pradāpayitā; he is called *tigmatejas* in TS I.1.9.c; (AV X.5.26 *vāyutejas*).

584. Vol. I, p. 98. TS V.5.1.1 : *tejo 'gner vāyus...tasmād yadriyaṃ vāyuḥ vāti tadriyaṅṅ agnir dahati.* TS II.1.1 : *sainaṃ īśvarā pradaha iti.*

585. TS V.5.1.3-4 : *vāyur vai paśūnāṃ priyaṃ dhāma...| yad vāyavyaḥ paśur bhavati tena vāyor naiti.* TBr III.2.1.3 : *vāyur vā antarikṣasyādhyakṣaḥ | antarikṣadevatyāḥ khalu vai paśavaḥ.* TMBr XXIII.13.2 : *etābhir vai vāyur āraṇyānāṃ paśūnām ādhipatyam āśnuta* (AV II.26.1 :*...paśavaḥ...ye pareyur, vāyur yeṣāṃ sahacāraṃ jujoṣa;* 34.4 : *ye grāmyāḥ paśavo viśvarūpāḥ...vāyuṣ tān agre pra mumoktu devaḥ prajāpatiḥ...*)

A *bhūtikāma* sacrifices a white animal *vāyave niyutvate*, for the latter is "the fastest deity," TS II.1.1; so does a *grāmakāma* "for Vāyu leads men tied by the nose" (just as one leads an animal by the nose), TS II.1.1.2; MS IV.3.3 (42.6); likewise a *prajākāma* (TS II.1.1.2) and *jyogāmayāvin* (II.1.1.3) One who is kept away from his throne for long should offer a cow to the sky and the earth and a calf to Vāyu. Vāyu is the calf of the two. The worlds turn away from him; people turn away from him (TS II.1.4.7). Of other animals, *inter alia*, *mṛga* TMBr I.8.13; *gomṛga* TS II.1.10.2; *tūpara* TS V.5.1.1; moreover *vehata* (i.e. *garbhaghātinī gauḥ*) comm. on TBr II.8.8.4, and a Cāṇḍāla TBr III.4.1.17. From TBr III.9.17.5, I cite the remark, *vāyavyā garbhāḥ*; this should not be understood like the dedication of a *garbha* to the Maruts because Vāyu impregnates.

586. With Savitṛ (*āgomucau*)—TS IV.7.15.g. Sacrifice for the two in TS VII.5.22. Hymn addressed to the two, AV IV.25. Identified with Savitṛ in TBr II.3.9.7 : *atha yad uttarato vāti savitaiva bhūtvottarato vāti saviteva svānāṃ bhavati.*

587. KŚS XXVI.6.1; VS XXXVIII.7-9 etc.

588. KŚS XVIII.6.1; VS XVIII.45 etc. Cf. *Rituallliteratur*, p. 164.

589. TBr II.3.9.5 ff. differentiates the winds according to the points of the compass, identifying them with Mātariśvan, Pavamāna and Savitṛ. In TS I.6.1.2 five winds, five ṛtus etc. are mentioned. More valuable is the distinction in ṚV X.137.2 between two winds, *á síndhor* and *á parāvátaḥ.*

590. On the distinction between Vāyu and Vāta in the Avesta, see Jackson, *Grundriss der iranischen Philologie*, II, p. 643 ff., Jarl Charpentier, *Kleine Beiträge*, p. 37. On Vāta's relation to Indra and on the connection between the Iranian Vāta and a great war-god Vərəgna, see B. Geiger, *Aməša Spəntas*, p. 19.

591. G. de Rialle, "Les déesses des eaux dans la ṚV," *Revue de Linguistique et de Philologie comparée*, IX, p. 46 ff.

592. Hirt, IF, I, p. 481, equates Parjanya with Fairguni and sees in him the "oak god"; against this identification, see Kögel, (GGA, 1897, p. 653, in the review of Golther) and von Grienberger, *Archiv für slavische Philologie*, XVIII, p. 12. According to Zupitza, Parjanya is "perhaps nothing but one who rains." Cf. Irish *arg*, "drops," Welsh *eira*, Breton *erc'h*, "snow"—DLZ, XVIII, p. 1488; cf. also Güntert, *Reimwortbildungen*, p. 203; In *Orient und Occident*, I, p. 214. Bühler has explained Parjanya as "thunder

cloud" (cf. Max Müller, *India*, p. 183 ff., SBE, XXXII, p. 92). In MS II.4.7 (44.11) *dyauḥ parjanya* is juxtaposed with *antarikṣa, pṛthivī*. We should reject the identification between Parjanya and Perkúnas. Kretschmer, *Einleitung in die Geschichte der griechischen Sprache*, p. 81; Much, *Festgabe für Heinzel*, 1898, p. 214.

593. Cf. also Bloomfield, JAOS, XVII, p. 173 ff.

594. IA, XXII, 1893, p. 293 : "the Nāgas, of whom the Nēwārs consider Karkoṭa the greatest, are worshipped on the fifth day (Nāgpañcamī) of the month of Sāvan (July) at the commencement of the rainy season, when the Nāgas (water-dragons) are thundering in the sky...Frogworship, on the other hand, is performed on the seventh day of the month of Kārttika (October) and usually at a pool, which is known to be frequented by frogs."

595. *Abhandlungen der Berliner Akademie der Wissenschaften*, 1898, pp. 1-69.

596. VII.49.2; cf. TBr III.1.2.3 : *yā divyā...yā antarikṣe uta pārthivīyāḥ ...kūpyāḥ...nādyāḥ samudriyāḥ...vaiśantīr prāsacīr*; II.7.15.3 ff.

597. ṚV III.22.3. TS IV.2.4f.

598. TS V.6.1.a etc.

599. Ibid., V.6.1.c.

600. Ibid., VI.4.2.3-4; ŚBr XIII.8.4.6.

601. Weber, *Rājasūya*, p. 33 ff. citing KŚS XV.4.22 ff.; TS I.8.11.1 (comm. II, p. 121).

602. ĀpŚS XX.11.17 ff.; TS VII.4.13. Cf. also the Ab-iṣṭakāḥ TS IV.3.1; TBr III.12.7; TĀr I.24.

603. ĀpŚS XXIV.2.9; KŚS I.10.14.

604. TS II.6.4.4 : *āpo vai rakṣoghnīḥ* etc.

605. PGS I.16.22.

606. TS I.3.11.e (comm. I, p. 551). Cf. Oldenberg, RdV, p. 520.

607. *Ritualliteratur*, p. 120; Caland, *Wenschoffers*, 6 (9).

608. On other ceremonies, see Oldenberg, RdV, pp. 359, 507; *Ritualliteratur*, p. 173 etc.; Caland, *Altindisches Zauberritual*, p. 140.

609. *Ritualliteratur*, p. 94 ff.; Caland, *Über die Totenverehrung bei einigen der indogermanischen Völker*, p. 44 ff.

610. ISt, XIII, p. 291; MŚS II.1.2.32, 36.

611. *Ritualliteratur*, p. 182.

612. Bloomfield, "Contributions II" (AJPh, XI), p. 24 ff.

613. Bloomfield, *loc. cit.*; among others, the *darbhāḥ* also; the TĀr (ed. BI), p. 524, cites *āpo vai darbhāḥ* as explanation for the rule (V.10.6) : *yatra darbha upadikasaṃtatāḥ syus tad udvāsayed vṛṣṭikāmasya / etā vā apām anūjjāvaryo nāma yad darbhāḥ...*

614. Cf. *inter alia*, Weber, *Rājasūya*, p. 12, n. 4; p. 104, n. 2; p. 109, n. 1; Oldenberg, RdV, p. 500; MS II.2.1 (15.13); 6.1 (64.6); III.1.3 (4.15); IV.3.1 (39.12); KŚS XXVI.1.6.

615. TĀr V.1.4. Cf. V.2.9 : *ūrjaṃ vā etaṃ rasaṃ pṛthivyā upadīkā uddihanti...yad valmīkavapāsaṃbhāro bhavati, ūrjam eva rasaṃ pṛthivyā avarundhe.* Comm. on TBr I.1.3.4 etc. Bloomfield, *Seven Hymns*, p. 18.

On the association of the mole and ant with the rain, see E. H. Meyer, *Indogermanische Mythen*, vol. II : Gandharven-Kentauren, p. 156 ff.

616. Magoun, JAOS, XIX, 2, p. 137 ff.; AJPh, XXI, p. 274 ff. (=chain-lightning); Gray, ARW, III, p. 18 ff., overrates the value of the Iranian *apām napā̊* for the explanation.

617. In the ritual of the Vasiṣṭhas, hymn VII.47 corresponds to X.30.

618. I.186.5 : *áhir budhnyà, síndhu, apā́ṃ nápāt...*
VI.49.14 : *áhir budhnyò adbhír arkaíḥ ..*
VII.34.16 : *abjā́m ukthaír áhiṃ gṛṇīṣe /*
budhné nadī́nāṃ rájassu ṣī́dan //
35.13 : *ajá ékapād, áhir budhnyàḥ, samudrá, apā́ṃ nápāt*
X.93.5 : *utá no náktam apā́ṃ vṛṣaṇvasū*
sū́ryāmā́sā sádanāya sadhanyā̀ /
sácā yát sā́dy eṣāṃ áhir budhnéṣu budhnyàḥ //
VS X.19.a. TS I.8.14.k:
samā́vavṛtrann adhirā́g údīcīr
áhiṃ budhníyam ánu saṃcárantīḥ /
tā́ḥ párvatasya vṛṣabhásya pṛṣṭhé
nā́vaś caranti svasica iyānā́ḥ //

619. ĀpŚS XI.15.1; TMBr I.4.11. In greater detail, ABr III.36.5 : *tāsu [prajāsu] ahinā budhnyena parokṣāt tejo 'dadhād eṣa ha vā ahir budhnyo yad agnir gārhapatyaḥ*, and TS I.5.4 : *bhūmir bhūmnā dyaur variṇety āhāśiṣaivainam ādatte / sarpā vai jīryanto 'manyanta / sa etaṃ Kasarṇīraḥ Kādraveyo mantram apaśyat / tato vai te jīrṇās tanūr apāghnata / sarparājñiyā ṛgbhir gārhapatyam ādadhāti / punarnavam evainam ajaram kṛtvādatte... yat sarparājñiyā ṛgbhir gārhapatyam ādadhāty annādyasyāvaruddhyai* (VII. 3.1). Elsewhere the Anvāhāryapacana is addressed thus : ĀpŚS VI.24.6 : *annaṃ me budhnya pāhi tan me gopāyāsmākaṃ punar āgamat* and the Āvasathya fire in TBr I.1.10; III.7.4.6; ĀpŚS V.27.10. Cf. also LŚS II.2.22 : *ahir iti prajahitam [upaṣṭheran], aja iti gārhapatyam;* TMBr I.4.11-12.

620. TS VII.3.1.3; TBr I.4.6.6; II.2.6.2; ABr V.23.1; TMBr IV.9.6 : *iyaṃ vai sarpato rājñī* or *sārparājñī.*

621. According to TBr III.1.5.11, a *bhūmikapāla* for Ahi. I see no grounds for Keith's assumption "that the god is nothing more than a personification of the writhing cloud" (p. 137); in the ṚV the clouds are no "serpents" !

622. *Arische Urzeit*, p. 147 f.

623. "Mythological Studies in the Ṛgveda," JRAS, 1893, XXV, pp. 419-96.

624. PJAOS, 1894, p. cxix; "Contributions VII," AJPh, XVII, p. 430 ff.

625. *Bidrag till Rigvedas tolkning*, p. 7 ff.; Johansson leaves the question about the original meaning quite open.

626. Geldner, VSt, III, p. 169. The legend of the well can be true but not necessary. The ṚV is familiar with a number of such legendary motifs. Besides Kutsa, also in the case of Bhujyu (I.116.4; 117.14; 118.6; 182.6; VII.68.7) of Rebha, Vandana (I.112.5; 116.24; 117.4; 119.6; X.39.

8-9), and Atri (I.116.8; 117.3). These apart, the legend of the buried disc, bowl or treasure may be mentioned. The origin might be varied and not always historical.

627. On ŚBr XIII.4.2.16, cf. Weber, *Rājasūya*, p. 114. I think that *āpya* is a secondary form (to be found also in the TBr) of Āptya.

628. ŚBr I.2.2.18; 3.1; TS I.1.8.q. VS I.23; cf. NVO, p. 43.

629. There is another legend in MS IV.1.9 (12). Cf. further the comm. on TĀr II.3.7 : *tritaḥ nāma kaścid puruṣaḥ / sa ca pauroḍāśikakāṇḍe aṅgāreṇodakapāvanād niṣpanna iti śrutaḥ* (v.1. : *dārśakāṇḍe aṅgāreṇodapātanāgniṣu utpannaḥ*). This recalls the legend of the Aṅgiras' emerging from the coals of Prajāpati's semen (Vol. I, p. 118). The example of the Aṅgiras' demonstrates that such tales do not detract from the historical character of the family; these are to be regarded as tribal legends.

630. Also Fick, VWB, 4th ed., I, p. 229, regards *dvitá* as a fiction.

631. The original meaning of the word Trita must remain uncertain. Its connection with the Old Irish *triath*, "ocean" (Fick, VWB, 4th ed., I, p. 63; Johansson, IF, IV, p. 143) appears as uncertain as the derivation from *tri*, "three."

632. Bartholomae, IF, I, p. 180; Johansson, *Bidrag till Rigvedas Tolkning*, p. 7.

633. The person of Traitana who cuts off the head of a demon and who appears only in one passage of the ṚV is not clear. Cf. B. Geiger, *Aməša Spəntas*, p. 65 ff.

634. Cf. the verses 9-11 in Macdonell. II.11.20; VIII.52.1; 12.16 :

yát sómam indra víṣṇavi yád vā gha tritá āptyé /
yád vā marútsu mándase sám índubhiḥ //

635. Macdonell, 12-14 : IX.32.2 :

ắd īṃ tritásya yóṣaṇo hárịṃ hinvanty ádribhiḥ /
índum índrāya pītáye //

34.4; 38.2; 102.2 (86.20 ?). "The maidens of Trita" are, like the daughters of Vivasvat (IX.14.5), the ten Harits etc., the ten fingers of the sacrificer. See below the section, Vivasvat and Yama. Macdonell, JRAS, XXV, p. 437. In IX.95.4 (discussed earlier on p. 23 above : *trito bibharti váruṇaṃ samudré*) also, where Varuṇa means Soma, Trita denotes the sacrificer, both the earthly and celestial ones. VIII.41. 6 is based on a misunderstanding of the poet.

636. Perhaps with the exception of

V.41.9 cd : *panitá āptyó yajatáḥ sádā no*
várdhān naḥ śáṃsaṃ náryo abhíṣṭau //

but *trita* occurs in the next verse 10 : *vṛ̥ṣṇo astoṣi bhūmyásya gárbhaṃ tritó*... Hence it is possible that here also the latter is meant.

637. Cf. also IX.102.3 : *mímīte asya* [*tritásya*] *yójanā ví sukrátuḥ*; V.54.2 :... *marutaḥ... sáṃ vidyútā dádhati vắśati tritáḥ* (cf. V.58.6 *krandatu dyaúḥ*; 59.8) *sváranty ắpo 'vánā párijrayaḥ*. But the other passages do not fit in. Hence I prefer the other explanation.

638. II.11.19; X.8.8; 48.2; 99.6. The Maruts help in II.34.10; VIII. 7.24.

639. I.52.5 (Vala); 187.1 (Vṛtra); X.99.6 (Varāha).

CHPTER VIII

VIṢṆU, PŪṢAN AND LESSER DEITIES

1. *Wörter und Sachen*, I, p. 80 ff.; Johansson, *Solfågeln*, p. 2; *Dhiṣaṇā*, p. 47; Jarl Charpentier, *Die Suparṇa Sage*, p. 329; against this Oldenberg, NGGW, 1915, p. 374 ff.; Güntert, *Der arische Weltkönig und Heiland*, p. 306. The etymology of *vi+sānu*, "surface, height,' accepted by the last two is much too reminiscent of Sāyaṇa.

2. *Kleine Beiträge*, p. 60.

3. Since related features are to be assumed between the Soma bird and the Iranian Vāregha, these do not belong in the Viṣṇu mythology.

4. II.1.3; 22.1; 34.11 } no vocative
III.54.14; 55.10 }

IV.3.7; 18.11 (one vocative).

V.3.3; 46.2 (vocative), 3, 4; 49.3; 51.9; 87.1, 8.

VI.17.11; 20.2; 21.9; 48.14; 49.13; 50.2; 69.8 (vocative).

VII.35.9; 36.9; 39.5; 40.5; 44.1; 93.8; 99.1-3, 6, 7 (vocative); 100.1,2 (vocative), 3, 4, 6.

VIII.3.8; 9.12; 12.16, 27; 15.9; 20.3; 25.12, 14; 27.8 (vocative); 31.10; 35.1, 14; 52.3; 54.4; 77.10 83.7 (vocative).

The occurrence in the other maṇḍalas is as follows : I (22 times in 9 hymns); IX (8 times in 8 hymns); X (11 times in 10 hymns).

5. II.1.3 : *tvám víṣṇur urugāyó namasyáḥ*
22.1 : *sómam apibad víṣṇunā sutáṃ yáthávaśat* /
34.11 : *tán vo mahó maruta evayávno*
víṣṇor eṣásya prabhṛthé havāmahe /
Or IV.3.7 : *...puṣṭimbharáya pūṣṇé...víṣṇave urugāyáya*
18.11 : *áthābravīd vṛtrám índro haniṣyán*
sákhe viṣṇo vitaráṃ ví kramasva

In addition to these, we find Indrāviṣṇu in 2.4 (an enumeration of gods) 55.4 (also an enumeration).

6. I.22.19; 61.7; 85.7; 155.1, 2; II.22.1; IV.2.4; 18.11; 55.4; VI.17.11; 20.2; 69; VII.99.4-6; VIII.3.8; 10.2; 12.16, 27; IX.56.4; 100.6; X.66.4; 113.2. Vālakhilya IV.3 including the association merely expressed through the dual number. Macdonell, p. 39.

Cf., e.g. 156.4: *vrajáṃ ca víṣṇuḥ sákhivāṅ̐ aporṇuté* //
5 : *á yó viváya sacáthāya daívyaḥ*
índrāya víṣṇuḥ sukṛ́te sukṛ́ttaraḥ /

The verse is composed by a Viṣṇuite who places his god higher than Indra. VIII.31.10 : *víṣṇoḥ sacābhúvaḥ* is more cautious.

7. *atha yā sahasratamy āsīt tasyām indraś ca viṣṇuś ca vyāyacchetāṃ*

sa indro 'manyatānayā vā idaṃ viṣṇuḥ sahasraṃ varkṣyata iti | tasyāṃ akalpetām | dvibhāga indras tṛtīye viṣṇuḥ. Cf. also VII.1.6.7.

8. On this, see apart from Holtzmann, also Dahlmann's remarks in *Das Mahābhārata*, pp. 236-37, about Indra's relation to Viṣṇu and Śiva.

9. TS I.7.5.4; V.2.1.1 : *viṣṇumukhā vai devāḥ.*

10. TS III.4.5.

11. I.61.7 : *asyéd u mātúḥ sávaneṣu sadyó*
maháḥ pitúṃ papivā́ñ cā́rv ánnā |
muṣāyád viṣṇuḥ pacatáṃ sáhīyān
vídhyad varāháṃ tiró ádrim ástā ||

VIII.69.14 : *átīd u śakrá ohata índro víśvā áti dvíṣaḥ |*
bhinát kanī́na odanáṃ pacyámānaṃ paro girā́ ||

77.6 : *nír ā́vidhyad giríbhya ā́ dhāráyat pakvám odanám |*
índro bundáṃ svā́tatam ||

10 : *viśvét tā́ víṣṇur ā́bharad urukramás tvéṣitaḥ |*
śatáṃ mahiṣā́n kṣīrapākám odanáṃ
varāhám índra emuṣám ||

(on b, cf. VI.17.11 : *várdhān yáṃ víśve marútaḥ sajóṣāḥ*
pácac chatáṃ mahiṣā́ñ indra túbhyam |)

VIII.96.2 : *átividdhā vithuréṇā vithureṇā cid ástrā*
tríḥ saptá sā́nu sáṃhitā girīṇā́m |

See also TS VI.2.4.2; MS III.8.9 (94.15 ff.); *Kāṭhaka* XXV.2 (see p. 356, n. 256 above); ŚBr XIV. 1.2.11 : *atha varāhavihitam iyaty agra āsīd itīyati ha vā iyam agre pṛthivy āsa prādeśamātrī tām emūṣa iti varāha ujjaghāna.* Cf. the story of Caraka Br. in Sāyaṇa's commentary on VIII. 77.10.

12. Geldner, VSt, III, p. 65ff., seeks to explain too much. There are several positive arguments against him. VIII.77.10 is not an "elliptical sentence." According to TS VI.2.4.2 Viṣṇu brings the boar also to Indra after the latter has killed it; accordingly the verse is to be translated without changing the subject : "he brought hither hundred buffaloes, rice gruel and the boar." This has been discussed anew by Charpentier, *Kleine Beiträge*, p. 49 ff., who believes, perhaps with justification, that there is an ancient folk tale here and explains, with L. von Schroeder, the rice gruel as the sun, the Varāha as the boar who holds the sun (*odana*) imprisoned and who is identical with Svarbhānu.

13. II.22.1; VIII.3.8; 12.16.

14. Cf. Macdonell, p. 38; more particularly his article in JRAS, 1895, p. 165 ff.

15. PJAOS, XVI, p. cxlviii : "of his solar character remain the three steps, indicated by *vi-kram*, 'step widely', one of which is located in the zenith and the others cannot be downward or upward (which *vi-kram* would not express) but across from horizon to horizon."

16. NVO, p. 171 f. Cf. TS I.7.6.1 : *pra vā eṣo 'smāl lokāc cyavate yaḥ viṣṇukramān kramate suvargāya hi lokāya viṣṇukramāḥ kramyante*; in the Ukhā ceremony, TS IV.2.1 : *pṛthivīm anu vi kramasva...antarikṣam anu*

vi kramasva...divam anu vi kramasva...diśo 'nu vi kramasva. TBr III.1.2.6 : *tredhā viṣṇur urugāyo vicakrame / mahīṃ divaṃ pṛthivīm antarikṣam.*

17. The ritualistic saga relates that with his three strides he won back the worlds from the Asuras. ABr VI.15.11 : *indraś ca ha vai viṣṇuś cāsurair yuyudhāte tān ha sma jitvocatuḥ kalpāmahā iti / te ha tathety asurā ūcuḥ / so 'bravīd indro yāvad evāyaṃ viṣṇus trir vikramate tāvad asmākam atha yuṣmākam itarad iti / sa imāṅl lokān vicakrame 'tho vedān atho vācam...*

18. I.155.4 : *yáḥ pā́rthivāni tribhír íd vígāmabhir*
urú krámiṣṭorugāyā́yā jīváse //

19. *trír deváḥ pṛthivī́m eṣá etā́ṃ ví cakrame śatárcasaṃ mahitvā́ /*

20. Cf. TS I.8.8, 17, TBr III.1.5.7; ABr I.1.7.

21. I.154.2 : *yásyorúṣu triṣú vikrámaṇeṣu*
adhikṣiyánti bhúvanāni víśvā //
(VIII.9.12 : *yád vā viṣṇor vikrámaṇeṣu tíṣṭhataḥ aśvinā*).

22. I.154.4 : *yásya trī́ pūrṇā́ mádhunā padā́ni*
ákṣīyamāṇā svadháyā mádanti /

23. The ritual enjoins that the footprint of the Somakrayaṇī, which is reminiscent of the *goḥ pādu* of the ṚV, should be treated in a specific cult form (see Vol. I, pp. 161-62). The horse's hoof plays a role in the installation of the fire and in the Agniciti (Vol. I, p. 61; *Rituallitteratur*, p. 162).

24. I.154.5 : *tád asya priyám abhí pā́tho aśyām*
náro yátra devayávo mádanti /
urukramásya sá hí bándhur itthā́
víṣṇoḥ padé paramé mádhva útsaḥ //
6 : *tā́ vāṃ vā́stūny uśmasi gámadhyai*
yátra gā́vo bhū́riśṛṅgā ayā́saḥ /
átrā́ha tád urugāyásya vṛ́ṣṇaḥ
paramáṃ padám áva bhāti bhū́ri //

On this cf. III.55.10 :
víṣṇor gopā́ḥ paramáṃ pāti pā́thaḥ priyā́ dhā́māny amṛ́tā dádhānaḥ.
(The dual *vām* in v. 6 above refers, as Macdonell correctly explains, to Indra-Viṣṇu to whom I.155 is addressed.)
X.1.3 : *viṣṇur itthā́ paramám asya vidvā́n* [*agnéḥ*]
jātó bṛhánn abhí pāti tṛtī́yam //
I.155.5; V.3.3; VII.99.1.

25. Besides I.154.6, cf. X.15.3; AV XVIII.1.45 :
ā́háṃ pitṝ́n suvidátrā́ṅ avitsi nápātaṃ ca vikrámaṇaṃ ca víṣṇoḥ. Hopkins, PJAOS, XVI, p. cxlvii.: "Viṣṇu is the first god to represent (what he continues to represent through later ages) the sunhome of souls." Does I.164.36 : *saptā́rdhagarbhā́ bhuvanasya réto víṣṇos tiṣṭhanti pradíśā vídharmaṇi*, belong here ? (Cf. Henry, *Actes du X. congrès*, I. 1, p. 43 ff.).

26. ABr I.1.1; 4.10; TS V.5.1.4; TBr II.4.3.3-4; III.3.7.6 etc. We may assume that the *dīkṣā*, to be derived in my view from *dah*, has been inherited from the Viṣṇu cult. Just as Viṣṇu is rather a stranger to the ṚV so is the *dīkṣā* which is consecrated to him. I explain it as a consecration for a voluntary suicide by burning, through which the Saṃnyāsin attains

Viṣṇu's place. The notion of the Brāhmaṇas that one who observes the consecration will become an embryo becomes thus intelligible. It is a constituent part of the Soma sacrifice but not an organic part and was added to it only at a later date. Besides the *dīkṣā*, Viṣṇu has practically no share in the Soma sacrifice.

27. AV V.26.7 : *viṣṇur yunaktu bahudhā́ tápāṃsy asmín yajñé.* Of the priests, the Agnīdh is occasionally closer to him. However, this passage which, on the other hand, connects Indra with the Brahman has perhaps no special value (TS VII.1.5.7).

28. I.155.6 : *catúrbhiḥ sākáṃ navatíṃ ca nā́mabhiḥ*
cakráṃ na vṛttáṃ vyátīṃr avīvipat | 4×90=360 days.

Cf. also X.181.1 : *dhātúr dyútānāt savitúś ca víṣṇo rathaṃtarám ā́ jabhāra.* Hopkins (PJAOS, XVI, p. cxlvii ff.) belongs to the most resolute advocates of the solar hypothesis.

29. VII.99.3 : *vy àstabhnā ródasī viṣṇav eté dādhártha pṛthivī́m abhíto mayū́khaiḥ* ||

30. *śipiviṣṭa* is apparently the oldest epithet and is known already to the seventh book of the ṚV. Cf. VII.100.6 :

kim ít te viṣṇo paricákṣyaṃ bhūt prá yád vavakṣé śipiviṣṭó asmi |
mā́ várpo asmád ápa gūha etád yád anyárūpaḥ samithé babhū́tha ||

The commentators themselves do not know any more how to explain this word. The comm. on TS VII.5.5.5 declares, *paśavaḥ śipir iti*, on II.5.5.2 : *śrutyantarāc chipiśabdaḥ paśuvācī*, the one on TMBr IX.7.8 : *śipayo raśmayas tair āviṣṭaḥ śipiviṣṭaḥ* (=Sāyaṇa). We find special oblations for Viṣṇu śipiviṣṭa in the Darśapūrṇamāsāyanas, ŚŚS III.2.2; TS II 5.5 : *ye* [*taṇḍulā*] *madhyamāḥ syus tān agnaye dātre puroḍāśam...kuryād, ye sthaviṣṭhās tān indrāya pradātre..., ye 'niṣṭhās tān viṣṇave śipiviṣṭāya śṛte carum.* Differently MS II.2.13 (25.10) during the Saṃsṛpāmiṣṭi-s (ŚŚS XV.14.4). Of the Yajñatanu-iṣṭakāḥ, one dedicated to Śipiviṣṭa is called *āsādita*, and the one to Viṣṇu is called *upāvahriyamāṇa* (TS IV.4.9). Johansson, *Solfågeln*, p. 12 ff. explains this obscure epithet *śipiviṣṭa* as the "one who is in the *liṅga*" and thinks that it is related to *śepa*, "penis" (cf., on this Charpentier, *Kleine Beiträge*, p. 54; but differently in KZ, XLVI, p. 32). This would be quite in keeping with Viṣṇu's association with birth and progeny. Güntert, *Der arische Weltkönig und Heiland*, p. 365, likewise connects the first part with *śepa* etc. and the second with *viṣṭí—*, *viṣṭíbhiḥ*, "changing" which is implicit in Irish *fecht*, "times," Old High German *wehsal.* "If we add *viṣṭá* to it, then the word can be interpreted in the sense of the swelling and diminishing of the phallus. Thus the phallic character of the god is clearly maintained in the word." All this is quite doubtful.

31. Thoroughly discussed by Macdonell, "Mythological Studies," JRAS, 1895, p. 168 ff.

32. Hemādri, 1378. Caland, *Altindischer Ahnenkult*, p. 188. In philosophical texts, the gods are thought of as *prādeśamātra* (ŚBr X.6.1.10).

33. TS I.8.8; 8.17; II.1.3.1 : *vaiṣṇavaṃ vāmanam ā labheta spardhamāno, viṣṇur eva bhūtvemāṃ lokān abhi jayati; viṣama ā labheta...*; 5.2; 8.3; TBr

I.2.5.1; 6.1.6; 7.2.3; MS II.5.3 (50.2; 51.1); 6.13 (72.14); IV.3.1 (40.5). This notion leads to a magical rite. According to *Ṛgvidhāna* I.17.4 ff., he inserts his thumb into the food with five Viṣṇu verses and thus wards of the Rakṣas'. Cf. Caland, *loc. cit.*

34. He states on p. 14 : "that from the beginning Viṣṇu is conceived primarily within the realm of animistic conceptions, and that only at a later point he was brought into association with a deity or was transformed into it under the influence, in particular, of the sacrificial technique which was developed in a Brahmanical way and of the fusion between the animistic elements and the more and more clearly developed concepts of celestial gods—a development which could not happen in later times so completely as not to reveal suddenly the original character through such traits which cannot possibly be of celestial or of solar character."

35. ABr I.15.4; KBr IV.2; TS II.1.8.3; TBr III.1.6.7; TMBr IX.7.5.8. It is also said that Viṣṇu is *yajñasya duriṣṭaṃ pāti...yathā vai matyam evaṃ yajñasya viṣṇuḥ* (ABr III.38.3).

36. TS VI.2.4.2; Sāyaṇa on ṚV VIII.77.10.

37. This is a custom of the Aitareyins (NVO, p. 84). There the two verses, ṚV I.22.17 and VII.99.7 serve as the Yājyā and the Puronuvākyā respectively (according to ŚŚS I.11.8). The employment of these verses here and elsewhere does not seem to be an original custom.

38. ŚŚS V.7.1; ĀpŚS X.30.1; TS I.2.10 etc.; a *navakapāla* during the Ātithyeṣṭi of the Soma sacrifice which is connected with the piling up of the altar (ŚŚS IX.24.7).

39. ĀpŚS XI.3.12.

40. ŚŚS VI.11.5. And also the verses of hymn I.154. (This hymn is employed elsewhere also, but by all appearances this is not the original custom).

41. ŚŚS VI.11.5. (I think it is superfluous to add quotations from other Sūtras). For this the verses of VI.69 are employed; incidentally these verses are recited elsewhere too.

42. E g. TS V.6.16 : *śuṇṭhās trayo vaiṣṇavā, adhīlodhakarṇās trayo viṣṇava urukramāya, lapsudinas trayo viṣṇava urugāyāya.*

43. IX.33.2; 34.2; 56.4; 63.3; 65.20; 90.5; 100.6. Cf. also VI.69.5. No special value should be attached to the fact that in IX.96.5 Soma is called *janitā́ matīnā́m, diváḥ, pṛthivyā́ḥ, agnéḥ, sū́ryasya, índrasya, víṣṇoḥ.*

44. ĀpSS XII.21.12. Cf. ŚBr IV.2.2.10 : *viṣṇus tvām indriyeṇa pātu, viṣṇuṃ tvaṃ pāhi.* Compare this with TBr III.2.3.12 : *viṣṇo hávyaṃ rakṣasva*; 7.4.18.

45. A few times Viṣṇu is identified with Soma; the path by which the theologians reached this idea is not clear. ŚBr III.6.3.19 : *yo vai viṣṇuḥ somaḥ saḥ.* Perhaps we should refer to III.5.3.2 for explanation.

46. KŚS X.7.11.

47. TS I.4.12.

48. Ibid., VI.5.1.3.

49. E.g. NVO, p. 23. With the mantra, "may Viṣṇu mount you," he

climbs up over the southern wheel. During the Vājapeya he says to the cart: *viṣṇoḥ kramo'si* (TS I.7.7. g).

50. Cf. ĀpŚS XI.7.3 : *vaiṣṇavam asi viṣṇus tvottabhnātv ity upastabhya divo vā viṣṇav ity adhvaryur dakṣiṇasya havirdhānasya dakṣiṇaṃ karṇātardam anu methīṃ nihanti* etc. TS III.1.6.1 : *vaiṣṇavyā havirdhānam abhimṛśet;* VI.2.9.4 : *vaiṣṇavaṃ hi devatayā havirdhānam.* TMBr I.1.8 : *viṣṇoḥ śiro 'si yośodhā* (comm. *havirdhānamaṇḍapo viṣṇudevatākatvāt...*).

51. TS II.2.9.2 ff. : *devatābhir eva devatāḥ praticaranti, yajñena yajñam;* 7. *kapālair eva cchandāṃsy āpnoti, puroḍāśaiḥ savanāni. Ritualliteratur,* p. 178.

52. I limit myself to pointing out other symbolizations the origins of which are obscure; for example, the *pṛṣadājya* is addressed thus : *viṣṇoṛ hṛdayam asi, ekam iṣa viṣṇus tvānu vi cakrame* (TS III.2.6). The Soma stones, boards, resonance holes and the skin on which the pressing is done belong to Viṣṇu, ĀpŚS XI.11.6; XII.2.15 etc. The Droṇakalaśa is addressed as follows : "you are Viṣṇu's body" (ĀpŚS XII.18.20). Thus we have a considerable number of allusions; but the key to their meaning is wanting.

53. TS II.2.9.1 ff. See also I.8.1.2; 8.8 etc.

54. Cf. TS V.6.14, 16.

55. TS II.1.4.4; ABr III.38.3; TMBr VIII.8.6.

56. AV VII.25.1-2; MS IV.14.6; TBr II.8.4.4. Cf. p. 309, n. 272 above.

57. Besides the passages cited on p. 378, n. 523, perhaps also the very cursory mention in ṚV I.85.7; X.65.1; 92.11. It is only patent that here the Maruts appear in some association or other with Viṣṇu, who takes Indra's place according to the views of some.

58. AV VII.46.3. Cf. also AV XIV.2.15 and Viṣṇu's connection to the progeny in AV VII.17.4; V.25.5 (=ṚV X.184.1).

59. III.52.7

60. ABr II.24.5. ĀpŚS XII.4.6. Ibid., XII.4.13 states on the Karambha : *manthaṃ saṃyutaṃ karambha ity ācakṣate.* The commentary explains thus : *saktavo manthaḥ | te tv adbhir ājyādinā vā saṃyutāḥ karambha ity ākhyāyante.* But the same commentary on VIII.5.37 states : *śamīpattramiśrāṇi karīrāṇi karambhāḥ.* KŚS V.3.2 : *karambho dadhnā saṃyutāḥ saktavaḥ.*

61. TS II.2.1.4. Cf. MS II.1.4 (6.5) : *saumāpauṣṇaṃ caruṃ nirvapen nemapiṣṭaṃ paśukāmaḥ | somo vai retodhāḥ pūṣā paśūnāṃ prajanayitā.*

62. ṚV VI.56.1 : *yá enam ādídeśati karambhád iti pūṣáṇam |*
ná téna deva ādíśe ||

63. ŚBr I.7.4.7. *Vāyupurāṇa* XXX.253 (cf. 256) : *bhaganetrāntakaś candraḥ pūṣṇo dantavināśanaḥ. karūḷatī* in ṚV IV.30.24 is obscure; Perry renders it as "broken-toothed."

64. Thus he is called in TS II.6.8.5 : *pūṣā prāśya dato 'rúṇat* etc.

65. KŚS VIII.8.26.

66. During the 12 Ratnahavis, offerings are made to him in the house

of the Bhāgadugha, the dakṣiṇā for it being a *śyāma*-coloured animal (TS I.7.9.6).

67. VI.54.5 ff.; Bergaigne, II, p. 430. Hence it is said in the later period also, *pūṣā paśubhiḥ*, TS I.5.1.2; TBr I.7.6.6; 8.1.1; MS II.2.4 (18.2); TĀr V.7.2. Even when one desires to recover what has been lost one invokes Pūṣan, ĀśvGS III.7.9.

68. VI.54.5 ff. He heals the lame animal also, TBr III.9.17.2 : *pūṣā vai śloṇyasya bhiṣak / sa evainaṃ bhiṣajyati.*

69. Cf. MS I.5.11 (80.4) : *pūṣā mādhipathipāḥ pātū, pūṣā mā paśupāḥ pātu.* The *pathyā* is regarded as his wife, MŚS II.2.4.11, and he grants the *pathyā́ svastí* (ṚV X.59.7; 17.5). Cf. Bergaigne, II, p. 430.

He is invoked when one goes on a business trip or when one wishes to undertake a long or dangerous journey. (ĀśvGS III.7.8, 10). According to MS I.5.14 (83.5), one who is about to undertake a journey says at the time of parting : *avinaṣṭān avihrutān pūṣainān abhirakṣatv āsmākam punar-āgamat.* On Pūṣan as the pioneer, see Gustav Herbig, "Zur Vorgeschichte der römischen Pontifices," KZ, XLVII, p. 211 ff. The identification of Pūṣan with the earth probably derives from his knowledge of the paths : *iyaṃ vai pūṣā* (TS VI.1.7.6).

70. VI.48.15. Cf. Bloomfield, SBE, XLII, p. 542. There is only one passage where the word does not denote the god. X.33.1 : *váhāmi sma pūṣáṇam ántareṇa*, "I drove without a patron." In my view this hymn is a lamentation of the poet for his late patron Kuruśravaṇa. Here Pūṣan means "patron, or one who feeds or maintains." Geldner, VSt, II, p. 184, is wrong.

71. ṚV VI.54.5, 6.

72. Ibid., X.26.6.

73. Ibid., I.138.4; VI.55.3 etc. : *ajā́śva;* 6 : *ájāso...ráthe janaśriyaṃ vahantu;* X.26.7 : *ā́ te ráthasya pūṣan ajā́ dhúraṃ vavṛtyuḥ;* AV XVIII.2.53 : *ágnīṣomāv úpa préṣyataṃ pūṣáṇaṃ yó váhāty ajayā́naiḥ pathíbhis tátra gacchatam.* The goat is regarded as the symbol of the fire (Vol. I, p. 62). According to TS IV.1.6.1; V.1.7.4, goat's milk is poured on the ukhā : *paramaṃ vā etat payo ajakṣīram*; the commentary says that goat's milk is the means for curing all diseases. Incidentally this is a notion prevalent also among us in the countryside.

74. TMBr I.8.12.

75. ṚV X.26.7.

76. Ibid., VI.55.2.

77. VI.53.9 : *yā́ te áṣṭrā gópaśā ...paśusā́dhanī*; 85.2 : *áṣṭrāṃ...śithirā́m udvā́rīvṛjat saṃcákṣāṇo bhúvanā...īyate.* The *áṣṭrā* occurs next to *vāhá, lā́ṅgala, varatrā́* in IV.57.4, a hymn addressed to the "lord of the field." On "lance" as a weapon of herdsmen, see Roscher, "Über den gegenwärtigen Stand der Forschung...", ARW, I, p. 63.

78. VI.53.5 : *pári tṛndhi paṇīnā́m ā́rāyā hṛ́dayā*, 6, 8. In the later period, according to the commentary on *Amarakośa* II.10.35, the *ārā* is a *carmakhaṇḍanārthaḥ śastrabhedaḥ.*

79. *The Cyclopedia of India*, s.v. Khoj (after *Calcutta Review*, No. LXXIII, September 1861, p. 11).

80. I have not been able to find anything on the Khojis in the sources available to me. I quote the following from a report from Kapurthala, printed in the *Kölnische Zeitung* of 14.2.1892, No. 123 (first supplement) : "These [scouts] are the terror not only of thieves but also of other criminals... There are families of scouts who can produce with assurance and pride a family-tree which would be looked at with envy by many a nobleman of Europe...Often the pursuit [of the criminal] is connected with great difficulties. While the Khoji exerts all his ingenuity to locate the criminal, the latter is equally clever and tries all the means to evade the pursuit. After he has gone awhile by foot, he wraps a piece of cloth around his feet, rides on an ox for some time, goes backwards or strides through a stream or a river. All this, however, should not confuse a good scout. Distances do not weigh with him...Once a scout set upon the pursuit of a criminal up to the banks of the river Beas. There he lost the trace because the Maharaja had crossed the river at that point with his entourage of two hundred men shortly before. With so many footprints it seemed next to impossible to find the trace which he had followed so far. Nevertheless the Khoji decided not to give up pursuit. In order to have a better picture of the traces in his mind, he followed them backwards for several miles, then returned to the bank, caused himself to be conveyed to the other shore, and there, among more than two hundred footprints, picked up really the traces of the fugitive whom he caught after a pursuit lasting more than eight days. It is also worth stating that a Khoji lives here who was paralyzed years ago and yet, armed with a long staff, he follows the traces..." Cf. *Mitteilungen der geographischen Gesellschaft zu Wien*, 1904, XLVII, p.351 ff.; Kauffmann, *Aus Indiens Dschungeln*, Leipzig 1911, p. 104.

81. Perry opines similarly in his "Notes on the Vedic deity Pūṣan" (*Classical Studies in Honour of Henry Drisler*, 1894), which contain good observations, p. 241: "...the Bhāradvāja-clan seems to have been most devoted to Pūṣan; and next to them comes the Clan of the Kāṇvas, the entire hymn ṚV I.42 being ascribed to Kaṇva Gaura and some halfdozen verses of Book I, with an equal number in Book VIII, the Kāṇvabook, to other members of that clan. It is accordingly not an unwarrantable supposition —though I admit the lack of cogent proof—that from these two clans his cult spread among the other tribes."

82. Hymn 57 is addressed to Indra-Pūṣan.

83. *Ritualliteratur*, p. 10.

84. Ibid., p. 170. VI.48.17 also probably accompanied a malevolent magic :

mā́ kākambī́ram úd vṛho vánaspátim áśastīr ví hí nī́naśaḥ /
mótá sū́ro áha evā́ etc.

85. E.g. VII.9.1-3=ṚV X.17.6, 5; VI.54.9.

86. v. 15 is not clear :

utó sá máhyam índubhiḥ
ṣáḍ yuktā̃n [ṛtū́n ?] anuséṣidhat |

87. VI.56.3 : *utā́dáḥ paruṣé gávi sū́raś cakrám hiraṇyáyam* |
ny aìrayad rathī́tamaḥ ||

88. VI.55.4, 5 : *mātúr didhiṣúm abravaṃ svásur jāráḥ śṛṇotu naḥ* |

89. VI.58.4 : *yáṃ devā́so ádaduḥ sūryā́yai*
kā́mena kṛtáṃ tavásaṃ svā́ñcam ||

according to Bergaigne, II, p. 437 f. See particularly Pischel, VSt, I, p. 21, who interprets him as son, which is doubtful. The passages do not offer adequate material to decide this.

90. VI.58.3 : *yā́s te pūṣan nā́vo antáḥ samudré*
hiraṇyáyīr antárikṣe cáranti |
tā́bhir yāsi dūtyā́ṃ sū́ryasya
kā́mena kṛta śráva icchámānaḥ ||

Pischel, *loc. cit.*, translates as "to Sūrya." I maintain that here also a definitive interpretation is not yet possible. Aśvins' relation to Pūṣan remains obscure. In this I see a late contamination of the two mythical cycles.

Perry, *loc. cit.*, p. 243, observes : "more significant are his relations to Sūryā, especially in the legend of Sūryā's marriage to the Aśvins, which has been so ably discussed by Pischel, VStud, I, 11-52. Here is doubtless a real myth—the result, I think, of the meeting of different streams of legend, in one of which Pūṣan, in the other Sūryā, plays the chief role."

91. X.5.5 : *antár yeme antárikṣe purājā́ icchán vavrím avidad pūṣaṇásya* is not clear.

92. X.17.3 : *pūṣā́ tvetáś cyā́vayatu prá vidvā́n*
ánaṣṭapaśur bhúvanasya gopā́ḥ |

93. Cf. also IX.67.10 : *avitā́ na ajā́śvaḥ pūṣā́ yāmaniyāmani* |
ā́ bhakṣat kanyā̀su naḥ ||

and X.85.37 : *tā́ṃ pūṣañ chivátamān érayasva*
yásyāṃ bī́jaṃ manuṣyā vápanti ||

94. On this, cf. X.16.4 from the hymn to the dead : *ajó bhāgás tápasā táṃ tapasva.*

95. I notice that Perry, *loc. cit.*, also interprets the dual as the sun and the moon. In the ritual, oblations are occasionally offered to both, caru-offerings as well as animal sacrifices. MS II.2.4.

96. VI.48.16; 53.3, 8, 9; 55.1,3. The qualities attributed to him in TĀr IV.16 are not clear : *śaras, narandhiṣa, aṅghṛṇi. naruṇa* and *sāketa.* There are still other epithets like *abhyardhayájvan* VI.50.5; *prátyardhir yajñā́nām* X.26.5. A further epithet is *vimuco napāt* in I.42.1 etc. Cf. Bloomfield, SBE, XLII, p. 526. The preceding words of the same verse support us when we translate *vimuco napāt* as the "son of liberation" : *sáṃ pūṣann ádhvanas tira vy áṃho vimuco napāt* |

97. On I.23.13 : *āgatadīptiyukta*; III.62.7 : *āgatadīptimant*; VI.48.16; 53.3, 8; VIII.4.17 : *āgatadīpte* etc. The explanation differs only in the commentary on I.138.4 : *sarvato vṛṣṭeḥ kṣārayitaḥ* | *yadvā haviṣām āhartaḥ, svīkartaḥ.* Oldenberg, RdV, 2nd ed., p. 236, n. 4, doubts the meaning

"glowing" but *gharmá, ghṛ́ṇi, ghraṃsá* (from the root 2, *ghar*) cannot be separated from the word and support the meaning.

98. Cf. Vol. I, p. 364, n. 52.

99. Sūrya :

I.24.8 : *urúṃ hí rā́jā váruṇaś cakā́ra*
sū́ryāya pánthām ánvetavā́ u / (VII.87.1).

71.9 : *máno ná yó 'dhvanaḥ sadyá éti*
ékaḥ satrā́ sū́ro vásva īśe /

100.2 : *yásya* [*índrasya*] *ánāptaḥ sū́ryasyeva yā́maḥ*

113.16 : *áraik pánthāṃ yā́tave sū́ryāya*

III.30.12 : *díśaḥ sū́ryo ná mināti prádiṣṭāḥ...*
sáṃ yád ā́naḷ ádhvana ā́d íd áśvair
vimócanaṃ kṛṇute tát tv àsya //

VII.60.4 : *...ā́ sū́ryo aruhac chukrám árṇaḥ*
yásmā ādityā́ ádhvano rádanti...//

Savitṛ :

I.35.11 : *yé te pánthāḥ savitaḥ pūrvyā́saḥ*
areṇávaḥ súkṛtā antárikṣe /

VII.76.1 : *úd u jyótir...savitā́ devó aśret* /

2 : *prá me pánthā devayā́nā adṛśran...*

Aryaman, see p. 47ff. above; Mitra :

V.64.3 : *yán nūnám aśyā́ṃ gátiṃ mitrásya yāyāṃ pathā́* /

I have noted the following from other texts.

AV XIII.2.14 : *ádhvāsya vítato mahā́n pū́rvaś cā́paraś ca yáḥ* [*sūryasya*].

VS V.33.b : *ádhvanām adhvapate prá mā tira svastí me 'smín pathí devayā́ne bhūyāt.*

MS IV.8.5 (112.9) : *eṣa vā apariparaḥ panthā arakṣasyo yenāsā āditya eti.*

TS VI.1.6.3 : *eṣá khálu vā́ árakṣohataḥ pánthā yò 'gnéś ca sū́ryasya.*
ĀśvŚS V.3.14 during the sun worship : *adhvanām adhvapate śreṣṭhaḥ svastyasyādhvanaḥ pāram aśiya* (Āditya). TMBr I.4.1.

Indra :

I.104.2 : *nū́ cit tā́n sadyó ádhvano jagamyāt* /

X.22.4 : *syántā pathā́ virúkmatā sṛjāná stoṣy ádhvanaḥ* //

Agni :

I.72.7 : *antarvidvā́ñ ádhvano devayā́nān*

VI.16.3 : *vétthā hí vedho ádhvanaḥ patháś ca...*

Soma :

IX.52.2 : *táva pratnébhir ádhvabhir* ... etc.

100. VI.57.4 : *yád indro ánayad apó vṛ́ṣantamaḥ* /
tátra pūṣā́bhavat sácā //

101. VI.57.2 : *sómam anyá úpāsadat pā́tave camvòḥ sutám* /
karambhám anyá icchati //

3 : *ajā́ anyásya váhnayo hárī anyásya sáṃbhṛtā* /
tā́bhyāṃ vṛtrā́ṇi jighnate //

102. ŚSS VI.11.1 lists the verses for an animal sacrifice for Indra-

Pūṣan. ṚV I.162.2 mentions a he-goat for them in the Aśvamedha, and the ritual also enjoins accordingly (cf. ŚŚS XVI.3.32; TBr III.8.23.2 etc.), likewise in the Rājasūya (ŚŚS XV.12.7). In the Aśvamedha they receive other joint animal sacrifices as well (*śyāmalalāmās tūparāḥ*).

103. Cf. VIII.54.4 : *pūṣā́ víṣṇur hávanaṃ me sárasvaty ávantu saptá síndhavaḥ* /

104. The Sarasvatī hymn VI.61 is separated from the preceding Pūṣan hymns by two addressed to Indrāgnī.

105. Cf. TS I.2.2.; VI.1.2.2 : *sarasvatyai pūṣṇe 'gnaye svāhā*; IV.1.11. ik : Yājyāpuronuvākye for Sarasvatī; lm : for Pūṣan; V.5.12 :...*dhātuḥ / sarasvatyai śāriḥ śyetā puruṣavāk, sarasvate śukaḥ śyetaḥ puruṣavāg, āraṇyo 'jo nakulā śakā te pauṣṇā vāce*...; VI.6.5.1 : *mithunaṃ sarasvatyā karoti retaḥ saumyena dadhāti pra janayati pauṣṇena.* TBr I.6.2.2 : *somo reto 'dadhāt, savitā prājanayat, sarasvatī vācam adadhāt, pūṣāpoṣayat*; 8.4.2 :... *sārasvataṃ caruṃ nirvapati / tasmāt prāvṛṣi sarvā vāco vadanti / pauṣṇena vyavasyanti*; II.1.7.1 : *pauṣṇam udantaṃ sārasvataṃ viṣyandamānam*; 5.3.3 : *pūṣā no gobhir avasā sarasvatī;* 5.7.4 : *pūṣā viśāṃ viṭpatiḥ...sarasvatī puṣṭiḥ puṣṭipatnī.* MS I.10.5 (145.16) : *sarasvaty eva sṛṣṭāsu vācam adadhāt pūṣaṇaṃ pratiṣṭhām abhy asṛjyanta / vāg vai sarasvatī, paśavaḥ pūṣā*; III.6.4 (64.1). ABr II.24.5 : *indraḥ pūṣaṇvān, indraḥ sarasvatīvān.*

106. Geiger, *Ostiranische Kultur im Altertum*, p. 364 ff.

107. TS II.1.2.6; ŚBr XIII.2.2.4; a ram in the Sautrāmaṇī; TBr II.6. 15.1.

108. Pischel, VSt, II, p. 210.

109. Zimmer, AIL, pp. 30 ff., 229.

110. Thornton, *Gazetteer of the Countries adjacent to India*, London 1844, I, p. 21 : "Should Afghanistan advance in cultivation...its wool would unquestionably become its most important element of wealth...The fine wool of Afghanistan is produced from goats and sheep...the fleeces are obtained at two seasons" etc., and later "the physiology of wool appears to be very little understood; it is produced of the finest quality, both in the sultry wilds of Kandahar and of Spain, and in the table-land of Pamir..."

111. Vol. I, pp 148, 352. This Sarasvatī is invoked in the Sautrāmaṇī also where, in the company of the Aśvins, she cures Indra who fell ill after consuming the Soma. Vol. I, pp. 148, 326. She is called *marútsakhā* in VII.96.2, *marútvatī* in II.30.8, and the Maruts are mentioned in direct association with her in III.54.13; VII.36.6, 7; 39.5. In the Yajus texts also she is glorified with formulas which are partly transferred to her from other gods. TBr I.7.5.5, during the Sārasvatagraha : *apām oṣadhīnāṃ rasa sthety āha /...sārasvataṃ grahaṃ gṛhṇāti, eṣā vā apāṃ pṛṣṭhaṃ yat sarasvatī*; II.4.6.1 : *uta naḥ priyā priyāsu saptasvasā sujuṣṭā* (=ṚV VI.61.10, cf. VII.36.6 : *saptáthī síndhumātā*); 5.8.6 etc. (cf. p. 119 above).

112. Sarasvatī does not occur in the fourth Maṇḍala.

113. Pūṣan is also associated with the *dhī*. He drives the *dhiyaḥ* of the singer as one drives the animals. IX.88.3 : *pūṣéva dhījávano 'si soma;* X.26.4.

114. Cf. I.3.11 : *codayitrī sūnṛtānāṃ cétantī sumatīnā́m* /
yajñáṃ dadhe sárasvatī //
12 : *dhíyo víśvā ví rājati* //
VII.35.11 : *sarasvatī sahá dhībhíḥ*
IX.67.32 : *pāvamānī́r yó 'dhyéti...* /
tásmai sárasvatī duhe kṣīráṃ sarpír mádhūdakám
X.65.13 : *víśve dévāsaḥ śṛṇavan vácāṃsi me*
sárasvatī sahá dhībhíḥ púraṃdhyā //
AV V.7.4 : *sárasvatīm ánumatim bhágaṃ yánto havāmahe* /
vā́caṃ juṣṭā́m avādiṣam... //
10.8 : *sárasvatyā vā́cam úpa hvayāmahe manoyújā*

I cannot quite see the reasons which led to the association between Vāc and Sarasvatī and to their total identification. One reason might be the cultivation of the traditions and of the sacred language on the banks of the river in the middle country and another might be of mythological nature. I cite the following passages also.

TBr I.8.1.1 : *sarasvatyā vācā dvitīye (prāyuṅkta)*; 4.2 : *sārasvataṃ caruṃ nirvapati* / *tasmāt prāvṛṣi sarvā vāco vadanti pauṣṇena vyavasyanti.* Does the association with the Atirātra (TMBr I.3.4.1 : *aindreṇa ṣoḍaśinastotraṃ sārasvatyātirātram*) belong here ?

TS VII.2.7.4 : *vāg vai sarasvatī* / *vācaivainam ati pra yuṅkte.* TMBr VI.7.7; ABr III.1.10; 2.10; MS III.6.4 (64.1).

ABr III.4.10 : *atha yat sphūrjayan vācam iva vadan dahati tad asya sārasvataṃ rūpam.*

TS II.1.2.6; TBr I.3.4.5 : *sārasvatīṃ meṣīm ālabheta ya īśvaro vāco vaditoḥ san vācaṃ na vadet...*/ *apannadatī bhavati* / *tasmān manuṣyāḥ sarvāṃ vācaṃ vadanti* /

115. *sárasvatīṃ yā́ṃ pitáro hávante dakṣiṇā́ yajñám abhinákṣamāṇāḥ* /

116. According to ĀśvŚS VI.10, verses 3-6 are recited at the death of a Dīkṣita; according to ŚŚS VI.10.4; ĀśvŚS III.7, verses 4 and 5 during the Aikādaśina Paśu for Pūṣan. The ritual employs these verses in this and in other cases in a way which is not original and to some extent, to judge from the content, inappropriate as well. What is more important is that v. 10 is employed, according to ŚŚS IV.15.4, during the death-ceremony, and vv. 3,5,4, according to the Taittirīyas, when the procession moves towards the cremation ground (Caland, *Die altindischen Todten- und Bestattungsgebräuche*, p. 23).

117. *Kauśika Sūtra* LXXXI. 35 ff. Caland, *op. cit.*, p. 64.

118. The ritual represents this in a slightly different manner. Seven pits are dug in the shape of a stream. During the Śāntikarman, the relatives must cross these pits obviously so that these streams lie between the departed person and themselves. Caland, *op. cit.*, p. 121.

119. Weber, ISt, I, pp. 398-9; Kuhn, KZ, II. p. 311 ff.; Lassen, IAK, 2nd ed., I, p. 674; (Pischel, VSt, II, p. 73); Scherman, *Visions-literatur*, p. 115.

120. The concept of a stream of the dead in the sky is quite widespread. Cf. Andree, *Ethnographische Parallelen*, p. 110.

121. *sarasvatyā vai devā ādityam astabhnuvan | sā nāyacchat | sābhyavlīyata | tasmāt sā nyubjimatīva | taṃ bṛhatyāstabhnuvan | sāyacchat | tasmād bṛhatī chandasāṃ vīryavattamā*..

122. AV VII.68.1 : *sárasvati vratéṣu te divyéṣu devi dhā́masu |*
juṣásva havyám ā́hutam ||

Incidentally, even already in hymn VI.61 (vv. 1-3 Jagatī, 4-12 Gāyatrī; 13 Jagatī, 14 Triṣṭubh) it is said of Sarasvatī in v. 11 : *āpaprúṣī pā́rthivāny urú rájo antárikṣam.* Does the verse originally belong here ? Besides the Sarasvatī, the *hotrā bhāratī* (Oldenberg, RdV, p. 243) and the *ilā* are mentioned. ṚV I.13.9; 142.9; 188.8; II.1.11; 3.8; III.4.8; IX.5.8; X.110.8; AV V.27.9; TS V.1.11.3. Just as the stream on the banks of which the Bharatas dwelt was transferred to the heavens so is their "sacrificial oblation."

123. This connection of the Sarasvatī with the New Moon remains quite unusal. TS III.5.1.4: *sārasvatau homau purastāj juhuyād, amāvāsyā vai sarasvaty anulomam evaināv ālabhate ... sarasvatyai carur bhavati sarasvate dvādaśakapālo 'māvāsyā vai sarasvatī pūrṇamāsaḥ sarasvān.* I know of no other ground than that both Sarasvatī and the New Moon are associated with the Manes.

124. Thus Ludwig.

125. Geldner, "who leads to different directions."

126. According to Sāyaṇa : "on the earth (in the shape of the plant), and in the atmosphere (as the moon)."

127. ṚV X.85.18.

128. MS II.5.10 (61.12); another reading in AV IX.4.5 : *somasya bhakṣam avṛṇīta śakraḥ* (that is Indra). Cf. also SV I.154 (ed. Benfey, p. 16):
sómaḥ pūṣā́ ca cetatur víśvāsāṃ sukṣitīnā́m |
devátrā rathyòr hitā́ ||

129. TS II.4.4.3 : *somo vai retodhāḥ | pūṣā paśūnāṃ prajanayitā | soma evāsmai reto dadhāti | pūṣā paśūn pra janayati.* MS II.2.4 (18.1, 7); 6.4 (65.17). According to MS II.5.5 (53.19) a eunuch is sacrificed to them.

130. III, 333 and V, 392 (on X.17).

131. I, p. 89 : "In fact the word *vivasvat* has become in later literature a name for the sun. I would even admit, if it comes to that, that he was called by this name from the earliest times. I would admit that the expression in X.39.12: 'the two days (day and night) of Vivasvat,' very naturally suggests that the sun is meant and in any case Vivasvat figures as a divine being in X.65.6 along with Varuṇa and the gods. It will still remain equally true that the conception of Agni, of whom the sun is only one of the forms, can alone account for the character of an ancient sacrificer, which is the dominant trait of Vivasvat in the ṚV."

132. I.44.1; 96.2; III.30.13; VII.9.3. However, in I.96.2 it can also be a substantive. Perhaps I.31.3. The case is not clear in I.187.7 (*pito... vivásva párvatānām*) and VIII.102.22 (*agním īdhe vivásvabhiḥ*). Roth's attempt (in *Verhandlungen des 7. Orientalisten-Kongresses*, p. 8) to equate *vivasva párvatānām* with *vivásvatāṃ párvatānām* seems doubtful to me as it does to Bartholomae (KZ, XXIX, p. 542, p. 1).

133. I.53.1; III.34.7; 51.3.

134. I.2.6 : *vā́yav índraś ca sunvatá ā́ yātam úpa niṣkṛtám / makṣv itthā́ dhiyā́ narā́*; II.41.2 : *gántāsi sunvató gṛhám*; III.58.9 : *táṃ pātam ā́ gataṃ duroṇé / rátho ha vām...sutā́vato niṣkṛtám ā́gamiṣṭhaḥ.*

135. VIII.6.39 : *mándasvā sú svàrṇara uténdra śaryaṇā́vati /*
mátsvā vívasvato matī́ //

"Become exhilerated, O Indra, in Svarṇara and at Śaryaṇāvat; delight in the hymn of Vivasvat (the sacrificer)."

136. IX.14.5 : *naptī́bhir yó vivásvataḥ śubhró ná māmṛjé yúvā /*
"he who is adorned by the fingers (cf. *dáśa yuvatáyaḥ, yóṣaṇaḥ, svásāraḥ*) of Vivasvat, like a handsome youth."

137. IX.99.2 : *yádi vivásvato dhíyo háriṃ hinvánti yā́tave //*
"when the sacrificer's skill sends the golden one on his journey."

138. IX.66.8 : *sám u tvā dhībhir asvaran*
hinvatī́ḥ saptá jāmáyaḥ /
vípram ājā́ vivásvataḥ //

139. It is not clear whether it is the god or the earthly sacrificer who is meant in X.65.6 : *sā́ [gaúr] prabruvāṇā́ váruṇāya dāśúṣe devébhyó dāśad dhavíṣā vivásvate.* I would think that it is the god.

140. See Ludwig, IV, p. 406 (No. 423, v. 7); Ehni, *Yama*, p. 25.

141. Vol. I, p. 172. Cf. also X.63.1 (see n. 172. below).

142. VS VIII.5. See PW; MS I.6.12 (105.6).

143. II.13.6 : *yó bhójanaṃ ca dáyase ca várdhanam...*
sá śevadhíṃ ní dadhiṣe vivásvati
víśvasyaika īśiṣe sā́sy ukthyàḥ //

144. VIII.3.8 : *asyéd índro vāvṛdhe vṛ́ṣṇyaṃ śávo máde sutásya víṣṇavi /*
12.16 : *yát sómam indra víṣṇavi yád vā gha tritá āptyé /*
yád vā marútsu mándase sám índubhiḥ //
X.113.2 : *tám asya [índrasya] víṣṇur mahimā́nam ójasā*
aṃśúṃ dadhanvā́n mádhuno ví rapśate /

145. IV.18.3; III.48.4.

146. MS III.8.10 (109.12) : *ta etāni dvitīyāni nāmāny adhatta* (?) *maṅgalecchāyai somapītho nā upanamād iti / tasmād ete dvināmānaḥ.* TS VI.3.1.3.

147. III.6.2.24 : *tasmād brāhmaṇo 'nṛdhyamāne dvitīyaṃ nāma kurvīta / rādhnoti haiva ya evaṃ vidvān dvitīyaṃ nāma kurute.* TS, *loc. cit. dvināmā brāhmaṇo 'rdhukaḥ.*

148. The only passage where one could look for an allusion to this is ṚV VII.33.13 : *satré jātáu* (Hauer, *Die Anfänge der Yogapraxis im alten Indien*, p. 71), but it is not so certain.

149. Similarly ŚBr III.2.2.10.

150. On the Dīkṣā itself, see Lindner, *Die Dīkṣā*, Leipzig 1878.

The consecration is not an original constituent of the Soma sacrifice but one of the many accretions which enriched the sacrifice in the course of the history of ritual.

The word is a desiderative formation. The ŚBr apparently derives the word from *dih* (III.2.2.30 : *sa vai dhīkṣate vāce hi dhīkṣate yajñāya hi dhīkṣate*; see Weber in PW, s.v. *dhīkṣ*, Eggeling, SBE, XXV, p. 47, n. 1) and the PW from *dakṣ*,. But the desiderative of *dih* as well as *dakṣ* ought to be quite different. On the analogy of *sah* and *sīkṣ*, *dabh* and *dhīps*, *dips*, we should trace *dīkṣ* back to *dah*, provided we did not have to expect *dhīkṣ*. The ṚV preserves two *s*-forms of *dah* which are valuable for the assessment of *dīkṣ*. These are listed already in the *Prātiśākhya* IV.41 (Benfey, *Kleinere Schriften*, ed. Bezzenberger, I, p. 308) and demonstrate the tendency of these roots to drop the aspiration from the initial consonant; these are *dakṣi* (Padapāṭha *dhakṣi*) in I.141.8; *dakṣu* (Padapāṭha *dhakṣu*) in II.4.4 and an aorist participle *dakṣat* in I.130.8; II.4.7 (which may be compared with the forms *adukṣat*, *dudukṣan* etc. of *duh*). It is not ruled out either that *dakṣat* in II.4.7 and *dakṣi* itself are verbal forms (see Ludwig, Nos. 252.13; 284.7). From this it follows that we do not commit any violence against Vedic grammar if we treat *dīkṣ*, with Whitney, *Sanskrit Grammar*, 2nd ed., § 1030, as the desiderative of *dah*, which in actual fact did not possess a desiderative in the Vedic period. Now there remains only the question how to reconcile the meaning of *dīkṣā*, "desire to burn oneself," with the common use of the word. On this we can state firstly that *tapas*, indisputably derived from the root *tap*, "to burn," is often associated with the *dīkṣā* (see PW, and Lindner, *op. cit.*, p. 15), hence the two concepts ought to complement one another roughly in the following manner : *dīkṣā* denotes "the desire to burn oneself" and *tapas* "the act of burning oneself." If we retain the usual meaning of "penance" or "asceticism" for *tapas*, then *dīkṣā* would denote the "desire for penance or asceticism." I think that this is almost the meaning of the word in the later period. The lords of the consecration for the Soma sacrifice, the *dīkṣāpālau*, are Agni the fire god (ABr I.4.10; Lindner, *op. cit.*, p. 14) and Viṣṇu the sun god. "Because he is consecrated he becomes Viṣṇu," states ŚBr III.2.1.17. Originally one may have consecrated oneself for these gods as well. Now from the statement which we have cited and others of the ŚBr we may conclude that it was believed that the consecrated person goes to the gods or becomes one of them. In other words, the consecration belonged originally in the ritual of voluntary death by burning. Such suicides were not uncommon in India. We know from the Greeks (Strabo, 712 ff.; Duncker, III, p. 323) that the wise men of India, when they became victims of disease, caused a funeral pyre to be built and let themself be burnt upon it without moving. One name especially is handed down to us : Kalanos of Takṣaśilā, who was in Alexander's entourage and died a voluntary death by burning. This custom was not approved of everywhere in India. *Yājñavalkya*, III.154, censures those who starve themselves to death or enter into the fire or jump into the water. There are some other factors which support the meaning proposed here for the Dīkṣaṇiyā-iṣṭi. After the Dīkṣā, an animal sacrifice for Agni-Soma is performed, which is included in the Agniṣṭoma. It appears that this animal sacrifice was substituted in the place of the human sacrifice for Agni-Viṣṇu.

For, MS III.7.8 (87.13) states : *yo dīkṣate sa vā etenaiva paśunātmānaṃ niṣkrīṇīte / sthūlaḥ pīvā syād ātmano niṣkrītyai / tasmād agniṣomīyasya paśor nāśitavyam / puruṣo hy etenātmānaṃ niṣkrīṇīte / tasmād agnīṣomīye saṃsthite yajamānasya gṛhe 'śitavyam / tarhi niṣkrīto 'nṛṇaḥ.* Likewise the ABr II.3.11 states *tad āhur nāgnīṣomīyasya paśor aśnīyāt / puruṣasya vā eṣo 'śnāti yo 'gnīṣomīyasya paśor aśnāti / yajamāno hy etenātmānaṃ niṣkrīṇīta iti,* and adds : *tattan nādṛtyam.* Cf. also KBr X.3.

With the relaxation in the harshness of the customs, the original significance of the Dīkṣā ceremony was forgotten. Now it was included in all major sacrifices as a sort of prelude and as merely symbolic consecration; *dīkṣā* as well as *tapas* acquired a sense conforming to the lenient customs of the later times. These arguments have been contested by Oldenberg, who explains *dīkṣā* as an example of those rites spread all over the earth whose purpose is to establish communication with gods or spirits by arousing a state of ecstasy. The standard means for this are, he goes on to say, contemplative sojourn at a solitary place, to isolate or hide oneself from disturbing spirits etc. Keith and Hauer (*Die Anfänge der Yogapraxis im alten Indien*, p. 65 ff.) are in agreement with him. I think that this explanation is not tenable; it introduces from ethnography a notion foreign to Indian thinking into Indian literature which understands the Dīkṣā differently. The derivation from *dakṣ* (instead of from *dah*) cannot be maintained linguistically. In my "Der freiwillige Feuertod in Indien und die Somaweihe" in SBKBAW, 1917, I have sought to thoroughly substantiate my interpretation on the basis of Indian customs. From this work one can also see that suicide was not of pessimistic nature in India (Keith, p. 303).

151. I.58.1 : *nū cit sahojā́ amṛ́to ni tundate*
hótā yád dūtó ábhavad vivasvataḥ /
ví sā́dhiṣṭhebhiḥ pathíbhī rájo mama
ā́ devátātā havíṣā vivāsati //

152. V.11.3 : *ásammṛṣṭo jāyase mātróḥ śúcir*
mandráḥ kavír úd atiṣṭho vivásvataḥ /
ghṛténa tvāvardhayann agna āhuta
dhūmás te ketúr abhavad diví śritáḥ //

153. VIII.39.3 : *ágne mánmāni túbhyaṃ káṃ ghṛtáṃ ná juhva āsáni /*
sá devéṣu prá cikiddhi
tváṃ hy ási pūrvyáḥ śivó dūtó vivásvataḥ...//

154. I.31.3 : *tvám agne prathamó mātaríśvana*
āvír bhava [ḥ] sukratūyā́ vivásvate /
árejetāṃ ródasī hotṛvū́rye
ásaghnor bhārám áyajo mahó vaso //

155. I, p. 55 f.

156. See also v. 1 : *tvám agne prathamó áṅgirā ṛ́ṣir devó devā́nām abhavaḥ śiváḥ sákhā /*

157. VI.8.4 : *apā́m upásthe mahiṣā́ agṛbhṇata*
víśo rā́jānam úpa tasthur ṛgmíyam /
ā́ dūtó agním abharad vivásvato
vaiśvānaráṃ mātaríśvā parāvátaḥ //

158. P.W., s.v.; Bergaigne, I, p. 52 ff. See ṚV I.93.6; cf. Vol. I, p. 154.

159. IV.7.4 : *āśuṃ dūtám vivásvato víśvā yáś carṣaṇīr abhí /*
ā́ jabhruḥ ketúm āyávo bhṛ́gavāṇaṃ viśé viśe //

160. Delbrück, *Altindische Syntax*, p. 449.

161. X.21.5 : *agnír jātó átharvaṇā vidád víśvāni kā́vyā |*
bhúvad dūtó vivásvato...ví vo máde...
priyó yamásya kā́myo vívakṣase ||

162. Besides II.13.6; VIII.72.9; IX.26.4; X.12.7, see pp. 217-18 above.

163. I.46.13 : *vāvasānā́ vivásvati sómasya pītyā́ girā́ |*
manuṣvác chambhū ā́ gatam ||

164. VIII.9.21 : *yán nūnáṃ dhībhír aśvinā pitúr yónā nisī́dathaḥ |*

165. X.39.12 : *ubhé áhanī sudíne vivásvataḥ.*

166. See among others, Bergaigne, II, p. 498 f.; Pischel, VSt, I, p. 29

167. X.39.12 : *ā́ téna yātaṃ mánaso jávīyasā*
ráthaṃ yáṃ vām ṛbhávaś cakrúr aśvinā |
yásya yóge duhitā́ jā́yate diváḥ
ubhé áhanī sudíne vivásvataḥ ||

On pāda d we should note that the sun creates the day and the night, as it indirectly follows from I.115.4 and from the Savitṛ hymns. Cf. ŚBr X.5.2.4 : *asau vā ādityo vivasvān eṣa hy ahorātre vivaste* (both are Vivasvat's wives).

168. VIII 67.20 : *mā́ no hetír vivásvata ā́dityāḥ kṛtrímā śáruḥ |*
purā́ nú jaráso vadhīt ||

Cf. ŚBr II.3.3.7.

169. ŚBr III.1.3.4 relates that Vivasvat is fashioned from Mārtaṇḍa, the eighth son of Aditi. In TBr I.1.9.3 Indra and Vivasvat are stated to be Aditi's sons.

170. I.96.2 : *vivásvatā cákṣasā dyā́m apáś ca* [*agnır ajanayat*].

There is nothing to prevent us from translating this as "with the sun, his eye."

171. I.139.1 : *yád dha krāṇā́ vivásvati nā́bhā saṃdā́yi návyasī |*

Hauer, *Die Anfänge der Yogapraxis im alten Indien* p. 147.

172. X.63.1 : *parāváto yé dídhiṣanta ā́pyam*
mánupritāso jánimā vivásvataḥ |
yayā́ter yé nahuṣyàsya barhíṣi
devā́ ā́sate té ádhi bruvantu naḥ ||

173. ŚBr XIII.4.3.3. ŚŚS XVI.21.; ĀśvŚS X.7.1.

174. Vol. I, p. 245.

175. *anu-ātatantha*, said of Soma in ṚV VIII.48.13; of Dawn in IV. 52.7 (without *anu*). See also I.35.7 : *kvedānīṃ sūryaḥ kaś ciketa katamāṃ dyāṃ raśmir asyā tatāna |*

176. ZDMG, IV, p. 425 ff.; ISt, XIV, p. 392.

177. "A kind of visionary description of hell from the Indian Middle Ages," in *Festschrift für K. Hofmann*, Erlangen 1890, p. 573 ff. This was elaborated later in the *Materialien zur Geschichte der Visionsliteratur*, Leipzig 1902, p. 13 ff. Hopkins agrees with him in the main points. He says in *The Religions of India*, pp. 134-5 : "Scherman's only error is in disputing the generally received opinion, one that is on the whole correct, that Yama in the early period is a kindly sovereign, and in later times becomes the dreaded king of horrible hells."

178. Thus we should read for *saparyata.*

179. On the difficulties raised by this verse, see the sound remarks of Ludwig in his *Über die Kritik des Ṛgvedatextes,*" p. 47.

180. ŚBr II.2.2.8; XI.1.2.12 : *martyā ha vā agre devā āsuḥ.* Other examples in Scherman, *op. cit.*, 134.

181. ABr VI.12.3 : *prajāpatir vai pita ṛbhūn martyān sato 'martyān kṛtvā.* ṚV IV.33.4 : *amṛtatvam āśuḥ.* 2 : *devānām upa sakhyam āyan* etc. Kaegi, *Ṛgveda*, 2nd ed., p. 54.

182. Roscher, *Ausführliches Lexikon*, I, p. 1159.

183. Probably with the exception of AV XI.6.11 : *pitṝn yamáśreṣṭhān brūmaḥ*; but this is perhaps the same as *yamárājñaḥ pitṝn* in AV XVIII.2.46.

184. X.15.8 : *tébhir [pitṝbhiḥ] yamáḥ saṃrarāṇo havī́ṃṣi*
uśánn uśádbhiḥ pratikāmám attu //

For X.135.1 see the note below.

185. X.135.1 : *yásmin vṛkṣé supalāśé devaiḥ sampibate yamáḥ /*
átrā no viśpátiḥ pitā́ purāṇā́n ánu venati //

Yet Ludwig, "Über Methode", p. 42, objected to the interpretation of *pitā* as Yama.

186. AV XVIII. 4.55: *yáthā yamā́ya harmyám ávapan páñca mānavā́ḥ /*
evā́ vapāmi harmyáṃ yáthā me bhūrayó 'sata //

"just as the five human races erected a palace for Yama so shall I build a palace so that more belong to me." Cf. another reading in TĀr VI.6.2 : *evam... yathāsāma jīvaloke bhūrayaḥ.*

187. This is corroborated by *Kauśika Sūtra* LXXXVI.11, according to which the mantra is used at the Śmaśāna, piled up during the Pitṛmedha. In the TĀr also the mantra occurs in the midst of verses which are patently devoted to the cult of the dead.

188. Roscher, *op. cit.*, I, p. 1034.

189. Ibid., p. 1165.

190. X.14.7 : *yamáṃ paśyāsi váruṇaṃ ca devám* has no significance (Hübschmann, *Jahrbücher für protestantische Theologie*, V, p. 206; Scherman, *op. cit.*, p. 580). From ṚV III.20.5 : *agním uṣásaṃ ca devī́m / bṛ́haspátiṃ savitā́raṃ ca devám* we may convince ourselves that no value should be attributed to such turns of expressions, for Agni and Bṛhaspati have as good a claim to be *devas* as Uṣas and Savitṛ have. Cf. also IV.51.11 : *dyauś ca dhattā́ṃ pṛthivī́ ca devī́.*

191. X.14.1 : *pareyivā́ṃsaṃ praváto mahī́r ánu*
bahúbhyaḥ pánthām anupaspaśānám /
2 : *yamó no gātúṃ prathamó viveda*

192. Zimmer, AIL, p. 415 (and following him Kaegi) sees an evidence favouring Roth's view in ṚV VII.33.12 : *yaména tatáṃ paridhíṃ vayiṣyánn apsarásaḥ pári jajñe vásiṣṭhaḥ;* I cannot at all see why.

193. Yamī was invented for Yama as Varuṇānī was invented for Varuṇa and Indrāṇī for Indra. (E. H. Meyer, *Gandharven-Kentauren*, p. 229). It is not apparant from the Vedic evidences whether she had a special significance. In VS XII.63 she appears in the highest heaven united with Yama.

I do not know why it is said in TS III.3.8.3 : *agnir vāva yama iyaṃ yamī.* The later literature explains Yamī as Yumunā.

194. Güntert himself wishes to see in the Aryan Yama a "primordial being of both genders," of whom I find no trace in the texts. Both the Yama-s have absolutely nothing to do with the creation of the world or with the human sacrifice. The cosmogony founded on human sacrifice is quite another thing.

195. VS XXIV.1 : *sauryayāmau śvetaś ca kṛṣṇaś ca.* ŚBr XIII.2.2.7.

196. Ehni, who can fight well against opposing views like those held by Bergaigne, thinks that Yama is a sun god (*Yama*, pp. 56, 109 : "rising sun or also the sun of the spring;" p. 64 ff. : "the sun who has set") for which notion there is absolutely no support. The following remark of his is far-fetched : "...thus by itself there would arise a sharp contrast between the visible sun with the world illuminated by him, and Yama, the invisible ruler with his realm in the other world" (p. 114). Later on Bergaigne has stated the same view as Ehni did (in the Lexicon of his *Manuel pour étudier le Sanscrit védique*, p. 283): "Yama, the incarnation of the setting or the nocturnal sun who sinks into the depth of the earth and is consequently the god of the dead."

197. X.85.19 : *návonavo bhavati jā́yamāno*; I.164.4 : *kó dadarśa prathamáṃ jā́yamānam.* Cf. the famous riddle (ŚŚS XVI.5.1 ff.) : *ka nu svij jāyate punaḥ*, and the answer : *candramā jāyate punaḥ.*

198. *Religions of the Primitive Peoples*, p. 140.

199. *Das Weltbild der Primitiven*, 1924, p. 47. Frazer cites the myths dealing with the death of the moon in *The Golden Bough*, III, p. 66 ff. (The Belief in Immortality). P. Ehrenreich. *Allgemeine Mythologie*, p. 116 : "...all the peoples regard the moon... as the lord of the dead." E. S. Hartland, in Hastings' ERE, IV, p. 412 b : "the phases of the moon naturally suggest death and restoration of life."

200. ŚBr II.4.2.2; MS IV.2.1; KBr I.2; see also Vol. I, p. 243 ff. I cannot agree with Johansson, who states in his *Solfågeln* p. 17 : "therefore, Yama's kingdom, the world of the ancestors, was originally not in the celestial regions."

201. ṚV VII.33.9 : *yaména tatáṃ paridhiṃ váyanto*
'psarása úpa sedur vásiṣṭhāḥ ||
12 : *yaména tatáṃ pariddhiṃ vayiṣyánn*
apsarásaḥ pári jajñe vásiṣṭhaḥ ||

202. Bṛhaspati is connected with the metres, MS I.9.2 (132.1). X.13.4 (like the whole hymn) is quite obscure : "they made Ṛṣi Bṛhaspati the victim; Yama surrendered his dear body." In this I see only a hint about his death which is treated here as sacrifice.

203. On "Yama's dogs," see Arbman, *Rudra*, p. 262, who seeks to explain these manifestations against a broader context. In his *Cerberus, the Dog of Hades*, Chicago 1905, Bloomfield makes an attempt to explain their original significance.

204. Yašt XIX.34 : *[āaṭ] yaṭ hīm aēm draogham vāčim*
[aŋhaithīm] činmānē paiti baraiti
vaēnəmnəm ahmaṭ hača xvarənō
mərəjahē kəhrpa frašūsaṭ.

205. In a different form in TS II.5.6.4; here Amāvāsyā and Paurṇamāsī are his neglected wives.

206. TS II.4.14.1; 3.5.3 (see Vol. I, p. 204). Cf. also MS II.2.7 (21.5).

207. Besides the TS, see *Kāṭhaka* XI.3 (Weber, ISt, III, p. 467; Max Müller, *Rgveda*, IV, Preface, p. lii; Weber, *Naxatra*, II, p. 275); furthermore, *Carakasaṃhitā* (ed. Jībānanda), p. 453 :

cikitsitaḥ śaśī tābhyām [aśvibhyāṃ] gṛhīto rājayakṣmaṇā
somān nipatitaś candraḥ kṛtas tābhyāṃ punaḥ sukhī ||

Suśruta II.445.7,20. Mallinātha's commentary on *Śiśupālavadha* II.96 contains the following quotation :

rājayakṣmā kṣayaḥ śoṣo rogarāḍ iti ca smṛtaḥ |
nakṣatrāṇāṃ dvijānāṃ ca rājño 'bhūd yad ayaṃ purā
yac ca rājā ca yakṣmā ca rājayakṣmā tato mataḥ ||

Vāyupurāṇa II.28.46 ff. etc.

208. *Viṣṇupurāṇa* IV.6. In *Vāyupurāṇa* II.28, it is related how Soma became insolent because of his being consecrated as king and seduced Tārā, the wife of Bṛhaspati. Thereupon, a battle took place between the gods and the demons who were on Soma's side. Finally Brahman himself brings the wife back to Bṛhaspati. This legend has probably a different meaning than the first one, but it is also characterized by the reference to Soma's insolence.

209. Geldner, KZ, XXV, p. 183, translates thus : "And Yima started out from among the stars and towards the path of the sun." Darmesteter, SBE, IV, p. 13 : "Then Yima stepped forward, towards the luminous space, southwards, to meet the sun." De Harlez : "Therefore Yima advanced to the brightest light of the day, at the hour of noon, following the path which the sun takes;"this is rather a loose translation because the correct shade of meaning is lost here; *hū paiti aδwanəm* means "towards the path of the sun." Fritz Wolff : "Then Yima advanced to the light [?] at noon towards the path of the sun." Geldner correctly treats the words *upa rapithwam* as a gloss since they do not fit into the metre, and translates the rest of the words appropriately as "towards the east." Cf. Lommel, ZII, II, p. 212, who does not put these two words in paranthesis.

210. On this, cf. the following remark of Darmesteter, SBE, IV, p. 13, n. 1 : "Thence [i.e. from the words *ā hū paiti aδwanəm*] is derived the following tradition recorded by G. du Chinon : 'with this they call that one who wandered every day in the sky of the sun, whence he brought back the science of the stars after having visited them from such close proximity. They call the great personage Gemachid' (*Relations nouvelles du Levant*, Lyon 1671, p. 478)."

211. The god who causes death can also naturally release one from it again. ṚV X.60.10; AV XVIII.3.63; MS IV.7.2 (95.7).

212. AV XIX.56.1: *yamásya lokā́d ádhy ā́ babhūvitha*
prámadā mártyān prá yunakṣi dhī́raḥ |
ékākinā sarátham yāsi vidvā́n svapnaṃ...

213. *varuṇānī te mātā yamaḥ pitā rarur nāmāsi*; v. 2 : *devajāmīnāṃ putro 'si yamasya karaṇaḥ.*

214. Bloomfield, "Contributions II," AJPh, XI, p. 36. AV VI.110.2 : *yamásya mūlabárhaṇāt pári pāhy enam.*

215. He is mentioned in a magic formula in AV VI.133.3. He is invoked in a Daurbhāgyakaraṇa, see AV I.14.2 (*Kauśika Sūtra* XXXVI.15).

216. AV V.30.6 (*dūtau*); VIII. 2.11; 8.11.

217. ṚV X.14.10-12.

218. Ibid., X.165.4.

219. Vol. I, pp. 308-9.

220. X.135.7 : *idáṃ yamásya sā́danaṃ devamānáṃ yád ucyáte* |
iyám asya dhamyate nāḷī́r ayáṃ gīrbhíḥ páriṣkṛtaḥ ||

221. AV II.12.7: *saptá prāṇā́n aṣṭaú majjñás tā́ṃs te vṛścāmi bráhmaṇā* |
áyā yamásya sā́danam agnídūto áraṃkṛtaḥ ||

See Bloomfield, *Seven Hymns*, p. 11.

222. AV VI.118.2 : *ṛṇā́n no nárṇám értsamāno yamásya loké ádhirajjur ā́yat.* In another passage which is not quite intelligible because of the word *virāṣā́ṭ* (ṚV I.35.6), it is said : *tisró dyā́vaḥ savitúr dvā́ upásthā́n ékā yamásya bhúvane virāṣā́ṭ.*

223. AV XVIII.2.56: *imaú yunajmi te váhnī ásunītāya vóḍhave* |
tā́bhyāṃ yamásya sā́danaṃ sámitīś cā́va gacchatāt ||

See also TĀr VI.1.

224. AV III. 29.1: *yád rā́jāno vibhájanta iṣṭāpūrtásya ṣoḍaśáṃ*
yamásyāmī́ sabhāsádaḥ |

On its use, see *Kauśika Sūtra* LXIV.2. Cf. TĀr VI.3.8 ff.

225. AV XVIII.3.70: *púnar dehi vanaspate yá eṣá níhitas tváyi* |
yáthā yamásya sā́dana ā́sātai vidáthā vádan ||

The preceding and the following verses show that this is about a funeral. v.71 : *śarī́ram asya sáṃ daha* [*agne*].

226. ṚV X.114.10 : *yadā́ yamó bhavati harmyé hitáḥ*, is not clear to me.

227. See Ludwig, "Über die Methode," p. 42 ff.

228. E.g. TĀr VI.7.14; 9.1.

229. The only verse which could suggest this, viz., I.116.2 does not prove much: *tád rā́sabho nāsatyā sahásram ājā́ yamásya pradháne jigāya* || "the new donkey, O Nāsatyas, won thousandfold wages in the contest for the price of Yama," or "in Yama's contest."

230. Besides Bergaigne and Oldenberg, see L. von Schroeder, *Griechische Götter und Heroen*, p. 112 ff., Ehni, *Yama*, p. 4 ff.

231. I.20.6 : *utá tyáṃ camasáṃ návaṃ tváṣṭur devásya níṣkṛtam* |
ákarta catúraḥ púnaḥ ||

110.3 : *tyám cic camasám ásurasya bhákṣaṇam*
ékaṃ sántam akṛṇutā cáturvayam ||
5 : *kṣétram iva ví mamus téjanenām̐*
ékaṃ pā́tram ṛbhávo jéhamānam |
161.4 : *yadā́vā́khyac camasā́ñ catúraḥ kṛtā́n*
ā́d ít tvā́ṣṭā gnā́sv antár ny ā̀naje ||
5 : *hánāmainām̐ íti tvā́ṣṭā yád ábravīc*
camaśaṃ yé devapā́nam ánindiṣuḥ |
IV.33.5 : *jyeṣṭhá āha camasā́ dvā́ karéti*
kánīyān trī́n kṛṇavāméty āha |
kaniṣṭhá āha catúras karéti
tvā́ṣṭa ṛbhavas tát panayad váco vaḥ ||
6 : *satyám ūcur nára evā́ hí cakrúr*
ánu svadhā́m ṛbhávo jagmur etā́m |
vibhrā́jamānāṁś camasā́m̐ áheva
ávenat tvā́ṣṭā catúro dadṛśvā́n

The Vaśā brought the Soma in three bowls, AV X.10.2.

232. At this place Tvaṣṭṛ is said to carry several bowls. The older concept is doubtless the one quoted in the preceding note, namely that he carries one and the Ṛbhus several bowls.

233. Zimmer, AIL, p. 352.

234. *ṚV*, III, p. 333.

235. Geldner, "a child who is carried around."

236. I.80.14 : *abhiṣṭané te adrivo yát sthā́ jágac ca rejate* |
tvā́ṣṭā cit táva manyáva
indra vevijyáte bhiyā́...||
III.48.4 : *tvā́ṣṭāram índro janúṣābhibhū́ya*
āmúṣyā sómam apibac camū́ṣu |
IV.18.3 : *tvā́ṣṭur gṛhé apibat sómam índraḥ*
śatadhanyàṃ camvòḥ sutásya |

To this we may add the legend, which occurs very often in the Brāhmaṇas, that Indra kills Tvaṣṭṛ's son and takes the Soma by force and, to be sure, is punished for it.

237. VII.54.1, 2; 55.1.

238. ṚV III.22.1 refers to Agni : *ayáṃ só agnír yásmin sómam índraḥ sutáṃ dadhé jaṭháre vāvaśānáḥ.*

239. Perry, "Indra in the Ṛgveda," JAOS, XI, p. 56 ff.

240. Ibid., p. 74 ff.

241. V.33.4 : *tatakṣé sū́ryāya cid ókasi své*
vṛ́ṣā samátsu dāsásya nā́ma cit ||

242. *Über die Erwähnung von Sonnenfinsternissen...*, p. 9 : "He with the strength of an ox caused the name of a Dāsa for Sūrya in the course of a battle even in his own house." Cf. IV.18.3 (n. 236 above). Does IV.28.2 also belong here ?

tvā́ yujā́ ní khidat sū́ryasya
índraś cakrám sáhasā sadyá indo /

"allied with you, O Indu, Indra seized the wheel of the sun by force."

243. Lubbock, *The Origin of Civilisation*, 5th ed., p. 319: "In hot countries the sun is generally regarded as an evil, and in cold as a beneficient being." p. 340 : "a Northern people is apt to look on the sun as a beneficient deity, while to a tropical race it would suggest drought and destruction."

244. X.49.10: *ahám tád āsu dhārayam yád āsu ná*
deváś caná tváṣṭādhārayad rúśat /
spārhám gávām ū́dhassu vakṣáṇāsv ā́
mádhor mádhu śvā́tryam sómam āśiram //

"I preserved in them what no god, not even Tvaṣṭṛ, preserved; the bright and the much-sought-after [milk] of the cows in the udders, in the teats, which is sweeter than honey (?), the tasteful Soma, the Āśir."

245. See also II.11.19.

246. Thus Ludwig.

247. X.76.3: *góarṇasi tvāṣṭré áśvanirṇiji*
prém adhvaréṣv adhvarā́ñ aśiśrayuḥ /

Perhaps we should add III.7.4 also (in which the word *tvāṣṭra* is explained by the PW as the power of procreation) :

máhi tvāṣṭrám ūrjáyantīr ajuryám
stabhūyámānam vaháto vahanti /
vy áṅgebhir didyutānáḥ sadhástha
ékām iva ródasī ā viveśa //

"the streams, growing mightily, carry forth Tvaṣṭṛ's youthful son who is leaning heavily," but the verse is not very clear. It is also possible that we should add *mádhu* here.

248. Vāyu and Tvaṣṭṛ are mentioned side by side in ṚV X.65.10; AV III.20.10; VI.141.1; IX.4.10 also. In MS III.6.9 (73.6) Vāyu is the *gopā*, Tvaṣṭṛ the *adhipati* and Pūṣan the *pratigrahītṛ*.

249. Vol. I, p. 436, n. 175.

250. X.46.9; 2.7. In the first passage Tvaṣṭṛ is juxtaposed with the sky and earth, Āpas and Mātariśvan; in the second with sky, earth and Āpas. We can safely ignore II.1.

251. X.2.1 : *ṛtū́ñr ṛtupate yajehá.* 3 : *sed u hótā só adhvarā́n sá ṛtū́n kalpayāti* (cf. X.85.18 : *ṛtū́ñr anyó vidádhaj jāyate púnaḥ*).. 5 : *devā́ñ ṛtuśó yajāti.* 6 : *víśveṣām hy àdhvarā́ṇām ánīkam citrám ketúm jánitā tvā jajñá* (cf. IX.86.7 : *yajñásya kétuḥ*, see Vol. I, p. 442, n. 251). 7 : *pánthām ánu pravidvā́n pitṛyā́ṇam agne...samidhānó ví bhāhi* /

252. TS VI.5.8.4 : *devā vai tvaṣṭāram ajighāmsan sa patnīḥ prāpadyata taṃ na prati prāyacchan.*

253. I.22.9 : *ágne pátnīr ihā́ vaha devā́nām uśatī́r úpa tváṣṭāram sómapītaye*; II.1.5; 31.4 : *tváṣṭā gnā́bhiḥ sajóṣāḥ*; 36.3.: *tváṣṭā devébhir jánibhiḥ sumádgaṇaḥ*; VI.50.13 : *tváṣṭā devébhir jánibhiḥ sajóṣāḥ*; VII.34.20 : *ā́ yán naḥ pátnīr gámanty ácchā tváṣṭā supāṇír dadhātu vīrā́n*; 22 : *várūtrībhiḥ suśaraṇó no astu tváṣṭā sudátro;* 35.6: *śám nas tváṣṭā gnā́bhiḥ*; X.64.10 : *utá*

mātá bṛhaddivá śṛṇotu nas tváṣṭā devébhir jánibhiḥ; 66.3 : *tváṣṭā no gnábhir... jinvatu.* MS II.5.5 (54.14); IV.14.9 (228.1ff.). ŚBr I.9.2.10-11 etc.

254. KZ, I, p. 448.

255. ṚV I.23.17 : *amúr yá úpa sū́rye yábhir vā sū́ryaḥ saha |*
V.45.10 : *á sū́ryo aruhac chukrám árṇaḥ:..*
udná ná návam anayanta dhírā
áśṛṇvatīr ápo arvág atiṣṭhan |
VII.47.4 : *yáḥ sū́ryo raśmíbhir āttatána |*
(VIII.72.16 : *ádhukṣat pipyúṣīṃ íṣam ū́rjaṃ saptápadīm aríḥ |*
sū́ryasya saptá raśmíbhiḥ ||)

IV.38.10; MS II.4.8 (46.2) : *agnir vā ito vṛṣṭim īṭṭe maruto 'mutaś cyāvayanti tāṃ sūryo raśmibhir varṣati.*

256. In ṚV V.44.7 Sūrya is called *jánivant.*

257. E.g. ĀpŚS XII.5.2. 3, 13, 14; XIII.14.11; 15.1 ff.; KŚS X.6.20 ff.; ŚBr IV.4.2.17 ff. etc.

258. Cf. Vol. I, p. 331. ṚV II.5.5 speaks of Neṣṭṛ's cows; this recalls Tvaṣṭṛ's cows.

259. He must sit for some time on the lap of the Neṣṭṛ, TS VI.5.8.6; ŚBr IV.4.2.18; see Vol. I, p. 470, n. 32. According to another rule (ĀpŚS XIII.15.1), he should be castrated when he does this. In MS I.9.4 (133.4) Tvaṣṭṛ is designated as Agnīdh; according to 9.2 (132.3) he has a samidh.

260. MS III.11.11 (158.14). ŚBr XIII.1.8.7.

261. AV IX.4.3 (cf. v. 6).

262. VS XX.44; MS III.11.1 (140.13).

263. MS IV.13.2 (201.4).

264. VS XXVIII.32.

265. ṚV X.18.6.

266. ṚV I.142.10; MS IV.14.9 (228.12) : *yonau reto dadhad asme nu tvaṣṭā.* He is also invoked in AV VI.8.3; this hymn is recited during pregnancy. In AV VI.78.3 he creates the wife and then a husband for her and grants them (as in ṚV X.18.6) long life. In ṚV X.17.1-2 he himself is the bride's father. In AV XIV.1.53 he arranges the garment. (Cf. TBr III.8.17.5 : *sauryaṃ retaḥ*).

267. Similarly *tváṣṭā* is juxtaposed with *savitá* in IX.81.4 (*tváṣṭā savitá*), X.10.5 (*devás tváṣṭā savitá viśvárūpaḥ*). In view of the occasional use of the word *savitṛ́* as an appellative, it is hard to decide here whether *savitṛ́* denotes merely the "Tvaṣṭṛ, the vivifier," or whether it designates the sun god himself.

268. Savitṛ's chariot and also the earth, among others, are called *viśvárūpa* (AV XII.1.11). Hence the meaning "having many forms" as proposed by the PW may be correct. Besides these, Tvaṣṭṛ has also the epithet *purúrūpa* in MS IV.13.2 (201.4); ŚBr XIII.1.8.7.

269. Cf. III.4.9; VII.34.20; VIII.102.8; X.10.5 etc. AV II.26.1; 29.2; V.25.11; 26.8; IX.4.6 : *tváṣṭā rūpáṇāṃ janitá paśū́nām*; XI.8.18 : *yadá tváṣṭā vyátṛṇat pitá tváṣṭur yá úttaraḥ | gṛháṃ kṛtvá mártyaṃ deváḥ púruṣam áviśan.*

(This, in my knowledge, is the only passage which speaks of a father of Tvaṣṭṛ, who, I think, is a pure abstraction. AV XI.8.8-9 : *kútas tvā́ṣṭā sámabhavat | tvā́ṣṭā ha jajñe tvā́ṣṭur* can demonstrate how one arrived at this abstraction). XII.3.33; VS XXIX.9; XXXI.17; MS IV.14.9 (228.4); ŚBr V. 4.5.2., XIII.1.8.7 : *tvaṣṭā vai paśūnāṃ mithunānāṃ rūpakṛt; Kauśika Sūtra* CXXIV.1 : *tvaṣṭā rūpāṇi bahudhā vikurvan* etc. Thus Tvaṣṭṛ comes close to another sun-god, the herdsman Pūṣan, of whom the Yajus literature says that he is *paśūnāṃ prajanayitā* (e.g. MS IV.3.7 (46.5 ff.)). Numerous other examples can be seen in the PW. *lomasakthau* are stated to be animals belonging to Tvaṣṭṛ. MS III.13.2 (168.12); VS XXIV.1; ŚBr XIII.2.2.8; VS XXIV.24; MS III.14.5 : *kaulīka*; 10 : *uṣṭra*; 12 : *kalaviṅkaḥ puṣkarasādo lohitāhis* (TS V.5.14; VS XXIV.28 etc.). See also MS II.6.13 (72.12); TS II.1.8.3 etc. The creator of men and beasts confers wealth through these gifts just as ultimately every other god does. It is not necessary to cite specific passages in support of this point.

270. ṚV I.85.9; III.54.12; VI.49.9; VII.34.20.

271. See PW, *Harivaṃśa* 12146.

272. In AV XII.3.33 : *tvā́ṣṭreva rūpā́ṃ súkṛtaṃ svádhityā* also *tvā́ṣṭṛ* is probably a proper noun and not an appellative.

273. II.1.5 and VS XX.44; MS IV.13.2 (201.4) etc. respectively. Apart from the horse, the sheep also belongs to him. MS II.7.17 (102.6). TS IV.2.10.9 etc. : *tvaṣṭur varūtrīṃ varuṇasya nābhim aviṃ jajñānāṃ rajasaḥ parasmāt*. He sends a he-goat to heaven along with the sacrificial horse, ṚV I.162.3.

274. VS XXIX.9; AV VI.92.1.

275. ṚV II.31.4.

276. ṚV I.13.10; AV XI.6.3.

277. ṚV IX.5.9 : *tvā́ṣṭāram agrajā́ṃ gopā́ṃ puroyā́vānam ā́ huve |*
índur índro vṛ́ṣā hárih pávamānaḥ prajā́patiḥ ||

Pādas cd look like a fragment of a dictionary containing synonyms for Agni.

278. MS IV.14.9 (228.5).

279. MS IV.14.9 (228.6).

280. IV.42.3 : *tvā́ṣṭeva víśvā bhúvanāni vidvā́n*. He is identified with Vāc in ABr II.4.13 : *vāg vai tvaṣṭā | vāg ghīdaṃ sarvaṃ tāṣṭīva.*

281. It is likely that ṚV V.42.13 alludes, as Ehni believes, to an incest by Tvaṣṭṛ (who, incidentally, is not mentioned) with his daughter. There is nothing we can do with the fragments of a myth which is handed down to us in an incomplete form.

282. This legend occurs again in V.5.4.2; TS II.4.12.1. Cf. also ŚBr I.2.3.2; XII.7.1.1; 8.3.1; XIV.5.5.22; MS II.4.1 ff. For other passages, see PW, s.v. *tvāṣṭra.*

283. II.11.19 : *asmábhyaṃ tát tvāṣṭrā́ṃ viśvárūpam*
árandhayaḥ sākhyásya tritā́ya |

284. *devo narāśaṃsas triśīrṣā ṣaḍakṣaḥ| śatam id enaṃ śitipṛṣṭhā ādadhati |*

285. See p. 222 above.

286. See Vol. I, p. 442, n. 251.

287. *viśvarūpo vai tvāṣṭraḥ purohito devānām āsīt svasrīyo 'surāṇām.*
288. See also Bergaigne, III, p. 65, n. 1.
289. Quoted by Oldenberg, RdV, 2nd ed., p. 193.
290. I.105.18 : *aruṇo mā sakṛd vṛkaḥ pathā yantaṃ dadarśa hi /*
uj jihīte nicāyyā taṣṭeva pṛṣṭyāmayī...// (cf. I.105.11)

291. Yāska, V.20, reading *māsakṛd* in ṚV I.105.18, explains thus : *māsakṛd vṛkaś candramā bhavati vivṛtajyotiṣko vā vikṛtajyotiṣko vā vikrāntajyotiṣko vā*; Sāyaṇa and the modern scholars, on the other hand, read *mā sakṛd* (cf. *Nirukta* III.101 at the end). While in Yāska's explanation one does not see what the substantive should be which belongs to *pathā yantam,* in the separation of *mā sakṛt* the second word gives rise to difficulties. These difficulties are increased by the wording of the other half of the verse for which I know of no satisfactory explanation, nor can I propose one.

292. Cf. TS VI.4.8.1 ff. The sentence "Soma was Vṛtra" does not occur here.

293. On this, cf. also ŚBr V.2.3.7 : *tasya [agnīṣomīyasya puroḍāśasya utsṛṣṭo gaur dakṣiṇotsarjaṃ vā amuṃ candramasaṃ ghnanti / paurṇamāsenāha ghnanty āmāvāsyenotsṛjanti.*

294. One may perhaps miss a discussion about the Vasus. A scrutiny of all relevant Ṛgvedic verses convinces me that there is nothing to add to what my predecessors have stated. The concept of the Vasus is vague in the ṚV. The word is applied sometimes to the gods in general or to those who have been just invoked, and sometimes it is connected as an adjective to single groups like the Ādityas or the Maruts. A specific class of gods as the later literature knows them was only in the process of formation and is rarely encountered in the *Ṛgveda.* The tenth book already contains nine such cases, exhibiting thus a distinct advance in comparison to the other maṇḍalas.

295. PJAOS, XVI, p. cxlv ff.

296. Oldenberg, RdV, p. 255 ff. can be consulted on this point. Of older works, cf. G. de Rialle, "La déesse des bois," *Revue de Linguistique et de Philologie comparée*, V, p. 273.

297. Ed. Bühler, 3rd ed., III, p. 51.

298. On this point I agree with Oldenberg, RdV, p. 259.

299. The parallel passage in *Viṣṇupurāṇa* V.10.29, 30 reads thus :

vidyayā yo yayā yuktas tasya sā daivataṃ mahat /
saiva pūjyārcanīyā ca saiva tasyopakārikā //
36 : *kim asmākaṃ mahendreṇa gāvaḥ śailāś ca devatāḥ //*
37 : *mantrayajñaparā viprāḥ sīrayajñāś ca karṣukāḥ /*
girigoyajñaśīlāś ca vayam adrivanāśrayāḥ //

300. Hillebrandt, *Tiere und Götter im vedischen Ritual*, Breslau 1905. (Off-print from the 83. *Jahresbericht der Schlesischen Gesellschaft für vaterländiche Kultur*).

301. Weber, *Omina und Portenta*, p. 382.

302. *Festgruss an Böhtlingk*, p. 40 ff. *Veda interpretation*, pp. 17-18.

303. ṚV I.163.6.

304. Sieg, *Die Sagenstoffe des Ṛgveda*, I, p. 97 ff.; Hillebrandt, GGA, 1903, pp. 243-44 (review of Sieg's work).

305. Foy, KZ, XXXIV, p. 266. Cf. Jarl Charpentier, *Die Suparṇa Sage*, p. 326.

306. Occasionally the commentaries identify *bradhna* with the "sun." Cf. TMBr XVIII.7.13; XIX.10.12; XXIII.19.3. ABr IV.4.7 : *svargo bradhnasya viṣṭapam.* TS V.3.3.5 : *āditvo bradhnasya viṣṭapam.* TBr III.9.4.1 : *asau vā āditvo bradhnaḥ.*

307. See my *Vedische Mythologie* (Kleine Ausgabe), p. 71.

308. ṚV III.54.20 : *śṛṇvántu no vṛ́ṣaṇaḥ párvatāso dhruvákṣemāsa iḷayā mádantaḥ*; IV.55.5 : *á párvatasya marutām ávāṁsi devásya trātúr avri bhágasya*; V.41.9 : *tujé nas táne párvatāḥ santu svaitavo yé vásavo ná vīrā́ḥ* (see p. 108 ff. above); VI. 49.14; VIII.18.16; X.158.3 (cf. also v. 11). Now and then the Soma stones are styled as the "mountains."

309. Keith objects to the expression "abstract gods," perhaps with justification, but so far no better word was found. However, Keith is mistaken when he states that "the idea of the deification of an abstraction inevitably suggests that the god was the production of priestly speculation" (p. 202). This need not necessarily be so.

310. Cf. X.65; 66.5.

311. Bloomfield, *The Symbolic Gods*, Baltimore 1902, p. 41.

312. The abstractions *urúr adhvā* (VIII.31.11); *urú vyácas* (X.92.4), *kṣétrasyapati, vā́stoṣpati, ūrjā́ṃ pati* etc. do not belong to the same category because they at any rate go back to a real basis and are not much different from such gods who are abstractions based on natural phenomena just as the genius or the god is an abstraction from the sun.

313. I do not deny the utility of a study of the origin and development of such manifestations as Prajāpati, who need not necessarily be as young as the appearances might suggest. But I think I should confine myself since these manifestations hardly belong still in mythology.

314. B. Geiger, *Aməša Spəntas*, p. 236. But it would be far-fetched to assign to her a fixed position in the midst of the set of conceptions about the Ādityas and to seek to find in her a connecting link between the Ādityas and the *Aməšas.*

315. I think ṚV VII.37.7 refers to a king who was expelled from his kingdom, i.e., who fell prey to Nirṛti :

abhí yáṃ deví nírṛtiś cid íśe...
ásvaveśaṃ yáṃ kṛṇávanta mártāḥ || Cf. X.39.6.

316. B. Geiger, *op. cit.*, p. 200 ff.; von Negelein, *Weltanschauung*, §15, p. 97.

317. HGS I.6.5.

318. Manu III.87 ff. enjoins offerings to Indra, Antaka (Yama), Appati (Varuṇa) and Indu with their entourage, to the Maruts, waters, Vanaspati, to Śrī (at the head of the bed), to Bhadrakālī (at the foot of the bed) and so on. In AV XI.9 Arbudi, Nyarbudi, Trisandhi with a host of assistants help in the battle.

319. PGS II.17.13 ff.; GGS IV.4.27. In the context of various agricultural sacrifices, Gobhila mentions, besides specific gods, also *sītā, āśā, araḍā* and *anaghā*.

320. GGS IV.8.4.

321. Caland, *Die altindischen Todten- und Bestattungsgebräuche*, p. 62.

322. *The Symbolic Gods*, p. 42 ff.

323. On this, see Sütterlin, ARW, IX, p. 533 ff. : "Mother earth."

324. Cf. III.48.2 : *táṃ te mātā́ pári yóṣā jánitrī*
mahá́ḥ pitúr dáma ā́siñcad ágre ||
VII.20.5 : *vṛ́ṣā jajāna vṛ́ṣaṇaṃ ráṇāya*
tám u cin nā́rī náryaṃ sasūva |
98.3 : *prá te mātā́ mahimā́nam uvāca* |
VIII.45.4 : *jātáḥ pṛcchad ví mātáram* |
5 : *práti tvā śavasī́ vadat* (cf. 20 : *śavasas pate*)

I.61.7; II.30.2; VIII.77.1; X.54.3; 73.1; 134.2. He made his mother a widow (IV.18.12); she hides him *avadyám iva* and so on. I think it is futile to look for deeper reasons; the poetic speculation has already set in here.

325. As far as I can see, there are three possibilities. 1. The father is a pure fiction (abstraction etc.) : Indra as the son of Prajāpati, of the Puruṣa etc. (see Macdonell, p. 57), son of *śavas, sahas*. 2. He is a natural phenomenon : *dyaúḥ* (ṚV IV.17.4). 3. As a result of the syncretic nature of Vedic mythology, he is combined with another cycle of myths : Tvaṣṭṛ's son or Aditi's son. Cf. Perry, "Indra in the Ṛgveda," JAOS, XI, p. 9 ff.

326. E. Sidney Hartland, *The Legend of Perseus*, I, p.71 ff.; Oldenberg, ṚdV, p. 134, n. 3; Andrew Lang, *Mythes, cultes et religion*, p. 426.

327. Bloomfield, ZDMG, XLVIII, p. 548 ff. Here I agree particularly with the author's remarks about *śacī*. An oblation for Indrāṇī is mentioned, for instance, in TS II.2.8.1 : *indrāṇyai caruṃ...yasya senāsaṃśiteva syāt* | *indrāṇī vai senāyai devatā* and so on.

328. Nārāyaṇa on GGS IV.4.32 explains Indrāṇī as Indra's mother (see Knauer). This is not surprising in view of the commingling of conceptions.

329. ṚV I.82.5; IV.24.8. At times it may be Indrāṇī.

330. Johansson, *Dhiṣaṇā*, p. 69 ff., has divided the goddesses, "a group of [demon-like) powers who can most conveniently be described as fertility powers," into different groups. 1. With names like *gnā́s*, (*deva-*) *pátnīs*, *jánanyaḥ*, these chiefly represent their character as wives of gods, as feminine counterparts to one or several gods; generally speaking, these are not conceived individually...When called *gnās* the sexual fertility is stressed in them, and as a class they are especially close to Tvaṣṭṛ who is, so to say, their masculine counterpart *par excellence*... 2. Chiefly as protectresses they bear the name *varūtrīs*... 3. Through *dhiṣaṇā* probably that aspect in them which grants nourishment—and wealth—and abundance is emphasized. Also the specifically nourishing (motherly) side of the great (*mahī*) Vegetation-Goddess is probably expressed especially in this name.

331. NVO, p. 155.

332. V.41.19 : *nadíbhir urváśī*; X.95.17 : *antarikṣaprā́m rájaso vimā́nīm urváśīm.* Cf. Bloomfield, JAOS, XX, p. 181. TS I.3.7.k (firesticks); VS V.2; KŚS V.1.30.

CHAPTER IX

MANES, DEMONS AND ASURAS

1. According to TS II.5.11.1, *nivīta* is for men, *prācīnāvīta* for the Manes and *upavīta* for the gods; similarly according to 9.6, *īḍenya* for men, *namasya* for the Manes and *yajñiya* for the gods.

2. Caland, *Die altindischen Todten- und Bestattungsgebräuche*, p. 172, where additional material can be found.

3. Tuxen, *Foréstillingen om sjaelen i Rigveda* (Kopenhagen 1919), p. 23 : "...the very strong emphasis on the totality of the person, coupled with the negative fact that not a single allusion refers to a soul, indisputably supports, to a large extent, the conclusion to which the preceding investigation of the conceptions like *manas, asu* and *ātman* has led."

4. See below Section B. Demons; Caland, *Über die Totenverehrung bei einigen der indogermanischen Völker* p. 44.

5. *Ritualliteratur*, p. 130 and note 35. ABr VII.34.2 : *ūmā vai pitaraḥ prātaḥsavana, ūrvā mādhyaṃdine, kāvyās tṛtīyasavane.*

6. X.154.1 : *sóma ékebhyaḥ pavate ghṛtám éka upāsate |*
yébhyo mádhu pradhā́vati etc.

7. See also Abegg, *Pretakalpa*, pp. 191-92. With this classification Manu draws also the individual castes into association with the Manes and gives the following genealogy which can hardly be accounted for.

Virāj	Somasad	Sādhya-s
Marīci	Agniṣvātta	Deva-s
Atri	Barhi ṣad	Daitya-s, Dānava-s, Yakṣa-s, Gandharva-s etc.
Kavi	Somapa	Viprāḥ (brahmins)
Aṅgiras	Havirbhuj	Kṣatriya
Pulastya	Ājyapa	Vaiśya
Vasiṣṭha	Sukālin	Śūdra

TBr I.6.9.6 defines thus : *ye vai yajvāno te pitaro barhiṣadaḥ..ye vā ayajvāno gṛhamedhinas te pitaro 'gniṣvāttāḥ.*

8. *Ritualliteratur*, pp. 118, 160. ŚBr II.6.1.4, 7.

9. Caland, *Altindischer Ahnenkult*, p. 94.

10. Ibid., p. 182 ff.

11. ABr III.37.11 lists the Kāvyas between the gods and the Manes; they are supposed to be lower than the gods but higher than the Manes.

12. Cf. also ŚPr III.6.1.14 : *pitṛdevatyaṃ vā asyā etad bhavati yan nikhātam.* TS I.3.1.e; VI.2.10.4. *Ritualliteratur*, p. 95.

13. *Ritualliteratur*, p. 88; Oldenberg, RdV, p. 545 ff.

14. See also Caland, *Die altindischen Todten- und Bestattungsgebräuche*, p. 78, n. 288.

15. TMBr IX.8.5 : *tṛtīye hi loke pitaraḥ*; TBr I.6.8.7 : *tṛtīye vā ito loke pitaraḥ*; TĀr II.6.2 : *yatra suhārdaḥ sukṛto madante vihāya rogaṃ tanvāṃ svāyām / aśloṇāṅgair ahṛtā svarge tatra paśyema pitaraṃ ca putrām //*

16. X.15.3 : *ā́hám pitṝ́n suvidátrā̃n avitsi nápātaṃ ca vikrámaṇaṃ ca viṣṇoḥ.*

17. Cf. the rich collection of material in Ludwig, *Der Rigveda*, VI, p. 196.

18. Cf. I.164.50 (=X.90.16) : *té [devā́ḥ] ha nā́kaṃ mahimā́naḥ sacanta yátra pū́rve sādhyā́ḥ sánti devā́ḥ*; TMBr VIII.3.5 : *sādhyā vai nāma devā āsan*; XXV.8.2 : *sādhyā vai nāma devebhyo devāḥ pūrva āsan*; TS VI.3.4.8 : *sādhyā vai devā yajñam aty amanyanta*; 3.5.1 : *sādhyā vai devā asmiṅ loka āsan*; in 5.6.1 Aditi, longing for sons, cooks Brahmaudana for them. In ABr VIII.12.4 they are mentioned along with the Āptyas between the Vasus, Rudras, Viśvedevāḥ on the one side and the Maruts and Aṅgirases on the other. In 14.3 they are drawn into association with the Kuru-Pañcālas. HGS II. 19.1 lists the Sādhyas between Sūrya, Candramas, Ādityas, Viśvedevāḥ on the one side and Ṛbhus, Bhṛgus, Maruts, Atharvans etc. on the other.

19. ṚV IV.51.11 : *pūṣā́ bhágo áditiḥ páñca jánāḥ /*
suśármāṇaḥ svávasaḥ sunīthā́
bhávantu naḥ sutrātrā́saḥ sugopā́ḥ //

X.60.4 : *divī́va páñca kṛṣṭáyaḥ.* TS I.7.12.1.d : *grahāḥ pañcajanīnāḥ.*

20. Manu III.284. According to III.201, from the Ṛṣis sprang the Manes and from the Manes the gods and the Dānavas. The Manes are the first of the deities (III.192) and have the qualities of being *akrodhana, śauca-para, satataṃ brahmacārin, nyastaśastra, mahābhāga*. In the ceremonies in honour of the Manes, great care should be exercised in selecting the brahmin to be invited (III.149).

21. WZKM, XIII, p. 289.

22. Weber, *Naxatra*, II, p. 268 ff.; Scherman, "Die Sterne im indogermanischen Seelenglauben," *Urquell*, VI, p. 5 ff.; Foy, ARW, VIII, pp. 539, 544; X.134.

23. Tr. Sachau, II, p. 94. On Rohiṇī, see ibid., II, p. 96.

24. Cf. *Raghuvaṃśa* IV.21; Weber, *Verzeichnisse der Sanskrit Handschriften* (*Die Handschriftenverzeichnisse der königlichen Bibliothek zu Berlin*), II, p. 103. A study of the statements of the later texts, Graheṣṭis etc. should yield much information on the beliefs about the stars in the Vedic period.

25. Hiraṇyakeśin (II.19.1) enumerates Viśvāmitra, Jamadagni, Bharadvāja, Gautama, Atri, Vasiṣṭha and Kaśyapa as the seven Ṛṣis. Arundhatī stands between the last two, Agastya is separated from the others.

26. ŚBr II.1.2.4 : *ṛkṣāṇāṃ ha vā etā agre patnya āsuḥ saptarṣīn u ha sma vai purarkṣā ity ācakṣate tā mithunena vyārdhyantāmī hy uttarāhi saptarṣaya udyanti pura etāḥ.* Cf. ṚV I.24.10 : *amī́ yá ṛ́kṣā níhitāsa uccā́*; ŚBr XIII.8.1.9 : *eṣo ha jīvānāṃ dig antareṇa saptarṣīṇāṃ codayanam ādityasya*

cāstamayanam; JUBr IV.26.12 : *atha yatraite sapta ṛṣayas tad divo madhyam.*

27. NVO, pp. 18, 75; ĀpŚS VI.8.11.

28. KŚS IV.14.27. When a comet obscures them, it means danger, see Weber, *Omina und Portenta*, p. 396.

29. X.109.4 : *devā́ etásyām avadanta pū́rve*
sapta-ṛṣáyas tápase yé niṣedúḥ /

30. III.7.7 : *adhvaryúbhiḥ pañcábhiḥ saptá víprāḥ*
priyáṃ rakṣante níhitaṃ padáṃ véḥ /
prā́ñco madanty ukṣáṇo ajuryā́
devā́ devā́nām ánu hí vratā́ gúḥ //

31. X.35.10 : *ā́ no barhíḥ sadhamā́de bṛhád diví*
devā́ñ īḷe sādáyā saptá hótṝn /
VI.22.2 : *tám* [*índram*] *u naḥ pū́rve pitáro návagvāḥ*
saptá víprāso abhí vājáyantaḥ //

IV.1.12. TĀr I.11.2 : *asataḥ sad ye tatakṣuḥ* / *ṛṣayaḥ saptātriś ca yat sarve trayo* (?) *agastyás ca nakṣatraiḥ śaṅkṛto 'vasan.*

32. III.31.5 : *vīḷaú satī́r abhí dhī́rā atṛndan*
prācā́hinvan mánasā saptá víprāḥ /

33. X.63.7 . *yébhyo hótrāṃ prathamā́m āyejé mánuḥ*
sámidhāgnir mánasā saptá hótṛbhiḥ /

34. In verses other than these mentioned above, i.e. in III.10.4; VIII. 60.16; IX.10.7; 92.2; X.130.7, it would be more appropriate to interpret the seven Hotṛs as those of the sacrificial place.

35. But not the names in any case. The mantras with which they are consecrated read thus : Hotṛ—*vahnir asi havyavāhana*; Maitrāvaruṇa—*śvātro 'si pracetāḥ;* Brāhmaṇācchaṃsin : *tutho 'si viśvavedāḥ*; Potṛ—*uśig asi kaviḥ*; Neṣṭṛ—*aṅghāriḥ*; Acchāvāka —*avasyur duvasvān;* Āgnīdhra—*vibhur asi pravāhaṇaḥ*, TMBr I.4.5; *Srautapadārthanirvacana*, p. 314 ff.

36. The Adhvaryu is called *iṣirá* in III.5.4; V.3.12 : *grā́vā...yásya jīrám adhvaryávaś cáranti.*

37. *amī́ ye páñcokṣáṇo mádhye tasthúr mahó diváḥ.* What Sāyaṇa states on this is useless. According to him, "these five constellations" are Indra, Varuṇa, Agni, Aryaman and Savitṛ, or Agni, Vāyu, Sūrya, Candramas and Vidyut !

38. Cf. the relation between the late Vedic Nejameṣa and Naigameṣa of Suśruta and Nemeso of the Mathurā inscription (Bühler, ed. *Epigraphia Indica*, II, p. 316, and Winternitz, JRAS, 1895, p. 149 ff.).

39. PGS III.7.3.

40. Ibid., I.9.5.

41. See below the section, Rudra's Names. Somewhat differently Weber, *Omina und Portenta*, p. 400.

42. PGS III.15.20. TĀr IV.29 ff. Cf. Oldenberg, RdV, 2nd ed., p. 264 ff.

43. PGS I.11.4. GDS XXVI.16, for example, mentions gods, "momentary gods" and demons of all kinds.

44. Bloomfield, *The Atharva Veda and the Gopatha Brāhmaṇa*. p. 9. The ŚBr puts the Bahvṛcas next to the Yātuvidas.

45. Cf. also Manu III.204, 238.

46. Cf. *inter alia*, NVO, p. 171.

47. Rohde, *Psyche*, 2nd ed. I, p. 272, n. 1.

48. ŚBr III.7.1.2.

49. ĀpŚS XI.11.6 etc.

50. Caland, *Altindischer Ahnenkult*, p. 26. On the Piśācas, see Jarl Charpentier, *Kleine Beiträge*, p. 1 ff. He proceeds from the first meaning "Jack-o'-lantern" and the additional meaning "glow-worm" as proposed by Roth. He says that the Piśācas have become a sort of demons already in the Vedic period and more so in later times. However, now and then they make their appearance as rather harmless creatures, but mostly as hideous-looking flesh-eating monsters (?).

51. VS I.26; TS I.1.9.i ff.; MS I.1.10; IV.1.10; TBr III.2.9.4.

52. Among the demons there is one called Makha. He seems to be particularly well known in the circle of the Bhṛgus as ṚV IX. 101.13 (*ápa svā́nam arādhásaṃ hatā́ makháṃ na bhṛ́gavaḥ*) shows. His name occurs often in the mantras of the YV, where Agni, Indra and Rudra are styled *makhahan* (cf. TS III.2.4). He stands next to the gods but he is unmistakably opposed to them. According to TMBr VII.5.6 (cf. MS IV.5.9) the splendour (*yaśas*) reaches him first. He runs away with it and remains standing, leaning against his bow. The bow-string snaps and severes Makha's head which becomes the Pravargya. As elsewhere it is said here that Makha is the sacrifice. It is also related that ants gnawed at the bow-string and as a reward for this they received the boon that wherever they dig they would find water (see Comm. on TMBr VII.5.6; TBr; MS IV.5.9. The variant readings in the last mentioned text are important; the ants reply to Indra : *abhimṛtāyām [jyāyāṃ] vā asyāṃ na śakṣyāmo jīvitum*). However, it is not always Makha who plays this role. According to TĀr I.5.2, it is Rudra whose head is torn off by the snapping end of the bow and it is Indra who gnaws at the bow-string in the shape of an ant (*vamrirūpeṇa*). In ŚBr XIV. 1.1.1 it is Viṣṇu whose head is cut off by the ends of the bow (cf. also TĀr V.1.2 and Rājendra Lāla Mitra, Introduction, p. 27; comm. p. 372). Like Makha, Viṣṇu is also well known as the "sacrifice." I have not been able to understand the meaning of this legend. In VS XI.57; TS IV.1.5 the lump of clay with which the Ukhā is formed is addressed thus : *makhasya śiro 'si*. This is in conformity with the fact that during the Pravargya the Mahāvīra vessel is similarly regarded as *makhasya śiraḥ* (VS XXXVII.7 ff.; TĀr V.3.2). The same form of address is employed, however, in the case of the roundish lump of food also which is used for the puroḍāśa (TS I.1.8.g; TBr III.2.8.3) and in the case of the remains of the Āghāra (TS I.1.12. p) where its significance is less obvious.

53. Ed. Trenckner, p. 272 : *kīṭa- kimi-, kipillika-, pataṃgavaṇṇa* etc.

54. PGS I.16.23; ĀpGS XVIII.1; *Mantrapāṭha* II.16.1 ff. The demon crowd is still more varied in HGS II.3.7 (*Rituallitératur*, pp. 181-82) :

pramṛśant, kūṭadanta, vikleśa, lambastana, uraspeśa etc. Cf. Caland, *Das rituelle Sūtra des Baudhāyana*, p. 31.

55. PGS I.16.24; HGS II.7.3.

56. HGS I.6.5 : *kaṣakāya tvā paridadāmi, antakāya tvā paridadāmi, aghorāya..., gadāya..., yamāya..., makhāya...* etc.

57. PGS II.6.10.

58. Justi, GGA, 1866, p. 1446 ff.; rejoinder by Dr M. Haug, p. 22 ff. (On this question cf. also Spiegel, *Eranische Altertumskunde*, pp. 231-273; Weber, IStr, II, pp. 445, 469 ff.).

59. B. Geiger, *Aməša Spəntas*, p. 225: "I think...that the old hypothesis of Haug, which had been rejected unanimously, did after all prove to be correct in the main points." Kshetreśa Chandra Chaṭṭopādhyāya has rejected Haug's view all too rashly (*Proceedings of the Fourth Oriental Conference*, p. 11 ff.).

60. The identity of the names can, by no means, be dismissed. Indra is probably the same as the Iranian *indro* as Geldner (on Vendidād X.9; XIX. 43) writes. *nåŋhaithya*, the hostile demon, cannot be separated from *nāsatyau* which is the name of two good gods. Since apparently many connecting links are lost, we are not able to recognize in each case the reason and history of the semantic change. It would be erroneous to think that the circumstances in Iran are the complete opposite of the Indian state of affairs or vice versa. Likewise *saurva* and *śarva* may perhaps be connected though there are difficulties of formal nature (Bloomfield also supports the connection, PJAOS, 1894, p. clix : "*śáru, śárv : śūr* 'crush'; the strong anteconsonantal *śáru-s* 'missile'; antevocalic *śārv-á*, Avestan *saurva* 'god of destruction.' ")

61. *Ormazd et Ahriman*, p. 268.

62. Ibid., p. 266 : "... transfer into that environment where Ahura and the Yazata have secured for themselves the whole divinity, transfer some invocations which are addressed to Ahura or to a Yazata and which are similar to those in which the Vedic heroes implore the gods 'that they may not be affected by *the trouble which emanates from men or by that which emanates from the deva*' (*deva-kṛtam, martyakṛtam aṃhas*)...'that nothing of *the anger of the devas or of men* may strike him' (*heḍo devānām uta martyānām*)... that there may be a stronghold against the attacks of the devas or of men'... then you will have the origin and the ancient significance of the constant prayers of the Avestan heroes, in which they beseech the favour of the gods for the triumph over the hatreds 'of the devas and of men' (*daēvanām uta martyānām*); formulas which are the true reproductions, the true echo, of the Indo-Iranian prayers, but where the word *deva*, having become obscure and denoting only a being who does evil deeds, had certainly reached the stage of assuming a demoniacal colour."

63. Ibid., p. 266.

64. When it is said in passages like I.24.14 : *áva te héḷo varuṇa...asura*, the *héḍo* is connected with Varuṇa not because he is an Asura but because he is a dangerous god on his own and yet Varuṇa has

never become a demon. When Darmesteter states, *op. cit.*, p. 269, that "images of terror have consequently come together under this name (Varuṇa); the greatest of the Asuras won the distinction of having joined the ranks of *terrible* gods," this is also wrong, because in the ṚV precisely the designation of Asura does not impart anything demoniacal to the one thus designated, and when the Asuras became demons at a later stage Varuṇa did not remain an Asura any longer. The hostility of the Brāhmaṇa period is not directed to the Asura Varuṇa who does not play any role in Iran but to the more general class of the Asuras. Varuṇa himself did not contribute to this development. Proceeding from the use of the word *māyā*, Oldenberg (RdV, 2nd ed., p. 161) states that in reality the purport of the word *asura*, which has a hostile colouring, is contained already in its essence in the oldest available meaning and that it has outgrown with use, but the change which really took place consists in the fact that '"gradually" the word went out of vogue for the gods and thus remained exclusively for the evil beings. What I have said against Tiele earlier applies to Oldenberg as well. Cf. incidentally. B. Geiger, *Aməša Spəntas*, p. 224. The history of the Asura cannot be compared with that of Gr. *daimon* (Scheftelowitz, ZII, IV, p. 336).

65. *Geschichte der Religion im Altertum bis auf Alexander den Grossen*, II, pp. 82, 84. *asura* does not mean, as Tiele remarks on p. 83, "just as often the divine as the demoniacal." The ratio is quite different and it varies depending on the branch of literature concerned.

66. Ludwig, *Der Rigveda*, IV, p. xviii.

67. von Bradke, *Dyaus Asura*, p. 106 : "Thus we must rule out the possibility that a transition from the concept of "asura=highest god" to the concept of the *asurā adevāḥ* could have taken place within the Indo-Brahmanical evolution. Accordingly what remains is the assumption that the younger *asurā adevāḥ* have been imported into the Brahmanical world from outside."

68. Ibid., p. 90 ff.

69. For a formal explanation of the passage, cf. Johansson, IF, III, p. 237.

70. ŚŚS XV.15.11; *Gobhila Śrāddha Kalpa* III.7 (Caland, *Über die Totenverehrung bei einigen der indogermanischen Völker*, p. 32).

71. Bartholomae, *Grundriss der iranischen Philologie*, I, p. 103.

72. Cf. also Yasna IX.18 : *nī taṭ yatha taurvayēni*
vīspanąm ṭbiš̆vatąm ṭbaēšå
daēvanąm mašyānąm ča
yāthvąm pairikanąm ča
sāthrąm kaoyąm karafnąm ča...

XXXII.15; XLVI.11; XLVIII.10; LI.14. Geldner, BKIS, XII, p. 98; XIV, pp. 3-4. Bartholomae, IF, I, p. 192 ff.

73. Cf. Wilhelm, "Priester und Ketzer im alten Erān," ZDMG, XLIV, p. 144; West, SBE, XLVII, p. 19, n. 2; Jackson, *Zoroaster, The Prophet of Ancient Iran*, p. 28.

74. This word (at times in the singular and at others in the plural) is the name of a priestly gotra and of its mythical progenitor who presses the Soma and enjoys the friendship of Indra. He is at par with Kutsa, Aṅgiras and Gautama. TS VI.3.6.1 : *ṛtvijə vai vahnaya uśijaḥ.*

75. Spiegel, *Die arische Periode*, p. 282 ff.

76. TMBr VII.5.20; see below.

77. Darmesteter errs also in the assumption that "all the deities and all the basic ideas of Mazdaism are Indian as well as Iranian," *Ormazd et Ahriman*, p. 262. He is wrong in tracing both Varuṇa and Ahuramazda back to the same source, likewise in his identification of the Ādityas with the Aməša Spəntas. As early as in the ṚV, Mitra had very little significance and in the Brāhmaṇas he became a mere shadow. His partner Varuṇa, recognizable in Iran only in some dual forms (see p. 6ff. above), is regarded in India as one of the greatest gods and as the creator of the world. Ahuramazda is totally absent in India; he exists only in some phrases like *ásurasya māyáyā* (see WZKM, XIII, p. 320) or as *pitṛ́ ásura.* The differences are actually large enough. But in addition there is, in the realm of the ritual, first the total abandonment of bloody sacrifices in Iran and then the exposure of the dead. We should not expect, as I said before, that the circumstances in Iran form the exact opposite of those in India or vice versa. Religious schisms do not lead to a complete abandonment of all that is common in the cult but only to a change of scene in the foreground. I think it is not at all a question of "a change in four or five ceremonies" (Darmesteter, *op. cit.* p. 262) but of a much deeper difference. The chief characters change while the minor ones remain in their posts.

Segerstedt, *Revue de l'histoire des religions*, LVII, p. 163 ff., proceeds from quite a different viewpoint. He ascribes the difference between the Asuras and the Devas to racial difference, particularly to the difference between the original inhabitants and the Aryans. He remarks that "Asura was the name not only of the original inhabitants of India but also of their gods. And it seems that we have a right to conclude that the last usage was the original usage" (p. 166). About Varuṇa he observes on p. 197 (and elsewhere) that "at the beginning Varuṇa was a stranger in the Aryan cult." I think the question of the demonization of the Asuras cannot be separated from that of the Devas. The explanation must be the same for both the cases; if not it would miss its mark. Even when the designation *asura* was given in the later period to the native gods and demons of India, this does not prove the least against the original meaning "lord." That they formed a class of gods who were different from the Devas, that *māyā* and *ṛta* were pre-eminent in their realm, and that they belonged to a different tribe is demonstrated by their conflict with the Devas. But they were not the gods of the aboriginal tribes of India. For further remarks, see my *Vedische Mythologie* (smaller edition), p. 189.

77a. Cf. my review of Hopkins, *The Religions of India*, in AISAK, IX, p. 16.

78. Cf. Ludwig, *Der Rigveda*, IV, p. xvii; TS I.6.6.r; from the Pāli

Jātakas, IV, 273, v. 146 (comm. : *asurajeṭṭhako sakko*). Wenzel, "Some Contributions to Pāli Lexicography," *Academy*, 1890, 30th August, p. 178.

79. My review of Hopkins, *The Religions of India*, *loc. cit.*

80. Here I agree partly with Tiele, *op. cit.*, II, p. 85 : "...The Vedic as well as the Zarathustran religions emerged only after a long period after this separation. Neither of them has directly emerged from the beliefs of the eastern branch of Aryans. Between their emergence and the split in the ancient Aryan peoples a long time must have elapsed, during which the old religion continued its course of evolution in various and often lively divergent directions.. " etc.

81. It is appropriate to remember von Bradke whose views are similar to those of Haug, but come quite close to the correct answer. In *Dyaus Asura*, p. 108, von Bradke says : "the only Aryans of whom we know positively that they worshipped the Asuras and loathed the Devas are the Iranians of the Avesta. Hence the demonization of the Asuras among the Brahmanical Indians has been traced back to the conflict between the latter and the followers of Zarathustra, as I think, with justification. Only we should not place this conflict in the Aryan antiquity. There is no doubt that the Iranians lived for a long time separated from the Indians, who had tribal affinities with the former, before Zarathustra began his reformatory activity. ...Consequently, we may trace the emergence of the *asurā adevāḥ* among the Vedic Indians to their opposition to the Iranians of the Avesta. ..." Here only the expressions "with the followers of Zarathustra" and "the Iranians of the Avesta" are wrong. B. Geiger (*Aməša Spəntas*, p. 225 n) thinks quite rightly "that the old hypothesis of Haug, which had been rejected unanimously, did after all prove to be correct in the main points." He goes on to say : "we may, above all, be permitted to ask why we must assume an enmity towards the Iranian Ahura worshippers when the Vedic Indians themselves possessed in their midst an Asura cult which was highly developed and was closely related to the Iranian cult. And the employment of the expressions *ásurasya vīrā́ḥ* and *ásurasya māyā́* for gods and demons leads us to conclude that the enmity was directed rather against the Indian Asura worshippers." However, the parallel process of transformation of the *devāḥ* into the "devil in Iran" permits us to recognize a connection between the two processes as Geiger also assumes (*op. cit.*, p. 224). I do not deny that the Indian Asura worshippers also might have been opposed by the Deva followers (cf. ṚV X. 124). But in the ṚV the animosity against the Asura is just in its beginnings and it is only afterwards, after the period of the ṚV, that we can notice hostility to all that goes by the name Asura. Hence I draw the line of demarcation in India in the period between the ṚV and the Brahmaṇas, during which the Asura cult was dislodged and the Deva cult gained the upper hand (perhaps politically also) and created a sharp distinction against the Iranian belief.

I cannot agree with Sten Konow (*Festschrift für Jacobi*, p. 263) who treats the opposition between the Devas and the Asuras as "a natural consequence of the difference in the historical development of the Indian Aryans and the

Iranian Aryans, but not as the result of ancient battles between the two peoples;" different historical developments usually take place even today without wars. Moreover, II.30.4; VI.22.4; VII.99.5; X.138.3 speak clearly enough, cf. p. 364, n. 381, 384 and 385 above.

Nor do the allusions to the *māyā́* of the Asuras prove anything. Indra himself employs *māyā́* upon them and yet he is opposed to the Asuras. Indians were not so averse to *māyā́*; WZKM, XIII, p. 316 ff.

82. II.30.4 : *bṛ́haspate...vidhya vṛ́kadvaraso ásurasya vīrā́n.* On this von Bradke (*Dyaus Asura*, p. 96) notes that *dvaras* looks like an Iranian form of Sanskrit *dhvaras*. Hence *vṛkadvaras* could be a semi-Sanskritized form of the Iranian proper name *vehrkadvaraṅh*. But ultimately it seemed more obvious to him to suppose, with the PW, that *vṛkadvaras* is a corrupt form of the Indian *vṛkadhvaras*. Wackernagel, SBKPAW, 1918, pp. 406-7, on the contrary, cites the late Avestan *dvar* ("running like a wolf") and maintains that "such an epithet is specially appropriate to the Asura host. In the Avesta *dvar* denotes...the running of the Daeva beings." Brunnhofer, *Iran and Turan*, p. 127, thinks of the inhabitants of the Shand desert. In v. 8 these enemies are called Śaṇḍikas.

VII.99.5 : *śatáṃ varcínaḥ sahásraṃ ca sākáṃ*
hathó apraty ásurasya vīrā́n ||

Since Śambara, as I have shown, should be located in the western countries because of his enmity with Divodāsa, the designation Asura does not seem to be accidental. The other two passages are X.138.3 : *dṛḷhā́ni pípror ásurasya māyína índro vy àsyat* (Pipru is close to Varcin and Śambara) and X.124.5 (see p. 41 ff above). The AV contains the singular in this sense three times (VIII.6.5; XIII. 4.42; XIX.56.1). See von Bradke, *op. cit.*, p. 101 ff.

83. VIII.96.9 : *asurāḥ adevāḥ*; 97.1 (in contrast to VIII.25.4 : *devā́v ásurau*). The other passages belong to the first book and more predominantly to the tenth (53.4; 82.5; 124.5; 151.3; 157.4). *āsurá* occurs in hostile sense in ṚV V.40.5, 9 (Svarbhānu) and X.131.4 (Namuci). *asurahán* occurs in VI.22.4; VII.13.1; X.170.2. The meaning of "demons" is generally on the increase in the tenth book, hence, it is closer to the period of the Brāhmaṇas. The hymns which refer to the Asuras in hostile sense provide thus a criterion to say that they belong to the Brāhmaṇa-stratum or, to put it more cautiously, to the groups whose notions were continued in the Brāhmaṇas. In the AV, the plural *asurāḥ* in the sense of demons occurs already thirty times (see von Bradke, *op. cit.*, p. 86).

84. Once (in hostile sense) in *asurahán* in VI.22.4. Cf. my review of McCrindle's *The Invasion of India by Alexander the Great* in GGA, 1894, p. 650. The word *asuryà* escaped from being outlawed and occurs four times in friendly sense in book VI (20.2; 30.2; 36.1; 74.1); it seems to have been saved from semantic change probably through the difference in accent and in the ending. Otherwise, *asura* occurs four times in book II (but in hostile sense in II.30.4), six times in book III (including *asuratva*), twice in

book IV, eleven times in book V, never in book VI, seven times in book VII and eight times in book VIII.

85. Neisser, WB, p. 143, correctly observes that *ásura* appears originally as one of the highest gods who are worshipped as the creators of the worlds and who precede the *dévas* in genealogy. Neisser's remark about the position of the word in the verse is important.

86. In VI.22.4 he is called *asurahán*; in VII.99.5 the *ásurasya vīrā́ḥ* are opposed to him and to Viṣṇu. Cf. also VIII.96.9; 97.1.

87. E.g. ABr II.16.4; IV.5.1; VI.4.2; 14.10; 32.25; 36.14; TS II.3.7; 4.2; VII.3.7.1; TBr I.1.2.4-5; 2.3.3; .3.10.1; III.3.5.1; ŚBr II.1.2.14; TMBr XX.14.2; *Jātaka* I.31 etc. (see Scheftelowitz, ZII, IV, p. 337). Other gods are also mentioned as the enemies of the Asuras but not so often as Indra. For example, Mitra-Varuṇa in ABr VI.4.1; Indra-Viṣṇu in ABr III.50.3; VI.15.10; Indra-Varuṇa in III.50.1; Viṣṇu in MS I.4.7 (54.18).

88. And also *asurahán* in VII.13.1.

89. That *déva* in *mū́radeva* (VII.104.24) has a bad sense is, as Tiele (*op. cit.*, II, p. 83, n. 1) assumes, true but that is due to the addition of *mūra* and therefore justifies no conclusion.

90. ŚBr III.2.1.23; Vol. I of this work, p. 336.

91. Nöldke, *Grundriss der iranischen Philologie*, II, p. 178, n. 1.

92. Cf. Weber, *Über die Magavyakti des Kṛṣṇadāsa Miśra*, Berlin 1879. *Über zwei Parteischriften zugunsten der Maga*, Berlin 1880. Haraprasād Śāstrī, PJASB, 1901, p. 75 ff. Weber draws attention also to the names in the lists of teachers in the *Vaṃśabrāhmaṇa* which "point to Iran" (ISt, IV, p. 375 ff.).

93. Cf. ĀpŚS I.8.7 : *apayantv asurāḥ pitṛrūpāḥ*. Donner, *Piṇḍapitṛyajña*, p. 19.

94. After they have been transformed into demons (partly in the ṚV already, e.g. X.157.4), other motifs whether young or old have been attached to them (Kuhn, *Über Entwicklungsstufen der Mythenbildung*, p. 129; Eggeling, SBE, XII, p. 286, n. 2). But Vincent Smith goes too far with the assumption that "the whole conception of the Asuras and their conflicts with the gods was borrowed from the Greek legends of the Gigantomachia (JASB, 1889, p. 133; 1892, p. 60). In such a case already TBr I.1.2.4 ff. and even parts of the ṚV would have been influenced by the Greeks.

95. The majority of the Deva-Asura legends are likely to be mere justifications of certain ritual practices and might have been freely invented. However, we do not know all the "Asuras" with whom Indians were in conflict, and it can be assumed, at least in principle, that hidden among these may be also conflicts that took place between the Purohitas of different clans. The legends of the MBh require a special study.

96. MS IV.6.3 (81.1); ŚBr IV.2.1.6; comm. on TBr, I, p. 6, etc. See also Vol. I, p. 307.

97. TS II.5.8.5; ŚŚS XIV.27.1. Geldner, VSt, II, p. 166.

98. Comm. : *uśanā nāma kaveḥ putraḥ asurāṇāṃ virocanādīnām purohitaḥ....*

99. Although the material is not adequate to define his characteristics more closely, we may nevertheless recognize that he is to be regarded as an ancestor who became mythical as Kutsa and others did.

100. Of the recent writings, cf. Spiegel, *Die arische Periode*, p. 284 ff.; Tiele, *op. cit.*, II, p. 72; Nöldke, *Grundriss der iranischen Philologie*, II, p. 190. n. 2. Contra Bartholomae, *Altiranisches Wörterbuch*.

101. Comm. : *kayādhusaṃjñitāyā hiraṇyakaśipubhāryāyāḥ putraḥ prahrādaḥ svakīyaṃ putraṃ virocanam asurasainyasvāminaṃ yuddhabhūmer apanīya.*

102. In the later period, besides Vepacitti and Śambara (*Saṃyuttanikāya*, I.225), Virocana is also regarded as *asurinda*.

103. Darmesteter, *Le Zend Avesta, Traduction nouvelle...*, II, p. 399; III, p. lviii.

104. Comm. : *kirātā mlecchāḥ*. They do not know the ritual of cooking correctly. Cf. Weber, ISt, X, p. 33 n.; Max Müller, "the Hymns of the Gaupāyanas," JRAS, NS, II, p. 426 ff. : *na ha smānagnau nidhāyaudanaṃ pacataḥ, agnau māṃsam / athāsurānnaṃ jagdhvekṣvākavaḥ parābabhūvuḥ /*

105. Comm. : *evamnāmāno 'surāḥ, makhasaṃjñakā yātisaṃjñakāś ca.*

106. Here it is to do with an old mistake in recitation, *etad u* instead of *idam u*, which was probably the sole starting point of this personification.

107. The legend of these Asuras who construct a fire altar is specially remarkable because it recalls the story of Otos and Ephialtes (Kuhn, *Über Entwicklungsstufen der Mythenbildung*, p. 129). Here altar bricks are substituted for mountains. See Eggeling, SBE, XII, p. 286, n. 2.

108. TS VI.2.5.3 : *trivrato vai manur āsīt dvivratā asurā ekavratā devāḥ prātar madhyaṃdine sāyam tan manor vratam āsīt...prātaś ca sāyaṃ cāsurāṇām nirmadhyam, kṣudho rūpam / tatas te parābhavan / madhyaṃdine madhyarātre devānām tatas te 'bhavan...*

109. Of the other differences, the following may be emphasized.

i. Those concerning the metre. TMBr XII.13.27 : *ekākṣaraṃ vai devānām avamaṃ chanda āsīt, saptākṣaraṃ paramam/ navākṣaram asurāṇām avamaṃ chanda āsīt, pañcadaśākṣaraṃ paramam* (cf. *ṚV Prātiśākhya* 866; Weber, ISt, VIII, p.75). This statements at once seems to be worthless since there is hardly any correspondence in the metres. Hence, Weber has rejected, I think, quite rightly Haug's conjecture (*Essays on the Parsis*, p. 229) that *gāyatrī āsurī, uṣṇiḥ āsurī, paṅkti āsurī* go back to the metres of the Avestan Gāthās, as "no doubt ingenious but absolutely untenable conjecture" (ISt, VIII, p. 232). But only an analysis of the Avestan and Vedic metres can decide how far a faint historical core is contained in it.

ii. The gods say *eka* and the Asuras form the feminine *ekā* and so on until finally the Asuras cannot form the feminine for *pañca*, TMBr XXI.13.2; ŚBr I.5.4.7 ff.

iii. According to some law books, the *āsura* form of marriage is allowed, as is well known, only to the Śūdras and Vaiśyas.

iv. In the battle between the Devas and the Asuras, Śibi Auśinara wins and receives a gift from Indra (Eggeling, *Catalogue of the Sanskrit Mss. in the Library of the India Office*, I, 87 a).

v. Māyā is attributed to the Asuras. Like Ṛta, it belongs to their realm.

vi. Āsuri is the name of a well-known teacher of Veda, ŚBr II.1.4.27; 3.1.9; 4.1.2 etc.

110. Some more examples are given in my *Vedische Mythologie* (smaller ed.), p. 189.

CHAPTER X

RUDRA

1. *rudro vai krūro devānām*, TS VI.1.7.8; 2.3.2; MS III.8.1 (92.16). He is a *varāha*, and about the *varāha* TBr I.7.9.4 declares : *paśūnāṃ vā eṣa manyuḥ yad varāhaḥ*.

2. ṚV X.92.5.

3. Rājendra Lāla Mitra, *Chāndogya Upaniṣad*, tr., p. 9. See Muir, CST, IV, p. 316.

4. KŚS I.10.4; ŚBr I.7.4.9; II.6.2.18; *Ritualliteratur*, p. 112.

5. Arbman, *Rudra : Untersuchungen zum altindischen Glauben und Kultus*, 1922; see my review in *Asia Major*, II, p. 612 ff.

6. Enthoven, *Folklore of Bombay*, p. 76; W. Crooke, *Religion and Folklore of Northern India*, p. 56.

7. TBr I.7.8.5; TS I.8.14.1 and the comm., p. 153.

7a. TS II.6.6.5 : *yad agnaye sviṣṭakṛte 'vadyati bhāgadheyenaiva tad rudraṃ sam ardhayati | sakṛtsakṛd ava dyati | sakṛd iva hi rudraḥ | uttarārdhād ava dyati | eṣā vai rudrasya dik | svāyām eva diśi rudraṃ niravadyate*. Cf. MS I.4.12 (63.10); TBr III.9.11.3; ŚBr I.7.3.20.

8. TS III.1.9.4 ff. Further on it is stated : "Manu divided his property among his sons but excluded Nābhānediṣṭha who was a student. He came to him and asked : 'Why did you exclude me ?' 'I did not exclude you. The Aṅgirases are holding a sacrificial session here; but they cannot find heaven. Tell them the magic formula. When they reach heaven, they will give you their cattle.' He told it to them. When they went to heaven, they gave him their cattle. As he went about in the place of sacrifice with the animals (that were left after the sacrifice, in order to lead them to his dwelling) Rudra approached him and said : 'These are my cattle.' 'But they gave these to me.' He replied : 'They cannot do that. Whatever is left on the sacrificial place is mine.' Hence one should not enter the sacrificial place. He said : 'Give me a share in the sacrifice. Then I shall not waylay your cattle.' He offered him the remnants of the Manthin. Hence Rudra did not waylay his cattle. Wherever one who knows thus offers the remnants of the Manthin, Rudra does not waylay the cattle" (cf. ĀpŚS XII.23.11.)

9. Comm. on the TS, II, p. 153. Weber, *Rājasūya*, p. 55. Other examples in Oldenberg, RdV, 2nd ed., pp. 218, 303.

10. TBr I.7.8.5. He is called *vāstavya* in ŚBr I.7.3.7 etc. I do not understand the designation Vāstoṣpati in TS III.4.10.3; TBr III.7.9.7; ĀpŚS XIII.20.1.

11. TS VI.5.6.3. TMBr VII.9.16 : "the gods divided the animals among themselves. They excluded Rudra. During the Vāmadevyastotra, he had his eyes on these..."

12. TS II.6.8.3. Cf. also ŚBr I.7.4.1 ff.

13. When Rudra saw, (narrates the MBh), that the gods had excluded him from the sacrifice, he made a bow for himself; filled with anger, Mahādeva went to the place where the gods were performing the sacrifice jointly. When they saw the imperishable one, the Brahmacārin...the divine earth trembled and the mountains shook ... overwhelmed, the gods lost their senses. The sacrifice lost its splendour; the gods were frightened. With a terrible arrow he shot at the heart of the sacrifice. Changing itself into a gazelle, the sacrifice ran away with the fire and when it reached the sky pursued by Rudra, it shone in the firmament. When the sacrifice fled away, consciousness did not return again to the gods. ...Enraged, Tryambaka destroyed, with the end of his bow, Savitṛ's arms, Bhaga's eyes and Pūṣan's teeth. The gods ran away from there and so did the individual parts of the sacrifice. Some of them, tottering to and fro, looked as if dead. ... But the hue and cry of the gods, it is said further, caused Rudra's bow-string to be torn off. The bow snapped asunder and the gods came near the "most beautiful of the gods" who was thus disarmed. They came along with the sacrifice for protection. The mighty one showed mercy and threw his anger into the water. This became the fire which incessantly causes the water to dry up. He gave the eyes back to Bhaga, arms to Savitṛ, teeth to Pūṣan and returned the sacrifice. "Then the whole world was happy once again." (Compare this with the Purāṇic legend of Rudra destroying Dakṣa's sacrifice, *Viṣṇupurāṇa*, tr. Wilson, p. 61 ff.). If a mythological conception underlies these legends, then I would think that the Rudra who throws his anger into the water, the "weeping" Rudra who flees with the wealth of the gods (cf. p. 288 below) and the *mīḷhvaṃs* or *jalāṣabheṣaja* ("whose medicine is urine" according to Bloomfield; but according to Scheftelowitz, KZ, LIII, p. 267, "having a medicine consisting of medicinal herbs") of the ṚV are mythological synonyms, that is to say, they are based on the same fundamental mythological notion, which is expressed in three different ways.

14. TS II.2.10.1 ff.; MS II.1.4 ff. (6.8 ff.). In the case of the caru for a sick person, the Hotṛ is led blindfolded into the forest and then the bandages are removed (MS, p. 82); a caru for Brahmavarcas, for which the milk of a white cow with a white calf is used, is offered behind an enclosure (TS).

15. Cf. also I.6.7.4; VI.3.9.3; 5.7.1; 8.5; TBr III.7.2.6; MS I.6.11 (103.17).

16. Cf. e.g., ŚŚS VII.18.2.

17. TBr III.7.8.1; ŚŚS III.20.2.

18. ŚŚS IV.17.1; comm. on HGS II.8.1.

19. See n. 110 below.

20. Arbman, *Rudra*, pp. 270, 273.

21. KŚS XXV.2.1.

22. *Ritualliteratur*, p. 78.

23. Just as Rudra is accommodated at the end so was it said earlier (n. 13 above) that "he shot at the heart of the sacrifice." We may interpret this, I suppose, in the sense that with the commencement of his regime, the year, or at least the sacrificial year, comes to an end.

24. On the *traiyambaka apūpa*, see also LŚS V.3. In Āpastamba's text the portion from *yāvantaḥ* up to *tāvantaḥ* is doubtless an old gloss for *pratipuruṣam*.

25. According to TBr I.6.10 the first ones for the already existing offspring whom he redeems (*niravadayate*) from Rudra with these and the single one is for those to be born in future.

26. According TBr I.6.10 the Abhighāraṇa is forbidden because with it one may bring about "that Rudra would sneak in between," i.e. the terrible god who brings ill-luck would penetrate into the house and obstruct us (TS I.8.6, comm. II, p. 84).

27. Ākhu is mentioned as an impure animal in a similar context on another occasion also without, however, Rudra being mentioned along with it. To the sacrificial posts called *upaśaya*, which can be neither cut not buried, one assigns mentally "an animal of the forest, an *ākhu* or his enemy." See *Ritualliteratur*, p. 136. VS XXIV.26 : *bhūmyā ākhūn ālabhate*. The comm. on TS, II, p. 85, (Lāṭyāyana 368) explains *ākhu* as *mūṣaka*, "mouse, rat." Kuhn, *Die Herabkunft des Feuers und des Göttertrankes*, 2nd ed., p. 178, makes an attempt at naturalistic explanation. Perhaps it is just in Rudra's season that the animal proves to be specially destructive to the produce of the fields. An offering to the Ākhurāja in GGS IV.4.31 at the earth dug up by mice can be accounted for in the context of the other agricultural sacrifices described there. (In TS V.5.14 *ākhu* is styled as *maitra*). Agni is regarded as a mole, TBr I.1.3.3; 2.1.2. Cf. ĀpŚS V.1.7; 9.8. See Vol. I, p. 393, n. 264; p. 394, n. 275.

28. Again here a symbolic allusion to the "end." The TBr states : "one should offer only with the last leaf. At the end he appeases Rudra with this."

29. We should note that there is *svāhā* and not *svadhā*, that is to say, in the view of the ritualists this act is not related to the cult of the Manes.

30. TS, II, p. 87 : *amba "pārvati."*

31. The name which is current in the later literature as well is explained in the comm. on TS, II, p. 87 as *triṇy ambakāni netrāṇi yasya*. *Vāyupurāṇa* XXXI.46 has a different explanation :

> *...tribhir eva kapālais tu tryambakair oṣadhikṣaye*
> *ijyate bhagavān yasmāt...*

ŚBr II.6.2.9 interprets him as *stri-ambakā*. The correct explanation is provided by Charpentier, WZKM, XXIII, p. 177 ff.; Johansson, *Dhiṣaṇā*, p. 88; Hopkins, *Epic Mythology*, p. 220, n. 1, who regard *tri* as the correct reading and refer to the three Ambikās, the three "god-wives" or "god-mothers" of Rudra-Śiva. See now Arbman, *Rudra*, pp. 295, 297.

32. PW, s.v. *bhaga*, cites *Kāṭhaka Saṃhitā*, XXXVI.14 : *ambhā vai strī bhaganāmnī.*

33. I think that the *saṃnayatyaḥ* in this Sūtra should be treated as an irregular feminine genitive singular form. Likewise now Caland, ZDMG, LII, p. 428.

34. TBr I.6.10.5 : "just as we prepare provisions for the journey for one who is going abroad, so is this."

35. Comm. on the TS, II, p. 89 : *pinākahasta*, i.e., *pinākanāmakaṃ dhanur haste gṛhītvā.*

36. Hence, the other cardinal points of the sacrifice are also shifted; what is usually north becomes east here, east becomes south and so on. The commentary mentions various kinds of deviations in the cult.

37. *Rituallitteratur*, p. 99.

38. ŚBr II.6.2.7: "He makes the offering on a road for the god moves on a road; he makes an offering on the cross-roads for those are known to be his favourite haunt." Eggeling compares this passage with TBr I.6.10.3. However, in the Gṛhya Sūtras cross-roads are not the only special haunt of his.

39. Like here, one dances to the left and to the right also in the Mahāvrata, the solstice-festival (ŚŚS XVII.14.16). Hence, the dance is not a special feature of the cult of the Manes, though a symbolic significance cannot be ignored.

40. The cow which smells it would fall ill, the comm. on VS III.61.

41. Similarly in the *baudhyavihāra* (*Rituallitteratur*, p. 84) a basket made of leaves with a ball of rice in it is suspended from a tree on the other side of the pasture land, while uttering the formula : "touch (pl) ! O [you who are] armed with quiver, the one [accusative] who is armed with quiver, svāhā !" (Note *svāhā* here also). Fastening gifts to the trees is customary elsewhere too. Tylor (*Anfänge der Kultur*, II, p. 224) reports that the Dajaks tie rags from their clothes to the trees at the cross-roads and if this practice is neglected they are afraid for their health. Cf. the section on "Lappenbäume" (trees with rags) in Andree, *Ethnographische Parallelen*, I, p. 59 ff.

42. *Rājasūya*, p. 24.

43. Cf. e.g. MS I.8.5 (121.18); III.3.4 (36.14); 3.10 (43.15).

44. Cf. Muir, OST, II, p. 352; Vol. I of this work, pp. 155-57. In the MBh also Mūjavat is said to be Rudra's seat; in X.17.26 he performs penance at the foot of the Mūjavat.

45. *śarad vā asyāmbikā svasā || tayā vā eṣā hinasti yaṃ hinasti | tayaivainaṃ saha śamayati*; cf. comm. on VS X.57.

46. Comm. on the TS, II, p. 85 : *bhaginīvad dhitakāriṇyāmbikayā pārvatyā saha.*

47. MS I.10.20 (160) : *śarad vai rudrasya yoniḥ | svasāmbikā | etāṃ vā eṣo 'nvabhyavacarati | tasmāñ śaradi bhūyiṣṭhaṃ hanti | tayaivainaṃ saha niravadayate ... girir vai rudrasya yonir ato vā eṣo 'nvabhyavacāraṃ prajāḥ śamayate | svenaivainaṃ bhāgadheyena svaṃ yoniṃ gamayati.* He lives after all on the "other side of the Mūjavat."

48. Cf. *avatatadhanvan, pinākahasta.* AV XI.2.12 : *dhánur bibharṣi*

háritaṃ hiraṇyáyaṃ sahasraghním śatávadhaṃ; ṚV VII.46.1 : *sthirádhanvan, kṣipréṣu, tigmáyudha.* His missile is called *hetí*, also *devahetí* in AV VI. 59.3; XI.2.19; XII.4.52; *śáru* in AV XII.2.47; in isolated passages *matyà* (club), AV XI.2.19. Cf. TS V.5.7.2. *tasya tisraḥ śaravyāḥ pratīcī tiraścī anūcī| tābhyo vā eṣa ā vṛścyate yo 'gniṃ cinute, 'gniṃ citvā tisṛdhanvan ayācitaṃ brāhmaṇāya dadyāt.*

49. Distinction is made in TMBr XXI.14.19 between the death caused by Rudra and other kinds of death.

50. Cf. *Kauśika Sūtra* XXXVI.15 : *īśānahatā*; comm. *jvarahatā.*

51. ŚŚS III.4.8; ŚGS V.6.1; ĀpGS IV.8.40; cf. HGS II.8.1 and the comm. on it etc. In AV VI.57.1 Rudra's arrow with one-shaft and hundred tips is in reality a boil the remedy for which is supposed to be urine. Cf. Bloomfield, SBE, XLII, p. 489.

52. Cf. also the comm. on the TS, II, p. 86 : *śaratkālo hi pīnasajvarādyutpādanena hiṃsakaḥ| tadvad iyam ambikā hiṃsikā, tataḥ śarad ity ucyate| eṣa rudraḥ tayaiva sahāyabhūtayā prāṇinaṃ hinasti.*

53. *Report of the Secretary to the Agricultural Department in India*, cited by Hunter, *India*, 3rd ed., p. 616. Cf. TMBr VI.9.9 : *viṣeṇa vai tāṃ samāṃ oṣadhayo 'ktā bhavanti yāṃ samāṃ mahādevaḥ paśūn hanti.* Cf. also *Missionsbilder*, Calw-Stuttgart, Heft 3, p. 25; Heft 4, p. 7. Garbe, *Indische Reiseskizzen*, p. 180.

54. *A Practical Guide to the Climates and Weather of India*, etc., p. 129.

55. For further information see W. Crooke, *The Tribes and Castes of North-Western Provinces*, p. 149, and the Report of F. W. Growse, ibid., on the fever-epidemic in the autumn of 1879 which reduced the population of Bulandshahar from 937,427 (1871) to 924,882 (1881), and of 1885 when 1,124,150 people died in the North-Western Provinces, chiefly in the Duāb and Rohilkhand.

56. The period might vary according to the regions of India. It is however striking that autumn, *śarad*, is described in two texts as the season in which Rudra kills mostly. In the south-eastern part of India the rains commence in September-October and last till December-January. Perhaps Rudra's association with *śarad* has its origin there, for *śarad* there is the same as *varṣāḥ* with a shift in the meaning just as in Ceylon *vas* denotes the most pleasant season of the year.

57. Pischel, ZDMG, XL, p. 120; VSt, I, p. 57. Arbman, *Rudra*, p. 274. Red as the colour of magic, death and ill-luck, see Zachariae, WZKM, XVII, p. 211 ff.

58. TS I.2.11.e : *yā te agne rudriyā tanūḥ*; I.3.3.r : *raudreṇānīkena pāhi māgne*; II.2.2.3 : *agnaye rudravate...aṣṭākapālam...abhicaran eṣā vā asya ghorā tanūr yad rudraḥ;* II.2.10.3 : *somāraudraṃ caruṃ...prajākāmaḥ; somo vai retodhā agniḥ prajānāṃ prajanayitā*; II.2.10.4: *saumyo vai devatayā puruṣa, eṣa rudro yad agniḥ;* II.6.6.6.; III.1.3.1: *sa* [*agnir*] *īśvaro rudro bhūtvā prajāṃ paśūn yajamānasya śamayitoḥ;* III.4.10.3 : *rudraḥ khalu vai vāstoṣpatir yad ahutvāvāstoṣpatīyaṃ prayāyād rudra enaṃ bhūtvāgnir anūtthāya hanyāt* (comm. : *gārhapatyāgniḥ krūro bhūtvā*); III.5.5.e; V.5.7.4; V.7.3.b; VI.3.5.1;

5.6.4; VII.5.15.1 : *athaiṣa rudro yaś cīyate;* TBr I.1.6.6; III.9.11.3; TMBr XII.4.24 : *agnir vai krūro rudro' gniḥ* (comm. : *rudro tīkṣṇo rudrātmako vā agniḥ*); MS I.6.11 (103.7); III.1.3 (4.5) etc.; KBr XIX.4; TĀr I.12.1.2,3 : *vārādaṃ janayāgre 'gniṃ ya eko rudra ucyate / asaṃkhyātā sahasrāṇi / smaryate na ca dṛśyate.* TĀr IV.22 explains Agni's *ghorās tanuvaḥ* as *kṣuc ca tṛṣṇā ca, asnuk cānāhutiś ca, aśanāyā ca pipāsā ca* etc. Cf. also ISt, XVII, p. 327; Macdonell, p. 75. Arbman rejects the identification saying that it was brought about by the priests and sees in the "formation Rudra-Agni no product of normal evolution but only an ephemeral creation of theological speculation." But placed against the above context the state of affairs looks different.

59. Bergaigne, III, p. 37 f. E.g. ṚV IV.3.1. : *á vo rā́jānam adhvarásya rudrám hótāraṃ satyayájaṃ ródasyoḥ;* but separated from him in v. 6. Cf. von Bradke, *Dyaus Asura*, p. 54. See also AV XIX.55.5 : *annādā́yā́nnapataye rudrā́ya námo agnáye;* VII.87.1 : *yó agnaú rudró yó apsv àntár yá óṣadhīr vīrudha āvivéśa / yá imā́ viśvā bhúvanāni cākḷpé tásmai rudrā́ya námo astv agnáye.* Cf. also MBh III.228.27.

60. Cf. TS VII.1.18 : *rudrebhir devebhir devatayā traiṣṭubhena tvā chandasā yunajmi grīṣmeṇa tvartunā haviṣā dīkṣayāmi.* In TĀr I.5, in a legend the elements of which are not clear to me, he is drawn into association with the Pravargya : *rudrasya tveva dhanurārtniḥ śira utpipeṣa sa pravargyo 'bhavat tasmād yaḥ sapravargyeṇa yajñena yajate rudrasya sa śiraḥ pratidadhāti* etc. On the meaning of the Pravargya, see *Ritualliteratur*, p. 136.

61. KŚS XV.3.12; Weber, *Rājasūya*, p. 20; *Ritualliteratur*, p. 144.

62. In view of the close inner relation between the sacrificial fee and the sacrifice, we may draw attention to the three dakṣiṇās connected with the gruel-offering, although their significance is still obscure to me; the dakṣiṇās are firstly an ox with white (or black) forelegs or with white (or black) tail, secondly a sword in the shape of a claw and thirdly a dice board bound with a belt made of tail-hair, Weber, *Rājasūya*, p. 24 (see p. 278 above); Weber, *loc. cit*, mentions the departures in the *Kāṭhaka* text.

63. *Ritualliteratur*, p. 164.

64. MS III.3.4 (37) : *uttarārdhe jaghanārdhe śroṇiḥ.*

65. MS III.3.4 (37) : *arkaparṇena juhoti / arkeṇa vā etad arkam avayajati / yat pātreṇa juhuyād rudraṃ prajāsv anvavanayet / tasmād āraṇyena juhoti.*

66. KŚS XVI.8.28.

67. KŚS XVIII.1.2 ff. Cf. MS III.3.4 (36.15 ff.).

68. Weber, ISt, II, p. 32 ff.; Muir, OST, IV, p. 267 ff.; Deussen, *Sechzig Upaniṣads des Veda*, p. 731 ff.; Eggeling, SBE, XLIII, p. 150 ff.

69. Cf. also MS II.9 (119 ff.); VS XVI.1. ff. *Svetāśvatara Up.* III.5.

70. Comm. on the TS, IV, p. 514 : [*asau*] *maṇḍalasthādityarūpa*; TBr II.7.12.4 : *vaidyutāgni.*

71. Cf. MS I.10.20 (160.17) : *anvabhyavacāram* (see n. 47 above).

72. WZKM, IX, p. 248.

73. Hopkins, PAOS, 1894, p. cl ff.; Macdonell, JRAS, 1895, p. 957;

Vedic Mythology, p. 77 : "not the thunderstorm pure and simple, but rather its baleful side in the destructive agency of lightning."

74. Oldenberg, RdV, p. 216 ff., agreeing with him, Winternitz, AISAK, VIII, p. 38; Arbman, *loc. cit.*

75. See p. 278 above; Arbman, *Rudra*, p. 42 ff. But it is not conclusive, for it is merely said there "go beyond the Mūjavat." One can, after all, wish that so-and-so be banished to a particular place without, however, implying that that place is also his native home. The authors of the YV probably meant it in such a sense.

76. MS II.9.1 (119); VS and TS, *loc. cit.*

77. Quite similarly he is called in HGS I.16.8 ff.: *pathi-, paśu-, sarpa-, antarikṣa, apsuṣad;* PGS III.15.7 : *pathi-, catuṣpatha-, vana-, giri-, pitṛ-, śakṛt-, piṇḍasad,* with the addition in III.15.16 : *yatra cānyatrāpi namo rudrāyety eva brūyāt / rudro hy evedaṃ sarvam iti śruteḥ.* To Rudra belong, of course, the animals of the forest (AV XI.2.24), but also the acquatic animals (v. 25) and "cow, horse, man, goat, sheep" (v. 9). According to ĀpŚS XIII. 20.1 he is *vāstoṣpati.* I see a clear allusion to his being a mountain-deity only in *Kauśika Sūtra* LI.7-8 and in its commentary in connection with a Svastyayana ceremony. 7 : "with *brahma jajñānam* and *bhavāśarvau* he makes an offering to a [nearby] mountain in the forest. 8 : In the case of another [mountain], he makes offerings separately to Bhava, Śarva, Paśupati, Ugra, Rudra, Mahādeva and Īśāna." Commentary : "these are seven mountain-deities. In case of fear from tigers, thieves, wild animals, elephants, wild bulls etc. the ceremony of auspicious journey."

78. *tvám agne rudró ásuro mahó divás* (=TBr III.11.2).

79. On *varāha*, cf. TBr I.7.9.1 (n. 1 above).

80. V.41.3 : *utá vā divó ásurāya mánma prā́ndhāṃsīva yájyave bharadhvam;* VIII.20.17 : *yáthā rudrásya sūnávo divó váśanty ásurasya vedhásaḥ*; VII.46.3 : *yā́ te didyúd ávasṛṣṭā divás pári kṣmayā́ cárati*; I.122.1 (?); X.92.6. Bergaigne, III, p. 35 f. Further TĀr X.10.20 (=*Svetāśvatara Up.* III.9) : *vṛkṣa iva stabdho divi tiṣṭhaty ekaḥ.*

81. Hopkins, PAOS, 1894, p. clii : "One may indulge in any speculation as to his pre-Vedic nature without affecting the Ṛg-Vedic conception of him; and one may interpret the later Śarva-Bhava-Śiva mixture as one chooses, but the Vedic Rudra is not this conglomerate."

82. The intrinsic magical relationship between the sacrifice and the sacrificial beast explains why animals of the forest, as far as I can see, are not sacrificed. "If he were to conclude the sacrifice with animals of the forest," declares TBr III.9.1.2 on one occasion, "then father and son would become estranged, paths would become wrong paths, boundaries of the villages would become very remote from one another (because vast forests would grow between them), bears, tiger-like men, highwaymen, bands of robbers and rogues would appear in the forest. Forest animals are no animals. If he were to attempt to conclude the sacrifice with them, then the sacrificer would be carried dead into the forest." As stated above on p. 275, Rudra is appeased with an "enemy" who is assigned to him as a sacrificial victim, or with an *ākhu.* "If he does not have an enemy, let him say, 'the

mole is your animal.' " "He should not kill the animals of the village, nor the animals of the forest," declare TS VI.6.4.6; TBr I.6.10.3. But *ākhu* is not the only animal dedicated to him. In TS V.5.19 a *ruru*, a kind of deer, is assigned to Rudra. The colour of his animals is given in TS V.6.11 as *babhru, aruṇababhru, śukababhru,* in MS III.13.4 (169.5); VS XXIV.3 as *śyeta, śyetākṣa, aruṇa*—a range of colours that is in harmony even with the ancient description of the god. According to TS II.1.7.2; TBr II.8.6.8 (comm. on p. 884) *rohiṇī vaśa* belongs to him (cf. n. 77 above). Arbman (*Rudra*, p. 118) sees in the employment of tree leaves a custom that is directly borrowed from folk cult, from the Bali sacrifice, and hence this emphasizes not Rudra's association with the wilderness but rather the popular rustic nature of the god. This is quite true as far as the form of offering is concerned. But the offering of the wild plants distinguishes him.

83. Arbman, *Rudra*, p. 154 : "Through the exclusiveness of the Vedic priestly circles who alone are decisive in the old texts, the concept of *devāḥ* underwent a contraction."

84. ŚŚS X.6.18.

85. Ibid., XI.13.16. A verse is recited for Rudra in the Agnimāruta-śastra (ŚŚS VII.6.3), that is to say, again at the end of a sacrifice. Cf. KBr. XVI.7; XXV.12.

86. As Rudriyas VI.62.8.

87. Rudriyas III.26.5.

88. According to I.43.5; II.33.3, he is the most beautiful of the gods KBr XXV.13 : *rudro vai jyeṣṭhaś ca śreṣṭhaś ca devānām.* The AV, on the contrary, describes him (or his chariot) as *śyāvāśva, kṛṣṇa, asita* (XI.2.18).

89. I.114.5 : *háste bíbhrad bheṣajā́ vā́ryāṇi*; II.33.4 : VII.46.2. Bloomfield, "Contributions IV" p. 425, and Hopkins, PAOS, 1894, p. cl ff., understand the remedies as rain, which Arbman (*Rudra*, p. 19) doubts. The *Rudrādhyāya* hardly speaks of his remedies.

90. Cf. Macdonell, pp. 75-76; Barth, *Journal des Savants*, 1896, p. 399.

91. ĀśvGS IV.8.23-24; ŚŚS IV.20.2.

92. Hauer, *Anfänge der Yogapraxis*, p. 136; Arbman, *Rudra*, p. 298.

93. Cf. Bloomfield, SBE, XLII, p. 618. To the literature cited there we may now add, Macdonell, p. 75; Winternitz, *Mantrapāṭha*, II.18. Among the names, we do not yet find *bhūtapati* which is given to *bhavāśarvau* in AV XI.2.1 and which later becomes a designation of Rudra. Arbman (*Rudra*, p. 165) interprets it as the king of demons. (He takes demons not only in hostile sense, see ibid., p. 212).

94. IV.28; X.1.23.

95. *yāv araṇye patayato vṛkāu jañjabhatāv iva.* Compare this with AV XI.2.30 : *rudrásyailabakā́rebhyo 'saṃsūktagilébhyaḥ | idáṃ mahā́syebhyaḥ śvábhyo akaraṃ námaḥ*; VS XVI.27 : *námo śvanībhyaḥ mṛgayúbhyaś ca vo námaḥ |*

96. Cf. *inter alia*, MS IV.2.12 (35.13).

97. *yāṃ samāṃ mahādevaḥ paśūn hanyāt* (cf. also VI.9.9). In the Aśvamedha, oblations are made to the individual names; TS I.4.36 : *bhavaṃ*

yaknā, rudraṃ tanimnā etc.; VS XXXIX.8; TĀr III.5; cf. also *Kauśika Sūtra* LI. 7—8 cited in n. 77, above. There is one more name which occurs very rarely. Its reading is uncertain (VS X.20.c *krivi;* TS I.8.14.1 *krayī;* MS IV.4.2 (51.17) *giriparaṃ nāma*) and does not permit any definite conclusion. *Krivi* would recall the old name of the Pāñcālas.

98. ABr III.33.1 (ed. BI, II, p. 149) : "Prajāpati waylaid his own daughter—the sky as some say or Dawn as others say. Changing himself into a he-goat he approached her who became an antilope. The gods saw him and declared : 'Prajāpati is committing an outrage.' They looked for one who is to punish him but found none among themselves. They put the most dreadful of their shapes together and these together became the 'god' (comm. : Rudra is indicated through *eṣa* while pointing to him with the hand). Hence his name contains the word *bhūta*. 2 : Whosoever knows this name of his 'becomes' (*bhavati*; comm. : *bhūtimān eva saṃpadyate*). 3 : The gods said to him : 'Prajāpati committed an outrage. Pierce him.' 'Yes,' he replied. 'I shall request a gift from you.' 'Do so.' He desired for himself the overlordship of the cattle...5 : He bent his bow and pierced Prajāpati. Thus pierced, the latter flew upwards. One calls him *mṛga* (comm. the *mṛgaśīrṣanakṣtra* between Rohiṇī and Ārdrā); *mṛgavyādha* is 'he' (i.e. Rudra), the antelope is Rohiṇī, his arrow with three parts is the *iṣus trikāṇḍa*." Cf. also MS IV.2.12 (35.11 ff.); ŚBr I.7.4.1 and the comm.; II.1.2.8; KBr VI.1; TMBr VIII.2.10. Mṛgavyādha is mentioned as one of the eleven Rudras in *Atharvaveda Pariśiṣṭas* XLV.5. Cf. Wilson, tr., *Viṣṇupurāṇa*, p. 121; Weber, *Omina und Portenta*. p. 366.

In the *Rudrādhyāya* verses, *asau yas tāmro* (TS IV.5.1.g), *asau yo 'vasarpati* (h), the word *asau* might have been chosen so that his name could be avoided. Geldner looks for a similar nameless reference to Rudra in ṚV X.10.1 (see *Festgruss für Weber*, p. 21).

99. See Vol. I, p. 34 f.

100. According to *Vāyupurāṇa* XXX.122 ff., Bhagavat creates from his mouth the Bhūta "who is like the fire of anger, with thousand heads, feet, eyes, hammers, arrows, with the conch and club etc." Cf. also IX.64 : *rudraṃ roṣātmasaṃbhavam*.

101. Similarly in *Vāyupurāṇa* XXVII.1 ff., where Brahman gives the names Rudra, Śiva etc. to the constantly weeping *kumāra nīlalohita* upon the latter's request. Cf. also the *Mārkaṇḍeyapurāṇa*, cited by Muir, OST, IV, p. 285. Rudra's weeping is spoken of in another context also. TS I.5.1 states : "...Agni ran away with the wealth of the gods. The gods ran after him in order to hold him back. They wanted to take their wealth away from him by force. Then he wept. Hence Rudra is called 'Rudra.' The tear that was shed became silver." MS IV.2.12 (35.15). Cf. n. 13 above.

102. In the ṚV, *rudra* is still used as an adjective; at least, words like *rudravartanī* cannot be explained in a different way than Pischel, *loc. cit.*, does. However, the Aśvins who mostly bear this name are also called

indratamā, maruttamā, śambhaviṣṭhā; even so I do not think that *rudra* in *rudravartanī* can be a proper name.

103. I imagine that the relationship would be as in the Italian churches where the Christian saint is combined with an original local godling.

104. "Fierce Orion," Virgil, *Aeneis*, VII.719. See Horace, *Epodon*, XV.7 : *dum pecori lupus et nautis infestus Orion turbaret hibernum mare*, "as long as the wolf should be hostile to the flock, as long as Orion, the sailors' foe, should toss the wintry sea" (Horace, *Odes and Epodes*, with an English translation by C. E. Bennett, London 1914, p. 401).

105. *kṛśā́num ástṝn tiṣyàṃ sadhástha ā́ / rudráṃ rudréṣu rudríyaṃ havāmahe.*

106. According to Ludwig, *astṝn* is genitive plural and Tiṣyam is identical with Kṛśānu; I doubt it.

107. TĀr X.10.3.19 : *yo devānāṃ prathamam purastāt*
viśvādhiko rudro maharṣiḥ /
hiraṇyagarbhaṃ paśyata jāyamānam
sa no devaḥ śubhayā smṛtyā saṃyunaktu //
20 : *yasmāt paraṃ nāparam asti kiṃcid*
yasmān nāṇīyo na jyāyo 'sti kiṃcid /
vṛkṣa iva stabdho divi tiṣṭhaty ekas
tenedaṃ pūrṇaṃ puruṣeṇa sarvam //

These verses occur also in *Śvetāśvatara Up.* III.9.

108. On Mṛgavyādha as Sirius, see the PW.

109. Thus the Śūlagava according to ĀśvŚS IV.8.1 ff. (see above); the Āgrahāyaṇī ceremony (see *Rituallіteratur*, p. 78) with the Pratyavarohaṇa (oblations for Mṛgaśiras etc.); the ceremony concerned with the well-being of cattle during which, among others, Rudra or Paśupati is invoked (*Ritualliteratur*, p. 77); according to MGS II.3.5. Agni, Rudra, Īśāna, Tryambaka, Śarad, Pṛṣātaka and Gāvaḥ are invoked.

110. In TBr I.5.1 the *bāhū*, i.e. according to the commentary the Ārdrānakṣatra, is mentioned in association with Rudra, Mṛgayu being above it and Vaksāra being below. On the Ārdrā, cf. also TBr III.1.1.3; ŚGS I. 26.4.

111. For reasons which are obvious from my treatment of Rudra, I cannot agree with Siecke (ARW, I, pp. 113 ff., 209 ff.).

CONCORDANCE OF TRANSLATED PASSAGES

TBr

TMBr

ĀpŚS

KŚS

GENERAL BIBLIOGRAPHY

ABEGG, EMIL. *Der Pretakalpa des Garuḍapurāṇa. Eine Darstellung des hinduistischen Totenkults und Jenseitsglaubens.* Berlin 1921; 2nd ed. 1956.

AL BERUNI. *Alberuni's India.* tr., E. C. Sachau. 2 vols. London 1888; 2nd ed. Delhi 1964.

ALABASTER, HENRY. *The Wheel of the Law. Buddhism illustrated from Siamese Sources by a modern Buddhist, a Life of Buddha and an Account of the Phrabat.* London 1871.

ALSBERG, MORITZ. *Anthropologie mit Berücksichtigung der Urgeschichte des Menschen allgemein fasslich dargestellt.* Stuttgart 1887.

ANDREE, RICHARD. *Ethnographische Parallelen und Vergleiche.* Leipzig 1889.

"Die Plejaden im Mythus und in ihrer Beziehung zum Jahresbeginn und Landbau." *Globus*, LXIV.

ANQUETIL-DUPERRON, ABRAHAM HYACINTHE. *Zend-Avesta. Ouvrage de Zoroaster.* Paris 1771.

Exposition des usages civils et religieux des Parses. Paris 1834.

ARBMAN, ERNST. *Rudra. Untersuchungen zum altindischen Glauben und Kultus.* Uppsala 1922.

ARRIAN. *Arrian's History of Alexander's Expedition.* tr., John Rooke. 2 vols. London 1814.

Anabasis. tr., E. Iliff Robson. (The Loeb classical Library, Vol. 269). London 1933; reprint 1958.

AUFRECHT, THEODOR. *Die Hymnen des Rigveda.* 2 vols. Berlin 1861, 1863; 2nd ed. Bonn 1877; reprint, 1973.

BALFOUR, EDWARD. *The Cyclopedia of India and of Eastern and Southern Asia.* 3 vols. Madras 1877; 3rd ed. London 1885; reprint, Graz 1967.

BARNETT, S. D. *Hindu Gods and Heroes.* London 1922.

BARTH, AUGUSTE. *Les religions de l'Inde.* Paris 1879. (=*The Religions of India.* tr., J. Wood. London 1882).

Oeuvres. 5 vols. Paris 1914-1927.

BARTHOLOMAE, CHRISTIAN. *Handbuch der altiranischen Dialekte. Kurzgefasste vergleichende Grammatik, Lesestücke und Glossar.* Leipzig 1883; reprint, Wiesbaden 1968.

Altiranisches Wörterbuch. Strassburg 1904; reprint, Berlin 1961.

Die Gathas des Awesta. Strassburg 1905.

Zum altiranischen Wörterbuch. Nacharbeiten und Vorarbeiten. (Beiheft zu IF, XIX) Strassburg 1906.

Zarathustras Leben und Lehre. Heidelberg 1924.

Vorgeschichte der iranischen Sprachen, and, Awesta Sprache und Altpersisch. In : *Grundriss der iranischen Philologie.* ed. by Wilhelm Geiger and Ernst Kuhn. vol. I, part 1. Strassburg 1895-1901.

BAUNACK, J. and TH. *Studien auf dem Gebiet der griechischen und der arischen Sprachen,* I. Leipzig 1888.

BEAL, SAMUEL. *Si Yu Ki. Buddhist Records of the Western World.* tr. from the Chinese of Hiuen Tsiang. London 1888; reprint, Delhi 1969.

BENFEY, THEODOR. *Vedica und Verwandtes.* Strassburg, London 1877.

Kleinere Schriften, Ausgewählt und hrsg. von Adalbert Bezzenberger. 2 vols. Berlin 1890-92.

BERGAIGNE, ABEL. *La religion védique d'après les hymnes du Rig-Veda.* 3 vols. Paris 1878, 1881, 1883. vol. 4 : Index by Maurice Bloomfield. Paris 1897. (= *Vedic Mythology according to the Hymns of the Ṛgveda.* tr., V. G. Paranjpe. 4 vols. Poona 1969, 1971, 1973, 1972).

Manuel pour étudier la langue sanscrite. Paris 1884.

Quarante hymnes du Rig-Véda. trad. et commentés. Paris 1895.

"Études sur le lexique du Ṛg-Veda." JA, 1883-84.

"La syntaxe des comparaisons védiques." *Mél. Renier,* 1886.

"Recherches sur l'histoire de la liturgie védique. La forme métrique des hymnes du Ṛg-Veda." JA, 1889.

BERGAIGNE, ABEL and HENRY, VICTOR. *Manuel pour étudier le Sanscrit védique. Grammaire. Chrestomathie. Lexique.* Paris 1890.

BHANDARKAR, R. G. *Vaiṣṇavism, Śaivism and Minor Religious Systems.* (Grundriss der indo-arischen Philologie und Altertumskunde, III, 6) Strassburg 1913.

— *Commemorative Essays presented to Sir Ramkrishna Gopal Bhandarkar.* Poona 1917.

BIELENSTEIN, H. "Die deeva dēli (Gottessöhne) des lettischen Volksliedes." *Magazin*, hrsg. von der Lettisch-literarischen Gesellschaft, XIX, 4. 1896.

BLANFORD, HENRY FRANCIS. *A Practical Guide to Climates and Weather of India, Ceylon and Burmah and the Storms of Indian Seas*. London 1889.

The Indian Meteorologist's Vademecum. (I: Instructions to the Observers; II: Meteorology of India). Calcutta 1877.

BLOCH, J. "Buddha worshipped by Indra." PASB, 1898.

BLOCH, TH. "Über einige altindische Götternamen." *Wörter und Sachen*, I.

BLOOMFIELD, MAURICE. *Hymns of the Atharva-Veda, together with extracts from the ritual books and the commentaries*. tr. (SBE, XLII) Oxford 1897.

The Atharva Veda and the Gopatha Brāhmaṇa. (Grundriss der indo-arischen Philologie und Altertumskunde II, 1 b) Strassburg 1899.

The Symbolic Gods. Baltimore 1902.

Cerberus, the Dog of Hades. The History of an Idea. Chicago 1905.

"Contributions to the Interpretation of the Veda." I: AJPh, VII; II: AJPh, XI; III: JAOS, XV; IV: AJPh, XII; V: JAOS, XVI; VI: ZDMG, XLVIII; VII: AJPh, XVII.

"Seven Hymns of the Atharva-Veda." Same as "Contributions," I.

— *Studies in Honor of Maurice Bloomfield*. New Haven 1920.

BOHNENBERGER, KARL. *Der altindische Gott Varuṇa*. Tübingen 1893.

BÖHTLINGK, OTTO VON. *Sanskrit Chrestomathie*. St. Petersburg 1845; 2nd ed. St. Petersburg 1870-73; reprint, Osnabrück, Wiesbaden 1966.

Indische Sprüche. 3 vols. St. Petersburg 1863-65.

Sanskrit-Wörterbuch in kürzerer Fassung. 3 vols. St. Petersburg 1879-89; 2nd ed. St. Petersburg 1923-25; reprint, Graz 1959.

— *Festgruss an Otto von Böhtlingk zum Doktor-Jubiläum... 1888 von seinen Freunden*. Stuttgart 1888.

BÖHTLINGK, OTTO VON and ROTH, RUDOLPH VON. *Sanskrit-Wörterbuch*. 7 vols. St. Petersburg 1852-1875; reprint, Osnabrück, Wiesbaden 1966.

BORNMÜLLER. "Reisebriefe aus Persien." *Mitteilungen des Thüringer Botanischen Vereins,* NF, Heft 3-4, 1893.

BRADKE, PETER VON. *Dyaus Asura, Ahura Mazda und die Asuras. Studien und Versuche auf dem Gebiete alt-indogermanischer Religionsgeschichte.* Halle 1885.

BRANDES, E. *Ushas og Ushashymnerne i Ṛgveda.* Mytologisk monografi. Kopenhagen 1880.

BRINTON, DANIEL GARRISON. *The Myths of the New World: A Treatise on the Symbolism and Mythology of the Red Race of America.* New York 1868.

Rig Veda Americanus. Sacred Sayings of the ancient Mexicans. Philadelphia 1890.

Religions of the Primitive Peoples. London 1897; reprint, New York 1969.

BRUGMANN, KARL and DELBRÜCK, BERTHOLD. *Grundriss der vergleichenden Grammatik der indogermanischen Sprachen.* 5 vols. Strassburg 1886-1900.

BRUNNHOFER, HERMANN. *Urgeschichte der Arier in Vorder- und Centralasien. Historisch-geographische Untersuchungen über den ältesten Schauplatz des Rigveda und Avesta.* 3 vols. (I: Iran und Turan; II: Vom Pontus bis zum Indus; III: Vom Aral bis zur Gaṅgā) Leipzig 1889, 1890, 1892.

Arische Urzeit. Forschungen auf dem Gebiete des ältesten Vorder- und Zentralasiens nebst Osteuropa. Bern 1910.

BÜHLER, GEORG. *Detailed Report of a Search of Sanskrit Manuscripts made (in 1975-76) in Kashmir, Rajputana, and Central India.* Bombay, London 1877.

Indische Paleographie von ca. 350 a. Chr.—ca. 1300 p. Chr. (Grundriss der indo-arischen Philologie und Altertumskunde, I, 11) Strassburg 1896.

CALAND, WILLEM. *Über Totenverehrung bei einigen der indogermanischen Völker.* Amsterdam 1888.

Altindischer Ahnenkult. Das Śrāddha nach den verschiedenen Schulen mit Benutzung handschriftlicher Quellen. Leiden 1893.

Die altindischen Todten- und Bestattungsgebräuche, mit Benutzung handschriftlicher Quellen. Amsterdam 1896.

Een indogermaansch lustratie-gebuik. Amsterdam 1898.

Altindisches Zauberritual. Probe einer Übersetzung der wichtigsten Teile des Kauśika-Sūtra. Amsterdam 1900.

Over de "Wenschoffers," bijdrage tot de kennis van den Veda. Amsterdam 1902.

Über das rituelle Sūtra des Baudhāyana. Leipzig 1903.

CALAND, WILLEM and HENRY, VICTOR. *L'Agniṣṭoma. Description complète de la forme normale du sacrifice de Soma dans la culte védique.* Paris 1906-7.

CHARPENTIER, JARL. *Kleine Beiträge zur indo-iranischen Mythologie.* Uppsala 1911.

Die Suparṇa-Sage. Untersuchungen zur altindischen Literatur- und Sagengeschichte. Uppsala 1920.

CHILDERS, ROBERT CAESAR. *A Dictionary of Pali Language.* 4th ed. London 1909.

CHINON, G. DU. *Relations nouvelles de Levant.* Lyon 1671.

COLINET, P. "La nature primitive d'Aditi." *Transactions of the ninth international congress of orientalists,* I, pp. 390-410.

CROOKE, WILLIAM. *The Popular Religion and Folklore of Northern India.* 2 vols. Westminster 1896. The same work was issued later under the new title, *Religion and Folklore of Northern India,* prepared for the press by R. E. Enthoven. London 1926.

The Tribes and Castes of North-Western Provinces and Oudh. 4 vols. Calcutta 1896.

"The Holi." *Folklore,* XXV.

CUMONT, FRANZ. *La théologie solaire.* 1909.

CUNNINGHAM, ALEXANDER. *The Ancient Geography of India.* London 1871; reprint ed. S. Majumdar. Calcutta 1924.

DAHLMANN, JOSEPH. *Das Mahābhārata als Epos und Rechtsbuch. Ein Problem aus Altindiens Cultur- und Literaturgeschichte.* Berlin 1895.

DARMESTETER, JAMES. *Haxrvatāṭ et Ameretāṭ. Essai sur la mythologie de l'Avesta.* Paris 1875.

Ormazd et Ahriman, leurs origines et leur histoire. Paris 1877.

The Zend-Avesta. tr. 2 vols. (SBE IV, XXIII) Oxford 1880, 1883.

Chants populaires des Afghans. Paris 1888-90.

Le Zend Avesta. Traduction nouvelle avec commentaire historique et philologique. 3 vols. Paris 1892-1893.

DELBRÜCK, BERTHOLD. *Altindische Syntax.* Halle 1888; reprint, Darmstadt 1968.

See also under BRUGMANN.

DEUSSEN, PAUL. *Sechzig Upanischads des Veda.* Leipzig 1897; 3rd ed. 1921.

Allgemeine Geschichte der Philosophie. 6 vols. Leipzig 1920-21.

DONNER, O. *Piṇḍapitṛyajña, das Manenopfer mit Klössen bei den Indern. Abhandlung aus dem vedischen Ritual.* Berlin 1870.

DRISLER, HENRY.—*Classical Studies in Honour of Henry Drisler.* New York 1894.

DRURY, HEBER. *The useful Plants of India, with Notices of their economic Value in Commerce, Medicine and the Arts.* Madras 1858; 2nd ed. London 1873.

DUBOIS, JEAN ANTOINE. *Hindu Manners, Customs and Ceremonies.* tr., H. K. Beauchamp. 2 vols. Oxford 1897.

DUNCKER, MAX. *Geschichte des Altertums.* 5th ed. Leipzig 1878.

EGGELING, JULIUS. *The Śatapatha-Brāhmaṇa according to the text of the Mādhyandina school.* tr. 5 vols. (SBE, XII, XXVI, XLI, XLIII, XLIV) Oxford 1882, 1885, 1894, 1897, 1899.

Catalogue of the Sanskrit Manuscripts in the Library of the India Office. 4 vols. London 1887-1904.

EGGERS, A. *Der arische (indo-iranische) Gott Mitra. Eine sprach- und religionsgeschichtliche Studie.* Dorpat 1894.

EHNI, J. *Der vedische Mythus des Yama, verglichen mit den analogen Typen der persischen, griechischen und germanischen Mythologie.* Strassburg 1889.

EHRENREICH, PAUL. *Die allgemeine Mythologie und ihre ethnologischen Grundlagen.* Leipzig 1910.

ENTHOVEN, R. E. *Folklore of Bombay.* Oxford 1924.

FEER, L. "Vritra et Namoutchi dans le Mahābhārata." *Revue de l'histoire des religions*, XIV, 1886.

FICK, A. *Vergleichendes Wörterbuch der indogermanischen Sprachen, sprachgeschichtlich angeordnet.* Göttingen 1874-76.

FICK, RICHARD. *Die soziale Gliederung im nordöstlichen Indien zu Buddhas Zeit.* Kiel 1897. (=*Social Organisation in North-East India in Buddha's Times.* tr., Sisirkumar Maitra. Calcutta 1920).

FORMICI, C. *Pensiero religioso nell'India.* Bologna 1926.

FOY, WILLY. *Die königliche Gewalt nach den altindischen Rechtsbüchern, den Dharmasūtren und älteren Dharmaśāstren.* Leipzig 1895.

FRAZER, JAMES GEORGE. *The Golden Bough. A Study in Magic and Religion.* 9 vols. London 1894; reprint 1966.

GAEDICKE, C. *Der Akkusativ im Veda.* Breslau 1880.

GARBE, RICHARD VON. *Indische Reiseskizzen.* 2nd ed. Munich 1925.

— *Aus Indiens Kultur. Festgabe Richard von Garbe, dem Forscher und Lehrer, zu seinem 70. Geburtstag dargebracht von seinen Freunden, Verehrern und Schülern.* Erlangen 1927.

GEIGER, BERNHARD. *Amǝša Spǝntas. Ihr Wesen und ihre urspüngliche Bedeutung.* Vienna 1916.

GEIGER, WILHELM. *Ostiranische Kultur im Altertum.* Erlangen 1882. (= *Civilization of the Eastern Iranians in ancient Times.* tr., Darab Dastur Peshotan Sanjana. 2 vols. London 1885-86).

GEIGER, WILHELM and KUHN, ERNST. ed. *Grundriss der iranischen Philologie.* 2 vols. Strassburg 1895-1904.

GELDNER, KARL FRIEDRICH. *Studien zum Avesta.* Strassburg 1882.

Über die Metrik des jüngeren Avesta. Nebst Übersetzungen ausgewählter Abschnitte. Tübingen 1877.

Der Rigveda in Auswahl. 2 vols. Stuttgart 1907, 1909.

Der Rigveda, übersetzt und erläutert, I: erster bis vierter Liederkreis. Göttingen 1923.

GELDNER, KARL FRIEDRICH and PISCHEL, RICHARD. *Vedische Studien.* 3 vols. Stuttgart 1889, 1892, 1901.

GELZER. "Zur armenischen Götterlehre." SBKSGW, XLVIII, 1896.

GRÄBNER, FRITZ. *Das Weltbild der Primitiven. Eine Untersuchung der Urformen weltanschaulichen Denkens bei Naturvölkern.* Munich 1924.

GRASSMANN, HERMANN. *Wörterbuch zum Rigveda.* Leipzig 1873.

GRIERSON, GEORGE ABRAHAM. *Bihar Peasant Life, being a discursive Catalogue of the Surroundings of the People of that Province.* Calcutta 1885.

GRILL, JULIUS. *Hundert Lieder des Atharva Veda.* Tübingen 1879; 2nd ed. 1888.

GRIMM, JACOB. *Deutsche Mythologie.* Göttingen 1835; 2nd ed. 1844.

GRISWOLD, H. D. *God Varuṇa in the Ṛgveda.* Ithaka 1910.
The Religion of the Ṛgveda. Oxford 1923.

GRÜNWEDEL, ALBERT. *Mythologie des Buddismus in Tibet und der Mongolei.* Leipzig 1900.

GRUPPE, OTTO. *Die griechischen Kulte und Mythen in ihren Beziehungen zu den orientalen Religionen.* Leipzig 1887.

GUBERNATIS, A. DE. *Lettura sopra la mitologia vedica.* 1874.
La mythologie des plantes. 2 vols. Paris 1878, 1882.

GÜNTERT, HERMANN. *Über arische Reimwortbildungen.* Heidelberg 1913.
Der arische Weltkönig und Heiland. Halle 1924.

GUTSCHMIDT, ALFRED VON. *Geschichte Irans und seiner Nachbarländer von Alexander dem Grossen bis zum Untergang der Arsaciden.* Tübingen 1888.
Kleine Schriften. hrsg. Franz Rühl. 5 vols. Leipzig 1889-94.

HALÉVY, J. *Considerations critiques sur quelques points de l'histoire ancienne de l'Inde.* Paris 1899.

HANN, JULIUS. *Handbuch der Klimatologie.* Stuttgart 1897.
Lehrbuch der Meteorologie. 2nd ed. Leipzig 1906.

HANUŠ, IGNAC JAN. *Die Wissenschaft des slavischen Mythus.* Lemberg 1842.

HARDY, EDMUND. *Die vedisch-brahmanische Periode der Religion des alten Indiens.* Münster in Westfalen 1893.

HARLEZ, CHARLES DE. *Avesta, livre sacré du Zoroastrisme. Trad. du texte Zend.* Liége 1875-77; 2nd ed. Paris 1881.
De l'exégèse et de la correction des textes Avestiques. Leipzig 1883.

HARTLAND, EDWIN SIDNEY. *The Legend of Perseus. A study of Tradition in Story, Custom and Belief.* 1894.

HASTINGS, JAMES. ed. *Encyclopaedia of Religion and Ethics.* 12 vols. Edinburg 1908-21.

HAUER, JACOB WILHELM. *Die Anfänge der Yogapraxis im alten Indien. Eine Untersuchung über die Wurzeln der indischen Mystik nach Ṛgveda und Atharvaveda.* Berlin 1922.
Die Religionen. Ihr Werden, ihr Sinn, ihre Wahrheit. Berlin 1923.
Der Vrātya. Untersuchungen über die nichtbrahmanische Religion Altindiens. Stuttgart 1927.

HAUG, MARTIN. *Essays on the Parsis.* 3rd ed. edited and enlarged by E. W. West. London 1884.

HAVELL, E. B. "What is Soma?" JRAS, 1920.

HEHN, VICTOR. *Kulturpflanzen und Haustiere in ihrem Übergang aus Asien nach Europa.* Edited by O. Schrader. Berlin 1902.

HEINZEL, RICHARD.—*Forschungen zur neueren Literaturgeschichte. Festgabe für Richard Heinzel.* Weimar 1898.

HENRY, VICTOR. *Les hymnes Rohitas. Livre XIII de l'Atharva-Véda. Traduction et commentaire.* Paris 1891.

Atharva-Véda. Traduction et commentaire. Le livre VII: Paris 1892; les livres VIII et IX: Paris 1894; les livres X, XI et XII: Paris 1896.

"Vedica." 2e sér. MSL, IX.

See also under BERGAIGNE and CALAND.

HERBIG, GUSTAV. "Zur Vorgeschichte der römischen Pontifices." KZ, XLVII.

HERTEL, JOHANNES. *Die Weisheit der Upanischaden. Eine Auswahl aus den älteren Texten, aus dem Sanskrit übersetzt.* Munich 1920.

Die Himmelstore im Veda und im Avesta. Leipzig 1924.

Die arische Feuerlehre, I. Leipzig 1925.

HOFMANN, K.——*Festschrift für K. Hofmann.* Erlangen 1890.

HOLTZMANN, ADOLF. *Agni nach den Vorstellungen des Mahābhārata.* *Strassburg* 1878.

Das Mahābhārata und seine Teile. 4 vols. Kiel 1892-95.

"Indra nach den Vorstellungen des Mahābhārata." ZDMG, XXXII.

HOPKINS, EDWARD WASHBURN. *The Religions of India.* Boston, London 1895.

Epic Mythology. (Grundriss der indo-arischen Philologie und Altertumskunde, III, 1b) Strassburg 1915.

"The Ocean in Sanskrit Epic Poetry." AJPh, XXI, 1900.

"The social and military Position of the ruling Caste in ancient India as represented by the Sanskrit Epic." JAOS, XIII, 1888.

"Prāgāthikāni." JAOS, XVII.

"The Punjab and the Ṛgveda." JAOS, XIX.

"The Fountain of Youth." JAOS, XXVI, 1905.

HÜBSCHMANN, HEINRICH. *Armenische Grammatik.* (Bibliothek indogermanischer Grammatiken, Bd. VI. 1) Leipzig 1897.

HULTZSCH, EUGEN. ed. *South Indian Inscriptions*. Madras 1890-1903.

HUNTER, WILLIAM WILSON. *Atlas of India, containing sixteen Maps & complete Index with an Introduction.* Edinburgh 1894.

India. In: *The History of Nations*. ed. H. C. Lodge. vol. V. Philadelphia 1906.

HÜSING, GEORG. *Die iranische Überlieferung und das arische System.* (Mythologische Bibliothek, Bd. 2, Heft 2) Leipzig 1909.

JACKSON, ABRAHAM VALENTIN WILLIAMS. *An Avestan Grammar in Comparison with Sanskrit.* Stuttgart 1892.

Zoroaster, the Prophet of Ancient Iran. New York 1899. reprint, New York 1965.

Die iranische Religion. In: *Grundriss der iranischen Philologie.* ed. Wilhelm Geiger and Ernst Kuhn. vol. II, part 3. Strassburg 1896-1904.

JACOB, G. A. *Upaniṣadvākyakośa. A Concordance to the principal Upanishads and the Bhagavadgitā.* Bombay 1891.

JACOBI, HERMANN. *Ausgewählte Erzählungen in Mahārāṣṭrī, zur Einführung in das Studium des Prakrit. Grammatik, Text, Wörterbuch.* Leipzig 1886; reprint, Darmstadt 1967.

— *Beiträge zur Literatur und Geistesgeschichte Indiens. Festschrift für Hermann Jacobi.* Bonn 1926.

JACOBSOHN, H. *Arier und Ugrofinnen.* Göttingen 1922.

JENSEN, PETER. *Hittiter und Armenier*, Strassburg 1893.

JOHANSSON, KARL FERD. *Bidrag till Rigvedas tolkning*. Uppsala 1897.

Solfågeln i Indien. En religionshistorisk-mythologisk Studie. Uppsala 1910.

Über die altindische Göttin Dhiṣáṇā und Verwandtes. Beiträge zum Fruchtbarkeitskultus in Indien. Uppsala 1917.

Etymologisches und Wortgeschichtliches. Uppsala 1927.

JUSTI, FERDINAND. *Iranisches Namensbuch.* Marburg 1895; reprint, Hildesheim 1963.

Geschichte Irans von den ältesten Zeiten bis zum Ausgang der Sasaniden. In: *Grundriss der iranischen Philologie*. ed. Wilhelm Geiger and Ernst Kuhn. vol. II, part 3. Strassburg 1896-1904.

Empire of the Persians. In: *The History of Nations*, II. Philadelphia and New York 1905.

KAEGI, ADOLF. *Der Rigveda, die älteste Literatur der Inder.* Leipzig 1878-79; 2nd ed. 1881.

KAUFFMANN. *Aus Indiens Dschungeln.* Leipzig 1911.

KEITH, ARTHUR BARRIEDALE. Indian Mythology. In: *Mythology of all Races.* Boston 1917.

The Age of the Ṛgveda, and, The Period of the Later Saṃhitās, the Brāhmaṇas, the Āraṇyakas and the Upaniṣads. In: *The Cambridge History of India,* I: Ancient India. Cambridge 1922.

The Religion and Philosophy of the Veda and Upanishads. (HOS, XXXI, XXXII) Cambridge (Mass) 1925.

KIEPERT, HEINRICH. *Lehrbuch der alten Geographie.* Berlin 1878.

KIRFEL, WILLIBALD. *Die Kosmographie der Inder.* Bonn, Leipzig 1920.

KNAUER, F. "Über Varuṇas Ursprung." *Actes du XIVe Congrès international des Orientalistes,* I.

KONOW, STEN. *The Aryan Gods of the Mitanni People.* Kristiania 1921.

KOULIKOVSKI, D. "Les trois feux sacrès du Rig-Veda," *Revue de l'histoire des religions XX.*

KREK, GREGOR. *Einleitung in die slavische Literaturgeschichte und Darstellung ihrer ältesten Perioden.* Graz 1874; 2nd ed. Graz 1887.

KRETSCHMER, PAUL. *Einleitung in die Geschichte der griechischen Sprache.* Göttingen 1896.

KRICHENBAUER, ANTON. *Theogonie und Astronomie.* Vienna 1881.

KUHN, ADALBERT. *Die Herabkunft des Feuers und des Göttertrankes.* Berlin 1859; 2nd ed. Gütersloh 1886; reprint, Darmstadt 1968.

Mythologische Studien. 2 vols. Gütersloh 1886, 1912.

"Zur ältesten Geschichte der indogermanischen Völker." *Indische Studien,* I, 1845.

"Über Entwicklungsstufen der Mythenbildung." *Abhandlungen der Berliner Akademie der Wissenschaften,* 1873.

KUHN, ERNST. *Beiträge zur Pali Grammatik.* Berlin 1875.

— *Aufsätze zur Kultur und Sprachgeschichte vornehmlich des Orients. E. Kuhn zum 70. Geburtstag gewidmet.* Munich 1916. See also under GEIGER, WILHELM.

LA VALLÉE POUSSIN, L. DE. *Indo-Européens et Indo-Iraniens. L'Inde jusque vers 300 avant J.-C.* Paris 1824.

LAGARDE, PAUL DE. *Gesammelte Abhandlungen.* Leipzig 1866.

LANG, ANDREW. *Custom and Myth.* London 1884; New York 1885; 2nd ed. London 1885; new ed. London 1893.
Myth, Ritual and Religion. 2 vols. London 1887; reprint, 1899. (=*Mythes, cultes et religion.* tr. into French by Mariller, 1896).
Modern Mythology. London 1897.
The Making of Religion. London 1898.

LANGLOIS, A. *Rig-Veda, ou livre des hymnes. trad. du sanscrit.* 4 vols. Paris 1848-51.

LANMAN, CHARLES ROCKWELL. "A statistical Account of Noun-inflection in the Veda." JAOS, 1878.

LASSEN, CHRISTIAN. *Indische Altertumskunde.* 4 vols. Leipzig 1858-74.

LEIST, BERNHARD WILHELM. *Altiranisches jus gentium.* Jena 1887.

LINDENAU, MAX. *Bhāsa-Studien. Ein Beitrag zur Geschichte des altindischen Dramas.* Leipzig 1918.

LINDNER, BRUNO. *Die Dīkṣā.* Leipzig 1878.
Altindische Nominalbildung nach den Saṃhitās dargestellt. Jena 1878.

LITTROW, JOHANN JOSEPH. *Wunder des Himmels oder gemeinfassliche Darstellung des Weltsystems.* 3 vols. Stuttgart 1834-37.

LUBBOCK, JOHN. *The Origin of Civilisation and the Primitive Condition of Man. Mental and Social Condition of Savages.* London 1870; 7th ed. London 1912.

LÜDERS, HEINRICH. *Das Würfelspiel im alten Indien.* Berlin 1907.

LUDWIG, ALFRED. *Die Nachrichten des Rig und Atharva Veda über Geographie, Geschichte, Verfassung des alten Indiens.* Prag 1875.
Der Rigveda oder die heiligen Hymen der Brāhmaṇa. Zum ersten Male vollständig ins Deutsche übersetzt. Mit Commentar und Einleitung. 6 vols. Leipzig 1876-88.
Über die Erwähnung von Sonnenfinsternissen im Ṛgveda. Prag 1885.
Über die Kritik des Ṛgveda-Textes. Prag 1889.
Über Methode bei Interpretation des Rigveda. Prag 1890.
Über die neuesten Arbeiten auf dem Gebiet der Ṛgveda-Forschung. Prag 1893.

LÜNING, OTTO. *Die Natur, ihre Auffassung und poetische Verwendung in der altgermanischen und mittelhochdeutschen Epic.* Zürich 1888.

MACDONELL, ARTHUR ANTHONY. *Vedic Mythology.* (Grundriss der indo-arischen Philologie und Altertumskunde, III, 1a) Strassburg 1897.

"The God Trita." JRAS, XXV.

"Mythological Studies in the Ṛgveda." JRAS, 1893.

"Mythological Studies." JRAS, 1895.

MAGOUN, H. W. *Early Religion of the Hindus.* 1897-98.

MARQUARDT, J. *Untersuchungen zur Geschichte von Eran.*

MARQUARDT, KARL JOACHIM and MOMMSEN, THEODOR. *Handbuch der römischen Alterthümer.* 7 vols. Leipzig 1881-88.

MAX MÜLLER, FRIEDRICH. *A History of ancient Sanskrit literature, as far as it illustrates the primitive religion of the Brahmans.* London 1859; reprint, 1860.

Lectures on the Science of Language. London 1861. (= *Vorlesungen über die Wissenschaft der Sprache.* tr. into German by Bōttger. 2 vols. 1863; 2nd ed. 1870; 3rd ed. 1875).

Rig-Veda-Saṁhita. The Sacred Hymns of the Brahmans. Translated and explained. London 1869.

Essays. tr. into German by Franke. 2nd ed. 1881.

India : What can it teach us. London 1883.

Biographies of Words and the Home of the Aryas. London 1888; 2nd ed. 1898.

Vedic Hymns, I : Hymns to the Maruts, Rudra, Vāyu and Vāta. (SBE, XXXII) Oxford 1891.

Physical Religion. London 1892; reprint, 1898. (= *Physische Religion.* tr. into German by Franke. 1892).

Chips from a German Workshop. new ed. London 1895.

Contributions to the Science of Mythology. 2 Vols. London 1897.

"The Hymns of the Gaupāyanas and the legend of king Asamāti." JRAS, NS, II.

"Ūber Todtenbestattung und Opfergebräuche bei den Brahmanen." ZDMG, IX.

MERK, J. N. *Acht Vorträge über das Pandschab.* Bern 1869.

MEYER, ELARD HUGO. *Indogermanische Mythen.* I : Gandharven-Kentauren, II : Achilles. Berlin 1883, 1887.

Deutsche Volkskunde. Strassburg 1898.

MEYER, JOHANN JACOB. *Über das Wesen der altindischen Rechtsschriften und ihre Verhältnis zu einander und zu Kauṭilya.* Leipzig 1927.

MILLER, V. *Očerki arijskoj mifologii v svjazis drevnejšej kulturoj.* I : Aśviny-Dioskury. Moscow 1876.

MINAYEFF, J. *Grammaire Palie.* tr. from Russian by Stanislas Guyard. Paris 1874.

MOGK, EUGEN. *Germanische Mythologie.* Leipzig 1906; 2nd ed. Strassburg 1907.

MONE, FRANZ JOSEPH. *Schauspiele des Mittelalters.* Mannheim 1852.

MONIER-WILLIAMS, MONIER. *Brahmanism and Hinduism, or religious Thought and Life in India, as based on the Veda and other Books of the Hindus.* London 1887.

MUIR, JOHN. *Original Sanskrit Texts on the Origin and History of the People of India, their Religion and Institutions.* 5 vols. London 1868-73.

MYRIANTHEUS, L. *Die Aśvins oder arischen Dioskuren. Ein Beitrag zur vergleichenden Mythologie.* Munich 1876.

NARIMAN, G. K. et al. *Priyadarśikā, a Sanskrit Drama by Harṣa,* translated into English by G. K. Narimann, A. V. Williams Jackson and Charles J. Ogden. (Columbia University Indo-Iranian Series, X) New York 1923; reprint, New York 1965.

NEGELEIN, JULIUS VON. *Weltanschauung des indogermanischen Asiens.* Erlangen 1924.

"Die Seele als Vogel." *Globus,* LXXIX, 1901.

NEISSER, WALTER. *Zum Wörterbuch des Rigveda.* Heft 1, 2. Leipzig 1924, 1930.

NÖLDKE, THEODOR. Das iranische Nationalepos. In : *Grundriss der iranischen Philologie.* ed. Wilhelm Geiger and Ernst Kuhn. vol. II, part 2. Strassburg 1896-1904.

OERTEL, HANS. "Contributions from the Jaiminīya Brāhmaṇa to the History of the Brāhmaṇa Literature." I : JAOS, XVIII; II : JAOS, XIX; III : *Congrès des orientalistes,* I; IV : JAOS, XXIII; V : JAOS, XXVI; VI : JAOS, XXVIII; VII : *Transactions of Conn. Academy,* XX.

OLDENBERG, HERMANN. *Buddha, sein Leben, seine Lehre, seine Gemeinde.* Berlin 1881; 6th ed. 1914; new ed. 1926.

Die Hymnen des Rigveda. I : Metrische und textgeschichtliche Prolegomina. Berlin 1888.

Die Religion des Veda. Berlin 1894; 2nd ed. 1913; 3rd ed. 1923.

Aus Indien und Iran. Gesammelte Aufsätze. Berlin 1899.

Ṛgveda. Textkritische und exegetische Noten. 2 vols. (I : first to sixth book; II : seventh to tenth book). Berlin 1909, 1912.

Reden des Buddha. Lehre, Verse, Erzählungen. Munich 1922.

PAGVEE, N. BH. *The indigenous far-famed Soma and the Aryan Autochthones in India.* Poona 1921.

PATRUBANY. "Armenische Beiträge." *Ethnologische Mitteilungen aus Ungarn.* V, no. 6.

Beiträge zur armenischen Ethnologie.

PERRY, E. D. "Indra in the Ṛgveda." JAOS, XI, 1882.

"Notes on the Vedic Deity Pūṣan." In : *Classical Studies in Honour of Henry Drisler.* New York 1894.

PETERSSON, H. "Einige Bemerkungen zu den Götternamen Mitra und Varuṇa." In : *Studier tillegnade Esaias Tegner.* 1918.

PISCHEL, RICHARD. "Die Hofdichter des Lakṣmaṇasena." *Abhandlungen der königlichen Gesellschaft der Wissenschaften zu Göttingen,* XXXIX, Historisch-philologische Klasse. Göttingen 1894.

See also under GELDNER.

PREUSS, K. TH. "Das Problem der Mondmythologie." ARW, XXIII.

"Die Naturbeobachtungen in den Religionen des mexikanischen Kulturkreises." *Zeitschrift für Ethnologie,* 1900.

"Phallische Fruchtbarkeitsdämonen." *Archiv für Anthropologie,* NF, I, 1903.

RAPSON, E. J. ed. *The Cambridge History of India.* I : Ancient India. Cambridge 1922.

RATZEL, FRIEDRICH. *Völkerkunde.* 3 vols. Leipzig 1885-1888.

"Der Ursprung und das Wandern der Völker geographisch betrachtet." SBKSGW, L, 1898.

RAWLINSON, GEORGE. *The History of Herodotus.* A new English version, edited with copious notes and appendices. 4 vols. London 1858-60.

REICHELT, HANS. "Der steinerne Himmel." IF, XXXII.

RENEL, CH. *L'évolution d'un mythe. Aśvins et Dioscures.* Paris 1896.

REULING, C. *Die comische Figur in den wichtigsten deutschen Dramen, bis zum Ende des XVI Jahrhunderts.* Stuttgart 1870.

RHYS DAVIDS, THOMAS WILLIAM. *Buddhist Birth Stories* (*Jātaka Tales*). London 1880.

RIALLE, GIRARDE DE. "La déesse mystérieuse des bois dans le Rig-veda." *Revue de linguistique et de philologie comparée*, V.
"Les déesses des eaux dans le Rig-Véda." *Revue de linguistique et de philologie comparée*, IX.

ROHDE, ERWIN. *Psyche. Seelenkult und Unsterblichkeitsglaube der Griechen.* Freiburg, Leipzig 1890-94.

ROSCHER, WILHELM HEINRICH. *Ausführliches Lexikon der griechischen und römischen Mythologie.* Leipzig 1921.
Über Selene und Verwandtes. Leipzig 1890.
"Über den gegenwärtigen Stand der Forschung." ARW, I.

ROTH, RUDOLPH VON. *Zur Literatur und Geschichte des Weda.* Stuttgart 1846.
Der Atharvaveda in Kaschmir. Tübingen 1875.
"Über den Soma." ZDMG, XXXV.
"Wo wächst der Soma?" ZDMG, XXXVIII.

— *Festgruss an Rudolph von Roth zum Doktor-Jubiläum, 24. August 1893, von seinen Freunden und Schülern.* Stuttgart 1893. See also under BÖHTLINGK.

RYDER, A. W. *Die Ṛbhus im Ṛgveda.* Gütersloh 1901.

SASTRI, S. M. NATESA. *Hindu Feasts, Fasts and Ceremonies.* Madras 1903.

SAUSSURE, F. DE. *Memoire sur le système primitif des voyelles dans les langues indo-européennes.* Leipzig 1879. Reprinted in *Recueil des publications scientifiques de F. de. Saussure.* Geneva 1922.

SCHERMAN, LUCIEN. *Philosophische Hymnen aus der Rig- und Atharva-Saṃhitā, verglichen mit den Philosophemen der älteren Upaniṣads.* Strassburg 1887.
Materialien zur Geschichte der indischen Visionsliteratur. Leipzig 1892.
"Die Sterne im indogermanischen Seelenglauben." *Urquell,* VI, 1895.
"Zum indischen Neujahresfest." *Einkehr*, 1920, Nr. 51; 1921, Nr. 1.

SCHLAGINTWEIT, EMIL. *Reisen in Indien und Hochasien.*

SCHMIDT, I. J. *Forschungen im Gebiete . . der Völker Mittelasiens.* St. Petersburg 1824.

SCHRADER, O. *Reallexikon der indogermanischen Altertumskunde.* Strassburg 1901.

Sprachvergleichung und Urgeschichte. I : Geschichte und Methode der linguistisch-historischen Forschung. Jena 1906.

SCHROEDER, LEOPOLD VON. *Indiens Literatur und Cultur in historischer Entwicklung*. Leipzig 1887.

Griechische Götter und Heroen. Eine Untersuchung ihres ursprünglichen Wesens mit Hilfe der vergleichenden Mythologie. Berlin 1887.

Mysterium und Mimus im Rigveda. Leipzig 1908.

Arische Religion. 2 vols. Leipzig 1914, 1916.

"*Lihgo*—Refrain der lettischen Sonnenwendlieder." *Mitteilungen der anthropologischen Gesellschaft zu Wien*, XXXII.

SCHULZE, FRITZ. *Psychologie der Naturvölker*.

SCHULZE, W. "Beiträge zur Wort- und Sittengeschichte III." SBKPAW, 1918.

SCHWAB, J. *Das altindische Thieropfer*. Erlangen 1886.

SIEG, EMIL. *Die Sagenstoffe des Ṛgveda und die indische Itihāsa-Tradition*. Stuttgart 1902.

SIMON, RICHARD. *Beiträge zur Kenntnis der vedischen Schulen*. Kiel 1889.

SMYTH, BROUGH. *The Aborigines of Victoria*.

SÖDERBLOM, NATHAN. *Das Werden des Gottesglaubens. Untersuchungen über die Anfänge der Religion*. Deutsche Bearbeitung hrsg. von Rudolf Stübe. Leipzig 1916.

SORENSEN, S. "Til spoergsmålet om Āditya'erne." In : *Festskrift til Vilhelm Thomsen*. 1894.

SPEYER, JACOB SAMUEL. *Vedische und Sanskrit Syntax*. (Grundriss der indo-arischen Philologie und Altertumskunde, I, 6) Strassburg 1896.

SPIEGEL, FRIEDRICH. *Die traditionelle Literatur der Parsen in ihrem Zusammenhange mit den angränzenden Literaturen*. Leipzig 1860.

Die alt-persischen Keilinschriften. Die Grundtexte mit Übersetzung, Grammatik und Glossar. Leipzig 1862.

Eranische Altertumskunde. 3 vols. Leipzig 1871-78.

Die arische Periode und ihre Zustände. Leipzig 1887.

— *Spiegel Memorial Volume*. Bombay 1908.

STEIN, MARC AUREL. *Zoroastrian Deities on Indo-Scythian Coins*. London 1887.

Memoir on Maps illustrating the ancient Geography of Kaśmīr. Calcutta 1899.

"Some River Names in the Ṛgveda." JRAS, 1917.

STEINEN, K. VON DEN. *Unter den Naturvölkern Zentral-Braziliens*. Berlin 1894.

STEVENSON, J. *Translation of the Saṁhitā of the Sāmaveda*. London 1842.

STRASS, OTTO. *Bṛhaspati im Veda*. Leipzig 1905.

STREITBERG, WILHELM. —*Stand und Aufgaben der Sprachwissenschaft. Festschrift für Wilhelm Streitberg*. Heidelberg 1924.

THIBAUT, G. *Astronomie, Astrologie und Mathematik*. (Grundriss der indo-arischen Philologie und Altertumskunde, III, 9) Strassburg 1899.

THOMAS, E. "The Rivers in the Vedas." JRAS, NS, XV, 1883.

THORNTON, EDWARD. *Gazetteer of countries adjacent to India on the North-West, including Sind, Afghanistan, Beloochistan, the Punjab and the neighbouring States etc.* 2 vols. London 1844.

TIELE, C. P. *Geschichte der Religion im Altertum bis auf Alexander den Grossen*. Deutsche autorisierte Ausgabe von G. Gehrich. Gotha 1898.

TILAK, BAL GANGADHAR. *The Orion or Researches into the Antiquity of the Vedas*. Bombay 1893.

TUXEN, POUL. *Forestéllingen om sjaelen i Rigveda*. Kopenhagen 1919.

TYLOR, EDWARD BARNETT. *Anfänge der Cultur. Untersuchungen über die Entwicklung der Mythologie, Philosophie, Religion, Kunst und Sitte*. 2 vols. Leipzig 1873.

Researches into the early History of Mankind and the Development of Civilization. London 1865; 3rd ed. London 1878.

UNGNAD, ARTHUR. *Die ältesten Völkerwanderungen Vorderasiens*. Breslau 1923.

USENER, HERMANN. *Götternamen. Versuch einer Lehre von der religiösen Begriffsbildung*. Bonn 1896.

Die Sintflutsagen. Bonn 1899.

VODSKOV, H. S. *Syaeledyrkelse og naturdyrkelse. Bidrag til bestemmelsen af den mytologiske metode*. I : Rig-Veda og Edda eller den komparative mytologi. Kopenhagen 1890-97.

WACKERNAGEL, JAKOB. *Altindische Grammatik.* 3 vols. Göttingen 1896, 1905, 1930.

WALLIS, H. W. *The Cosmology of the Rig-Veda. An Essay.* London 1887.

WEBER, ALBRECHT. ed. *Indische Studien. Beiträge für die Kunde des indischen Alterthums.* 1845 ff.

Akademische Vorlesungen über indische Literaturgeschichte. Berlin 1852, 2nd ed. 1876 (= *The History of Indian Literature.* tr. John Mann and Theodor Zachariae. London 1878; 6th ed. Varanasi 1961).

Verzeichnis der Sanskrit und Prakrit Handschriften der königlichen Bibliothek zu Berlin. 4 vols. Berlin 1853-92.

Indische Skizzen. Berlin 1857.

Zwei vedische Texte über Omina und Portenta. Das Adbhutabrāhmaṇa des Sāmaveda und der Adbhutādhyāya des Kauśikasūtra. Berlin 1859.

Die vedischen Nachrichten von den Naxatra. Berlin 1860-62.

Indische Streifen. 3 vols. Berlin 1868, 1869, 1879.

Über die Magavyakti des Kṛṣṇadāsa Miśra. Berlin 1879.

Über zwei Parteischriften zugunsten der Maga. Berlin 1880.

Über die Königsweihe, den Rājasūya. Berlin 1893.

"Episches im Vedaritual" SBKPAW, 1891.

"Über den Vājapeya." SBKPAW, 1892.

"Vedische Beiträge." SBKPAW, 1894-1901.

— *Festgruss für Weber.*

WEINHOLD. "Die Verehrung der Quellen in Deutschland." *Abhandlungen der Berliner Akademie der Wissenschaften,* 1898.

WENZEL, HEINRICH. "Some Contributions to Pāli Lexicography." *Academy,* 30 August 1890.

WEST, E. W. *Pahlavi Texts.* 5 vols. (SBE V, XVIII, XXIV, XXXVII, XLVII) Oxford 1880, 1882, 1885, 1892, 1897.

WHITNEY, W. D. *A Sanskrit Grammar, including both the classical language and the older dialects of Veda and Brāhmaṇa.* Leipzig 1879; 2nd revised ed. 1889.

WILAMOWITZ-MOELLENDORF, U. VON. *Euripides Herakles, erklärt von..* 2 vols. Berlin 1889; 2nd ed. 1895; 3rd ed. 1909.

WILHELM. "Priester und Ketzer im alten Indien." ZDMG, XLIV.

WILSON, HORACE HAYMANN. *The Viṣṇu Purāṇa.* tr. London 1840.

Rig-Veda-Saṃhitā. A Collection of ancient Hindu Hymns. tr. 6 vols. London 1850-1888.

Religious Festivals of the Hindus. In : *Essays,* vol. II. London 1862.

Selected Works. London 1864.

WINDISCH, ERNST. *Māra und Buddha.* Leipzig 1895.

Buddhas Geburt und die Lehre von der Seelenwanderung. Leipzig 1908.

WINDISCHMANN, FRIEDRICH. *Die persische Anāhitā, der Anaïtis. Ein Beitrag zur Mythengeschichte des Orients.* Munich 1856.

Mithra. Ein Beitrag zur Mythengeschichte des Orients. Leipzig 1857.

Zoroastrische Studien. Abhandlungen zur Mythologie und Sagengeschichte des alten Iran. Berlin 1863.

WINTERNITZ, MORITZ. *Das altindische Hochzeitsrituell nach dem Āpastambīya-Gṛhya-Sūtra und einigen anderen verwendbaren Werken. Mit Vergleichung der Hochzeitsgebräuche bei den übrigen indogermanischen Völkern.* Vienna 1892.

Geschichte der indischen Litteratur. 3 vols. Leipzig 1908-20.

"Der Sarpabali. Ein altindischer Schlangenkult." *Mitteilungen der anthropologischen Gesellschaft zu Wien,* XVIII, 1888.

WIRTH, LUDWIG. *Die Oster- und Passionsspiele bis zum XVI Jahrhundert. Beiträge zur Geschichte des deutschen Dramas.* Halle 1889.

WOLFF, FRITZ. *Avesta, die heiligen Bücher der Parsen, übersetzt auf der Grundlage von Chr. Bartholomaes Altiranischem Wörterbuch.* Strassburg 1910.

WUNDT, WILHELM. *Völkerpsychologie.* 10 vols. Leipzig 1900 ff.

ZIMMER, HEINRICH. *Altindisches Leben. Die Cultur der vedischen Arier, nach der Saṃhitā dargestellt.* Berlin 1879.

BIBLIOGRAPHY

OF ALFRED HILLEBRANDT'S WORKS ON THE VEDA

BOOKS

Über die Göttin Aditi (vorwiegend im Ṛgveda). Breslau 1876.

Varuṇa und Mitra. Ein Beitrag zur Exegese des Veda. Breslau 1877.

Das altindische Neu- und Vollmondsopfer in seiner einfachsten Form mit Benutzung handschriftlicher Quellen dargestellt. Jena 1880; reprint, Graz 1977.

Vedainterpretation. Breslau 1885.

Veda-Chrestomathie für den ersten Gebrauch bei Vorlesungen, hrsg. und mit einem Glossar versehen. Berlin 1885.

The Śrauta Sūtra of Śāṅkhāyana (with the commentaries of Varadattasuta Ānartīya and Govinda). 4 vols. (Bibliotheca Indica). Calcutta 1885-99.

Vedische Mythologie. 3 vols. Breslau 1891, 1899, 1902; 2nd revised ed. 2 vols. Breslau 1927, 1929; reprint. Hildesheim 1965.

Rituallitteratur. Vedische Opfer und Zauber. (Grundriss der indo-arischen Philologie und Altertumskunde, III, 2). Strassburg 1897; reprint Graz 1981.

Alt-Indien. Kulturgeschichtliche Skizzen. Breslau 1899.

Vedische Mythologie. Kleine Ausgabe. Breslau 1910.

Lieder des Ṛgveda. tr. (Quellen der Religionsgeschichte, Bd. 5, Gruppe 7). Göttingen, Leipzig 1913.

Aus Brāhmaṇas und Upanischaden. Gedanken altindischer Philosophen. Jena 1921; new ed. under the title, *Upanischaden, Altindische Weisheit.* Düsseldorf 1958; Cologne 1968.

Aus Alt- und Neu-Indien. Gesammelte Aufsätze. Breslau 1922.

ARTICLES

"Zu ṚV V.2.1-6." ZDMG, XXXIII, 1879.

"nikante, uskante, anuskante. Vendidād 3, 8, 36, 7, 48." BKIS, VII, 1883.

"Zu ṚV I.162." ZDMG, XXXVII, 1883.

"Spuren einer älteren Ṛgveda-Recension." BKIS, VIII, 1884.
"Die beiden arischen Accentsysteme." Breslau 1885.
"Bemerkungen zum Avesta." BKIS, IX, 1885.
"uktham madaś ca śasyate." BKIS, IX, 1885.
"Eine Miscelle aus dem Vedaritual." ZDMG, XL, 1886.
"Nationale Opfer in Alt-Indien." In : *Festgruss an Otto von Böhtlingk*. Stuttgart 1888.
"Die Sonnenwendfeste in Alt-Indien." *Romanische Forschungen*, V, 1889.
"On the Origin and Import of the oldest Sāmans." *Trübn. Rec.* 1889.
"Vedica." WZKM, III, 1889.
"Zarathustra und der Zendavesta." *Nord und Süd*, LIX, 1891.
"Die Götter des Ṛgveda, eine euhemeristische Skizze." (under the pseudonymn Fritz Bonsens). Breslau 1894.
"Vedische Einzelheiten." ZDMG, XLVIII, 1894.
"Die Beziehungen des Brahmanismus zur indischen Volksreligion." *Mitteilungen der Schlesischen Gesellschaft für Volkskunde*, I, 1894.
"Zu Oldenbergs Religion des Veda." ZDMG, IL, 1895.
"Brahmanen und Śūdras." In : *Festschrift für Weinhold* (*Germanistische Abhandlungen*, XII), 1896.
"Indra und Vṛtra." ZDMG, L, 1896.
"Māyā." WZKM, XIII, 1899.
"ví vo máde." WZKM, XIV, 1900.
"antaraiś cakraiḥ." WZKM, XV, 1901.
"Vedisch arkásāti und medhásāti." In : *Album Kern*, 1903.
"Das sogenannte Śāṅkhāyanaprātiśākhya." WZKM, XIX, 1905.
"Tiere und Götter im vedischen Ritual." Offprint from the *83. Jahresbericht der Schlesischen Gesellschaft für vaterländische Kultur*, Breslau 1905.
"Zur Bedeutung von Gandharva." Offprint from the *84. Jahresbericht der Schlesischen Gesellschaft für vaterländische Kultur*. Breslau 1906.
"What to learn from Vedic Mythology." *Transactions of the III international Congress of History of Religions*, II, 1908.
Articles on Birth (Hindu, literary); Brahman; Death and disposal of the dead (Hindu); Dyaus; Mysticism (Hindu); Worship (Hindu). In : *Encyclopaedia of Religion and Ethics*. Edinburgh 1908-1921.

"Über die Anfänge des indischen Dramas." SBKBAW, IV, 1914.
"Zum altindischen Königsrecht." ZDMG, LXX, 1916.
"Die Paṇis im Ṛgveda." ZDMG, LXX, 1916.
"Die Heimat des Ṛgveda." OMO, XVI, 1916.
"Der freiwillige Feuertod in Indien und die Somaweihe." SBKBAW, VIII, 1917.
"Zum vedischen Sandhi." In : *Stand und Aufgaben der Sprachwissenschaft, Festschrift für Wilhelm Streitberg*. Heidelberg 1924.
"Zur vedischen Mythologie und Völkersiedlung." ZII, III, 1924.
"Der Nachtweg der Sonne." ZB, VI, 1925.
"Vedisch dhāman." IF, XLIV, 1926.
"Bemerkungen zur vedischen Mythologie." ZII, IV, 1926.
"bráhman." In : *Beiträge zur Literatur und Geistesgeschichte Indiens. Festschrift für Hermann Jacobi*. Bonn, 1926.
"Vedisch yakṣá." In: *Aus Indiens Kultur. Festgabe Richard von Garbe*. Erlangen 1927.
"Das Maskulinum brahmán im Ṛgveda." ZII, V, 1927.
"Die Anschauungen über das Alter des Ṛgveda." ZDMG, LXXXI, 1927.
"pañca janāḥ." ZII, VI, 1928.

Except the contributions to the ERE, all other articles listed here are reprinted in: Rahul Peter Das (ed.). Alfred Hillebrandt: *Kleine Schriften*. Sluttgart 1987.

INDEX

A

C

D

E

N

O

P

R

S